HANDBOOK OF RESEARCH ON STEM EDUCATION

D1609124

The Handbook of Research on STEM Education represents a groundbreaking and comprehensive synthesis of research and presentation of policy within the realm of science, technology, engineering, and mathematics (STEM) education. What distinguishes this Handbook from others is the nature of integration of the disciplines that is the founding premise for the work—all chapters in this book speak directly to the integration of STEM, rather than discussion of research within the individual content areas.

The Handbook of Research on STEM Education explores the most pressing areas of STEM within an international context. Divided into six sections, the authors cover topics including: the nature of STEM, STEM learning, STEM pedagogy, curriculum and assessment, critical issues in STEM, STEM teacher education, and STEM policy and reform. The Handbook utilizes the lens of equity and access by focusing on STEM literacy, early childhood STEM, learners with disabilities, informal STEM, socio-scientific issues, race-related factors, gender equity, cultural-relevancy, and parental involvement. Additionally, discussion of STEM education policy in a variety of countries is included, as well as a focus on engaging business/industry and teachers in advocacy for STEM education.

The Handbook's 37 chapters provide a deep and meaningful landscape of the implementation of STEM over the past two decades. As such, the findings that are presented within provide the reader with clear directions for future research into effective practice and supports for integrated STEM, which are grounded in the literature to date.

Carla C. Johnson is Professor of Science Education and Associate Dean in the College of Education, and Executive Director of the Friday Institute for Educational Innovation at North Carolina State University, USA.

Margaret J. Mohr-Schroeder is Professor of STEM Education and Associate Dean at University of Kentucky, USA.

Tamara J. Moore is Professor of Engineering Education and Interim Executive Director of INSPIRE Research at Purdue University, USA.

Lyn D. English is Professor of STEM Education at Queensland University of Technology, Australia.

HANDBOOK OF RESEARCH ON STEM EDUCATION

Edited by Carla C. Johnson, Margaret J. Mohr-Schroeder, Tamara J. Moore and Lyn D. English

Routledge
Taylor & Francis Group

NEW YORK AND LONDON

First published 2020
by Routledge
52 Vanderbilt Avenue, New York, NY 10017

and by Routledge
2 Park Square, Milton Park, Abingdon, Oxon, OX14 4RN

Routledge is an imprint of the Taylor & Francis Group, an informa business

© 2020 Taylor & Francis

The right of Carla C. Johnson, Margaret J. Mohr–Schroeder, Tamara J. Moore, and Lyn D. English to be identified as the authors of the editorial material, and of the authors for their individual chapters, has been asserted in accordance with sections 77 and 78 of the Copyright, Designs and Patents Act 1988.

Library of Congress Cataloging-in-Publication Data
A catalog record for this book has been requested

ISBN: 978-0-367-07560-6 (hbk)
ISBN: 978-0-367-07562-0 (pbk)
ISBN: 978-0-429-02138-1 (ebk)

Typeset in Bembo
by Apex CoVantage, LLC

In the spirit of lifelong learning and the pursuit of solutions to the most pressing educational challenges, both of which we hope that this Handbook will serve a unique purpose for many of the readers, the editorial team would like to individually provide a dedication to those who have pushed our thinking forward in regard to integrated STEM education research. We are grateful for all the authors who contributed to this very first volume of the Handbook of Research on STEM Education. They each have their own stories on how they came to be the experts in their areas within STEM education, and we appreciate their insights, fortitude, and passion for STEM.

Carla C. Johnson—I have had the great fortune of working with several talented scholars across my career and have found that the best source of inspiration for my work are those people who push my thinking forward, challenge my ideas, and are excited about making a difference in this world. I dedicate this Handbook to those individuals who have made me a better researcher and provided the spark to continue forward each day. This group includes the editors and chapter authors on this Handbook, as well as my great research partners and STEM Road Map team, and my dear friend and mentor, Dr. Piyush Swami.

Margaret J. Mohr-Schroeder—My journey into STEM integration came early and unexpectedly when I finally found an institution that would allow me to double major in mathematics and biology—Thank you, Pittsburg State University (Kansas)! I would like to thank Bruce Walcott for his inspiration and mentorship as we forged an unexpected partnership between the Colleges of Education and Engineering when I first came to the University of Kentucky. Our partnership together propelled us into the world of integrated and transdisciplinary STEM education. Finally, I want to thank my STEM Rocks research team—Christa Jackson, Craig Schroeder, Thomas Roberts, Ashley Delaney, Sarah B. Bush, and Cathrine Maiorca. Our courageous conversations, innovative thinking, strategic planning, and mad research skills have helped shape me into the STEM advocate and enthusiast I am today.

Tamara J. Moore—My journey into STEM integration has been a culmination of many different scholars that have contributed to my thinking. People such as Dick Lesh, Heidi Diefes-Dux, Tom Post, and Kathy Cramer, to name a few, have had a major impact on the ways I think about STEM. In particular, I would like to thank Karl Smith, who has been my mentor, champion, confidant, and all-around go-to person for many years.

CONTENTS

CONTRIBUTORS

Jennifer Adams
Tier 2 Canada Research Chair of Creativity and STEM
Associate Professor
The University of Calgary, Canada
Her research focuses on the intersection between creativity and STEM teaching and learning in postsecondary contexts. She has scholarly expertise in STEM teaching and learning in informal science contexts including museums, national parks and everyday learning. She was awarded a National Science Foundation Early CAREER Award to study informal learning contexts and formal/informal collaborations for STEM teacher education. Her research portfolio also includes youth learning and identity in informal science contexts, with a focus on underrepresented youth and place/identity in transnational communities and environmental education. Her work emphasizes critical and sociocultural frameworks and participatory, qualitative, poststructural approaches. She has also worked as an educator and researcher in New York City public schools and the American Museum of Natural History.

Robin Adams
Professor in the School of Engineering Education
Purdue University, USA
Robin Adams holds a PhD in Education, an MS in Materials Science Engineering, and a BS in Mechanical Engineering. Her research is in three areas: cross-disciplinary thinking, acting, and being; design cognition and learning; and translating research to practice.

Juan Carlos Andrade
Project Manager
Innovación en la Enseñanza de la Ciencia (INNOVEC) A.C., Mexico
His research and professional experience has been linked to professional development of Teachers on Inquiry Based Science Education and STEM methodologies.

Mollie H. Appelgate
Assistant Professor
Iowa State University, USA

Mollie H. Appelgate's research focuses on teacher learning in mathematics and STEM education. She examined teachers' instruction and curriculum use and the development of standard-based STEM curriculum materials. She is a co-author on an integrated STEM curriculum.

Paul A. Asunda
Associate Professor of Engineering and Technology Teacher Education, and Curriculum & Instruction Purdue University, Purdue Polytechnic Institute, USA
Dr. Asunda's research focuses on supporting integrated STEM practices and learning across the professional continuum; career and technical education, and initiatives in career and college success; and assessment and evaluation in STEM environments

Courtney K. Baker
Assistant Professor of Mathematics Education Leadership
George Mason University, USA
Courtney K. Baker's research centers on mathematics teacher leader preparation. She examines how pre-K–12 teachers and leaders integrate STEM and use mathematics in STEM initiatives via model-eliciting activities.

Chantal Barriault
Director of the Science Communications program
Master Lecturer
Laurentian University, Canada
Chantal Barriault is the Director of the Science Communication Graduate program, offered jointly by Science North and Laurentian University in Sudbury, Ontario. Her research focuses on understanding and assessing the impact of science communication strategies in informal learning environments.

Martín Bascopé
Assistant Professor
Pontificia Universidad Católica de Chile, Chile
Martín Bascopé's research focuses on teacher training and policy focus on citizenship education and education for sustainable development.

James D. Basham
Associate Professor
University of Kansas, USA
James D. Basham is the Senior Director of Learning and Innovation at CAST. Dr. Basham studies learning, innovation, and implementation of Universal Design for Learning.

Margaret Blanchard
Professor of Science Education
North Carolina State University, USA
Margaret Blanchard is Professor of Science Education at North Carolina State University. Her research focuses on analyzing models of teacher professional development to support engagement and learning in STEM, and college and career potential, particularly in rural, low-wealth districts.

Mildred Boveda
Assistant Professor of Special Education
Arizona State University, USA
Dr. Mildred Boveda uses the term intersectional competence to describe teachers' understanding of diversity and how multiple sociocultural markers intersect in complex and nuanced ways.

Jonathan M. Breiner

Associate Professor of STEM Education

University of Cincinnati, USA

Dr. Jonathan M. Breiner's primary efforts and research focus on STEM teaching practices, inclusivity, and social justice in science classes for pre-service teachers.

Kimberly Brenneman

Program Officer, Education

Heising-Simons Foundation, USA

Kimberly Brenneman is a program officer at the Heising-Simons Foundation. At Rutgers University she led projects to develop resources to foster STEM learning for children in school and home settings. She consults to develop educational media for children and families.

Gayle A. Buck

Associate Dean and Professor

Indiana University Bloomington, USA

Gayle A. Buck is the Associate Dean for Research and Professor of Science Education in the School of Education at Indiana University-Bloomington. Her research explores populations traditionally underserved in science education and neglected epistemological assumptions in teaching and learning.

Timothy Burg

Professor

Director, Office of STEM Education

The University of Georgia, USA

Dr. Burg has extensive experience in industry and academia. He is spearheading the University-level effort to implement peer mentoring in challenging undergraduate courses and is using biomedical research as a platform to induce broader impacts, including mentoring undergraduates at risk.

Thomas J. Bussey

Assistant Teaching Professor

University of California, San Diego, USA

Dr. Thomas J. Bussey received his Bachelors of Science in Biochemistry and Music from the University of Wisconsin-Madison. He went on to receive his Master in Education in Secondary Science with an Emphasis in Technology and PhD in Chemistry with a research focus in Chemical Education from the University of Nevada, Las Vegas. His research explores students' understandings of non-experiential, abstract, and/or emergent scientific phenomena.

Sarah B. Bush

Associate Professor of K-12 STEM Education

University of Central Florida, USA

Sarah B. Bush's scholarship includes deepening student and teacher understanding of mathematics through transdisciplinary STE(A)M instruction and STE(A)M education professional development effectiveness. She is currently a member of the National Council of Teachers of Mathematics Board of Directors.

Secil Caskurlu

Visiting Assistant Professor

Purdue University, USA

Dr. Secil Caskurlu is a visiting assistant professor in the learning design and technology program at Purdue University. Dr. Caskurlu's research focuses on designing and developing meaningful learning experiences, specifically in online learning environments, and systematic reviews in educational research.

Esra Ceran
Visiting Scholar, San Francisco State University
Research Assistant, Istanbul University, Turkey
Esra Ceran is a doctoral candidate in the Educational Science program at Marmara University in Istanbul, Turkey. She has an appointment as a research assistant at Istanbul University and was a visiting scholar at San Francisco University.

Javier Barrera Cervantes
Executive director
Latino/a Youth Collective of Indiana, USA
Javier Barrera Cervantes is the Executive Director of the Latino/a Youth Collective of Indiana. As a digital media strategist, his work revolves around exploring the intersection of marketing and education and their effect on identity formation.

Douglas H. Clements
Distinguished University Professor
Kennedy Endowed Chair
Co-Executive Director, Marsico Institute for Early Learning and Literacy
Co-Director, James C. Kennedy Institute for Educational Success
University of Denver, USA
Marsico Institute for Early Learning and Literacy
Douglas H. Clements is Distinguished University Professor and Kennedy Endowed Chair in Early Education at the University of Denver. He has directed 35 funded projects and published over 160 refereed research studies, 27 books, 100 chapters, and 300 additional works.

Geraldine L. Cochran
Assistant Professor of Professional Practice
Rutgers University, USA
Dr. Cochran, a physics education researcher, is passionate about teaching physics and supporting efforts to broaden participation in STEM fields. Cochran's research focuses on creating, quantifying, and visualizing inclusive environments and using an intersectional approach to broadening participation in physics

Sandi Cooper
Professor of Mathematics Education
Baylor University, USA
For over 30 years, Sandi Cooper has been a mathematics educator, preparing the next generation of elementary teachers. She has coordinated several collaborative STEM projects, and her research is focused on early childhood mathematics, integrating children's literature, and informal learning.

Amy Corp
Assistant professor
Texas A&M University-Commerce, USA
Amy Corp prepares elementary educators by teaching elementary science, mathematics, technology, and early childhood courses, and by supervising student teachers in the field. She also facilitates online master's classes in mathematics education at Texas A&M University-Commerce.

Digna Couso
Associate Professor
Universitat Autònoma de Barcelona, Spain
Dr. Digna Couso is Associate Professor in the Faculty of Education at Universitat Autònoma de Barcelona and director of the Research Center for Science and Mathematics Education (CRECIM). Dr. Couso's research focuses on scientific practices and modeling and equity and gender balance in STEM including the analysis of interest, self-efficacy and aspirations in STEM

Jennifer Cribbs
Associate Professor of Teaching, Learning & Educational Sciences
Oklahoma State University, USA
Dr. Cribbs's research focuses on students' mathematics identity development and its connection to students' persistence in STEM fields.

Elizabeth A. Crotty
University of Minnesota, USA
Elizabeth A. Crotty taught K-12 mathematics and science for several years before completing her PhD. She earned her PhD in STEM Education from the University of Minnesota in 2018 and completed her K-12 Principal and Administrative license in 2019.

Charlene M. Czerniak
Distinguished University Professor
The University of Toledo, USA
Charlene M. Czerniak has authored articles, book chapters, books, and grants focused on teacher professional development, project-based learning, and elementary science teaching. She served as President of NARST and SSMA.

Ashley Delaney
Science Curriculum Consultant
Heartland Area Education Association, USA
Ashley Delaney is a Science Consultant in Iowa. She taught for 12 years before becoming a consultant. Ashley teaches mathematics and science methods, and courses focused on special populations. Ashley's research interests are focused on STEM education and equity.

Jaime M. Diamond
Assistant Professor of Mathematics Education
University of Georgia, USA
Jaime M. Diamond's work focuses on the unique intersection of teachers' practices and student learning, which involves the transfer of learning and algebraic reasoning.

Remy Dou
Assistant Professor
Florida International University, USA
Dr. Remy Dou is an assistant professor with dual appointments in the Department of Teaching & Learning and the STEM Transformation Institute at Florida International University, contributing to research on the development and impact of teacher leaders in policy arenas.

Kerrie A. Douglas
Assistant Professor of Engineering Education
Purdue University, USA

Dr. Kerrie A. Douglas's research seeks to advance holistic and ethical approaches to validation and inferences of student learning in integrated STEM and engineering environments.

Mauricio Ismael Duque
Professor
Universidad de los Andes in Bogotá, Colombia
STEM-Academia of the Academia Colombiana de Ciencias
Mauricio Ismael Duque is responsible for academic and evaluation dimensions of the STEM-Academy program of the Colombian Academy of Sciences. He has worked for 20 years in the training of teachers in service in STEM education.

Richard A. Duschl
Executive Director, Caruth Institute Engineering Education
Southern Methodist University, USA
Chair, NRC (2007) synthesis report *Taking Science to School*; Co-chair NGSS Earth/Space Sciences Writing Team; Recipient, NARST Distinguished Career in Research Award; Research: learning progressions, formative assessments, design of learning environments for epistemic reasoning and development of science practices.

David Ellis
Lecturer in Digital, Design and Technology Education
Southern Cross University, Australia
David Ellis started his teaching technology education in Australian High Schools in 1992. Since 2009, he has been working in Teacher Education. His interests in STEM education reside in teacher expertise and authentic pedagogies that enhance student engagement.

Mary C. Enderson
Associate Professor
Old Dominion University, USA
Mary C. Enderson is an Associate Professor of Mathematics Education and Co-Director of the MonarchTeach STEM teacher preparation program at Old Dominion University. Her research focuses on STEM teacher preparation, STEM literacy, and modeling and simulation in teacher education.

Lyn D. English
Faculty of Education
Queensland University of Technology, Australia
Lyn D. English holds a PhD (mathematics education; cognitive psychology), an MEd in mathematics education, a BEd, and a DipT. She is the Faculty Professor of STEM Education. Her areas of research include mathematics education, engineering education, integrated STEM learning, mathematical modelling, problem solving/posing, and statistics education.

Coskun Erden
PhD Candidate
Iowa State University, USA
Coskun Erden was a high school mathematics teacher in the Philippines, Albania, Turkey, and Kosovo. His research interest includes mathematics teachers' STEM and statistical knowledge and its influence on teaching practices.

Melanie Fields
Assistant Professor
Texas A&M University-Commerce, USA
Melanie Fields prepares secondary STEM educators by teaching STEM pedagogy, integration, technology, providing early field experiences, and supervising student teachers in the field. She also facilitates online master's classes in curriculum education at Texas A&M University-Commerce.

Marilyn Fleer
Laureate Professor
Monash University, Australia
Marilyn Fleer holds the Foundation Chair of Early Childhood Education and Development. She was awarded the 2018 Kathleen Fitzpatrick Laureate Fellowship by the Australian Research Council.

Dionne Cross Francis
Associate Professor
Indiana University Bloomington, USA
Dionne Cross Francis's research focuses on examining the psychological constructs that influence teachers' instructional decision-making and the design features of professional development that allows teachers to flourish, specifically within the mathematics classroom.

Terrie M. Galanti
Adjunct Professor
George Mason University, USA
Terrie M. Galanti is an electrical engineer, high school teacher, and adjunct professor in Mathematics Education Leadership at George Mason University. She studies how hyper-acceleration of Algebra I to Grade 7 or earlier is related to STEM identity and persistence.

Brian D. Gane
Assistant Research Professor
Learning Sciences Research Institute
University of Illinois at Chicago, USA
Brian D. Gane's research interests include developing and validating assessments that can promote student learning, particularly in science and engineering disciplines.

Aran W. Glancy
PhD Candidate
University of Minnesota, USA
Aran W. Glancy is a PhD candidate in STEM education with a focus on mathematics education at the University of Minnesota.

Allison Godwin
Assistant Professor of Engineering Education
Purdue University, USA
Allison Godwin studies the factors influence diverse students to choose engineering and stay in engineering through their careers and how different experiences within the practice and culture of engineering foster or hinder belongingness and identity development.

Lynn Goldsmith
Distinguished Scholar
Education Development Center, USA

Dr. Goldsmith leads studies that provide insights into effective approaches to interdisciplinary STEM learning and strategies to help teachers become more thoughtful and effective in their instruction. Recent research includes integrating computational thinking into elementary subject areas and arts/STEM learning.

Melva R. Grant
Associate Professor
Old Dominion University, USA
Melva R. Grant, Associate Professor of Mathematics Education, is a STEM professional with degrees from Coppin State University, University of Maryland, and Ohio State University. Her research focuses on broadening participation in STEM, problem solving, and self-based research methodologies.

Daryl Greenfield
Professor of Psychology & Pediatrics
University of Miami, USA
Daryl Greenfield works at the interface of research, policy and practice broadly focused on school readiness with at-risk and dual language learners, with a more specific focus on early science education.

Preeti Gupta
Director of Youth Learning and Research
American Museum of Natural History, USA
Dr. Preeti Gupta is responsible for strategic planning, program development, human capital development and research and evaluation for out-of-school time youth initiatives at the American Museum of Natural History.

Kristie Gutierrez
Assistant Professor of Science Education
Old Dominion University, USA
Kristie Gutierrez is Assistant Professor of Science Education at Old Dominion University. Her areas of interest include informal STEM education, integration of engineering and computer science into elementary teacher preparation and professional development, and preparation of culturally competent STEM educators.

S. Selcen Guzey
Associate Professor
Purdue University, USA
Dr. Guzey is Associate Professor of Science Education at Purdue University. She earned a MS and PhD in science education from the University of Minnesota. Her work includes teacher professional development and curriculum development in integrated STEM education.

Bobby Habig
NSF Postdoctoral Fellow
American Museum of Natural History
Queens College, USA
Bobby Habig's research interests include informal science education, museum education, and factors that impact youths' awareness, interest, and engagement in STEM majors and STEM careers.

Helen Hadani

Director of Research

Bay Area Discovery Museum, USA

As director of research at the Bay Area Discovery Museum, Dr. Helen Hadani applies her knowledge of early childhood and creativity development to design and evaluate experiences that promote children's curiosity, inquiry, and love of learning.

Kyounggun Han

Professor in the Department of Special Education

Dankook University, South Korea

Kyoung Gun Han is also the vice president of Korean Society of Special Education. His research is focused on severe and multiple disabilities, curriculum and instruction, Universal Design For Learning, and life-long learning.

Alexandria Hansen

Assistant Professor

California State University-Fresno, USA

Alexandria Hansen is an Assistant Professor of Science Teacher Education in the College of Science and Mathematics at Fresno State University. Hansen's research focuses on preparing teachers to engage diverse classrooms in creative and authentic STEM learning experiences.

Susanna Hapgood

Associate Professor

The University of Toledo, USA

Susanna Hapgood is an Associate Professor in the Department of Teacher Education at the University of Toledo. Her research interests include the design of texts and experiences that foster young learners' content area literacies, particularly in STEM disciplines.

Danielle B. Harlow

Professor and Associate Dean

University of California Santa Barbara, USA

Danielle B. Harlow is a professor in the Department of Education at UC-Santa Barbara. Harlow's research focuses on STEM learning in schools, museums, and afterschool programs, and on how formal and informal educators learn to guide learning.

Rebecca Hite

Assistant Professor

Texas Tech University, USA

Rebecca Hite's research focuses on K-12 STEM education, specifically the ways K-12 STEM teachers participate in STEM advocacy efforts and develop policy-based leadership.

Margret A. Hjalmarson

Professor of Mathematics Education Leadership

George Mason University, USA

Hjalmarson's research has focused on engineering education and mathematics education with emphasis on STEM faculty development and mathematics teacher leadership design-based research frameworks for STEM education.

Lisa Hoffman

Associate Professor of Graduate Education

Indiana University Southeast, USA

Lisa Hoffman is recipient of the IUS Trustees Teaching Award. Her research focuses on immigrant acculturation or teaching and learning with English language learners.

Nancy Holincheck

Assistant Professor of STEM Education

George Mason University, USA

Holincheck's research interests include teacher education, teacher research, inquiry instruction, physics education, problem solving, science teaching and learning, STEM teaching and learning, and problem-based learning.

Soo-Young Hong

Alan T. Seagren Associate Professor in Education

University of Nebraska-Lincoln, USA

Soo-Young Hong has expertise in early childhood science teaching and learning. Her primary research goal is to define effective ways to incorporate science talk in the interactions between teachers and young children while enhancing teachers' reflective practices in science teaching.

Ann House

Senior Researcher

Center for Education Research and Innovation

SRI Education, USA

Dr. House explores the topics of science education in both formal and informal learning settings. Her research and publications focus on primary and secondary STEM school models, science in afterschool, and curriculum design for deeper learning.

Cassandra L. Hunt

Doctoral Candidate

University of Kansas, USA

Ms. Hunt conducts research in the measurement and implementation of Universal Design for Learning.

Christa Jackson

Associate Professor

Iowa State University, USA

Christa Jackson's research centers on equity issues, teachers' knowledge and conceptions of equity in the teaching and learning of mathematics and STEM. She also focuses on the development, use, and implementation of STEM curriculum. She has co-authored integrated STEM curriculum.

Carla C. Johnson

Professor of Science Education and Associate Dean

North Carolina State University, USA

Dr. Johnson's research is primarily focused on enabling opportunity and access in STEM for all students. A main thread of this research is examining the implementation of STEM education policy, including STEM teaching and learning, STEM professional development, STEM schools/programs, and STEM networks and/or partnerships. Her research informs policy investments, new STEM models and frameworks, and STEM curriculum development.

Amanda C. Johnston
PhD Candidate
Purdue University, USA
Amanda C. Johnston is a PhD candidate in engineering education at Purdue University.

Cindy Jong
Associate Professor
University of Kentucky, USA
Cindy Jong is an Associate Professor in the STEM Education Department at the University of Kentucky where she teaches a graduate course on Equity in STEM Education. Her research intersects equitable mathematics teaching practices, professional noticing, and identity.

Kari Jurgenson
PhD Candidate
Iowa State University, USA
Kari Jurgenson is a mathematics education doctoral candidate at Iowa State University. She primarily researches the teaching and learning of mathematics as well as STEM education.

Shakhnoza Kayumova
Assistant Professor of STEM Education and Teacher Development
University of Massachusetts Dartmouth, USA
Dr. Kayumova's research examines how social constructs such as class, gender, race, ethnicity, and language get implicated in science identity development.

Donna King
Faculty of Education
Queensland University of Technology, Australia
Donna King is associate dean, teaching and learning, in the Faculty of Education. Her recent research in STEM education spans three interconnecting fields, namely, context-based science, engineering education, and the emotional engagement of students in science classes.

Vance Kite
Doctoral Student in STEM Education
North Carolina State University, USA
Vance Kite is a third-year doctoral student focusing on research in CT in K-12 education, in particular effective professional development of CT integration for science teachers. Before returning to graduate school, Mr. Kite was a high school science teacher.

Hunkar Korkmaz
Professor of Education
Haccettepe University, Turkey
Hunkar Korkmaz's research focuses on science curriculum and instruction and students' images of science and scientist in context-based science instruction.

Kadir Kozan
Research Associate
Purdue University, USA
Dr. Kadir Kozan is a research associate in the School of Engineering Education at Purdue University with a current focus on predicting undergraduate engineering students' academic success. Dr. Kozan holds a PhD in Learning Design and Technology from Purdue University.

Jia Li
PhD student
Capital Normal University, China
Jia Li is a PhD candidate from Capital Normal University and a visiting scholar of The Education University of Hong Kong. Her research currently focuses on STEM education, especially STEM curriculum development and STEM teacher development. She has rich experience in designing and teaching STEM courses, and is also devoted to running training programs for STEM teachers in China.

Stanley M. Lo
Assistant Teaching Professor
University of California San Diego, USA
Dr. Stanley M. Lo received his undergraduate degree from Yale University and his PhD in Biochemistry from Harvard University. He was a Research Associate at Northwestern University. His research aims to understand how higher education faculty develop and change their teaching.

Christine G. Lord
Graduate Assistant
University of Florida, USA
Christine G. Lord's research interests focus on science teacher professional development, inquiry-based science pedagogical practices, and teaching and learning science in rural districts.

Julie A. Luft
Athletic Association Professor of Mathematics and Science Education
University of Georgia, USA
For over 25 years, Julie A. Luft has studied the professional learning of STEM teachers. Her expertise resides in the area of professional development programming and newly hired teachers.

Tian Luo
PhD student
The Education University of Hong Kong, China
Tian Luo's research mainly focuses on STEM education, especially STEM learning for primary and secondary students. She has also co-organized and designed a STEM summer camp for students and STEM professional development workshops for teachers.

Paula A. Magee
Clinical Professor of Science Education
Indiana University-Purdue University Indianapolis, USA
Dr. Magee's work focuses on using inquiry and Culturally Relevant Pedagogy as frameworks for teaching science in urban schools.

Cathrine Maiorca
Assistant Professor, Mathematics Education
California State University, Long Beach, USA
Cathrine Maiorca's research includes Model-Eliciting Activities, preservice teachers' and students' perceptions of integrated STEM, and equity in STEM.

Matthew T. Marino
Professor of Exceptional Student Education
University of Central Florida, USA

Dr. Marino's research focuses on the design, implementation, and assessment of technology-enhanced STEM curricular materials.

Mandy McLean
Senior Researcher
Guild Education, USA
Mandy McLean is a Senior Researcher at Guild Education, a fast-growing startup helping to increase economic mobility for working adults. McLean's research focuses on the retention of adult learners in higher education.

Jeff Milbourne
Independent Researcher
San Luis Obispo, CA, USA
Jeff Milbourne is an independent researcher who focuses on teacher leadership in the policy/advocacy space, 21st-century school design, and complex problem solving. He is a former K-12 science instructor and a former Congressional staffer.

Margaret J. Mohr-Schroeder
Professor of STEM Education & Associate Dean
University of Kentucky, USA
Margaret J. Mohr-Schroeder's research interests include investigating ways to broaden participation in STEM, especially of underrepresented populations and the effects these mechanisms have on their STEM literacy. Through this work, she has focused on creating opportunity and access to STEM experiences for each and every participant who studies their effects.

Melinda Williams Moore
Public Service Assistant
Carl Vinson Institute of Government
University of Georgia, USA
Melinda Williams Moore directs qualitative and quantitative methodologies for evaluation and research.

Tamara J. Moore
Professor, Engineering Education and Interim Executive Director, INSPIRE Research
Institute for Pre-College Engineering
Purdue University, USA
Tamara J. Moore is a Professor of Engineering Education and the Interim Executive Director of the INSPIRE Research Institute for Pre-College Engineering at Purdue University. Her research is centered on the integration of STEM concepts in K–16 classrooms.

Mayte Morales
General Director
Instituto Apoyo, Peru
Mayte Morales is also a Chevening Fellow of the UK with MSc. The Instituto APOYO contributes to education through innovation projects, articulation, awareness, dissemination and strengthening of educative public policy.

Samuel D. Museus
Professor of Education Studies
University of California, San Diego, USA

Samuel D. Museus is Founding Director of the National Institute for Transformation and Equity (NITE). His research agenda is focused on diversity and equity in education.

Gilbert Naizer
Professor
Texas A&M University-Commerce, USA
Gilbert Naizer primarily teaches graduate courses in elementary education with emphasis on science education. He has conducted multiple mathematics and science teacher professional development grants for elementary teachers.

Jasmine Nation
Postdoctoral Scholar
University of California, Irvine, USA
Jasmine Nation is a postdoctoral scholar working with university scientists and teacher-researchers to implement inclusive science curriculum. She supports Research-Practice Partnerships that promote personally relevant and equitable science experiences for Latinx students both in and out of school.

Suzanne M. Nesmith
Associate Professor of Science Education
Baylor University, USA
Suzanne M. Nesmith has been involved in STEM education for over 30 years at every educational level. Her specializations, research interests, and numerous publications include topics related to literacy integration in STEM, early childhood engineering, and inquiry-based science in elementary classrooms.

Knut Neumann
Professor and Director of the Department of Physics Education
Leibniz-Institute for Science and Mathematics Education, Germany
Knut Neumann's research interests include the assessment of student competence and the development of student competence in science.

Megan Nickels
Faculty Director, UCF's PedsAcademy at Nemours Children's Hospital
Assistant Professor of STEM Education
University of Central Florida, USA
Megan Nickels's research agenda centers around mathematical thinking and learning through disruptive technologies—utilizing robotics and immersive virtual reality, and STEM(M), the holistic examination of STEM education and medical outcomes for children with chronic and complex medical issues.

Gwen Nugent
Research Professor
Nebraska Center for Research on Children, Youth, Families and Schools
University of Nebraska, Lincoln, USA
Gwen Nugent leads research projects focusing on the development and delivery of STEM instruction and training to improve student learning and teacher competencies. She is currently principal investigator for the National Science Foundation and the U.S. Department of Education grants.

David Owens

Assistant Professor of Science Education

Georgia Southern University, USA

David Owens's research focuses on the characteristics of learning environments that enhance learners' motivation and ability to understand science and take informed positions when considering socio-scientific issues.

Soonhye Park

Associate Professor

North Carolina State University, USA

Dr. Park's research interests focus on teacher pedagogical content knowledge (PCK), teacher professional identity, and teacher change. She has led numerous funded grant projects on teacher professional development that explicitly seek effective ways to advance science teachers' knowledge, skills, and practices.

James W. Pellegrino

Professor and Co-Director of Learning Sciences Research Institute

University of Illinois at Chicago, USA

James W. Pellegrino's research and development interests include applications of cognitive and psychometric research and theory to advancement of STEM teaching, learning and assessment.

Erin E. Peters-Burton

Donna R. and David E. Sterling Endowed Professor in Science Education

George Mason University, USA

Dr. Peters-Burton investigates STEM school models, the use of educational psychology to promote diversity in STEM, supporting student science and engineering practices with self-regulated learning tactics, integration of computational thinking and data practices, and K-12 STEM curriculum.

Vanessa Peters

Senior Learning Sciences Researcher

Digital Promise, USA

Dr. Peters's research focuses on how emergent uses of technology can create opportunities for teaching and learning, particularly in science. She applies an interdisciplinary lens to her research with design-based, qualitative, and mixed-methods research approaches. Current research interests include alternative educational models including competency-based curriculum and digital badging.

Chanda Prescod-Weinstein

Assistant Professor

University of New Hampshire, USA

Dr. Chanda Prescod-Weinstein is an assistant professor in the Department of Physics and Astronomy and Core Faculty in Women's and Gender Studies at the University of New Hampshire. She is an expert in particle physics and feminist science studies.

Jeremy Price

Assistant Professor of Technology, Innovation, and Pedagogy

Indiana University-Purdue University Indianapolis, USA

Dr. Price's work focuses on using technology to support culturally relevant and sustaining teaching and learning.

Christen Priddie
Research Associate
Indiana University, USA
Christen Priddie is a doctoral student in the Higher Education program at Indiana University, Bloomington. She currently serves as a research project associate for the National Survey of Student Engagement. Her research agenda is focused on underrepresented minorities in STEM.

Rose M. Pringle
Associate Professor
University of Florida, USA
Rose M. Pringle's research agenda includes science teachers' professional learning and how teachers' knowledge becomes translated into effective and culturally relevant pedagogical practices that challenge assumptions and the status quo and lead to increased participation of marginalized learners in science.

Annie Prud'homme-Généreux
Director, Continuing Studies and Executive Education
Capilano University, Canada
A founder at Quest University, Annie designed the innovative Bachelor of Arts & Sciences. She then led the science departments of one of Canada's largest science centres. Now, she blends formal and informal learning, leading a school of continuing studies.

Javier Pulgar
Professor
University of Bio Bio, Chile
Javier Pulgar is a professor in the Physics Department at the University of Bio Bio, Chile. Pulgar's research focuses on creating teaching and learning environments where students can engage in solving problems, creative thinking and social networks for collaboration.

Chris Rasmussen
Professor
San Diego State University, USA
Dr. Chris Rasmussen received his BA, MA and PhD from the University of Maryland in Mechanical Engineering, Mathematics, and Mathematics Education, respectively. His research interests include inquiry-oriented approaches to the undergraduate mathematics teaching and learning and departmental change.

Carina M. Rebello
Assistant Professor of Practice
Purdue University, USA
Dr. Rebello's research focuses on scientific argumentation. Specifically, she investigates the use of argumentation prompts in physics problem solving in courses for future engineers as well as in engineering design problems in courses for future elementary teachers.

Philip A. Reed
Professor
Old Dominion University, USA
Philip A. Reed is a professor and technology teacher education program leader with degrees from Old Dominion University, the University of South Florida, and Virginia Tech. His research focuses on curriculum development and assessment in career and technical education.

Kristina Reiss

Dean of School of Education

Technical University of Munich, Germany

Kristina Reiss is also the director of PISA in Germany. Her main research interest is focused on competence development in STEM education.

Julie Remold

Senior Education Researcher

Center for Technology in Learning

SRI Education, USA

Dr. Julie Remold, is a senior education researcher at SRI International. Trained as an anthropologist, her work focuses on STEM education, professional development, networked communities for educators, and learning in informal environments.

Léonie J. Rennie

Emeritus Professor in Science and Technology Education

Curtin University, Australia

Léonie has published extensively about research in learning in science and technology, particularly in integrated and out-of-school settings. In 2009, she received the Distinguished Contributions to Science Education Through Research Award from the National Association for Research in Science Teaching.

Pilar Reyes

Executive Director of the Inquiry Based Science Education Program

Universidad de Chile, Chile

The line of research is dedicated both to teaching and learning inquiry science for general education and professional development for science teachers from K through 12.

Jeffrey Robert

Collegiate Assistant Professor of Real Estate

Virginia Polytechnic & State University, USA

Jeffrey Robert's teaching and research interests include real estate price externalities, state and local land use policy, and real estate development. Additionally, he researches topics in student achievement and classroom outcomes.

Thomas Roberts

Assistant Professor

Bowling Green State University, USA

Thomas Roberts teaches mathematics education courses in the Inclusive Early Childhood Program at Bowling Green State University. His research interests include informal STEM learning environments, early childhood and elementary STEM education, and preservice teacher preparation.

Claudia Robles

Coordinator

Innovación en la Enseñanza de la Ciencia A.C., Mexico

Claudia Robles is Coordinator at Innovación en la Enseñanza de la Ciencia, A.C. (INNOVEC), a non-profit organization that promotes Inquiry Based Science Education (IBSE) in Public Education Schools in Mexico.

Gillian H. Roehrig

Institute on the Environment Fellow
Professor of STEM Education
University of Minnesota, USA

Dr. Roehrig's research interests center on understanding how teachers translate science standards into their classroom practices. Of particular interest is how teachers implement integrated STEM instruction and how professional development programs can influence teachers' knowledge, beliefs, and classroom practices.

Nancy Romance

Professor, Science Education
Director, FAU STEM Collaborative
Florida Atlantic University, USA

Dr. Romance is a science educator specializing in early science and literacy learning as well as post-secondary curricular reform and pedagogical practices of College STEM faculty. Her research has been funded by NSF and the USDOE Institute of Education Sciences.

Troy D. Sadler

Thomas James Distinguished Professor of Experiential Learning
University of North Carolina at Chapel Hill, USA

Troy D. Sadler's research focuses on how students negotiate complex socio-scientific issues and how these issues may be used as contexts for science learning.

Julie Sarama

Distinguished University Professor
Kennedy Endowed Chair
University of Denver, USA

Julie Sarama, Kennedy Endowed Chair and Distinguished University Professor, has taught early to high school mathematics. She has directed 30 projects funded by the NSF, IES, etc., and authored over 80 refereed articles, 7 books, 60 chapters, and over 100 additional publications.

Christina Schwarz

Professor
Michigan State University, USA

Christina Schwarz is a professor at Michigan State University in the Department of Teacher Education. She works with teachers and students to study PK-16 science teaching and learning. She focuses on science and engineering practices that foster equitable disciplinary sense-making.

Tredina D. Sheppard

8th Grade Science Instructor
P.K. Yonge Developmental
Research School
PhD Student
University of Florida, USA

Tredina D. Sheppard's research includes science teacher professional development, inquiry-based science teacher practices, and STEM integration in middle school.

Cristina Simarro

Adjunct Professor
Universitat Autònoma de Barcelona, Spain

Dr. Cristina Simarro is adjunct professor in the Faculty of Education at Universitat Autònoma de Barcelona and researcher at the Research Center for Science and Mathematics Education (CRE-CIM). Dr. Simarro's research focuses on engineering education and the promotion of STEM aspirations in students.

Ron Skinner
Director of Education
MOXI, The Wolf Museum of Exploration + Innovation, USA
Ron Skinner created and oversees the education department at MOXI, The Wolf Museum of Exploration + Innovation. Skinner's research focuses on developing and studying practice-based facilitation methods to engage learners in STEM practices.

John F. Smith
Doctoral Student, Learning Sciences
Northwestern University, USA
John F. "Trey" Smith teaches science, social studies, and engineering in Philadelphia public schools and is a doctoral student at Northwestern University in Learning Sciences. He studies science learning intersecting with social, cultural, historical, political, community contexts and questions.

Winnie Wing Mui So
Professor
Director of the Centre for Education in Environmental Sustainability
Associate Dean of the Graduate School
The Education University of Hong Kong, China
Winnie Wing Mui So was the President of the Asia Pacific Educational Research Association (APERA) during 2014–2016 and a serving executive member of the World Education Research Association (WERA). Professor So's main research areas are STEM education, science and environmental education.

Alexis Spina
PhD Student
University of California, Santa Barbara, USA
Alexis Spina is a fourth-year PhD student at the University of California, Santa Barbara. Spina's research focuses primarily on preparing preservice mathematics teachers, as well as providing professional development to in-service mathematics and science teachers.

Timothy Spuck
Director of Education & Public Engagement
Associated Universities Inc., USA
Dr. Timothy Spuck is the Director of Education and Public Engagement at Associated Universities Inc., where he develops and manages innovative STEM education programs for astronomy and earth-space sciences, making STEM accessible through authentic engagement, network building, and policy development.

Emily K. Suh
Assistant Professor of Developmental Literacy
Texas State University, USA
Dr. Emily K. Suh's dissertation on the experiences of adult-arrival immigrants in developmental education won the dissertation award from the American Association for Applied Linguistics. She is the recipient of the Emergent Scholar Award from the International Society for Language Studies.

Kristina M. Tank

Assistant Professor of Science Education and Materials Science Engineering

Iowa State University, USA

Kristina M. Tank is a teacher educator and researcher in elementary science and engineering education. Her research centers around how to better support and prepare educators to integrate STEM in a way that supports teaching and learning across multiple disciplines.

David Tanner

Associate Director, Carl Vinson Institute of Government

University of Georgia, USA

With two decades of work in government, David Tanner addresses issues related to workforce and economic development and improving decision making with data analytics.

Julie Thomas

Professor and Interim Associate Dean for Research

University of Nebraska-Lincoln, USA

Julie Thomas has developed expertise in elementary science education—and the nexus of learning for children, teachers, and parents. Her primary research goals focus on (a) improving elementary teachers' knowledge and confidence in science content and (b) enhancing home-school connections.

Juliana Utley

Professor and Morsani Chair of Mathematics and Science Education

Oklahoma State University, USA

Juliana Utley directs the Center for Research on STEM Teaching and Learning. Her research interests include beliefs and attitudes of teachers related to STEM content areas, mathematical knowledge of teachers, and engineering education.

Beth Dykstra VanMeeteren

University of Northern Iowa, USA

Associate Professor

Director of the Iowa Regents' Center for Early Developmental Education

Beth Dykstra VanMeeteren is Director of the Iowa Regents' Center for Early Developmental Education at the University of Northern Iowa. She conducts research and designs and delivers professional learning on early engineering and integrative STEM and literacy.

Grady Venville

Professor

Australian National University, Australia

Grady Venville is Pro Vice-Chancellor, Education at the Australian National University. She is responsible for the quality of teaching and learning and for special education projects. Her research interests focus on curriculum integration, conceptual change and cognitive acceleration.

Rebecca E. Vieyra

Doctoral Student

University of Maryland, College Park, USA

Rebecca E. Vieyra is a program manager at a multilateral diplomatic organization that promotes STEM teacher leadership in the Americas. She collaborates on physics education projects funded by the U.S. Department of State, NASA, and the National Science Foundation.

John Wallace

Professor Emeritus

Ontario Institute for Studies in Education, University of Toronto, Canada

John Wallace is Professor Emeritus at the Ontario Institute for Studies in Education of the University of Toronto, Canada. He has published extensively in the fields of curriculum integration, science education and qualitative inquiry.

Janet B. Walton

Senior Research Scholar

North Carolina State University

William and Ida Friday Institute for Educational Innovation, USA

Dr. Janet B. Walton is a senior research scholar on the STEM Education Policy Research Team at North Carolina State University's William and Ida Friday Institute for Educational Innovation. Her research focuses on mixed-methods research methodologies and evaluation, educational policy, and cross-sector collaboration.

Hui–Hui Wang

Assistant Professor of Agricultural Sciences Education and Communication, and Curriculum & Instruction

Purdue University, USA

Dr. Wang's research focuses on STEM integration, inquiry-based instruction, and project-based learning in science and agricultural education across formal and non-formal settings.

Karen Webber

Associate Professor of Higher Education

Institute of Higher Education

The University of Georgia, USA

Karen Webber publishes on a number of issues related to institutional effectiveness in higher education, including student success in STEM education.

P. John Williams

Professor of Education

Director of Graduate Research in the School of Education

Curtin University, Western Australia

Professor Williams researches and supervises students in STEM, technology education, PCK and digital assessment. He is the series editor of Springer Technology Education and is on the editorial board of six journals, and he has authored or contributed to over 250 publications.

Dorothy Y. White

Associate Professor of Mathematics and Science Education

University of Georgia, USA

For over 15 years, Dr. White has studied professional learning communities among mathematics teachers. Her expertise includes equity in mathematics education and professional development models for teachers.

Eric Wiebe

Professor in the STEM Education Department

North Carolina State University, USA

Dr. Wiebe's research has focused on technology integration in K-12 STEM instructional settings. This work has ranged from individual student to whole school district research studies. For the past seven years, he has focused on CT/CS K-12 education.

Kerrie Wilkins-Yel
Assistant Professor
University of Massachusetts Boston, USA
Kerrie Wilkins-Yel's research examines the influential factors that enhance academic and career persistence among women of color enrolled in science, technology, engineering, and mathematics (STEM) disciplines.

Craig J. Willey
Associate Professor of Mathematics Education and Teacher Education
Indiana University, Purdue University Indianapolis, USA
Dr. Willey uses the theoretical and analytical frameworks of Culturally Relevant Pedagogy and Whiteness to understand teachers' interpretations of schooling contexts and their instructional decision-making processes.

Jian-Xin Yao
Associate Professor
National Institute for Curriculum and Textbook Research,
Ministry of Education, P. R. of China, China
Jian-Xin Yao received his PhD from Beijing Normal University, China and Leibniz Institute for Science and Mathematics Education (IPN), Germany. He conducts research on students' progression of scientific understanding and practices, and international comparative studies of science curricula. Recently he has an increasing interest in STEM education and is participating as an associate editor in the development of a K–9 STEM book series.

Chunlei Zhang
Lecturer
East China Normal University, China
Chunlei Zhang received his PhD in College of Life Sciences of Beijing Normal University. His research interests include teacher knowledge and professional development of STEM teachers.

Alan Zollman
Professor of Mathematics Education
Indiana University Southeast, USA
Dr. Zollman is Past President of School Science and Mathematics Association (SSMA) and a Past Vice President of Research Council of Mathematics Learning (RCML). Dr. Zollman has received numerous teaching, research and service awards, and his research focuses on the teaching and learning of STEM education.

PREFACE

The first *Handbook of Research on STEM Education* is a collection of the most relevant and imperative topics that permeate the field of STEM education across the world today. The *Handbook* editorial team is comprised of researchers with background in fields including science education, mathematics education, and engineering education whose scholarship intersects within and across the STEM disciplines. This publication comes at an important time for our field of STEM education. Although there have been great advances in STEM education over nearly two decades, there is still a dearth of venues, outlets, and academic journals which provide a forum for discourse and dissemination of findings related to STEM education—beyond those which are tailored for the individual disciplines. Additionally, the volume of literature that examines STEM education topics has grown substantively—warranting a synthesis to ground future research studies. Our team conceptualized the *Handbook* as a way to pull together the insightful and rigorous interdisciplinary and integrated STEM education research in a manner that could be leveraged to move the field forward.

The content of the *Handbook* was solicited through an open call which yielded over 200 chapter proposals. Through a thorough and rigorous review process, the resulting internationally grounded *Handbook* contents and author teams were determined—six themes that are represented by each section and 37 chapters across the themes. The six themes include: the nature of STEM; STEM learning; STEM pedagogy, curriculum and assessment; critical issues in STEM; STEM teacher education; and STEM policy and reform. A key feature of this *Handbook* is that the chapters focus on the integration of the STEM disciplines as the frame for the STEM education work and research. In addition, the *Handbook* includes several chapters which provide both a historical and current lens into STEM education policy in countries around the globe who are engaged in STEM work. Moreover, it is the desire of the *Handbook* contributors that scholars in the field will utilize this resource as a launchpad for generating new questions to be explored, as well as a base to continue to build the research within the realm of STEM education.

Carla C. Johnson and Margaret J. Mohr-Schroeder

SECTION 1

The Nature of STEM

1

STEM INTEGRATION

A Synthesis of Conceptual Frameworks and Definitions

Tamara J. Moore, Amanda C. Johnston and Aran W. Glancy

Introduction

The calls to increase STEM (i.e., Science, Technology, Engineering, and Mathematics) education efforts around the world have led to new and different models of STEM instruction. Integrating the STEM subjects is gaining a foothold as one of the ways in which to help students make meaning out of and gain interest in the STEM subjects and careers that are heavily STEM related. There are many different ways in which researchers and educators look at STEM integration and what it entails. STEM integration has been defined at a variety of grade levels, including at the pre-school level (Aldemir & Kermani, 2017), primary school level (e.g., Baker & Galanti, 2017), middle school level (e.g., Burrows, Lockwood, Borowczak, Janak, & Barber, 2018; Kloser, Wilsey, Twohy, Immonen, & Navotas, 2018), high school level (e.g., Bell & Bell, 2018; Berland, 2013; Berland, Steingut, & Ko, 2014), and in teacher education programs (e.g., Brown & Bogiages, 2019; Burrows & Slater, 2015; Lupinacci & Happel-Parkins, 2017; Thibaut, Knipprath, Dehaene, & Depaepe, 2018a). STEM integration has been researched internationally and calls for more integrated STEM learning are prevalent, including in the United States (Johnson, 2013; National Academy of Engineering and National Research Council, 2014), Canada (e.g., Sengupta & Shanahan, 2017), the United Kingdom (Council for Science and Technology, 2013), Australia (Office of the Chief Scientist, 2015), Taiwan (e.g., Lou, Shih, Diez, & Tseng, 2011), Indonesia (e.g., Blackley, Rahmawati, Fitriani, Sheffield, & Koul, 2018), Turkey (e.g., Ong et al., 2016), Japan (e.g., Saito, Gunji, & Kumano, 2015), Egypt (e.g., El-Deghaidy, 2017), Saudi Arabia (e.g., El-Deghaidy, Mansour, Alzaghibi, & Alhammad, 2017), and Thailand (e.g., Thananuwong, 2015), to name a few. Within this literature base, the language used to describe STEM integration differs among authors and between contexts. For example, different researchers use different terms for STEM integration. The most common terms are STEM integration and integrated STEM, but other terms that are also used are integrative STEM and interdisciplinary STEM.

The manner in which subjects of STEM are included or not, how concepts from other non-STEM disciplines are added, the length of the integrated STEM learning episode, and the purpose of the learning within a STEM integration setting all make a difference in how STEM integration is defined and used. This chapter looks at the different conceptual underpinnings of how STEM integration is defined, bringing together commonalities and differences among these frameworks and definitions. To do this, we aimed to answer the research question: How is STEM integration defined, conceptualized, or operationalized within the current literature?

Methods

In order to present the different conceptual underpinnings of STEM integration, we conducted an in-depth integrative literature review (Torraco, 2005) of conceptual frameworks and definitions for STEM integration. For our initial search, we limited our criteria to keywords, titles, and abstracts in peer-reviewed research articles and books that were printed in English. We used the search terms "STEM integration," "integrated STEM," and "integrative STEM." We searched the databases Education Source, PsychINFO, PsychArticles, Education Full Text, Educational Administration Abstracts, and ERIC. For each database, we included all sources found. Additionally, we searched Google Scholar and included all sources that were relevant to STEM education until we reached an entire page without relevant sources. We also looked through the reference lists of our sources to include sources that were commonly cited but that did not appear in our searches described previously. After removing duplicates, we had a total of 170 sources. From each of these sources, we extracted the conceptual framework of STEM integration, if there was one, and compiled all the definitions. These definitions ranged in length from a few sentences to entire book chapters. Throughout this process, we eliminated sources that did not have a definition or conceptual framework for STEM integration. In a few cases, the definitions of STEM integration within one article used another article in such a way that we added the cited article to our sources. In the end, our total number of sources included in the final review was 109. From here, we extracted the key aspects and points of each framework by using open coding (Saldaña, 2016; Schreier, 2012). All three authors worked collaboratively to do this, focusing on reading and commenting on the definitions individually, with frequent interaction with the other authors to remain consistent. Then, we did a second round of open coding on the key aspects and points extracted through our first round of open coding. From these comments, we developed themes and coded each comment based on which theme or themes it fell into, again working collaboratively. This process yielded the themes that we describe in the remainder of this chapter. While not all sources will be cited in this chapter due to space limitations, all sources were used as primary data.

Results

Review of the different definitions and conceptual frameworks for STEM integration revealed several common themes among how scholars conceptualize STEM integration. Within these themes, however, we found variation in how authors incorporated them into their definitions and the degree to which they were emphasized. One of the most common themes was that STEM integration should be centered on real-world problems or context. We describe the ways that authors envision incorporating the real world into integrated STEM lessons, and we also describe the varied justifications for why this is appropriate and beneficial. Many authors also argued for STEM integration because the STEM disciplines themselves are connected by big ideas and common skills and practices. Another theme we identified within the conceptual frameworks for STEM integration is that there is a significant amount of variation in the degree to which authors believe the disciplines should be integrated. Although it is agreed that STEM integration requires at least two disciplines, some authors stop there while others require more or more specific subjects. Additionally, many scholars acknowledged this variation and described different ways of categorizing or differentiating types of STEM integration. We describe several of those schemas in this chapter. The final theme we identified was that authors frequently describe structures for supporting integration. Within this theme, we noticed differences in how scholars conceptualize the role of each discipline, and we describe the pedagogies that are commonly described in conjunction with STEM integration. These themes provide a broad overview of the similarities and differences among definitions of STEM integration within the literature.

STEM Problems and Lessons Should Be Based on the Real World

A theme that runs throughout many conceptualizations of STEM integration is that integrated STEM activities should be realistic or focused on real-world problems. Many authors recommend that STEM problems in the classroom be "authentic" in that the problems students engage with in the classroom parallel problems addressed by scientists, engineers, or applied mathematicians in the real world (Barth, Bahr, & Shumway, 2017; Burrows et al., 2018; Dare, Ellis, & Roehrig, 2018; El-Deghaidy et al., 2017; Felix & Harris, 2010; Kloser et al., 2018; Meyrick, 2011). Similarly, scholars also emphasize that STEM lessons and STEM problems should have rich contexts that reflect the complexity of real-world problems (Berland & Steingut, 2016; Bybee, 2013; Johnson, 2013; Moore, Stohlmann et al., 2014; Nadelson & Seifert, 2013). Others advocate that problems be realistic so that they provide a compelling purpose for engaging with the problem and the content (Guzey, Moore, & Harwell, 2016; Kloser et al., 2018). The real-world nature of STEM integration is also thought to help make explicit the connection between school and STEM careers (Radloff, 2015; Roehrig, Moore, Wang, & Park, 2012; Ryu, Mentzer, & Knobloch, 2018).

Some scholars also argue that not only should STEM problems be connected to the real world, but that STEM lessons and STEM problems should be explicitly connected to the community of the students. Specifically, centering the students' community during STEM lessons can help to make the STEM concepts more socially and culturally relevant (Johnson, 2011) and help students see both opportunities for themselves in STEM careers and the ways in which STEM disciplines can impact their lives (Meyrick, 2011; Moore & Smith, 2014; Ryu et al., 2018; Uğraş & Genç, 2018). Sias, Nadelson, Juth, and Seifert (2017) explicitly argue for involving the students' families in STEM activities.

Embedding STEM content in real-world activities that are relevant to students' lives has the additional benefit, many argue, of making the STEM lessons and activities more motivating and engaging for the students. Some focus on the context itself as being engaging (Breiner, Harkness, Johnson, & Koehler, 2012; Corlu & Aydin, 2016; Guzey et al., 2016; Johnson, Peters-Burton, & Moore, 2016; Stubbs & Myers, 2015). Wasserman and Rossi (2015) state that this engaging context has the potential to engage a broader, more diverse group of students. Others argue that integration of the subjects, rather than the context itself, makes the subjects and the problems they can address seem more interesting and applicable to students (Berland & Steingut, 2016; Corlu & Aydin, 2016; Lou et al., 2011; Uğraş & Genç, 2018).

STEM integration is often portrayed as a more modern approach to education in a more modern world. Real-world, integrated activities are thought by some to help develop STEM literacy and *21st-century skills*, among which are listed characteristics such as creativity, curiosity, collaboration, and critical thinking (Bybee, 2013; Carter, Beachner, & Daugherty, 2015; Shahali, Halim, Rasul, Osman, & Zulkifeli, 2017; Sias et al., 2017; Uğraş & Genç, 2018; Wang & Knobloch, 2018). Others argue that STEM integration not only helps students learn about the existence and relevance of STEM careers, but also increases student interest in STEM careers (Karahan, Canbazoglu Bilici, & Unal, 2015; Ryu et al., 2018; Shahali et al., 2017; Swafford, 2018).

STEM Disciplines Are Connected by Ideas and Skills

One main reason for integrating the STEM disciplines is that they share many big ideas, conceptual structures, and practices that, when integrated, allow students to apply their knowledge in an array of ways and make connections that allow them to tranfer that knowledge across disciplines (Capraro, Capraro, & Morgan, 2013; Myers, 2015; Nathan et al., 2013; Ryan, Gale, & Usselman, 2017). For example, science, technology, engineering, and mathematics share "specialized vocabulary and representational systems . . . digital media . . . raw materials . . . and designed objects, tools, and measurement instruments" (Nathan, Wolfram, Srisurichan, Walkington, & Alibali, 2017, p. 272). Chalmers,

Carter, Cooper, and Nason (2017) divide these "Big Ideas" into three major themes: (1) "within-discipline big ideas that have application in other disciplines," such as applying science concepts as the context for learning design; (2) "cross–discipline big ideas (e.g., variables, patterns, models, computational thinking, reasoning and argument, transformations, nature of proof)"; and (3) "encompassing big ideas." This last point includes *conceptual encompassing of big ideas*, for which they gave representations, conservation, systems, coding, relationships, and change as examples, and *content encompassing big ideas* that can be grand challenges, such as "how human activity is perturbing the six nutrient cycles of carbon, oxygen, hydrogen, nitrogen, sulfur, and phosphorus" (p. 32). The big ideas of STEM play a role in many conceptual frameworks of STEM integration. STEM integration allows students to engage in the practices associated with the STEM disciplines in new ways and to use new skills that they would not get experience with if the disciplines were isolated (Brown & Bogiages, 2019; Bybee, 2013). STEM integration fosters students' conceptual understanding and their understanding of applications of STEM to solve complex problems (Karahan et al., 2015; Lou et al., 2011). Even subjects that traditionally fall outside of the four disciplines of STEM share some of these big ideas and can be integrated effectively with STEM (e.g., Bell & Bell, 2018; Carter et al., 2015).

Some authors take this a step further, however, arguing that the STEM disciplines do not just share big ideas but are fundamentally interconnected. Son, Mackenzie, Eitel, and Luvaas (2017), for example, point out that in the real world, the STEM disciplines must work together to solve problems and by doing so they are able to achieve more than if they worked in isolation. Vasquez (2014) argues that the barriers between the disciplines in schools are artificial and that STEM integration has the potential to remove those barriers, and Wang and Knobloch (2018) advocate that integrating STEM disciplines helps students to see the connections between the disciplines. Ryu et al. (2018) refer to STEM integration as a "blending" of the disciplines, and for Slykhuis, Martin-Hansen, Thomas, and Barbato (2015), a lesson is not truly STEM integration unless it "combines all aspects of STEM: science, technology, engineering, and mathematics in a unique way that is dependent upon all of the fields" (p. 255). Similarly, Stohlmann, Moore, McClelland, and Roehrig (2011) discuss STEM integration as more like a new interdisciplinary field unto itself rather than a combination of four distinct disciplines, while Nathan et al. (2013) sum up this view nicely, stating that "STEM integration curriculum reveals a synergy that goes beyond the constituent parts" (p. 82).

The STEM disciplines are also connected by certain professional skills, and scholars point to integrated STEM activities as a way to develop these skills. Solving more realistic, more complex problems requires students to work together; thus integrating STEM is thought to afford opportunities to develop teamwork (Bybee, 2013; Guzey et al., 2016; Hong, Lin, Chen, & Chen, 2018; Johnson et al., 2016; Kloser et al., 2018; Meyrick, 2011; Shaughnessy, 2013; Swafford, 2018; Walker, Moore, Guzey, & Sorge, 2018). Similarly, working in teams encourages the development of communications skills (Asunda & Mativo, 2017; Meyrick, 2011; Moore, Guzey, & Brown, 2014). Additionally, certain content–related ideas recur frequently within different definitions of STEM integration. For many scholars, for an activity to truly be considered STEM integration, the activity must provide students with the opportunity to apply concepts from mathematics and science (Johnson et al., 2016; Meyrick, 2011; Moore, Guzey et al., 2014; Nadelson & Seifert, 2017; Shaughnessy, 2013; Wang & Knobloch, 2018). Similarly, Bybee (2013) and Walker et al. (2018) encourage the use of data and data analysis techniques within STEM integration. Other researchers point to the opportunities in STEM integration to engage in engineering practices and habits of mind (Guzey et al., 2016; Hauze & French, 2017) and systems thinking (Bybee, 2013).

Degrees of Integration

Number of Disciplines. The literature varies in how it defines the number of disciplines that need to be included in the learning experiences to be considered STEM integration. Many define STEM integration as integrating any two of the disciplines (e.g., Barth et al., 2017; Brown & Bogiages, 2019; Capraro & Nite, 2014; Debs & Kelley, 2015; El-Deghaidy et al., 2017; Hong et al., 2018; Kelley & Knowles, 2016; Kloser et al., 2018; Ntemngwa & Oliver, 2018; Thibaut, Knipprath, Dehaene, & Depaepe, 2018b). Most commonly, these two subjects are science and engineering (e.g., Barth et al., 2017; Berland & Steingut, 2016). On the other hand, other researchers argue that true STEM integration does not happen unless all four disciplines are integrated together in ways that require knowledge from all disciplines that are dependent on each other (e.g., Aldemir & Kermani, 2017; Burrows et al., 2018; Chandan, Magana, & Vieira, 2019; McCulloch & Ernst, 2012; Moore & Smith, 2014; Norhaqikah Mohamad & Kamisah, 2017; Ong et al., 2016; Slykhuis et al., 2015). Some reach further to define STEM integration as integrating any two subjects, even if one of those subjects falls outside of science, technology, engineering, or mathematics, such as social science or consumer science (Bell & Bell, 2018; Stubbs & Myers, 2016). These authors make the case that integrating disciplines outside STEM adds to the learning by bringing in even more opportunities for students to make connections to their lives and community (Carter et al., 2015; Meyrick, 2011).

Implementation Strategies. Many authors define STEM integration as combining the disciplines into a single class, unit, or lesson with the focus on learning standards for multiple disciplines (Bell & Bell, 2018; Moore & Smith, 2014; Shahali et al., 2017; Stohlmann et al., 2011; Stohlmann, Moore, & Roehrig, 2012). For example, Bell and Bell (2018) stated that

> integration means that both subjects are being taught at the same time, which not only provides efficiency in the use of class time, but also helps students to avoid seeing subjects in isolation, and can potentially engage students who are more attracted to one of the integrated elements than the other.
>
> *(p. 152)*

However, the conceptual frameworks of STEM integration are not limited to integrating within one classroom. Some describe how STEM integration should involve teachers working across courses to align their teaching to allow students to learn and apply their ideas without strict boundaries between courses (Asunda & Mativo, 2017; Thibaut et al., 2018a). Asunda and Mativo (2017) argue that a successful integrated approach "would require close collaboration among the science, mathematics, engineering, and technology teachers, their commitment to the integrative approach, and administrative support" (p. 15). In addition to the benefits for students, close collaboration between the teachers in different subject areas has the potential to alleviate some of the challenges teachers face to implement STEM integration (Ryu et al., 2018). One case study demonstrated STEM integration units within classrooms where there was co-teaching (teachers of different disciplines in the same classroom), team teaching (teachers of different disciplines planning a unit together and focusing on the disciplinary aspects of the overall project within the disciplinary classrooms), team planning with individual teachers implementing the entire unit within their own classrooms, and individual planning and implementation of the entire unit (Roehrig et al., 2012).

Defining Levels of Integration. These different approaches are not necessarily at odds with each other. Rather than specifying specific prescriptions for what counts as STEM integration, some scholars instead describe different levels or categories that can be used for classifying types of STEM integration. Each of these individual levels describes a different approach to tackling the challenges of STEM integration, and each approach has pros and cons. For example, Moore, Stohlmann, et al. (2014) differentiate between context integration and content integration. In context integration, instruction in one discipline uses a problem from another discipline as the context, but only attempts to achieve learning goals in the primary discipline; content integration does the same while trying also to achieve learning goals in multiple disciplines. In a later publication, Moore and Hughes (2018) add the idea of tool or application integration, which looks a little different from context integration in that the main discipline to be taught is supported by a tool from another discipline (such as learning mathematics with a technological tool like Desmos or using DNA sequencing techniques to learn about genetic engineering).

In many of these categorizations, authors describe a continuum of STEM integration that goes from little to no integration on one end to fully integrated, authentic project- or problem-based learning on the other. For example, Saito, Anwari, Mutakinati, and Kumano (2016) describe three methods of integration, "within single disciplines, across several disciplines, and within learners and across networks of learners" (p. 52), where the third level allows learners to make the most meaningful connections across the different STEM disciplines and their lives. Burrows and Slater (2015) describe five levels (Levels 0 to 4) of STEM integration. At Level 3, students engage in engineering projects, and Level 4 is full STEM integration. Nadelson and Seifert (2013, 2017) define a "STEM Continuum" that goes from traditional instruction in separated disciplines to "fully integrated" STEM instruction categorized by "complex, ill-structured problems found in business and industry" (2013, p. 245). Wang and Knobloch (2018) describe levels of STEM integration as *disciplinary*, *multidisciplinary*, *interdisciplinary*, and *transdisciplinary*. The disciplinary level is not considered STEM integration, while at the highest, transdisciplinary level, students make deep connections between the disciplines, real-world STEM careers and problems, and their communities. Wang, Moore, Roehrig, and Park (2011) also discuss the differences between multidisciplinary and interdisciplinary, comparing them to chicken noodle soup, where ingredients retain their separate identities, and tomato soup, where all ingredients are blended smoothly together. Rennie, Wallace, and Venville (2012) acknowledge these ways of creating levels on a continuum but caution that these levels imply a hierarchy. Instead they describe six approaches to integration without attempting to judge the relative merits of each approach: synchronized approach (identifying big ideas in more than one discipline and showing parallels), thematic (organized around a particular topic), project-based (based on an engineering design project), cross-curricular (a topic is talked about in more than one subject), school specialized, and community focused. Although these ways of defining levels of STEM integration are not new, they have become more refined. For example, in the early 1990s, Fogarty (1991) had proposed 10 ways of integrating separate disciplines: *Fragmented, Connected, Nested, Sequenced, Shared, Webbed, Threaded, Integrated, Immersed*, and *Networked*. In more recent years, frameworks for STEM integration continue to reflect a diversity in ways of approaching integration, but systems that describe a continuum, or degrees of integration, are much more common.

Structures for Integrating the Disciplines

Role of Individual Disciplines. Although science, technology, engineering, and mathematics share many connections that support their integration, they are varied and diverse fields that each play a role in how they are integrated in classrooms. The ways in which they can each be used play an important role in the conceptual frameworks of STEM integration. Most often, especially with the conceptual frameworks that define STEM integration as including all four disciplines, STEM integration is achieved by framing a STEM integration unit or lesson around an engineering design challenge that necessitates the application of science and mathematics concepts to create a technology, treating engineering as the glue that holds the STEM disciplines together (e.g., Bartholomew, 2017; Berland, 2013; Berland et al., 2014; Blackley et al., 2018; Cavlazoglu & Stuessy, 2017; Dare et al., 2018; English, King, & Smeed, 2017; Felix & Harris, 2010; Guzey et al., 2016; Hudson, English, Dawes, King, & Baker, 2015; Johnson et al., 2016; McCulloch & Ernst, 2012; Moore & Smith, 2014; Nathan et al., 2013; Roehrig et al., 2012; Shaughnessy, 2013; Thibaut et al., 2018b; Walker et al., 2018; Walkington, Nathan, Wolfgram, Alibali, & Srisurichan, 2014; Wang & Knobloch, 2018). For example, Berland (2013) developed a unit called Pinholes to Pixels in which students applied their learning of mathematical modeling, scientific principles, and mechanical and chemical engineering to design a solution to capturing images. Guzey et al. (2016) analyzed teacher-developed units, such as "Chill Out," which applied heat transfer concepts to solve the problem of transporting vaccines. In these units, each of the mathematics and science activities was connected to the design project from "day one" of the unit, and the mathematics and scientific concepts that the students had learned through the unit were necessary for the development of the solution. Not only does this approach allow students to experience all four STEM disciplines, it has also been shown to increase students' science learning and improve their motivation (Berland & Steingut, 2016). Additionally, this approach allows students to apply their knowledge in more real-life contexts and in more complex problems that may further their understanding of each individual discipline and help them transfer skills and knowledge across disciplines (Hudson et al., 2015). Engineering design challenges also offer students a chance to learn from failure, an important skill not often supported in other disciplines (Guzey et al., 2016; Johnson et al., 2016; Moore & Smith, 2014; Walker et al., 2018). Integrating engineering into science classes also meets the requirements of many standards documents that call science teachers to integrate engineering into their courses (Capobianco & Rupp, 2014). This approach requires teachers to have at least a basic knowledge of each of the STEM disciplines and understand how they work together. In order for this approach to STEM integration to be most successful, each discipline must be given equal importance and be needed for the completion of the project or problem (Baker & Galanti, 2017; Berland, 2013; Shaughnessy, 2013).

Other conceptual frameworks explain the role of each individual discipline by describing the methods or procedures from that discipline that should be applied by students as they engage in STEM integration activities (e.g., Johnson, 2013; Lou, Liang, & Chung, 2017; Meyrick, 2011), including scientific inquiry, mathematical analysis, problem solving, discovery, and engineering design and emphasizing the importance of each of these practices to their respective disciplines. Some of these examples identify that the practices of each discipline should be treated with equal importance, rather than raising the importance, for example, of scientific inquiry above that of engineering design or vice versa (Ames, Reeve, Stewardson, & Lott, 2017).

Some of the conceptual frameworks argue that STEM integration should not treat STEM as four discrete disciplines with separate learning goals, because "expertise is built iteratively across all subjects" and for future job success, students need to be able to understand "interaction of knowledge from within each and also across STEM disciplines" (Capraro & Slough, 2013, p. 2). These authors take the position that STEM integration does not always need to focus equally on each of the disciplines, but that STEM integration learning environments should require students to use critical thinking and problem-solving skills to work across the disciplines (Akgun, 2013; Nadelson & Seifert, 2017; Thananuwong, 2015; Vasquez, 2014). However, these approaches are not universally agreed upon. For example, Chien (2017) makes the claim that "STEM knowledge should first be explored separately" (p. 2942) and then integrated together to integrate the knowledge and build competency.

In addition to the four STEM disciplines, other subjects, including language arts, social studies, consumer science, and visual and fine arts have roles to play in STEM integration as a way to contextualize problems and make further connections for students of the interconnectedness of their learning experiences (Carter et al., 2015; Johnson, 2013; Johnson et al., 2016; Meyrick, 2011; Pryor, Pryor, & Kang, 2016; Sanders, 2008; Satchwell & Loepp, 2002). Additionally, the inclusion of agriculture education is sometimes included as a science discipline and sometimes as its own entity, although advocating for the importance of integrating agriculture education with STEM is common, both to provide engaging contexts to learn other STEM subjects as well as to improve agricultural education itself (e.g., Ryu et al., 2018; Stubbs & Myers, 2015; Swafford, 2018; Wang & Knobloch, 2018). The integration of the arts with science, technology, engineering, and mathematics is often described with the acronym STEAM and provides further opportunities to encourage creativity, communication, and teamwork (Bell & Bell, 2018; Tillman, An, & Boren, 2015). Similarly, literacy and reading can also be integrated with STEM. An example of this is the PictureSTEM curriculum (www. picturestem.org), which uses picture books to help K–2 students learn engineering, mathematics, science, and computational thinking, as well as reinforcing reading skills (Tank et al., 2018).

Specific Pedagogies. The ways in which STEM integration is taught plays a significant role in the conceptual frameworks of STEM integration in much of the literature. The literature calls for "teachers [to] act as facilitators" (El-Deghaidy et al., 2017, p. 2462) and go "beyond traditional lecture and laboratory instruction, by incorporating rich integrated STEM learning opportunities" (Hauze & French, 2017, p. 484) to more authentically "expose students to meaningful learning experiences that enrich their deep content understanding in the STEM disciplines and then establish connections to everyday life experiences" (El-Deghaidy et al., 2017, p. 2462). Myers (2015) goes so far as to say that effective STEM integration requires a "shift in the philosophical framework for teaching and learning" (p. xv). Some of the literature specifically explains that these ideas are based on social constructivism and the work of Dewey (Corlu & Aydin, 2016; Moore & Smith, 2014; Thibaut et al., 2018a).

In the literature, the pedagogies for teaching STEM integration that are foundational for the conceptual frameworks often include active learning, student-centered pedagogies (e.g., Aldemir & Kermani, 2017; Guzey et al., 2016; Johnson et al., 2016; Ring, Dare, Crotty, & Roehrig, 2017; Saito et al., 2015) that are focused on problem- or project-based learning (e.g., Asunda & Mativo, 2017; Baker & Galanti, 2017; Berland & Steingut, 2016; Norhaqikah Mohamad & Kamisah, 2017; Wang & Knobloch, 2018). The uses of problem- and project-based learning are not consistent, with some literature using problem-based learning and project-based learning almost synonymously (Guzey et al., 2016; Nadelson & Seifert, 2017; Tseng, Chang, Lou, & Chen, 2013) and others distinguishing project-based learning as different from problem-based learning (e.g., Capraro et al., 2013). Additionally, some of the literature further describes that STEM integration should be design-oriented (e.g., Hong et al., 2018; Sandall, Sandall, & Walton, 2018) and focus on ill-defined problems (Kloser et al., 2018; Nadelson & Seifert, 2017). In order for these learning experiences to most effectively integrate STEM disciplines, the content knowledge from each discipline must be necessary for the project or problem at hand (Nadelson & Seifert, 2013, 2017; Ntemngwa & Oliver, 2018). Some of the literature described that these activities should be hands-on, allowing students to create physical prototypes and physically explore scientific phenomena (Berland & Steingut, 2016; Capraro et al., 2013; Carter et al., 2015; Chien, 2017; Stubbs & Myers, 2015). Additionally, much of the literature emphasizes the necessity of classroom environments that have students work collaboratively in teams (Hong et al., 2018; Kloser et al., 2018; Meyrick, 2011). Some of the literature also identifies that teachers need to go beyond their classrooms to reach the community, using pedagogical strategies such as bringing STEM professionals into the classroom (Myers, 2015).

Often, each definition of STEM integration includes multiple aspects of these pedagogies that must be utilized in conjunction with each other to authentically teach STEM integration. For example, Thibaut et al. (2018a) define five key features that STEM integration should have, namely, integration of the content, "problem-centered learning," "inquiry-based learning," "design-based learning," and "cooperative learning" (p. 633). Shaughnessy (2013) identifies "three necessary ingredients for any STEM activity: . . . it must have a problem to solve . . . significant mathematics involved in the problem . . . [and] require teamwork that draws on knowledge and approaches from several disciplines" (p. 324).

Conclusion

One of the challenges of making progress in STEM education is that a single, consensus definition of STEM integration does not yet exist. Thus, claims made about the benefits of or challenges to STEM integration are highly dependent on the specifics of the definition being used by the person making the claim. That being said, this review shows that although there is still much variation in how scholars conceptualize and define STEM integration, most definitions do share many commonalities. Regardless of their definitions, a majority of the papers we reviewed emphasized the need for complex, authentic, or real-world problems within STEM integration; thus it seems that grounding STEM integration in rich, realistic problems is a foundational, crosscutting idea. Additionally, the frequency with which authors referred to the shared practices, skills, and concepts across disciplines as a motivation for integrating those disciplines implies that the similarities and connections between the disciplines are also an important unifying idea across the literature. There also seems to be a similar consensus around the most effective pedagogies for supporting STEM learning through STEM integration. Although authors formulate the specifics in different ways, conceptualizations of STEM integration very frequently encourage or even require student-centered teaching strategies and classroom structures, and collaboration and teamwork appear to be essential ingredients in STEM integration as well.

The literature is less clear about the degree to which disciplines are integrated or how specifically that integration should be structured within schools or classrooms. While some authors consider putting problems in one discipline in the context of one other discipline as sufficient to be called STEM integration, others require a much deeper level of integration, while still others describe a range in between. This variation will inevitably persist; however, moving toward a consistent and agreed-upon language and vision for this variation will help facilitate forward progress in research and practice. Continuums, such as those described by English (2016) or Nadelson and Seifert (2013) or the framework described by Moore and colleagues (Moore & Hughes, 2018; Moore, Stohlmann, et al., 2014), are important steps in this direction to better define consistent language and ways of thinking about different types of STEM integration.

References

Akgun, O. E. (2013). Technology in STEM project-based learning. In R. M. Capraro, M. M. Capraro, & J. R. Morgan (Eds.), *STEM project-based learning: An integrated science, technology, engineering, and mathematics (STEM) approach* (2nd ed., pp. 65–76). Rotterdam, The Netherlands: Sense Publishers.

Aldemir, J., & Kermani, H. (2017). Integrated STEM curriculum: Improving educational outcomes for head start children. *Early Child Development & Care, 187*(11), 1694–1706. http://doi.org/10.1080/03004430.2016.1185102

Ames, T. R., Reeve, E., Stewardson, G., & Lott, K. (2017). Wanted for 21st century schools: Renaissance STEM teacher preferred. *Journal of Technology Education, 28*(2), 19–30. http://doi.org/10.21061/jte.v28i2.a.2

Asunda, P. A., & Mativo, J. (2017). Integrated STEM: A new primer for teaching technology education. *Technology & Engineering Teacher, 76*(5), 14–19.

Baker, C., & Galanti, T. (2017). Integrating STEM in elementary classrooms using model-eliciting activities: Responsive professional development for mathematics coaches and teachers. *International Journal of STEM Education, 4*(1), 1–15. http://doi.org/10.1186/s40594-017-0066-3

Barth, K., Bahr, D., & Shumway, S. (2017). Generating clean water. *Science and Children, 55*(4), 32–37. http://doi.org/10.2505/4/sc17_055_04_32

Bartholomew, S. R. (2017). Integrated STEM through tumblewing gliders. *K-12 STEM Education, 3*(1), 157–166. http://doi.org/10.14456/k12stemed.2017.2

Bell, J., & Bell, T. (2018). Integrating computational thinking with a music education context. *Informatics in Education, 17*(2), 151–166. http://doi.org/10.15388/infedu.2018.09

Berland, L. K. (2013). Designing for STEM integration. *Journal of Pre-College Engineering Education Research, 3*(1), 22–31. http://doi.org/10.7771/2157-9288.1078

Berland, L. K., & Steingut, R. (2016). Explaining variation in student efforts towards using math and science knowledge in engineering contexts. *International Journal of Science Education, 38*(18), 2742–2761. http://doi.org/10.1080/09500693.2016.1260179

Berland, L. K., Steingut, R., & Ko, P. (2014). High school student perceptions of the utility of the engineering design process: Creating opportunities to engage in engineering practices and apply math and science content. *Journal of Science Education & Technology, 23*(6), 705–720. http://doi.org/10.1007/s10956-014-9498-4

Blackley, S., Rahmawati, Y., Fitriani, E., Sheffield, R., & Koul, R. (2018). Using a makerspace approach to engage Indonesian primary students with STEM. *Issues in Educational Research, 28*(1), 18–42. http://doi.org/10.1016/j.tate.2013.04.001.

Breiner, J. M., Harkness, S. S., Johnson, C. C., & Koehler, C. M. (2012). What is STEM? A discussion about conceptions of STEM in education and partnerships. *School Science and Mathematics, 112*(1), 3–11. https://doi.org/10.1111/j.1949-8594.2011.00109.x

Brown, R. E., & Bogiages, C. A. (2019). Professional development through STEM integration: How early career math and science teachers respond to experiencing integrated STEM tasks. *International Journal of Science and Mathematics Education, 17*(1), 1–18. http://doi.org/10.1007/s10763-017-9863-x

Burrows, A., Lockwood, M., Borowczak, M., Janak, E., & Barber, B. (2018). Integrated STEM: Focus on informal education and community collaboration through engineering. *Education Sciences, 8*(4). http://doi.org/10.3390/educsci8010004

Burrows, A., & Slater, T. F. (2015). A proposed integrated STEM framework for contemporary teacher preparation. *Teacher Education & Practice, 28*(2/3), 318–330.

Bybee, R. W. (2013). *The case for STEM education: Challenges and opportunities.* Arlington, VA: National Science Teachers Association.

Capobianco, B. M., & Rupp, M. (2014). STEM teachers' planned and enacted attempts at implementing engineering design-based instruction. *School Science & Mathematics, 114*(6), 258–270. http://doi.org/10.1111/ssm.12078

Capraro, M. M., & Nite, S. B. (2014). STEM integration in mathematics standards. *Middle Grades Research Journal, 9*(3), 1–10.

Capraro, R. M., Capraro, M. M., & Morgan, J. R. (Eds.). (2013). *STEM project-based learning: An integrated science, technology, engineering, and mathematics (STEM) approach.* Rotterdam, The Netherlands: Sense Publishers.

Capraro, R. M., & Slough, S. W. (2013). Why PBL? Why STEM? Why now? An introduction to STEM project-based learning: An integrated science, technology, engineering, and mathematics approach. In R. M. Capraro, M. M. Capraro, & J. R. Morgan (Eds.), *STEM project-based learning: An integrated science, technology, engineering, and mathematics (STEM) approach* (2nd ed., pp. 1–6). Rotterdam, The Netherlands: Sense Publishers.

Carter, V., Beachner, M., & Daugherty, M. K. (2015). Family and consumer sciences and STEM integration. *Journal of Family & Consumer Sciences, 107*(1), 55–58.

Cavlazoglu, B., & Stuessy, C. L. (2017). Identifying and verifying earthquake engineering concepts to create a knowledge base in STEM education: A modified Delphi study. *International Journal of Education in Mathematics, Science and Technology, 5*(1), 40–52. http://doi.org/10.18404/ijemst.60674

Chalmers, C., Carter, M., Cooper, T., & Nason, R. (2017). Implementing "big ideas" to advance the teaching and learning of science, technology, engineering, and mathematics (STEM). *International Journal of Science & Mathematics Education, 15*(Suppl 1), 25–43. http://doi.org/10.1007/s10763-017-9799-1

Chandan, D., Magana, A. J., & Vieira, C. (2019). Investigating the affordances of a CAD enabled learning environment for promoting integrated STEM learning. *Computers & Education, 129*, 122–142. http://doi.org/10.1016/j.compedu.2018.10.014

Chien, Y.-H. (2017). Developing a pre-engineering curriculum for 3D printing skills for high school technology education. *EURASIA Journal of Mathematics, Science & Technology Education, 13*(7), 2941–2958. http://doi.org/10.12973/eurasia.2017.00729a

Corlu, M. A., & Aydin, E. (2016). Evaluation of learning gains through integrated STEM projects. *International Journal of Education in Mathematics, Science and Technology, 4*(1), 20–29. http://doi.org/10.18404/ijemst.35021

Council for Science and Technology (Producer). (2013). *Science, technology, engineering and mathematics education: Update.* Retrieved from https://assets.publishing.service.gov.uk/government/uploads/system/uploads/attachment_data/file/230509/13-1131-stem-education.pdf

Dare, E., Ellis, J., & Roehrig, G. (2018). Understanding science teachers' implementations of integrated STEM curricular units through a phenomenological multiple case study. *International Journal of STEM Education, 5*(4), 1–19. http://doi.org/10.1186/s40594-018-0101-z

Debs, L., & Kelley, T. (2015). Gathering design references from nature. *Technology and Engineering Teacher, 75*(1), 10–14.

El-Deghaidy, H. (2017). STEAM methods: A case from Egypt. In A. Sickel & S. Witzig (Eds.), *Designing and teaching the secondary science methods course: An international perspective.* Amsterdam, The Netherlands: Sense Publishers.

El-Deghaidy, H., Mansour, N., Alzaghibi, M., & Alhammad, K. (2017). Context of STEM integration in schools: Views from in-service science teachers. *EURASIA Journal of Mathematics, Science & Technology Education, 13*(6), 2459–2484. http://doi.org/10.12973/eurasia.2017.01235a

English, L. D. (2016). STEM education K-12: Perspectives on integration. *International Journal of STEM Education, 3*(1), 3. http://doi.org/10.1186/s40594-016-0036-1

English, L. D., King, D., & Smeed, J. (2017). Advancing integrated STEM learning through engineering design: Sixth-grade students' design and construction of earthquake resistant buildings. *The Journal of Educational Research, 110*(3), 255–271. https://doi.org/10.1080/00220671.2016.1264053

Felix, A., & Harris, J. (2010). A project-based, STEM-integrated alternative energy team challenge for teachers. *Technology Teacher, 69*(5), 29–34.

Fogarty, R. (1991). Ten ways to integrate curriculum. *Educational Leadership, 49*(2), 61–65.

Guzey, S. S., Moore, T. J., & Harwell, M. (2016). Building up STEM: An analysis of teacher-developed engineering design-based STEM integration curricular materials. *Journal of Pre-College Engineering Education Research (J-PEER), 6*(1), 11–29. https://doi.org/10.7771/2157-9288.1129

Hauze, S., & French, D. (2017). Technology-supported science instruction through integrated STEM guitar building: The case for STEM and non-STEM instructor success. *Contemporary Issues in Technology & Teacher Education, 17*(4), 483–503.

Hong, H.-Y., Lin, P.-Y., Chen, B., & Chen, N. (2018). Integrated STEM learning in an idea-centered knowledge-building environment. *The Asia - Pacific Education Researcher,* 1–14. https://doi.org/10.1007/s40299-018-0409-y

Hudson, P., English, L., Dawes, L., King, D., & Baker, S. (2015). Exploring links between pedagogical knowledge practices and student outcomes in STEM education for primary schools. *Australian Journal of Teacher Education, 40*(6). http://doi.org/10.14221/ajte.2015v40n6.8

Johnson, C. C. (2011). The road to culturally relevant science: Exploring how teachers navigate change in pedagogy. *Journal of Research in Science Teaching, 48(2),* 170–198.

Johnson, C. C. (2013). Conceptualizing integrated STEM education. *School Science & Mathematics, 113*(8), 367–368. https://doi.org/10.1111/ssm.12043

Johnson, C. C., Peters-Burton, E. E., & Moore, T. J. (2016). *STEM road map: A framework for integrated STEM education.* New York, NY: Routledge.

Karahan, E., Canbazoglu Bilici, S., & Unal, A. (2015). Integration of media design processes in science, technology, engineering, and mathematics (STEM) education. *Eurasian Journal of Educational Research,* (60), 221–240. http://doi.org/10.14689/ejer.2015.60.15

Kelley, T. R., & Knowles, J. G. (2016). A conceptual framework for integrated STEM education. *International Journal of STEM Education, 3*(11), 1–11. http://doi.org/10.1186/s40594-016-0046-z

Kloser, M., Wilsey, M., Twohy, K. E., Immonen, A. D., & Navotas, A. C. (2018). "We do STEM": Unsettled conceptions of STEM education in middle school S.T.E.M. classrooms. *School Science & Mathematics, 118*(8), 335–347. https://doi.org/10.1111/ssm.12304

Lou, S.-J., Liang, C.-P., & Chung, C.-C. (2017). Effectiveness of combining STEM activities and PBL: A case study of the design of fuel-efficient vehicles. *International Journal of Engineering Education, 33*(6A), 1763–1775.

Lou, S.-J., Shih, R.-C., Diez, C. R., & Tseng, K.-H. (2011). The impact of problem-based learning strategies on STEM knowledge integration and attitudes: An exploratory study among female Taiwanese senior high school students. *International Journal of Technology & Design Education, 21,* 195–215. http://doi.org/10.1007/s10798-010-9114-8

Lupinacci, J., & Happel-Parkins, A. (2017). Ecocritcally (re)considering STEM: Integrated ecological inquiry in teacher education. *Issues in Teacher Education, 26*(3), 52–64.

McCulloch, A. W., & Ernst, J. V. (2012). Estuarine ecosystems: Using T & E signature approaches to support STEM integration. *Technology & Engineering Teacher, 72*(3), 13–17.

Meyrick, K. M. (2011). How STEM education improves student learning. Meridian K-12 School. *Computer Technologies Journal, 14*(1), 1–6.

Moore, T. J., Guzey, S. S., & Brown, A. (2014). Greenhouse design to increase habitable land: An engineering unit. *Science Scope, 37*(7), 51–57. https://doi.org/10.2505/4/ss14_037_07_51

Moore, T. J., & Hughes, J. E. (2018). Chapter 12: Teaching and learning with technology in science, engineering, and mathematics. In M. D. Roblyer & J. E. Hughes (Eds.), *Integrating educational technology into teaching* (8th ed.). New York, NY: Pearson.

Moore, T. J., & Smith, K. A. (2014). Advancing the state of the art of STEM integration. *Journal of STEM Education: Innovations & Research, 15*(1), 5–10.

Moore, T. J., Stohlmann, M. S., Wang, H.-H., Tank, K. M., Glancy, A. W., & Roehrig, G. H. (2014). Implementation and integration of engineering in K-12 STEM education. In Ş. Purzer, J. Strobel, & M. Cardella (Eds.), *Engineering in precollege settings: Research into practice* (pp. 35–60). West Lafayette, IN: Purdue University Press.

Myers, A. (2015). *The STEM shift: A guide for school leaders.* Thousand Oaks, CA: Corwin.

Nadelson, L. S., & Seifert, A. L. (2013). Perceptions, engagement, and practices of teachers seeking professional development in place-based integrated STEM. *Teacher Education and Practice, 26*(2), 242–265.

Nadelson, L. S., & Seifert, A. L. (2017). Integrated STEM defined: Contexts, challenges, and the future. *The Journal of Educational Research, 110*(3), 221–223. https://doi.org/10.1080/00220671.2017.1289775

Nathan, M. J., Srisurichan, R., Walkington, C., Wolfgram, M., Williams, C., & Alibali, M. W. (2013). Building cohesion across representations: A mechanism for STEM integration. *Journal of Engineering Education, 102*(1), 77–116. http://doi.org/10.1002/jee.20000

Nathan, M. J., Wolfgram, M., Srisurichan, R., Walkington, C., & Alibali, M. W. (2017). Threading mathematics through symbols, sketches, software, silicon, and wood: Teachers produce and maintain cohesion to support STEM integration. *The Journal of Educational Research, 110*(3), 272–293. https://doi.org/10.1080/00220671.2017.1287046

National Academy of Engineering and National Research Council. (2014). *STEM integration in K-12 education: Status, prospects, and an agenda for research*. Washington, DC: The National Academies Press.

Norhaqikah Mohamad, K., & Kamisah, O. (2017). STEM-21CS module: Fostering 21st century skills through integrated STEM. *K-12 STEM Education, 3*(3), 225–233. http://doi.org/10.14456/k12stemed.2017.8

Ntemngwa, C., & Oliver, J. S. (2018). The implementation of integrated science technology, engineering and mathematics (STEM) instruction using robotics in the middle school science classroom. *International Journal of Education in Mathematics, Science and Technology, 6*(1), 12–40. http://doi.org/10.18404/ijemst.380617

Office of the Chief Scientist (Producer). (2015). *Transforming STEM teaching in Australian primary schools: Everybody's business*. Retrieved from https://www.chiefscientist.gov.au/wp-content/uploads/Transforming-STEM-teaching_FINAL.pdf

Ong, E. T., Ayob, A., Ibrahim, M. N., Adnan, M., Shariff, J., & Ishak, N. (2016). The effectiveness of an in-service training of early childhood teachers on STEM integration through project-based inquiry learning (PIL). *Journal of Turkish Science Education, 13*(Special Issue), 44–58. http://doi.org/10.12973/tused.10170a

Pryor, B. W., Pryor, C. R., & Kang, R. (2016). Teachers' thoughts on integrating STEM into social studies instruction: Beliefs, attitudes, and behavioral decisions. *Journal of Social Studies Research, 40*(2), 123–136. http://doi.org/10.1016/j.jssr.2015.06.005

Radloff, J. D. (2015). Give the students science: Creation and implementation of a fourth grade STEM unit. *Purdue Journal of Service-Learning and International Engagement, 2*(1). http://doi.org/10.5703/1288284315695

Rennie, L., Wallace, J., & Venville, G. (2012). Exploring curriculum integration: Why integrate? In L. Rennie, G. Venville, & J. Wallace (Eds.), *Integrating science, technology, engineering, and mathematics* (pp. 1–11). New York, NY: Routledge.

Ring, E. A., Dare, E. A., Crotty, E. A., & Roehrig, G. H. (2017). The evolution of teacher conceptions of STEM education throughout an intensive professional development experience. *Journal of Science Teacher Education, 28*(5), 444–467. http://doi.org/10.1080/1046560X.2017.1356671

Roehrig, G. H., Moore, T. J., Wang, H.-H., & Park, M. S. (2012). Is adding the E enough? Investigating the impact of K-12 engineering standards on the implementation of STEM integration. *School Science and Mathematics, 112*(1), 31–44. http://doi.org/10.1111/j.1949-8594.2011.00112.x

Ryan, M., Gale, J., & Usselman, M. (2017). Integrating engineering into core science instruction: Translating NGSS principles into practice through iterative curriculum design. *International Journal of Engineering Education, 33*(1B), 321–331.

Ryu, M., Mentzer, N., & Knobloch, N. (2018). Preservice teachers' experiences of STEM integration: Challenges and implications for integrated STEM teacher preparation. *International Journal of Technology and Design Education*, 1–20. http://doi.org/10.1007/s10798-018-9440-9

Saito, T., Anwari, I., Mutakinati, L., & Kumano, Y. (2016). A look at relationships (part I): Supporting theories of STEM integrated learning environment in a classroom – A historical approach. *K-12 STEM Education, 2*(2), 51–61. http://doi.org/10.14456/k12stemed.2016.2

Saito, T., Gunji, Y., & Kumano, Y. (2015). The problem about technology in STEM education: Some findings from action research on the professional development & integrated STEM lessons in informal fields. *K-12 STEM Education, 1*(2), 85–100. http://doi.org/10.14456/k12stemed.2015.16

Saldaña, J. (2016). *The coding manual for qualitative researchers* (3rd ed.). Los Angeles, CA: Sage.

Sandall, B. K., Sandall, D., L., & Walton, A. L. J. (2018). Investigating educators' perceptions of STEM integration: A phenomenological study. *Journal of STEM Teacher Education, 53*(1), 27–42. http://doi.org/10.30707/JSTE53.1Sandall

Sanders, M. E. (2008). STEM, STEM education, STEMmania. *The Technology Teacher, 68*(4), 20–26.

Satchwell, R. E., & Loepp, F. L. (2002). Designing and implementing an integrated mathematics, science, and technology curriculum for the middle school. *Journal of Industrial Teacher Education, 39*(3), 41–66.

Schreier, M. (2012). *Qualitative content analysis in practice*. Los Angeles, CA: Sage.

Sengupta, P., & Shanahan, M.-C. (2017). Boundary play and pivots in public computation: New directions in STEM education. *International Journal of Engineering Education, 33*(3), 1124–1134.

Shahali, E. H. M., Halim, L., Rasul, M. S., Osman, K., & Zulkifeli, M. A. (2017). STEM learning through engineering design: Impact on middle secondary students' interest towards STEM. *EURASIA Journal of Mathematics, Science & Technology Education, 13*(5), 1189–1211. http://doi.org/10.12973/eurasia.2017.00667a

Shaughnessy, J. M. (2013). Mathematics in a STEM context. *Mathematics Teaching in the Middle School, 18*(6), 324. http://doi.org/10.5951/mathteacmiddscho.18.6.0324

Sias, C. M., Nadelson, L. S., Juth, S. M., & Seifert, A. L. (2017). The best laid plans: Educational innovation in elementary teacher generated integrated STEM lesson plans. *The Journal of Educational Research, 110*(3), 227–238. https://doi.org/10.1080/00220671.2016.1253539

Slykhuis, D. A., Martin-Hansen, L., Thomas, C. D., & Barbato, S. (2015). Teaching STEM through historical reconstructions: The future lies in the past. *Contemporary Issues in Technology and Teacher Education (CITE Journal), 15*(3), 254–264.

Son, J. S., Mackenzie, S. H., Eitel, K., & Luvaas, E. (2017). Engaging youth in physical activity and STEM subjects through outdoor adventure education. *Journal of Outdoor & Environmental Education, 20*(2), 32–44. http://doi.org/10.1007/BF03401012

Stohlmann, M., Moore, T. J., McClelland, J., & Roehrig, G. H. (2011). Impressions of a middle grades STEM integration program: Educators share lessons learned from the implementation of a middle grades STEM curriculum model. *Middle School Journal, 43*(1), 32–40. http://doi.org/10.1080/00940771.2011.11461791

Stohlmann, M., Moore, T. J., & Roehrig, G. H. (2012). Considerations for teaching integrated STEM education. *Journal of Pre-College Engineering Education Research, 2*(1), 28–34. http://doi.org/10.5703/1288284314653

Stubbs, E. A., & Myers, B. E. (2015). Multiple case study of STEM in school-based agricultural education. *Journal of Agricultural Education, 56*(2), 188–203. http://doi.org/10.5032/jae.2015.02188

Stubbs, E. A., & Myers, B. E. (2016). Part of what we do: Teacher perceptions of STEM integration. *Journal of Agricultural Education, 57*(3), 87–100. http://doi.org/10.5032/jae.2016.03087

Swafford, M. (2018). STEM education at the nexus of the 3-circle model. *Journal of Agricultural Education, 59*(1), 297–315. http://doi.org/10.5032/jae.2018.01297

Tank, K. M., Moore, T. J., Dorie, B. L., Gajdzik, E., Sanger, M. T., Rynearson, A. M., & Mann, E. F. (2018). Engineering in early elementary classrooms through the integration of high-quality literature, design, and STEM+C content. In L. English & T. Moore (Eds.), *Early engineering learning* (pp. 175–201). Singapore: Springer.

Thananuwong, R. (2015). Learning science from toys: A pathway to successful integrated STEM teaching and learning in Thai middle school. *K-12 STEM Education, 1*(2), 75–84. https://doi.org/10.14456/k12stemed.2015.22

Thibaut, L., Knipprath, H., Dehaene, W., & Depaepe, F. (2018a). How school context and personal factors relate to teachers' attitudes toward teaching integrated STEM. *International Journal of Technology & Design Education, 28*(3), 631–651. http://doi.org/10.1007/s10798-017-9416-1

Thibaut, L., Knipprath, H., Dehaene, W., & Depaepe, F. (2018b). The influence of teachers' attitudes and school context on instructional practices in integrated STEM education. *Teaching and Teacher Education, 71*, 190–205. http://doi.org/10.1016/j.tate.2017.12.014

Tillman, D. A., An, S. A., & Boren, R. L. (2015). Assessment of creativity in arts and STEM integrated pedagogy by pre-service elementary teachers. *Journal of Technology & Teacher Education, 23*(3), 301–327.

Torraco, R. J. (2005). Writing integrative literature reviews: Guidelines and examples. *Human Resource Development Review, 4*(3), 356–367. https://doi.org/10.1177/1534484305278283

Tseng, K.-H., Chang, C.-C., Lou, S.-J., & Chen, W.-P. (2013). Attitudes towards science, technology, engineering and mathematics (STEM) in a project-based learning (PjBL) environment. *International Journal of Technology and Design Education, 23*(1), 87–102. http://doi.org/10.1007/s10798-011-9160-x

Uğraş, M., & Genç, Z. (2018). Investigating preschool teacher candidates' STEM teaching intention and the views about STEM education. *Bartın University Journal of Faculty of Education, 7*(2), 724–744. http://doi.org/10.14686/buefad.408150

Vasquez, J. A. (2014). STEM beyond the acronym. *Educational Leadership, 72*(4), 10–15.

Walker, W. S., III, Moore, T. J., Guzey, S. S., & Sorge, B. H. (2018). Frameworks to develop integrated STEM curricula. *K-12 STEM Education, 4*(2), 331–339. http://doi.org/10.14456/k12stemed.2018.5

Walkington, C., Nathan, M. J., Wolfgram, M., Alibali, M. W., & Srisurichan, R. (2014). Bridges and barriers to constructing conceptual cohesion across modalities and temporalities: Challenges of STEM integration in the precollege engineering classroom. In Ş. Purzer, J. Strobel, & M. Cardella (Eds.), *Engineering in precollege settings: Research into practice* (pp. 183–210). West Lafayette, IN: Purdue University Press.

Wang, H.-H., & Knobloch, N. A. (2018). Levels of STEM integration through agriculture, food, and natural resources. *Journal of Agricultural Education, 59*(3), 258–277. https://doi.org/10.5032/jae.2018.03258

Wang, H.-H., Moore, T. J., Roehrig, G. H., & Park, M. S. (2011). STEM integration: Teacher perceptions and practice. *Journal of Pre-College Engineering Education Research (J-PEER), 1*(2), 1–13. https://doi.org/10.5703/1288284314636

Wasserman, N. H., & Rossi, D. (2015). Mathematics and science teachers' use of and confidence in empirical reasoning: Implications for STEM teacher preparation. *School Science and Mathematics, 115*(1), 22–34. https://doi.org/10.1111/ssm.12099

2

STEM EDUCATION THROUGH THE EPISTEMOLOGICAL LENS

Unveiling the Challenge of STEM Transdisciplinarity

Digna Couso and Cristina Simarro

Introduction

There are several reasons why an integrated vision of STEM education has gained relevance in recent years (see Chapter 1, this volume). From claims on equipping students to address real-world problems, to concerns regarding how to prepare them for their future jobs, there is no doubt that integrated STEM education lies at the heart of multiple discussions among the educational community (National Academy of Engineering [NAE] & National Research Council [NRC], 2014). Multidisciplinary, interdisciplinary, transdisciplinary or meta-disciplinary approaches to STEM education are indistinctly presented by STEM education scholars as a way of improving the STEM educational field (An, 2013; Barakos, Lujan, & Strang, 2012; Brown, Brown, Reardon, & Merrill, 2011; Ejiwale, 2013; Henriksen, 2014; Jenlink, 2015; Kennedy & Odell, 2014; Merrill & Daugherty, 2009; Vasquez, 2015), with the transdisciplinary approach as the most acclaimed in the literature.

In this context of global interest and recognition for STEM integrative approaches, however, important challenges to this proposal have also been found. These are mostly related to two factors: the need to deepen students' learning and the need to guarantee a balanced impact regarding the learning of different STEM disciplines (Becker & Park, 2011; English, 2016). According to research, the learning of in-depth STEM knowledge is an obstacle to many integrated STEM curricula (Chalmers, Carter, Cooper, & Nason, 2017). Moreover, research points to teachers' difficulties in tackling such integration in STEM education due to several different reasons. For example, a lack of school administration support (Clark & Ernst, 2007), difficulties in the mutual understanding and collaboration among different STEM teachers (Zubrowski, 2002) and, more importantly, limited interdisciplinary understandings (Ryu, 2019) are challenges and tensions identified in the literature of integrative STEM, particularly in secondary and college education. Regarding the latter, research has highlighted teachers' limited backgrounds in terms of disciplinary practices, the nature of reasoning in disciplines other than their own, as well as relations among STEM disciplines. For example, in their study following a science teacher trying to integrate engineering into his lessons, Guzey and Ring-Whalen (2018) found tensions in reconciling his identity as science teacher with the needs presented by an integrated curriculum. As the authors point out, integrating science and engineering is challenging since it requires science teachers to have a strong understanding of engineering.

In our opinion, the problems outlined in the previous paragraph are related to STEM integration based on the idea of a STEM literacy or competence that goes *easily* beyond each of the scientific, engineering and mathematical literacies and competences. But the perspective of a sort of global competence area (Surr, Loney, Goldston, Rasmussen, & Anderson, 2016), if not well addressed, could result in an amalgam of the different well-researched scientific, engineering, or mathematic literacies that have not yet been developed or tested (Williams, 2011). This is because the conceptualization of STEM as a meta-discipline (Kennedy & Odell, 2014; Morrison & Raymond Bartlett, 2009), which unites the normally separated disciplines to create new knowledge, forces us to establish connections to bridge the gap between disciplines that are closely related but fundamentally different in nature. As such, well-defined STEM integrative approaches (such as those presented in this handbook) are needed.

While we acknowledge that in real-world contexts STEM problems are tackled in an integrative way and that, in fact, STEM disciplines share important commonalities that allow this integrative approach (see Chapter 1), we highlight the fact that STEM disciplinary practices are also epistemologically different, and that there are educational benefits associated with this fact. When proposing rich and high-quality STEM integrative approaches, these commonalities and differences both should be borne in mind, as there is a lot of educational potential in exploring and embracing them. This is why, in this chapter, we advocate including an explicit epistemological perspective in STEM integration, specifically for science and engineering.

Establishing the Need for an Epistemological Perspective in STEM Education

An epistemological lens could guide how we face the challenges of STEM integration. By reflecting on the idiosyncratic epistemic features of the different STEM disciplines, some of the problems that STEM education research has identified in relation to STEM integration (such as restricted in-depth knowledge, the unbalanced presence of STEM disciplines or the limited interdisciplinary understanding of teachers) could be more easily problematized, detected and better equipped for a quality integrative STEM education.

An even more important argument for including an epistemological lens in STEM education is that epistemic knowledge and competence are in fact learning objectives of STEM education. The inclusion of epistemic knowledge and competence has been agreed internationally in the new PISA framework (OECD's Program for International Student Assessment), and it has been explicitly introduced in most curricula internationally, including the Next Generation Science Standards (NGSS) in the United States. As such, nowadays there is global recognition that a disciplinary competence refers not only to the conceptual knowledge and body of practices of that discipline, but also to the epistemic objectives and values underpinning those practices (Duschl & Grandy, 2012; Osborne, 2014). In other words, one cannot be considered competent in science or engineering if she or he does not know what science or engineering is about. Hence, a good STEM education curriculum that encompasses students' entire education should ensure students' competence in each of the STEM fields, which includes having a mastery of the core ideas and prototypical practices of these fields (National Research Council, 2012), as well as having the (often neglected) epistemic competence in it. This entails an epistemological approach that allows clarification of the particularities of each of the STEM disciplines in terms of their nature and value system and realizes the similarities as well as the differences among them. Such a clarification is useful for designers, adapters, implementers and reviewers of STEM education approaches in terms of ensuring the provision of a full STEM curriculum where integration of knowledge and practices of different STEM disciplines benefits from epistemological reflection.

An Epistemological Lens for STEM Education: A Model Inspired by the Family Resemblance Approach

Epistemology, or the nature of the scientific disciplines in broad terms, encapsulates the range of practices, methodologies, aims and values, knowledge and social norms that characterize the disciplines, and which have to be acknowledged when teaching those disciplines (Erduran & Dagher, 2014). Epistemology is largely discussed in the literature on the nature of science (NOS) and to a lesser extent on the nature of engineering/technology (NOE/T). The idea behind including epistemology as a learning objective of STEM education is that students should be able to grasp the ways of thinking and valuing, as well as the social contexts in which science, engineering or mathematics are developed and used.

In this regard, we find it interesting to epistemologically compare the constituent STEM disciplines. In particular, we focus on science and engineering, which are often considered together and share crosscutting concepts (NRC, 2012) but also have significant differences in domains of knowledge. For years, authors have argued different positions regarding the integration of science and engineering. From the contested "engineering as an applied science", to that of engineering and science sharing certain characteristics (such as methods) but differing strongly in others (such as aims [Sinclair, 1993]), epistemic underpinnings of science and engineering have largely been discussed in terms of the philosophy and epistemology of both disciplines. Interestingly, these arguments have not been fully taken into account when proposing integrative approaches to STEM education.

In order to account for these arguments, we present a model inspired by the well-known framework of the Family Resemblance Approach (FRA) to NOS (Erduran & Dagher, 2014) as a basis for highlighting the epistemic similarities and differences between science and engineering. FRA presents the possibility of considering STEM as a cognitive, epistemic, and social-institutional system whereby each constituent discipline is contrasted relative to aims, values, practices, norms, knowledge, methods, and social context. Erduran and Dagher (2014) represented the system visually and captured the various categories in a holistic and interactive manner. Their framework allows comparing and contrasting of the constituent disciplines of STEM as members of a "family" that share particular features, but it also highlights domain-specificity where particular knowledge and practices are specific to the respective discipline. For example, even though all sciences rely on evidence, the precise nature of this evidence can be very different between different sciences. Astronomy, for instance, relies on historical data collected from stars that are light years away. Chemistry, on the other hand, can involve the direct manipulation of data to generate evidence in the laboratory.

We extend this discussion to the contrast of science and engineering (see the next section, "Epistemic Features of Science and Engineering"). Since a broad range of new scientific disciplines have emerged, some of a dual science and engineering nature, the discussion will focus on epistemic differences that can be found when pursuing scientific or engineering aims. This is despite the fact that this could be done within "purely" scientific or engineering activities, but also from mixed disciplines such as nanotechnology or bioengineering. In addition, some of the aspects discussed in the FRA are truly controversial and polysemic (for instance, there is not an agreed definition regarding which are engineering practices, with some proposals referring to certain "habits of mind" [Lucas, Hanson, & Claxton, 2014], and others to particular engineering processes). For the sake of comparison, we will refer to each of these aspects (values, practices, etc.) at the abstract level necessary to illustrate epistemic contrast among disciplinary fields, rather than make a concrete or final definition of each of them.

Epistemic Features of Science and Engineering

The model inspired by FRA to NOS of Erduran and Dagher (2014) that we propose to use for the purpose of epistemic characterization of science and engineering in STEM education is shown in Figure 2.1.

In this model, the aim of science and engineering is at the core of the figure, as the crucial differential characteristic of both disciplines in which all the other epistemic aspects rely on. In the inner circle, closely connected to the aim of each discipline, we found four core characteristics: the

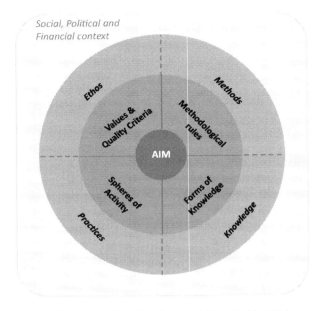

Figure 2.1 Epistemic features of science and engineering: model inspired by FRA.

spheres or core forms of activity that characterize the activity that takes place in each discipline; the core forms of knowledge that are both the basis of and the result of this activity; the core methodological rules that apply to the activity that takes place and the way different forms of knowledge are used and/or produced; and finally, the core values and quality criteria that are used to ethically value and judge the activity taking place, the way of doing it (methodological rules) and the forms of knowledge being used and/or produced. All of the four core characteristics mentioned influence each other in profound ways. Finally, in an outer circle that is more affected by the social, political and financial context than the previous ones, we find the particular practices, knowledge, methods and ethos of each of the disciplines. These are the particular or concrete kinds of practices, sets of knowledge, lists of methods, and professional characteristics (ethos) that scientists or engineers deploy in particular socio-political and historical contexts, such as the ones they use today. These change quickly according to societal interests, technical possibilities or funding available, but they always rely on the deeper, core characteristics that make these practices, knowledge, methods and ethos either scientific or from engineering.

The justification for a model like the one presented in Figure 2.1 is based on epistemological grounds that have been summarized in Table 2.1. At the center of our proposal of using an epistemological lens, the *Aims* of each discipline are highlighted as the main distinctive characteristic of disciplines because we agree with Sinclair (1993) when he states that "*the essential difference between science and engineering lies . . . in the goals of their respective activities*" (p. 360; emphasis added). Several authors argue that science focuses on constructing reliable explanatory frameworks for the natural world in order to develop a set of theoretical descriptions and interpretations. Engineering, on the contrary, has as a primary aim the construction of human-made solutions that are optimal. This means that the engineering objects of knowledge are human-made artifacts, its study in functional terms and its construction (Boon, 2006; Bunge, 2017; Hansson, 2007, 2015; NRC, 2012; Sharp, 1991). Despite the fact that both activities are done with the final aim of serving human needs, the nature of both aims is fundamentally different. Ontologically, for instance, engineering solutions not only are physical but need to be able to produce something real, either as a program, protocol or tool that can be "put to

Table 2.1 Epistemic Features of Science and Engineering

		Science	Engineering
AIM	Main purpose of the discipline	Construct reliable explanations of natural phenomena	Construct of human-made optimal solutions
Spheres of Activity	Main areas of activity or fields of action of the discipline carried out to pursue its aim	Inquiry, argumentation and modeling	Test, argumentation and creation
Forms of Knowledge	Types of products generated by and used for the activities of the discipline to give answer to the discipline's aim	Theories, laws, models, etc.	Technologies, processes, etc.
Values and Quality Criteria	Epistemic objectives of the discipline that ensure its value and quality	Accuracy, objectivity, universality, theoretical consistency, coherence, simplicity, empirical adequacy, validity and reliability	Practical success of a technical solution: applicability, effectiveness and efficiency
Methodological Rules	Main rules that guide the way activities are done and knowledge is generated and used within the discipline	Hypothesis should be testable (theoretically or with real experiments). There has to be convergence of variety of evidences supporting a claim.	Solutions should be testable (no room for idealization). Solutions need to be comparable in terms of applicability, efficiency and efficacy.
Methods	Processes and techniques used within the discipline that comply with its methodological rules	Control of variables, experimental design, statistical analysis, etc.	Control of variables, experimental design, statistical analysis, etc.
Ethos	Norms that guide professionals' work and their interaction with others according to the values and quality criteria of the discipline	Research integrity, ethical concerns regarding human data and applications, environmental awareness, etc.	Professional integrity, ethical concerns regarding user experience and design impact, sustainability of production, etc.
Practices	Cognitive, social and discursive practices carried out within the activity of the discipline	Asking scientific questions, planning and carrying out investigations, constructing explanations, etc. (NRC, 2012)	Defining engineering problems, planning and carrying out tests, designing solutions, etc. (NRC, 2012)
Knowledge	Conceptual products generated by and used for the activity of the discipline	Core scientific ideas, such as the idea of matter made of parts or the evolution of life beings	Core engineering ideas, such as the idea of machines to reduce human effort or gears to transfer movement

practice." In the engineering field, a solution needs to be operational and feasible today. A scientific explanatory framework such as a theory or model, on the other hand, despite its many possible mathematical, argumentative or graphical representations, can only be conceptual. It would never become physical. In addition, it does not have more operational demands than to describe and explain what happens, at a certain level, and predict what could happen under certain conditions. Furthermore, despite the importance of its connection to reality and evidence-based nature (a model or theory has to be in agreement with the data we obtain from the world), this connection can be delayed in time. For instance, some theories are proposed based on thought experiments or mathematical possibilities, with many years between their proposition and the gathering of the required experimental evidence.

Seeking to give answer to these aims, both science and engineering undertake their respective activities with their own characteristics. Different *Spheres of Activity* are identified for science and engineering that follow their respective aims. Scientific activity, for instance, is characterized by three different and interconnected fields of action that involve the socio-discursive and reasoning processes of inquiry, modeling and argumentation (Duschl & Grandy, 2012; Osborne, 2014). Engineering practices take place in the creation (problem scoping and solution generation), the evaluation (assessment and selection) and the realization (making and bringing ideas to life) spaces (Dym, Agogino, Eris, Frey, & Leifer, 2005).

As a result of these core activities, scientific and engineering *Forms of Knowledge* are specific. In science, principles, theories, laws, models and facts are recognized forms of knowledge that work together in generating and validating scientific explanations (Erduran & Dagher, 2014). In engineering, less work has been done in NOE in order to establish the forms of knowledge that are important for this field, but one can find certain curricular references to mechanisms, processes and technologies that could be understood as the way knowledge is encapsulated in engineering, both as a source and product of the engineering activity.

Also related to the core aim of each discipline, *Values and Quality Criteria* are again specific aspects that characterize science and engineering. For instance, the descriptions and interpretations constructed by science intend to be accurate, universal, simple, coherent, mutually consistent and, perhaps the most contested value and quality criterion, based on evidence in an adequate, valid and reliable way. In science, then, explanatory, descriptive and predictive frameworks are successful as far as they are adjusted to these values (even theoretically) regardless of their immediate practical application. In contrast, engineering success is measured by the extent to which a technical solution provides an answer to a problem addressed in an optimal way, in terms of applicability, reliability, effectiveness and efficiency (Boon, 2006; Erduran & Dagher, 2014; NRC, 2012). In engineering, the values to be applied are closely connected to the practical feasibility and success of the engineered solution.

Influenced by the characteristics of other dimensions, both science and engineering follow specific *Methodological Rules* that meet the values and quality criteria just described. In science, there have been many philosophical discussions regarding what these methodological rules are, particularly regarding what role is given to evidence, theory and societal/historical factors. Important contributions studied in any NOS course refer to the well-known Popper claim that scientific hypotheses should be testable, or the widely recognized post-Kuhnian evolutionary/revolutionary view of science where theories can be both gradually and radically displaced by newer ones that comply better with values and quality characteristics or, more recently, the cognitively based and semanticist-oriented views of science, where building meaning drives the scientific activity (Adúriz-Bravo, 2013). These authors and many others contribute different but essentially compatible methodological rules, which in science basically refer to the sophisticated ways in which theory, data and evidence should be coordinated. In engineering, where there is less room for idealization, other methodological rules apply. Of particular importance is the need for actual testing of the diverse proposed solutions (Hansson, 2007; NAE & NRC, 2009).

All these dimensions—spheres of activity, forms of knowledge, values and quality criteria, and methodological rules—influence the more visible and recognizable characteristics of science and engineering which, in turn, are those more easily influenced by the changing contexts in which we live. While the inner circle dimensions are more dependent on the disciplines, the outer circle ones are more context-dependent (historically, socially, politically and financially). An example could be the *Practices* dimension. While the three spheres of activity (modeling, inquiry and argumentation) are those essential for science since its origins, the specific scientific practices (NRC, 2012; Osborne, 2014) within these spheres of action vary more over time and in connection with available technology. For instance, computational modeling was not a scientific practice some years ago, and the citizens' participation in scientific development could soon, under the Responsible Research and Innovation (RRI) paradigm, be a scientific practice that becomes included. The same happens with methodological rules and methods: the methods are quite up to date (see nowadays CRIS-PR techniques), but the methodological rule that different methods should provide compatible results to be considered adequate remains unalterable whatever the technology or new techniques used.

The outer circle of Figure 2.1 refers not only to those characteristics of a discipline that are more influenced by contextual factors, but also to those less idiosyncratic of the discipline. In this sense, the more we move away from the center of Figure 2.1, the more likely it is that some overlap exists in the way we define these characteristics in different disciplines. Not surprisingly, in curriculum proposals, particularly for primary school, scientific and engineering *Practices* are commonly presented in parallel (NRC, 2012). The same happens with *Methods*, with both science and engineering basing them on techniques rooted in experimental design, control of variables or statistical analysis that they borrow from each other. Each discipline, however, will follow its own methodological rules when applying these methods. Also, despite important attempts to define the core ideas of each discipline (see, for example, Harlen [2010], "big ideas of Science"), some of the knowledge produced and used in both science and engineering commonly overlap, which sometimes makes it difficult to identify the nuances of the *Knowledge* of each discipline. For instance, knowledge of parallel electrical circuits can be used to challenge your understanding of voltage or to build a technological solution for lighting a house. Finally, our proposal also includes the *Ethos* dimension, which refers to the norms that guide professionals' work and their interaction with others. Again, today the ethos of both disciplines are built around agreed pillars, such as sustainability or professional integrity, that affect their professional identities (Erduran & Dagher, 2014; Panofsky, 2010).

The epistemic analysis of science and engineering in Table 2.1 shows how both disciplines have idiosyncratic and quite different central epistemic features, particularly aims, which are helpful to understanding the different roles they play in our human attempts to act upon the world. At the same time, in terms of outer epistemic characteristics such as concrete techniques or particular concepts, there is some overlap and also commonalities that allow for certain integration. However, if we explicitly consider an educational aim the mastery of the epistemic competence, there is much greater learning potential in STEM activities that emphasize the different approaches that science and engineering can contribute to a problem.

Epistemic Features in STEM Education School Projects

There is more to inclusion of an epistemological lens in STEM education than just increasing our students' epistemic knowledge. When we shift an activity from a scientific to an engineering focus, fundamental aspects change. This is important for both teachers and designers of STEM activities. As such, we will describe here some real examples of STEM school projects and teaching and learning sequences we have come across when participating in STEM educational research and teacher continuing professional development programs. The idea is to share how applying an epistemological lens to STEM education can help to guide STEM design and classroom practice.

One example is a middle school (sixth grade) STEM project on a boat competition. Introduced as a school interdisciplinary STEM project, designers of the activity did not find it necessary to closely guide the activity and provided only its general structure. That is, teachers were asked to define how to launch the challenge, what sources of information they could use, what restrictions they would establish (for instance, regarding time, use of materials or how to judge the best boat), how classroom management would be organized (for instance, using group work), and how they would evaluate the process and/or outcome.

The openness of this project is, of course, its major attraction, as teachers can decide which orientation to give to it—in other words, which "disciplinary glasses" can be useful for approaching the boat competition challenge. For instance, one science teacher in a school applied this STEM project by focusing mostly on the scientific activity of modeling floatation, using the boat competition as a context to extensively develop explanatory frameworks regarding how and why things float. Other teachers, however, focused on the engineering practice of building a real solution by designing, constructing and testing different boats that float with recycled materials. In these other cases, however, not all teachers relied on the science of floating and sinking as their primary source of knowledge. While some based their boat designs on a very simplistic descriptive model of floatation that could be summarized as "things denser than water need to have air inside to float," others just analyzed the materials and shapes of different types of existing boats to inspire their designs. Finally, another pair of teachers employed a mix of both approaches by focusing on investigating which boat floats better and having students try to figure out why. Although in this latter approach it seems that the scientific practice of inquiry guides the activity, the action was actually addressed by testing different boats and finding engineering problems in them, rather than understanding the relation among the variables involved in floating.

The approaches outlined in this section of a school STEM project can be considered sound STEM education depending on how they were implemented and evaluated in the classroom. In fact, we consider it not a problem that different, either more scientific or engineering approaches, emerged in the context of this STEM challenge. Furthermore, although none of the teachers thought so, we believe that students could have actually benefited a lot in their learning about science and engineering by changing the focus of the project from "addressing the problem as scientists do" (for instance, trying to understand floatation) to "addressing the problem as engineers do" (for instance, testing to find engineering problems in the designed boats). However, it is very important that the teachers behind such projects realize what actual practices, knowledge, methodological rules, quality criteria and ethos can be learned or not in their classrooms depending on the actual orientation to the STEM project they are promoting.

For instance, if an integrated STEM education curriculum proposal is based only on engineering design challenges (designing, building and testing solutions) without explicit promotion of other STEM practices such as imagining *why* or investigating *how*, then one must be aware that in STEM education proposals, science (and also mathematics) are applied in real contexts, but not constructed in depth. As such, one could argue that within this engineering-based approach to integrated STEM education, further scientific teaching and learning are needed for students to master all the scientific practices at an adequate level. Examples of these include students' learning to ask scientific questions, modeling scientific phenomena or differentiating between scientific research and solution testing. In such a curriculum, the introduction of other challenges where science guides the action would be important for those students to understand science as something more profound than just offering a knowledge base for the development of engineering solutions and technological products. The same would happen regarding learning about the nature of science and how science is done.

In an analogous way, when the focus of an integrated STEM education proposal is mostly scientific, the engineering practice could be reduced to "build" something in a quite amateur manner to allow the desired research to be conducted. This could happen by building boats as simply as possible to investigate the effect of the variables "type of material" and "shape." In this second case, for instance, the level of sophistication given to the selection and measurement of variables does not compare to the one given to the selection of building materials, the materialization of the solution, or the optimization of the construction process. Again, the epistemic analysis of the teaching and learning activity posed to students allows us to see the potential but also the limits of our proposal, and realize what other educational actions are needed in order to develop a more balanced STEM curriculum that allows development of an epistemically rich STEM competence.

Of course, "doing it all" in every single school STEM project takes a lot of time and is not actually feasible in real school contexts: there is a limited number of ideas and practices one can build with an adequate depth in a time-framed school project. In addition, there are "differences in how scholars conceptualize the role of each discipline" in STEM education, as the authors of Chapter 1 point out (p. XXX, this volume). As a consequence, rather than a transdisciplinary STEM education approach, what we usually find in real practice is an amalgam of disciplinary STEM project proposals, where scientific or engineering aims lead the action and in which there are more or less superficial connections with other disciplines.

These different ways of conceptualizing STEM integration are not problematic per se. In the aforementioned examples, the disciplinary focus taken by different teachers would become problematic only if this approach is the focus given to every STEM project in a school or curriculum both horizontally (along each academic year) and vertically (along schooling); and if no other engineering, scientific or mathematical education is promoted. Our claim in this chapter is that applying an epistemological lens to STEM education can help us realize which epistemic features we are promoting and which we are not in every single project. This is done in order to achieve a longer-term, more balanced STEM education where all the science and engineering practices, knowledge bases, methods and quality criteria can be learnt at some point, as well as an environment where students do learn *about* science and engineering in addition to their learning *of* science and engineering.

Conclusions and Implications

Discussions on what counts as STEM integrated education, why to embrace an integrative approach to STEM education, and how to do so in practice are prevalent in the literature. When discussing these important issues, however, there is generally a lack of epistemic sensitivity and a certain neglect of the important body of literature regarding the teaching and learning of epistemic knowledge and competences.

We agree with other authors that the "appealing but still somewhat intuitive notion [that concepts and practices from different STEM disciplines can be learned in concert] *is not yet strongly supported by findings from research*" (NAE & NRC, 2014, p. 136; emphasis added). In fact, we challenge the assumption that transdisciplinary integration is the intrinsic and most important characteristic of STEM education by introducing an epistemological lens into these discussions. As we have discussed, complete integration of STEM disciplines is not often happening in real school projects for very different reasons. What can often be seen is engineering or scientific aims taking a leading role, either by centering the activity in the use of technology or by posing design challenges solved using scientific knowledge, or even by doing scientific practices (inquiring, for instance) with rather poor mathematical reasoning. In all these approaches, some disciplines are portrayed as tools to solve problems rather than different, legitimate, and interesting ways of thinking about those problems. The result is an epistemic malpractice that could communicate a poor view of the nature of each of the STEM disciplines. More importantly, the result is a limitation of the most important potentiality we associate with the integrated STEM education approach: to offer a pedagogical context to use, argue, reflect, and value the different epistemologies that scientific, engineering and also mixed disciplines contribute. We conceive integrated STEM education not necessarily as a transdisciplinary approach that goes beyond the disciplines, but as an approach that allows and benefits from the epistemic comparison, selection and evaluation of different STEM disciplines. These disciplines can be seen as related but diverse and complementary bodies of knowledge, practices and systems of values that students need to know about and be able to use in real contexts. Therefore, we do not imply that the integrated STEM educational approach is not a useful one with clear benefits. On the contrary, we agree with Honey and colleagues on acknowledging the "exciting potential of leveraging the natural connections between and among the four STEM subjects for the benefit of students" (NAE & NRC, 2014, p. viii). However, we believe that the existing integration frameworks where the epistemic dimension does not play a role could strongly benefit from including it.

An epistemic emphasis on the curriculum and helping teachers, and therefore students, to be able to identify and master such epistemic differences may help to guarantee that integrated STEM education offers a comprehensive and more realistic view of the STEM fields, improving students' understanding and knowledge both *of* and *about* STEM. In terms of a well-used definition by Balka, "STEM literacy is the ability to identify, apply, and integrate concepts from science, technology, engineering, and mathematics to understand complex problems and to innovate to solve them" (Balka, 2011, p. 11). Despite the limits we find in this concept-focused and value-free definition that we have tried to overcome in an alternative definition published elsewhere (Couso, 2017), we agree with the author that being able to differentiate and integrate concepts, but also processes and epistemic practices of the different STEM disciplines, is the desirable outcome of a sound STEM education, which would not happen adequately without a clear epistemological approach to it.

These limitations, due to holding poor epistemological grounds in STEM education, also apply today to the widely acclaimed STEAM education. For instance, the aspects commonly associated with the "A" in STEAM include creativity, design, aesthetics or even just crafts, and can also be related to a non-recognition of the epistemic value and contribution of the liberal arts and the arts as proper epistemic disciplines. To think on what counts as art and what artists actually do will encourage teachers in STEAM to go beyond the colorful, beautiful and crafting productions that fill any online search of STEAM activities. Understanding that there is creativity in all STEM disciplines without the need to introduce music or drama as a context, and that these creativities take different disciplinary forms, would give much greater meaning to creativity by working with students in terms of what being creative in science versus being creative in engineering or art is. The same occurs regarding certain approaches to teaching science, such as the STS (Science, Technology and Society) approach or the SSI (Socio-Scientific Issues) tradition, which could be considered STEAM approaches where the disciplinary knowledge, practices and epistemic values of the humanities and social sciences are developed together with scientific ones, by posing ethical, moral, political, economic and societal challenges.

Due to space limitations and lack of enough expertise from the authors, in this chapter we have not referred explicitly to mathematics as the other important discipline in STEM that could benefit from an epistemological lens to an integrative approach to STEM education. However, we believe that in the case of mathematics, it is even more important to advocate for this epistemic focus, as most STEM education projects we have come across use mathematics, in fact only mathematical calculus, in a completely applied way that does not promote sound mathematical reasoning. It is very rare that mathematical activity drives the action in a STEM project. This puts mathematics at risk of losing identity and learning potential: mathematical reasoning goes beyond the mathematics that are useful in science and engineering, so either extra mathematical reasoning is promoted out of the STEM curriculum, or within a STEM curriculum we include STEM projects that are led by mathematics, such as a mathematical challenge.

Finally, we want to share that in this chapter we have not aimed to clarify each of the epistemic features that help to characterize a discipline. In fact, we find it problematic to identify some of them, particularly for engineering where less philosophical and educational developments can be found in the literature compared to scientific ones. Examples of these are core engineering ideas. We think, in fact, that the characterization of the discipline in epistemic features is perhaps one of the important tasks that engineering education should undertake in the future. This would otherwise risk a poor understanding of the discipline with important educational consequences: for instance, that all engineering education focus only on the engineering process as the only subject-matter knowledge to be learnt.

Acknowledgements

We want to thank the collaboration of scholars Sibel Erduran and Ebru Kaya in earlier versions of this paper. Research funded by the Spanish Government (PGC2018-096581-B-C21), within the ACELEC research group (2017SGR1399).

References

Adúriz-Bravo, A. (2013). A "Semantic" view of scientific models for science education. *Science & Education, 22*(7), 1593–1611. http://doi.org/10.1007/s11191-011-9431-7

An, D. (2013). *A meta-analysis of the effectiveness of STEM-programs in the United States* (Doctoral dissertation). Retrieved from https://engagedscholarship.csuohio.edu/etdarchive/75

Balka, D. (2011). Standards of mathematical practice and STEM. In *Math-Science connector newsletter*. Stillwater, OK: School Science and Mathematics Association.

Barakos, L., Lujan, V., & Strang, C. (2012). *Science, technology, engineering, and mathematics (STEM): Catalyzing change amid the confusion.* Portsmouth, NH: RMC Research Corporation, Center on Instruction.

Becker, K., & Park, K. (2011). Effects of integrative approaches among science, technology, engineering, and mathematics (STEM) subjects on students' learning: A preliminary meta-analysis. *Journal of STEM Education, 12*(5), 23–38. http://doi.org/10.1037/a0019454

Boon, M. (2006). How science is applied in technology. *International Studies in the Philosophy of Science, 20*(1), 27–47. http://doi.org/10.1080/02698590600640992

Brown, R., Brown, J., Reardon, K., & Merrill, C. (2011). Understanding STEM: Current perceptions. *Technology and Engineering Teacher, 70*(6), 5–9. http://doi.org/10.1136/bjsports-2011-090606.55

Bunge, M. (2017). *Philosophy of science: Volume 1, from problem to theory* (Revised ed.). London, UK: Routledge.

Chalmers, C., Carter, M. L., Cooper, T., & Nason, R. (2017). Implementing "big ideas" to advance the teaching and learning of science, technology, engineering, and mathematics (STEM). *International Journal of Science and Mathematics Education, 15*(Suppl 1), 25–43. http://doi.org/10.1007/s10763-017-9799-1

Clark, A. C., & Ernst, J. V. (2007). A model for the integration of science, technology, engineering, and mathematics. *Technology Teacher, 66*(4), 24–26. Retrieved from https://www.learntechlib.org/p/99897/

Couso, D. (2017). Per a què estem a STEM? Definint l'alfabetització STEM per a tothom i amb valors. *Revista Ciències. Revista del Professorat de Ciències d'Infantil, Primària i Secundària, 34*, 22–28. https://doi.org/10.5565/rev/ciencies.403

Duschl, R. A., & Grandy, R. (2012). Two views about explicitly teaching nature of science. *Science and Education, 22*(9), 2109–2139. http://doi.org/10.1007/s11191-012-9539-4

Dym, C. L., Agogino, A., Eris, O., Frey, D. D., & Leifer, L. J. (2005). Engineering design thinking, teaching, and learning. *Journal of Engineering Education, 94*(1), 103–120. https://doi.org/10.1002/j.2168-9830.2005.tb00832.x

Ejiwale, J. A. (2013). Barriers to successful implementation of STEM education. *Journal of Education and Learning, 7*(2), 63–74. http://doi.org/10.1007/978-3-319-24436-5_20

English, L. D. (2016). STEM education K-12: Perspectives on integration. *International Journal of STEM Education, 3*(1), article 3. http://doi.org/10.1186/s40594-016-0036-1

Erduran, S., & Dagher, Z. R. (2014). *Reconceptualizing the nature of science education for science education: Scientific knowledge, practices and other family categories.* Dordrecht, The Netherlands: Springer.

Guzey, S. S., & Ring-Whalen, E. A. (2018). Negotiating science and engineering: An exploratory case study of a reform-minded science teacher. *International Journal of Science Education, 40*(7), 723–741. https://doi.org/10.1080/09500693.2018.1445310

Hansson, S. O. (2007). What is technological science? *Studies in History and Philosophy of Science Part A, 38*(3), 523–527. http://doi.org/10.1016/j.shpsa.2007.06.003

Hansson, S. O. (2015). Science and technology: What they are and why their relation matters. In S. O. Hansson (Ed.), *The role of technology in science: Philosophical perspectives* Dordrecht: Springer (pp. 11–24). http://doi.org/10.1007/978-94-017-9762-7

Harlen, W. (Ed.). (2010). *Principles and big ideas of science education*. Hatfield, England: Association for Science Education. Retrieved from https://www.interacademies.org/File.aspx?id=25103

Henriksen, D. (2014). Full STEAM ahead: Creativity in excellent STEM teaching practices. *The STEAM Journal, 1*(2), article 15. http://doi.org/10.5642/steam.20140102.15

Jenlink, P. M. (2015). STEM teacher education—Imagining a metadisciplinary future. *Teacher Education and Practice, 28*(2/3), 197–207.

Kennedy, T. J., & Odell, M. R. L. (2014). Engaging students in STEM education. *Science Education International, 25*(3), 246–258. Retrieved from https://files.eric.ed.gov/fulltext/EJ1044508.pdf

Lucas, B., Hanson, J., & Claxton, G. (2014). *Thinking like an engineer: Implications for the education system. A report for the Royal Academy of Engineering Standing Committee for Education and Training*. Retrieved from http://www.raeng.org.uk/publications/reports/thinking-like-an-engineer-implications-summary

Merrill, C., & Daugherty, J. (2009). *The future of TE masters degrees: STEM*. Paper presented at the Meeting of the International Technology Education Association, Louisville, KY.

Morrison, J., & Raymond Bartlett, V. (2009). STEM as curriculum. *Education Week, 23*(March 4), 28–31.

National Academy of Engineering, & National Research Council. (2009). *Engineering in K-12 education: Understanding the status and improving the prospects*. Washington, DC: The National Academies Press. https://doi.org/10.17226/12635.

National Academy of Engineering, & National Research Council. (2014). *STEM integration in K-12 education: Status, prospects, and an agenda for research*. Washington, DC: The National Academies Press. https://doi.org/10.17226/18612.

National Research Council. (2012). *A framework for K-12 science education: Practices, crosscutting concepts, and core ideas*. Washington, DC: The National Academies Press. https://doi.org/10.17226/13165.

Osborne, J. (2014). Teaching scientific practices: Meeting the challenge of change. *Journal of Science Teacher Education, 25*(2), 177–196. http://doi.org/10.1007/s10972-014-9384-1

Panofsky, A. (2010). A critical reconsideration of the ethos and autonomy of science: Sociology of science and sociology as science. In C. Calhoun (Ed.), *Robert K. Merton: Sociology of science and sociology as science* (pp. 140–163). New York, NY: Columbia University Press. http://doi.org/10.7312/calh15112-007

Ryu, M. (2019). Preservice teachers' experiences of STEM integration: Challenges and implications for integrated STEM teacher preparation. *International Journal of Technology and Design Education, 29*(3), 493–512. http://doi.org/10.1007/s10798-018-9440-9

Sharp, J. J. (1991). Methodologies for problem solving: An engineering approach. *The Vocational Aspect of Education, 42*(114), 147–157. http://doi.org/10.1080/10408347308003631

Sinclair, M. (1993). On the differences between the engineering and scientific methods. *International Journal of Engineering Education, 9*(5), 358–361.

Surr, W., Loney, E., Goldston, C., Rasmussen, J., & Anderson, K. (2016). *From career pipeline to STEM literacy for all: Exploring evolving notions of STEM*. Washington, DC: American Institutes for Research.

Vasquez, J. A. (2015). STEM: Beyond the acronym. *Educational Leadership, 72*(4), 10–15.

Williams, P. J. (2011). STEM education: Proceed with caution. *Design and Technology Education: An International Journal, 16*(1), 26–35.

Zubrowski, B. (2002). Integrating science into design technology projects: Using a standard model in the design process. *Journal of Technology Education, 13*(2). https://doi.org/10.21061/jte.v13i2.a

3

MOVING TOWARD AN EQUITY-BASED APPROACH FOR STEM LITERACY

Margaret J. Mohr-Schroeder, Sarah B. Bush,
Cathrine Maiorca and Megan Nickels

Introduction

The complexities of today's world require all people to be equipped with a new set of core knowledge and skills to solve difficult problems, gather and evaluate evidence, and make sense of information they receive from varied print and, increasingly, digital media.

(U.S. Department of Education, 2016, p. i)

An overarching goal of the reform efforts in STEM education, especially since 2013, has been to prepare a STEM-literate workforce; one that will bolster the social and economic well-being (e.g., Committee on STEM Education National Science and Technology Council, 2013; Kennedy & Odell, 2014; National Science Board, 2015) of countries across the world in STEM areas. However, groups historically underrepresented in STEM continue to be at risk of disengaging from STEM (e.g., Beasley & Fischer, 2012; Morgan, Farkas, Hillemeier, & Maczuga, 2016; Museus, Palmer, Davis, & Maramba, 2011). While many educators and educational researchers approach work with underrepresented students through a problem-solving framework to develop their positive STEM socio-academic identities, it is less common that attention to the cognitive-linguistic and affective dimensions of students' STEM transitions take center stage. In this chapter, we review the most recent decade of literature on STEM literacy, especially in, but not limited to, integrated STEM environments. We begin with a brief history of STEM literacy, then provide context and urge for consensus on a definition for STEM literacy, and finally, discuss characteristics of STEM literacy. The articles we reviewed with international perspectives were limited to STEM literacy as opposed to a siloed approach of mathematics, science, engineering, or technology literacy. In total, we reviewed 112 empirical studies, conceptual or research-informed practice-oriented articles, book chapters, syntheses, or reports published since 2009 that examined STEM literacy within an integrated STEM context. While there were many blog and news-media publications regarding STEM literacy, we chose not to include them so as to focus on research-based evidence of STEM literacy.

Integrated STEM, as defined by Moore and colleagues in Chapter 1 of this handbook, and Gutiérrez's (2008) four dimensions of equity—access, power, identity, and achievement—were our guiding analytical framework for the review. *Access* relates to what resources are available to participants (e.g., supplies, quality teaching, rigorous curriculum experiences). *Achievement* relates to student outcomes and the measurement of them. *Identity* not only relates to addressing students' pasts, but also balances the opportunities to self-reflect and to reflect with others as part of a learning experience. *Power* relates to social transformations at multiple points and levels (e.g., voice in the classroom, opportunity). All four dimensions are non-negotiable when truly embodying an equitable mindset. While a single, consensus definition of integrated STEM still does not exist, certain characteristics have been shown to be important in integrated STEM. These include (a) the need to address a complex, authentic, or real-world problem; (b) shared skills, practices, and concepts from across disciplines; (c) student-centered teaching strategies, including an emphasis on collaboration and teamwork; and (d) integration of at least two or more disciplines. Alongside the importance of integrated STEM is the opportunity and access to such educational opportunities (Flores, 2007). Equity must remain an integral and regular part of conversations to ensure each and every student experiences the distribution of power (Gutiérrez, 2008), especially as it relates to STEM literacy. We present findings from our review as a way to come to a shared understanding of what STEM literacy is, how it can be defined, and what it means to be STEM literate. For all students to become STEM literate, each and every student must have access to quality STEM learning experiences where STEM literacy is a focus. A clear understanding of what STEM literacy is and what it aims to do is necessary to design and implement integrated learning experiences.

History of STEM Literacy

In order to obtain a clearer understanding of STEM literacy, we need to first understand disciplinary literacies (e.g., Shanahan & Shanahan, 2012) as a definition and then examine the disciplinary literacies as they currently exist. Whereas literacy is the ability to read, write, spell, listen, and speak, disciplinary literacy refers to reading, writing, and communicating in the context of a given field (e.g., mathematics). In this section, we briefly discuss disciplinary literacies related to STEM, but in their individual contexts (i.e., science, technology, engineering, mathematics). The purpose is to understand the individual disciplinary literacies in order to build an understanding of how STEM literacy was derived.

Science Literacy

Historically, there are differing viewpoints on science literacy. One refers to how science is used in society, and the other refers to an individual's scientific knowledge (Holbrook & Rannikmae, 2008). The American Association for the Advancement of Science (AAAS, 1989) defined science literacy to include not only mathematics and technology but also the social and natural sciences. According to AAAS, a scientifically literate person understands that science, mathematics, and technology are interconnected human endeavors with both strengths and weaknesses. A scientifically literate person also has the thinking skills and scientific knowledge to use mathematics, science, and technology at both personal and societal levels. "Thus scientific, mathematical, and technological processes are important factors in improving society, along with thinking skills and scientific knowledge" (AAAS, 1989, p. 20). This definition reflects how science, technology, and mathematics are interconnected as well as the importance of being able to apply scientific knowledge and thinking. The National Research Council [NRC] (2012) defined science literacy as not only having scientific knowledge but being educated consumers of the technology and science which permeates everyday lives. The NRC also states that a scientifically literate person should appreciate the wonder and beauty of science and have the skills to continue to learn science outside of schools for either pleasure or a future career, regardless of the field. The NRC (2012) used this definition to develop the framework for the United States Next Generation Science Standards (NGSS Lead States, 2013) in which the science and engineering practices are introduced. These practices include:

1. Asking questions (for science) and defining problems (for engineering)
2. Developing and using models
3. Planning and carrying out investigations
4. Analyzing and interpreting data
5. Using mathematics and computational thinking
6. Constructing explanations (for science) and designing solutions (for engineering)
7. Engaging in argument from evidence
8. Obtaining, evaluating, and communicating information

The Board on Science Education in the U.S. further refined science literacy to define aspects, including:

- an understanding of scientific practices;
- content knowledge (knowledge of basic facts, concepts, and vocabulary); and
- an understanding of science as a social process (National Academies of Sciences, Engineering, and Medicine, 2016).

It is important for individuals to be scientifically literate for economic, personal, democratic, and cultural reasons (National Academies of Sciences, Engineering, and Medicine, 2016). Economically, scientifically literate people can participate in society by pursuing either science-related jobs or jobs that require some scientific knowledge. Personally, an understanding of science helps individuals make knowledgeable decisions and actions that will lead to healthier and richer lives. Democratically, scientifically literate people are informed members of a democratic society that can participate in government decision-making that will impact problems that humanity faces. Culturally, "the sciences are important cultural activities that offer a powerful way to understand the world" (National Academies of Sciences, Engineering, and Medicine, 2016, p. 26). Science and technology shape the ever-changing world around us.

Technology Literacy

Technology refers to "the act of making or crafting, but more generally it refers to the diverse collection of processes and knowledge that people use to extend human abilities and to satisfy human needs and wants" (International Technology Education Association [ITEA], 2007, p. 2) and being able to use, understand, and develop technology is vital to our society. Bybee (2010) suggested, "there are very few other things that influence our everyday existence more and about which citizens know less" (p. 30). Technology literacy is essential in enhancing the education of other subjects, which is vital for individuals to gain and maintain employment, as well as to participate in our ever-changing technological society.

Engineering Literacy

According to Moore et al. (2014), "Engineering requires that application of mathematics and science through the development of technologies, it can provide a way to integrate the STEM disciplines meaningfully" (p. 2). Engineering also provides real-world contexts that can used to teach mathematics and science through the engineering design process (Maiorca & Stohlmann, 2016). Engineering is an essential tool that can be used to integrate science, technology, and mathematics (Grubbs & Strimel, 2016; Moore et al., 2014). Therefore, it is increasingly important for teachers to be able to implement quality engineering design problems. The K-12 framework for quality K-12 engineering education focuses on students using the engineering design process to solve relevant problems, what an engineer is and does, and how they can impact the world (Moore et al., 2014). This framework includes 12 indicators for quality engineering problems: process of design (problem and background, plan and implement, and also test and evaluate), apply science, engineering and mathematics, engineering thinking, conceptions of engineers and engineering, engineering tools issues, solutions and impacts as well as ethics, teamwork, and communication related to engineering. Based on this framework, an engineering-literate person should know what engineers do, how engineering can be used to solve the challenges of today and make a better future for tomorrow. They also should be able to use the engineering design process to solve real-world problems that incorporate mathematics, science, and technology. The inclusion of engineering in the Next Generation Science Standards (NGSS) is "an unmistakable policy statement that science, technology, engineering and mathematics (STEM) integration is a desired outcome" (Roehrig, Moore, Wang & Park, 2012, p. 41).

Mathematical Literacy

In order to participate in society, individuals have always needed to have mathematical literacy, also more commonly referred to internationally as quantitative literacy (e.g., Steen, 2001). In 2003, the Program for International Student Assessment (PISA) stated that a mathematically literate person can use mathematics outside of the classroom in their personal and private lives (as cited in Kaiser & Willander, 2005). Steen, Turner and Burkhardt (2007) defined mathematical literacy as having the ability to use one's knowledge and understanding of mathematics in everyday life. Similarly, the Organisation for Economic Co-Operation and Development (OECD) defines mathematical literacy as the "capacity to formulate, employ, and interpret mathematics in a variety of contexts. It includes reasoning mathematically and using mathematics concepts, procedures, facts, and tools to describe, explain, and predict phenomena" (2016, p. 28). Mathematical literacy provides students with the knowledge to apply mathematics in other content areas and to their daily lives. The U.S. National Council of Teachers of Mathematics (2018) argues that in today's world, "mathematical literacy is needed more than ever to filter, understand, and act on the enormous amount of data and information that we encounter every day" (p. 1). In *Charting a Course for Success: America's Strategy for STEM Education* (Committee on STEM Education of the National Science and Technology Council, 2018), mathematics is rightfully positioned as foundational to success across the STEM fields and the importance of mathematical literacy as well as computational literacy and thinking are prioritized.

Summary

STEM disciplines have similar desired outcomes, and therefore, there should be some commonality across definitions of literacy for the subject areas. For example, disciplinary literacy approaches in science, technology, engineering, and mathematics all address problem solving in some way. For example, with technology literacy and engineering literacy, students design problems, create solutions, and evaluate design by considering effects on other technology or solving real-world problems (ITEA, 2007). Scientifically literate individuals formulate hypotheses, design and conduct experiments, make arguments with scientific evidence, consider alternate hypotheses, and interpret results (NRC, 2012). Mathematically literate students make conjectures, explore, justify conclusions with counter examples and evaluate the reasonableness of results (National Governors Association Center for Best Practices & Council of Chief State School Officers (CCSSO), 2010). To promote disciplinary literacy, individuals need to be given the opportunity and access to engage in authentic problems, and this requires the integration of different content areas (Cavalcanti, 2017). Because of this integration, STEM literacy should be considered not as siloed content literacies but as an integrated literacy (Zollman, 2012). These kinds of learning experiences promote not only literacy in the individual content areas but also integrated STEM literacy.

What Is STEM Literacy?

While there is no agreed-upon definition of STEM literacy, it is not because there have not been multiple attempts. This is likely due to the dynamic nature of the STEM field, and subsequently STEM literacy (Cavalcanti, 2017; Cavalcanti & Mohr-Schroeder, 2019; Zollman, 2012). However, the definition must remain dynamic and responsive to reflect the ever-changing society in which we live (Cavalcanti, 2017). Table 3.1 provides a non-exhaustive list of current, commonly used definitions of STEM literacy.

As one can see from the definitions in Table 3.1, there are a variety of interpretations. In a comparison study of the disciplinary literacies of STEM, Tang and Williams (2019) found similarities and differences, arguing that the following similarities can and should be used as a basis for a common STEM literacy definition:

- The creation, use, and conversion of codified multimodal representations.
- The mastery of common visual resources such as annotated diagrams and geometric drawings.
- The application of cognitive and metacognitive strategies involving problem identification, planning, and evaluation and self-monitoring.

The commonalities across the STEM disciplines and across the definitions provided in the literature reveal a unique tool set, especially as it relates to the ability to create and use knowledge in integrated STEM. The goal of any participant in an integrated STEM experience is to master the related outcomes as they learn how to create, communicate, and use knowledge within and across STEM. As Cavalcanti (2017) argues,

> Using the substantive literature on literacy within the STEM disciplines, it may behoove stakeholders to place more targeted attention to the themes of utility, social responsibility, response to change, communication, decision-making, and knowledge to define STEM literacy in a way that can be understood and applied across a variety of contexts.
>
> *(p. 65)*

In this light, we offer a dynamic, process, equitable and content-oriented definition of STEM literacy that holistically captures previously published work, is outcomes- and process-oriented, and honors the individual strengths each of the STEM disciplines brings, while focusing on integrated STEM as the cornerstone.

> *STEM literacy is the dynamic process and ability to apply, question, collaborate, appreciate, engage, persist, and understand the utility of STEM concepts and skills to provide solutions for STEM-related personal, societal, and global challenges that cannot be solved using a single discipline.*

Regardless of how you define STEM literacy, a basic understanding of the STEM disciplines is necessary to be an informed decision-maker and member of a democratic and ever-changing society. Research has shown that greater exposure to a variety of STEM opportunities has a long-term effect on individuals (e.g., Wai, Lubinski, Benbow, & Steiger, 2010) and in formal and informal settings (e.g., Maiorca et al., 2020; Mohr-Schroeder et al., 2014; Roberts et al., 2018).

Table 3.1 Current, Commonly Used Definitions of STEM Literacy

Reference	Definition
National Governors Association (2007, p. 7)	STEM literacy refers to an individual's ability to apply his or her understanding of how the world works within and across four interrelated domains.
	STEM literacy is an interdisciplinary area of study that bridges the four areas of science, technology, engineering, and mathematics. STEM literacy does not simply mean achieving literacy in these four strands or silos.
Bybee (2010, p. 31)	STEM literacy includes the conceptual understandings and procedural skills and abilities for individuals to address STEM-related personal, social, and global issues. STEM literacy involves the integration of STEM disciplines and four interrelated and complementary components. STEM literacy refers to the following:
	• Acquiring scientific, technological, engineering, and mathematical knowledge and using that knowledge to identify issues, acquire new knowledge, and apply the knowledge to STEM-related issues.
	• Understanding the characteristic features of STEM disciplines as forms of human endeavors that include the processes of inquiry, design, and analysis.
	• Recognizing how STEM disciplines shape our material, intellectual, and cultural world.
	• Engaging in STEM-related issues and with the ideas of science, technology, engineering, and mathematics as concerned, affective, and constructive citizens.
Balka (2011, p. 7)	STEM literacy is the ability to identify, apply, and integrate concepts from science, technology, engineering, and mathematics to understand complex problems and to innovate to solve them. To understand and address the challenge of achieving STEM literacy for all students begins with understanding and defining its component parts and the relationships between them.
National Research Council (2011, p. 5)	STEM literacy is the knowledge and understanding of scientific and mathematical concepts and processes required for personal decision-making, participation in civic and cultural affairs, and economic productivity for all students.
Zollman (2012, p. 18)	STEM literacy is a dynamic process that spotlights the three strata in the STEM literacy process: educational objectives of the content areas; cognitive, affective, and psychomotor domains from learning theory; and economic, societal and personal needs of humanity.
Mohr-Schroeder, Cavalcanti, & Blyman (2015); Jackson & Mohr-Schroeder (2018, p. 43)	STEM literacy is the ability to apply concepts from science, technology, engineering, and mathematics to solve problems that cannot be solved using a single discipline.
Cavalcanti (2017, pp. 66–67)	STEM literacy may be defined as the conceptual understandings and procedural skills and abilities for individuals to address STEM-related personal, social, and global issues (Bybee, 2010, p. 31); the ability to engage in STEM specific discourse; a positive disposition toward STEM (e.g., Wilkins, 2000, 2010, 2015), including a willingness to engage and persist in STEM-related areas (e.g., Wilkins, 2000, 2010, 2015); an understanding of the utility of applying STEM concepts to solve real world problems; and, an appreciation of how the processes and practices of STEM areas change as technologies and demands of modern society change.

Critical Need for a STEM-Literate Society

STEM policy reports (such as Committee on STEM Education of the National Science & Technology Council, 2018; National Research Council, 2011; U.S. Department of Education, 2016) speak to the critical need and urgency of fostering STEM literacy in each and every student so that they can develop foundational knowledge in STEM regardless of whether or not they pursue a STEM career (for a critical review, see Bush, 2019). STEM literacy prepares students for adulthood and empowers them as informed members of a democratic society that can understand and make sound decisions on topics such as mortgages and investments; comparison shopping; interpreting medical documents; preserving the environment; analyzing a news report; and completing a home improvement project (Bush, 2019). National education professional organizations, such as the National Council of Teachers of Mathematics (2018), have highlighted areas of STEM literacy, such as mathematical and statistical literacy, for the same reason of helping our students become adults who are informed decision makers. Further, as described earlier in the science literacy section, the National Academies of Sciences, Engineering, and Medicine (2016) describes how individuals should be scientifically literate for four different reasons: economic, personal, democratic, and cultural. We contend that this idea geared at scientific literacy can be extended to STEM literacy and serve as a guide for schools, districts, and all STEM stakeholders as we consider in what ways do our students need to be STEM literate. As a field, we must ensure each and every student has opportunities to engage in a variety of experiences which will build their STEM literacy as they relate to economic, personal, democratic, and cultural considerations.

It is clear that students need more applicable, integrated, and authentic learning experiences. Our work centers on fostering STEM literacy specifically from that integrated approach, as we know that to solve complex problems in our communities and, more broadly, the world, knowledge from multiple disciplines must be applied. These integrated and authentic STEM experiences cannot simply be left to chance. Planning the best STEM experiences requires carefully considering the on-grade-level content and practices of focus and maintaining the integrity of the standards (Larson, 2017; NCSM/NCTM, 2018). Only through such intentional planning can we move away from disjointed integrated STEM "activities" which are often not authentic in nature (e.g., build a bridge, but for what purpose?) or which are fun and might even be engaging but do not align to grade-level learning goals (Bush & Cook, 2019).

Further, each and every student must have access to rich content-based authentic STEM experiences (Bush & Cook, 2019; Roberts et al., 2018). This includes in both formal and informal learning settings, with a push for STEM learning to become a foundational part of a student's school career, akin to reading, rather than a special, add-on, or enrichment program. Research and resources (e.g., Bush & Cook, 2019; Johnson, Peters-Burton, & Moore, 2016; Sahin & Mohr-Schroeder, 2019) are becoming more available to provide guidance to schools, districts, and states as they begin to develop long-term sustained STEM infrastructures to create systemic ways to ensure each and every student develops STEM literacy.

Conclusions

To be clear, we contend that STEM, and the development of STEM literacy, should become as natural a part of the school experience as literacy. STEM literacy *is* literacy. We argue that STEM literacy is not an option, as no matter a student's future career choice, each and every student should leave high school STEM literate so that they can be an informed consumer and decision maker in our ever-increasing information and data-rich society. As the recent report by the Committee on STEM Education of the National Science & Technology Council (2018) states, "A STEM-literate public will be better equipped to conduct thoughtful analyses and to sort through problems, propose innovative solutions, and handle rapid technological change, and will be better prepared to participate in civil society as jurors, voters, and consumers" (p. 5). The learning experiences that students receive to build their STEM literacy will impact the quality of their entire adult lives. In essence, STEM literacy is a vehicle through which to develop the 21st Century Learning Skills (as described by the National Education Association, 2012) while honing rich disciplinary content learning: critical thinking and problem solving, communication, collaboration, and creativity and innovative thinking. Even more important are opportunities to participate in problem solving that provides STEM literacy input and opportunities for output to scaffold and support mastery of the repertoire of practice. Experiences aimed at participants becoming STEM-literate "are shaped by and contribute to social practices, purposes, and contexts" (Moje, Collazo, Carrillo, & Marx, 2001, p. 472). For these reasons, it is critical that students are provided opportunity, access, and meaningful exposure to a STEM literacy community in which to participate, practice, and belong.

References

American Association for the Advancement of Science (AAAS). (1989). *Science for all Americans: A project 2061 report on literacy goals in science, mathematics, and* technology. (AAAS Publication 89–01S). Washington, DC: Author.

Balka, D. (2011, Summer). *Standards of mathematical practice and STEM. Math-Science Connector Newsletter* (pp. 6–8). Stillwater, OK: School Science and Mathematics Association. Retrieved from http://ssma.play-cello.com/wp-content/uploads/2016/02/MathScienceConnector-summer2011.pdf

Beasley, M. A., & Fischer, M. J. (2012). Why they leave: The impact of stereotype threat on the attrition of women and minorities from science, math and engineering majors. *Social Psychology of Education, 15*(4), 427–448.

Bush, S. B. (2019). National reports on STEM education: What are the implications for K–12? In A. Sahin & M. Mohr-Schroeder (Eds.), *STEM education 2.0 myths and truths: What has K-12 STEM education research taught us?* (pp. 72–90). Leiden, The Netherlands: Brill Publishing.

Bush, S. B., & Cook, K. L. (2019). *Step into STEAM: Your standards-based action plan for deepening mathematics and science learning.* Thousand Oaks, CA: Corwin and Reston, VA: National Council of Teachers of Mathematics.

Bybee, B. R. W. (2010, September). Advancing STEM education: A 2020 vision. *Technology and Engineering Teacher,* 30–36.

Cavalcanti, M. A. L. (2017). *Assessing STEM literacy in an informal learning environment* (Unpublished doctoral dissertation). Lexington, KY: University of Kentucky. Retrieved from https://uknowledge.uky.edu/edsc_etds/22/

Cavalcanti, M., & Mohr-Schroeder, M. J. (2019). Toward a common vision of STEM literacy. In A. Sahin & M. J. Mohr-Schroeder (Eds.), *STEM education 2.0. myths and truths: What did 10 years of STEM education research in K12 teach us?* (pp. 3–21). Leiden, The Netherlands: Koninklijke Brill NV. doi: 10.1163/9789004405400

Committee on STEM Education National Science and Technology Council. (2013). *Federal science, technology, engineering, and mathematics (STEM) education 5-year strategic plan: A report from the Committee on STEM Education National Science and Technology Council.* Washington, DC: Executive Office of the President National Science and Technology Council.

Committee on STEM Education of the National Science & Technology Council. (2018). *Charting a course for success: America's strategy for STEM education.* Washington, DC: Executive Office of the President National Science and Technology Council.

Flores, A. (2007). Examining disparities in mathematics education: Achievement gap or opportunity gap? *The High School Journal, 91*(1), 29–42. doi:10.1353/hsj.2007.0022

Grubbs, M., & Strimel. (2016). Engineering design: The great integrator. *Journal of STEM Teacher Education, 50*(1), 77–90.

Gutiérrez, R. (2008). Framing equity: Helping students "play the game" and "change the game". *Noticias de TODOS, 4*(1), 1–3.

Holbrook, J., & Rannikmae, M. (2008). The meaning of scientific literacy. *International Journal of Environmental and Science Education, 4*(3), 275–288.

International Technology Education Association (ITEA). (2007). *Standards for technological literacy: Content for the study of technology* (3rd ed.). Reston, VA: Author.

Jackson, C. D., & Mohr-Schroeder, M. J. (2018). Increasing stem literacy via an informal learning environment. *Journal of STEM Teacher Education, 53*(1), Article 4. https://doi.org/10.30707/JSTE53.1Jackson

Johnson, C., Peters-Burton, E., & Moore, T. (2016). *STEM road map.* New York: Routledge.

Kaiser, G., & Willander, T. (2005). Development of mathematical literacy: Results of an empirical study. *Teaching Mathematics and its Applications, 24*(2–3), 48–60.

Kennedy, T. J., & Odell, M. R. L. (2014). Engaging students in STEM education. *Science Education International, 25*(3), 246–258.

Larson, M. (2017). Math education *is* STEM education! *NCTM President's Message.* Retrieved from https://www.nctm.org/News-and-Calendar/Messages-from-the-President/Archive/Matt-Larson/Math-Education-Is-STEM-Education!/

Maiorca, C., Roberts, T., Jackson, C., Bush, S., Delaney, A., Mohr-Schroeder, M., & Yao, S. (2020). Informal learning environments and impact on interest in STEM careers. *International Journal of Science and Mathematics Education.* doi:10.1007/s10763-019-10038-9

Maiorca, C., & Stohlmann, M. (2016). Inspiring students in integrated STEM education through modeling activities. In *Annual perspectives in mathematics education 2016: Mathematical modeling and modeling mathematics.* Reston, VA: NCTM.

Mohr-Schroeder, M. J., Cavalcanti, M., & Blyman, K. (2015). STEM education: Understanding the changing landscape. In A. Sahin (Ed.), *A practice-based model of effective science, technology, engineering and mathematics (STEM) education teaching: STEM Students on the State (S.O.S) model* (pp. 3–14). Rotterdam, The Netherlands: Sense.

Mohr-Schroeder, M. J., Jackson, C., Miller, M., Walcott, B., Little, D. L., Speler, L., Schooler, W., & Schroeder, D. C. (2014). Developing middle school students' interests in STEM via summer learning experiences: See Blue STEM Camp. *School Science and Mathematics – STEM Special Issue, 114*(6), 291–301. doi:10.1111/ssm.12079

Moje, E. B., Collazo, T., Carrillo, R., & Marx, R. W. (2001). "Maestro, what is 'quality'?": Language, literacy, and discourse in project-based science. *Journal of Research in Science Teaching, 38*(4), 469–498.

Moore, T., Glancy, A., Tank, K., Kersten, J., Smith, K., & Stohlmann, M. (2014). A framework for quality K-12 engineering education: Research and development. *Journal of Pre-college Engineering Education Research, 4*(1), 1–13. doi:10.7771/2157-9288.1069

Morgan, P. L., Farkas, G., Hillemeier, M. M., & Maczuga, S. (2016). Science achievement gaps begin very early, persist, and are largely explained by modifiable factors. *Educational Researcher, 45*(1), 18–35.

Museus, S. D., Palmer, R. T., Davis, R. J., & Maramba, D. C. (2011). *Racial and ethnic minority students' success in STEM education.* San Francisco: Jossey-Bass Incorporated.

National Academies of Sciences, Engineering, and Medicine. (2016). *Science literacy: Concepts, contexts, and consequences.* Washington, DC: National Academies Press.

National Council of Supervisors of Mathematics and National Council of Teachers of Mathematics. (2018). *Building STEM education on a sound mathematical foundation.* A joint position statement. Aurora, CO: Author.

National Council of Teachers of Mathematics. (2018). *Catalyzing change in high school mathematics: Initiating critical conversations.* Reston, VA: Author.

National Education Association. (2012). *Preparing 21st century students for a global society: An educator's guide to "the four Cs."* Washington, DC: Author. Retrieved from http://www.nea.org/assets/docs/A-Guide-to-Four-Cs.pdf

National Governors Association Center for Best Practices & Council of Chief State School Officers (CCSSO). (2010). *Common core state standards.* Washington, DC: Authors. Retrieved from www.corestandards.org

National Governors Association. (2007). *Innovation America: A final report.* Retrieved from http://files.eric.ed.gov/fulltext/ED504101.pdf

National Research Council. (2011). *Successful K-12 STEM education: Identifying effective approaches in science, technology, engineering, and mathematics.* Washington, DC: National Academies Press.

National Research Council. (2012). *A framework for K-12 science education: Practices, crosscutting concepts, and core ideas.* Washington, DC: National Academies Press.

National Science Board. (2015). *Revisiting the STEM workforce: A companion to science and engineering indicators 2014.* Arlington, VA: National Science Board.

NGSS Lead States. (2013). *Next generation science standards: For states, by states.* Washington, DC: The National Academies Press. Retrieved from www.nextgenscience.org/overview-dci

Organisation for Economic Co-operation and Development (OECD). (2016). *PISA 2015 results (Volume I): Excellence and equity in education.* Paris: OECD Publishing.

Roberts, O. T., Jackson, C., Mohr-Schroeder, M. J., Bush, S. B., Maiorca, C., Cavalcanti, M., Schroeder, D. C., Delaney, A., Putman, L., & Cremeans, C. (2018). Students' perceptions of STEM learning after participating in a summer informal learning experience. *International Journal of STEM Education, 5*(35). doi:10.1186/s40594-018-0133-4

Roehrig, G., Moore, T., Wang, H., & Park, M. (2012). Is adding the E enough? Investigating the impact of K-12 engineering standards on the implementation of STEM integration. *School Science and Mathematics, 112*(1), 31–44. doi:10.1111/j.1949-8594.2011.00112.x

Sahin, A., & Mohr-Schroeder, M. J. (Eds). (2019). *STEM education 2.0. Myths and truths: What did 10 years of STEM education research in K12 teach us?* Leiden, The Netherlands: Brill Publishing. doi: 10.1163/9789004405400

Shanahan, T., & Shanahan, C. (2012). What is disciplinary literacy and why does it matter? *Topics in Language Disorders, 32*(1), 7–18.

Steen, L. A. (Ed.). (2001). *Mathematics and democracy: The case for quantitative literacy.* National Council on Education and the Disciplines. Princeton: Woodrow Wilson Foundation.

Steen, L. A., Turner, R., & Burkhardt, H. (2007). Developing mathematical literacy. In W. Blum, P. L. Galbraith, H. W. Henn, & M. Niss (Eds.), *Modelling and applications in mathematics education: The 14th ICMI study* (pp. 285–294). New York, NY: Springer.

Tang, K., & Williams, J. P. (2019). STEM literacy or literacies? Examining the empirical basis of these constructs. *Review of Education, 7*(3), 675–697.

U.S. Department of Education. (2016). *STEM 2026: A vision for innovation in STEM education.* Washington, DC: Author.

Wai, J., Lubinski, D., Benbow, C. P., & Steiger, J. H. (2010). Accomplishment in science, technology, engineering, and mathematics (STEM) and its relation to STEM education dose: A 25-year longitudinal study. *Journal of Educational Psychology, 102*(4), 860–871.

Wilkins, J. L. (2000). Special issue article: Preparing for the 21st century: The status of quantitative literacy in the United States. *School Science and Mathematics, 100*(8), 405–418.

Wilkins, J. L. M. (2010). Modeling quantitative literacy. *Educational and Psychological Measurement, 70*(2), 267–290. doi:10.1177/0013164409344506

Wilkins, J. L. M. (2015). A two-tier full-information item factor analysis model with applications. *Psychometrika, 75*(4), 581–612. doi:10.1177/0013164409344506

Zollman, A. (2012). Learning for STEM literacy: STEM literacy for learning. *School Science and Mathematics, 112*(1), 12–19.

4

A WORLDLY PERSPECTIVE
Applying Theory to STEM Education

Léonie J. Rennie, Grady Venville and John Wallace

Introduction

In recent years the acronym and phrase "STEM education" have captured attention as a curriculum approach that promises to improve school students' academic success and their broader educational outcomes. Exploring how this improvement might occur requires strong theoretical underpinnings; yet, as earlier chapters have illuminated, STEM education is notoriously under-theorized by educators, administrators, and researchers. In this chapter we articulate a STEM education theory entitled the Worldly Perspective, developed in the context of international literature and two decades of research and thinking about integrated STEM curricula. Rennie, Venville, and Wallace (2012a) described the development of the theory in full; here we argue in brief that a powerful STEM curriculum has, at its core, two dimensions: a balance between disciplinary and integrated knowledge, and connection between local and global contexts. We illustrate these two dimensions—balance and connection—through analysis of three international case studies that show how the Worldly Perspective operates in practice across STEM education programs at elementary and secondary levels. We explore how the Worldly Perspective can potentially be employed to bring together other STEM knowledge systems, for example, Western and Aboriginal worldviews, life and work, the particular and the general.

The Worldly Perspective on STEM Education

In developing the Worldly Perspective, we systematically reviewed international literature about integrated curriculum, including seminal works by Beane (1995), Clark (1997), Drake (1998), Hargreaves, Earl, and Ryan (1996), and Jacobs (1989), supplemented by multiple case studies of STEM education in practice, exploring the diversity of approaches and their outcomes. In synthesizing those findings (Venville, Wallace, Rennie, & Malone, 2002), we resisted the notion of separate discipline-based and integrated paradigms, favoring a single, "worldly" perspective of curriculum incorporating both paradigms. Our view of the structure of knowledge is a holistic one; we see integrated knowledge and disciplinary knowledge as overlapping and complementary, rather than separate, allowing for a pragmatic approach to STEM education. The Worldly Perspective is based on the notion of "balance" between disciplinary and integrated knowledge—we propose that a high-quality STEM curriculum brings the disciplines together in an integrated manner to help understand and analyze real-world, complex problems. A high-quality STEM curriculum also respects the powerful learning that can be contributed by individual disciplines, utilizing the disciplinary conventions and special ways of knowing to address the problems and issues under consideration. This interplay, and ultimately the balance between integrated and disciplinary knowledge, is critical to the quality and power of the student learning in STEM contexts (Rennie et al., 2012a).

In early case studies, we investigated teachers' views of how they were integrating STEM curriculum and what students were learning in their classrooms. By theoretically triangulating our research findings, we expanded on the "knowledge dimension," using Bakhtin's (1981) metaphor of centripetal and centrifugal thinking about knowledge and curriculum; concepts somewhat parallel to Roberts' Visions I and II of science curriculum (Roberts, 2007). This metaphorical approach demonstrated that

> within a balanced curriculum, students can be encouraged to reflect on and critique subject-specific knowledge, understand the limitations of that knowledge, particularly in applied situations, and recognize when creativity, lateral thinking, adaptive help-seeking, and trial and error play a role in the knowledge-building process.
> *(Rennie, Venville, & Wallace, 2011, pp. 157–158)*

For example, we found that 10th-grade students who were set the open-ended task of building a solar-powered boat could use specialized knowledge from the contributory disciplines, like the angle of the sun required to align their solar panel. However, when they tested their boat, students found that theoretical knowledge was inadequate because in the real world, other variables are involved. They sought contextual knowledge from parents and others beyond their classroom, thus blending their disciplinary knowledge with other, more integrated knowledge to successfully complete their boat.

Figure 4.1 depicts a balance between disciplinary knowledge and integrated knowledge, with the horizontal arrows indicating that the contribution from each STEM discipline, and the point of balance, will vary according to the curriculum context. Also, although not shown, other disciplines, such as the arts and social sciences, may contribute to the integrated curriculum, as the curriculum context demands.

The findings about what and how students learned enabled us to articulate the "locality dimension" of the Worldly Perspective. The significance of locality was clear in our data; one way or another, successful STEM programs had explicit links to their local community. We postulated that when the real-world problems and issues that underpin STEM curricula were considered at the local level, this enhanced relevance and engagement for students. By interacting with specific issues in their community, students made connections between the local knowledge they were gaining with more global knowledge; the "big ideas" that underpin the physical and life sciences, such as energy transfer and evolution. Knowing and understanding issues relevant at the local level enabled students to abstract the important principles and apply them to other situations in multiple, global contexts. We argued that the knowledge students thus gained was powerful because the emphasis on conceptual learning moved to "a more balanced focus among things conceptual, epistemic, and social" (Duschl, 2008, p. 283).

Figure 4.1 illustrates how the appropriate balance between disciplinary and integrated knowledge exists within the local context but allows abstraction to more global contexts. The connection between local and global contexts is dynamic.

Our research also illuminated the factors that enabled or hindered the implementation and success of an integrated STEM curriculum. In overview, enabling factors include stable learning environments, where at least two teachers work together to provide learning activities linked to the classroom and intended curriculum. Supportive within-school leadership that provides teachers with in-school planning time and a flexible timetable that allows classes to come together, or to go outside of school, are important to promote connection to and participation with community resources.

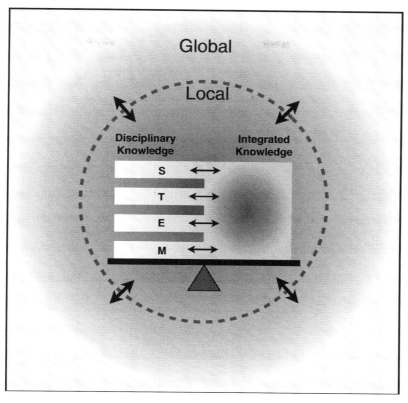

Figure 4.1   The dimensions of the Worldly Perspective: balance between disciplinary and integrated knowledge and connection between local and global contexts.

These factors are consistent with those identified in the review by Pang and Good (2000), in more recent research including Holmlund, Lesseig, and Slavit (2018) and LaForce et al. (2016), and in other chapters in this volume.

In sum, and as represented in Figure 4.1, the Worldly Perspective provides a balanced view of curriculum, allowing all participants—students, teachers, and researchers—to use the cognitive and practical tools of disciplinary knowledge while also engaging in the integrated knowledge that better reflects the real-world problems and issues that can be explored in a more holistic way. Similarly, by illuminating the connection between local problems and broader, more abstract global issues, this view of curriculum provides students with knowledge that is useful and relevant to them, and, we believe, it is powerful knowledge. The point of balance and the degree of connection will, of course, depend on the particular context and desired outcomes of any integrated STEM curriculum.

The Worldly Perspective in Practice

The Worldly Perspective proved a useful tool to understand the effectiveness and outcomes of the integrated STEM curricula explored in our research (for examples, see case studies in Rennie, Venville, & Wallace, 2012b). We test its generalizability by drawing on integrated programs from different countries and different education sectors to examine the balance between disciplinary and integrated knowledge, and the connection between local and global contexts. We begin with an elementary school program based on the ecological and cultural importance of freshwater sources in drought-affected South Australia. At the secondary level we recount two very different programs; an astronomy education program offered to students in 6th to 11th grade in Perth, Western Australia, then recount a STEM project relating to pregnancy awareness delivered to teenagers at a Brazilian Science Center.

Fresh Water Literacies: A Transdisciplinary Program at Elementary Schools

South Australia is the driest state in Australia, and the ramifications of this impact all walks of society and the environment. A team of researchers with expertise in science, mathematics, English, Aboriginal studies, citizen science, and environmental education obtained funding for a pilot study based on transdisciplinary curriculum and a futures-based pedagogy. *Fresh Water Literacies* (Paige et al., 2018a) was a one-year, place-based investigation involving fifth-grade students and their teachers in one urban and two rural schools located near a wetland, lake, or river. The project aimed to build "students' understanding of the importance and finite availability of natural resources" (p. 4), in this case, fresh water.

The integrated curricular approach endeavored to connect explicitly to "students' personal and collective futures using a futures methodology which is inclusive of individual and community, material and cultural needs, and cognizant of planetary boundaries" (Paige et al., 2018b, p. 50). The futures-thinking, pedagogical approach aimed to raise awareness and understanding of local environmental issues, and enable students to feel both responsible and empowered to take action toward making a better community. Although each school's curriculum focus varied according to its water context, the central theme related to the environmental health and cultural importance of fresh water.

Over the year, teachers participated in six days of professional learning, had access to considerable resources and support funding, and worked closely with the research team. They collaboratively developed

> transdisciplinary units of work around water . . . [including] the *Science* of water quality (measuring salinity, turbidity, pH), the *Mathematics* of data collection (locating middle of data, mean, mode and median), the *English* of constructing future scenarios and the *Art* of accurately depicting and recording local animal and plant species.
>
> *(Paige et al., 2018b, p. 52; original emphasis)*

Details of the practitioner-focused action research design that underpinned the program and teachers' professional learning, and the comprehensive data set collected, are presented in Paige et al. (2018a, 2018b). Here we draw examples from these reports to describe how *Fresh Water Literacies* reflected the knowledge and locality dimensions of the Worldly Perspective approach to STEM integration.

The Knowledge Dimension While disciplinary knowledge underpinned the designed curriculum, the contextual implementation allowed subjects to flow together in an integrated way. Teachers commented: "The science was connected to the English, the geography was connected to the math, the technology was connected to the art, etc." (Paige et al., 2018a, p. 19). In one school, students decided a measure of water salinity must be an error because the salt level was higher than expected. This revealed a misunderstanding: Students did not recognize the decimal point, so teachers explicitly taught decimals beyond the year level curriculum expectations. This helped students to understand the correct recording, graphing, and analysis of salinity measures as well as the importance of questioning data. Because students' science disciplinary knowledge about salinity was contextualized in terms of the wetland, it led naturally to the need for further depth in their mathematics disciplinary knowledge, an illustration of the dynamic balance between integrated and disciplinary knowledge.

Paige et al. (2018b) noted that student assessments by the school and education system usually value cognitive learning most highly; however, this project recognized the importance of knowledge growth in both cognitive and affective domains. Growth in cognitive knowledge is expected over a year, but teachers stated that not only had students' "skills increased, their inquiry skills were there, they took responsibility for this outdoor education center. We saw improvement in reading; I saw amazing changes in science and of their ability in numeracy" (Paige et al., 2018a, p. 19). Reported examples of teachers' reflections and students' comments demonstrate students' developing social conscience and sense of ecojustice based on their growing understanding of the wetland ecology and its social and cultural relationship to the community. Clearly, students' scientific disciplinary learning about ecology has supported interdisciplinary learning about ecojustice and social justice, a valued balance in this project.

The Locality Dimension. Students developed deep connections with their freshwater locality and seized opportunities to broaden their sphere of knowledge. One student described how, in looking at the sustainability of the wetlands, her class had learned that the water enters the lake from gutters and stormwater drains, and that rain carries the litter into the wetlands. Teachers helped students to use their audit data to prepare a brochure about the need for clean gutters and stormwater drains. With their knowledge and commitment to preservation, students also prepared guides to the wetland, its macroinvertebrates, and its birds. Students actively "shared their knowledge and passion for looking after the wetlands" (Paige et al., 2018b, p. 56) by presenting their brochures at the local shopping mall.

A teacher gave this class a "stimulus proposal" suggesting that the council wanted to redevelop the wetlands. She explained that by late in the project

> the students had had experience in taking action and were familiar with the local and state government bodies that they could approach in protest to this happening. They also knew so much about their wetlands that they could use their knowledge and experience to discuss and argue against the stimulus proposal confidently.
>
> *(p. 56)*

In this school, taking their brochures to the local mall and talking with the wider community, together with the role-play in making their protests to the local council, helped students to connect their knowledge and understanding of the local wetland to a more global perspective. They realized the need for community commitment to safe-guard and ensure the future of the wetland and its ecology.

At another school, teachers commented that "Our students learn best when they're actually connected, they were connected to the lake" (Paige et al., 2018a, p. 19). When they talked about the history of flooding in the lake, it had meaning for them. Students' knowledge of historical flood levels empowered them to connect their local, contemporary understanding to a more global view in an historic sense, applying their learnings to a broader context in terms of time.

As these examples showed, students were able to see beyond the disciplinary science and mathematics in their classroom using powerful, integrated knowledge about the ecology of their freshwater source. They were also prepared to take action to protect and maintain the water source for the benefit of the local community and beyond, demonstrating "the capacity to apply it to significant matters in the interest of democracy and social justice. . . . truly powerful knowledge" (Wrigley, 2018, p. 22). As Paige et al. (2018a) summarized:

> Water literacy curriculum is about more than the cognitive and more than knowing. It is transdisciplinary, and uses different lenses to explore an issue in depth. What has also been very powerful in this project was the integral work the students and teachers did in the community; they have written letters to politicians, engaged with local council and set up displays in the main street and in shopping centers. They have made a difference!
>
> *(p. 53)*

An Astronomy Program at Secondary Schools

This case study concerns an astronomy education program offered to students from 6th to 11th grade in two schools in Perth, Western Australia (Heary, 2019). The program encouraged students to learn how to locate, image, and analyze asteroids, as if they were scientists. They gathered ephemerides from the Minor Planet Center, used *Stellarium* software to place their object in the night sky, and the remote Zadko Robotic Telescope to request and view an image and search for asteroids. Here we explore the case study from the two dimensions of the Worldly Perspective. For the knowledge dimension we explore the developing disciplinary and interdisciplinary knowledge of eighth-grade student Mark, who was particularly interested in the potential for humans living permanently in space stations. For the locality dimension, we provide insight from local and global perspectives of ninth-grade student Peta, whose special interests were finding a previously undiscovered asteroid and the potential of asteroids to cause damage on impact with Earth.

The Knowledge Dimension. Data from the case study, especially concept maps, showed that Mark significantly improved his knowledge related to asteroids as he progressed through the astronomy program. Aside from asteroids, Mark had a passion for SpaceX, an organization based in California that manufactures and launches advanced rockets and spacecraft. When established in 2002, one of SpaceX's stated goals was to "revolutionize space travel, with the ultimate goal of enabling people to live on other planets" (http://www.spacex.com/about). Mark was soon linking his new knowledge about asteroids to the SpaceX goal of mining asteroids. In Week 5 of the program, another student reported hearing a news report that asteroid mining was to be listed on the stock exchange. Students were initially amazed that money could be made in this way and discussed asteroid research from the perspective of the economics discipline. This included discussion of issues related to the cost and logistics of removing, transporting, and processing minerals from the asteroids.

To gauge the depth of Mark's understanding, during an interview he was asked to elaborate on his classroom talk about using asteroids as fuel stations. Mark clearly articulated that water was thought to be in abundance on asteroids in the asteroid belt and could be used as a source of drinking water, or it could be split into hydrogen for fuel and valuable oxygen. He weighed up the expense of transporting water and fuel from Earth to a space station compared with the challenges of mining water from asteroids, evoking complex concepts from economics. Further, he stated that SpaceX planned to set up the equipment necessary on asteroids so it could be accessed by spacecraft as a fueling station.

Mark did not elaborate on the details of the asteroid mining process, which he read about in Dunnill and Phillips (2016). However, Mark's understanding that water could be split into hydrogen and oxygen and could also be used as a water source for further space travel was valid and indicated an applied understanding of the chemistry of water, the biology of living things, and some of the factors they need to live in space. This is indeed cutting-edge multidisciplinary science happening in the real world, and beyond.

The flexible nature of the astronomy program that allowed students to explore issues related to a number of disciplines enabled the students, like Mark, to go well beyond learning facts and information about asteroids. We argue this case study demonstrates balance in the knowledge dimension. The participating students were able to gain depth from their disciplinary focus on astronomy and asteroids and breadth by explorations of other disciplines like economics, chemistry, and biology by bringing ideas from those disciplines to contribute to their consideration of astronomy-related problems.

The Locality Dimension. The potential risk of asteroids impacting Earth has resulted in the growth of international centers dedicated to early warning systems and minimizing the potential impact (http://www.nasa.gov/planetarydefense/aida). Of particular interest to the students in this case study was that both ground optical and radio telescopes mostly cover the sky in the Northern Hemisphere, leaving the Southern Hemisphere largely uncovered. The students were able to use a software program, *Sky Coverage*, to determine which parts of Earth were and were not being surveyed for near-Earth objects including asteroids.

Peta's journal entries showed that she began to formulate questions that would help her select sites for imaging quite early on in the program. She wrote,

> I was thinking about the telescopes being used and . . . are any areas in the sky that we can see asteroids from down here [in Perth] that telescopes up north [in the Northern Hemisphere] can also see, like a "crossing over zone" where we take responsibility for looking at that asteroid?
>
> *(Journal #3, Peta)*

By Week 5 students had selected and mapped sections of the sky as part of their individual projects. The images loaded onto the school's server were from the Zadko Robotic Telescope and in black and white. The students were a little disappointed at first but eventually came to understand that not all images would have an asteroid in them. This was because images were being taken in areas that most northern telescopes could not reach. The decision to do this was made on the basis that it would increase their chances of finding a new asteroid rather than confirming known asteroids.

Though they could choose any area of sky that could be imaged by the Zadko, Peta wavered between looking at the asteroid belt and areas too far south for northern telescopes to reach.

> First of all, looking in the asteroid belt would probably have a higher likelihood of observing an asteroid or two that hadn't been discovered or named before, because it's an area where there are lots and lots of them. But, at the same time, if they are able to view the asteroid belt from up north, then it's quite possible that the majority of them have been mapped and looked at already. But, wouldn't it be rather unlikely that we'd find asteroids in other locations anyway? So wouldn't that make it better to look at the asteroid belt because the chances of finding something there are more likely?
>
> *(Journal #6, Peta)*

Peta's thinking was highly sophisticated, and her journal demonstrates that she was able to make in-depth connections between her local, place-based work on searching for asteroids in the Southern Hemisphere from Australia and global scientific knowledge about asteroids and other near-Earth objects. Peta's journal notes illustrated the connection between local and global knowledge inherent in the astronomy program, and provided evidence of metacognitive reflection on her knowledge of Universal Time and an awareness that she found it difficult to comprehend this concept. Moreover, Peta weighed up the advantages and disadvantages of searching for asteroids in different parts of the sky and demonstrated an understanding of how any possible discoveries might contribute to the global knowledge of near-Earth objects.

Preventing Youth Pregnancy: A Program for Teenagers

In this case study we examine the science museum exhibit *Preventing Youth Pregnancy* displayed at the Museu Catavento in São Paulo, Brazil. This exhibit was mounted in the context of increasing concern in Brazil about youth pregnancy and the health risks associated with sexual activity among young people, particularly among marginalized groups, and was co-sponsored by the Kaplan Institute for Sexual Education, the São Paulo State Secretary of Education, and the Museu Catavento. In 1998, the Brazilian National Curricular Parameters designated the topic of sexuality education as one of its cross-curricular themes. Here we draw on the descriptions provided by Navas Iannini and Pedretti (2017) to detail the elements of the exhibit display and the pedagogical sequence of the related curriculum activities.

The installation utilized a variety of passive and interactive displays and pedagogies—including information brochures and panels, drama, fictional narratives, and debates—to engage participants with topics such as STDs, teenage pregnancy, and sexual practices. The sequence of activities began when participants (older than 13 years) entered a room containing puff seats (similar to beanbag seats). They were invited to relax in the seats and encouraged to share with a sex educator, and with one another, why they chose to attend the exhibit and what their expectations were for their visit. The sex educator then showed a video to help participants imagine a trip to their futures.

In the next phase, the room was transformed into a venue for a party. Seating was removed and the room became a labyrinth with walls and display panels emerging from the ceiling. Lights were lowered and music played to simulate a party atmosphere, and participants were exposed to fictional scenarios and situations related to sexual practices and asked to make personal decisions about what she or he would do in that situation. Decisions made by the participants led to different outcomes and potential consequences, causing them to think about their actions in different ways.

In the concluding phase of the program, the room was restored to its original formation with the puff seats in the middle. The sex educator asked the participants about their experiences in the exhibit, their doubts, and their concerns. Participants were invited to revisit their personal dreams and plans for the future and think about how they might be enacted. The discussion finished with an examination of some practical options for contraception (e.g., putting a condom on a dildo, taking condoms home).

In their analysis of this program, Pedretti and Navas Iannini (2018) highlighted how the program helped build connections across formal and informal communities, and with youth culture, and established possible pathways for change. The program was designed to create connections and work with the wider community, including schools. It built on the theme of sexual orientation that is part of the Brazilian National Curricular Parameters and cuts across science, technology, and society.

The program was innovative in that it did not simply transmit information through a one-way communication model, but rather invited participants to read and recount stories and enact dramatizations. Thus, it created the potential for "multi-directional, open-ended knowledge co-production" (Pedretti & Navas Iannini, 2018, p. 39). In the words of one staff member:

> We enter a creative process, the one about dramatisation through the notion of psycho-drama . . . it is important to put the subject [participant] in that dramatization. . . . The rest part [of the exhibit] is the introduction where we ask young people to project into the future, that is the technique. (Interview, female, 30s, museum curator)
>
> *(Pedretti & Navas Iannini, 2018, pp. 41–42)*

The *Preventing Youth Pregnancy* program sought to educate, challenge, and promote social change and understandings. As the following comment suggests, students' active participation, followed by opportunities for reflection, have the potential to help participants to make informed decisions about their own sexual practices and to develop a sense of agency:

> To have them [the teenagers] using condoms, learning how to use them, critically facing the issue of gender inequalities, calls them to dramatize this experience by acting, doing, being in the place of this experience, reflecting. . . . We always tell them to take condoms with them. Some of them empty the box while others are shy and they take just one. (Interview, male, 20s, museum sex educator)
>
> *(Pedretti & Navas Iannini, 2018, p. 43)*

The authors concluded their findings with the following observation about the impact of the program on the participants.

> *Preventing Youth Pregnancy* promotes learning about action through: (i) engaging visitors in debates around critical and complex issues (such as youth pregnancy, abortion, prevention of sexually transmitted diseases); (ii) creating opportunities for visitors to experience dissent and conflict (e.g., when preconceptions about sexism are exposed); (iii) connecting visitors with their personal stories and narratives; and (iv) challenging visitors' beliefs and emotions.
>
> *(Pedretti & Navas Iannini, 2018, pp. 43–44)*

The Knowledge Dimension. The authors conducted this study as part of an international examination of controversial exhibits in science centers and museums (Pedretti & Navas-Iannini, in press). Controversial exhibits are by their very nature integrated across the different elements of the various STEM disciplines—we see the application of scientific knowledge of the human body, knowledge of the technologies of birth control, and mathematical knowledge of time scales and probability—as well as having important socio-cultural-political dimensions. *Preventing Youth Pregnancy* placed an explicit (and sometimes implicit) emphasis on the importance of making informed decisions about sexual activity, setting the context for those decisions, explaining the consequences of those decisions, challenging stereotypes, and providing the knowledge and tools to help young people to take appropriate action. To inform decision-making, participants were provided with information on specific topics such as sexual practices, prevention of teenage pregnancy, and risk and prevention of STDs, as well as technologies for avoiding pregnancy. As such the program was both integrated and disciplinary—decisions about engaging in sexual activity, for example, are best made with scientific/biological knowledge of how pregnancy occurs, mathematical knowledge about timeframes, and technological knowledge about contraceptive devices (as well as the cultural context within which such activity occurs). In this case we see how the knowledge dimension does not favor one form of knowledge over another but demonstrates how integrated knowing and disciplinary knowing work together in a powerful and synergetic way to produce the best outcomes.

The Locality Dimension. The locality dimension stresses the importance of moving back and forth between locales, seeing the relevance of a topic in the local setting and being able to apply it more broadly.

Preventing Youth Pregnancy is an excellent example of how this dimension applies to STEM curricula. The exhibit was established to encourage participants to examine how the topic of youth pregnancy applied to them in a very personal way, by imagining futures, personal storying, role playing, etc.—but also to look at the notion of otherness—leading to important discussions about youth inclusion and groups who are economically disadvantaged and/or marginalized in Brazil and elsewhere.

The students were able to pivot back and forth between personal and local experiences of sexual activity and the consequences, and the wider implications of the topic for groups (particularly marginalized groups) across the country. In this case, we see the importance and power of the locality dimension. Local and personal knowledge, combined with more global knowledge, has the potential to build connections, understandings, and support change within communities and across communities.

Discussion and Conclusions

These three case studies exemplify integrated STEM curricula that were designed for very different purposes; they had very different content and engaged quite different populations. Yet all three demonstrated the important roles played by the two dimensions of the Worldly Perspective: balance between integrated and disciplinary knowledge (the knowledge dimension) and connection between local and global contexts (the locality dimension).

Fresh Water Literacies was aimed at fifth-grade elementary students as a place-based program, involving the use of the local community and its environments as a starting point for the teaching of discipline concepts in the school curriculum. But more than that, as Deringer (2017) emphasized, by engaging students through connection with their community, place-based education has themes relating to environmental and social justice. In *Fresh Water Literacies*, through the community connection, students were able to explore the environmental aspects of their freshwater source, but also they had opportunities to touch on the ways in which it had cultural significance to the local Aboriginal people (Paige et al., 2018a). Thus, not only was the balance between disciplinary and interdisciplinary knowledge important to the students' learning, the connection with their community opened opportunities to build more global perspectives about their water source, in terms of time and differences in worldviews.

The second case study was also place-based, but a very different place: the asteroid belt within Earth's Solar System. In this case, high school students experienced in-depth, disciplinary learning about astronomy, including how to obtain images of sections of the sky and make explorations relating to asteroids. Through two students' journeys, we saw how they were able to build cross-disciplinary knowledge to achieve the aims of their personal projects, as well as moving between local, "earthly knowledge" to more global or space perspectives. Researching the potential of asteroid mining, for example, involved Mark using knowledge from several other disciplines in his futuristic thinking about the possibilities of living in space, but also making connections with living on Earth. Peta's interest in the potential threat to Earth of asteroid impact, and her wish to discover new asteroids in "her piece" of the sky, involved making sophisticated connections between parts of Earth and varying telescope "coverage" of parts of the sky. An important corollary of programs such as this, where students are able to pursue their own sub-projects, is the making of links between life and work, in this case, the work of astronomers.

Our final case study was not school-based, although it had its foundations in the Brazil school curriculum. *Preventing Youth Pregnancy* was an ambitious, and doubtless controversial, exhibit developed at the Museu Catavento. Rather than being based in a "place," this program was based squarely in a significant community concern; the problem of youth pregnancy and associated health risks. Further, because family is the fundamental unit of every society, the topic of this case study has very real and personal importance to everyone. The primary audience was school groups, but the exhibition was open to members of the public, and thus had the capacity to make connections not only with school students but with non-school youth and adults as well. Although this program was implemented in a short time frame, its potential effects were long term due to the underpinning techniques of provoking participants to think about themselves, the significance of the decisions they make about pregnancy and contraception, and their futures. By encouraging participants to consider their choices and responsibilities in their own future, we see how particular knowledge about biology can be balanced with more general social and cultural knowledge about youth pregnancy and contraception. Participants' experience in the program provided a balance of knowledge and revealed the connection between the personal, or local, perspective and the global, or wider, community perspective about this important issue.

This chapter documented how the Worldly Perspective operates in practice across three very different STEM education programs, and explored their effects through the dimensions of balance between disciplinary and integrated knowledge, and connection between local and global contexts. We demonstrated that integrated STEM curricula can have important outcomes in terms of students' ability to think about real-world issues and explore how they impact their life outside of the classroom. We also saw how students found relevance in the STEM curriculum because they were able to make connections to the outside world (see Rennie, Venville & Wallace, 2018, for further exploration of relevance in STEM curricula).

We believe that the power of the Worldly Perspective in STEM education lies in its capacity to *bridge* different knowledge systems. In this chapter, we emphasized the importance of balance—between disciplinary and integrated knowledge—and connection—between local and global contexts. But as our examples have shown, the Worldly Perspective can also be employed as a bridge across other STEM knowledge systems; for example, Western and Aboriginal worldviews in *Fresh Water Literacies*, life and work in the astronomy case study, and the particular and the general in *Preventing Youth Pregnancy*. We chose these cases to illustrate the importance of working across boundaries. In our attempt to implement some underlying theory to the STEM education movement, we have deliberately used the term *Worldly* as a metaphor for striving for a higher level of wisdom. Such wisdom is attained, we believe, by balancing, connecting, and building bridges across the different knowledge systems of science, technology, engineering, and mathematics.

Acknowledgements

The research that underpinned the development of the Worldly Perspective was funded by an Australian Research Council Collaborative Grant (C59700325) with the Education Department of Western Australia, an Australian Research Council Discovery Grant (DP0451818), and a Canadian Social Science and Humanities Research Council Standard Grant (410–2006–2443).

The authors respectfully acknowledge the researchers whose original work formed the basis of the case studies. We are very grateful to Kathryn Paige and her colleagues (Fresh Water Literacies Case), Auriol Heary (Astronomy Case), and Ana Maria Navas Iannini and Erminia Pedretti (Youth Pregnancy Case) for giving permission for us to re-analyze their work in terms of the Worldly Perspective. The opinions expressed are entirely those of the authors.

References

Bakhtin, M. M. (1981). *The dialogic imagination: Four essays* (C. Emerson & M. Holmquist, Trans.). Austin, TX: University of Texas Press.

Beane, J. A. (1995). Curriculum integration and the disciplines of knowledge. *Phi Delta Kappan, 76*(8), 616–622.

Clark, E. T., Jr. (1997). *Designing and implementing an integrated curriculum*. Brandon, VT: Holistic Education Press.

Deringer, S. A. (2017). Mindful place-based education: Mapping the literature. *Journal of Experiential Education, 40*(4), 333–348. https://doi.org/10.1177/1053825917716694

Drake, S. M. (1998). *Creating integrated curriculum: Proven ways to increase student learning*. Thousand Oaks, CA: Corwin Press.

Dunnill, C. W., & Phillips, R. (September 28, 2016). Making space rocket fuel from water could drive a power revolution on Earth. *The Conversation*. https://theconversation.com/making-space-rocket-fuel-from-water-could-drive-a-power- revolution-on-earth-65854

Duschl, R. (2008). Science education in three-part harmony: Balancing conceptual, epistemic, and social learning goals. *Review of Research in Education, 32*, 268–291. https://doi.org/10.3102/0091732X07309371

Hargreaves, A., Earl, L., & Ryan, J. (1996). *Schooling for change: Reinventing education for early adolescents*. London: Falmer.

Heary, A. (2019). *An investigation of the impact of an authentic astronomy program and school students' understanding of and attitudes towards science*. Perth, Australia: University of Western Australia.

Holmlund, T. D., Lesseig, K., & Slavit, D. (2018). Making sense of "STEM education" in K–12 contexts. *International Journal of STEM Education, 5*(32). https://doi.org/10.1186/s40594-018-0127-2

Jacobs, H. (Ed.). (1989). *Interdisciplinary curriculum: Design and implementation*. Alexandria, VA: Association for Supervision and Curriculum Development.

LaForce, M., Nobel, E., King, H., Century, J., Blackwell, C., Holt, S., . . . Loo, S. (2016). The eight essential elements of inclusive STEM high schools. *International Journal of STEM Education, 3*(21). https://doi.org/10.1186/s40594-016-0054-z

Navas Iannini, A., & Pedretti, E. (2017). Preventing youth pregnancy: Dialogue and deliberation in a science museum exhibit. *Canadian Journal of Science, Mathematics and Technology Education, 17*(4), 271–287. https://doi.org/10.1080/14926156.2017.1381285

Paige, K., Caldwell, D., Elliott, K., O'Keeffe, L., Osborne, S., Roetman, P., . . . Gosnell, S. (2018a). *Fresh water literacies: Transdisciplinary learning for place and eco justice*. Adelaide, Australia: University of South Australia.

Paige, K., Lloyd, D., Caldwell, D., Comber, B., O'Keeffe, L., Osborne, S., & Roetman, P. (2018b). Futures in primary science education—connecting students to place and ecojustice. *Visions for Sustainability, 9*, 49–59. https://doi.org/10.13135/2384-8677/2773

Pang, J. S., & Good, R. (2000). A review of the integration of science and mathematics: Implications for further research. *School Science and Mathematics, 100*(2), 73–82. https://doi.org/10.1111/j.1949-8594.2000.tb17239.x

Pedretti, E., & Navas Iannini, A. (2018). Pregnant pauses: Science museums, schools and a controversial exhibition. In D. Corrigan, C. Bunting, A. Jones, & J. Loughran (Eds.), *Navigating the changing landscape of formal and informal science learning opportunities* (pp. 31–49). Dordrecht, The Netherlands: Springer. https://doi.org/10.1007/978-3-319-89761-5_3

Pedretti, E., & Navas-Iannini, A. (in press). *Controversy in science museums: Re-imagining exhibition spaces and practice*. New York and London: Routledge.

Rennie, L. J., Venville, G., & Wallace, J. (2011). Learning science in an integrated classroom: Finding balance through theoretical triangulation. *Journal of Curriculum Studies, 43*(2), 139–162. https://doi.org/10.1080/00220272.2010.509516

Rennie, L. J., Venville, G., & Wallace, J. (2012a). *Knowledge that counts in a global community: Exploring the contribution of integrated curriculum*. London: Routledge.

Rennie, L. J., Venville, G., & Wallace, J. (Eds.). (2012b). *Integrating science, technology, engineering, and mathematics: Issues, reflections and ways forward*. New York, NY: Routledge.

Rennie, L., Venville, G., & Wallace, J. (2018). Making STEM curriculum useful, relevant, and motivating for students. In R. Jorgensen & K. Larkin (Eds.), *STEM in the Junior Secondary: The state of play* (pp. 91–109). Dordrecht, The Netherlands: SpringerNature. https://doi.org/10.1007/978-981-10-5448-8_6

Roberts, D. A. (2007). Scientific literacy/science literacy. In S. K. Abell & N. G. Lederman (Eds.), *Handbook of research on science education* (pp. 729–780). Mahwah, NJ: Lawrence Erlbaum.

Venville, G., Wallace, J., Rennie, L. J., & Malone, J. (2002). Curriculum integration: Eroding the high ground of science as a school subject. *Studies in Science Education, 37*, 43–84. https://doi.org/10.1080/03057260208560177

Wrigley, T. (2018). Knowledge, curriculum and social justice. *The Curriculum Journal, 29*(1), 4–24. https://doi.org/10.1080/09585176.2017.1370381

5

THEORETICAL FRAMEWORKS FOR STEM EDUCATION RESEARCH

Thomas J. Bussey, Stanley M. Lo and Chris Rasmussen

Introduction

There are considerable workforce needs to produce more and better-prepared science, technology, engineering, and mathematics (STEM) graduates (PCAST, 2012). Meeting these needs is arguably more effectively done when efforts are aligned with research that is theoretically informed, grounded in the existing literature, and methodologically rigorous. But to what extent is there commonality in the use of various theoretical perspectives, literature reviews, and methodologies across the STEM fields? In this chapter, we address this question by examining different fields of STEM education research to present a review of the research published in the peer-reviewed journals of each field. This analysis provides an overview of the general practices of each field and compares the use of theoretical perspectives, literature reviews, and methodologies across fields.

The chapter begins with a reflection on the enterprise of discipline-based education research (DBER) in general, followed by an organizational framing that enables us to compare and contrast trends in the different DBER fields. We then examine publications in integrated STEM journals, followed by discipline-specific reviews in undergraduate mathematics education research, engineering education research, physics education research, chemical education research, and biology education research. We conclude with a call for transcending the compartmentalization of these different areas of research.

The Humanity (and Messiness) of Research

Scientific research is a human enterprise (Reiss & Sprenger, 2017). The researchers involved in STEM education research are human beings, and their work relies on human subjects—instructors and students—and the environments and artifacts they create. "In improving the quality of practice [in education], complexity and the messiness of practice-in-context cannot be fantasized away" (Lather, 2004, p. 768). Therefore, it is essential to acknowledge the complexity of the human experience for both the researcher(s) and the subject(s).

> Humans are complex beings, and modeling their behavior, belief systems, actions, character traits, location in culture, and volition is intrinsically complicated. Research challenges arise in large part because social scientists lack the high degree of control over their subjects that is typical in the [other areas of science].
>
> *(NRC, 2002, p. 48)*

A breaker full of molecules is much more well behaved than a classroom full of students (NRC, 2002). First, the numbers of molecules in the sample are orders of magnitude larger than the numbers of human subjects in any education research project. Additionally, the molecules do not leave the beaker after eight hours (e.g., of a school day) and introduce a variety of confounding variables in between measures. This is not to discount the veracity of STEM education research, but to acknowledge the intricacies and array of obstacles faced by the education researcher as well as the variety of paradigms and approaches employed to explore the richness and density of teaching and learning in STEM disciplines.

The perspective of the researcher in traditional STEM disciplines is often discounted or diminished under the guise of objectivity. In reality, the disciplinary training of a field generates a set of norms and expectations for how research is carried out, interpreted, and communicated within the field (Reiss & Sprenger, 2017). As such, disciplinary disparities exist between fields. A geneticist sees the world differently from an engineer. A mathematician views argumentation differently from a physicist. The traditions, language, and cultures of the various STEM disciplines influence how they view the world and, in turn, define and limit how they understand and explore this world. Similarly, education researchers draw upon a variety of theoretical frameworks to define a particular worldview. Given the complexity of the human experience, the choice of particular theoretical frameworks allows the researcher to make explicit the lens through which they are framing their work. These choices denote certain assumptions about and limitations of their work (Bodner & Orgill, 2007).

The Framing Triangle

In the course of developing this chapter, we observed that research published in various fields in STEM education utilize a broad range of stated theoretical frameworks. However, there does not seem to be a single set of theoretical frameworks from which all STEM education research is conducted. Moreover, some research did not present an explicit statement of their theoretical perspective at all. Instead, the background literature provided much of the framing and backing for the content and direction of the work described; other research further framed their theoretical rationale utilizing their choice and justification of methodology. Ideally, the theoretical perspective of the researcher should inform and situate their work within a body of literature and set of methods. The alignment of these framing conditions are further positioned within the disciplinary practice of the field. Given the diversity and variation in the use of theoretical frameworks across the domains of STEM education research, we have chosen instead to describe what we refer to as a "framing triangle", as depicted in Figure 5.1.

Inspired by the instruction triangle of Ball and colleagues (Cohen, Raudenbush, & Ball, 2003; Ball & Forzani, 2007), the framing triangle conveys the relationship between the theoretical perspective of the researcher, the body of literature within which their work is situated, and their choice of methodology. The framing parameters constituted by these three vertices are influenced by the unique disciplinary practices of a given field and can be informed by practices across fields.

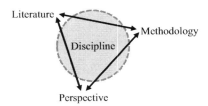

Figure 5.1 The framing triangle positions literature, methodology, and perspective influences in constituting the theoretical framework for STEM education research.

Use of Theoretical Frameworks in STEM Education Research

In an attempt to evaluate the use of theoretical frameworks in the STEM education literature, we began by looking to the peer-reviewed published work in the field. However, in this effort we were met with two main obstacles: (1) there are very few journals in which STEM education research (and integrated STEM education research for that matter) are published, and (2) even in such journals, most of the published work is discipline-specific. We began by creating a historical review of the work published in the newly created *International Journal of STEM Education* from 2014 to 2018. A total of 49 articles were classified as education research, i.e., scholarly work that focused on the processes, contexts, social dynamics, or resources that influence the learning and/or teaching of STEM. Of the 49 articles, slightly less than half, only 23 (46.9%), identified STEM as the context of the study. The remaining 53.1% of the articles presented discipline-specific education research in various subdisciplines of science, engineering, or mathematics. We observed that no technology education research was presented in this journal.

Given the lack of STEM education journals or published work in the area of integrated STEM education, we then turned to three major science education journals (*Journal of Research in Science Teaching, Science Education,* and *International Journal of Science Education*) to see if work was presented in an integrated science context. Given the range of DBER present in the *International Journal of STEM Education,* we hoped that perhaps the more established science education journals might publish work that captured an integrated approach. The science education journals we examined represent an established research field across global contexts with a longer history compared to the *International Journal of STEM Education.* We noted that the range of education research presented in the science education journals included a wider range of educational context; whereas the research presented in the *International Journal of STEM Education* was almost exclusively focused on undergraduate education. In order to maintain a more focused comparison to the STEM education research previously reported, we decided to look only at science education articles in these journals from 2000 to 2018 that were conducted in a higher education context. A total of 407 articles were examined: 165 (40.5%) from the *Journal of Research in Science Teaching,* 72 (17.7%) from *Science Education,* and 170 (41.8%) from the *International Journal of Science Education.* Across these three journals, only 165 articles (35.6%) were contextualized as science (95 articles), STEM (39 articles), science education (9 articles), science and mathematics (1 article), or interdisciplinary science (1 article). The majority of the work presented in these journals (64.4%) were discipline specific. As such, we noted that relatively little integrated science or STEM education research is being published. The vast majority of STEM-related education research continues to be conducted as DBER and may speak to a larger need to promote cross-disciplinary conversations about the research and, subsequently, the theoretical underpinnings of the work being conducted in these areas.

While the specific theoretical frameworks varied from discipline to discipline, there were some common themes across both the STEM and science education journals as shown in Figure 5.2. Cognitive frameworks were predominantly used in STEM education (63%) and science education (50%) in the articles that we examined. Some examples of commonly used cognitive frameworks include argumentation, conceptual change, constructivism, information processing, learning progressions, nature of science, etc. Social frameworks, such as community of practice, critical theory, cultural historical activity theory, and situated cognition, make up about 10% of the STEM education and science education articles. Interestingly, the three science education journals have different distributions or proportions of cognitive versus social frameworks. *Journal of Research in Science Teaching* has the highest proportion of social frameworks (17%), compared to *Science Education* (14%) and *International Journal of Science Education* (3%). Correspondingly, for cognitive frameworks, *Journal of Research in Science Teaching* has the lowest proportion (42%), followed by *Science Education* (54%) and *International Journal of Science Education* (56%).

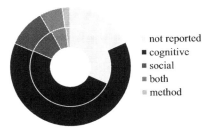

Figure 5.2 Distribution of frameworks in various integrated STEM and science education journals. The inner
ring is STEM education, and the outer ring is science education.

The use of theoretical frameworks in DBER shapes how members of those communities view
their disciplines, influences how they enact curriculum and pedagogies within their fields, and influences how they view and conceptualize the integration of STEM concepts and practices. From our
initial analysis, we concluded that most education research is still done within clearly defined DBER
communities. Therefore, if we are to make any headway in producing a better understanding of an
integrated STEM perspective, we should start by understanding how the different disciplines are
using theoretical frameworks in their own research fields. In this way, we can learn from one another
and ultimately better understand how teaching and learning occurs across the various iterations of
STEM education. As such, we then set out to map how the various subdisciplines of STEM have
used theoretical frameworks over the past decade. The goal of the subsequent analysis is to initiate
cross-disciplinary conversations about the recent historical use and variety of theoretical frameworks
across STEM education research.

Research in Undergraduate Mathematics Education

Over the past several years, the field of research in undergraduate mathematics education (RUME)
has experienced considerable growth. This growth is evident by three major milestones. In 2011, a
dedicated university mathematics education working group at the biennial Congress of the European Society for Research in Mathematics Education was established. In 2015, there was the birth of
a new international journal focused solely on RUME, and in 2016 we saw the start of the biennial
International Network for Didactic Research in University Mathematics conference. This growth
builds on two long-standing conferences on RUME, each which began in the late 1990s. One of
these is held annually in the United States, and the other is biennial and takes place in various countries throughout the Southern Hemisphere.

Recognizing this tremendous growth and need to take stock of where the field has been and
where it is going, the RUME community has recently produced six reviews that synthesize early
research and highlight developments and trends in the field, including theoretical and methodological shifts and advances (Artigue, 2016; Biza, Giraldo, Hochmuth, Khakbaz, & Rasmussen, 2016;
Larsen, Marrongelle, Bressoud, & Graham, 2017; Rasmussen & Wawro, 2017; Winsløw & Rasmussen, 2018; Winsløw, Gueudet, Hochmuth, & Nardi, 2018). We therefore begin our survey of the use
of different theoretical perspectives in RUME by highlighting what these scholars have found in
their comprehensive reviews. We conclude this section with insights from our own review of *Educational Studies in Mathematics*, which is one of the top mathematics education journals that frequently
publishes RUME, as well as studies that focus on the elementary and secondary levels.

One thing that stands out in all six of these reviews on RUME is the focus on different theoretical perspectives (as opposed to methodology or literature). That is, in terms of our framing triangle,
perspective is the core vertex that RUME uses to characterize the state of the field. This makes good

sense when one recognizes that the shift from predominantly quantitative methods to the embracing of qualitative methods happened several decades ago. A second thing that stands out in all six reviews is that they highlight the marked shift from the use of cognitive perspectives that strive to understand student conceptions of and difficulties with particular mathematical concepts to the use of a broader range of sociocultural, institutional, and discursive theoretical perspectives that seek to understand the complex social aspects of learning and teaching.

This shift in the dominant theoretical perspectives used by researchers in RUME reflects a "turn to social theories" (Lerman, 2000, p. 20) that characterizes the broader field of research in mathematics education. Indeed, Inglis and Foster (2018) recently analyzed over 50 years of mathematics education research and systematically documented the dominance of cognitive theories such as constructivism in the late 1980s, which has steadily declined to the current day, giving rise to the pervasive use of various social theories including the theory of didactical situations, communities of practice, emergent perspective, commognition, semiotics, embodied cognition, discursive theories, and instrumental and documentational approaches. Another notable shift in the field regards the object of inquiry. Rather than focusing primarily on the cognition of individual learners, the field has moved toward analyses of teaching practices, teacher knowledge, and classroom and institutional norms and practices, to name just a few lines of research that go beyond individual student cognition. Methodologically, such analyses necessitate researchers to immerse themselves into the experiences of students and teachers, including ethnographic approaches and design-based classroom research.

In our targeted review of the last 18 years of *Educational Studies in Mathematics* (2000–2018), we identified 105 articles that focused on RUME and used some form of qualitative approach. Of these 105, over half (56) took primarily a cognitive perspective, while 49 made us of various social perspectives. This breakdown does not immediately reflect the "turn to the social" identified by Lerman and further documented by Inglis and Foster. We therefore looked at these studies by decade, grouping those that were published between 2000 and 2009 and those that were published between 2010 and 2018. While the pattern is somewhat similar, there is a definite shift toward the use of social theories. In particular, of the 71 RUME studies published between 2010 and 2018, 34 of these made use of a cognitive perspective, while 37 adopted a social perspective. Thus, we see two notable trends. First, the number of RUME publications that used a qualitative approach more than doubled from 2000–2009 to 2010–2018 (34 studies to 71 studies). Second, across these same two time periods, the percent of studies that used some variation of a social theory increased from 35% to 52%. Both these trends are consistent with the growth in RUME research in general and the greater prominence of social perspectives.

Engineering Education Research

The field of engineering education research (EER) is, compared to mathematics education research and physics education research, a relatively young discipline. The emergence of EER as a discipline, both across North America and Europe, is documented and described in the article "The Emergence of Engineering Education Research as an International Connected Field of Inquiry" by Borrego and Bernhard (2011). As is the case with any emerging discipline, there is the reliance on established approaches from the broader field of education research. In the early days or EER, quantitative research methods were the norm (Koro-Ljungberg & Douglas, 2008). The use of qualitative research methods, however, is on the rise and, as argued by Case and Light (2011), qualitative researchers in EER are embracing a range of different methodologies. These researchers further argue that the following methodologies, while not yet widely embraced in EER, show considerable promise: case study, grounded theory, ethnography, action research, phenomenography, discourse analysis, and narrative analysis. Case and Light (2011) define a methodology as "the theoretical arguments that researchers use in order to justify their research methods and design". In terms of our framing triangle, we see that methodology (as opposed to perspective or literature) is the core vertex in how the field of EER defines itself and judges the quality of research (Walther et al., 2017).

In their meta-analysis of all articles published in 2005–2006 in the *Journal of Engineering Education*, Koro-Ljungberg & Douglas (2008) reviewed 48 articles, only nine of which used qualitative approaches and six were mixed methods. Of the remaining articles, 30 were quantitative studies, and three were not empirical studies. Koro-Ljungberg and Douglas (2008) applied a generous definition of qualitative, including any study under this umbrella that used text-based or descriptive data. For the nine studies that used qualitative approaches, Koro-Ljungberg and Douglas (2008) further identified those that had a clearly defined theoretical perspective. Perhaps not surprising given EER's focus on methodology, only four of these nine articles had clearly defined theoretical perspectives. All four of these studies made use of social theories, including social constructivism, phenomenology, and gender studies. The remaining three qualitative studies had less clearly articulated theoretical perspectives, two of which were classified simply as post-positivist and one as constructivist.

To complement this brief review of the EER literature, we conducted a review of all 135 articles in the *Journal of Engineering Education* (JEE) from 2010 to 2018. We chose this time period for review because it reflects a period of growth in qualitative EER. In our review of published studies during this time period that took a qualitative approach, we were interested in learning the extent to which articles in this leading journal leaned toward the use of social theories more so than cognitive theories, or vice versa. This interest was in part motivated by the clear turn toward the social in RUME. Interestingly and somewhat surprisingly (to us), we found that of the 54 papers reviewed with clearly identifiable theoretical perspectives, 28 used some form of social perspective, and 26 used some form of a cognitive perspective. Recall that in our review of RUME research, we found that 52% of the studies used a social perspective during this same time period. Thus, we see a striking similarity between RUME and EER in terms of the perspectives being used.

Physics Education Research

Of the science education research fields addressed in this chapter (e.g., physics, chemistry, and biology), physics education research (PER) is generally recognized as the oldest of these subdisciplines, beginning in the 1970s (Docktor & Mestre, 2014; Cummings, 2011). Arising from the disciplinary focus of physics education researchers, several discipline-specific journals including the *American Journal of Physics* and the *European Journal of Physics* have occasionally published PER. However, in responding to the growth of the field, several PER-specific journals have emerged (*Physical Review Special Topics—Physics Education Research, American Journal of Physics PER Supplement, The Physics Teacher, Physics Education*, and the *European Journal of Physics Education*). In addition to the growth in journals for and publications of PER, the field has also developed three major PER conferences. Beginning in the 1990s with the Physics Education Research Conference, the field grew in 2000 to include the Gordon Research Conference on Physics Research and Education, and again in 2005 with the Foundations and Frontiers in Physics Education Research conference. This growth reflects a robust PER community.

Two major reviews of the PER literature have been conducted. Cummings (2011) described the historical development of PER, and Docktor and Mestre (2014) categorized and characterized the PER literature. Both of these reviews were commissioned for the National Academies Board on Science Education's study of the Status, Contributions, and Future Directions of Discipline Based Education Research. Cummings (2011) describes a general Piagetian influence in PER through the use of clinical interviews and a focus on concept development. This cognitive focus is further characterized by a variety of theoretical frameworks identified by the field ranging from Vygotsky's social constructivism to diSessa's conceptual change perspective of "knowledge in pieces".

Cummings (2011) specifically addressed the question "What theoretical frameworks have guided the development of physics education?" and notes that

> I was struck by the range and nature of responses that I received in regard to this question. There were several very knowledgeable physics education researchers who answered along the lines of "what is a theoretical framework?" when I asked this question of them. Perhaps the lack of any consensus on this issue is an indication that [. . .] we have no theoretical frameworks in the field of PER.

This comment is interesting in that it suggests the perception that the theoretical perspective with regard to the framing triangle is either not of importance or significantly varied amongst the PER community.

More recently, the 2014 report by Docktor and Mestre presents a comprehensive review of the PER literature. This report organizes the PER literature around six topic areas: (1) conceptual understanding, (2) problem solving, (3) curriculum and instruction, (4) assessment, (5) cognitive psychology, and (6) attitude and beliefs about teaching and learning. All six topic areas are described in terms of the methodologies used—primarily interviews, self-reports, and quantitative measures. This suggests that methodology is the primary vertex of PER. While all topic areas are also characterized in terms of "theoretical frameworks", this was found to refer primarily to framing literature rather than theoretical perspectives. The PER literature draws on a variety of previous work in the areas of information processing, problem solving, expertise, transfer, metacognition, and language. Thus, the literature vertex also appears to be robust. Very few topic areas in this report address theoretical perspectives in PER, and of those, "constructivism and its associated theories, such as situated, socio-cultural, ecological, everyday, and distributed cognition" are primarily addressed (Docktor & Mestre, 2014, p. 14). In contrast to RUME and EER, PER displays a significant cognitive perspective.

Chemical Education Research

Chemical education research (CER) developed alongside PER in response to calls for an exploration and better understanding of how students learn science (Bodner, 2011). The focus on science education has given way to the focus on discipline-specific research in chemistry education. This has been supported by the publication of this work in several journals including the *Journal of Chemical Education, Chemical Education Research and Practice* (formerly *University Chemistry Education*), and *The Chemical Educator*, and the presentation of CER at the American Chemical Society's national, regional, and local meetings, the Biennial Conference on Chemical Education, the Gordon Research Conference on Chemical Education Research and Practice, and the International Conference on Chemistry Education.

To date, three meta-analyses of the CER literature have been conducted. Kornhauser (1979) published the first review of some 250 articles primarily from 1975 to 1977. Kornhauser describes a focus on evaluating the chemistry curricula and notes that "the development of integrated teaching-learning theories, based on the nature of the chemical sciences, on psychological and sociological knowledge, and acknowledging the interactions between chemistry, curriculum, student, teacher and society, is now favoured" (1979, p. 23). More recently, Towns and Kraft (2011) conducted a more systematic and rigorous evaluation of 379 peer-reviewed CER manuscripts from 2000 to 2010, and Teo and colleagues (2014) presented a content analysis of 650 empirical CER articles from 2004 to 2013. Towns and Kraft (2011) identified six major categories of research: (1) pedagogies, (2) misconceptions, (3) particulate nature of matter (PNOM), (4) instrument development, (5) student achievement, and (6) miscellaneous. Similarly, Teo et al. (2014) identified nine categories adapted from Tsai and Wen (2005): (1) teacher education, (2) teaching, (3) learning (students' conceptions and conceptual change); (4) learning (classroom contexts and learner characteristics); (5) goals and policy, curriculum, evaluation, and assessment; (6) cultural, social, and gender issues; (7) history, philosophy, and nature of chemistry; (8) educational technology; and (9) informal learning. Both recent reviews contain a primary focus on cognitive perspectives and a lesser extent on social perspectives in CER.

Both Towns and Kraft (2011) and Teo et al. (2014) include an explicit analysis of general methodologies rather than theoretical perspectives. Qualitative studies constitute 29.8% (Towns & Kraft, 2011) and 21.7% (Teo et al., 2014), quantitative studies constitute 51.7 % (Towns & Kraft, 2011) and 26.3% (Teo et al., 2014), and mixed-methods studies constitute 18.5% (Towns & Kraft, 2011) and 52.0% (Teo et al., 2014). The shift in quantitative to mixed methods is likely not a significant shift in the research methodologies used in CER but rather reflects the larger pool of manuscripts analyzed in the Teo et al. (2014) study. This emphasis on the methodology vertex of the framing triangle is likely reflected in the guidelines for authors from these journals, many of which contain explicit requirements for inclusion and discussion of methods and data analysis grounded in relevant research practices. More recently, changes in the guidelines for authors for the *Journal of Chemical Education* and *Chemical Education Research and Practice* now include calls for theoretical perspectives and research questions that are grounded in the conceptual frameworks of the prior literature.

Biology Education Research

The field of biology education research (BER) has embraced theoretical and methodological traditions from DBER and science education research, as well as other social science fields, to study the learning and teaching of biology (NRC, 2012). The growth of BER is evidenced by the increasing number of journals. The *Journal of Biological Education*, founded in 1967 by the Royal Society of Biology in the UK, is the first dedicated BER journal across a wide range of educational settings. More specifically for undergraduate BER, other journals emerged from various professional societies for research in the biological sciences, such as *Biochemistry and Molecular Biology Education* in 1972, *Advanced in Physiology Education* in 1989, *Journal of Microbiology and Biology Education* in 2000, *Life Sciences Education* (*LSE*) in 2002, and *Anatomical Sciences Education* in 2008. As an example of the growth of BER, the number of articles in *LSE* increased from 26 in 2002 to 60 in 2015. In parallel, the Society for the Advancement of Biology Education Research (SABER) was founded in 2011 and saw a rapid increase in the number of presentations from 94 in 2011 to 192 in 2015. A second conference dedicated to undergraduate BER, the Gordon Research Conference, was established in 2015. Together, these numbers highlight the increase in BER scholarship.

Four recent reviews of BER in the existing literature complement one another and create a holistic view of the field that is inclusive of international and global context. DeHaan (2011) traced the origins of BER primarily in the United States from 1920 to 1989. Dirks (2011) described BER studies at the undergraduate level in publications across the world from 1990 to 2010. Gul (2016) and Lo (2019) examined trends and changes in BER in predominantly European journals from 1997 to 2014 and in US-based journals and conferences from 2002 to 2015 respectively.

In the literature corner of the framing triangle, BER tends to foreground literature reviews of the topics being studied while utilizing theoretical frameworks sparingly. DeHaan (2011) found that from 1920 to 1989, BER studies focused on either the investigation of instructional strategies or examination of student reasoning. DeHaan (2011) also identified constructivism and conceptual change theory as the two main theoretical frameworks, with constructivism emerging in the 1960s followed by conceptual change theory in the 1980s. Similarly, Dirks (2011) identified three main topics of studies in undergraduate BER from 1990 to 2010: student learning and performance, student attitudes and beliefs, and development of concept inventories and validated instruments. Most of these studies did not have explicitly stated theoretical frameworks, and the remaining few studies are most commonly situated in the traditions of cooperative or constructivist learning, including various learning cycles. For studies on student attitudes and beliefs, Dirks (2011) attributed the affective domain from Bloom's *Taxonomy of Educational Objectives* as the main theoretical framework. Gul (2016) found that the most common areas of investigation were learning (21%), teaching (19%), and attitudes (17%), mirroring what Dirks (2011) described for undergraduate BER studies from an overlapping but not identical period of time. Neither Gul (2016) nor Lo (2019) dealt explicitly with theoretical frameworks.

For methodology, Gul (2016) analyzed articles in eight major academic journals from 1997 to 2014, with the majority of the data coming from European journals such as *Journal of Biological Education* (31%) and *International Journal of Science Education* (24%). These articles comprised of a wide range of study populations, with the most studied populations being secondary school students (34%) undergraduates (23%), and primary school students (20%). Gul (2016) identified qualitative methodologies as the majority mode of investigation (53%), with descriptive studies (18%) and case study approaches (17%) being the most common. Quantitative methodologies accounted for 43% of these BER studies, again with descriptive studies being the most common (11%), followed by quasi-experimental approaches (9%). Few BER studies in this review used mixed methodologies (4%). In contrast, Lo (2019) analyzed the US-based journal *LSE* and SABER conference and found that *LSE* articles were most commonly guided by descriptive research questions, whereas SABER abstracts were most commonly guided by causal research questions. Research at both venues prioritize undergraduate classrooms as the study context and quantitative methodologies.

Lo (2019) attributed these trends to the historical development of biologists pursuing education research. As these researchers are crossing disciplinary boundaries from the biological sciences, they may be predictably relying on the data sources and research methodologies that are most prevalent in their (post)-positivist perspectives. As a focal example of the larger trends, we analyzed work in *LSE* from 2002 to 2015 and found that nearly 75% of the articles with identifiable perspectives follow a positivist or post-positivist perspective. Furthermore, over half of all the articles (53%) did not explicitly state a theoretical framework. The remaining articles were mostly based on cognitive frameworks (40%) such as constructivism, conceptual change, Bloom's taxonomy, metacognition, and various active, cooperative, or inquiry-based learning, with a small number using social frameworks (3%) and both cognitive and social frameworks (3%). In contrast to the social turn observed in RUME, BER seems to be undergoing a cognitive turn. The social turn in RUME was preceded by an increase in the number of articles using cognitive frameworks as their theoretical basis, so perhaps this trend in BER is indicative of its development as a DBER field.

Conclusion: The Promise of Networking

Our review of the DBER literature across STEM disciplines suggests an abundance of guiding theoretical frameworks that inform research. In contrast to the global call and research for integrated STEM learning and pedagogy (Chapter 1), the STEM education research literature uses a divergence of theoretical frameworks. From our review, we found that the individual DBER fields emphasize different vertices of our framing triangle: literature, methodology, and perspective. RUME foregrounds perspective, whereas EER highlights methodology, and PER, CER, and BER focus on literature. As each of the different DBER fields grow and develop with "deep grounding in the discipline's priorities, worldview, knowledge, and practices" (Gul, 2016, p. 1632), this diversity in theoretical frameworks is a natural consequence and also an untapped source of richness. However, there is the danger that the different DBER fields become so compartmentalized that communication among researchers becomes problematic, which could ultimately have negative impacts on the ability of DBER to coherently and effectively impact and improve learning and teaching in STEM.

We argue that the DBER communities would benefit by engaging in what mathematics education researchers Prediger, Bikner-Ahsbahs, and Arzarello (2008) describe as theoretical networking

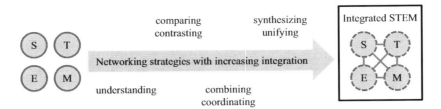

Figure 5.3 Networking strategies to promote integrated STEM.

strategies: a framework for different ways that theories can be related and mutually leveraged. In particular, they put forth a continuum of different networking strategies from simply understanding different approaches, to comparing and contrasting, to combining and coordinating, to synthesizing and unifying. While developing a grand, unifying theory across STEM disciplines is both unlikely and of questionable value, we postulate that connecting different theoretical frameworks from various DBER fields at the other three levels of the networking strategies has a number of potential affordances, including the promotion of discourse among colleagues from related disciplines; an increase in descriptive, explanatory, or prescriptive power; and a condensed number of theoretical frameworks that can facilitate and integrate understanding across STEM.

The recent book edited by Bikner-Ahsbahs and Prediger (2014), *Networking of Theories as a Research Practice in Mathematics Education*, opens up a dialogue on ways in which networking theories might constitute a new form of research practice in mathematics education. As the various DBER fields move forward collectively and in parallel, we see a similar opportunity to establish an analogous networking of the theoretical frameworks used across research in STEM education (Figure 5.3). Therefore, we hope that our results and discussion here would serve as a call for thoughtful introspection and that this chapter would provide the necessary information for our communities to reflect on how to move toward an integration of theoretical frameworks in STEM education research.

While such an undertaking will undoubtably be a challenge, we argue that it will be worth the effort, both for the research and ultimately for student learning in STEM. Indeed, if the field is going to meet the call for improvement laid out in the PCAST report, a concerted effort that brings coherence across the various DBER fields is needed.

Acknowledgements

We would like to thank the numerous collaborators who have helped to make this work possible. Thank you to Adriana Corrales, Song Wang, and Colin McGrane from San Diego State University and the University of California, San Diego, for their work on the STEM and science education, chemistry education, and mathematics and engineering education framework analysis, respectively. We would also like to thank Grant Gardner, Joshua Reid, Velta Napoleon-Fanis, Penny Carroll, and Emily Smith from Middle Tennessee State University for their help with the analysis of theoretical frameworks in biology education research.

References

Artigue, M. (2016). Mathematics education research at university level: Achievements and challenges. In E. Nardi, & C. Winsløw (Eds.), *Proceedings of the first conference of INDRUM* (pp. 11–27). Montpellier: INDRUM and Université de Montpellier.

Ball, D. L., & Forzani, F. M. (2007). 2007 Wallace foundation distinguished lecture—What makes education research "Educational"? *Educational Researcher, 36*(9), 529–540. https://doi.org/10.3102/0013189x07312896

Bikner-Ahsbahs, A., & Prediger, S. (Eds.). (2014). *Networking of theories as a research practice in mathematics education.* Heidelberg, Germany: Springer.

Biza, I., Giraldo, V., Hochmuth, R., Khakbaz, A., & Rasmussen, C. (2016). Research on teaching and learning mathematics at the tertiary level: State-of-the-art and looking ahead. In *Research on teaching and learning mathematics at the tertiary level* (pp. 1–32). Cham, Switzerland: Springer.

Bodner, G. M. (2011). *The development of research in chemical education as a field of study.* Paper presented at the Second Committee Meeting on the Status, Contributions, and Future Directions of Discipline-Based Education Research, Washington, DC, October 18–19, 2010. Retrieved from https://sites.nationalacademies.org/cs/groups/dbassesite/documents/webpage/dbasse_072579.pdf

Bodner, G. M., & Orgill, M. (2007). *Theoretical frameworks for research in chemistry/science education.* Upper Saddle River, NJ: Prentice Hall.

Borrego, M., & Bernhard, J. (2011). The emergence of engineering education research as an internationally connected field of inquiry. *Journal of Engineering Education, 100*(1), 14–47. https://doi.org/10.1002/j.2168-9830.2011.tb00003.x

Case, J. M., & Light, G. (2011). Emerging research methodologies in engineering education research. *Journal of Engineering Education, 100*(1), 186–210. https://doi.org/10.1002/j.2168-9830.2011.tb00008.x

Cohen, D. K., Raudenbush, S. W., & Ball, D. L. (2003). Resources, instruction, and research. *Educational Evaluation and Policy Analysis, 25*(2), 119–142. https://doi.org/10.3102/01623737025002119

Cummings, K. (2011). *A developmental history of physics education research.* Paper presented at the Second Committee Meeting on the Status, Contributions, and Future Directions of Discipline-Based Education Research, Washington, DC, October 18–19, 2010. Retrieved from http://sites.nationalacademies.org/cs/groups/dbassesite/documents/webpage/dbasse_072580

DeHaan, R. L. (2011). *Education research in the biological sciences: A nine-decade review.* Paper presented at the Second Committee Meeting on the Status, Contributions, and Future Directions of Discipline-Based Education Research, Washington, DC, October 18–19, 2010. Retrieved from http://sites.nationalacademies.org/dbasse/bose/dbasse_080124

Dirks, C. (2011). *The current status and future direction of biology education research.* Paper presented at the Second Committee Meeting on the Status, Contributions, and Future Directions of Discipline-Based Education Research, Washington, DC, October 18–19, 2010. Retrieved from http://sites.nationalacademies.org/dbasse/bose/dbasse_080124

Docktor, J. L., & Mestre, J. P. (2014). Synthesis of discipline-based education research in physics. *Physical Review Special Topics-Physics Education Research, 10*(2), 020119. https://doi.org/10.1103/physrevstper.10.020119

Gul, S., & Sozbilir, M. (2016). International trends in biology education research from 1997 to 2014: A content analysis of papers in selected journals. *Eurasia Journal of Mathematics, Science & Technology Education, 12*(6), 1631–1651. https://doi.org/10.12973/eurasia.2015.1363a

Inglis, M., & Foster, C. (2018). Five decades of mathematics education research. *Journal for Research in Mathematics Education, 49*(4), 462–500. https://doi.org/10.5951/jresematheduc.49.4.0462

Kornhauser, A. (1979). Trends in research in chemical education. *European Journal of Science Education, 1*(1), 21–50. https://doi.org/10.1080/0140528790010104

Koro-Ljungberg, M., & Douglas, E. (2008). State of qualitative research in engineering education: Meta-analysis of JEE articles, 2005–2006. *Journal of Engineering Education, 97*(2), 163–175. https://doi.org/10.1002/j.2168-9830.2008.tb00965.x

Larsen, S., Marrongelle, K., Bressoud, D., & Graham, K. (2017). Understanding the concepts of calculus: Frameworks and roadmaps emerging from educational research. In J. Cai (Ed.), *Compendium for research in mathematics education* (pp. 526–550). Reston, VA: National Council of Teachers of Mathematics.

Lather, P. (2004). Scientific research in education: A critical perspective. *British Educational Research Journal, 30*(6), 759–772. https://doi.org/10.1080/0141192042000279486

Lerman, S. (2000). The social turn in mathematics education research. In J. Boaler (Ed.), *Multiple perspectives on mathematics teaching and learning* (pp. 19–44). Westport, CT: Ablex.

Lo, S. M., Gardner, G. E., Reid, J., Napoleon-Fanis, V., Carroll, P., Smith, E., & Sato, B. K. (2019). Prevailing questions and methodologies in biology education research: A longitudinal analysis of research in CBE-Life sciences education and at the society for the advancement of biology education research. *CBE-Life Sciences Education, 18*(1), ar9. https://doi.org/10.1187/cbe.18-08-0164

National Research Council. (2002). *Scientific research in education.* Washington, DC: The National Academies Press.

National Research Council. (2012). *Discipline-based education research: Understanding and improving learning in undergraduate science and engineering.* Washington, DC: The National Academies Press.

Prediger, S., Bikner-Ahsbahs, A., & Arzarello, F. (2008). Networking strategies and methods for connecting theoretical approaches: First steps towards a conceptual framework. *ZDM—The International Journal on Mathematics Education, 40*(2), 165–178. https://doi.org/10.1007/s11858-008-0086-z

President's Council of Advisors on Science and Technology. (2012). *Engage to excel: Producing one million additional college graduates with degrees in science, technology, engineering, and mathematics.* Washington, DC: Author.

Rasmussen, C., & Wawro, M. (2017). Post-calculus research in undergraduate mathematics education. In J. Cai (Ed.), *Compendium for research in mathematics education* (pp. 551–581). Reston, VA: National Council of Teachers of Mathematics.

Reiss, J., & Sprenger, J. M. (2017). Scientific objectivity. In E. N. Zalta (Ed.), *The Stanford encyclopedia of philosophy* (Winter 2017 Ed.). Retrieved from https://plato.stanford.edu/archives/win2017/entries/scientific-objectivity/

Teo, T. W., Goh, M. T., & Yeo, L. W. (2014). Chemistry education research trends: 2004–2013. *Chemistry Education Research and Practice, 15*(4), 470–487. https://doi.org/10.1039/c4rp00104d

Towns, M. H., & Kraft, A. (2011). *Review and synthesis of research in chemical education from 2000–2010.* Paper presented at the Second Committee Meeting on the Status, Contributions, and Future Directions of Discipline-Based Education Research, Washington, DC, October 18–19, 2010. Retrieved from http://sites.nationalacademies.org/cs/groups/dbassesite/documents/webpage/dbasse_072594

Tsai, C. C., & Wen, M. L. (2005). Research and trends in science education from 1998 to 2002: A content analysis of publication in selected journals. *International Journal of Science Education, 27*(1), 3–14. https://doi.org/10.1080/0950069042000243727

Walther, J., Sochacka, N. W., Benson, L. C., Bumbaco, A. E., Kellam, N., Pawley, A. L., & Phillips, C. M. (2017). Qualitative research quality: A collaborative inquiry across multiple methodological perspectives. *Journal of Engineering Education, 106*(3), 398–430. https://doi.org/10.1002/jee.20170

Winsløw, C., Gueudet, G., Hochmuth, R., & Nardi, E. (2018). Research on university mathematics education. In T. Dreyfus, M. Artigue, D. Potari, S. Prediger, & K. Ruthven (Eds.), *Developing research in mathematics education—twenty years of communication, cooperation and collaboration in Europe* (pp. 60–74). Oxon, UK: Routledge.

Winsløw, C., & Rasmussen, C. (2018). University mathematics education. In S. Lerman (Ed.), *Encyclopedia of mathematics education.* Cham, Switzerland: Springer. https://doi.org/10.1007/978-3-319-77487-9_100020-1

SECTION 2

STEM Learning

6

INTEGRATED STEM PEDAGOGIES AND STUDENT LEARNING

S. Selcen Guzey, Secil Caskurlu and Kadir Kozan

Over the past 25 years, as the research on STEM education has moved forward, the focus has shifted from individual disciplines to a more integrated or interdisciplinary approach to teaching and learning. Recent education reforms throughout the world have emphasized the important role of integrated STEM education and called for revision of curriculum, assessment, and teaching practices to teach STEM in an integrated fashion (English, 2017). This integrated STEM education approach includes the teaching of science and mathematics through engineering or technological design (Moore et al., 2014). Today, many K–12 students are engaged in integrated STEM education in formal and informal settings, and recent research has demonstrated the impact of integrated approaches on various student outcomes, such as learning and achievement, development of STEM identity, and interest in pursuing a STEM-related career (e.g., Burrows, Breiner, Keiner, & Behm, 2014; Fan & Yu, 2017; Guzey, Harwell, Moreno, Peralta & Moore, 2017). Research has also shown that integrated STEM experiences can provide invaluable opportunities to students to engage in activities that allow them to make connections across the STEM subjects (National Academy of Engineering [NAE] & National Research Council [NRC], 2009, 2014). Being able to make connections and apply knowledge across STEM disciplines is critical since "the most transformative discoveries and innovations take place at the junctures of where disciplines converge" (National Science & Technology Council, 2018, p. 15). Although their efforts largely focus on disciplinary or transdisciplinary learning, some studies have attempted to highlight the contributions of the integrated STEM education to the development of a wide range of 21st-century skills, such as critical and analytical thinking, problem solving, and communication (e.g., Guzey & Aranda, 2017). Research findings on the impact of integration on learning and achievement in STEM and STEM-related interest and identity development highlight the importance of implementing integrated experiences.

Looking across studies, integrated STEM education includes a range of experiences (NAE & NRC, 2014). Duration, setting, size, and level of integration change from program to program. Students may engage in integrated STEM education in formal or informal settings, while in formal settings it may occur in one or multiple class periods or throughout one course or several courses. Duration and context are closely related to the goals, purposes, and resources of integrated STEM education programs and the scope of the integration (NAE & NRC, 2014). With respect to implementation of effective integrated STEM experiences, successful implementation requires educators to use effective pedagogical approaches. While there is no widespread agreement of what pedagogical strategies teachers should use when implementing integrated STEM education, there is recognition that some pedagogical practices most likely lead to more interdisciplinary teaching. The following section presents existing pedagogical approaches to integrated STEM education.

Pedagogical Approaches to Integrated STEM Education

The latest research on integrated STEM education has shown that many pedagogical approaches and strategies are employed by teachers when teaching integrated STEM in K-12 schools (NAE & NRC, 2014). These approaches are primarily student-centered and overlap with one another in several ways. In the context of integrated, interdisciplinary learning, for example, these approaches promote authentic learning of science and/or mathematics content and also aim at enhancing students' understanding of the relationship between STEM subjects. In this review, we largely focus on integrated STEM teaching and learning in science classes.

Scientific Inquiry, Science and Engineering Practices

Inquiry is central to science, and teaching science as inquiry has a long history in science education research and reform (Anderson, 2002). In many countries, education reform efforts have called on science teachers to employ inquiry pedagogy. However, today, inquiry in science classrooms is still rare (Crawford, 2014). Many science teachers struggle to teach science as inquiry, and thus use strategies that are didactic or teacher-centered. Studies have shown challenges teachers face in teaching science as inquiry (Crawford, 2007; Fletcher & Luft, 2011). These challenges range from availability of time and resources to lack of confidence about teaching science. Among the different challenges to teaching science as inquiry, research has shown that there has not been an agreement on the definition of inquiry in science education. Defining teaching science as inquiry in different ways has created misunderstandings about how to implement inquiry and contributed to the rare implementation. According to the National Science Education Standards (NRC, 1996)

> Scientific inquiry refers to the diverse ways in which scientists study the natural world and propose explanations based on the evidence derived from their work. Inquiry also refers to the activities of students in which they develop knowledge and understanding of scientific ideas, as well as an understanding of how scientists study the natural world.
>
> *(p. 23)*

More specifically, teaching science as inquiry involves engaging students in the following practices: asking scientifically oriented questions, giving evidence in responding to questions, formulating explanations from evidence, connecting explanations to scientific knowledge, and communicating and justifying explanations (NGSS Lead States, 2013). Over the past decades, instructional models have been developed to help teachers use inquiry pedagogy so that their students engage in the aforementioned scientific practices. Bybee's (2009) 5E instructional model consists of five stages: engage, explore, explain, elaborate, and evaluate. According to Bybee, each phase has a specific function and ensures that classroom activities allow students to engage in critical practices. The 5E model highlights that teaching science as inquiry is more than just hands-on laboratory activities. The activities should be designed intentionally to include a wide array of scientific practices.

The most recent reform document in the United States, the Next Generation Science Standards (NGSS Lead States, 2013), puts greater emphasis on some of the practices such as scientific modeling and argumentation while still focusing on providing opportunities for students to engage in science. The authors of NGSS, however, limit the use of the term "inquiry" and instead use scientific and engineering practices. K-12 students are expected to "actively engage in scientific and engineering practices and apply cross-cutting concepts to deepen their understanding of the core ideas in these fields" (NRC, 2012, pp. 8–9). The term "engineering" in these documents is used in a broad sense to mean "any engagement in a systematic practice of design to achieve solutions to particular human problems" (NRC, 2012, p. 11). The intent is to encourage more K–12 students to explore engineering design, learn about the interconnection of science and engineering, and apply science knowledge and skills to solve engineering challenges presented in science classes. In this new vision of science education, engineering does not replace inquiry, but rather supplies an additional range of practices which enrich the teaching of science.

Project- and Problem-Based Science

Problem- and project-based learning approaches are often used interchangeably. Here, we briefly identify and characterize these two pedagogical approaches; readers interested in learning more detail about problem- and project-based learning may consult Blumenfeld et al. (1991) and Hmelo-Silver (2004). Both problem- and project-based learning approaches focus on providing hands-on experiences and can be considered as variations of teaching science as inquiry (Barron et al., 1998). According to Marx and colleagues (1994), "project-based science focuses on student-designed inquiry that is organized by investigations to answer driving questions, includes collaboration among learners and others, the use of new technology, and the creation of authentic artifacts that represent student understanding" (p. 341). However, the question that drives a project is critical since it should be carefully drafted to allow students to understand the connections between the project activities and focal science concepts (Barron et al., 1998). For example, Petrosino (1998) designed and implemented a model rocket project that asked a group of sixth-grade students to build and launch rockets. Petrosino found that simply asking students to design and launch rockets did not really help them learn the underlying science concepts. The revised version of the project included specific driving questions. Consequently, students better understood the purpose of the activity, learned scientific methods, and designed controlled experiments. Similarly, using project-based activities, Krajcik et al. (1998) found that students learned to plan and design experiments. Teachers' constructive feedback and instructional support helped students in the study to generate better questions and carry out their investigations.

Kolodner et al. (2003) defined problem-based learning "as a cognitive apprenticeship approach that focuses on learning from problem-solving experience and promotes learning of content and practices at the same time" (p. 497). Problem-based learning involves the use of authentic, rich, real-world problems that students explore collaboratively (Hmelo-Silver & Barrows, 2006). Since most problems are ill-defined, students need to conduct research to find information needed to solve the problem and conduct scientific investigations. Thus, engaging in problem-based learning allows students to apply target science concepts to authentic situations (Gijbels, Dochy, Bossched, & Segers, 2005).

Engineering Design-Based Science

While inquiry is "the diverse ways in which scientists study the natural world and propose explanations based on the evidence derived from their work" (NRC, 1996, p. 23), design is a core engineering practice and refers to a systematic and iterative decision-making process (NAE, 2009; NRC, 2012). Scientific inquiry and engineering design are closely related, and curriculum materials that include both can help students make connections among these two disciplines and improve learning in science and engineering.

Engineering design as a pedagogical approach means systematically emphasizing and reinforcing connections among science and engineering. At the heart of the engineering design pedagogy is the student solving an engineering design problem by using scientific inquiry to collect and analyze data that can inform design decisions. In other words, through engineering design pedagogy, "all scientific knowledge and problem-solving skills are constructed in the context of designing artifacts as particular instances of solving ill-defined, real-world problems" (Fortus, Dershimer, Krajcik, Marx, & Mamlok-Naaman, 2004, p. 1082). For example, students are asked to design vehicles following an iterative design process in which they first design a prototype, experiment with the variables to discover ways to design a better prototype, and redesign.

Research has shown the benefits of engineering design pedagogy: improved learning in science and mathematics, increased awareness of what engineering is and what engineers do, and enhanced understanding of and the ability to engage in engineering design (NAE, 2009). For example, in a study by Fortus et al. (2004), students engaged in a series of design activities in which they designed a structure for extreme environment, a battery that is better for the environment, and a cellular phone that is safer to use. Analysis of pre- and post-tests and student design artifacts demonstrated that substantial learning gains occurred during the enactments of all three units. In another study, Penner, Lehre, and Schauble (1998) designed and studied a unit focused on the biomechanics of the human arm. In this unit, students generated data on biomechanical principles, which informed their design models of the human elbow. Study findings demonstrated that investigations fostered students' understanding of the biomechanics of the human arm. In these curriculum projects and many others (e.g., Roth, 1996), design is presented as a problem-solving strategy that places students in a cycle of planning, testing, and evaluating; and requires that students apply focal science concepts to their design.

Here it is important to note that simply implementing one or more of the aforementioned pedagogical approaches does not guarantee successful implementation of integrated STEM experiences. Inquiry is the centerpiece for learning science and understanding how science is done; problem- and project-based learning experiences are critical for practicing science and engineering; and engineering design is necessary to engage in engineering practices and apply science. The following section presents a brief synthesis of main student learning outcomes in integrated STEM contexts.

Student Learning Highlights in Integrated STEM Contexts

This section focuses on selected recent (2008 to present) and comprehensive research on integrated STEM in K-12 from a student learning perspective based on different outcomes ranging from attitudes to actual learning results. The review also let us dig deeper into the characteristics of effective integrated STEM learning contexts that contribute to all those student outcomes. Specifically, what follows is a descriptive review of highlighted outcomes emanating from students' science and/or mathematics learning through engineering and/or technology-enabled design tasks in integrated STEM learning contexts. Overall, it showed that engineering or technology design tasks might enhance student outcomes including attitudes toward STEM, engagement, interest, actual learning, and perceived learning.

First, existing research indicates that engineering design-based integrated STEM content focusing on science leads to improved student attitudes and learning (e.g., Guzey, Moore, Harwell, & Moreno, 2016). Unsurprisingly, previous studies also revealed increased interest and engagement in pursuing STEM-related careers or degrees (e.g., Hsu, Lin, & Yang, 2017; Shahali, Halim, Rasul, Osman, & Zulkifeli, 2017) and in STEM content or fields (e.g., Grant, MacFadden, Antonenko, & Perez, 2017; Guzey, Moore, & Morse, 2016; John, Bettye, Ezra, & Robert, 2016). Further, research revealed that learning itself can be a crucial component here. In other words, there has been research pointing at both enhanced learning and interest (e.g., Burrows et al., 2014; Fan, Yu, & Lou, 2017; Guzey et al., 2016; Hirsch, Berliner-Heyman, & Cusack, 2017; Moreno, Tharp, Vogt, Newell, & Burnett, 2016; Toma & Greca, 2018) or engagement (e.g., Hudson, English, Dawes, King, & Baker,

2015; Mativo et al., 2017) suggesting that it is not only whether learning experiences are attractive but also that engagement in learning can lead to increased learner attitude and interest. This point is crucial for making STEM education sustainable and accountable, since only a learning experience that promotes both actual learning and interest would persuade all stakeholders that it is worthy of investment.

Some other recent studies referred to improved learning outcomes (e.g., Crotty et al., 2017; Fan & Yu, 2017; Guzey et al., 2017; Wilhelm, Jackson, Sullivan, & Wilhelm, 2013; Yoon, Dyehouse, Lucietto, Diefes-Dux, & Capobianco, 2014). Not only actual learning, but students' perceptions of learning also seem to increase as a result of learning in integrated STEM contexts (e.g., Blackley, Rahmawati, Fitriani, Sheffield, & Koul, 2018; Ntemngwa & Oliver, 2018). This result aligns with the increased actual learning findings noted earlier in that it shows that students are or become aware of their increasing learning levels in integrated STEM learning contexts. Further, these two findings promote the accountability of integrated STEM learning from both perceived and actual learning perspectives. After all, perception of better learning outcomes strongly suggests a high level of metacognitive awareness that is an essential component of any given learning experience. Combined with increased interest or engagement, higher perceived and actual learning importantly suggests that integrated STEM learning experiences driven by engineering- or technology-enabled design tasks may enrich education from multiple dimensions. Therefore, it is not surprising to find studies reporting enhanced 21st-century skills (e.g., problem solving, collaboration, teamwork, communication, teamwork, and creative thinking) in integrated STEM learning contexts (e.g., Husin et al., 2016; Ntemngwa & Oliver, 2018; Sheffield, Koul, Blackley & Maynard, 2017).

Research suggests that diverse and varying numbers of STEM disciplines have been incorporated in integrated STEM instruction. Some studies, for instance, involved all four disciplines (e.g., Fan et al., 2017; Fan & Yu, 2017; Grant et al., 2017; Toma & Greca, 2018), while others included three disciplines (e.g., Crotty et al., 2017; Guzey et al., 2017; Hirsch et al., 2017; Wilhelm et al., 2013) or two disciplines (e.g., Burrows et al., 2014; Guzey et al., 2016; Moreno et al., 2016). Independent of what disciplines were included in learning contexts, it seems that certain student outcomes including learning and interest were achieved, suggesting that integrated STEM instruction has been successful at promoting student outcomes no matter what combinations of disciplines it employed. This conclusion further suggests the flexibility of integrated STEM learning as long as main design tasks, challenges, inquiries, or focus points are intriguing enough for learners and encourage their actual learning.

To conclude, literature suggests several aspects of student impact and learning resulting from integrated STEM learning contexts, including promoting positive attitudes toward STEM and interest in both STEM content and careers, improving both student learning and interest, and enhancing students' perceptions of their learning. Importantly, these benefits may be accomplished by specific strategies such as explicitly integrating STEM fields (e.g., Crotty et al., 2017; Toma & Greca, 2018), supporting students' learning of each field in addition to interconnections between and among them (e.g., Kopcha et al., 2017; Tank, Moore, Babajide, & Rynearson, 2015), encouraging learners to provide explanations and/or justifications for their efforts including design decisions (e.g., Dare, Ellis, & Roehrig, 2018), and employing authentic or real-life contexts including hands-on inquiry-based approaches (e.g., Hirsch et al., 2017).

Suggestions for Teacher Education

The structure of this section is based around two areas: (a) pre-service teacher learning, and (b) in-service teacher learning. The literature demonstrates how pre- and in-service teachers learn and implement integrated STEM education approaches. In particular, the recent literature explores complex learning of integrated STEM in teacher education programs and professional development programs and challenges to implementation of integrated STEM (Ring, Dare, Crotty, & Roehrig, 2017). Clearly, it is challenging for many teachers to not only learn integrated STEM approaches but also align their learning with their instructional practices.

There have been recent calls for teacher education programs to focus more on integrated practices (NRC, 2012). Teaching science as envisioned by the new education reforms requires that teachers have a well-developed understanding of integrated STEM education. However, methods courses for teaching rarely offer pre-service teachers opportunities to develop understandings about the pedagogical approaches to integrated STEM education. O'Brien et al. (2014) reviewed preservice teacher education programs at the elementary and secondary levels and found that engineering is rarely required in teacher education programs and that integration of engineering content into teacher education courses is uncommon. As a consequence, most pre-service teachers do not develop knowledge in the engineering design process and practices and do not feel comfortable designing instruction based on engineering.

Given the benefits of explicit STEM integration (e.g., Crotty et al., 2017; Toma & Greca, 2018), and lack of deeper insights into how to prepare teachers to teach integrated STEM or interdisciplinary content (Hsu et al., 2017), pre-service teacher education programs should strive to incorporate integrated STEM learning experiences more explicitly. Such an incorporation may come in the form of either a required or elective interdisciplinary course focusing on teaching and learning of science and mathematics through engineering- or technology-enabled design tasks. Previous studies have already suggested undergraduate integrated STEM coursework as a solution (e.g., Ntemngwa & Oliver, 2018) and provided examples of how to infuse integrated STEM-related work into existing undergraduate coursework (e.g., Novak & Wisdom, 2018). Further, ensuring the interdisciplinary nature of pre-service teacher coursework may be crucially important since this provides the opportunity for pre-service teachers from various disciplines (i.e., science, engineering education, mathematics, and technology education or instructional/educational technology) to form STEM learning communities in which they enhance each other's learning. Even more, pre-service teachers from non-STEM fields such as English language education may participate in such courses. For instance, content and language integrated learning already includes teaching both subject content and target language in the same learning experience. Consequently, integrated STEM learning experiences can even help pre-service teachers learn and teach a target foreign language and STEM content simultaneously. This example illustrates that it may even be possible to combine social sciences with integrated STEM efforts while designing, developing, and implementing effective learning contexts. It is important to note that although integrated STEM is relatively new, integrating multiple disciplines into curriculum is a practice with a longer history (Dare et al., 2018).

Moreover, one common criticism for teacher education is the gap between theory and practice (Broekkamp & Van Hout-Wolters, 2007; Hennissen, Beckers, & Moerkerke, 2017). In other words, even though theory is essential for teacher education, it is not often well integrated into teaching practice (Hennissen et al., 2017). Regular practice seems to be learning theory first and then applying theoretical insights later in an isolated manner, which is ineffective (Hennissen et al., 2017). To address this issue, and given that quality teaching occurs through quality practice together with support and feedback (Benedict, Holdheide, Brownell, & Foley, 2016), some teacher education programs have switched to a more practice-based approach (McDonald, Kazemi, & Kavanagh, 2013). Moreover, since integrated STEM approaches encourage employing authentic, real-life, or inquiry-based challenges, using such approaches pre-service teacher education has the potential to increase the quality of teaching practice for pre-service teachers. Further, integrated STEM practice can form a rich context in which different theoretical insights can be examined and learned from multiple perspectives or content areas much more effectively, thereby leading to better teaching practice.

In response to the recent calls for integrated teaching approaches, a great number of curriculum resources and professional development opportunities have been offered to in-service teachers.

Research conducted around these professional development programs has revealed promising results for student learning and interest in STEM (Buxton, Cardozo Gaibisso, Li, & Xia, 2017; Guzey et al., 2017; Lachapelle, Cunningham, & Davis, 2017). For example, when teachers' understanding of integrated STEM increases (Ring et al., 2017), and when subsequently they purposefully and meaningfully integrate engineering into their instruction, studies have shown increases in student achievement and interest in science and engineering (Lachapelle et al., 2017; Silk, Schunn, & Cary, 2009). It is important to note, however, that teacher professional development programs are costly and offered only to limited numbers of in-service teachers. A more cost-effective and broader-reaching approach is to prepare pre-service teachers with skills to integrate engineering into science.

Accordingly, another interesting possibility would be forming teaching communities where groups of pre-service teachers from different fields can collaborate to design, develop, and implement integrated STEM learning experiences. Professional learning communities can also become a part of in-service teachers' professional life, providing ongoing support to teachers in their efforts to integrated STEM in their classrooms. This way, two important barriers to the successful implementation of integrated STEM, lack of content knowledge and knowledge of how to integrate STEM into existing standards (Ntemngwa & Oliver, 2018), may be addressed effectively. Such strategies are important since, even though professional development or training is a common solution offered for in-service teacher learning, (e.g., Ntemngwa & Oliver, 2018), there is some evidence that even after long-term professional development programs, teachers may still struggle to achieve integration (e.g., Tank et al., 2015). Likewise, there is also evidence that professional development programs may impact teachers' in-class performance at varying levels (e.g., Guzey et al., 2017).

Finally, employing integrated STEM learning communities for pre-service and in-service teachers may require systematic adjustments to attend to factors such as teachers' workload, administrative support, and resources. Likewise, sustainable and continuous support and available resources are also important (Toma & Greca, 2018). Further, collaborative approaches for both pre-service and in-service teachers may also require a similar level of collaboration for teacher educators. In other words, interdisciplinary integrated STEM undergraduate courses can be designed and offered by teacher educators from different fields collaboratively. Finally, as Tank et al. (2015) highlighted, it is also essential to investigate implementation of integrated STEM in the classroom and how teacher educators can enhance its success.

Suggestions for Future Research

Further understanding of research designs, assessment, and teaching and learning practices are necessary in order to advance teacher preparation for and implementation of integrated STEM education. Here, we present three research areas that would contribute to improved understanding of integrated STEM education and our goal of widespread implementation of integrated approaches.

Research Designs

The review of the literature about integrated STEM teaching and learning suggests the need for large-scale quantitative impact studies. Researchers should clearly report the treatment and control conditions and specify student outcomes. Previous work (e.g., Shahali, Halim, Rasul, Osman, & Zulkifeli, 2017; Toma & Greca, 2018) also pointed to a strong need for more robust research designs including not only true experimental and control groups but also active control groups. By employing alternative instructional approaches to integrated STEM, active control groups can also make it possible to compare and contrast different instructional approaches with integrated STEM in terms of effectiveness and efficiency. For instance, a possible instructional approach would be to employ regular class activities (e.g., Mativo et al., 2017), or extracurricular ones, and the comparison of these two approaches can be a topic for future research. Likewise, further research should examine impact of different pedagogies and types of STEM integration (Crotty et al., 2017; Guzey et al., 2016) as well as the effect of the degree of integration (Dare et al., 2018). Future research also needs to pay attention to the long-term effects of integrated STEM interventions (Guzey et al., 2016; Shahali et al., 2017) in addition to how and when to address existing or possible misconceptions (e.g., Novak & Wisdom, 2018). Closely related to running stronger research designs focusing on different pedagogies or instructional approaches, further research can also report research details including methods and results more robustly. For instance, adding practical significance insights to statistical significance can provide deeper insights into the strength of findings, and more details can make it easier to run future replication studies if needed.

Assessment

Development of appropriate and novel assessments to measure student outcomes of integrated STEM education and research employing these assessments is crucial for continuous and meaningful improvement of integrated STEM. What and how to assess seem to be crucial concerns for future research, too. For instance, assessing successful task performance is not enough, and attention can also be paid to gaining insights into learning processes (e.g., Savard & Freiman, 2016). A possible alternative to individual assessment is collective or collaborative assessment that can also align more with integrated STEM pedagogy. Unsurprisingly, researchers presented assessment of collaborative team performance as an option (e.g., Savard & Freiman, 2016). Similarly, formal versus informal assessment (Savard & Freiman, 2016) is important to gauge integrated STEM interventions employed by future research. Another research topic for further studies is the impact of systemic changes and what sort of resources and/or help should be provided to teachers (Toma & Greca, 2018) in addition to curriculum-related changes entailed by integrated STEM efforts. Another aspect is what kind of evidence can be used for assessment purposes (e.g., Tank et al., 2015), which also waits for further research.

Successful assessment is also closely connected to the instruments to be developed to gauge STEM competencies (Hsu et al., 2017) and objective measurement instead of anecdotal insights (Novak & Wisdom, 2018). Ensuring the high quality of assessment items is a critical area for research (Yoon et al., 2014). Timing or duration of instruction and grade level (Dare et al., 2018; Lambert, Cioc, Cioc, & Sandt, 2018; Yoon et al., 2014) is also an area in need of further research focused on assessing learning outcomes. Students' performance in integrated STEM assessments can also depend largely on feedback provided, which also entails further research-based insights to the role of teachers while assessing student learning and guiding them through an integrated STEM task (Savard & Freiman, 2016). Not only learning outcomes, but also learners' emotions, cognition, and skills can be a target of research regarding integrated STEM assessment (e.g., Hsu et al., 2017).

Teacher Learning and Practices

Learning and implementation of integrated STEM education approaches is challenging. Research should examine different formats and structures of teacher education and professional development programs and the impact of those on teacher learning and practices of integrated STEM. Specifically, what type of follow-up support teachers require is an area for future research (e.g., Lambert et al., 2018).

In this respect, as stated earlier in the "Suggestions for Teacher Education" section, future research should address interdisciplinary integrated STEM learning communities in teacher education programs and integrated STEM teaching communities. After all, if we assume that integrated STEM is based on collaboration of STEM fields, and one single teacher may not be knowledgeable enough about each STEM field, it is reasonable to research teaching communities where more than one teacher can design, develop, and implement integrated STEM learning experiences.

References

Anderson, R. (2002). Reforming science teaching: What research says about inquiry. *Journal of Science Teacher Education, 13*(1), 1–12.

Barron, B., Schwartz, D., Vye, N., Moore, A., Petrosino, A., Zech, L., & Bransford, J. (1998). Doing with understanding: Lessons from research on problem- and project-based learning. *Journal of the Learning Sciences, 7,* 271–311.

Benedict, A., Holdheide, L., Brownell, M., & Foley, A. M. (2016). *Learning to teach: Practice-based preparation in teacher education.* Special Issues Brief. Washington, DC: American Institutes for Research.

Blackley, S., Rahmawati, Y., Fitriani, E., Sheffield, R., & Koul, R. (2018). Using a makerspace approach to engage Indonesian primary students with STEM. *Issues in Educational Research, 28*(1), 18–42.

Blumenfeld, P. C., Soloway, E., Marx, R. W., Karjcik, J. S., Guzdial, M., & Palinscar, A. (1991). Motivating project-based learning: Sustaining the doing, supporting the learning. *Educational Psychologist, 26,* 369–398.

Broekkamp, H., & Van Hout-Wolters, B. (2007). The gap between educational research and practice: A literature review, symposium, and questionnaire. *Educational Research and Evaluation, 13,* 203–220.

Burrows, A. C., Breiner, J. M., Keiner, J., & Behm, C. (2014). Biodiesel and integrated STEM: Vertical alignment of high school biology/biochemistry and chemistry. *Journal of Chemical Education, 91,* 1379–1389.

Buxton, C., Cardozo Gaibisso, L., Li, J., & Xia, Y. (2017). How perspectives from linguistically diverse classrooms can help all students unlock the language of science. In L. Bryan & K. Tobin (Eds.), *13 Questions: Reframing education's conversation: Science* (pp. 273–291). New York, NY: Peter Lang.

Bybee, R. (2009, January). *The BSCS 5E: Instructional model and 21st century skills.* Presentation for The National Academies, Washington, DC.

Crawford, B. (2007). Learning to teach science as inquiry in the rough and tumble of practice. *Journal of Research in Science Teaching, 44,* 613–642.

Crawford, B. (2014). From inquiry to scientific practices in the science classroom. In N. Lederman & S. Abell (Eds.), *Handbook of research on science education* (Vol. II, pp. 515–544). New York, NY: Taylor and Francis Group.

Crotty, E. A., Guzey, S. S., Roehrig, G. H., Glancy, A. W., Ring-Whalen, E. A., & Moore, T. J. (2017). Approaches to integrating engineering in STEM units and student achievement gains. *Journal of Pre-College Engineering Education Research (J-PEER), 7*(2), 1–14.

Dare, E. A., Ellis, J. A., & Roehrig, G. H. (2018). Understanding science teachers' implementations of integrated STEM curricular units through a phenomenological multiple case study. *International Journal of STEM Education, 5*(4), 1–19.

English, L. D. (2017). Advancing elementary and middle school STEM education. *International Journal of Science and Mathematics Education, 15*(1), 5–24.

Fan, S. C., & Yu, K. C. (2017). How an integrative STEM curriculum can benefit students in engineering design practices. *International Journal of Technology and Design Education, 27*(1), 107–129.

Fan, S. C., Yu, K. C., & Lou, S. J. (2017). Why do students present different design objectives in engineering design projects? *International Journal of Technology and Design Education, 28,* 1039–1060.

Fletcher, S. S., & Luft, J. A. (2011). Early career secondary science teachers: A longitudinal study of beliefs in relation to field experiences. *Science Education, 95,* 1124–1146.

Fortus, D., Dershimer, R. C., Krajcik, J., Marx, R. W., & Mamlok-Naaman, R. (2004). Design-based science and student learning. *Journal of Research in Science Teaching, 41,* 1081–1110.

Gijbels, D., Dochy, F., Bossched, P., & Segers, M. (2005). Effects of problem-based learning: A meta-analysis from the angle of assessment. *Review of Educational Research, 75*(1), 27–61.

Grant, C. A., MacFadden, B. J., Antonenko, P., & Perez, V. J. (2017). 3-D fossils for K–12 education: A case example using the giant extinct shark carcharocles megalodon. *The Paleontological Society Papers, 22,* 197–209.

Guzey, S. S., & Aranda, M. (2017). Student participation in engineering practices and discourse: An exploratory case study. *Journal of Engineering Education, 106,* 585–606.

Guzey, S. S., Harwell, M., Moreno, M., Peralta, Y., & Moore, T. J. (2017). The impact of design-based STEM integration curricula on student achievement in engineering, science, and mathematics. *Journal of Science Education and Technology, 26,* 207–222.

Guzey, S. S., Moore, T. J., Harwell, M., & Moreno, M. (2016). STEM integration in middle school life science: Student learning and attitudes. *Journal of Science Education and Technology, 25,* 550–560.

Guzey, S. S., Moore, T. J., & Morse, G. (2016). Student interest in engineering design–based science. *School Science and Mathematics, 116*, 411–419.

Hennissen, P., Beckers, H., & Moerkerke, G. (2017). Linking practice to theory in teacher education: A growth in cognitive structures. *Teaching and Teacher Education, 63*, 314–325.

Hmelo-Silver, C. E. (2004). Problem-based learning: What and how do students learn? *Educational Psychology Review, 16,* 235–266.

Hmelo-Silver, C. E., & Barrows, H. (2006). Goals and strategies of a problem-based learning facilitator. *Interdisciplinary Journal of Problem-Based Learning, 1*(1). https://doi.org/10.7771/1541-5015.1004

Hirsch, L. S., Berliner-Heyman, S., & Cusack, J. L. (2017). Introducing middle school students to engineering principles and the engineering design process through an academic summer program. *International Journal of Engineering Education, 33*, 398–407.

Hsu, Y-S., Lin, Y-H., & Yang, B. (2017). Impact of augmented reality lessons on students' STEM interest. *Research and Practice in Technology Enhanced Learning, 12*(2), 1–14.

Hudson, P., English, L., Dawes, L., King, D., & Baker, S. (2015). Exploring links between pedagogical knowledge practices and student outcomes in STEM education for primary schools. *Australian Journal of Teacher Education (Online), 40*(6), 134–151.

Husin, W. N. F. W., Arsad, N. M., Othman, O., Halim, L., Rasul, M. S., Osman, K., & Iksan, Z. (2016). Fostering students' 21st century skills through project oriented problem based learning (POPBL) in integrated STEM education program. *Asia-Pacific Forum on Science Learning and Teaching, 17.*

John, M., Bettye, S., Ezra, T., & Robert, W. (2016). A formative evaluation of a Southeast High School integrative science, technology, engineering, and mathematics (STEM) academy. *Technology in Society, 45*, 34–39.

Kolodner, J. L., Camp, P. J., Crismond, D., Fasse, B., Gray, J., Holbrook, J., Puntambekar, S., & Ryan, M. (2003). Problem-based learning meets case-based reasoning in the middle-school science classroom: Putting learning by design into practice. *Journal of the Learning Sciences, 12*, 495–547.

Kopcha, T. J., McGregor, J., Shin, S., Qian, Y., Choi, J., Hill, R., Mativo, J., & Choi, I. (2017). Developing an integrative STEM curriculum for robotics education through educational design research. *Journal of Formative Design in Learning, 1*(1), 31–44.

Krajcik, J., Blumenfeld, P., Marx, R., Bass, K., Fredricks, J., & Soloway, E. (1998). Learning through problem solving. *The Journal of the Learning Sciences, 7*, 313–350.

Lachapelle, C. P., Cunningham, C. M., & Davis, M. (2017). Middle childhood education: Engineering concepts, practices, and trajectories. In M. J. de Vries (Ed.), *Handbook of technology education* (pp. 1–17). Switzerland: Springer International Publishing.

Lambert, J., Cioc, C., Cioc, S., & Sandt, D. (2018). Making connections: Evaluation of a professional development program for teachers focused on stem integration. *Journal of STEM Teacher Education, 53*(1), 2.

Marx, R. W., Blumenfeld, P. C., Krajcik, J., Blunk, M., Crawford, B., Kelly, B., & Meyer, K. (1994). Enacting project–based science: Experiences of four middle grade teachers. *Elementary School Journal, 94*, 499–516.

Mativo, J. M., Hill, R. B., Kopcha, T. J., McGregor, J., Shin, S., & Choi, I. (2017, June). *Lessons learned in teaching science using an integrative approach that used engineering design process.* Paper presented at the American Society for Engineering Education Annual Conference.

McDonald, M., Kazemi, E., & Kavanagh, S. S. (2013). Core practices and pedagogies of teacher education a call for a common language and collective activity. *Journal of Teacher Education, 64*, 378–386.

Moore, T. J., Stohlmann, M. S., Wang, H. H., Tank, K. M., Glancy, A. W., & Roehrig, G. H. (2014). Implementation and integration of engineering in K-12 STEM education. In S. Purzer, J. Strobel, J., & M. E. Cardella (Eds.), *Engineering in pre-college settings: Synthesizing research, policy, and practices* (pp. 35–60). West Lafayette, IN: Purdue University Press.

Moreno, N. P., Tharp, B. Z., Vogt, G., Newell, A. D., & Burnett, C. A. (2016). Preparing students for middle school through after-school STEM activities. *Journal of Science Education and Technology, 25*, 889–897.

National Academy of Engineering and National Research Council. (2009). *Engineering in K-12 education: Understanding the status and improving the prospects.* Washington, DC: The National Academies Press. https://doi.org/10.17226/12635

National Academy of Engineering and National Research Council. (2014). *STEM Integration in K-12 Education: Status, Prospects, and an Agenda for Research.* Washington, DC: The National Academies Press. https://doi.org/10.17226/18612

National Research Council. (1996). *National science education standards.* Washington, DC: National Academy Press.

National Research Council. (2012). *A framework for K-12 science education: Practices, crosscutting concepts, and core ideas.* Washington, DC: The National Academies Press. https://doi.org/10.17226/12635

National Science & Technology Council. (2018). *Charting a course for success: America's strategy for STEM education*. A report by the committee on STEM education of the National Science & Technology Council. Retrieved from https://www.whitehouse.gov/wp-content/uploads/2018/12/STEM-Education-Strategic-Plan-2018.pdf

NGSS Lead States. (2013). *Next generation science standards: For states, by states*. Washington, DC: National Academies Press.

Novak, E., & Wisdom, S. (2018). Effects of 3D printing project-based learning on preservice elementary teachers' science attitudes, science content knowledge, and anxiety about teaching science. *Journal of Science Education and Technology, 27*, 412–432.

Ntemngwa, C., & Oliver, S. (2018). The implementation of integrated science technology, engineering and mathematics (STEM) instruction using robotics in the middle school science classroom. *International Journal of Education in Mathematics, Science and Technology, 6*(1), 12–40.

O'Brien, S., Karsnitz, J., Sandt, S., Bottomley, L., & Parry, E. (2014). Engineering in pre-service teacher education. In S. Purzer, J. Strobel, & M. Cardella (Eds.), *Engineering in pre-college settings: Synthesizing research, policy, and practices* (pp. 277–299). West Lafayette, IN: Purdue University Press.

Penner, D., Lehre, R., & Schauble, L. (1998). From physical models to biomechanics: A design-based modeling approach. *Journal of the Learning Sciences, 7*, 429–449.

Petrosino, A. (1998). *The use of reflection and revision in hands-on experimental activities by at-risk children* (Unpublished doctoral dissertation). Vanderbilt University, Nashville, TN.

Ring, E. A., Dare, E. A., Crotty, E. A., & Roehrig, G. H. (2017). The evolution of teacher conceptions of STEM education throughout an intensive professional development experience. *Journal of Science Teacher Education, 28*, 444–467.

Roth, W. (1996). Art and artifact of children's designing: A situated cognition perspective. *The Journal of the Learning Sciences, 5*, 129–166.

Savard, A., & Freiman, V. (2016). Investigating complexity to assess student learning from a robotics-based task. *Digital Experiences in Mathematics Education, 2*(2), 93–114.

Shahali, E. H. M., Halim, L., Rasul, M. S., Osman, K., & Zulkifeli, M. A. (2017). STEM learning through engineering design: Impact on middle secondary students' interest towards STEM. *EURASIA Journal of Mathematics, Science and Technology Education, 13*, 1189–1211.

Sheffield, R., Koul, R., Blackley, S., & Maynard, N. (2017). Makerspace in STEM for girls: A physical space to develop twenty-first-century skills. *Educational Media International, 54*, 148–164.

Silk, E. M., Schunn, C. D., & Cary, M. S. (2009). The impact of an engineering design curriculum on science reasoning in an urban setting. *Journal of Science Education and Technology, 18*(3), 209–223.

Tank, K., Moore, T., Babajide, B., & Rynearson, A. M. (2015, June). *Evidence of students' engineering learning in an elementary classroom*. Paper presented at the American Association of Engineering Education Annual Conference.

Toma, R. B., & Greca, I. M. (2018). The effect of integrative STEM instruction on elementary students' attitudes toward science. *Eurasia Journal of Mathematics, Science and Technology Education, 14*, 1383–1395.

Wilhelm, J., Jackson, C., Sullivan, A., & Wilhelm, R. (2013). Examining differences between preteen groups' spatial-scientific understandings: A quasi-experimental study. *The Journal of Educational Research, 106*, 337–351.

Yoon, S. Y., Dyehouse, M., Lucietto, A. M., Diefes-Dux, H. A., & Capobianco, B. M. (2014). The effects of integrated science, technology, and engineering education on elementary students' knowledge and identity development. *School Science and Mathematics, 114*, 380–391.

7

DESIGN LEARNING IN STEM EDUCATION

Lyn D. English, Robin Adams and Donna King

Design and design thinking have become more prominent in recent years, with design now being applied to a range of fields as diverse as business and medicine (Dorst, 2011; Glen, Suciu, & Baughn, 2014). As van der Bijl-Brouwer and Dorst (2017) emphasized, design these days refers not just to the creation of physical objects but increasingly to the development of any form of intervention that changes current situations into preferred ones, including delivering services, applying procedures and strategies, and developing policies. Expressed simply, design may be defined as dealing with "the ways in which human beings modify their environments to better satisfy their needs and wants" (Kangas & Seitamaa-Hakkarainen, 2018, p. 597). Applying design in this way is often referred to as design-led or design-driven innovation. Design thinking, an important component of complex problem solving, entails the processes of problem identification, brainstorming ideas for solution, generating proto-types, and testing and refining outcomes (Chin et al., 2019).

Design is currently practised in qualitatively different ways across a variety of disciplines (Daly, Adams, & Bodner, 2012; van Kuijk, Daalhuizen, & Christiaans, 2019) and is considered to be multifaceted, with not just one but several forms of thinking including rational, analytical, and creative thought (Lawson & Dorst, 2009). Unfortunately, design is also used and misused in everyday communications including the media, with the result that the term, *design*, has become confusing and, indeed, problematic for the development of both the design professions and design education (cf. Lawson & Dorst, 2009).

Design education is a much-researched field with myriad articles appearing in the literature (Bartholomew & Strimel, 2018; Chin et al., 2019; Crismond & Adams, 2012; Daly et al., 2012; Jonassen, 2011; Strimel, Kim, Grubbs, & Huffman, 2019; Sung & Kelley, 2019). The central role of design in technology and engineering education is widely acknowledged where a basic understanding of how design within these disciplines impacts on the world and ultimately shapes our personal lives is considered essential (de Vries, 2009; Haupt, 2018; ITEA, 2007; Kangas & Seitamaa-Hakkarainen, 2018). Indeed, technology is viewed as "incomplete without design" (McCracken, 2000, p. 87) and that "neither design nor technology can be fully appreciated without an understanding of the other" (Kangas & Seitamaa-Hakkarainen, 2018, p. 598). Likewise, design is considered central to engineering education (Moore & Smith, 2014; Moore et al., 2014), where design thinking is generally viewed as a set of iterative processes of understanding a problem and developing an appropriate solution.

Policy documents for K-12 STEM education in several nations have strongly advocated STEM integration rather than compartmentalized, siloed learning of the respective disciplines (e.g., Canada 2067 (2017); Education Council, 2015; International Technology and Engineering Educators

Association, 2007; National Science & Technological Council, 2018). It is beyond the scope of this chapter to consider the wide range of design interpretations and studies; rather, we focus on design learning in K–12 STEM education, specifically integrated STEM-based problem solving, through the lenses of learning *about* and learning *through* design.

Learning *About* and *Through* Design

A popular approach to teaching students about design and engaging them in design processes is design-based learning. This approach is a means for students to learn theoretical concepts while developing the design of innovative products or systems in solving open-ended problems (Gómez Puente, van Eijck, & Jochems, 2011) and is considered to promote integrated learning in a project-oriented setting (Grubbs & Strimel, 2015; Mehalik, Doppelt, & Schunn, 2008). Engineering design is typically the focus of design-based learning in schools, with its concepts and problem-solving practices being regarded as key components of both technology and engineering education (Asunda & Hill, 2007; Daugherty & Carter, 2018; Daugherty, Dixon, & Merrill, 2018), as well as science education (Next Generation Science Standards, 2013). Design is also a powerful tool in integrative STEM-based pedagogical approaches (Bartholomew & Strimel, 2018; English, 2018).

In examining design in K–12 STEM education, we first consider two key forms of design learning, namely learning *about* design and learning *through* design. Learning about design in solving complex problems focuses primarily on *design processes*. Learning *through* design is concerned with disciplinary concept development during the application of design processes in solving complex problems. Of course, both concept development and design process learning should not be divorced during problem solving (van Breukelen, de Vries, & Schure, 2017), but frequently one learning goal takes precedence over the other. As Kangas and Seitamaa-Hakkarainen (2018) highlighted, design can be the focus of an investigation, a means of investigation, or both.

With the wide range of perspectives on design, it is not surprising that Kangas and Seitamaa-Hakkarainen (2018) claim that design education lacks a common framework. Given that design education is a core component of integrated STEM learning, a commonly accepted framework would likely contribute to a greater recognition of, and focus on, design-based learning experiences. Neither learning *about* design nor learning *through* design in STEM education has received the attention required, especially in today's design-focused world. We first examine learning about design during design-based learning experiences and then consider STEM concept development through design, while at the same time acknowledging their interaction. Our presentation of these two aspects in separate sections is to highlight the key features of each form of learning, either one of which can be neglected in STEM-based problem solving, especially if teachers lack the important design pedagogical content knowledge (Crismond & Adams, 2012).

Learning *About* Design During STEM-Based Problem Solving

Design has historically been a core feature of technology and engineering education (e.g., Crismond & Adams, 2012; Dym, Agogino, Eris, Frey, & Leifer, 2005; Moore et al., 2014). The role of design processes has been explored increasingly in mathematics and science learning, more so in the high school years than in the elementary grades (Fan & Yu, 2017; Jones, Buntting, & de Vries, 2011; Kelley, Brenner, & Pieper, 2010). Even the high school years remain under-researched in students' learning about design during complex problem solving (Mentzer, Becker, & Sutton, 2015). As Mentzer et al. lamented, we know little about the design processes of high school students as most studies focus on the design processes of college-level engineering students or of professional engineers. Furthermore, the literature frequently claims that engaging in design processes is beyond young children's capabilities and that teachers lack knowledge and confidence in implementing design-based problems, as educators such as Bagiati and Evangelou (2018) and McFadden and Roehrig (2018) have noted. Yet research over the last decade has clearly indicated how elementary school children can engage in design processes and display sophisticated thinking in doing so (e.g., see English & Moore, 2018). At the same time, students' design learning can be hindered by teachers' lack of pedagogical knowledge about design and design processes (Haupt, 2018; Yasar, Baker, Robinson-Kurpius, Krause, & Roberts, 2006). Professional development is thus a key component in any endeavour to develop students' learning about design, where teachers' concerns and lack of confidence in teaching design can be addressed (Lee & Strobel, 2014).

Engineering design has become an integral component of STEM-based problem solving. There appears to be no single, agreed-upon definition of engineering design (Daugherty et al., 2018), although Dym et al.'s (2005) definition is frequently cited, namely, "a systematic, intelligent process in which designers generate, evaluate, and specify concepts for devices, systems, or processes whose form and function achieve clients' objectives or users' needs while satisfying a specified set of constraints" (p. 104). The Accreditation Board for Engineering and Technology (2015) currently defines engineering design as:

> the process of devising a system, component, or process to meet desired needs. It is a decision-making process (often iterative), in which the basic sciences, mathematics, and the engineering sciences are applied to convert resources optimally to meet these stated needs.
>
> *(p. 4)*

When applied to STEM-based problem solving in K-12 education, design learning is usually described in terms of a number of iterative processes, including (a) problem framing or scoping, where problem boundaries, goals, and constraints are identified; (b) generation of ideas for planning and potential construction, in contrast to focusing on the development of just a single idea; (c) balancing of benefits and trade-offs in considering design ideas; (d) designing and constructing, involving design sketching, and transforming a design into a product; (e) testing and reflecting on outcomes, where attainment of the problem goal(s) is checked and constraints adhered to; (f) redesigning and reconstructing, where reflections on the initial design help identify improvements, with a subsequent redesign developed; and (g) reflecting on and communicating the overall design processes applied (Crismond & Adams, 2012; Lucas, Claxton, & Hanson, 2014; Tank et al., 2018; Wendell & Kolodner, 2014).

With design now playing a prominent role across a broader array of fields, issues pertaining to design learning have become paramount. As emphasized by Nielsen, Brænne, and Maus (2015),

> We regard education at many different levels [Kindergarten to PhD] as important in securing a sustainable future for the design of everyday life solutions. For that, we need qualified and reflective decision makers with a consciousness for quality of design and solutions.
>
> *(p. 1)*

The question of how best to develop design learning across grades K-12, however, has not received adequate attention. This is perhaps not surprising given that comparatively few studies have investigated the design thinking of grades 6–12 and even fewer across the elementary years (Kelley & Sung, 2017; Strimel, Bartholomew, Kim, & Zhang, 2018).

The use of think-aloud protocols has been a popular approach to identifying students' design thinking and the products generated for a STEM-based problem, with the intent of improving students' learning about design (e.g., Kelley & Sung, 2017; Kelley, Capobianco, & Kaluf, 2015; Strimel et al., 2018). In one study using think-aloud protocols to identify iterative patterns of design thinking, Sung and Kelley (2019) examined the cognitive activities of fourth-grade science students as they worked an engineering design problem. It was argued that addressing patterns of design processes can assist students in coping with the complex nature of design problems by "conceptualizing successful pathways to problem solving" (p. 286; online only at present). Their analysis confirmed that when students generate ideas, designing is a central point of the entire iterative process, often followed by sketching, predicting, or questioning. Their findings agree with Dorst and Cross's (2001) perspective that design involves an ongoing process of developing and refining ideas. Students' use of sketching reinforces previous findings that sketching is an important tool to externalize cognitive images. It was also found that the students tended to operate within the problem space, iterating between designing and predicting.

A focus on students' design conversations was undertaken by Aranda, Lie, and Guzey (2019) in an effort to identify the thought processes used by sixth-grade students while engaging in a complex design activity. Building on Guilford's (1956) theory of productive thinking, Aranda et al. were interested in how these students applied different modes of thinking when working on the design activity. In planning their initial design, students applied "Cognitive Memory, Divergent Thinking, and Evaluative Thinking" as they recalled scientific knowledge in initially justifying their design decisions. As they finalized and subsequently conveyed their design decisions, students employed higher forms of thinking. It was concluded that students' use of divergent forms of thinking indicates how engineering design-based units can provide a rich avenue for developing students' creativity, an important skill in our increasingly design-focused world.

In another study investigating students' thinking as they developed and designed a product during an engineering design task, Strimel et al. (2018) compared the design processes of kindergarten and fourth-grade students. Significant differences between the two grade levels were found with respect to the times the various design thinking processes were applied. Fourth-grade students devoted significantly more time than their kindergarten counterparts to the processes of defining problems, creating, measuring, and testing. Furthermore, it appeared that more time devoted to the process of managing could be a significant predictor of lower achievement in design. It was concluded that potential areas for improving learning can be gleaned from students' thinking processes at different grade levels and from the quality of their design work.

The extensive research of Cunningham and her colleagues (e.g., Cunningham, 2018; Cunningham, Lachapelle, & Davis, 2018), as well as that of Elkin, Sullivan, and Bers (2018) has shown that even very young children are capable of engaging in early engineering design when provided with appropriate opportunities. Elkin et al., for example, used robotics in early childhood classrooms to introduce foundational engineering design processes. The study illustrated how these young learners kept engineering design journals and engaged in design processes as they engineered creative solutions to each of the challenges presented to them. It seems somewhat paradoxical that foundational engineering design processes are a natural part of young children's inquiry about their world, yet this important component has been largely ignored in these informative years. The sentiments of Lippard, Lamm, and Riley (2017) are worth highlighting in this regard, namely, "Pre-kindergarten children are primed for engineering thinking" (p. 455).

Research on high school students' learning about design includes the studies of Mentzer and his colleagues (e.g., Mentzer, Becker, & Sutton, 2015). In one study, Mentzer et al. (2015) explored the differences in design processes between high school engineering students and expert engineers, as well as between high school freshmen who had studied one engineering course and seniors who had taken a suite of engineering courses. Among their findings was that freshmen spent significantly less time in generating ideas than seniors and experts. Both freshmen and seniors devoted significantly less time than the experts in determining the feasibility of their ideas, evaluating alternative ideas, and making decisions. Given Mentzer et al.'s (2015) conclusions that high school students apply design thinking with limited understanding of a problem's client base and also appear reluctant to compare alternative solutions, the need to foster core facets of design learning throughout K–12 is clearly evident.

More recent insights into students' application of design processes appear in a meta-synthesis of primary and secondary students' cognition in the practices of design (Strimel et al., 2019). Their analysis entailed synthesizing findings from multiple design cognition studies that used different coding schemes. Across the multiple studies analysed, findings revealed students' tendency to overlook the importance of problem framing, instead moving immediately to the stage of idea generation or developing a solution. Students' tendency not to devote time to understand, analyse, define, and scope a given design challenge is of concern. Likewise, when meeting an unanticipated problem or an undesirable solution, students usually tried to correct the situation through trial and error rather than through a more informed and analytical process. Of concern is that opportunities to develop these design skills appear to be lacking in elementary and secondary classrooms. Strimel et al. (2019) concluded that educators need more support in developing their students' design skills, with a focus on the key design elements highlighted in their meta-synthesis.

STEM Concept Development *Through* Design

In contrast to learning *about* design, learning *through* design has received considerably greater research attention, but more so in the middle and high school years. Learning through design typically occurs in integrated STEM problem solving, where engineering/technology design serves as a disciplinary linking tool. Concept development is facilitated as students apply design processes to problem formulation and solution development. Before reviewing learning through design, it is worth first considering briefly some of the debates surrounding STEM integration in problem-solving projects.

STEM integration has been variously interpreted, ranging from a single discipline perspective through to multidisciplinary, interdisciplinary, and transdisciplinary approaches (Adams, Mann, Jordan, & Daly, 2009; English, 2017; Lattuca, 2003; Lattuca, Knight, & Bergom, 2013; Vasquez, Sneider, & Comer, 2013). Proponents of STEM integration cite the increasing challenges of multidisciplinary problems in today's world and maintain that students from the youngest grades require some experiences in solving integrated STEM-based problems (Daugherty & Carter, 2018; English, 2016, 2017; Honey, Pearson, & Schweingruber, 2014; Park, Park, & Bates, 2018; Rennie, Venville, & Wallace, 2018). In contrast, counter-arguments to STEM integration have continued for a number of years, with the main issues involving the nature and extent of integration (Bybee, 2013; Daugherty & Carter, 2018), inadequate content coverage, and thus limited conceptual development (English, 2016, 2017; Guzey, Ring-Whalen, Harwell, & Peralta, 2019; Honey et al., 2014; Langman et al., 2019; Shaughnessy, 2013). This lack of content learning has been reported in mathematics, where concerns have been expressed that the discipline is not receiving the required attention in integrated STEM projects, despite its foundational role across the disciplines (Doig & Jobling, 2019; Fitzallen, 2015; Honey et al., 2014; Lyons, 2018; National Council of Supervisors of Mathematics & the National Council of Teachers of Mathematics, 2019). Likewise, technology educators have indicated that many students fail to develop an understanding of how mathematics and science knowledge supports their use of design processes and their subsequent solutions (Fan & Yu, 2017; Mativo & Wicklein, 2011).

On the other hand, numerous studies have revealed how the application of design processes in an integrative STEM problem can assist middle and high school students in developing new knowledge and capabilities, as well as making connections among the STEM disciplines (e.g., Burghardt & Hacker, 2004; Bybee, 2013; English & King, 2015; Fan & Yu, 2017; Guzey et al., 2019; King & English, 2017; Kolodner et al., 2003; Penner, Lehrer, & Schauble, 1998; Roth, 1996; Wendell et al., 2014). Several studies have shown how elementary and middle school students apply STEM concepts in designing and constructing various physical artifacts. King and English (2017), for example, gave fifth-grade students the problem of designing and building an optical instrument that enabled them to see around corners. During their design phases, students were observed to apply scientific concepts of light, mathematical understandings pertaining to geometry, angles and measurement, and technology concepts related to how light travels through a system. In an earlier study, Penner et al. (1998) reported on students' designed models of the human elbow, where they applied mathematics to analyze data that led to science understandings about force and the location of the attachment point of biceps. In yet another study by Kolodner et al. (2003), middle school students learned about forces and motion by designing and redesigning vehicles and their propulsion systems.

In a three-year longitudinal study on how different approaches to engineering integration impacted on student learning and interest, Guzey et al. (2019) analyzed a middle school life science teacher's implementation of three design-focused life science units. It was found that the design and implementation of each unit reflected a unique approach to engineering integration, namely, "add on, implicit, and explicit" (p. 23). Teachers' approaches to discussing engineering also varied among each curriculum unit. Analyses of pre- and post-test results in disciplinary content learning, as well as student interest surveys and videotaped classroom lessons, revealed that explicit engineering integration and engineering language use in the classroom lessons yielded higher student learning gains in science and engineering. However, no significant effects on students' interest in science and engineering were found. The importance of incorporating engineering design and practice into science programs was highlighted, with the cautionary note that teachers require support in developing the necessary expertise to successfully implement engineering experiences.

A different approach to STEM-based problem solving and learning was adopted by Langman et al. (2019) in their study of high school students' disciplinary learning from a real-world engineering context. Student groups completed modules that included a model-eliciting activity (Lesh & Zawojewski, 2007) involving iterative design processes. They were to interpret, assess, and compare images of blood vessel networks grown in scaffolds, develop a procedure or tool for measuring (or scoring) this vessel growth, and demonstrate how to apply their procedure to the images, as well as to any image of a blood vessel network. The results showed how students designed a range of mathematical models of varying levels of sophistication to evaluate the quality of blood vessel networks and developed a knowledge of angiogenesis in doing so. Comparisons of students' science knowledge before and after the module completion indicated that they knew almost nothing about angiogenesis before commencing the module but were able to describe important aspects of angiogenesis on module completion.

Not surprisingly, fewer studies have explored learning through design during STEM-based problem solving by the younger grades, as noted by Tank, Rynearson, and Moore (2018). In a recent study, Tank et al. investigated how an engineering design-based STEM integration unit was enacted across three kindergarten classrooms. Their findings suggested that kindergarten children were able to engage meaningfully in, and with, multiple phases of an engineering design process while also developing an understanding of scientists and engineers. Through multiple instances of student-initiated talk, student-student interactions, and the use of explicit engineering language, the students were observed to make connections to their prior learning. The research further indicated that activities with engineering design in the early school years should incorporate multiple aspects of engineering and engineering design, together with interdisciplinary content and a context for STEM integration. It was concluded that kindergarten students are able to complete long-term, multi-component engineering design projects that include integrated STEM lessons, and that students can develop high levels of understanding and engagement. The researchers warned, however, that teachers need to facilitate and guide students in their learning during an engineering design-based project, but not constrain them.

In sum, a key factor in creating and implementing problems that focus on learning through design is to ensure that the core STEM concepts are central to the design process. Unfortunately, as Burghardt and Hacker lamented, design projects can often end up with the learner focusing on the product rather than on the core concepts to be developed. Without a concomitant development of content and design, students can simply resort to trial-and-error problem solving that can be devoid of any conceptual growth.

Concluding Points

This chapter has explored research on design and design thinking in STEM education through two fundamental lenses of learning *about* design and learning *through* design. Despite the increased role of design across many varied fields today, there appears an inadequate number of studies exploring design learning throughout the school years, especially during the elementary grades. Many of the STEM-based education studies have focused on science as the primary learning discipline, which is perhaps not surprising, given the inclusion of engineering design within the NGSS (2013). Mathematics learning, however, appears to have received less attention, as has technology, in integrated STEM projects (e.g., de Vries, 2018; Haupt, 2018; National Council of Supervisors of Mathematics & the National Council of Teachers of Mathematics, 2019). Maintaining the integrity of the respective disciplines in learning through design remains a concern and is in need of further research. Likewise, learning about design is increasingly important in a world where design is essential to so many industries, businesses, and the professions more broadly.

Design education needs to commence early. Nielsen (2013), for example, maintained that an aptitude for, and interest in, design is developed from the kindergarten years and continues through to the primary and into the secondary grades. Chin et al.'s (2019) recent study involving sixth-grade students provided timely evidence that the application of design processes may improve learning and problem solving well beyond the school years. Furthermore, instruction in design thinking may improve the chances of lower-achieving students applying these processes in a range of novel problem situations. Effective teacher education programs are essential to advancing design learning in STEM education programs (Nadelson, Callahan, Pyke, Hay, Dance, & Pfiester, 2013). STEM education across K-12 cannot ignore the contributions of design and design thinking in enhancing learning and complex problem solving. Indeed, many of our students' future careers will demand design thinking and design dispositions in meeting the demands of innovation (Chin et al., 2019) and in keeping abreast of digital disruption.

References

Accreditation Board for Engineering and Technology, Engineering Accreditation Commission. (2015). *Criteria for accrediting engineering programs: Effective for reviews during the 2016–2017 accreditation.* Retrieved from http://www.abet.org/accreditation/accreditation-criteria/criteria-for-accrediting-engineering-programs-2016-2017/

Adams, R., Mann, L., Jordan, S. S., & Daly, S. (2009). Exploring the boundaries: Language, roles, and structures in cross-disciplinary design teams. In J. McDonnell & P. Lloyd (Eds.), *About: Designing—Analysing design meetings (pp.* 339–358). London: Taylor & Francis.

Aranda, M. L., Lie, R., & Guzey, S. S. (2019). Productive thinking in middle school science students' design conversations in a design based engineering challenge. *International Journal of Technology and Design Education.* doi:10.1007/s10798-019-09498-5

Asunda, P. A., & Hill, R. B. (2007). Critical features of engineering design in technology education. *Journal of Industrial Teacher Education, 44*(1), 25–48.

Bagiati, A., & Evangelou, D. (2018). Identifying engineering in a PreK classroom: An observation protocol to support guided project-based instruction. In L. D. English & T. Moore (Eds.), *Early engineering learning* (pp. 83–111). Berlin: Springer.

Bartholomew, S. R., & Strimel, G. J. (2018). Factors influencing student success on open-ended design problems. *International Journal of Technology and Design Education, 28,* 753–770.

Burghardt, D., & Hacker, M. (2004). Informed design: A contemporary approach to design pedagogy as a core process in technology. *The Technology Teacher, 64*(1), 6–8.

Bybee, R. W. (2013). *The case for STEM education: Challenges and opportunities.* Arlington, VA: NSTA Press.

Canada 2067. (2017). *Global shapers report: Shaping the future of K-12 STEM education.* Retrieved from https://canada2067.ca/app/uploads/2017/12/Canada-2067-Global-Shapers-Report.pdf

Chin, D. B., Blair, K. P., Wolf, R. C., Conlin, L. D., Cutumisu, M., Pfaffman, J., & Schwartz, D. L. (2019). Educating and measuring choice: A test of the transfer of design thinking in problem solving and learning. *Journal of the Learning Sciences,* online. doi:10.1080/10508406.2019.1570933

Crismond, D. P., & Adams, R. S. (2012). The informed design teaching and learning matrix. *Journal of Engineering Education, 101,* 738–797.

Cunningham, C. M. (2018). *Engineering in elementary STEM education: Curriculum design, instruction, learning, and assessment.* New York, NY: Teachers College Press.

Cunningham, C. M., Lachapelle, C. P., & Davis, M. E. (2018). Engineering concepts, practices, and trajectories for early childhood education. In L. D. English, & T. Moore (Eds.), *Early engineering learning,* (pp. 135–174). Singapore: Springer.

Daly, S., Adams, R. S., & Bodner, G. (2012). What does it mean to design? A qualitative investigation guided by design professionals' experiences. *Journal of Engineering Education, 101,* 187–219.

Daugherty, J., Dixon, R., & Merrill, C. (2018). Research evidence of the impact of engineering design on technology and engineering education students. *Journal of Technology Education, 30*(1), 46–65.

Daugherty, M. K., & Carter, V. (2018). The nature of interdisciplinary STEM education. In M. J. de Vries (ed.), *Handbook of Technology Education* (pp. 159–169). Cham: Springer International. doi:10.1007/978-3-319-44687-5_48

de Vries, M. (2009). The developing field of technology education: An introduction. In M. de Vries & A. Jones (Eds.), *International handbook of research and development in technology education* (pp. 1–9). Rotterdam: Sense.

de Vries, M. (2018). Philosophy of technology: Themes and topics. In M. J. de Vries (Ed.), *Handbook of technology education* (pp. 7–16). Cham: Springer International. doi:10.1007/978-3-319-44687-5_48

Doig, B., & Jobling, W. (2019). Inter-disciplinary mathematics: Old wine in new bottles? In B. Doig, J. Williams, D. Swanson, R. Borromeo Ferri, & P. Drake (Eds.), *Interdisciplinary mathematics education: The state of the art and beyond.* ICME-13 Monographs (pp. 245–255). Springer Open. https://doi.org/10.1007/978-3-030-11066-6_15

Dorst, K. (2011). The core of design thinking and its application. *Design Studies, 32,* 521–532.

Dorst, K., & Cross, N. (2001). Creativity in the design process: Co-evolution of problem—Solution. *Design Studies, 22,* 425–437.

Dym, C. L., Agogino, A. M., Eris, O., Frey, D. D., & Leifer, L. J. (2005). Engineering design thinking, teaching, and learning. *Journal of Engineering Education, 94*(1), 103–120.

Education Council (December, 2015). *National STEM school education strategy.* Retrieved from www.educationcouncil.edu.au

Elkin, M., Sullivan, A., & Bers, M. U. (2018). Books, butterflies, and 'bots: Integrating engineering and robotics into early childhood curricula. In L. D. English & T. Moore (Eds.), *Early engineering learning* (pp. 225–248). Singapore: Springer.

English, L. D. (2016). STEM education K–12: Perspectives on integration. *International Journal of STEM Education, 3*(3), 1–8. doi:10.1186/s40594-016-0036-1.

English, L. D. (2017). Advancing elementary and middle school STEM education. *International Journal of Science and Mathematics Education* (special issue: STEM for the Future and the Future of STEM), *15*(1), 5–24.

English, L. D. (online first, 2018). Learning while designing in a fourth-grade integrated STEM problem. *International Journal of Technology and Design Education.* doi:10.1007/s10798-018-9482-z

English, L. D., & King, D. T. (2015). STEM learning through engineering design: Fourth—grade students' investigations in aerospace. *International Journal of STEM Education, 2*(14), 1–18.

English, L. D., & Moore, T. (Eds.). (2018). *Early engineering learning.* Singapore: Springer.

Fan, S., & Yu, K. (2017). How an integrative STEM curriculum can benefit students in engineering design practices. *International Journal of Technology and Design Education, 27*(1), 107–129.

Fitzallen, N. (2015). *STEM education: What does mathematics have to offer?* Paper presented at the Annual Meeting of the Mathematics Education Research Group of Australasia (38th, Sunshine Coast, Queensland, Australia, 2015)

Glen, R., Suciu, C., & Baughn, C. (2014). The need for design thinking in business schools. *Academy of Management Learning and Education, 13,* 653–667.

Gómez Puente, S. M., van Eijck, M., & Jochems, W. (2011). Towards characterising design-based learning in engineering education: A review of the literature. *European Journal of Engineering Education, 36,* 137–149. doi: 10.1080/03043797.2011.565116.

Grubbs, M., & Strimel, G. (2015). Engineering design: The great integrator. *Journal of STEM Teacher Education, 50*(1), 77–90.

Guilford, J. P. (1956). Structure of intellect. *Psychological Bulletin, 53*, 267–293.

Guzey, S. S., Ring-Whalen, E. A., Harwell, M., & Peralta, Y. (2019). Life STEM: A case study of life science learning through engineering design. *International Journal of Science and Mathematics Education, 17*(1), 23–42.

Haupt, G. (2018). Design in technology education: Current state of affairs. In M. J. de Vries, (ed.), *Handbook of technology education* (pp. 643–659). Springer International. doi:10.1007/978-3-319-44687-5_48

Honey, M., Pearson, G., & Schweingruber, A. (2014). *STEM integration in K-12 education: Status, prospects, and an agenda for research*. Washington, DC: National Academies Press.

International Technology and Engineering Educators Association (ITEA/ITEEA). (2007). *Standards for technological literacy: Content for the study of technology* (3rd ed.). Reston, VA: ITEEA.

Jonassen, D. H. (2011). *Learning to solve problems: A handbook for designing problem-solving learning environments*. New York, NY: Routledge.

Jones, A., Buntting, C., & de Vries, M. (2011). The developing field of technology education: A review to look forward. *International Journal of Technology and Design Education, 23*. doi:10.1007/s10798-011-9174-4

Kangas, K., & Seitamaa-Hakkarainen, P. (2018). Collaborative design work in technology education. In M. J. de Vries (Ed.), *Handbook of technology education* (pp. 597–609). Springer International. doi:10.1007/978-3-319-44687-5_48.

Kelley, T. R., Brenner, D. C., & Pieper, J. T. (2010). Two approaches to engineering design: Observations in Stem education. *Journal of STEM Teacher Education, 47*. doi:10.30707/JSTE47.2

Kelley, T. R., Capobianco, B. M., & Kaluf, K. J. (2015). Concurrent think–aloud protocols to assess elementary design students. *International Journal of Technology and Design Education, 25*, 521–540.

Kelley, T. R., & Sung, E. (2017). Examining elementary school students' transfer of learning through engineering design using think–aloud protocol analysis. *Journal of Technology Education, 28*(2), 83–108.

King, D. T., & English, L. D. (2017). Engineering design in the primary school: Applying stem concepts to build an optical instrument. *International Journal of Science Education, 38*, 2762–2794.

Kolodner, J. L., Camp, P. J., Crismond, D., Fasse, B., Gray, J., Holbrook, J., Puntambeker, S., & Ryan, M. (2003). Problem-based learning meets case-based reasoning in the middle school science classroom. Putting Learning by Design™ curriculum into practice. *Journal of the Learning Sciences, 12*, 495–547.

Langman, C., Zawojewski, J., McNicholas, P., Cinar, A., Brey, E., Bilgic, M., & Mehdizadeh, H. (2019). Disciplinary learning from an authentic engineering context. *Journal of Pre-College Engineering Education Research, 9*, 77–94.

Lattuca, L. R. (2003). Creating interdisciplinarity: Grounded definitions from college and university faculty. *History of Intellectual Culture, 3*(1), 1–20.

Lattuca, L. R., Knight, D., & Bergom, I. (2013). Developing a measure of interdisciplinary competence. *International Journal of Engineering Education, 29*, 726–739.

Lawson, B., & Dorst, K. (2009). *Design expertise*. New York, NY: Routledge.

Lee, J. B., & Strobel, J. (2014). Teachers' concerns in implementing engineering into elementary classrooms and the impact of teacher professional development. In S. Purzer, J. Strobel, & M. E. Cardella (Eds.), *Engineering in pre-college settings: Synthesizing research, policy, and practice* (pp. 163–182). West Lafayette, IN: Purdue University Press.

Lesh, R., & Zawojewski, J. S. (2007). Problem solving and modeling. In F. Lester (Ed.), *Second handbook of research on mathematics teaching and learning* (pp. 763–804). Charlotte, NC: Information Age Publishing.

Lippard, C. N., Lamm, M. H., & Riley, K. M. (2017). Engineering thinking in pre-kindergarten children: A systematic literature review. *Journal of Engineering Education, 106*, 454–474.

Lucas, B., Claxton, G., & Hanson, J. (2014). *Thinking like an engineer: Implications for the education system*. Report for the Royal Academy of Engineering Standing Committee for Education and Training. London: Royal Academy of Engineers.

Lyons, T. (2018). Helping students make sense of STEM. *Teaching Science, 64*(3), 37–43.

Mativo, J., & Wicklein, R. (2011). Learning effects of design strategies on high school students. *Journal of STEM Teacher Education, 48*(3), 8.

McCracken, J. (2000). Design: The creative soul of technology. In E. Martin (Ed.), *Technology education for the 21st century: 49th yearbook*. Council on Technology Teacher Education. Peoria, IL: Glencoe/McGraw Hill.

McFadden, J., & Roehrig, G. (2018). Engineering design in the elementary science classroom: Supporting student discourse during an engineering design challenge. *International Journal of Technology and Design Education, 29*, 231–262. https://doi.org/10.1007/s1079 8-018-9444-5

Mehalik, M. M., Doppelt, Y., & Schunn, C. D. (2008). Middle-school science through design–based learning versus scripted inquiry: Better overall science concept learning and equity gap reduction. *Journal of Engineering Education, 97*, 71–85.

Mentzer, N., Becker, K., & Sutton, M. (2015). Engineering design thinking: High school students' performance and knowledge. *Journal of Engineering Education, 104,* 417–432.

Moore, T. J., Glancy, A. W., Tank, K. M., Kersten, J. A., Smith, K. A., & Stohlmann, M. S. (2014). A framework for quality K-12 engineering education: Research and development. *Journal of Pre-College Engineering Education Research* (J-PEER), *4.* https://doi.org/10.7771/2157-9288.1069

Moore, T. J., & Smith, K. A. (2014). Advancing the state of the art of STEM integration. *Journal of STEM Education, 15*(1), 5–10.

Moore, T. J., Stohlmann, M. S., Wang, H. H., Tank, K. M., Glancy, A. W., & Roehrig, G. H. (2014). Implementation and integration of engineering in K-12 STEM education. In S. Purzer, J. Strobel, & M. E. Cardella (Eds.), *Engineering in pre-college settings: Synthesizing research, policy, and practice* (pp. 183–210). West Lafayette, IN: Purdue University Press.

Nadelson, L. S., Callahan, J., Pyke, P., Hay, A., Dance, M., & Pfiester, J. (2013). Teacher STEM perception and preparation: Inquiry-based STEM professional development for elementary teachers. *The Journal of Educational Research, 106,* 157–168.

National Council of Supervisors of Mathematics and the National Council of Teachers of Mathematics. (2019). *Building STEM education on a sound mathematical foundation. A joint position statement on STEM from the National Council of Supervisors of Mathematics and the National Council of Teachers of Mathematics.* Retrieved from https://www.mathedleadership.org

National Science & Technological Council. (2018). *Charting a course for success: America's strategy for STEM education.* Committee on STEM Education of the National Science & Technological Council. Retrieved from https://www.whitehouse.gov/wp-content/uploads/2018/12/STEM-Education-Strategic-Plan-2018.pdf

NGSS Lead States. (2013). Next generation science standards: For states, by states. Washington, DC: The National Academic Press.

Nielsen, L. M. (2013). Design learning for tomorrow. Design education from kindergarten to PhD. In J. B. Reitan, P. Lloyd, E. Bohemia, L. M. Nielsen, I. Digranes, & E. Lutnæs (Eds.), *Design learning for tomorrow. Design education from kindergarten to PhD.* Proceedings from the *2nd International Conference for Design Education Researchers* (Vol. 1, pp. i–iii). Oslo: ABM-media.

Nielsen, L. M., Brænne, K., & Maus, I. G. (2015). Editorial: Design learning for tomorrow. FOR*Makademisk.* org, *8*(1), 1–5.

Park, D.-Y., Park, M.-H., & Bates, A. B. (2018). Exploring young children's understanding about the concept of volume through engineering design in a STEM activity: A case study. *International Journal of Science and Mathematics Education, 16,* 275–294.

Penner, D., Lehrer, R., & Schauble, L. (1998). From physical models to biomechanics: A design-based modelling approach. *Journal of the Learning Sciences, 7,* 427–449. doi:10.1080/10508406.1998.9672060

Rennie, L., Venville, G., & Wallace, J. (2018). Making STEM curriculum useful, relevant, and motivating for students. In R. Jorgensen & K. Larkin (Eds.), *STEM education in the junior secondary* (pp. 91–109). Berlin: Springer.

Roth, W-M. (1996). Learning to talk engineering design: Results from an interpretive study into a grade 4/5 classroom. *International Journal of Technology and Design Education, 6,* 107–135.

Shaughnessy, M. (2013). By way of introduction: Mathematics in a STEM context. *Mathematics Teaching in the Middle School, 18,* 324.

Strimel, G. J., Bartholomew, S. R., Kim, E., & Zhang, L. (2018). An investigation of engineering design cognition and achievement in primary school. *Journal for STEM Education Research, 11.* https://doi.org/10.1007/s41979-018-0008-0.

Strimel, G. J., Kim, E., Grubbs, M. E., & Huffman, T. J. (2019). A meta-synthesis of primary and secondary student design cognition research. *International Journal of Technology and Design Education.* https://doi.org/10.1007/s10798-019-09505-9

Sung, E., & Kelley, T. R. (2019). Identifying design process patterns: A sequential analysis study of design thinking. *International Journal of Technology and Design Education, 29,* 283–302.

Tank, K. M., Moore, T. J., Dorie, B. L., Gajdzik, E., Sanger, M. T., Rynearson, A. M., & Mann, E. F. (2018). Engineering in early elementary classrooms through the integration of high-quality literature, design, and STEM+C content. In L. D. English & T. J. Moore (Eds.), *Early engineering learning* (pp. 175–202). Singapore: Springer.

Tank, K. M., Rynearson, A. M., & Moore, T. J. (2018). Examining student and teacher talk within engineering design in kindergarten. *European Journal of STEM Education, 3.* https://doi.org/10.20897/ejsteme/3870

van Breukelen, D. H. J., de Vries, M. J., & Schure, F. A. (2017). Concept learning by direct current design challenges in secondary education. *International Journal of Technology and Design Education, 27,* 407–430.

van der Bijl-Brouwer, M., & Dorst, K. (2017). Advancing the strategic impact of human-centred design. *Design Studies, 53,* 1–23. https://doi.org/10.1016/j.destud.2017.06.003

van Kuijk, J., Daalhuizen, J., & Christiaans, H. (2019). Drivers of usability in product design practice: Induction of a framework through a case study of three product development projects. *Design Studies, 60*, 139–179. https://doi.org/10.1016/j.destud.2018.06.002

Vasquez, J., Sneider, C., & Comer, M. (2013*). STEM lesson essentials, grades 3–8: Integrating science, technology, engineering, and mathematics*. Portsmouth, NH: Heinemann.

Wendell, K. B., Kendall, A., Portsmore, M., Wright, C., Jarvin, L., & Rogers, C. (2014). Embedding elementary school science instruction in engineering design problem solving. In S. Purzer, J. Strobel, & M. E. Cardella (Eds.), *Engineering in pre-college settings: Synthesizing research, policy, and practice* (pp. 143–162). West Lafayette, IN: Purdue University Press.

Wendell, K. B., & Kolodner, J. L. (2014). Learning disciplinary ideas and practices through engineering design. In A. Johri & B. M. Olds (Eds.), *Cambridge handbook of engineering education research* (pp. 243–263). New York, NY: Cambridge University Press.

Yasar, S., Baker, D., Robinson-Kurpius, S., Krause, S., & Roberts, C. (2006). Development of a survey to assess K-12 teachers' perceptions of engineers and familiarity with teaching design, engineering, and technology. *Journal of Engineering Education, 95*, 205–216.

8

THE IMPORTANCE OF EARLY STEM EDUCATION

*Susanna Hapgood, Charlene M. Czerniak, Kimberly Brenneman,
Douglas H. Clements, Richard A. Duschl, Marilyn Fleer,
Daryl Greenfield, Helen Hadani, Nancy Romance, Julie Sarama,
Christina Schwarz and Beth VanMeeteren*

Introduction

Science, Technology, Engineering, and Mathematics (STEM) are often discussed using the familiar STEM acronym (e.g., McClure et al., 2017; Spaepen et al., 2017), as subject-specific learning and as integrated use of the subjects to solve real-world problems. Despite often being interpreted as an interdisciplinary endeavor, there is disagreement regarding how STEM integration is defined, conceptualized, or operationalized; and few research-based early childhood exemplars exist that blend science, technology, engineering, and mathematics. *Integrated*, *interdisciplinary*, and *thematic* have been used synonymously, and there are concerns that some forms of integration, often seen in early childhood classrooms around "themes," lack meaningful STEM content (Czerniak, Weber, Sandmann, & Ahern, 1999). Robust programs that integrate STEM subjects are limited in schools and in teacher preparation programs (Czerniak & Johnson, 2014). Where integration has been successfully implemented, it tends to focus on a real-life question or problem using a project- or problem-based instructional approach (Krajcik & Czerniak, 2014; Mitchell, Foulger, Wetzel, & Rathkey, 2009; Venville, Wallace, Rennie, & Malone, 1998) or an engineering design approach (e.g., English & Moore, 2018; Tank et al., 2018) with connections to reading and social studies (Portsmore & Milto, 2018). For this chapter, we include integrated examples when found, but because of the limited examples of STEM integration in EC, we do not limit our review of STEM in EC to those that demonstrate integration.

Calls for STEM in early years have come from educators and policymakers alike (e.g., Katz, 2010). Reflecting this, this chapter explores STEM in early childhood across five areas: (1) the state of research; (2) teacher preparation and teacher professional development; (3) available tools for evaluating learning and issues in measuring learning; (4) policy issues; and (5) a summary of continuing struggles and promising future directions for EC-STEM education.

State of the Research in EC-STEM

Research in EC-STEM typically examines the cognitive capacities young children bring to those opportunities and the role of play in shaping early STEM learning. Research has also examined the impact of STEM on lifelong learning.

Play-Based Learning. Play is a critical context and tool for EC-STEM learning (Bulunuz, 2013). Playful learning often emerges in children's curiosity about what is in the world and how it works (Fleer, 2013; Shulz & Bonawitz, 2007). Play provides space for children to collaborate to build scientific and mathematical knowledge (Vogt, Hauser, Stebler, Rechsteiner, & Urech, 2018), to engage in engineering design and problem solving, and to deploy and strengthen science and engineering practices such as asking questions and communicating understandings (Kane, 2015). In play, children's emotional responses to and attitudes about STEM are further developed through experiences in settings where STEM thinking and habits of mind are promoted (Blake & Howitt, 2012).

Preschool and home settings afford many opportunities for STEM learning (Gomes & Fleer, 2017; Sarama & Clements, 2009), but adults are needed to maximize this potential (Sikder & Fleer, 2015). For example, when educators use a "Conceptual PlayWorld" model, they craft a story-based imaginary-play STEM adventure in which children use STEM concepts to solve problems (Fleer, 2017). Similarly, in home settings, parents and other caregivers can support children's talk about STEM while engaging with them in imaginative and dramatic play and everyday practices, such as riding a bike on different surfaces (Hao & Fleer, 2016) or while building with blocks (Ferrara, Hirsh-Pasek, Newcombe, Golinkoff, & Lam, 2011). "Guided" play lays the conceptual foundations for lifelong learning and creates conditions for continued development of cognitive capacities needed for STEM inquiry (Weisberg, Hirsh-Pasek, & Golinkoff, 2013).

Young Children's STEM Cognitive Strengths. Beginning in infancy, children have intuitive theories about the world and reasoning skills that likely form the foundations of STEM learning (Gopnik, 2012; Goswami, 2015). Capacities to recognize changes in the quantity of objects and relationships between a sample and a population begin in infancy (Xu & Garcia, 2008). These abilities may contribute to probabilistic reasoning and learning statistics and to the development of scientific inquiry skills, such as prediction of probabilistic outcomes (Cook, Goodman, & Schulz, 2011). Children as young as two can infer physical causal relationships based on patterns of evidence about covariation (Gopnik, Sobel, Schulz, & Glymour, 2001), and by six or seven years old are capable of revising their interpretations on the basis of counter-evidence (Bonawitz, van Schijndel, Friel, & Schulz, 2012). Causal learning can be promoted by asking children to explain what they observe (Walker, Lombrozo, Legare, & Gopnik, 2014).

Children's language and communication skills that permeate STEM learning capacities undergo tremendous development during the early childhood years. For example, children's use and comprehension of mathematically important words such as *many*, *most*, *few*, and *fewest* reveal deep connections between language and mathematics concept learning (Purpura, Napoli, & King, 2019) as well as how various languages differ in terms of everyday use of such language (Kung et al., 2019). Developing science knowledge and the capacity to produce external representations of it seem to be mutually reinforcing, as when K and first graders' representations of their understandings about how honeybees collect nectar became more relevant and accurate (Danish & Phelps, 2011).

Building on decades of research (e.g., Gelman & Markman, 1986), we continue to learn about how capacities for sorting, categorizing, and sequencing, which are foundational to learning across STEM domains, begin to develop early in children's lives (Sarama, Brenneman, Clements, Duke, & Hemmeter, 2017). For example, Collins and Laski (2019) found a strong relationship between preschoolers' symbolic mapping and relational reasoning and their early literacy and mathematics competencies. Recent research also suggests strong links between STEM-related skills and children's cognitive and emotional self-regulatory skills including executive function and executive control (Clements, Sarama, & Germeroth, 2016; Morgan et al., 2019) and between science skills and positive approaches to learning (Bustamante, White, & Greenfield, 2018).

The Impact of STEM on Lifelong Learning. Mathematical knowledge and skills in kindergarten and growth in these skills across the K-1 years have been identified as the strongest correlates of elementary achievement in math and reading (e.g., Duncan et al., 2007; Sarama, Lange, Clements, & Wolfe, 2012). Correlations between early math skills and later achievement have been found through high school (Casey, Nuttall, & Pezaris, 1997; Watts, Duncan, Siegler, & Davis-Kean, 2014).

The spatial reasoning children's block building demands, predicts math and science achievement in middle and high school (Casey et al., 2008; Wolfgang, Stannard, & Jones, 2001) as well as later aptitude for STEM success in mathematics (Casey et al., 1997), engineering (McGarvey, Luo, Hawes, & Spatial Reasoning Study Group, 2018), and physics (Kozhevnikov, Motes, & Hegarty, 2007). Whether these correlations are indicative of causal relationships has been questioned.

Correlations have also been found between early science and social studies knowledge and later science skills, reading, and mathematics achievement (Grissmer, Grimm, Aiyer, Murrah, & Steel, 2010; Morgan et al., 2016; Paprzycki et al., 2017), likely because real-world knowledge and vocabulary are associated with comprehension (Duke & Carlisle, 2011; Neuman & Roskos, 2005). Similarly, longitudinal outcomes related to measures of executive function in the early grades (Morgan et al., 2019), suggest that less robust executive function when children are six or seven years old is related to later academic difficulties.

Effective Curricula for EC-STEM. Worldwide, there is growing recognition of the importance of STEM in EC curricula. Many Asian countries are incorporating robotics and coding education beginning in preschool. In Singapore, for example, these curricular initiatives include the use of tangible and programmable materials (e.g. KIBO robot kits) that do not involve screen time (Sullivan & Bers, 2017). Similar initiatives are being implemented in Malaysia (Ismail, Hashim, Anis, Ismail, & Ismail, 2017) and Hong Kong, Korea, and China (Lee & Seo, 2011; Lau, Ho, & Lam, 2015). In Japan there are small-scale programs to systematically introduce preschool children to STEM inquiry activity (Sumida, 2015). In the United States, Boston Public Schools combined evidence-based literacy and math curricula with supports for social skills and found strong learning effects (Weiland & Yoshikawa, 2013). An interdisciplinary curriculum that combines math, science, literacy, and social-emotional learning shows promising pilot results for science understanding, vocabulary, phonological awareness, and some math concepts (e.g., Sarama et al., 2017). Research from Northern Ireland demonstrates the value of curricular materials that encourage teachers to engage in "early number talk" and to invite children to create their own representations of abstract ideas (Moffet & Eaton, 2018). Additionally, roleplay and story-based practices and approaches offer promise for increasing the amount of science taught (Varelas & Pappas, 2013; Bulunuz, 2013; Fleer, 2017).

Technology curriculum for young children should not be assumed to necessarily include the use of digital or electronic technology (Clements, Guernsey, & McClure, 2016). Technology is "the process by which humans modify nature to meet their needs and wants" (National Academy of Engineering [NAE] & National Research Council [NRC], 2002, p. 2); thus electronic technology is but one form. A broader perspective within EC curricula regarding how young children can "modify nature to meet their needs and wants," reveals ways children engaging in inquiry and engineering may design their own tools and technology while examining how materials interact (science) and arranging the materials in different configurations (spatial thinking and mathematics). Though a robust curriculum is important, effective enactment to foster learning requires that EC professionals have sufficient knowledge and skills, which we address next.

Teacher Preparation and Professional Development

This section summarizes challenges in EC teacher education and in-service teacher education. The discussion includes linking STEM teacher education in an integrated fashion and evidence-based models.

Preservice Teacher Preparation. There are many challenges in the preparation of effective EC-STEM teachers with candidates often acknowledging their own inadequate background knowledge and lack of confidence and interest in STEM domains (Nadelson et al., 2013; Gresham & Burleigh, 2019). Though particularly acute in the United States (Epstein & Miller, 2011), this issue is worldwide (e.g., Thiel, 2010; Ng, 2011).

Multiple studies have demonstrated that teacher candidates' self-efficacy for teaching science can be increased through science teaching methods coursework (Avery & Meyer, 2012; Del Greco, Bernadowski, & Parker, 2017; Hechter, 2011; Menon & Sadler, 2016), but much of the extant research on teacher preparation is piecemeal, examining discrete approaches to improving teacher candidates' STEM knowledge and pedagogical skill. Though many EC teachers report being better prepared to teach life science (Banilower et al., 2013), EC teacher candidates often lack understanding of engineering, physical science, and technology. These gaps in teachers' background content knowledge are unfortunately rarely ameliorated, as many early childhood licensure programs do not provide teachers with adequate subject matter expertise to know how to integrate across STEM subjects (Czerniak & Johnson, 2014).

Despite their rarity, there are promising approaches for elementary STEM teacher preparation that include practice-based approaches that adhere to recommendations from professional organizations and many countries' educational stakeholders (e.g. Australian Government, 2017; National Association for the Education of Young Children [NAEYC], 2019; NRC, 2012). Integration of STEM disciplines is one aspect of some preservice teaching initiatives (Tsybulsky & Oz, 2019) as is attention to academic language and STEM (Jung & Brown, 2016) and culturally responsive pedagogy (Arreguín-Anderson & Alanis, 2017). Such work will contribute to more comprehensive models of teacher preparation that yield positive results (Lippard, Tank, Walter, Krogh, & Colbert, 2018).

Evidence-Based Professional Development Models. Researchers worldwide recognize professional development as a priority for improving EC-STEM learning (e.g. Murphy, Mac-Donald, Danaia, & Wang, 2018; Stylianidou et al., 2018; Symaco & Daniel, 2018), particularly for those who serve children from low socioeconomic backgrounds (Hamlin & Wisneski, 2012). Some evidence-based models for preK-3 teacher professional development exist (Borko, Jacobs, & Koellner, 2010; Clements, Greenfield, Landry, & Sarama, 2015; Sarama, Clements, Wolfe, & Spitler, 2016; Romance & Vitale, 2017; Paprzycki et al., 2017). Features these efforts share include teacher learning of content, active engagement, conceptual coherence and cumulative learning, adequate program duration and collective participation, participants' physical and psychological comfort, and curricular materials supporting teacher and student learning (Klieckmann, Trobst, Jonen, Vehmeyer, & Moller, 2015). Yet, even with best efforts, teacher practices have not substantially changed, nor have they been sustained, likely because, despite the need for it, professional development of this kind remains relatively infrequently available to early childhood educators (DeJarnette, 2012). Still, examples of effective PD models can provide direction for future endeavors.

Several interdisciplinary instructional models for teacher professional development have demonstrated positive achievement outcomes in science, mathematics, and literacy, including transfer effects to later grade levels. With a strong track record of effectiveness, the Science IDEAS model for early elementary is characterized by sustained standards-based PD linking reading and writing in support of students' science learning (cf. Romance & Vitale, 2012, 2017). The NURTURES model also consisted of a sustained Framework-aligned PD with emphasis on building teacher content and pedagogical knowledge and helping teachers engage parents and caregivers in STEM learning leading to increased opportunities for classroom discourse, early literacy, computational and mathematical thinking experiences, and scientific reasoning. The combined elements of the NURTURES science-based PD model have demonstrated effectiveness in terms of proximal and distal student achievement outcomes with significant gains in early literacy, reading, mathematics, and science (see Kaderavek et al., submitted; Paprzycki et al., 2017; Tuttle et al., 2016).

Transforming knowledge of children's mathematical thinking into professional development through *learning trajectories* has also been recognized as effective (Sztajn, Confrey, Wilson, & Edgington, 2012). Learning trajectories (LTs) have three interconnected parts (Clements & Sarama, 2018): a goal (subject-matter students should learn); a developmental progression regarding how students' thinking sophistication increases; and instructional tasks and strategies to foster learning and elucidate what effective teachers must know and be able to do. Use of LTs support teachers to (a) understand mathematical content more deeply than often presented in texts or standards (e.g., Ma, 1999), (b) appreciate the way that their students think and learn mathematics (Ball & Forzani, 2011; Clements & Sarama, 2014), and (c) better assess children's learning. This approach has been effective in improving teaching *and* learning—and it *sustains through many years* (Sarama & Clements, 2018; Sarama et al., 2016).

Issues in Measuring Early STEM Learning

While STEM learning opportunities have been demonstrated to aid young children's development of numerous skills in early childhood, research on EC-STEM learning is impacted by the measures used to examine it. Measurement tools for this age group are limited, and they are most often subject specific rather than focused on integrated STEM.

Assessing Classroom Environments and Teaching. The primary influences on EC-STEM learning are teachers and classroom environments (Pianta, Belsky, Vadergrift, Houts, & Morrison, 2008). Although several general instruments are available to assess classrooms (e.g., ECERS, ECERS-R, CLASS), their association with STEM child outcomes is weak to moderate, and they do not identify specifically what is supporting STEM learning (e.g., Anders et al., 2012; Brunsek et al., 2017; Pianta et al., 2005). A review by Kilday and Kinzie (2009) identified nine instruments designed to measure mathematics (some also science) teaching quality. Through analyses of their theoretical bases, foci, psychometrics, and EC appropriateness, three were deemed of high quality: the Classroom Observation of Early Mathematics–Environment and Teaching (COEMET) (Clements & Sarama, 2000/2019), the Reformed Teaching Observation Protocol (RTOP) (Sawada et al., 2002) and the Inside the Classroom Observation Protocol (Weiss, Pasley, Smith, Banilower, & Heck, 2003). The latter two were designed for grades K-12, with only the COEMET appropriate for PreK and designed specifically for EC settings. Specifically for science, the Preschool Science Observation Measure (PSOM) (Vitiello, Whittaker, Mulcahy, Kinzie, & Helferstay, 2018) assesses science content and teaching quality in preschools. Psychometrics for the PSOM are adequate although associations with child outcomes were limited, they indicate some evidence for predictive validity. Designed for use in PreK-third grade classrooms, the Systematic Characterization of Inquiry Instruction in Early LearNing Classroom Environments (SCIIENCE) (Kaderavek et al., 2015) was designed to capture teacher behaviors aligned with the K-12 conceptual framework for science education (NRC, 2012). To date, data on SCIIENCE is limited to concurrent validity with eight preschool through third-grade teachers.

Measuring Child Outcomes. Few assessments of EC-STEM student outcomes for specific domains, and even fewer examining integrated STEM learning currently exist. A recent review identified and evaluated 16 mathematics-specific instruments for PreK-second grade preschool on a wide variety of features including psychometrics (Clements, Sarama, Germeroth, & Day-Hess, 2019). For use with children ages four to seven, the REMA (Clements, Sarama, & Liu, 2008), includes items representing 17 of 21 (81%) topics of early childhood math. Though limited to use with preschool-aged children, Every Child Ready–Math (ECR-M) (AppleTree Institute for Education Innovation, 2010) includes 48% of EC math topics. Addressing 43% math topics and designed to guide teachers' instruction, the Early Math Diagnostic Assessment (EMDA) (Pearson, 2003) evaluates the mathematics skills of PreK-third grade learners. The remaining assessments addressed only number-related topics. Providing item-level analysis of nearly 2000 items on 14 of the 16 instruments, the full review aligns the level of thinking assessed along research-based learning trajectories.

For science, an adaptive assessment based on the K-12 framework (NRC, 2012) and delivered on touch-screen devices for preschool-aged children is being used across multiple sites and projects (Greenfield, 2015). Measures of early technology learning are scarce, but an engineering observation protocol for examining early engineering and project-based design is available (Bagiati & Evangelou, 2018), and Purzer and Douglas (2018) call for a multifaceted approach for assessing early engineering skills.

Policy in EC-STEM

The success of EC-STEM initiatives around the world is contingent upon implementation of good policies. The impetus for policy reforms regarding STEM education comes from multiple directions. Cross-national tests of children's academic achievement (e.g., PISA & TIMSS) have been an impetus for numerous policy reforms worldwide (e.g., Korean Science & Engineering Foundation, 2019; Rothman, 2017). Research identifying the societal and economic value of starting STEM in EC contexts is also influencing policies to include STEM in EC care and education (Azzi-Lessing, 2009; Lynch, 2007; Mahony & Hayes, 2006; Tietze & Cryer, 2004). There are also calls to increase the coordination between preschool and primary grade approaches to STEM education to create a smoother transition for children (Black et al., 2017; Early Childhood STEM Working Group, 2017).

Adequate training for EC teachers in STEM is of central importance. Policies addressing high-quality early STEM experiences and curriculum in EC care and education will need an educated EC workforce to ensure proper implementation. Such policies currently exist. The Organisation for Economic Co-operation and Development proposed five policy levers for improving child development and learning (OECD, 2019). One lever focuses on caregiver and educator qualifications training, and working conditions. Six participating European countries have frameworks and policies supporting professional learning and development of EC caregivers and educators. In the United States, the Institute of Medicine (IOM) and National Research Council (NRC) provided a blueprint for establishing a unifying foundation for consistent and cumulative support for early learning. The blueprint recommends actions geared toward (1) improving higher education and ongoing professional learning; (2) strengthening qualification requirements based on knowledge and competencies; and (3) promoting evaluation that leads to continuous improvements in professional practices (Achieve, 2013; NRC, 2015.)

Continuing Struggles and Promising Future Directions

This chapter summarizes important findings regarding EC-STEM education and the many benefits of STEM education for children. We conclude with a list of recommended steps or conditions needed to develop high-quality EC-STEM curriculum and programs in the future:

Research

- Research should examine the STEM content and skills that, when strengthened early on, serve as powerful foundations for future learning, and additional work should explore endogenous and exogenous factors contributing to the stability of STEM achievement over time (e.g., Watts, Duncan, Clements, & Sarama, 2018).
- Integrated STEM curriculum (made available on the commercial market) needs to be developed and researched to ascertain its effectiveness. This could also include examination of STEM curriculum integration with reading, social studies, and the arts.
- Although programs exist that focus on technology and engineering education in early grades (e.g., McClure et al., 2017), including work on coding and robotics with young children, additional research is needed in these areas.
- There should be increased research regarding the coordination between preschool and primary grade approaches to STEM education to create a smoother transition for children (Black et al., 2017; EC-STEM Working Group, 2017).

- Additional research should examine the impact of informal, out-of-school science opportunities for their ability to enhance EC-STEM learning that carries over to K–12 learning (Marcus, Haden & Uttal, 2018).
- It is important to understand cultural differences related to STEM education (Vogt et al., 2018), so future research should study this in early grades. A potential starting point is a culturally-relevant preschool STE curriculum co-constructed by Head Start teachers, researchers, and (largely) immigrant families (http://rise.as.tufts.edu).
- Although K–12 STEM schools have taken hold in some countries, we found no solid research studies to determine the impact on student achievement with young students. Future research should examine the impact of these specialized STEM schools at the early grades.

Teacher Preparation and Professional Development

- Decades of research demonstrate the lack of EC teacher preparation in and comfort with STEM disciplines. The pattern of findings suggest that a major challenge will be to design newer models of preservice PreK–3 teacher preparation and teacher professional development programs in support of early STEM. Promising work in mathematics professional development incorporates knowledge of children's mathematical thinking into professional development through *learning trajectories* (Sarama et al., 2016; Sztajn et al., 2012). A learning trajectories approach may prove beneficial in science, technology, and engineering as well.
- Technology offers a promising direction for increasing educators' access to PD. For example, a study in Finland of a Massive Open Online Course (MOOC) about coding and computational thinking with over 500 participating primary school teachers, found that teachers were receptive to both the content of the course and the MOOC platform (Toikkanen & Leinonen, 2017).

Measurement of STEM Learning

- To move the field forward, we need assessments or combinations of assessments of *classrooms and teaching* and of *child outcomes* in all four STEM domains that acknowledge the unique components of each STEM domain as well as their overlap in young children's learning. The strong push for a greater focus on STEM learning opportunities for young children requires building an evidence base of effective programs and best practices. Such evidence requires a strong companion set of valid and reliable assessment tools for both assessment of component skills in each STEM area as well as their integrated application in the lives of young children.
- Although progress has been made in measuring science and mathematics teaching and learning, there is a serious gap in strong evidence-based measures for technology and engineering.

Policy for EC-STEM

- Children have few opportunities to engage with STEM of any form in most EC education classrooms (e.g., Banilower et al., 2013; Greenfield et al., 2009). Policymakers can find recommendations in recent National Research Council synthesis research reports (e.g., 2014a, 2014b); the Organisation for Economic Co-operation and Development (OECD, 2019); scholarly works (e.g., Clements, Guernsey, & McClure, 2016; Early Childhood STEM Working Group, 2017; Greenfield, Alexander, & Frechette, 2017; McClure et al., 2017); and the National Science Teachers Association (NSTA) Early Childhood Science Education Position Statement (2014).
- Policies that empower and enable caregivers and teachers to merge STEM learning with familiar experiences, objects, and the perspectives of the child's world will be more meaningful and facilitate the formation of STEM identities.

- Around the world, there is too often a false dichotomy created between policies in EC care and policies in education, with care as a response to physical needs and education as a response to instructional needs. Yet, a healthy, developing child is dependent upon an environment that is both physically and intellectually nurturing (Haddad, 2006).
- Policies that focus on EC–STEM learning should complement each other. In the United States, for example, the focus of federal policy is on EC literacy with success measured by standardized test scores despite the NAEYC's cautions of using standardized tests with young children (2003); such tests narrow the curricular experiences of young learners and nearly eliminate STEM (Center on Education Policy, 2017).
- STEM opportunities are not available for all children. For example, children in Sub-Saharan Africa are the least likely in the world to have access to early education. Recognizing that massive growth in brain development occurs by age five, national and regional organizations, academia, entrepreneurs, and the private sector should collaborating to improve outcomes (e.g., Africa Early Childhood Network [AfECN], 2018). In the United States, Head Start is a an example program that could provide strong early STEM background (e.g., Aldemir & Kermani, 2017).
- It is imperative that the EC workforce receive stronger coursework in STEM disciplines. The starting point for this STEM development rests with teacher licensure agencies that develop and oversee policies guiding teacher education and EC workforce requirements.

References

Achieve. (2013). *Next generation science standards*. Retrieved from http://www.nextgenscience.org

AfECN. (2018). *Africa early childhood network*. Retrieved from https://africaecnetwork.org

Aldemir, J., & Kermani, H. (2017). Integrated STEM curriculum: Improving educational outcomes for head start children. *Early Child Development and Care, 187*(11), 1694–1706.

Anders, Y., Rossbach, H-G., Weinert, S., Ebert, S., Kuger, S., Lehrl, S., & von Maurice, J. (2012). Home and preschool learning environments and their relations to the development of early numeracy skills. *Early Childhood Research Quarterly, 27*, 231–244. doi:10.1016/j.ecresq.2011.08.003

AppleTree Institute for Education Innovation. (2010). *Every child ready: Math assessment*. Washington, DC: AppleTree Institute.

Arreguín-Anderson, M. G., & Alanis, I. (2017). Oral academic language by design: Bilingual pre-service teachers' purposeful infusion of paired strategies during science instruction. *Journal of Classroom Interaction, 52*(2), 31–44.

Australian Government. (2017). *Department of education and training restoring focus on STEM in schools initiative*. Retrieved from https://www.education.gov.au/support-science-technology-engineering-and-mathematics

Avery, L. M., & Meyer, D. Z. (2012). Teaching science as science is practiced: Opportunities and limits for enhancing preservice elementary teachers' self-efficacy for science and science teaching. *School Science and Mathematics, 112*(7), 395–409.

Azzi-Lessing, L. (2009). Quality support infrastructure in early childhood: Still (mostly) missing. *Early Childhood Research and Practice, 11*(1).

Bagiati, A., & Evangelou, D. (2018). Identifying engineering in a PreK classroom: An observation protocol to support guided project-based instruction. In L. English & T. Moore, *Early engineering learning* (pp. 83–111). Singapore: Springer. doi:10.1007/978-981-10-8621-2

Ball, D. L., & Forzani, F. M. (2011). Building a common core for learning to teach, and connecting professional learning to practice. *American Educator, 35*(2), 17–21, 38–39.

Banilower, E. R., Smith, P. S., Weiss, I. R., Malzahn, K. A., Campbell, K. M., & Weis, A. M. (2013). *Report of the 2012 national survey of science and mathematics education*. Horizon Research, Inc., NJ.

Black, M., Walker, S. P., Fernald, L. C. H., Andersen, C. T., DiGirolamo, A, M., Lu, C., . . . Grantham-McGregor, S. (2017). Early childhood development coming of age: Science through the life course. *The Lancet, 389*, 77–90.

Blake, E., & Howitt, C. (2012). Science in early learning centres: Satisfying curiosity, guided play or lost opportunities? In K. C. D. Tan & M. Kim (Eds.), *Issues and challenges in science education research* (pp. 281–300). Dordrecht, The Netherlands: Springer.

Bonawitz, E. B., van Schijndel, T. J., Friel, D., & Schulz, L. (2012). Children balance theories and evidence in exploration, explanation, and learning. *Cognitive Psychology, 64*, 215–234.

Borko, H., Jacobs, J., & Koellner, K. (2010). Contemporary approaches to teacher professional development. *International Encyclopedia of Education, 7*, 548–556.

Brunsek, A., Perlman, M., Falenchuk, O., McMullen, E., Fletcher, B., & Shah, P. S. (2017). The relationship between the early childhood environment rating scale and its revised form and child outcomes: A systematic review and meta-analysis. *PLoS ONE, 12*(6). doi:10.1371/journal.pone.0178512

Bulunuz, M. (2013). Teaching science through play in kindergarten: Does integrated play and science instruction build understanding? *European Early Childhood Education Research Journal, 21*, 226–249. doi:10.1080/13 50293x.2013.789195

Bustamante, A. S., White, L. J., & Greenfield, D. B. (2018). Approaches to learning and science education in Head Start: Examining bidirectionality. *Early Childhood Research Quarterly, 44*, 34–42. doi:10.1016/j.ecresq.2018.02.013

Casey, B. M., Andrews, N., Schindler, H., Kersh, J. E., Samper, A., & Copley, J. (2008). The development of spatial skills through interventions involving block building activities. *Cognition and Instruction, 26*(3), 269–309.

Casey, M. B., Nuttall, R. L., & Pezaris, E. (1997). Mediators of gender differences in mathematics college entrance test scores: A comparison of spatial skills with internalized beliefs and anxieties. *Developmental Psychology, 33*, 669–680. doi:10.1037/0012-1649.33.4.669

Center on Education Policy, (2017). *The legacy of more & better learning time: Grantee and stakeholder reflections.* Policy Report. Retrieved from https://www.cep-dc.org/cfcontent_file.cfm?Attachment=FrizzellRentner KoberBraunFerguson%5FReport%5FLegacyMBLT%5F1%2E24%2E17%2Epdf

Clements, D. H., Greenfield, D. B., Landry, S. H., & Sarama, J. (2015). Assessment using technology: Formative assessment with young children. In O. Saracho (Ed.), *Contemporary perspectives on research in assessment and evaluation in early childhood education* (pp. 339–371). Charlotte, NC: Information Age Publishing.

Clements, D. H., Guernsey, L., & McClure, E. (2016). *Fostering STEM trajectories: Background, challenges, & opportunities for change.* Paper presented at Fostering STEM Trajectories: Bridging ECE Research, Practice, & Policy Conference, New America/Sesame Workshop, Washington, DC.

Clements, D. H., & Sarama, J. (2000/2019). *COEMET: The classroom observation of early mathematics environment and teaching instrument.* Denver, CO: University of Denver.

Clements, D. H., & Sarama, J. (2014). *Learning and teaching early math: The learning trajectories approach* (2nd ed.). New York, NY: Routledge.

Clements, D. H., & Sarama, J. (Producer). (2018). *Learning and teaching with learning trajectories (LT²).* Retrieved from http://LearningTrajectories.org

Clements, D. H., Sarama, J., & Germeroth, C. (2016). Learning executive function and early mathematics: Directions of causal relations. *Early Childhood Research Quarterly, 36*, 79–90. doi:10.1016/j.ecresq.2015.12.009

Clements, D. H., Sarama, J., Germeroth, C., & Day-Hess, C. (2019). Review of assessments of early childhood mathematics competencies. *Submitted for publication.*

Clements, D. H., Sarama, J., & Liu, X. (2008). Development of a measure of early mathematics achievement using the Rasch model: The research-based early math assessment. *Educational Psychology, 28*(4), 457–482. doi:10.1080/01443410701777272

Collins, M. A., & Laski, E. V. (2019). Digging deeper: Shared deep structures of early literacy and mathematics involve symbolic mapping and relational reasoning. *Early Childhood Research Quarterly, 46*, 201–212.

Cook, C., Goodman, N. D., & Schulz, L. E. (2011). Where science starts: Spontaneous experiments in preschoolers' exploratory play. *Cognition, 120*, 341–349. doi:10.1016/j.cognition.2011.03.003

Czerniak, C. M., & Johnson, C. C. (2014). Interdisciplinary science and STEM teaching. In N. G. Lederman & S. K. Abell (Eds.), *Handbook of research on science education* (2nd ed.). Mahwah, NJ: Lawrence Erlbaum Associates, Inc.

Czerniak, C. M., Weber, W., Sandmann, A., & Ahern, J. (1999). A literature review of science and mathematics integration. *School Science and Mathematics, 99*(8), 421–430.

Danish, J. A., & Phelps, D. (2011). Representational practices by the numbers: How kindergarten and first-grade students create, evaluate, and modify their science representations. *International Journal of Science Education, 33*(15), 2069–2094.

DeJarnette, N. K. (2012). America's children: Providing early exposure to STEM Initiatives. *Education, 133*(1), 77–84.

Del Greco, R., Bernadowski, C., & Parker, S. (2017). Using illustrations to depict preservice science teachers' self-efficacy: A case study. *International Journal of Instruction, 11*(2), 75–88.

Duke, N. K., & Carlisle, J. (2011). The development of comprehension. In M. L. Kamil, P. D. Pearson, E. B. Moje, & P. Afflerbach (Eds.), *Handbook of reading research* (Vol. 4, pp. 199–228). London: Routledge.

Duncan, G. J., Dowsett, C. J., Claessens, A., Magnussen, K., Huston, A. C., Klebenov, P., & Japel, C. (2007). School readiness and later achievement. *Developmental Psychology, 43*, 1428–1466.

Early Childhood STEM Working Group. (2017). Early STEM matters: Providing high-quality STEM experiences for all young learners. *Policy Report.*

English, L., & Moore, T. (2018). *Early engineering learning.* Gateway East, Singapore: Springer. doi:10.1007/978-981-10-8621-2

Epstein, D., & Miller, R. T. (2011). *Slow off the mark: Elementary school teachers and the crisis in science, technology, engineering, and math education.* Washington, DC: Center for American Progress.

Ferrara, K., Hirsh-Pasek, K., Newcombe, N. S., Golinkoff, R. M., & Lam, W. S. (2011). Block talk: Spatial language during block play. *Mind, Brain and Education, 5*(3), 143–151.

Fleer, M. (2013). Affective imagination in science education: Determining the emotional nature of scientific and technological learning of young children. *Research in Science Education, 43*, 2085–2106. doi:10.1007/s11165-012-9344-8

Fleer, M. (2017). Scientific playworlds: A model of teaching science in play-based settings. *Research in Science Education*, 1–22. doi:10.1007/s11165-017-9653-z

Gelman, S. A., & Markman, E. M. (1986). Categories and induction in young children. *Cognition, 23*, 183–209. doi:10.1016/0010-0277(86)90034-X

Gomes, J., & Fleer, M. (2017). The development of a scientific motive: How preschool science and home play reciprocally contribute to science learning. *Research in Science Education*, 1–22. doi:10.1007/s11165-017-9631-5

Gopnik, A. (2012). Scientific thinking in young children: Theoretical advances, empirical research, and policy implications. *Science, 337*, 1623–1627. doi:10.1126/science.1223416

Gopnik, A., Sobel, D. M., Schulz, L. E., & Glymour, C. (2001). Causal learning mechanisms in very young children: Two-, three-, and four-year-olds infer causal relations from patterns of variation and covariation. *Developmental Psychology, 37*, 620–629. doi:10.1037/0012-1649.37.5.620

Goswami, U. (2015). *Children's cognitive development and learning* (CPRT Survey 3). Retrieved from Cambridge Primary Review Trust website: http://www.cprt.org.uk

Greenfield, D. B. (2015). Assessment in early childhood science education. In K. C. Trundle & M. Saçkes (Eds.), *Research in early childhood science education* (pp. 353–380). New York, NY: Springer Publishing.

Greenfield, D. B., Alexander, A., & Frechette, L. (2017). Unleashing the power of science in early childhood: A foundation for high-quality interactions and learning. *Zero to Three, 37*(5), 13–21.

Greenfield, D. G., Jirout, J., Dominguez, X., Greenberg, A., Maier, M., & Fuccillo, J. (2009). Science in the preschool classroom: A programmatic research agenda to improve science readiness. *Early Education & Development, 20*, 238–264. doi:10.1080/10409280802595441

Gresham, G., & Burleigh, C. (2019). Exploring early childhood preservice teachers' mathematics anxiety and mathematics efficacy beliefs. *Teaching Education, 30*(2), 217–241. doi:10.1080/10476210.2018.1466875

Grissmer, D., Grimm, K. J., Aiyer, S. M., Murrah, W. M., & Steel, J. S. (2010). Fine motor skills and early comprehension of the world: Two new school readiness indicators. *Developmental Psychology, 46*, 1008–1017. doi:10.1037/a0020104

Haddad, L. (2006). Integrated policies for early childhood education and care: Challenges, pitfalls and possibilities. *Cadernos de Pesquisa, 36*(129), 519–546. doi:10.1590/S0100-15742006000300002

Hamlin, M., & Wisneski, D. B. (2012). Supporting the scientific thinking and inquiry of toddlers and preschoolers through play. *Young Children, 67*(3), 82.

Hao, Y., & Fleer, M. (2016). Creating collective scientific consciousness: A cultural-historical study of early learning about earth and space in the context of family imaginary play. *Asia-Pacific Journal of Research in Early Childhood Education, 10*, 93–124.

Hechter, R. P. (2011). Changes in preservice elementary teachers' personal science teaching efficacy and science teaching outcome expectancies: The influence of context. *Journal of Science Teacher Education, 22*(2), 187–202.

Ismail, I. M., Hashim, S., Anis, K., Ismail, A., & Ismail, M. E. (2017). Implementation of a development in cognitive, psychomotor and socio emotional elements through games to achieve national preschool curriculum standards. *2017 IEEE 9th International Conference on Engineering Education (ICEED)*, Kanazawa, Japan (pp. 143–148). doi:10.1109/ICEED.2017.8251182

Jung, K. G., & Brown, J. C. (2016). Examining the effectiveness of an academic language planning organizer as a tool for planning science academic language instruction and supports. *Journal of Science Teacher Education, 27*(8), 847–872. doi:10.1007/s10972-016-9491-2

Kaderavek, J., North, T., Rotshtein, R., Dao, H., Liber, N., Milewski, G., Molitor, S., & Czerniak, C. (2015). SCIIENCE: The creation and pilot implementation of an NGSS-based instrument to evaluate early childhood science teaching. *Studies in Educational Evaluation, 45*, 27–36.

Kadervaek, J., Paprzycki, P., Czerniak, C. M., Hapgood, S., Mentzer, G., Molitor, S., & Mendenhall, R. M. (Submitted). Longitudinal impact of early childhood science instruction on 5th grade science achievement. *International Journal of Science Education.*

Kane, J. M. (2015). The structure-agency dialectic in contested science spaces: "Do earthworms eat apples?" *Journal of Research in Science Teaching, 52*(4), 461–473.

Katz, L. G. (2010). STEM in the early years. *Early Childhood Research and Practice, 12*(2), 11–19.

Kilday, C. R., & Kinzie, M. B. (2009). An analysis of instruments that measure the quality of mathematics teaching in early childhood. *Early Childhood Education Journal, 36,* 365–372.

Klieckmann, T., Trobst, S., Jonen, A., Vehmeyer, & Moller, K. (2015). The effects of expert scaffolding in elementary science professional development on teachers' beliefs and motivations, instructional practices and student achievement. *Journal of Educational Psychology, 108*(1), 21–42.

Korean Science and Engineering Foundation. (2019). *STEAM.* Retrieved March 30, 2019 from https://steam.kofac.re.kr/?page_id=11269.

Kozhevnikov, M., Motes, M. A., & Hegarty, M. (2007). Spatial visualization in physics problem solving. *Cognitive Science, 31,* 549–579. doi:10.1080/15326900701399897

Krajcik, J., & Czerniak, C. M. (2014). *Teaching science to children: A project-based science approach.* New York, NY: Routledge.

Kung, M., Schmitt, S. A., Zhang, C., Witeman, S. D., Yang, F., & Purpura, D. J. (2019). The role of mathematical language in mathematics development in China and the US. *International Journal of Educational Research, 95,* 131–142. doi:10.1016/j.ijer.2019.02.008.

Lau, K., Ho, E. S., & Lam, T. Y. (2015). Effective classroom pedagogy and beyond for promoting scientific literacy: Is there an East Asian model? In M. S. Khine (Ed.), *Science education in East Asia* (pp. 16–40). Switzerland: Springer International.

Lee, Y. S., & Seo, H. (2011). A basic study for the development of R–learning curriculums in the Early Childhood school system. *8th International Conference on Ubiquitous Robots and Ambient Intelligence (URAI), Incheon* (pp. 699–700).

Lippard, C. N., Tank, K., Walter, M. C., Krogh, J., & Colbert, K. (2018). Preparing early childhood preservice teachers for science teaching: Aligning across a teacher preparation program, *Journal of Early Childhood Teacher Education, 39*(3), 193–212. doi:10.1080/10901027.2018.1457578

Lynch, R. G. (2007). *Enriching children, enriching the nation: Public investments in high-quality prekindergarten.* Washington, DC: Economic Policy Institute.

Ma, L. (1999). *Knowing and teaching elementary mathematics: Teachers' understanding of fundamental mathematics in China and the United States.* Mahwah, NJ: Erlbaum.

Mahony, K., & Hayes, N. (2006). *In search for quality. Multiple perspectives. Final report.* Dublin, Ireland: Centre for Early Childhood Development and Education.

Marcus, M., Haden, C., & Uttal, D. H. (2018). Promoting children's learning and transfer across informal science, technology, engineering, and mathematics learning experiences. *Journal of Experimental Child Psychology, 157,* 80–95.

McClure, E. R., Guernsey, L., Clements, D. H., Bales, S. N., Nichols, J., Kendall–Taylor, N., & Levine, M. H. (2017). *STEM starts early: Grounding science, technology, engineering, and math education in early childhood.* Joan Ganz Cooney Center at Sesame Workshop. Retrieved from https://eric.ed.gov/?id=ED574402

McGarvey, L., Luo, L., & Hawes, Z., & Spatial Reasoning Study Group. (2018). Spatial skills framework for young engineers. In L. English & T. Moore (Eds.), *Early engineering learning* (pp. 53–81). Singapore: Springer.

Menon, D., & Sadler, T. D. (2016). Preservice elementary teachers' science self-efficacy beliefs and science content knowledge. *Journal of Science Teacher Education, 27*(6), 649–673.

Mitchell, S., Foulger, T. S., Wetzel, K., & Rathkey, C. (2009). The negotiated project approach: Project–based learning without leaving the standards behind. *Early Childhood Education Journal, 36*(4), 339.

Moffett, P., & Eaton, P. (2018). The impact of the promoting early number talk project on the development of abstract representation in mathematics. *European Early Childhood Education Research Journal, 26*(4), 547–561. doi:10.1080/1350293X.2018.1487166

Morgan, P. L., Farkas, G., Hillemeier, M. M., & Maczuga, S. (2016). Science achievement gaps begin very early, persist, and are largely explained by modifiable factors. *Educational Researcher, 45,* 18–35. doi:10.3102/0013189X16633182

Morgan, P. L., Farkas, G., Wang, Y., Hillemeier, M. M., Oh, Y., & Maczuga, S. (2019). Executive function deficits in kindergarten predict repeated academic difficulties across elementary school. *Early Childhood Research Quarterly, 46,* 20–32.

Murphy, S., MacDonald, A., Danaia, L., & Wang, C. (2018). An analysis of Australian STEM education strategies. *Policy Futures in Education, 17*(2), 122–139.

Nadelson, L. S., Callahan, J. C., Pyke, P., Hay, A., Dance, M., & Pfiester, J. (2013). Teacher STEM perception and preparation: Inquiry-based STEM professional development for elementary teachers. *Journal of Educational Research, 106*(2), 157–168.

National Academy of Engineering and National Research Council. (2002). *Technically speaking: Why all Americans need to know more about technology.* Washington, DC: National Academy Press.

National Association for the Education of Young Children. (2003). *Early childhood curriculum, assessment, and program evaluation: Building an effective accountable system in programs for children birth through age 8 (Position Statement).* Retrieved from www.naeyc.org/positionstatements/cape

National Association for the Education of Young Children. (2019). *NAEYC.* Retrieved from https://www.naeyc.org

National Research Council. (2012). *Framework for K-12 science education.* Washington, DC: The National Academies Press.

National Research Council. (2014a). *Literacy for science: Exploring the intersection of the next generation science standards and common core for ELA Standards: A workshop summary.* Washington, DC: The National Academies Press.

National Research Council. (2014b). *STEM integration in K-12 education: Status, prospects, and an agenda for research.* Washington, DC: The National Academies Press.

National Research Council. (2015). *Transforming the workforce for children birth through age 8: A unifying foundation.* Washington, DC: The National Academies Press.

National Science Teachers Association. (2014). *Early childhood science education* (NSTA position statement). Retrieved from http://www.nsta.org/about/positions/earlychildhood

Neuman, S. B., & Roskos, K. A. (2005). The state of state prekindergarten standards. *Early Childhood Research Quarterly, 20,* 125–145. doi:10.1016/j.ecresq.2005.04.010

Ng, D. (2011). Indonesian primary teachers' mathematical knowledge for teaching geometry: Implications for educational policy and teacher preparation programs. *Asia-Pacific Journal of Teacher Education, 39,* 151–164.

NGSS Lead States. (2013). *Next generation science standards: For states, by states.* Washington, DC: National Academies Press.

Organisation for Economic Co-operation and Development. (2019, February). *Starting strong III: A quality toolbox for quality early childhood education and care.* Retrieved from http://www.oecd.org/education/school/startingstrongiiipolicytoolboxtoencouragequalityinececcountrymaterials.htm

Paprzycki, P., Tuttle, N., Czerniak, C. M., Molitor, S., Kadervaek, J., & Mendenhall, R. M. (2017). The impact of a framework-aligned science professional development program on literacy and mathematics achievement of K-3 students. *Journal of Research in Science Teaching, 54*(9), 1174–1196.

Pearson. (2003). *Early math diagnostic assessment.* San Antonio, TX: Author.

Pianta, R. C., Belsky, J., Vadergrift, N., Houts, R., & Morrison, F. J. (2008). Classroom effects on children's achievement trajectories in elementary school. *American Educational Research Journal, 45,* 365–397.

Pianta, R. C., Howes, C., Burchinal, M. R., Bryant, D., Clifford, R. M., Early, D. M., & Barbarin, O. A. (2005). Features of pre-kindergarten programs, classrooms, and teachers: Do they predict observed classroom quality and child–teacher interactions? *Applied Developmental Science, 9,* 144–159.

Portsmore, M, & Milto, E. (2018). Novel engineering in early elementary classrooms. In L. English & T. Moore (Eds.), *Early Engineering Learning.* Singapore: Springer. doi:10.1007/978-981-10-8621-2

Purpura, D. J., Napoli, A. R., & King, Y. A. (2019). Development of mathematical language in preschool and its role in learning numeracy skills. *Mathematical Cognition and Learning, 5,* 175–193.

Purzer, S., & Douglas, K. A. (2018). Assessing early engineering thinking and design capacities in the classroom. In L. English & T. Moore (Eds.), *Early engineering learning* (pp. 113–132). Singapore: Springer. doi:10.1007/978-981-10-8621-2.

Romance, N. R., & Vitale, M. R. (2012). Expanding the role of K-5 science instruction in educational reform: Implications of an interdisciplinary model for integrating science and reading. *School Science and Mathematics, 112*(8), 506–515.

Romance, N. R., & Vitale, M. R. (2017). *Direct and transfer effects of a model integrating reading and science in grades 1–2: Results and policy implications.* Presented at the Annual Meeting of the Literacy Research Association, Tampa, FL.

Rothman, B. (2017). After the shock: The German education system in 2017. *National Center on Education and the Economy, Top of the Class Newsletter.* Retrieved March 30, 2019 at http://ncee.org/2017/09/after-the-shock-the-german-education-system-in-2017/.

Sarama, J., Brenneman, K., Clements, D. H., Duke, N. K., & Hemmeter, M. L. (2017). Interdisciplinary teaching across multiple domains: The C4L (Connect4Learning) curriculum. In L. B. Bailey (Ed.), *Implementing the Common Core State Standards across the early childhood curriculum* (pp. 13–65). New York, NY: Routledge.

Sarama, J., & Clements, D. H. (2009). Building blocks and cognitive building blocks: Playing to know the world mathematically. *American Journal of Play, 1,* 313–337.

Sarama, J., & Clements, D. H. (2018). Designing, scaling up, and evaluating comprehensive professional development based on learning trajectories. In P. Sztajn, P. H. Wilson, & C. Edgington (Eds.), *Learning trajectories-based professional development*. New York, NY: Teachers College Press.

Sarama, J., Clements, D. H., Wolfe, C. B., & Spitler, E. (2016). Professional development in early mathematics: Effects of an intervention based on learning trajectories on teachers' practices. *Nordic Studies in Mathematics Education, 21*, 29–55.

Sarama, J., Lange, A., Clements, D. H., & Wolfe, C. B. (2012). The impacts of an early mathematics curriculum on emerging literacy and language. *Early Childhood Research Quarterly, 27*, 489–502. doi:10.1016/j.ecresq.2011.12.002

Sawada, D., Piburn, M. D., Judson, E., Turley, J., Falconer, K., Benford, R., & Bloom, I. (2002). Measuring reform practices in science and mathematics classrooms: The reformed teaching observation protocol. *School Science and Mathematics, 102*, 245–253.

Schulz, L. E., & Bonawitz, E. B. (2007). Serious fun: Preschoolers engage in more exploratory play when evidence is confounded. *Developmental Psychology, 43*, 1045–1050. doi:10.1037/0012-1649.43.4.1045

Sikder, S., & Fleer, M. (2015). Small science: Infants and toddlers experiencing science in everyday family life. *Research in Science Education, 45*, 445–464. doi:10.1007/s11165-014-9431-0

Spaepen, E., Bowman, B., Day, C., Chen, J., Cunningham, C., Donohue, C., . . . Worth, K. (2017). *Early STEM matters: Providing high-quality STEM experiences for all young learners*. Chicago: Erikson Institute.

Stylianidou, F., Glauert, E., Rossis, D., Compton, A., Cremin, T., Craft, A, & Havu-Nuutinen, S. (2018). Fostering inquiry and creativity in early years STEM education: Policy recommendations from the creative little scientists project. *European Journal of STEM Education, 3*(3), 15.

Sullivan, A., & Bers, M. U. (2017). Dancing robots: Integrating art, music, and robotics in Singapore's early childhood centers. *International Journal of Technology and Design Education, 28*(2), 325–346.

Sumida, M. (2015). Kids science academy: Talent development in STEM from the early childhood years. In M. S. Khine (Ed.), *Science education in East Asia* (pp. 269–298). Switzerland: Springer International.

Symaco, L. P., & Daniel, E. G. S. (2018). Curriculum, pedagogy, teacher training and recent reforms in primary science education. In Y. J. Lee & J. Tan (Eds.), *Primary science education in East Asia* (pp. 215–228). Switzerland: Springer.

Sztajn, P., Confrey, J., Wilson, P. H., & Edgington, C. (2012). Learning trajectory based instruction: Toward a theory of teaching. *Educational Researcher, 41*, 147–156.

Tank, K. M., Moore, T. J., Dorie, B. L., Gajdzik, E., Sanger, M. T., Rynearson, A. M., & Mann, E. F. (2018). Engineering in early elementary classrooms through the integration of high-quality literature, design, and STEM+ C content. In L. English & T. Moore (Eds.), *Early engineering learning* (pp. 175–201). Singapore: Springer. doi:10.1007/978-981-10-8621-2

Thiel, O. (2010). Teachers' attitudes towards mathematics in early childhood education. *European Early Childhood Education Research Journal, 18*(1), 105–115. doi:10.1080/13502930903520090

Tietze, W., & Cryer, D. (2004). Comparisons of observed process quality in German and American infant/toddler programs. *International Journal of Early Years Education, 12*(1), 43–62.

Toikkanen, T., & Leinonen, T. (2017). The code ABC MOOC: Experiences from a coding and computational thinking MOOC for Finnish primary school teachers. In P. J. Rich & C. B. Hodges (Eds.), *Emerging research, practice, and policy on computational thinking* (pp. 239–248). Cham: Springer International.

Tsybulsky, D., & Oz, A. (2019). From frustration to insights: Experiences, attitudes, and pedagogical practices of preservice science teachers implementing PBL in elementary school. *Journal of Science Teacher Education, 30*(3), 259–279.

Tuttle, N., Kaderavek, J. N., Molitor, S., Czerniak, C. M., Johnson-Witt, E., Bloomquist, D., Namatovu, W., & Wilson, G. (2016). Investigating the impact of NGSS-Aligned professional development on PreK-3 teachers science content knowledge and pedagogy. *Journal of Science Teacher Education, 27*, 717–745.

Varelas, M., & Pappas, C. C. (2013). *Children's ways with science and literacy: Integrated multimodal enactments in urban elementary classrooms*. New York, NY: Routledge.

Venville, G., Wallace, J., Rennie, L. J., & Malone, J. (1998). The integration of science, mathematics, and technology in a discipline-based culture. *School Science and Mathematics, 98*(6), 294–302.

Vitiello, V. E., Whittaker, J. V., Mulcahy, C., Kinzie, M. B., & Helferstay, L. (2018). Reliability and validity of the Preschool Science Observation Measure. *Early Education and Development, 1–20*. doi:10.1080/10409289.2018.1544814

Vogt, F., Hauser, B., Stebler, R., Rechsteiner, K., & Urech, C. (2018). Learning through play: Pedagogy and learning outcomes in early childhood mathematics. *European Early Childhood Education Research Journal, 26*(4), 589–603. doi:10.1080/1350293X.2018.1487160

Walker, C. M., Lombrozo, T., Legare, C. H., & Gopnik, A. (2014). Explaining prompts children to privilege inductively rich properties. *Cognition, 133*, 343–357. doi:10.1016/j.cognition.2014.07.008

Watts, T. W., Duncan, G. J., Clements, D. H., & Sarama, J. (2018). What is the long-run impact of learning mathematics during preschool. *Child Development, 89,* 539–555. doi:10.1111/cdev.12713

Watts, T. W., Duncan, G. J., Siegler, R. S., & Davis-Kean, P. E. (2014). What's past is prologue: Relations between early mathematics knowledge and high school achievement. *Educational Researcher, 43,* 352–360. doi:10.3102/0013189X14553660

Weiland, C., & Yoshikawa, H. (2013). Impacts of a pre-kindergarten program on children's mathematics, language, literacy, executive function, and emotional skills. *Child Development, 84,* 2112–2130. doi:10.1111/cdev.12099

Weisberg, D. S., Hirsh-Pasek, K., & Golinkoff, R. M. (2013). Guided play: Where curricular goals meet a playful pedagogy. *Mind, Brain, and Education, 7*(2), 104–112.

Weiss, I. R., Pasley, J. D., Smith, P. S., Banilower, E. R., & Heck, D. J. (2003). *Looking inside the classroom: A study of K-12 mathematics and science education in the United States.* Chapel Hill, NC: Horizon Research.

Wolfgang, C. H., Stannard, L. L., & Jones, I. (2001). Block play performance among preschoolers as a predictor of later school achievement in mathematics. *Journal of Research in Childhood Education, 15,* 173–180.

Xu, F., & Garcia, V. (2008). Intuitive statistics by 8-month-old infants. *Proceedings of the National Academy of Sciences, 105,* 5012–5015. doi:10.1073/pnas.0704450105

9

ELEMENTARY STEM LEARNING

Suzanne M. Nesmith and Sandi Cooper

The foundational knowledge and experiences that students develop in science, technology, engineering, and mathematics (STEM) are shaped early during their K-12 schooling and promote their intellectual development, interests for future study, and potential choices of future careers (National Research Council [NRC], 2011b). Proponents of early exposure to these STEM disciplines have argued that foundational knowledge in STEM learning is best formed during the elementary years (e.g., NRC, 2007).

Additionally, these early experiences develop a student's capacity to make informed decisions as a citizen and about their own lives. According to a report from the NRC (2011b), "the solutions to some of the most daunting problems facing the nation will require not only the expertise of top STEM professionals but also the wisdom and understanding of its citizens" (p. 1). Furthermore, the report indicates that "literacy in STEM subjects is important both for the personal well-being of each citizen and for the nation's competitiveness in the global economy" (NRC, 2011b, p. 3).

This chapter addresses key issues concerning elementary STEM learning. The chapter begins with the rationale and purpose for including STEM learning in elementary grades. Next, it offers an overview of the identified benefits, drawbacks, and barriers to incorporating STEM in elementary classrooms. Finally, it provides a synopsis of reported impacts of STEM experiences on and the influence of associated programs, practices, and partnerships.

Rationale for Elementary STEM Learning

Early exposure to STEM opportunities makes a difference for students. According to a recent report, *Early STEM Matters* (Early Childhood STEM Working Group, 2017), educational experience in STEM should start early to promote the benefits and future engagement in the STEM fields. Despite a concerted national effort to promote effective early childhood education, the notion of STEM for early learners is rarely discussed (Early Childhood STEM Working Group, 2017).

Chen (2011) found that children who were exposed to STEM learning experiences at a young age actually perform better in science and mathematics than students lacking such opportunities. Emphasizing STEM learning at an early age has been found to contribute to positive academic and professional trajectories in the STEM fields (Ricks, 2012). Research also shows that an early STEM learning experience prepares students for more independent innovation and develops critical thinking skills (Chen, 2011).

Critical thinking, problem solving, and working collaboratively can be effectively nurtured through STEM learning. STEM learning experiences support the development of independent, critical thinkers who are capable of making good decisions while working collaboratively with others and provide opportunities for students to grow into responsible citizens (Isabelle, 2017). Proponents argue that STEM learning experiences provide students with these 21st-century skills, all necessary to become the next generation of innovative STEM professionals (Cotabish, Dailey, Robinson, & Hughes, 2013).

Recent studies have found that interest in STEM-related careers may be influenced at an early age (Foltz, Gannon, & Kirschmann, 2014; Wang, 2012). The National Science Board (2010) recommended early exposure to inquiry-based learning, peer collaboration, and open-ended, real-world problem solving, as well as engagement in STEM opportunities, in order to encourage students to consider STEM-related careers.

In the interest of developing future STEM innovators, changes in elementary science programs are necessary (Cotabish et al., 2013). Over two decades ago, Brandwein (1995) recommended that science learning begin in the early grades and include "evocative instruction, stimulating idea-enactive, inquiry-oriented behavior" (p. 41) to develop a strong disposition for science content. Keeley (2009) stressed the importance of science in the early grades to maximize the cumulative learning processes involved in developing science talent that could potentially lead more students to choose advanced science courses and science-related careers. More recently, Isabelle (2017) posited that the vision of the Next Generation Science Standards (NGSS) may not be achieved when many elementary schools across the nation allot a very limited time to the teaching of science. To develop a strong disposition toward science and STEM, science learning must be highly valued by school districts, to the degree that they support quality science instruction by dedicating more time for science in the elementary grades, providing science materials, and offering effective professional development (PD) opportunities for elementary teachers (Isabelle, 2017).

Walker (2012) advocated that even young learners are capable of understanding basic STEM concepts. Many educators feel STEM instruction in the early years of school can "boost overall learning, by tapping into children's natural curiosity and interest in experimentation and engineering" (Wheelcock College Aspire Institute, 2010, p. 9). Likewise, Lottero-Perdue, Lovelidge, and Bowling (2010) found that integrated STEM education focused on hands-on and inquiry-based strategies improved students' self-management skills as well as supported the development of STEM concepts. Finally, integrated STEM learning at the elementary level has the potential to support students in making meaningful connections, developing 21st-century skills, and building overall confidence (Claymier, 2014; Moore & Smith, 2014).

Perceptions of STEM Learning in Elementary Grades

Important to understanding how to cultivate early STEM learning is to consider the identified challenges, or perceived barriers, and benefits of STEM learning in the elementary grades.

Challenges or Perceived Barriers of STEM in Elementary Grades

Although many elementary classrooms are "self-contained", there is still this notion that content be taught separately (Shernoff, Sinha, Brassler, & Ginsburg, 2017). In addition, some elementary grade levels are "departmentalized" where one teacher is responsible for teaching one or two subject areas to rotating groups of students. This presents a primary challenge elementary schools face in teaching STEM subjects in an integrated way.

Moore and Smith (2014) asserted that school change is needed to support STEM integration. It is important for schools to work to allow students to learn how each of the STEM disciplines are interconnected in ways they might encounter in real-world problems. In a needs assessment conducted by Shernoff et al. (2017), teacher participants acknowledged that the school schedule greatly impacted any opportunities for collaborative planning as well as instructional time for STEM integration.

Sikma and Osborne (2014) examined teachers' experiences in the year preceding the launch of a new STEM magnet elementary school. Over the course of the year, the researchers examined the teachers' engagement with the activities required to establish and shape a new school and how this evolved as they negotiated this process amidst the realities of curricular and accountability pressures in literacy and mathematics instruction. As they developed a collected group vision, the teachers took ownership of the curriculum and the change process itself and were able to draw upon their own professional knowledge to create a STEM-focused curriculum aligned to standards and their own understanding of best practice. Unfortunately, throughout the process of shaping the STEM school, test score concerns were predominant, and these limitations set by the district were in conflict with the vision of a student-centered school with a meaningful and integrated curriculum.

Clearly, the testing environment diminishes time for the pedagogical approaches that STEM instruction requires (Shernoff et al., 2017). When teachers and students are in the context of high-stakes standardized testing, and the results of these tests determine school funding, school image, and teacher performance pay, it is understandable that priority is focused on the subject areas that are being tested, which are primarily mathematics and literacy (Blackley & Howell, 2015). Additionally, teachers have difficulty visualizing how to implement a cross-disciplinary STEM instructional approach while the accountability for within-subject content mastery remains a priority. It has been widely reported that this testing environment reduces the time for creative and innovative instructional approaches that many teachers desire (Shernoff et al., 2017).

Although pressure applied in the testing environment is a challenge for STEM integration, many teachers also explained that they simply did not know how to effectively integrate the STEM areas (Shernoff et al., 2017). Teaching integrated STEM requires some fundamental knowledge of how to facilitate an effective learning environment that supports the development of STEM concepts and how these are integrated. Consequently, teachers who have limited knowledge or who are not willing to learn the concepts are not likely to be willing or capable of supporting an integrated STEM approach to teaching and learning (Nadelson & Seifert, 2017).

In 2016, Bennett organized a study to explore potential differences in elementary teachers' sense of self-efficacy related to teaching integrated STEM. Results indicated that these teachers had a strong sense of self-efficacy with regard to teaching integrated STEM education in the elementary grades. However, the qualitative data gathered from the study revealed that teachers identified their need for more curricular support and training in STEM to increase their overall effectiveness.

Another area for consideration relative to challenges of quality STEM integration in elementary classrooms is initial teacher preparation. Currently, initial teacher education programs that prepare elementary teachers are not necessarily designed to include preparation specific to STEM integration. In most programs, there are discrete courses that specifically cover two of the subject areas, science and mathematics, and may include some technology applications, but engineering has not been a component included at this level (Blackley & Howell, 2015). According to Shernoff et al.'s (2017) study, strengthening preservice teachers' content knowledge in STEM fields and developing effective classroom management skills is an important element needed to efficiently facilitate integrated STEM lessons. Other suggestions from this study include the examination of model or exemplar STEM lessons, mentoring by teachers who are experienced in integrated approaches, and an emphasis on student-centered pedagogical approaches. Perhaps the most salient preliminary finding from this study was that current teacher education does not adequately prepare teachers and would need to be considerably reconceptualized for integrated STEM to flourish in schools.

Benefits of STEM in Elementary Grades

STEM experiences in the elementary grades offer more student-centered, meaningful, engaging, and less fragmented learning experiences that involve higher-level thinking and problem-solving skills (Stohlmann, Moore, & Roehrig, 2012). Moore and colleagues (2014) add that combining the disciplines of STEM is "based on connections between the subjects and real world problems," and more specifically entails "an effort by educators to participate in engineering design as a means to develop technologies that require meaningful learning and an application of mathematics and/or science" (p. 38). Furthermore, STEM learning can promote 21st-century transferable skills which include inventiveness, creativity, critical thinking, collaboration, and problem solving. Research has found that integrated STEM teaching encourages student-centered pedagogies (Roehrig, Moore, Wang, & Park, 2012), a more authentic application of mathematics and science content (Stohlmann et al., 2012), and a focus on interdisciplinary, contextualized, real-life problems (LaForce et al., 2016). These learning experiences can support students to become independent, critical thinkers who are able to make good decisions while working collaboratively with others.

STEM learning provides a more hands-on, inquiry-based approach that improves students' self-management, promotes more meaningful connections, allows students to learn concepts more deeply, and builds confidence. Research has shown that students who experience STEM learning early through hands-on experiences are best equipped to develop and maintain a greater understanding of STEM concepts as they advance through school. By introducing STEM in the elementary grades, students have the opportunity to establish a foundation of knowledge and skills necessary to become successful in the STEM fields (Wheelcock College Aspire Institute, 2010).

In a 2015 study conducted by Alumbaugh, six STEM teachers were interviewed, and they shared that students were much more interested in learning and applying STEM concepts when offered hands-on learning coupled with real-life experiences. Moreover, because STEM education promotes a more student-centered than teacher-centered environment, the students were more engaged in the lessons. Alumbaugh (2015) further determined that students were more willing to learn in numerous ways and were motivated to try to make sense through problem solving in a variety of ways.

Impact of STEM Learning on Elementary Students

The STEM For All initiative (Obama, 2009) affirms that all students, including those expressing diverse learning needs, should be included in quality STEM education that allows them to develop skills associated with STEM processes and expertise in STEM areas. However, global and national indicators such as Trends in International Mathematics and Science Study (TIMSS) and National Assessment of Educational Progress (NAEP) reveal that students in many countries continue to perform poorly in science and mathematics, and that both socioeconomic status and ethnicity continue to play significant roles in score variance (Baldi, Jin, Skemer, Green, & Herget, 2007; Darling-Hammond, 2010; NCES, 2015; US Department of Education, 2015, 2017). In light of these matters, it is certainly essential to explore the impact of STEM-focused processes and programs on the learning of all elementary students.

General Education Students

Several studies indicate that incorporating STEM opportunities in elementary classrooms yields positive outcomes for general education students, or those students not identified as having special learning needs. Becker and Park (2011) conducted a meta-analysis to explore the effects of integrative approaches among STEM subjects on students' learning. Ten percent of the studies included in the analysis occurred in elementary contexts with general education students, and comparisons of study effect size by grade level led the researchers to suggest that early exposure to integrative approaches may yield higher achievement scores in STEM subjects and, thus, the approaches may be better suited to young learners.

Though STEM education is appropriate and well suited at the elementary level, there are implications for teaching and curriculum design that must be considered when integrating STEM content in elementary classrooms. For example, Glancy, Moore, Guzey, and Smith (2017) exposed fifth-grade students to a STEM unit that included the application of data analysis and measurement skills in the contexts of science and engineering. Although the students struggled with the application of these skills, the authors cautioned against inferring that the integrated STEM content was too difficult because students experienced success in articulating conclusions consistent with the science and engineering concepts. Thus, the study highlights the importance of elementary teachers and curriculum writers considering appropriate STEM concepts and skills and developing age-appropriate STEM integrative approaches.

A 2018 study conducted by Acar, Tertemiz, and Taşdemir revealed that fourth-grade Turkish students exposed to authentic, problem-based integrated STEM lessons in classroom settings scored significantly higher than control group counterparts in tests of science and mathematics achievement. Results further indicated that students enjoyed the STEM experiences and developed positive attitudes towards STEM fields. Similar results were reported from an afterschool program that included elementary-age children (Leas, Nelson, Grandgenett, Tapprich, & Cutucache, 2017). The STEM lessons utilized in the program were designed to supplement and support the school day curricula, and examination of lesson observations revealed positive impacts on the students' excitement, attitudes about STEM, curiosity/inquiry, and understanding of STEM concepts (Leas et al., 2017).

Tolliver (2016) revealed somewhat different results from those previously delineated. Following implementation of a STEM curriculum in fifth-grade classrooms in an urban district, Tolliver compared the mathematics test scores for students in two demographically similar schools within the district, one implementing the STEM curriculum and the other utilizing a traditional curriculum. Results revealed no significant difference between the mathematics scores for the two groups.

Exceptionality Diverse Students

Scholars suggest that purposeful introduction and early exposure with learning experiences that focus on STEM curricula enhance the recognition and talent development of high-ability students (e.g., Dailey, Cotabish, & Jackson, 2018; Keeley, 2009). In support of this suggestion, Robinson, Dailey, Hughes, and Cotabish (2014) found that implementation of a biography-focused STEM curriculum alongside authentic problem-based science units increased gifted elementary students' achievement in science concepts, content, and process skills. Similarly, a study of high potential underrepresented minority students in grades 3–8 revealed that the incorporation of a long-term, problem-based, integrated supplemental STEM enrichment program reduced the mathematics and science achievement gap between disadvantaged high-potential minority and high-achieving majority students and improved student representation and participation in advanced placement high school courses (Olszewski-Kubilius, Steenbergen-Hu, Thomson, & Rosen, 2017). A 2017 study by Young, Young, and Ford explored the impact of gifted education on fourth-grade Black girls' achievement in STEM. Results revealed that Black girls who received gifted instruction significantly outperformed Black girls who do not receive gifted instruction in both science and mathematics. Moreover, though White girls who received gifted instruction also significantly outperformed White girls who did not receive gifted instruction, the mean difference effect size was almost twice as large for Black girls. In a study that explored the intersection of gifted education and gender, Kerr, Vuyk, and Rea (2012) reported that the small differences between gifted boys and girls in achievement, careers, and interests are often enhanced by gendered educational practices. With respect to STEM, these practices often fail to support gifted girls' interests in STEM careers and ultimately result in occupation choices that do not provide a sense of purpose (Kerr et al., 2012).

Students with disabilities often struggle in STEM-related courses and consistently underperform in STEM coursework, yet these students are capable of succeeding in STEM areas when their instructional needs are met (AccessSTEM, 2007). Israel, Maynard, and Williamson (2013) promote the integration of explicit literacy instruction within STEM education for elementary students with disabilities because the practice provides students with tools to meaningfully access and comprehend STEM text materials that often pose significant barriers to their learning. Other scholars suggest that early integration of computational thinking and computer programming within STEM education presents as a means of empowering students with disabilities (Israel, Wherfel, Pearson, Shehab, & Tapia, 2015). Though the integration of computing education requires consideration of necessary supports, technologies, and strategies to meet students' special needs, benefits include enhanced higher-order thinking skills, utilization of real-world applied contexts, and increased collaborative problem solving (Israel et al., 2015).

Gender Diverse Students

Gender research in STEM education has sought to explore gender gaps in STEM fields, gender-specific beliefs about STEM, and gender-based STEM educational practices. International studies and reports reveal that the gender achievement gap in STEM-related fields has shrunk over the last twenty years (Mullis, Martin, & Loveless, 2016), yet there remains a significant gender difference in choosing STEM professions (Blažev, Karabegović, Burušić, & Selimbegović, 2017). Additionally, Blažev and colleagues (2017) determined that gender-specific perceptions and stereotypes related to STEM attitudes and careers form at a very early age and likely shape future career preferences and choices.

Recent studies have explored the role of gender stereotyping and parental occupations in shaping STEM-based gender differences of elementary students. Bowden, Bartkowski, Xu, and Lewis (2018) examined the degree to which parental occupation impacted students' performance on standardized mathematics tests. Results revealed that students with STEM-employed parent(s) performed significantly better than students with non–STEM-employed parent(s), yet the advantage did not eliminate the gender mathematics gap (Bowden et al., 2018). Likewise, a study of the gender-STEM stereotyped beliefs of elementary Croatian students revealed that regardless of prior STEM achievement, the students endorsed the gender stereotyped belief that STEM-related subjects are more suitable to boys than to girls (Blažev et al., 2017).

Culturally and Linguistically Diverse Students

Linguistic mismatches contribute to educational opportunity gaps for linguistically diverse students (Villegas, 1998) and, in STEM contexts, the mismatches often negatively impact student achievement (Hyde & Mertz, 2009). Linguistic mismatches and resulting barriers are due in large part to the language used in STEM educational settings and STEM fields. Lee (2002) developed a research program to address these mismatches and thereby promote science learning and scientific inquiry among culturally and linguistically diverse students. Fourth-grade linguistically diverse students involved in the program experienced meaningful science and expressed enhanced science relevancy when their teachers attended to cultural congruence (Lee, 2002).

Strong relationships exist between low socioeconomic status (SES), underachievement of youth in STEM-related areas (Duodu, Noble, Yusuf, Garay, & Bean, 2017), and underrepresentation in STEM careers (Douglas & Strobel, 2015). A Canadian-based, community-focused STEM program for children in grades 3–8 revealed that the following factors contributed to the program's success and positive student outcomes: (1) community-based delivery, including attention to common accessibility and affordability barriers associated with low-income communities; (2) consistent, sustained engagement that allowed for positive group dynamics; and (3) engagement with STEM educators that allowed for positive youth-staff relationships (Duodu et al., 2017). Similar positive results revealed through an in-school STEM program for low SES students of color. Fifth-grade students in a campus with a predominantly low SES minority student population were provided opportunities to experience authentic integrated STEM activities and interact with community members and experts in STEM fields. Results from the annual statewide science assessment revealed a substantive increase in students' scores for the first time in many years (Molina, Borror, & Desir, 2016).

In 2015, Douglas and Strobel utilized a unique approach to explore STEM education in diverse urban communities of poverty through the lens of students' level of hope in relation to STEM careers. Recognizing that students' level of hope has been shown to influence students' academic success (Ciarrochi, Heaven, & Davies, 2007), Douglas and Strobel developed and utilized the Hopes and Goals Survey to assess the hope diverse elementary students in urban settings hold for their adult lives and the connections they draw between their efforts in STEM fields and a fulfilling life. Results revealed no significant mean difference between the racial groups of third- through fifth-grade students in any of the hope factors and further provided a valid instrument for researching students' hope in relation to STEM education.

Supporting Elementary STEM Educators

Elementary teachers are often referred to as the gatekeepers of future STEM innovators. However, few elementary teachers participate in the in-depth, theme-based STEM PD programs necessary to prepare them to effectively teach STEM curricula (NRC, 2011a). This problem is exacerbated by the recent inclusion of engineering into standards at all grade levels because there now exists a need to provide elementary teachers with opportunities to understand, experience, and incorporate content they have not previously encountered as students or educators. Moreover, though the number and types of STEM experiences for elementary preservice teachers vary greatly by program, most programs provide limited training in teaching mathematics and science and little to no training in teaching engineering and technology (Epstein & Miller, 2011). Taken together, these issues highlight the importance of exploring, developing, and providing elementary STEM educators with appropriate forms of support to assure quality STEM instruction at the elementary level.

Teacher Education Programs

Reports from Epstein and Miller (2011) and DeJarnette (2012) highlight the crisis in elementary STEM education and cite general recommendations specific to elementary preparation programs. These recommendations include increasing the selectivity of programs that prepare elementary educators; including additional mathematics and science content and pedagogy within elementary programs; providing methodology in inquiry, problem-based learning, engineering design, and technology; and requiring candidates to pass mathematics and science sections of licensure exams.

One specific approach utilized to support STEM preservice teachers is the incorporation of explicit components within traditional STEM courses. An afterschool STEM program for students in grades 3–5 provided elementary preservice teachers with opportunities to explore science pedagogy through iterative cycles of enactment, a process where preservice teachers plan, teach, and analyze lessons with children (Bottoms, Ciechanowski, & Hartman, 2015). The afterschool STEM club was embedded within a science methods course and situated within a culturally and linguistically diverse school community. Bottoms and colleagues (2015) determined that participation in the iterative cycles contributed to the preservice teachers' confidence in their ability to teach science and provided opportunities to plan lessons, enact specific practices with children, and collaboratively analyze, reflect, and respond to their developing science competence. Additionally, by situating the learning in context, the experience aided the preservice teachers in developing tools for culturally relevant science practices and supported their ability to adapt their instruction in situ (Bottoms et al., 2015).

An alternative means of meeting the needs of elementary STEM preservice teachers is through the development of specifically designed STEM programs. McIntyre et al. (2013) and DiFrancesca, Lee, and McIntyre (2014) describe and report results from a STEM-focused elementary teacher preparation program that included an extensive engineering component. The program combined general education courses, conceptually focused methods courses, extensive field work, and integration of the engineering design process within all required content area methods courses. Candidates reported recognizing the value of the program courses and appreciating the program structure, strong field experience component, and the integration between coursework and field experiences (McIntyre et al., 2013). Specific to engineering, program evaluation interviews revealed evidence of preservice teachers' positive attitudes toward engineering alongside their recognition that the inclusion of engineering in elementary school classrooms is a rarity (DiFrancesca et al., 2014).

Professional Development

A high-profile report, *Rising Above the Gathering Storm*, substantiated that high-quality, content-driven PD can have a significant impact on student achievement (Committee on Science, Engineering, and Public Policy, 2007). The impact was confirmed through a study conducted by Cotabish et al. (2013) that revealed a significant increase in science process skills, concepts, and content knowledge among elementary students whose teachers participated in an effective STEM PD program. The study further substantiated the importance of PD that is intensive, sustained, content-focused, well-defined, and effectively implemented and that provides opportunities for teachers to explore effective curricula and instructional models (Yoon, Duncan, Lee, & Shapley, 2008).

A comparison of elementary and secondary STEM teachers' views on and preferences for meeting STEM PD needs revealed that elementary teachers place greater importance on improving their teaching practices in terms of learning about new and innovative strategies, receiving feedback, and learning from experts in the field (Owens, Sadler, Murakami, & Tsai, 2018). Additionally, Owens and colleagues (2018) reported that elementary STEM teachers cited significantly less participation in STEM PD and indicated feeling less supported by their principals for pursuing STEM PD.

In a needs assessment study conducted by Shernoff et al. (2017), many teachers suggested that more PD was needed to help them better understand the integrated approaches to STEM education. In addition, these teachers and administrators reported that it would be helpful to review exemplar units that include key pedagogical strategies such as project-based learning, view video-recorded sessions of integrated STEM lessons taught by experienced teachers, and experience problem solving within an integrated STEM approach. (Shernoff et al., 2017).

A 2017 study conducted by Anderson and Moeed associated a STEM PD with successful implementation of the country's new curriculum. The PD experience incorporated a scientist-teacher partnership to address the misalignment between the aims and scope of the current New Zealand curriculum and primary teachers' science knowledge and pedagogy. Providing teachers with opportunities to work alongside scientists conducting authentic research has been shown to improve teachers' confidence in their understanding of contemporary science (Rennie, 2012) and improve understanding and incorporation of scientific inquiry (McLaughlin & MacFadden, 2014), yet elementary teachers are commonly not participants in the scientific community. Participation in the PD modified the teacher participants' beliefs about science and science education from a focus on science content to an emphasis on citizenship and informed decision-making—beliefs more closely aligned with the country's curriculum goal of developing science for citizenship.

It has been suggested that PD with a focus on engineering is essential to assure that elementary teachers are capable of implementing new standards that emphasize engineering practices (Roehrig et al., 2012), yet much of the PD in engineering design has been directed toward secondary teachers, and studies of elementary engineering PD report varying results. Capobianco and Rupp (2014) found that fifth- and sixth-grade teachers who participated in a science and engineering design program were able to plan effective engineering design lessons but sometimes struggled to enact all phases of the engineering design process and to apply scientific principles during instruction. Similarly, a 2014 study of teachers who planned and implemented engineering lessons in their third- through sixth-grade classrooms following a year-long engineering-focused PD revealed that about half of the lessons were complete engineering lessons, many were design-focused engineering lessons with a missing component, and a few of the lessons utilized the term "design" but were, in fact, science activities (Guzey, Roehrig, Tank, Moore, & Wang, 2014). In 2017, Estapa and Tank utilized an engineering design focus in their PD experience, but their analysis focused less on engineering design components and more on the integration of STEM concepts. Results revealed that the PD supported participants' identification of STEM content within engineering design activities but failed to fully support their planning and enactment of the content in an integrated manner.

Numerous studies utilized novel instruments to explore the impacts of elementary engineering PD experiences. Following a brief PD and the provision of a sample engineering lesson plan, Kendall and Portsmore (2013) observed three elementary teachers' implementations of the lessons through the lens of teacher attention to student thinking. Analysis of the observations and follow-up interviews using an attentional skills framework revealed that the elementary teachers sometimes struggled with deciding whether and how to deviate from the provided lesson plan, focused more on noting student ideas as opposed to interrogating their ideas, and varied their responses to student thinking depending on the stage of the engineering design process. The Level of Design Rubric was utilized by Nadelson, Pfiester, Callahan, and Pyke (2015) to classify engineering lessons with respect to levels of responsibility for student and teacher. Following participation in a STEM program that included an emphasis on engineering design, elementary teachers from kindergarten through fifth grade were observed implementing their teacher-designed engineering lessons via level of design analysis. Results revealed that, on average, the teachers implemented engineering design lessons in which they shared responsibility for the structure of the design elements with their students (Nadelson et al., 2015). The STEM Integration Curriculum Assessment (STEM-ICA) tool was developed to analyze the engineering design-based unit lessons developed by fourth- through eighth-grade teachers following their participation in a year-long STEM integration PD program (Guzey, Moore, & Harwell, 2016). Results revealed that the engineering challenge lessons focused on physical science utilized more engaging and motivating contexts that those focused on life science and earth science, and mathematics integration and communication of thinking did not strongly contribute to the quality of the lessons (Guzey et al., 2016).

Though less common than science and engineering-focused STEM PD experiences, researchers have attended to elementary STEM PD through the lenses of mathematics and linguistics. Recognition of both the typical supporting role that mathematics plays in STEM integration (Fitzallen, 2015) and the potential and challenges associated with incorporating mathematical modeling in elementary classrooms guided Baker and Galanti's (2017) development of an elementary PD built upon the design features of model-eliciting activities (MEAs). Participation in the PD allowed the teachers to broadly envision mathematics content within STEM integration and resulted in expressions of readiness to use MEAs in STEM integration. Similarly, researchers' desire to reduce the linguistic and cultural gaps in STEM pedagogy and practice caused by educators' demarcation between reading, literacy, writing, and communication and STEM instruction led to their development of a STEM PD built upon culturally and linguistically responsive approaches (Charity Hudley & Mallinson, 2017). Results revealed that participants learned "to view students' rich and varied identities not as a deficit but as a resource," recognized challenges to meeting students' linguistic and cultural needs, and felt prepared to begin incorporating strategies to support and incorporate students' diverse cultural backgrounds within STEM experiences (Charity Hudley & Mallinson, 2017, p. 656).

Partnerships

Many of the aforementioned projects represent STEM partnerships between formal educational entities including school districts, elementary campuses, universities, and education service centers as well as informal institutions such as museums. Additionally, some of these projects have received support from foundations, businesses, and community organizations. A report outlining criteria of effective STEM schools and programs indicated that the success of STEM partnerships should be determined based not on what is accomplished but, rather, on the convergence between the goals of the school/district and the partner. Ultimately, the success of all partnerships must be based on the degree to which the interests of the partners are served (NRC, 2011b).

A program that highlights elementary STEM is Engineering is Elementary (EiE). EiE is an engineering curriculum developed by the school curriculum division of the Museum of Science of Boston. A five-year study of EiE explored the efficacy of the program for over 14,000 students in grades 3–5 and found that the curriculum enabled learners of every level, gender, and background to improve in both science and engineering outcomes (Engineering is Elementary, 2018).

Conclusions

Certainly, building a STEM foundation in elementary grades can spark early interest and lead to future enrollment in advanced STEM courses and potentially choosing STEM careers, and research supports the need to expose children to appropriate STEM opportunities early in their education. Advocates for early exposure to STEM concepts have contended that it develops critical thinking and reasoning skills, supports overall academic growth, is vital for nurturing and stimulating elementary children's curiosity, and enhances future interest in STEM-related careers (NRC, 2011b). STEM education at the elementary thereby maximize the transformational power of STEM in the lives of young children.

References

Acar, D., Tertemiz, N., & Taşdemir, A. (2018). The effects of STEM training on the academic achievement on 4th graders in science and mathematics and their views on STEM training teachers. *International Electronic Journal of Elementary Education, 10,* 505–513. doi:10.26822/iejee.2018438141

AccessSTEM. (2007). *Building capacity to include students with disabilities in science, technology, engineering, and mathematics fields.* Seattle, WA: University of Washington. Retrieved from https://eric.ed.gov/?id=ED506543

Alumbaugh, K. M. (2015). *The perceptions of elementary STEM schools in Missouri* (Unpublished doctoral dissertation). Retrieved from ProQuest LLC. (Order No. 10031817)

Anderson, D., & Moeed, A. (2017). Working alongside scientists: Impacts on primary teacher beliefs and knowledge about science and science education. *Science & Education, 26,* 271–298. doi:10.1007/s11191-017-9902-6

Baker, C. K., & Galanti, T. M. (2017). Integrating STEM in elementary classrooms using model-eliciting activities: Responsive professional development for mathematics coaches and teachers. *International Journal of STEM Education, 4*(1), 1–15. doi:10.1186/s40594-017-0066-3

Baldi, S., Jin, Y., Skemer, M., Green, P. J., & Herget, D. (2007). *Highlights from Pisa 2006: Performance of U.S. 15-year-old students in science and mathematics literacy in an international context* (NCES 2008–016). Washington, DC: U.S. Department of Education, National Center for Education Statistics, Institute of Education Sciences. Retrieved from https://nces.ed.gov/pubs2008/2008016.pdf

Becker, K., & Park, K. (2011). Effects of integrative approaches among science, technology, engineering, and mathematics (STEM) subjects on students' learning: A preliminary meta-analysis. *Journal of STEM Education, 12*(5&6), 23–37.

Bennett, J. M. P. (2016). *An investigation of elementary teachers' self-efficacy for teaching integrated science, technology, engineering, and mathematics (STEM) education* (Unpublished doctoral dissertation). Regent University, Virginia.

Blackley, S., & Howell, J. (2015). A STEM narrative: 15 years in the making. *Australian Journal of Teacher Education, 40*(7), 8, 102–112. doi:10.14221/ajte.2015v40n7.8

Blažev, M., Karabegović, M., Burušić, J., & Selimbegović, L. (2017). Predicting gender-STEM stereotyped beliefs among boys and girls from prior school achievement and interest in STEM school subjects. *Social Psychology of Education, 20*, 831–847. doi:10.1007/s11218-017-9397-7

Bottoms, A. I., Ciechanowski, K. M., & Hartman, B. (2015). Learning to teach elementary science through iterative cycles of enactment in culturally and linguistically diverse contexts. *Journal of Science Teacher Education, 26*, 715–742. doi:10.1007/s10972-016-9447-6

Bowden, M., Bartkowski, J. P., Xu, X., & Lewis, R. L. Jr. (2018). Parental occupation and the gender math gap: Examining the social reproduction of academic advantage among elementary and middle school students. *Social Sciences, 7*(1), 6. doi:10.3390/socsci7010006

Brandwein, P. F. (1995). *Science talent in the young expressed within ecologies of achievement* (RBDM 9510). Storrs, CT: The National Research Center on the Gifted and Talented, University of Connecticut.

Capobianco, B. M., & Rupp, M. (2014). STEM teachers; planned and enacted attempts at implementing engineering design-based instruction. *School Science and Mathematics, 114*, 258–270. doi:10.1111/ssm.12078

Charity Hudley, A. H., & Mallinson, C. (2017). "It's worth our time": A model of culturally and linguistically supportive professional development for K-12 STEM educators. *Cultural Studies of Science Education, 12*, 637–660. doi:10.1007/s11422-016-9743-7

Chen, G. (2011). *The rising popularity of STEM: A crossroads in public education or a passing trend?* Retrieved from http://www.publicschoolreview.com/articles/408.

Ciarrochi, J., Heaven, P. C. L., & Davies, F. (2007). The impact of hope, self-esteem, and attributional style on adolescents' school grades and emotional well-being: A longitudinal study. *Journal of Research in Personality, 41*, 1161–1178. Retrieved from http://www.sciencedirect.com/science/article/pii/s009265660700207

Claymier, B. (2014). Integrating STEM in the elementary curriculum. *Children's Technology & Engineering, 18*. doi:10.1186/s40594-017-0058-3

Committee on Science, Engineering, and Public Policy. (2007). *Rising above the gathering storm: Energizing and employing America for a brighter economic future*. Washington, DC: National Academy Press. Retrieved from http://nap.edu/11463

Cotabish, A., Dailey, D., Robinson, A., & Hughes, G. (2013). The effects of a STEM intervention on elementary students' science knowledge and skills. *School Science & Mathematics, 113*, 215–226. doi:10.111/ssm12023

Dailey, D., Cotabish, A., & Jackson, N. (2018). Increasing early opportunities in engineering for advanced learners in elementary classrooms: A review of recent literature. *Journal for the Education of the Gifted, 41*(1), 93–105. doi:10.1177/0162353217745157

Darling-Hammond, L. (2010). *The flat world and education: How America's commitment to equity will determine our future*. New York, NY: Teachers College Press.

DeJarnette, N. K. (2012). America's children: Providing early exposure to STEM (science, technology, engineering, and math) initiatives. *Education, 133*(1), 77–84. Retrieved from https://www.researchgate.net/publication/281065932_America's_Children_Providing_early_exposure_to_STEM_Science_Technology_Engineering_Math_Initiatives

DiFrancesca, D., Lee, C., & McIntyre, E. (2014). Where is the "E" in STEM for young children? Engineering design education in an elementary teacher preparation program. *Issues in Teacher Education, 23*(1), 49–64. Retrieved from https://www.itejournal.org/back-issues/spring-2014/09difrancescaetal.pdf

Douglas, K. A., & Strobel, J. (2015). Hopes and goals survey for use in STEM elementary education. *International Journal of Technology and Design Education, 25*, 245–259. doi:10.1007/s10798-014-9277-9

Duodu, E., Noble, J., Yusuf, Y., Garay, C., & Bean, C. (2017). Understanding the delivery of a Canadian-based after-school STEM program: A case study. *International Journal of STEM Education, 4*(20), 1–11. doi:10.1186/s40594-017-0083-2

Early Childhood STEM Working Group. (2017). *Early STEM matters: Providing high-quality STEM experiences for all young learners: A policy report by the early childhood STEM Working Group*. Chicago, IL: UChicago STEM Education. Retrieved from https://50.erikson.edu/wp-content/uploads/2017/01/STEM-Working_Group_Report.pds

Engineering is Elementary. (2018, September 10). *EiE, the curriculum division of the Museum of Science, Boston, launches early childhood engineering effort with the release of two new curricula for use in pre-k and kindergarten*. https://www.eie.org/news/eie-curriculum-division-museum-science-boston-launches-early-childhood-engineering-effort

Epstein, D., & Miller, R. T. (2011). *Slow off the mark: Elementary school teachers and the crisis in STEM education*. Report from The Center for American Progress. Retrieved from https://files.eric.ed.gov/fulltext/ED536070.pdf

Estapa, A. T., & Tank, K. M. (2017). Supporting integrated STEM in the elementary classroom: A professional development approach centered on an engineering design challenge. *International Journal of STEM Education, 4*(6), 1–16. doi:10.1186/s40594-017-0058-3

Fitzallen, N. (2015). STEM education: What does mathematics have to offer? In M. Marshman (Ed.), *Mathematics education in the margins*. Proceedings of the 38th annual conference of the Mathematics Education Research Group of Australasia, Sunshine Coast, June 28—July 2 (pp. 237–244). Sydney: MERGA. Retrieved from https://files.eric.ed.gov/fulltext /ED572451.pdf

Foltz, L., Gannon, S., & Kirschmann, S. (2014). Factors that contribute to the persistence of minority students in STEM fields. *Planning for Higher Education Journal, 42*(4), 46–58.

Glancy, A. W., Moore, T. J., Guzey, S., & Smith, K. A. (2017). Students' successes and challenges applying data analysis and measurement skills in a fifth-grade integrated STEM unit. *Journal of Pre-College Engineering Education Research, 7*(1), 68–75. doi:10.7771/2157-9288.1159

Guzey, S. S., Moore, T. J., & Harwell, M. (2016). Building up STEM: An analysis of teacher-developed engineering design-based STEM integration curricular materials. *Journal of Pre-College Engineering Education Research, 6*(1), 10–29. doi:10.7771/2157-9288.1129

Guzey, S. S., Roehrig, G., Tank, K., Moore, T., & Wang, H-H. (2014). A high-quality professional development for teachers of grades 3–6 for implementing engineering into classrooms. *School Science and Mathematics, 114*(3), 139–149. doi:10.1111/ssm.12061

Hyde, J. S., & Mertz, J. E. (2009). Gender, culture, and mathematics performance. *Proceedings of the National Academy of Sciences of the United States of America, 106*, 8801–8807. doi:10.1073/pnas.0901265106

Isabelle, A. D. (2017). STEM is elementary: Challenges faced by elementary teachers in the era of the next generation science standards. *The Educational Forum, 81*(1), 83–91. doi:10.1080/00131725.2016.1242678

Israel, M., Maynard, K., & Williamson, P. (2013). Promoting literacy-embedded, authentic STEM instruction for students with disabilities and other struggling learners. *Teaching Exceptional Children, 45*(4), 18–25. doi:10.1177/004005991304500402

Israel, M., Wherfel, Q. M., Pearson, J., Shehab, S., & Tapia, T. (2015). Empowering K-12 students with disabilities to learn computational thinking and computer programming. *Teaching Exceptional Children, 48*(1), 45–53. doi:10.1177/0040059915594790

Keeley, P. (2009). Elementary science education in the K-12 system. *NSTA WebNews Digest*. Retrieved from http://www.nsta.org/publications/news/story.aspx?id=55954

Kendall, A., & Portsmore, M. D. (2013, June). *Teachers' attention to student thinking during the engineering design process: A case study of three elementary classrooms*. Paper presented at the American Society for Engineering Education, Atlanta, GA. Retrieved from https://peer.asee.org/teachers-attention-to-student-thinking-during-the-engineering-design-process-a-case-study-of-three-elementary-classrooms

Kerr, B. A., Vuyk, M. A., & Rea, C. (2012). Gendered practices in the education of gifted girls and boys. *Psychology in the Schools, 49*, 647–655. doi:10.1002/pits.21627

LaForce, M., Noble, E., King, H., Century, J., Blackwell, C., Holt, S., . . . Loo, S. (2016). The eight essential elements of inclusive STEM high schools. *International Journal of STEM Education, 3*(21), 1–11. doi:10.1186/s40594-016-0054-z.

Leas, H. D., Nelson, K. L., Grandgenett, N., Tapprich, W. E., & Cutucache, C. E. (2017). Fostering curiosity, inquiry, and scientific thinking in elementary school students: Impact of the NE STEM 4U intervention. *Journal of Youth Development, 12*(2), 103–120. doi:10.5195/jyd.2017.474

Lee, O. (2002). Chapter 2: Promoting scientific inquiry with elementary students from diverse cultures and languages. *Review of Research in Education, 26*(1), 23–69. doi:10.3102/0091732X026001023

Lottero-Perdue, P. S., Lovelidge, S., & Bowling, E. (2010). Engineering for all. *Science and Children, 47*(7), 24–27. Retrieved from http://www.jstor.org/stable/43175601

McIntyre, E., Walkowiak, T., Thomson, M., Carrier, S., Lee, C., Greive, E., . . . DiFrancesca, D. (2013). A STEM-focused elementary teacher preparation program: Candidate and alumni perceptions. *Teacher Education and Practice, 26*, 670–687.

McLaughlin, C. A., & MacFadden, B. J. (2014). At the elbows of scientists: Shaping science teachers' conceptions and enactment of inquiry-based instruction. *Research in Science Education, 44*, 927–947. doi:10.1007/s11165-014-9408-z

Molina, R., Borror, J., & Desir, C. (2016). Supporting STEM success with elementary students of color in a low-income community. *Distance Learning, 13*(2), 19–25.

Moore, T. J., & Smith, K. A. (2014). Advancing the state of the art of STEM integration. *Journal of STEM Education: Innovations & Research, 15*(1), 5–10. Retrieved from https://karlsmithmn.org/wp-content/uploads/2017/08/Moore-Smith-JSTEMEd-GuestEditorialF.pdf

Moore, T. J., Stohlmann, M., Wang, H. H., Tank, K. M., Glancy, A. W., & Roehrig, G. H. (2014). Implementation and integration of engineering in K-12 STEM education. In *Engineering in pre-college settings: Synthesizing research, policy, and practices* (pp. 35–60). West Lafayette, IN: Purdue University Press.

Mullis, I. V. S., Martin, M. O., & Loveless, T. (2016). *20 years of TIMSS: International trends in mathematics and science achievement, curriculum, and instruction.* Chestnut Hill, MA: Boston College, TIMSS and PIRLS International Study Center.

Nadelson, L. S., Pfiester, J., Callahan, J., & Pyke, P. (2015). Who is doing the engineering, the student or the teacher? The development and use of a rubric to categorize level of design for the elementary classroom. *Journal of Technology Education, 26*(2), 22–45. doi:10.21061/jte.v26i2.a.2

Nadelson, L. S., & Seifert, A. L. (2017). Integrated STEM defined: Contexts, challenges, and the future. *The Journal of Educational Research, 110*, 221–223. doi:10.1080/00220671.2017.1289775

National Center for Education Statistics. (2015). *Trends in international mathematics and science study (TIMMS).* U.S. Department of Education. Institute of Education Sciences.

National Research Council. (2007). *Taking science to school: Learning and teaching science in grades K–8.* Washington, DC: National Academies Press.

National Research Council. (2011a). *A framework for K-12 science education: Practices, crosscutting concepts, and core ideas.* Washington, DC: National Academies Press.

National Research Council. (2011b). *Successful K-12 STEM education: A workshop summary.* Washington, DC: The National Academies Press.

National Science Board. (2010). *Preparing the next generation of STEM innovators: Identifying and developing our nation's human capital.* NSB-10–33. Retrieved from http://www.nsf.gov/nsb/publications/2010/nsb1033.pdf

NGSS Lead States. (2013). *Next generation science standards: For states, by states.* Washington, DC: The National Academies Press.

Obama, B. (November 23, 2009). *Educate to innovate press conference.* Retrieved from http://www.whitehouse.gov/issues/education/educate-innovate.

Olszewski-Kubilius, P., Steenbergen-Hu, S., Thomson, D., & Rosen, R. (2017). Minority achievement gaps in STEM: Findings of a longitudinal study of project excite. *Gifted Child Quarterly, 61*(1), 20–39. doi:10.1177/0016986216673449

Owens, D. C., Sadler, T. D., Murakami, C. D., & Tsai, C. L. (2018). Teachers' views on and preferences for meeting their professional development needs in STEM. *School Science and Mathematics, 118*, 370–384. doi:10.1111/ssm.12306

Rennie, L. (2012). *Evaluation of the scientists in schools project.* Retrieved from http://www.scientistsinschools.edu.au/downloads/SiSEvaluationReport2011-2012.pdf

Ricks, E. D. (2012). *Cultivating early STEM learners: An analysis of mastery classroom instructional practices, motivation, and mathematics achievement in young children* (Unpublished doctoral dissertation). Howard University, Washington, DC.

Robinson, A., Dailey, D., Hughes, G., & Cotabish, A. (2014). The effects of a science-focused STEM intervention on gifted elementary students' science knowledge and skills. *Journal of Advanced Academics, 25*, 189–213. doi:10.1177/1932202X14533799

Roehrig, G. H., Moore, T. J., Wang, H.-H., & Park, M. S. (2012). Is adding the E enough? Investigating the impact of K-12 engineering standards on the implementation of STEM integration. *School Science and Mathematics, 112*(1), 31–44. doi:10.1111/j.1949-8594.2001.00112.x

Shernoff, D. J., Sinha, S., Brassler, D. M., & Ginsburg, L. (2017). Assessing teacher education and professional development needs for the implementation of integrated approaches to STEM education. *International Journal of STEM Education.* doi:10.1186/s40594-017-0068-1.

Sikma, L., & Osborne, M. (2014). Conflicts in developing an elementary STEM magnet school. *Theory Into Practice, 53*(1), 4–10. doi:10.1080/00405841.2014.862112

Stohlmann, M., Moore, T. J., & Roehrig, G. H. (2012). Considerations for teaching integrated STEM education. *Journal of Pre-College Engineering Education Research, 2*(1), 28–34. doi:10.5703/1288284314653.

Tolliver, E. R. (2016). *The effects of science, technology, engineering and mathematics (STEM) education on elementary student achievement in urban schools* (Unpublished doctoral dissertation). Grand Canyon University, Arizona.

U.S. Department of Education. (2015). National assessment of educational progress (Science).

U.S. Department of Education. (2017). National assessment of educational progress (Mathematics).

Villegas, A. M. (1998). School failure and cultural mismatch: Another view. *The Urban Review, 20*, 253–265.

Walker, T. M. (2012). Engaging elementary students in summer STEM camp. *Texas Science Teacher, 41*(1), 6–14.

Wang, X. (2012). Why students choose STEM majors: Motivation, high school learning, and postsecondary context of support. *American Educational Research Journal, 50*, 1081–1121. doi:10.3102/0002831213488622

Wheelcock College Aspire Institute. (2010). *Strengthening STEM education in the early years.* Retrieved from https://www.mass.gov/files/documents/2018/07/03/foundationforfuturereport.pdf

Yoon, K. S., Duncan, T., Lee, S., & Shapley, K. (2008). *The effects of teachers' professional development on student achievement: Findings from a systemic review of evidence.* Paper presented at the annual meeting of the American Educational Research Association, New York, NY. Retrieved from https://ies.ed.gov/ncee/edlabs/regions/southwest/pdf/REL_2007033.pdf

Young, J. L., Young, J. R., & Ford, D. Y. (2017). Standing in the gaps: Examining the effects of early gifted education on black girl achievement in STEM. *Journal of Advanced Academics, 28,* 290–312. doi:10.1177/1932202X17730549

10

SECONDARY STEM LEARNING

Rose M. Pringle, Christine G. Lord and Tredina D. Sheppard

Secondary education is an important period in which adolescents negotiate and develop their academic and career trajectories (Ogle, Hyllegard, Rambo-Hernandez, & Park, 2017; Nugent, Barker, Welch, Grandgenett, Wu, & Nelson, 2015). The burgeoning international interest in science, technology, engineering, and mathematics (STEM) spurred on by business and policy leaders has forged a strong connection into and influence on schooling. Many countries, as seen in their national policies and reports, have invested and promoted STEM as a pillar of secondary education. A report published in the United Kingdom (UK) identified STEM education as being central to their workforce development and key in the reduction of economic problems (National Audit Office, 2018). As a result, the UK now has a National STEM Education network with the goal of securing STEM education for all young people. In the United States (US), policymakers and stakeholders have argued for the expansion and improvement of STEM education as a critical component to developing and maintaining the nation's capacity for innovation (National Science and Technology Conference, 2018). The urgency to advance STEM is also evident in calls from the Office of the Chief Scientist (2014) and other groups and organizations concerned with Australia's status as a leader in education and having a substantive position in world economics and sustainability. The report from Australia identified a STEM workforce with critical thinking and problem-solving skills as pertinent to driving its economic prosperity and fostering creativity and innovative ideas (Timms, Moyle, Weldon, & Mitchell, 2018). Other countries such as Malaysia, Canada, Turkey, China, and nations in the European Union (EU) have instituted a range of policies to support the development of STEM education in their secondary schools (Freeman, Marginson, & Tytler, 2014). This international and heightened attention to secondary STEM education is a direct response to the need for an informed and literate citizenry and a continued supply of a workforce prepared with 21st-century skills to respond to global and economic challenges.

Secondary school experiences prepare students for post-secondary pathways that may include essential prerequisites to career technical training, advanced college and graduate studies, and technical skills for the workplace. For the purposes of this chapter, secondary education is defined as the period of formal schooling from grade 6 until the end of the secondary program. Globally, notable differences and trends exist across secondary grade level bands; specifically, lower secondary refers to grades 6–8, and "high schools" being from grade 9, with overlap in some places. Some students may choose to continue the study of STEM-related disciplines in post-secondary institutions. For others not pursuing such fields and who may enter vocational training, an effective STEM program in secondary education could foster the development of STEM literacy and 21st-century skills.

As noted in policy documents, these skills and competencies are important for the workplaces including the manufacturing industries.

A review of educational reforms and the enactment of STEM-focused curricula has revealed a range of initiatives and models. For example, in the US, documents such as the New Science Framework (NRC, 2012), Next Generation Science Standards (NGSS Lead States, 2013) and the Common Core Science Standards (CCSS) (National Governors Association, 2010) emphasize the importance of an interdisciplinary approach to STEM teaching and learning and call for incorporating contexts that reveal real-world issues. Furthermore, performance expectations outlined in the NGSS (NGSS Lead States, 2013) related to secondary education call for the development of knowledge across disciplines; demonstration of proficiencies in mathematical thinking; and obtaining, evaluating, and communicating information. These salient practices, when appropriately developed, support the achievement of STEM literacy described as the integration of the STEM disciplines and the tools and knowledge necessary to solve complex issues (Balka, 2011; Mohr-Schroeder, Bush, & Jackson, 2018). Australia, facing the challenge of a "crowded traditional curriculum," introduced the Australia Curriculum: Technologies focusing on systems thinking as a unifying approach and with intent that students from foundation to year eight in schools develop levels of proficiencies in design and digital technologies (Timms et al., 2018). In Korea, as reported by Freeman, Marginson, and Tytler (2015), the development of a STEM curriculum is driven by the relevance of science and technology in daily life and the public interests in new discoveries and awareness.

Secondary STEM education can be considered a single or multidisciplinary field (Holmlund, Lessig, & Slavit, 2018), but there seems to be a lack of consensus among educational stakeholders concerning its conceptualizations and approaches. Scholars embrace the notion that an interdisciplinary approach can foster students' STEM identity (Holmegaard, Madsen, & Ulriksen, 2014; Gonsalves, Silfver, Danielsson, & Berge, 2019), develop 21st-century workforce skills (Kennedy & Odell, 2014), and lead to well-rounded, scientifically literate global citizens (Bybee, 2013). In this chapter, we examine STEM learning in secondary schools and discuss the approaches, and challenges of integrating two or more disciplines. In addition, we highlight the personal and global economic benefits of secondary STEM education. Our discussion ends with a proposal for a research agenda that will secure the reduction of ambiguity in STEM education and from which will emerge a global cohesive vision as indicated in international policies along with strategies and best practices to support its continued enactment.

Current Landscape: STEM in Secondary Education

While goals for STEM education have been identified at the national levels and expressed in policy documents (Bybee, 2013; Kennedy & Odell, 2014), there is no agreed-upon national or international approach to curricular design for secondary education. Such decisions are usually left to school administrators and teachers (McNally, 2012; Roehrig, Moore, Wang, & Park, 2012). As a result, STEM in secondary education exists within a vast landscape of variability integrating two or more disciplines within the context of existing curricular frameworks (Moore, Johnson, Peters-Burton, & Guzey, 2016), as a program (Bicer & Caparo, 2018; Wiswall, Stiefel, Schwartz, & Boccardo, 2014), or as specialized courses of studies within schools classified as STEM schools (LaForce et al., 2016; Wiswall et al., 2014; Subotnik, Tai, Rickoff, & Almarode, 2009). This variability does not, however, detract from the general agreement that STEM within secondary education should involve all students in a rigorous curriculum, be applicable to real-world experiences, and include problem or project-based learning opportunities that contribute to the building of 21st-century skills (Bybee, 2013; Peters-Burton, Lynch, Behrend, & Means, 2014). In the report on STEM education in the US, *Charting a Course for Success: America's Strategy for STEM Education* (NSTC, 2018), the federal government identified three aspirational goals for the achievement of a high-quality STEM education:

(1) build strong foundations for STEM literacy, (2) increase diversity, equity, and inclusion in STEM, and (3) prepare the STEM workforce for the future. These goals confirm the importance of quality STEM education for all learners (particularly those who historically have been underserved and underrepresented), while also acknowledging that the nation's economic welfare is dependent upon increasing access and inclusivity in STEM education.

In secondary STEM education, combinations of the disciplines are taught within existing traditional school curricula as concepts or practices providing support or deepening learning in the core or host subject (Kelley, & Knowles, 2016; Asghar, Ellington, Rice, Johnson, & Prime, 2012). Described as "ad hoc infusion" (Katehi, Pearson, & Feder, 2009), these STEM-oriented curricula embed disciplinary processes and competencies such as problem solving, creativity, and critical thinking skills into a core subject. These pertinent skills and disciplinary content knowledge in secondary STEM education have been lauded as being instrumental in fostering and contributing to the development of functional citizens and ensuring the continued pipeline toward higher-level studies including research, mathematics, science, and engineering (Archer et al., 2012; Capraro & Nite, 2014).

Science and Engineering

Engineering concepts and skills and the alignment with science content standards, though not a novel idea (Grubb & Strimel, 2015), have been given much credence in increasing the pipeline with a talented workforce, capable of innovation and prepared to solve real-world problems through design, troubleshooting, and analysis activities (Brophy, Klein, Portsmore, & Rogers, 2008; Bybee, 2010; Cantrell, Pekcan, Itani, & Velasquez-Bryant, 2006; Chien & Chu, 2018; Grubb & Strimel, 2015). Globally, engineering design and practices are emerging as dynamic elements of science education. For example, in the Netherlands as well as in many other countries, there is increasing interest in integrating engineering as part of the general education (Kőycű & de Vries, 2016). In Malaysia, attempts at integration include the introduction of biotechnology into science curriculum (Yasin, Amin, & Hin, 2018). In the US, the New Science Framework (NRC, 2012) explicitly incorporates engineering practices, raising them to the same level as science practices within the three-dimensional approach to science learning. The three dimensions to science learning (NRC, 2012) include core science ideas, crosscutting concepts, and science and engineering practices.

Science investigation and engineering design together provide a structure in which students participate in science as a social enterprise and connect disciplinary concepts and principles to their own experiences and ideas (NSTC, 2018). While science usually serves as the host discipline with engineering-based problem solving (Goonatilake & Bachnak, 2012; Chien & Chu, 2018), research indicates that in such integration, engineering has the potential to occupy more than a "spectator" role. Engineering design, emphasis on problem solving and optimizing solutions using a variety of tools for modeling and analysis are integral to students' preparation for engaging in systematic processes to solve societal and environmental challenges (Brophy et al., 2008; Grubb & Strimel, 2015; NGSS Lead States, 2013). In a study examining the effects of engineering design-focused modules on student learning in lower secondary school science, Cantrell et al. (2006) concluded that engineering design experiences facilitated the development of science content knowledge and higher-order thinking skills such as analysis and synthesis. Their results also indicated that a curriculum that includes engineering design-based activities and in which students seek solutions to authentic real-world issues may reduce academic achievement gaps among underrepresented populations of learners.

Reports from integrating engineering into secondary education curricula reveal mixed results. In Mooney's and Laubach's (2002) Adventure Engineering program, students immersed in open-ended design experiences improved in achievement in mathematics and science but showed no significant change in knowledge about engineering (Mooney & Laubach, 2002). In another project, engineering was purposively integrated into science to enrich the regular school curricula including expanded opportunities for creativity and problem solving (Redmond, Thomas, High, Scott, Jordan, & Dockers, 2011). This program resulted in a significant impact on students' confidence, awareness of engineering, and interest in engineering as a potential career. Other work exploring the impact of integrating an engineering design-based science unit reported statistically significant achievement for life science among a group of special education students (Guzey, Moore, Harwell, & Moreno, 2016). Even with mixed results, an integrated science and engineering curriculum provides a rich context for bridging classroom lessons to real-world experiences, allowing students to develop knowledge and abilities necessary for fostering innovation and piquing their curiosity and motivation toward both disciplines (Brophy et al., 2008; Grubb & Strimel, 2015).

Using Technology as the Lens to Inform STEM

Technological advances have permeated many areas of life in the 21st century, thus igniting an even greater interest in pursuing the STEM enterprise as a field of study. In support of the global consensus that technology integration holds great promise for enhancing STEM learning, educators are now capitalizing on its potential to motivate students by connecting learning to digital cultures characteristic of real-world perspectives (Saavedra & Opfer, 2012; Basu et al., 2016; Dogan & Robin, 2015). For example, a study examining the impact of online forensic science games on secondary students' knowledge, attitudes, and science careers, Miller (2011) offered evidence to support the positive role of technology in knowledge acquisition, its motivational effects on learners, and its use as a means to foster the development of 21st-century skills. Upper-level secondary students in Malaysia experienced the positive impact of technology through a biotechnology-infused classroom that allowed them to apply and manipulate biological processes (Yasin et al., 2018). The researchers found that even though teachers were limited in their preparation to teach the subject, access to appropriate technologies, resources and simulations, and ease of communication impacted their teaching and facilitated students' learning.

Europe and the US have a long history of integrating technology into their formal school curricula, and this has expanded to other countries. In recent international reports, STEM integration has now become a central issue in educational reform in countries like Israel where digital technologies in science classes exist as both an instructional tool and a separate discipline with its own parameters (Valkanova & Watts, 2007). Emphasis on the incorporation of technology-rich STEM-based programs with secondary students has demonstrated how technological tools and methods have been used to foster collaborative learning environments and enhance student ownership and independence (Ardito, 2010; Clayton & Ardito, 2009; Ardito, Mosley, & Scollins, 2014; Capraro & Jones, 2013; Yasin et al., 2018). In other efforts, technology integration in STEM learning has impacted secondary learners' effectiveness, attitudes, and creativity (Lou, Chung, Dzan, Tseng, & Shih, 2013); achievement, and self-efficacy (Liu, Cho, & Schallert, 2006; Ketelhut, 2007); and student-directed scientific inquiry in real-world settings by improving their problem-solving abilities (Barak & Dori, 2005).

As technology becomes more indispensable, computer and network technologies are now contributing to experiential learning in STEM. In addition to computer science curricula and the integration of computational thinking skills, there is now much support for the inclusion of robotics as a viable platform for the application of STEM (Allen, 2013; Barak & Assal, 2018; Rihtarsic, Avsec, & Kocijancic, 2016). For example, Bowen, DeLuca, and Franzen (2016), in their study of content knowledge learning in a computer simulation modeling program, posited that students with less content knowledge can achieve certain goals if sufficiently engaged in simulation. Their findings also raise the issue of the extent to which students integrate content knowledge, procedural knowledge, experimental knowledge, and trial and error to achieve learning outcomes. While the interdisciplinary nature of computer simulation modeling raises questions about the nature and quality of content knowledge, it provides a unique opportunity for students to persevere through challenges and offers a platform from which the vision of STEM can be realized in secondary classrooms.

Science and Mathematics

When students learn mathematics and science simultaneously as in integration, they are likely to increase comprehension in both subjects, and the experiences could provide the intellectual excitement necessary to increase interest and engagement (Weinberg, & Sample McMeeking, 2017; Schroeder, Scott, Tolson, Huang, & Lee, 2007). Researchers in the fields of both mathematics education and science education have long asserted that the two disciplines are complementary (Lee, Chauvot, Plankis, Vowell, & Culpepper, 2011; Boboňová, Čeretková, Tirpáková, & Markechová, 2019; Schroeder et al., 2007). However, while some educators have lauded the usefulness of the mathematics-science integration (Becker & Park, 2011), others have indicated that the nature and level of learning appear to differ for the two disciplines and is less evident for mathematical outcomes (Shaughnessy, 2013; Boboňová et al., 2019).

In supporting the integration of mathematics and science, Treacy and O'Donoghue (2014) describe mathematics as a universal tool for evaluating a set of values in addition to modeling skills necessary for quantitative analysis of large data sets prevalent in science. The expression of the quantitative results can therefore lead to the discovery of new patterns or relationships (Michaels, Shouse, & Schweingruber, 2008). Mathematics and science integration allow students to learn organized knowledge structures drawn from both disciplines, explore the interconnectedness of the disciplines and heighten their understanding of the relevance and real-life applications of each discipline (Enderson, 2015; Huntley, 1998; McHugh, Kelly, & Burghardt, 2017).

An examination of existing models of integration shows a greater focus on science, with mathematics content integration that gives little regard to learning the discipline (Boboňová et al., 2019). They contend that simply adding mathematical concepts in science instruction is not necessarily supportive in providing a meaningful context for developing an understanding of mathematical principles. This observation has generated debates as educators invoke the call for mathematics to be made transparent and explicit and to occur within the context of a problem that requires significant mathematical skills (Shaughnessy, 2013; Weinberg & Sample McMeeking, 2017). Accordingly, the context of the problem should explicitly draw from both disciplines and be taught in a manner consistent with inquiry-based pedagogical strategies. Ideally in these strategies, the abstract concepts in mathematics are realized as students develop and use skills such as measurement and graphing in interpreting data which then become reinforced across the two disciplines. Stinson, Harkness, Meyer, and Stallworth (2009) also note that the ability to apply mathematics within a real-world context is at the core of quantitative reasoning where, as a universal language, mathematics provides scientists with another system for sharing, communicating, and understanding science concepts.

While many countries subscribe to a discipline-centered curriculum, over the last decade places like Slovakia have seen the rise of interdisciplinary curriculum in which mathematics is integrated into specific science disciplines such as the life sciences. This move toward mathematics integration according to Boboňová et al. (2019) has emerged in response to the need to improve overall quantitative skills required in secondary and post-secondary science learning. In the current reforms in the US, both the NGSS (NGSS Lead States, 2013) and the Common Core State Standards (CCSS, 2010) have affirmed the importance of integrating science and mathematics and the role each discipline plays in providing a context in which students can make connections across the two disciplines. Both US standards are grounded in the belief that the systematic inclusion of mathematics and science in instruction can satisfy the learning of important disciplinary concepts and skills as indicated in the respective curricular documents. The general consensus among educators is that science and mathematics integration will allow for improvement in the complexity and scope of student knowledge and comprehension (Treacy & O'Donoghue, 2014). However, at the heart of the debates around the integration is the need for a common understanding of how to utilize mathematical approaches while simultaneously employing scientific examples.

STEM Curriculum: Programmatic Approach

A promising approach to enacting STEM integration in secondary education has been the development of a cohesive course of studies in which learning is anchored in meaningful contexts. Project Lead the Way (PLTW, 2019) is one such program. This premier engineering education program in the US provides a STEM-focused curriculum that concentrates on the integration of engineering with science and mathematics within the context of real-world challenges. The program was developed in response to concerns over the diminishing number of students in the US choosing to enter science and engineering post-secondary education programs. PLTW specifically addresses the anticipated needs of the 21st-century workforce and provides students with a foundation and a pathway to college and careers in STEM-related fields. The sequence of engineering courses in PLTW encourages students to use their mathematics and science knowledge and skills to complete problems applicable to their everyday lives.

Research examining the effectiveness of PLTW on student science achievement has garnered some mixed results. PLTW in general has contributed to positive academic achievement on standardized measures and motivation in science and engineering (Tai, 2012). Additionally, studies have determined the significance of PLTW and its hands-on, project-based engineering curriculum as students demonstrated higher scores on state mathematics assessments, a higher percentage met the college-ready criterion, a higher percentage enrolled in higher education institutions, and non-college-bound PLTW students earned higher wages (Van Overschelde, 2013). Other studies, however, did not find significant differences when examining students' achievement in mathematics (Tran & Nathan, 2010). The discrepancies in the findings indicate the complex challenges engineering education programs like PLTW face as they seek to effectively integrate the disciplines in STEM in ways that support the construction of academic content and the development of the skills to a wide range of students.

Like PLTW, another approach to STEM integration and given much credit in the literature is STEM project based learning (PBL). As a pedagogical strategy, STEM PBL (Abbott, 2016; Capraro & Nite, 2014) offers a comprehensive and interdisciplinary approach to investigating authentic problems from which students develop critical thinking skills and values along with specific content knowledge. A hallmark of STEM PBL is its focus on learning in the context of real-world challenges that require developing and using skills, tools, and knowledge central to the disciplines. When PBL is carefully designed with attention to the content knowledge of each discipline and enacted accordingly, studies show increased academic achievement, student engagement, interest in pursuing STEM careers, and overall positive attitudes towards STEM (Newman, Dantzler, & Coleman, 2015; Guzey et al., 2016; Dorph, Bathgate, Schunn, & Cannady, 2018). Ideally the integration of a well–developed STEM PBL curriculum allows secondary students to experience the overlapping nature of disciplines leading to deep conceptual understanding.

Students engaged in STEM PBL confront global and local challenges as they master grade-level content knowledge and skills and habits of mind necessary for success (Abbott, 2016; Capraro & Jones, 2013; Korur, Efe, Erdogan, & Tunc, 2017; Newman et al., 2015). Due to its wide reach and authenticity in engaging learners, educators note the extent to which PBL curriculum seamlessly cuts across traditional content lines and integrates engineering and technological design, inquiry-based science, and mathematical reasoning in the process of developing a potential curricular prototype for the future (Johnson, Peters-Burton, & Moore, 2016). Students placed at the center of the learning process become motivated (Flores, 2018), and the emerging knowledge, both meaningful and relevant, can impact their academic choices as they contemplate high school studies and beyond. A well-designed PBL STEM curriculum according to Knezek, Christensen, Tyler-Wood, and Peri-athiruvadi (2013) can therefore be very effective during the secondary years of schooling. Other scholars have cited increases in science academic achievement (Newman et al., 2015) changes in attitudes (Guzey et al., 2016; Dorph et al., 2018), and positive impacts on the learning and engagement of students from underrepresented populations (Flores, 2018).

Another program, *STEM Road Map: A Framework for Integrated STEM Education*, is described by the editors, Johnson et al. (2016), as "a coordinated response to the need for addressing STEM learning in K–12" (p. 4). The program embraces the reform efforts presented by the new framework, NGSS, and the US national standards expressed in the common core. Organized around five real-world STEM themes—cause and effect, innovation and progress, the represented world, sustainable systems, and optimizing the human experience—the curriculum framework is spiraled and reinforced throughout the K–12 environment. One of the important features of the STEM Road Map is the ease of implementation supported by the authentic and facilitative learning environments in which students engage in real-world STEM projects (Johnson et al., 2016). Other unique features of the STEM Road Map framework include the distinctive roles for all the content areas; teachers working collaboratively across disciplines to implement the integrated curriculum; and students being immersed in authentic, project- and problem-based learning across traditional content areas, integrating technology, engineering, scientific inquiry, and mathematical reasoning. The learning experiences being personal, relevant and of interest to secondary students serve the multiple purposes of supporting the development of 21st-century competencies, STEM literacy, and laying the foundation for career choices that will secure a pipeline of STEM experts and innovators.

In addition to increasing STEM curricular developments, there has also been a growing number of STEM-focused schools (Scott, 2012). STEM-focused secondary schools are classified into three categories by the National Research Council (2012): selective, inclusive, or career and technical education (CTE) focused. Studies on STEM- focused schools and non-STEM focused schools have not shown significant differences in academic achievement, based on standardized test results (Bicer & Capraro, 2018; Wiswall et al., 2014). However, studies do indicate STEM-focused schools lessen the achievement gap between underrepresented student populations and their White counterparts (Bicer & Capraro, 2018; Wiswall et al., 2014). As summarized by Wiswall et al. (2014), for average students, the effects of attending a STEM high school are not significant, but STEM-focused schools have the potential to be a powerful tool for leveling the playing field among varying populations of learners and to mitigate student outflows into STEM.

Challenges to STEM Integration in Secondary Education

STEM learning in secondary education holds the undeniable promise of impacting the educational trajectory of learners as they graduate high school, yet there are many challenges to its enactment. Some of these challenges include the ambiguity of the meaning and interpretation of STEM and the lack of a consistent operational definition; teachers' preparedness to teach the principles, knowledge, and practices across the disciplines; access to a viable curriculum and related materials; and already crowded programs of studies that in many cases are tightly knitted to historical norms, procedures, and structures. Despite the crafting of the STEM acronym in the 1990s, and the dramatic momentum in the enterprise over the years (Asghar et al., 2012), there remains a pronounced lack of consensus on its meaning within the context of educational policies, programs, and curricular practices (Bybee, 2013; Sanders, 2009). This ambiguity in meaning diminishes the power of STEM as the conversations around goals and expectations project out from the national policies and translated into curricular practices (Sanders, 2009).

Teachers prepared to teach traditional single courses offer one of the main challenges to STEM integration (Stohlmann, Moore, McClelland, & Roehrig, 2011). This is compounded by the lack of an established STEM curriculum. While teachers will require learning opportunities in multiple disciplinary content knowledge and STEM-related pedagogies, some researchers responding to the lack of knowledge suggest that teachers could adopt new ways of collaborating and co-teaching to offset the existing deficit in content knowledge (Roehrig et al., 2012; Capraro & Nite, 2014; McNally, 2012). Embracing STEM learning in secondary education requires a shift in teachers' professional development along with significant implications for teacher preparation programs.

Curricular materials that purposefully identify and connect relevant practices and specific disciplinary knowledge are essential to support STEM education in secondary schools (Katehi et al., 2009; Rihtarsic et al., 2016). In addition, the curriculum should be responsive to the learning needs of historically underrepresented students in STEM disciplines, including students who are female, have low socioeconomic status (SES), and who represent certain ethnic minorities and indigenous groups. The curriculum should be culturally responsive, leveraging students' funds of knowledge (Ladson-Billings, 2014; Paris, 2012), and provide equitable access to each of the disciplines, thus holding the promise of broadening participation. Issues related to the curriculum also include the impact of high-stakes assessment, as what is tested dictates the value and attention ascribed to teaching. Furthermore, current structural organization of schools, access to viable curriculum and materials, and approaches to pedagogical practices offer challenges to the enactment of sustainable STEM programs for secondary education (Katehi et al., 2009) including attention to the organization of grade levels, teachers' assignments, and assessment policies. Moving forward, the continued evolution of STEM learning in secondary schools will require a curriculum with clear delineation of the disciplinary content knowledge and or specialized skills and dispositions from each of the four component disciplines—science, technology, engineering, and mathematics.

Looking Forward: A Research Agenda for the 21st Century

STEM learning in secondary education is important to increase students' achievement in science and mathematics, improve STEM literacy, and foster the development of skilled 21st-century workers and innovators to advance areas within STEM fields (Stohlmann et al., 2011; Navracsics, 2017; NRC, 2012; NSTC, 2018). The literature is replete with claims of the effectiveness of STEM learning that have emerged from pockets of research activities which, from our observation and consistent with those of other scholars, is lacking in substantive empirical evidence. To provide guidance going forward, what is needed is a definitive model of STEM education including its progression and articulation across K–12 schooling, and the extent to which it supports meaningful learning across all four disciplines. STEM education in secondary schools could be better informed by a universally accepted curricular framework that could be imported into traditional school structures. This framework would include best practices, relevant and appropriate assessments, and would be complemented with the preparation of a cadre of competent and dedicated STEM teachers and supportive school administrators. From our examination of the landscape of STEM education in secondary education, we propose a research agenda that includes unearthing and learning from the past and preparing for the future.

Despite the pockets of positive results highlighting the development of STEM-related interest and identity and the potential to foster learning across the four disciplines, there is a paucity of information on best strategies and approaches to inform classroom practices. This is further complicated by the many different approaches to STEM, each with its own implementation challenges and variant outcomes. We are therefore at a time in the history of STEM education that warrants a well-developed systematic analysis of the research that has occurred over the past nineteen or so years, and a mixed-methods longitudinal study to investigate trends in processes and practices. The proposed studies would be twofold. First, the systematic review would provide insights into past occurrences and would reveal possible questions and hypotheses to direct future research efforts. Perhaps most importantly, the systematic review would provide information to guide the development of a consistent operational definition of STEM. Second, the longitudinal study would respond to questions related to the impact of STEM education in secondary schools on students' choice of subjects and career trajectory. Furthermore, the findings could inform the refinement of models of best practices, including learning goals in the context of the individual subjects and across the four disciplines. Thus ending the concerns as to what should be contained in a STEM program in secondary education.

Conclusion

In the review of STEM education in secondary schools, the consensus is that an integrated approach has the potential to facilitate students' development of the necessary skills, knowledge, and dispositions to be functional 21st-century citizens. Furthermore, an integrated STEM education that provides real-world, relevant, and appropriate learning experiences can prepare students with college-readiness skills, increase the number and diversity pursuing a career in a STEM-related field, and provide a continuous supply of skilled and innovative workers necessary to maintain worldwide economic stability. Advocates for STEM education in secondary education (Krapp & Prenzel, 2011; Stohlmann et al., 2011) contend that teaching in ways that allow students to make connections to real-world issues and challenges can make the disciplines more relevant and improve academic achievement and students' interest. The successful achievement of the promise of STEM education in secondary schools hinges on the development of a cohesive definition, creation of real-world curricular materials, comprehensive STEM teacher preparation, and the alignment of secondary school practices with international goals for STEM education. Ultimately, increasing the access to and the quality of STEM education in secondary schools will foster creativity and ensure innovative solutions to current and future global dilemmas.

References

Abbott, A. (2016). Chemical connections: A problem–based learning, STEM experience. *Science Scope, 39*(7).

Allen, K. C. (2013). Robots bring math-powered ideas to life. *Mathematic Teaching in the Middle School, 18*(6), 340–347.

Archer, L., DeWitt, J., Osborne, J., Dillon, J., Willis, B., & Wong, B. (2012). Science aspirations, capital, and family habitus: How families shape children's engagement and identification with science. *American Educational Research Journal, 49*(5), 881–908.

Ardito, G. (2010). *The shape of disruption: XO laptops in the fifth-grade classroom.* White Plains, NY: Pace University.

Ardito, G., Mosley, P., & Scollins, L. (2014). WE, ROBOT: Using robotics to promote collaborative and mathematics learning in a middle school classroom. *Middle Grades Research Journal, 9*(3), 73–88.

Asghar, A., Ellington, R., Rice, E., Johnson, F., & Prime, G. M. (2012). Supporting STEM education in secondary science contexts. *Interdisciplinary Journal of Problem-Based Learning, 6*(2), 85–125.

Balka, D. (2011). Standards of mathematical practice and STEM. Stillwater, OK. *Math-science Connector Newsletter, 6–8.*

Barak, M., & Assal, M. (2018). Robotics and STEM learning: Students' achievements in assignments according to the P3 task taxonomy—practice, problem solving, and projects. *International Journal of Technology and Design Education,* (1), 121–144.

Barak, M., & Dori, Y. J. (2005). Enhancing undergraduate students' chemistry understanding through project-based learning in an IT environment. *Science Education, 89*(1), 117–139.

Basu, S., Biswas, G., Sengupta, P., Dickes, A., Clark, D., & Kinnebrew, J. (2016). Identifying middle school students' challenges in computational thinking-based science learning. *Research & Practice in Technology Enhanced Learning, 11*(1), 1–35.

Becker, K., & Park, K. (2011). Effects of integrative approaches among science, technology, engineering, and mathematics (STEM) subjects on students' learning: A preliminary meta-analysis. *Journal of STEM Education: Innovations & Research, 12,* 23–36.

Bicer, A., Capraro, R. M., & Capraro, M. M. (2018). Hispanic students' mathematics achievement in the context of their high school types as STEM and non-STEM schools. *International Journal of Mathematical Education in Science and Technology, 49*(5), 705–720.

Boboňová, I., Čeretková, S., Tirpáková, A., & Markechová, D. (2019). Inclusion of interdisciplinary approach in the mathematics education of biology trainee teachers in Slovakia. In *Interdisciplinary mathematics education* (pp. 263–280). Cham, Switzerland: Springer.

Bowen, B. D., DeLuca, V. W., & Franzen, M. M. S. (2016). Measuring how the degree of content knowledge determines performance outcomes in an engineering design-based simulation environment for middle school students. *Computers & Education, 117.*

Brophy, S., Klein, S., Portsmore, M., & Rogers, C. (2008). Advancing engineering education in P-12 classrooms. *Journal of Engineering Education,* 369–387.

Bybee, R. W. (2013). *The case for STEM education: Challenges and opportunities.* Arlington, VA: National Science Teachers Association Press.

Cantrell, P., Pekcan, G., Itani, A., & Velasquez-Bryant, N. (2006). The effects of engineering modules on student learning in middle school science classrooms. *Journal of Engineering Education, 95*(4), 301–309.

Capraro, M. M., & Jones, M. (2013). Interdisciplinary stem project-based learning. In R. M. Capraro, M. M. Capraro, & J. Morgan (Eds.), *Project-based learning: An integrated science, technology, engineering, and mathematics (STEM) approach* (2nd ed., pp. 47–54). Rotterdam, The Netherlands: Sense.

Capraro, M. M., & Nite, S. B. (2014). Stem integration in mathematics standards. *Middle Grades Research Journal, 9*(3), 1.

Chien, Y. H., & Chu, P. Y. (2018). The different learning outcomes of high school and college students on a 3D-printing STEAM engineering design curriculum. *International Journal of Science and Mathematics Education, 16*(6), 1047–1064.

Clayton, C., & Ardito, G. (2009). Teaching for ownership in the middle school science classroom: Towards practical inquiry in an age of accountability. *Middle Grades Research Journal, 4*(4), 53–79.

Common Core State Standards Initiative. (2010). *Common Core State Standards for mathematics.* Retrieved from http://www.corestandards.org

Dogan, B., & Robin, B. (2015). Technology's role in STEM education and the stem S.O.S. Model. In Sahin, A. (Ed.D.), *A practice-based model of STEM teaching: STEM students on the stage (SOS)* (pp. 77–94). Rotterdam, The Netherlands: Sense Publishing.

Dorph, R., Bathgate, M. E., Schunn, C. D., & Cannady, M. A. (2018). When I grow up: The relationship of "science learning activation" to STEM career preferences. *International Journal of Science Education, 40*(9), 1034–1057.

Enderson, M. C. (2015). Ready, aim, fire your cannons! *Teaching Children Mathematics, 21*(8), 502–506.

Flores, C. (2018). Problem-based science, a constructionist approach to science literacy in middle school. *International Journal of Child-Computer Interaction, 16*, 25–30.

Freeman, B., Marginson, S., & Tytler, R. (2015). *The age of STEM: Educational policy and practice across the world in Science, Technology, Engineering and Mathematics.* London: Routledge, Taylor & Francis.

Gonsalves, A. J., Silfver, E., Danielsson, A., & Berge, M. (2019). "It's not my dream, actually": Students' identity work across figured worlds of construction engineering in Sweden. *International Journal of STEM Education, 6*(1), 1–17.

Goonatilake, R., & Bachnak, R. A. (2012). Promoting engineering education among high school and middle school students. *Journal of STEM Education: Innovations & Research, 13*(1), 15–21.

Grubbs, M., & Strimel, G. (2015). Engineering design: The great integrator. *Journal of STEM Teacher Education, 50*(1), 77–90.

Guzey, S. S., Moore, T. J., Harwell, M., & Moreno, M. (2016). STEM integration in middle school life science: Student learning and attitudes. *Journal of Science Education and Technology, 25*(4), 550–560.

Holmegaard, H. T., Madsen, L. M., & Ulriksen, L. (2014). To choose or not to choose science: Constructions of desirable identities among young people considering a STEM higher education programme. *International Journal of Science Education, 36*(2), 186–215.

Holmlund, T., Lessig, K., & Slavit, D. (2018). Making sense of "STEM education" in K-12 contexts. *International Journal of STEM Education, 5*(32), 1–18.

Huntley, M. (1998). *Design and implementation of a framework for defining integrated mathematics and science education.* Hoboken: Blackwell Publishing Ltd.

Johnson, C., Peters-Burton, E., & Moore, T. (Eds.). (2016). *STEM road map: A framework for integrated STEM education.* New York, NY: Routledge.

Katehi, L., Pearson, G., & Feder, M. (2009). The status and nature of K-12 engineering education in the United States. *The Bridge, 39*(3), 5–10.

Kelley, T. R., & Knowles, J. G. (2016). A conceptual framework for integrated STEM education. *International Journal of STEM Education, 3*(1), 11.

Kennedy, T. J., & Odell, M. R. L. (2014). Engaging students in STEM education. *Science Education International, 25*(3), 246–258.

Ketelhut, D. J. (2007). The impact of student self-efficacy on scientific inquiry skills: An exploratory investigation in River City, a multi-user virtual environment. *Journal of Science Education and Technology, 16*(1), 99–111.

Knezek, G., Christensen, R., Tyler-Wood, T., & Periathiruvadi, S. (2013). Impact of environmental power monitoring on middle school student perceptions of STEM. *Science Education International, 24*(1), 98–123.

Korur, F., Efe, G., Erdogan, F., & Tunç, B. (2017). Effects of toy crane design-based learning on simple machines. *International Journal of Science and Mathematics Education, 15*(2), 251–271.

Köycü, Ü., & de Vries, M. J. (2016). What preconceptions and attitudes about engineering are prevalent amongst upper secondary school pupils? An international study. *International Journal of Technology and Design Education, 26*(2), 243–258.

Krapp, A., & Prenzel, M. (2011). Research on interest in science: Theories, methods, and findings. *International Journal of Science Education, 33*(1), 27–50.

Ladson-Billings, G. (2014). Culturally relevant pedagogy 2.0: Aka the remix. *Harvard Educational Review, 84*(1), 74–84.

LaForce, M., Noble, E., King, H., Century, J., Blackwell, C., Holt, S., . . . Loo, S. (2016). The eight essential elements of inclusive STEM high schools. *International Journal of STEM Education, 3*(21), 1–11. doi:10.1186/s40594-016-0054-z.

Lee, M. M., Chauvot, J., Plankis, B., Vowell, J., & Culpepper, S. (2011). Integrating to learn and learning to integrate: A case study of an online master's program on science–mathematics integration for middle school teachers. *The Internet and Higher Education, 14*(3), 191–200.

Liu, M., Cho, Y., & Schallert, D. (2006). Middle school students' self-efficacy, attitudes, and achievement in a computer-enhanced problem-based learning environment. *Journal of Interactive Learning Research, 17*(3), 225–242.

Lou, S., Chung, C., Dzan, W., Tseng, K., & Shih, R. (2013). Effect of using TRIZ creative learning to build a pneumatic propeller ship with applying STEM knowledge. *International Journal of Engineering Education, 29*(2), 365–379.

McHugh, L., Kelly, A. M., & Burghardt, M. D. (2017). Teaching thermal energy concepts in a middle school mathematics-infused science curriculum. *Science Scope, 41*(1), 43.

McNally, T. (2012). Innovative teaching and technology in the service of science: Recruiting the next generation of STEM students. *Journal of the Scholarship of Teaching and Learning, 12*(1).

Michaels, S., Shouse, A. W., & Schweingruber, H. A. (2008). *Ready, set, science!: Putting research to work in K-8 science classrooms*. Board on Science Education, Center for Education, Division of Behavioral and Social Sciences and Education. Washington, DC: National Academies Press.

Miller, L., Chang, C., Wang, S., Beir, M., & Klisch, Y. (2011). Learning and motivational impacts of a multimedia science game. *Computers and Education, 57*, 1425–1433.

Mohr-Schroeder, M., Bush, S. B., & Jackson, C. (2018). K12 STEM education: Why does it matter and where are we now? *Teachers College Record*. Retrieved February 3, 2018, from http://www.tcrecord.org ID Number: 22288.

Mooney, M. A., & Laubach, T. A. (2002). Adventure engineering: A design centered, inquiry-based approach to middle grade science and mathematics education. *Journal of Engineering Education, 91*(3), 309–318.

Moore, T. J., Johnson, C. C., Peters-Burton, E. E., & Guzey, S. S. (2016). The need for a STEM road map. In C. C. Johnson, E. E. Peters-Burton, & T. J. Moore (Eds.), *Stem road map: A framework for integrated STEM education*. New York, NY: Routledge.

National Audit Office. (2018). *Delivering STEM (science, technology, engineering and mathematics) skills for the economy*. Victoria and London: National Audit Press Office.

National Governors Association. (2010). *Common core state standards*. Washington, DC: Author.

National Research Council. (2012). *A framework for K-12 science education: Practices, crosscutting concepts, and core ideas*. Washington, DC: National Academies Press.

National Science and Technology Council. (2018). *Charting a course for success: America's strategy for STEM education: A report by the Committee on STEM Education of the National Science and Technology Council*. Retrieved from https://www.whitehouse.gov/wp-content/uploads/2018/12/STEM-Education-Strategic-Plan-2018.pdf

Navracsics, T. (2017). *Why STEM subjects and democratic citizenship go together.* Retrieved from https://ec.europa.eu/commission/commissioners/2014-2019/navracsics/announcements/why-stem-subjects-and-democratic-citizenship-go-together_en

Newman, J. L., Dantzler, J., & Coleman, A. N. (2015). Science in action: How middle school students are changing their world through STEM service-learning projects. *Theory into Practice, 54*(1), 47–54.

NGSS Lead States. (2013). *Next generation science standards: For states, by states.* Washington, DC: National Academies Press.

Nugent, G., Barker, B., Welch, G., Grandgenett, N., Wu, C., & Nelson, C. (2015). A model of factors contributing to STEM learning and career orientation. *International Journal of Science Education, 37*(7), 1067.

Office of the Chief Scientist. (2014). *Science, technology, engineering and mathematics: Australia's future.* Canberra: Australian Government.

Ogle, J. P., Hyllegard, K. H., Rambo-Hernandez, K., & Park, J. (2017). Building middle school girls' self-efficacy, knowledge, and interest in math and science through the integration of fashion and STEM. *Journal of Family & Consumer Sciences, 109*(4), 33.

Paris, D. (2012). Culturally sustaining pedagogy: A needed change in stance, terminology, and practice. *Educational Researcher, 41*(3), 93–97.

Peters-Burton, E., Lynch, S. J., Behrend, T. S., & Means, B. B. (2014). Inclusive STEM high school design: 10 critical components. *Theory into Practice*, (1), 64.

Project Lead the Way. (2019). *PLTW, state by state.* Retrieved from https://www.pltw.org/about-us/pltw-state-presence.

Redmond, A., Thomas, J., High, K., Scott, M., Jordan, P., & Dockers, J. (2011). Enriching science and math through engineering. *School Science and Mathematics, 111*(8), 399–408.

Rihtarsic, D., Avsec, S., & Kocijancic, S. (2016). Experiential learning of electronics subject matter in middle school robotics courses. *International Journal of Technology and Design Education*, (2), 205.

Roehrig, G. H., Moore, T. J., Wang, H., & Park, M. S. (2012). Is adding the E enough? investigating the impact of K-12 engineering standards on the implementation of STEM integration. *School Science and Mathematics, 112*(1), 31–44.

Saavedra, R. A., & Opfer, V. D. (2012). Learning 21st-century skills requires 21st-century teaching. *Phi Delta Kappan, 94*(2), 8–13.

Sanders, M. (2009). Integrative STEM education: Primer. *The Technology Teacher, 68*(4), 20–26.

Schroeder, C., Scott, T., Tolson, H., Huang, T-Y, & Lee, Y-H. (2007). A meta-analysis of national research: Effects of teaching strategies on student achievement in science in the United States. *Journal of Research and Science Teaching, 44*(10), 1436–1460.

Scott, C. (2012). An investigation of science, technology, engineering and mathematics (STEM) focused high schools in the US. *Journal of STEM Education: Innovations & Research, 13*(5).

Shaughnessy, J. M. (2013). By way of introduction: Mathematics in a STEM context. *Mathematics Teaching in the Middle School, 18*(6), 324.

Stinson, K., Harkness, S. S., Meyer, H., & Stallworth, J. (2009). Mathematics and science integration: Models and characterizations. *School Science and Mathematics, 109*(3), 153–161.

Stohlmann, M., Moore, T. J., McClelland, J., & Roehrig, G. H. (2011). Impressions of a middle grades STEM integration program: Educators share lessons learned from the implementation of a middle grades STEM curriculum model. *Middle School Journal, 43*(1), 32–40.

Subotnik, R. F., Tai, R. H., Rickoff, R., & Almarode, J. (2009). Specialized public high schools of science, mathematics, and technology and the STEM pipeline: What do we know now and what will we know in 5 years? *Roeper Review, 32*(1), 7–16.

Tai, R. H. (2012). *An examination of the research literature on Project Lead the Way.* Retrieved from http://citeseerx.ist.psu.edu/viewdoc/download?doi=10.1.1.361.548&rep=rep1&type=pdf

Timms, M., Moyle, K., Weldon, P., & Mitchell, P. (2018). *Challenges in STEM; earning in Australian schools: Literature and policy review.* Australian Council For Educational Research.

Tran, N. A., & Nathan, M. J. (2010). Pre-college engineering studies: An investigation of the relationship between pre-college engineering studies and student achievement in science and mathematics. *Journal of Engineering Education, 99*(2), 143–157.

Treacy, P., & O'Donoghue, J. (2014). Authentic Integration: A model for integrating mathematics and science in the classroom. *International Journal of Mathematical Education in Science and Technology, 45*(5), 703–718.

Valkanova, Y., & Watts, M. 2007. Digital story telling in a science classroom: Reflective self-learning (RSL) in action. *Early Child Development and Care, 177,* 793–807.

Van Overschelde, J. P. (2013). Project Lead the Way students more prepared for higher education. *American Journal of Engineering Education, 4*(1), 1–12.

Weinberg, A. E., & Sample McMeeking, L. B. (2017). Toward meaningful interdisciplinary education: High school teachers' views of mathematics and science integration. *School Science and Mathematics, 117*(5), 204–213.

Wiswall, M., Stiefel, L., Schwartz, A. E., & Boccardo, J. (2014). Does attending a STEM high school improve student performance? Evidence from New York City. *Economics of Education Review, 40,* 93–105.

Yasin, R., Amin, L., & Hin, K. (2018). Teaching & learning of 21st century biotechnology in secondary school additional science. *Teaching Science, 64*(3), 27–36.

11

CONSIDERING STEM FOR LEARNERS WITH DISABILITIES AND OTHER DIVERSE NEEDS

James D. Basham, Matthew T. Marino,
Cassandra L. Hunt and Kyounggun Han

Introduction

The first topical issue on STEM education in the field of special education emerged a decade ago. Published in the *Journal of Special Education Technology* (*JSET*), the issue recognized the importance of an integrated, transdisciplinary view of STEM education that focused on all learners. Within this perspective, learners across varied levels of academic, social-emotional, and other life domains could be provided with high-quality integrated STEM instruction. Basham and Marino (2010) identified the need to develop an educational structure that prepared all learners for citizenry in a society that was global, rapidly evolving, and pluralistic.

The World Economic Forum (WEF) (2016) recently highlighted the emerging Fourth Industrial Revolution and concurrent need for STEM education. This revolution is buttressed by the continual and rapid iteration of new technologies in combination with increased interdisciplinary research and development. According to Schwab (2016), globally there will be an integration of the physical, digital, and biological worlds. For example, day-to-day future existence will be an emergence of interdisciplinary innovations such as artificial intelligence, robotics, the Internet of Things, nanotechnology, information technology, biotechnology, and materials science. These coming changes will impact nearly all aspects of human life.

The Fourth Industrial Revolution requires a citizenship that is prepared for an undetermined, continually evolving, and potentially disruptive future (Schwab, 2016). Serving as a presage across the globe, countries have begun developing policies and infrastructure to support impending societal challenges. According to the WEF (2016), Bahrain, Brazil, China, Denmark, India, Japan, Rwanda, State of Maharashtra, State of Andhra Pradesh, United Arab Emirates, United Kingdom, and the United States currently have, or are planning, policies to prepare for the challenges of modernity. The global education system needs to develop a cohesive interdisciplinary framework so all learners, including those with disabilities, have the necessary knowledge and skills for success in the Fourth Industrial Revolution. According to the WEF (2016) and Schwab (2016, 2018), future learners will require foundational knowledge, technical and ethical understandings, as well as intrapersonal and interpersonal skills that will serve as the fundamental building blocks for global citizenry in a continuously evolving world.

For all learners, especially those with disabilities, this modernized perspective of education challenges the traditions of those who serve them. For instance, the field of special education traditionally views STEM across siloed content areas that are taught and assessed using conventional education methods such as textbook reading followed by lectured explanation. Within this approach, learners who have disabilities and other low-performing students are supported using interventions to catch up with their "average" learning peers. While interventions are being used to close the deficiency gap, the gap itself is widening because the "average" learners are also advancing, usually at a more rapid pace. Often students with disabilities cannot catch up (Reynolds & Shaywitz, 2009). This is not to question the necessity of providing students with disabilities with extra support, but to question how and what support might be provided.

Success is often attributed to special education when a student maintains, rather than declines, on test performance when compared to their grade level peers without disabilities (Office of Special Education Programs; OSEP, 2017). Additionally, an increasing number of emerging studies show an association with the current model of special education and unexpected side-effects. For instance, after controlling for multiple factors associated with low-performance, Chesmore, Ou, and Reynolds (2016) found that placement in special education associated with fewer years of education and greater rates of incarceration, depression, and drug misuse.

This unfortunate reality is the result of misunderstanding among STEM professionals and people with disabilities. For example, individuals with autism have difficulties with social communication and restrictive behavior that can vary along a continuum from mild to severe. Many of these individuals are underutilized members of the workforce who express attributes which make them uniquely qualified for STEM careers. These include: (1) sustained, hypersensitive attention to detail; (2) the ability to disassociate themselves from emotional attachment when completing tasks; (3) repetitive, systematic procedural knowledge and skills; and (4) the ability to conceptualize outcomes and solutions to complex STEM problems (White & Mitchel, 2013). Given these attributes, high-functioning individuals with autism have the potential to flourish in critical STEM careers such as computer science, data science, electrical engineering, and software development (National Science & Technology Council, 2018).

This chapter describes interdisciplinary STEM research related to the challenges and attributes of individuals with disabilities at the K-12 and postsecondary levels. The chapter begins with a discussion of Universal Design for Learning as a means to promote equity during instruction and assessment. This is followed with research at the K-12 level. Finally, research at the postsecondary level is presented. It is important to note that strategies for students with disabilities have also been shown to be beneficial to other students who may be considered at-risk.

Universal Design for Learning: A Foundation for Equity Driven STEM

Persons with disabilities have been underrepresented in the STEM fields for many years (Dunn, Rabren, Taylor, & Dotson, 2012; Leddy, 2010). Reasons for this include low expectations for students with disabilities, limited exposure to prerequisite courses, lack of role models, lack of mentoring experiences, and lack of access to individualized supports (Marino, 2010; National Science & Technology Council, 2018). Universal Design for Learning (UDL) is a framework for the design and implementation of learning environments (i.e., physical and digital) that meet the need of all learners by proactively circumventing barriers in the learning process (Rappolt-Schlichtmann, Daley, & Rose, 2012). This is accomplished through careful consideration of the broad range of needs, motivations, and strengths across all learners, including traditionally marginalized populations such as English language learners, those with disabilities, and students with diverse cultural backgrounds.

Different from a single approach or strategy, UDL is a goal-driven design framework that foundationally integrates the design of learning environments and experiences for all learners. From an instructional perspective, UDL frames instruction around three guiding principles: (a) multiple means of engagement (i.e., considering how to engage students through a variety of pathways), (b) multiple means of representation (i.e., providing content through multiple methods), and

(c) multiple means of action and expression (i.e., providing opportunities for students to demonstrate their understanding in multiple ways) (CAST, 2018). Each principle is further delineated by guidelines and subsequent checkpoints (see http://udlguidelines.cast.org). To support further understanding on research and implementation around UDL, a number of organizations recently launched a platform, Learning Designed, that includes resources for supporting growth in the field (https://www.learningdesigned.org).

The Future of STEM for Learners With Disabilities

An integrated approach to STEM education is critical to promote the success of individuals with disabilities in the 21st century (Basham & Marino, 2010). According to Sanders (2009), integrative approaches are defined as "approaches that explore teaching and learning between/among any two or more of the STEM subject areas, and/or between STEM subjects and one or more other school subjects" (p. 21). For example, technology education professionals have developed technology design projects to provide a context in which students can apply understandings they have developed in science, mathematics, and technology (Lewis, 2006). The engineering education profession has employed engineering design as a means of integrating STEM subjects (Apedoe, Reynolds, Ellefson, & Schunn, 2008). Additionally, Cantrell, Pekca, and Ahmad (2006) concluded that engaging students in engineering curriculum activities may diminish achievement gaps in science for some student populations (e.g., low-achieving students, minority students, students with disabilities). The educators in science education have supported the idea of integration through design-based learning (Mehalik, Doppelt, & Schuun, 2008). Overall, integrated approaches among STEM content areas can lead to advanced learning opportunities and outcomes for students with disabilities.

Becker and Park (2011) conducted a meta-analysis to synthesize the findings from existing research on the effects of integrative approaches among STEM subjects on students' learning. The meta-analysis was intended to facilitate a greater understanding of the effects of integrative approaches among STEM subjects. The authors had four primary research questions: (1) What is the effect of an integrative approach among STEM subjects? (2) How does the effect of integrative approaches among STEM subjects differ by grade levels? (3) What type of integrative approaches are more likely than others to lead to the improvement of student achievement? (4) What achievement score among STEM subjects is most improved through integrative approaches? With respect to the grade levels, the effects of integrative approaches showed the largest effect size at the elementary school level and the smallest effect size at the college level. Regarding the types of integration, STEM, the integration of four subjects, presented the largest effect size, and E-M and M-S-T showed the smallest effect size. In addition, concerning the achievement through integrative approaches, STEM achievement showed the highest effect size and mathematics achievement showed the smallest effect size. The results of this meta-analysis reveal that integrative approaches among STEM subjects have positive effects on the students' learning.

These effects have been identified across individual content areas as well. For example, integrative efforts in engineering education show that the engineering design process not only motivates students' learning in mathematics and science but also are beneficial to a variety of students with different characteristics. Mathematics educators have provided evidence that integrative approaches among STEM subjects are effective and necessary for success in mathematics (Elliott, Oty, McArthur, & Clark, 2001; Judson & Sawada, 2000). Integration of mathematics with science, technology, and engineering (STE) provides students with the context in which they can make meaningful connections between mathematics and STE subjects. Mathematics is already embedded in STE, and integrative approaches could bridge abstract concepts in mathematics to practices in STE.

STEM Research in the K-12 Special Education Literature

International policy guidelines call for an increased focus on crosscutting concepts, science and engineering practices, and disciplinary core ideas (e.g., Australian Council for Research in Education, 2018; Hoyle, 2016). Each dimension is designed to enhance inquiry-based learning. For example, the Next Generation Science Standards (2013) state, "students will develop an in-depth understanding of content and develop key skills—communication, collaboration, inquiry, problem solving, and flexibility—that will serve them throughout their educational and professional lives." However, these cognitive and interpersonal skills can be challenging for students with disabilities and other executive function deficits (Koch, 2016). Executive functions are defined as the process of physical, cognitive, and emotional self-control and self-regulation necessary to maintain an effective goal-directed behavior (Torske, Nærland, Øie, Stenberg, & Andreassen, 2018). They include several components such as working memory, flexibility, emotional control, initiation, planning, organization, and self-control (Diamond, 2013).

Executive dysfunction is often associated with neurologic impairments related to the medial frontal cortex (Hsuan-Chen, White, Rees, & Burgess, 2018; Miyake & Friedman, 2012). While this presents a clear challenge to effective STEM learning and assessment, executive function can be scaffolded. For example, smartphones can provide alerts for students to initiate tasks, transition to a new task, or contact a teammate (Koch, 2016). This can assist students while solving ill-structured problems that lack explicit instructions or rule sets (White, 2013).

Early STEM research related to students with disabilities focused on the types of inquiry approaches necessary to maximize student engagement and learning outcomes. For example, Scruggs and Mastropieri (2007), in an examination of constructed versus instructed learning, found strengths and limitations to each approach. They highlighted the need for student engagement, frequent progress monitoring, direct questions, and explicit instruction including step-by-step directions when necessary. In addition, they identified depth over breadth of learning with an emphasis on comprehension over factual recall. Finally, they noted the importance of coached elaborations (i.e., asking a series of leading questions) and mnemonic instruction (e.g., keyword method) as a means to enhance learning for students with disabilities. Their research extended more than two decades and influenced the field immeasurably.

Marino (2009) found the instructional supports Mastropieri and Scruggs identified could be administered using technology. In a study involving 1153 students across 62 inclusive (i.e., containing both general education and special education students) middle school science classrooms, students with disabilities were able to personalize instruction and benefit from cognitive tools embedded in their STEM curriculum at a rate more than double that of their general education peers. Basham, Hall, Carter, and Stahl (2016) found developing personalized learning experiences required a new educational architecture that values individual growth across a variety of domains. A personalized learning education system integrates individual, collaborative, face-to-face, as well as digital experiences to support holistically designed experiences for all learners (Basham, Stahl, Hall, & Carter, 2017). These personalized environments benefit students with and without disabilities by allowing students to learn at their own pace.

Later work by Marino, Black, Hayes, and Beecher (2010) identified significant gender-related discrepancies in student performance on traditional paper-based STEM assessments. Based on this finding, Marino, Basham, and Beecher (2011) examined video games as an alternative means to more accurately assess STEM performance. STEM education in many classrooms includes digitally based activities such as simulations and virtual laboratories. When such technologies are used during STEM assessments, a major challenge is to ensure the assessments are accessible so all students can show what they know and can do (Haertel et al., 2010; Hansen, Liu, Rogat, Hakkinen, & Darrah, 2016). In addition to implementing principles of UDL in assessment contexts, reasonable accommodations must be afforded to ensure accessibility. Accommodations can include extended time, alternate locations, and/or assistive technologies such as text-to-speech (Israel, Marino, Delisio, & Serianni, 2014).

All learners require meaningful STEM assessments. Research across the globe has demonstrated that preparation for a STEM career involves more than preparing students to take an exam. Learners need 21st-century knowledge and skills including authentic and dynamic problem solving, collaboration, executive functioning, and critical analysis skills (Schwab, 2016, 2018). Research in STEM education for students with disabilities often overlooks positive findings in immersive environments when students are unable to transfer their knowledge to traditional assessments such as paper-based multiple-choice tests (Marino et al., 2014). For example, a student may be able to complete every level of a STEM video game because she or he understands the content, but the student is unable to replicate the performance on a paper-based exam because of a reading (i.e., dyslexia) or writing (i.e., dysgraphia) disability. This perspective is antiquated and fails to recognize the reliability and validity technology provides.

STEM and Postsecondary Education for Learners With Disabilities

Research suggests students' experiences during the first two years of college are most critical for successful persistence in STEM courses (Light & Micari, 2013). Unfortunately, universities often present undergraduates with an array of institutional barriers that can be difficult to circumvent (Bettencourt, Kimball, & Wells, 2018; National Academy of Engineering, 2014). Introductory STEM courses are often taught in large lecture halls with more than 100 students. The students then participate in smaller lab experiences, where they are supposed to receive more personalized instruction. However, these labs are often staffed by graduate assistants who have little to no formal teacher training (Committee on Research Universities Board on Higher Education and Workforce Policy and Global Affairs, 2012). Language barriers add to the complexity as graduate assistants, who may be English learners, try to translate their understanding of the content to another language. The results can be disheartening for students, leaving them disenfranchised with STEM before they have an opportunity to gain success. As a result, only 40% of the students who intend to major in STEM careers persist until graduation as a result of the current education model (President's Council of Advisors on Science and Technology, 2012).

Persons with disabilities, along with women and members of ethnic and racial minority groups, are underrepresented in STEM across postsecondary and workforce settings (Burrelli & Falkenheim, 2011; National Science Foundation, 2013). There are three primary benefits to focusing on students with disabilities. First, they are widely recognized as experiencing the most significant challenges in postsecondary environments (Madaus et al., 2013). Second, they provide an ample and easily accessible population to target instruction. Third, STEM-related interventions that are efficacious for students with disabilities are also highly effective for other traditionally marginalized groups (Marino et al., 2010).

Traditional institutional reform efforts focus on system-level changes in instructor behaviors and supports. Several of these initiatives have indicated positive results. For example, Martin and colleagues (2011) and Stinson, Elliot, and Easton (2014) reported promising recruiting and retention practices for increasing the participation of students in STEM majors. Professional development programs for faculty and other service providers also show positive outcomes (Moon, Utschig, Todd, & Bozzorg, 2011; Soldner, Rowan-Kenyon, Inkelas, Garvey, & Robbins, 2012; Wei et al., 2014). Examples include SciTrain University programs developed in collaboration with the Center for Assistive Technology and Environmental Access and Georgia Tech. Unfortunately, current institutional reform efforts have not had an immediate wide-scale impact on the attrition rate of STEM majors (Beasley & Fischer, 2012; Chen, 2013; Johnson, 2012).

The STEM Persistence Framework by Graham, Frederick, Byars-Winston, Hunter, and Handelsman (2013) is a model focused on developing student agency, confidence, and self-efficacy. These constructs increase both confidence and motivation. Key elements of the framework include early research experiences, active learning strategies, and participation in learning communities. This led to increases in self-identification as a scientist and academic success (Graham et al., 2013). Another promising model is the BreakThru Theory of Change (Gregg, Chang, & Todd, 2012). BreakThru is a powerful learning community that connects students with disabilities and mentors in a unique way to promote universal learning and accessibility toward STEM-based degrees. BreakThru is a blended learning community that bridges the gap between the classroom and the virtual world to engage students in STEM-based curricula and resources. These projects increased students' motivation, persistence, and perceptions of themselves as scientists.

Other research identified effective accommodations that increase the accessibility of STEM content (e.g., Access STEM, 2008; Dunn et al., 2012; Graves, Asunda, Plant, & Goad, 2011; Leddy, 2010; Supalo, Isaacson, & Lombardi, 2014). Burgstahler and colleagues (2009, 2011) developed Do-IT and Access Technology Center, which supports transition from high school to college to careers for students with disabilities. DO-IT Scholars are college-bound high school students who face significant challenges in pursuing postsecondary studies and careers as a result of their disabilities. A longitudinal study of the program indicated college career preparation programs, mentoring, and internships were positively correlated with academic and employment outcomes. Importantly, the programs mentioned here are rooted in UDL principles.

Researchers have recently begun a second approach; focus on short-term individual-level interventions. For example, Izzo, Murray, Priest, and McArrell (2011) reported learning communities for students who were interested in pursuing STEM degrees showed promise for enhancing self-advocacy and career development skills. Another example with significant empirical support by Wolfe and Lee (2007) found positive outcomes when an automated pedagogical agent was personalized for each student. Gregg et al. (2012) suggested key factors essential to the success of their model Improving Undergraduate STEM Education were: virtual access, social networking tools, e-mentoring, persistence incentives, case-based reasoning resources, and universal design principles. These principles are supported by other research (e.g., Stamp, Banerjee, & Brown, 2014; Takahashi, Uyehara, Park, Roberts, & Stodden, 2018).

Considerations for the Future

The WEF (2016) recently implored leaders from across the globe to develop infrastructure for supporting the development of a future-focused society as we enter the Fourth Industrial Revolution. The coming revolution is directly associated with changes that will spur rapid and often disruptive innovation across an interdisciplinary and continually connected society. Schwab (2016) identified ongoing and rapid iteration across traditional and emergent industries as key business drivers in the coming age. These changes have the potential to extend the divide between those who can thrive in a dynamic and pluralistic global society and those who cannot (Harari, 2018).

There is little doubt that all learners, including those with learning differences and disabilities, require a future-focused education. A primary component of this education is the knowledge and skills associated with integrated STEM. Educators must design curricula, learning environments, and learner experiences that support global citizens who are prepared to work and thrive in the Fourth Industrial Revolution. Success in the future will require a variety of technical and ethical foundations along with diverse intrapersonal (e.g., executive functioning, complex problem solving, systems thinking) and interpersonal skills (e.g., interdisciplinary understanding, effective communication, collaboration). The UDL framework provides a foundation for developing these integrated STEM environments. Concurrently, it supports the design of dynamic learning challenges that lead to self-determination and lifelong participation in a global society.

Researchers, education leaders, and policymakers must overcome barriers associated with the current education system, shifting the focus from average learners to all learners. This consideration places value on the learner variability associated with each learner, rather than the learning of a few. To actualize this vision, future research should enhance the systematic integration of STEM content by developing educational systems, environments, and experiences that allow personalized learning pathways. Each of these environments and experiences should be reinforced by research-driven measurement models that enable personalized, holistic growth across cognitive and behavioral domains.

Conclusion

There is a clear need to promote interdisciplinary education and participation in the STEM workforce as we enter the Fourth Industrial Revolution. Individuals with disabilities can make a valuable contribution to the global STEM community. Scientists like Stephen Hawking, Temple Grandin, Thomas Edison, and Albert Einstein serve as examples. However, low expectations for students with disabilities, limited exposure to prerequisite courses, lack of role models, lack of mentoring experiences, and lack of access to individualized supports often lead to fewer years of education and greater rates of incarceration, depression, and drug misuse. This chapter provided research supporting the end of this cycle. It described current interdisciplinary STEM research at the K-12 and postsecondary levels. Research indicates UDL, in concert with technology, can lead to personalized learning experiences that have a positive impact on STEM learning outcomes. The chapter highlighted executive function as a critical area that can be supported and enhanced through the use of technology. In addition, it identified the need to consider a broader range of assessment practices when determining what students know and can do when solving interdisciplinary STEM challenges.

References

AccessSTEM. (2008). *The alliance for access to science, technology, engineering, and mathematics.* Retrieved from https://www.washington.edu/doit/programs/accessstem/accommodations

Apedoe, X. S., Reynolds, B., Ellefson, M. R., & Schunn, C. D. (2008). Bringing engineering design into high school science classrooms: The heating/cooling unit. *Journal of Science Education and Technology, 17*(5), 454–465.

Australian Council for Educational Research. (2018). *Challenges in STEM learning in Australian schools.* Retrieved from https://research.acer.edu.au/cgi/viewcontent.cgi?article=1028&context=policy_analysis_misc

Basham, J. D., Hall, T. E., Carter, Jr. R. A., & Stahl, W. M. (2016). An operationalized understanding of personalized learning. *Journal of Special Education Technology, 31*(3), 126–136.

Basham, J. D., & Marino, M. T. (2010). Introduction to the topical Issue: Shaping STEM education for all students. *Journal of Special Education Technology, 25*(3), 1–2. doi:10.1177/016264341002500301.

Basham, J. D., Stahl, S., Hall, T., & Carter, Jr. R. A. (2017). Establishing a student-centered environment to support all learners. In *Handbook of research on classroom diversity and inclusive education practice* (pp. 155–182). Hershey, PA: IGI Global.

Beasley, M. A., & Fischer, M. J. (2012). Why they leave: The impact of stereotype threat on the attrition of women and minorities from science, math and engineering majors. *Social Psychology of Education, 15*(4), 427–448.

Becker, K., & Park, K. (2011). Effects of integrative approaches among science, technology, engineering, and mathematics (STEM) subjects on students' learning: A preliminary meta-analysis. *Journal of STEM Education: Innovations and Research; Auburn, 12*(5/6), 23–37.

Bettencourt, G. M., Kimball, E., & Wells, R. S. (2018). Disability in postsecondary STEM learning environments: What faculty focus groups reveal about definitions and obstacles to effective support. *Journal of Postsecondary Education & Disability, 31*(4), 383–396.

Burgstahler, S., & Chang, C. (2009). Promising interventions for promoting STEM fields to students who have disabilities. *Review of Disability Studies: An International Journal, 5*(2), 29–47.

Burgstahler, S., Moore, & Crawford, L. (2011). *Report of the AccessSTEM/AccessComputing/DO-IT longitudinal tracking study (ALTS)*. Seattle: DO-IT, University of Washington.

Burrelli, J. S., & Falkenheim, J. C. (2011). *Diversity in the federal science and engineering workforce*. Washington, DC: National Science Foundation, Directorate for the Social, Behavioral, and Economic Sciences (NSF 11–303).

Cantrell, P., Pekca, G., & Ahmad, I. (2006). The effects of engineering modules on student learning in middle school science classrooms. *Journal of Engineering Education, 95*(4), 301–309.

CAST. (2018). *Universal design for learning guidelines version 2.1*. Wakefield, MA: Author.

Chen, X. (2013). *STEM attrition: College students' paths into and out of STEM fields*. National Center for Education Statistics, Institute of Education Sciences. Retrieved from https://nces.ed.gov/pubs2014/2014001rev.pdf

Chesmore, A., Ou, S., & Reynolds, A. (2016). Childhood placement in special education and adult well-being. *The Journal of Special Education, 50*(2), 109–120.

Committee on Research Universities Board on Higher Education and Workforce Policy and Global Affairs. (2012). *Research universities and the future of America: Ten breakthrough actions vital to our nation's prosperity and security*. Washington, DC: National Academies Press.

Diamond, A. (2013). Executive functions. *Annual Review of Psychology, 64,* 135–168. doi:10.1146/annurev-psych-113011-143750

Dunn, C., Rabren, K. S., Taylor, S. L., & Dotson, C. K. (2012). Assisting students with high-incidence disabilities to pursue careers in science, technology, engineering, and mathematics. *Intervention in School and Clinic, 48*(1), 47–54. doi:10.1177/1053451212443151

Elliott, B., Oty, K., McArthur, J., & Clark, B. (2001). The effect of an interdisciplinary algebra/science course on students' problem solving skills, critical thinking skills and attitudes towards mathematics. *International Journal of Mathematical Education in Science and Technology, 32*(6), 811–816.

Graham, M. J., Frederick, J., Byars-Winston, A., Hunter, A., & Handelsman, J. (2013). Increasing persistence of college students in STEM. *Science, 341,* 1455–1456.

Graves, L., Asunda, P. A., Plant, S. J., & Goad, C. (2011). Asynchronous online access as an accommodation on students with learning disabilities and/or attention-deficit hyperactivity disorders in postsecondary STEM courses. *Journal of Postsecondary Education and Disability, 24*(4), 317–330.

Gregg, N., Chang, Y., & Todd, R. (2012). Social media, avatars, and virtual worlds: Reimagine an inclusive learning environment for adolescents and adults with literacy barriers. *Procedia Computer Science, 14,* 336–342.

Haertel, G. D., DeBarger, A., Cheng, B., Blackorby, J., Javitz, H., Ructtinger, L., . . . Hansen, E. G. (2010). *Using evidence-centered design and universal design for learning to design science assessment tasks for students with disabilities* (Assessment for Students with Disabilities Technical Report 1). San Francisco, CA: SRI International.

Hansen, E. G., Liu, L., Rogat, A., Hakkinen, M. T., & Darrah, M. A. (2016). Designing innovative science assessments that are accessible for students who are blind. *Journal of Blindness Innovation and Research, 6,* 1–11. doi:10.5241/6-91

Harari, Y. N. (2018). *21 Lessons for the 21st century*. New York: Random House.

Hoyle, P. (2016). *Must try harder: An evaluation of the UK government's policy directions in STEM education*. Retrieved from https://research.acer.edu.au/cgi/viewcontent.cgi?article=1280&context=research_conference

Hsuan-Chen, W., White, S., Rees, G., & Burgess, P. U. (2018). Executive function in high-functioning autism: Decision-making consistency as a characteristic gambling behavior. *Cortex, 107,* 21–36.

Israel, M., Marino, M. T., Delisio, L., & Serianni, B. (2014). *Supporting content learning through technology for K-12 students with disabilities (Document No. IC-10)*. Retrieved from University of Florida, Collaboration for Effective Educator, Development, Accountability, and Reform Center (CEEDAR). Retrieved from http://ceedar.education.ufl.edu/tools/innovation-configurations/

Izzo, M. V., Murray, A., Priest, S., & McArrell, B. (2011). Using student learning communities to recruit STEM students with disabilities. *Journal of Postsecondary Education and Disability, 24*(4), 301–316.

Johnson, C. C. (2012). Implementation of STEM education policy: Challenges, progress and lessons learned. *School Science and Mathematics, 112*(1), 45–55.

Judson, E., & Sawada, D. (2000). Examining the effects of a reformed junior high school science class on students' math achievement. *School Science and Mathematics, 100*(8), 419–425.

Koch, A. (2016). *Project iCAN: An analysis of landmark college model of supports* (PhD dissertation). College of Education and Human Performance, Department of Child, Family, and Community Sciences. University of Central Florida.

Leddy, M. H. (2010). Technology to advance high school and undergraduate students in science, technology, engineering, and mathematics. *Journal of Special Education Technology, 25*(3), 3–8.

Lewis, T. (2006). Design and inquiry: Bases for an accommodation between science and technology education in the curriculum? *Journal of Research in Science Teaching, 43*(3), 255–281.

Light, G., & Micari, M. (2013). *Making scientists: Six principles for effective college teaching*. Cambridge, MA: Harvard University Press.

Madaus, J. W., Gelbar, N. W., Dukes, L. L., Faggella-Luby, M. N., Lalor, A. R., & Kowitt, J. (2013). Thirty-five years of transition: A review of CDTEI Issues from 1978–2012. *Career Development and Transition for Exceptional Individuals, 36*, 7–14.

Marino, M. T. (2009). Understanding how adolescents with reading difficulties utilize technology-based tools. *Exceptionality, 17*(2), 88–102.

Marino, M. T. (2010). Defining a technology research agenda for elementary and secondary students with learning and other high incidence disabilities in inclusive science classrooms. *Journal of Special Education Technology, 25*(1), 1–28.

Marino, M. T., Basham, J. D., & Beecher, C. C. (2011). Using video games as an alternative science assessment for students with disabilities and at-risk learners. *Science Scope, 34*(5), 36–41.

Marino, M. T., Black, A., Hayes, M., & Beecher, C. C. (2010). An analysis of factors that affect struggling readers' comprehension during a technology-enhanced STEM astronomy curriculum. *Journal of Special Education Technology, 25*(3), 35–48.

Marino, M. T., Gotch, C. M., Israel, M., Vasquez III, E., Basham, J. D., & Becht, K. (2014). UDL in the middle school science classroom: Can video games and alternative text heighten engagement and learning for students with learning disabilities?. *Learning Disability Quarterly, 37*(2), 87–99.

Martin, J. K., Stumbo, N. J., Martin, L. G., Collins, K. D., Hedrick, B. N., Nordstrom, D., & Peterson, M. (2011). Recruitment of students with disabilities: Exploration of science, technology, engineering, and mathematics. *Journal of Postsecondary Education and Disability, 24*(4), 285–299.

Mehalik, M. M., Doppelt, Y., & Schuun, C. D. (2008). Middle-school science through design based learning versus scripted inquiry: Better overall science concept learning and equity gap reduction. *Journal of Engineering Education, 97*(1), 71–85.

Miyake, A., & Friedman, N. P. (2012). The nature and organization of individual differences in executive functions: Four general conclusions. *Current Directions in Psychological Science, 21*(1), 8–14. doi:10.1177/09637 21411429458

Moon, N. W., Utschig, T. T., Todd, R. L., & Bozzorg, A. (2011). Evaluation of programmatic interventions to improve postsecondary STEM education for students with disabilities: Findings from SciTrain University. *Journal of Postsecondary Education and Disability, 24*, 331–349.

National Academy of Engineering. (2014). *Surmounting the barriers: Ethnic diversity in engineering education: Summary of a workshop*. Washington, DC: National Academies Press.

National Science Foundation, National Center for Science and Engineering Statistics. (2013). *Scientists and Engineers Statistical Data System (SESTAT)*. Retrieved from http://www.nsf.gov/statistics/sestat/

National Science and Technology Council. (2018). *Charting a course for success: America's strategy for STEM education*. Retrieved from https://www.whitehouse.gov/wp-content/uploads/2018/12/STEM-Education-Strategic-Plan-2018.pdf

NGSS Lead States. (2013). *Next generation science standards: For states, by states*. Washington, DC: The National Academies Press.

Office of Special Education Programs. (2017). *38th annual report to Congress on the implementation of the Individuals With Disabilities Education Act, 2016; 2017 ASI 4944-4.*

President's Council of Advisors on Science and Technology (PCAST). (2012). *Engage to excel: Producing one million additional college graduates with degrees in science, technology, engineering and mathematics*. Retrieved January 26, 2019 from, https://obamawhitehouse.archives.gov/sites/default/files/microsites/ostp/pcast-engage-to-excel-final_2-25-12.pdf

Rappolt-Schlichtmann, G., Daley, S. G., & Rose, T. L. (2012). *A research reader in universal design for learning*. Boston: Harvard Education Press.

Reynolds, C. R., & Shaywitz, S. E. (2009). Response to intervention: Ready or not? Or, from wait-to-fail to watch-them-fail. *School Psychology Quarterly, 24*(2), 130. doi:10.1037/a0016158.

Sanders, M. (2009). STEM, STEM education, STEM mania. *Technology Teacher, 68*(4), 20–26.

Schwab, K. (2016). *The fourth industrial revolution*. New York, NY: Crown Business.

Schwab, K. (2018). *Shaping the fourth industrial revolution*. New York: World Economic Forum.

Scruggs, T. E., & Mastropieri, M. A. (2007). Science learning in special education: The case for constructed versus instructed learning. *Exceptionality, 15*(2), 57–74.

Soldner, M., Rowan-Kenyon, H., Inkelas, K. K., Garvey, J., & Robbins, C. (2012). Supporting students' intentions to persist in STEM disciplines: The role of living-learning programs among other social-cognitive factors. *The Journal of Higher Education, 83*(3), 311–336.

Stamp, L., Banerjee, M., & Brown, F. (2014). Self-advocacy and perceptions of college readiness among students with ADHD. *Journal of Postsecondary Education and Disability, 27*(2).

Stinson, M. S., Elliot, L. B., & Easton, D. (2014). Deaf/hard of hearing and other postsecondary learners' retention of STEM content with tablet computer-based notes. *Journal of Deaf Studies and Deaf Education, 19*(2), 251–269.

Supalo, C., Isaacson, M. D., & Lombardi, M. V. (2014). Making hands-on science learning accessible for students who are blind or have low vision. *Journal of Chemical Education, 92*(2), 195–199.

Takahashi, K., Uyehara, L., Park, H. J., Roberts, K., & Stodden, R. (2018). Internship to improve postsecondary persistence for students with disabilities in the STEM pipeline (practice brief). *Journal of Postsecondary Education & Disability, 31*(2), 179–185.

Torske, T., Nærland, T., Øie, M. G., Stenberg, N., & Andreassen, Ö. A. (2018). Metacognitive aspects of executive function are highly associated with social functioning on parent-rated measures in children with autism spectrum disorder. *Frontiers in Behavioral Neuroscience, 11*, 258. doi:10.3389/fnbeh.2017.00258

Wei, X., Christiano, E. R., Jennifer, W. Y., Blackorby, J., Shattuck, P., & Newman, L. A. (2014). Postsecondary pathways and persistence for STEM versus non-STEM majors: Among college students with an autism spectrum disorder. *Journal of Autism and Developmental Disorders, 44*(5), 1159–1167. doi:10.1007/s10801-013-1978-5.

White, J. L., & Mitchell, S. K. (2013). Career certainty and persisting interest in STEM: An analysis of underrepresented groups. *Journal of Women and Minorities in Science and Engineering, 19*(1). doi:10.1615/JWomen MinorScienEng.2013004825.

White, S. J. (2013). The triple I hypothesis: Taking another('s) perspective on executive dysfunction in autism. *Journal of Autism Development Disorders, 43*, 114–121. doi:10.1007/s10803-012-1550-8

Wolfe, G. L., & Lee, C. (2007). Promising practices for providing alternative media to postsecondary students with print disabilities. *Learning Disabilities Research and Practice, 22*(4), 256–263.

World Economic Forum (WEF). (2016). *The fourth industrial revolution: What it means, how to respond.* Retrieved from https://www.weforum.org/agenda/2016/01/the-fourth-industrial-revolution-what-it-means-and-how-to-respond/

12

INFORMAL STEM PROGRAM LEARNING

Margaret Blanchard, Kristie Gutierrez, Bobby Habig,
Preeti Gupta, and Jennifer Adams

Informal STEM programs can take on different forms and have characteristics that distinguish them from formal STEM educational programs. For instance, informal STEM programs are usually held during out-of-school time hours, typically after school, on weekends, and during the summer (Bell, Lewenstein, Shouse, & Feder, 2009). In the United States, approximately 8.4 million students participate in out-of-school-time (OST) programs each year (Krishnamurthi, Ballard, & Noam, 2014), and there are a variety of OST STEM program formats around the globe (e.g., Banerjee, 2017). Some afterschool programs are school-site based and led by certified teachers with credentials (e.g., Blanchard, Gutierrez, Hoyle, Painter, & Ragan, 2018). Others involve field experiences through travel to museums, zoos, planetariums, and national parks (e.g., Adams, Gupta, & Cotumaccio, 2014). Still others may choose to take a more competitive approach through organizations such as robotics clubs, science fairs, and Science and Math Olympiads (e.g., Sahin, Ayar, & Adiguzel, 2013; Sahin, Gulacar, & Stuessy, 2014).

In contrast to formal STEM settings, informal STEM settings typically need to have a strong engagement portion, because attendance is not compulsory, and the programs are run by facilitators who may or may not have specialized teaching credentials (Barker, Nugent, & Grandgenett, 2014). The overarching goal for most informal STEM programs is not to improve grades or test scores, but rather to "increase involvement and exploration with STEM, decrease anxiety around STEM, and energize motivation" (Krishnamurthi et al., 2014, p. 7).

Informal STEM programs typically are not constrained by a mandated curriculum or local, state, and national mandates, although some countries strongly encourage them (e.g., Banerjee, 2017; NGSS Lead States, 2013). Thus, programs can take on many forms, including STEM clubs, informal STEM competitions (e.g., Science Olympiad, robotics competitions, Future City), youth research internships, and summer camps (Bell et al., 2009; McCreedy & Dierking, 2013). Integrated STEM can range from the interrelationship between two of the content areas or full integration across the STEM sub-fields (Thibaut, Knipprath, Dehaene, & Depaepe, 2018). These experiences are often comprised of "hands-on activity sessions, talks and outreach events, science weeks and ambassador visits" that help connect STEM sub-fields to careers and opportunities in the real world (Banerjee, 2017, p. 2014). This chapter provides an overview of some of the goals, benefits, and types of informal STEM programs, and theoretical underpinnings of some of the related research. The chapter concludes by proposing a conceptual framework for studying informal STEM education programs and recommendations.

Goals for Out-of-School Time

A wide range of goals are often desired in OST programs. These include encouraging students to actively participate in STEM learning activities; demonstrate curiosity about STEM topics, concepts, or practices; develop abilities to engage in STEM investigations; develop skills that are relevant to life or careers; understand the role STEM plays in societal issues; and gain an awareness of STEM professions (Krishnamurthi et al., 2014). These informal STEM education programs can be important vehicles for facilitating awareness, interest, and engagement in STEM courses, majors, and careers, especially for disciplines not typically introduced during students' formal education (Bell et al. 2009; McCreedy & Dierking, 2013; Young, Ortiz, & Young, 2017). Museums, science centers, botanical gardens, and zoos can provide exposure that may help students consider STEM majors and careers beyond the scope of a traditional education (e.g., Adams et al., 2014; Gupta & Siegel, 2008). In many cases, these opportunities provide experiences for females and for members of historically marginalized racial and ethnic groups by facilitating exposure to, and interest in, careers in which these groups have been underrepresented (e.g., Gutierrez, 2016; Hanks et al., 2007; Heo & Myrick, 2009) and thus hold the potential of diversifying the workforce. Indeed, in recent years considerable research on programs in informal settings has concentrated on how and to what extent these programs have impacted participants' awareness, interest, and engagement in STEM majors and careers (e.g., Fadigan & Hammrich, 2004; Habig, Gupta, Levine, & Adams, 2018; McCreedy & Dierking, 2013; Schumacher et al., 2009; Winkleby, Ned, Ahn, Koehler, & Kennedy, 2009).

Benefits of Informal STEM Education

Many benefits of informal STEM education have been identified: increases in STEM subject content knowledge that may result in better student standardized test scores; subtle gains in the STEM achievement gap of historically underrepresented students; intrinsic gains in STEM interest and future career goals; and more internal, personal changes in the self-efficacy, confidence, and behavior choices of students involved (Falk et al., 2016; Gottfried & Williams, 2013; Hartley, 2014; Krishnamurthi et al., 2014).

Types of Informal STEM Programs and Results

In the next sections, we provide an overview of the different types of informal STEM programs and experiences, and their associated benefits. The sections were organized based on whether the informal programs were mainly connected to schools, competitive-focused, community-based, or both school- and community-based.

Informal STEM Connected to Schools

Many schools and districts believe that offering a supplementary afterschool STEM club, in addition to traditional STEM coursework, will help students to be more engaged, learn more content, and help students seriously consider STEM majors in college (Bell et al., 2009). Activities in an afterschool club may range from individual or group activities, conversations and socializing, to tinkering with objects, science hobbies, or reading science fiction/non-fiction books (Maltese & Tai, 2010). Mannion and Coldwell (2008) found that students had greater interest in scientific topics if they were presented in an afterschool STEM club instead of the traditional classroom, even if the topic was not initially the learners' direct interest. A study of afterschool STEM clubs at four rural US middle schools (Blanchard et al., 2018) analyzed interviews of over 100 students to gain an understanding of what motivated student participation, based on expectancy-value theory constructs (Eccles, 1994).

Informal Competitive STEM Experiences

A qualitative study by Sahin et al. (2013) focused on middle and high school students who had participated in at least two afterschool STEM activities, including mathematics, robotics, science fair, Science Olympiad, and University Interscholastic League. These activities, which involved collaboration, student commitment and ownership, and building a community, helped "students to learn from each other, develop skills, and shift their interest toward STEM fields" (p. 319). The authors also believed that this engagement with open-ended and real-world problems helped cultivate STEM literacy and develop 21st-century skills.

A survey of nearly 650 college students and adults who were involved with Science Olympiad in middle or high school believed the Science Olympiad had an impact on their career choices, increased their learning and interest in science and STEM areas, and enhanced their 21st-century skills (Wirt, 2011). Similarly, Sahin et al. (2014) studied participants of the International Science Olympiad, and found that 80% of high school students who participated in this competitive STEM experience indicated that their participation reinforced or positively changed their decision to engage in a STEM career pathway.

Community-Based Informal STEM Experiences

The goal of many museums and science centers is to use their exhibits and resources as a basis of exposing students to STEM. The desired outcomes range from sparking curiosity and developing interests to fostering a STEM major and/or career pathway. For the latter, the programs aim to engage students in STEM practices through interaction with STEM professionals and field experiences that allow them to collect and analyze authentic data, thus participating in or contributing to scientific endeavor. Adams et al. (2014) found that girls in a museum-based afterschool program built a collective identity, established an identification with the museum, and gained broad exposure to science careers and topics that helped with their persistence in science when they moved on to college.

Burrows, Lockwood, Borowczak, Janak, and Barber (2018) conducted an integrated STEM action research project to investigate how the STEM sub-fields strengthen and support one another. Girl Scouts (similar to Girl Guides, internationally), parents, leaders, and faculty and students in higher education worked together to uncover water quality issues and propose necessary action steps for a locally restored river in the US state of Wyoming. Analyses of participant reflections indicated that authentic projects with an engineering focus may be best suited for fully integrating the STEM subject areas. Science content was visible throughout the project and was particularly evident in the content within the culminating poster presentation. Technology was used to gather samples of river invertebrates, weigh samples, and create a visual display of their findings. Engineering was evident through many aspects of the engineering design process (e.g., asking a question, designing solutions, evaluating evidence), and mathematical and computational thinking was evident as participants modeled, analyzed, and interpreted data.

Denson, Stallworth, Hailey, and Householder (2015) studied the Mathematics, Engineering, Science Achievement (MESA) program, which has been offered on multiple college campuses and informal spaces in California (US) since the 1970s. The authors wanted to gain an understanding of what program components led to effective and appealing informal learning environments for underrepresented student populations. Analyses of focus group data revealed that participants benefited from informal mentoring. Positive outcomes included exposure to new opportunities, time management skills, and the ability to apply math and science to their lives. Participants also reported increased confidence and camaraderie as a result of their participation. A related quantitative study by Denson (2017) found that hands-on activities were strongly correlated to students' self-efficacy, positive perceptions, and interest in engineering, and that significantly stronger results were found for students who participated in MESA competitions.

Informal STEM in Schools and in the Community

Makerspaces are places to provide opportunities to tinker with materials, build foundational skills, and facilitate independent making. According to Preddy (2013) "A makerspace is a community destination where students—sometimes alongside staff, parents and mentors—can create, problem solve, and develop skills, talents, thinking and mental rigor" (p. 1). In a four-year study led by Barton and Tan (2018), 48 youth "makers" in the US created and designed prototypes of products to solve problems plaguing their local communities. Not only did youth construct authentic prototypes, they also worked with community mentors to help address historical injustices they personally experience. In this way, these adolescent "makers" used STEM content and skills to make their learning more culturally relevant.

The citizen science movement began as a means to assist actual scientists in data collection through an increase in personnel and as a way to "collect information that would otherwise not be affordable" (Tulloch, Possingham, Joseph, Szabo, & Martin, 2013, p. 128). However, more recent efforts have morphed citizens into scientists through co-creation of knowledge (Dickinson et al., 2012; Lakshminarayanan, 2007). Technology and the interconnected nature of the world afforded by the internet has increased the ease of accessibility and social visibility of citizen science projects worldwide (Bonney et al., 2014). As a result, citizen scientists are able to interact with projects that are both of scientific and personal interest for their local environment and health (Burgess et al., 2017) (e.g., air and water pollution, climate change impacts, resource conservation; Brulle & Pellow, 2006; Leung, Yen, & Minkler, 2004). Not only has participation in citizen science helped to increase public scientific awareness and knowledge, it has also led toward movement in community mobilization and political action around social and environmental justice issues (Brulle, Carmichael, & Jenkins, 2012; Conrad & Daoust, 2008). Community mobilization/action projects have been supported via a wide range of data collection tools used by citizen scientists, including personal computers, mobile devices, and sensors (e.g., phones, tablets, GPS, digital compass, microphones, cameras) (Jennett et al., 2016). A range of curriculum-based computer science (CS) projects (e.g., BirdSleuth, Monarch in the Classroom, Nature's Notebook, Vital Signs, LIMPETS, GLOBE) are more directly connected to and used by schools (Bonney, Phillips, Ballard, & Enck, 2016; Taber, Ledley, Lynds, Domenico, & Dahlman, 2012). Museums have had active collaborations with the public through a wide range of citizen science projects (e.g., ebirds, emammal) (McShea, Forrester, Costello, He, & Kays, 2016). A study of 44 citizen science programs across three museums in the US and the United Kingdom documented the contribution of these programs to conservation, as well as indirect benefits to research, education, and policy (Ballard et al., 2017).

GLOBE connects stakeholders (e.g., scientists, teachers, students, citizens) from around the world in efforts to increase interest and awareness about local and global environments (Bonney et al., 2016). Along with an increase in basic content knowledge, observation, and communication skills, Butler and MacGregor (2003) noted that GLOBE participation increased students' local environmental awareness and decision-making skills. A study of the Coastal Observation and Seabird Survey Team (COASST) found that place-based local experiences led to an increase in both individual and collective action, and increased scientific literacy (Haywood, Parrish & Dolliver, 2016). Resonant with Haywood et al. (2016), Groulx, Brisbois, Lemieux, Winegardner, and Fishback (2017) found that participant learning about invasive species and bird biology was greatly enhanced if the context of the study is germane to the local area, or place-based, and research is conducted in real-world, relevant places. In their Motivation, Learning, and Creativity (MLC) model, Jennett et al. (2016) acknowledge participant identity development (e.g., self-confidence, contribution to research, belonging to community) to be contributing factors to both participant motivation and creativity. The more invested and involved participants became, the more likely they were to persist. Tulloch et al. (2013) found that participants' motivations lie in their potential to "contribute to 'real' science, public information, and conservation" (p. 129).

Theoretical Underpinnings of Research on Informal STEM Education

Sociocultural theory, a dominant theoretical framework guiding many studies of informal STEM programs, is based on the concept that learning is social and mediated by one's cultural and historical experiences (Vygotsky, 1978). Five related theoretical frameworks used to understand these programs are: (1) identity development-related constructs (Gee, 2000; Stetsenko, 2008); (2) communities of practice (Lave & Wenger, 1991); (3) expectancy value theory (Wigfield & Eccles, 2000); (4) social cognitive career theory (Lent, Brown, & Hackett, 1994); and (5) possible selves theory (Markus & Nurius, 1986).

Identity Theory

Gee (2000) defines identity as being perceived as a certain "kind of person" within a given context. Adams et al. (2014) describe identity in the context of informal science learning experiences and argue that participation in informal STEM programs afford youth opportunities to access science in personally meaningful ways. For instance, in doing science, youth begin to see themselves as someone who can do science. Equally important, youth gain confidence as they get recognized by others as someone who can do science. Through these authentic learning experiences, youth develop a "science-affinity" identity (Gray, 2013), which contributes to their trajectories with science. Several informal programs have used identity development theory or variants of this theory (e.g., social identity theory: Hogg, 2003; Tajfel & Turner, 2004; domain identification theory: Osborne & Jones, 2011) to guide their research on how youth participation in an informal context fosters a STEM identity, interest, and motivation for a career in STEM. These studies have been conducted in a variety of informal contexts, including a six-year weekend/summer program at a science museum (Adams et al., 2014), an afterschool program at a Boys and Girls Club (Schnittka, Brandt, Jones, & Evans, 2012), a summer camp at a university (Farland-Smith, 2009), a Saturday program at a science museum (Cole, 2012), and a summer camp at an environmental learning center (Riedinger, 2011). Whether science-affinity identities, or potentially mathematics-affinity or engineering-affinity identities that develop through participation in an informal program, have long-term or "cascading effects" (McCreedy & Dierking, 2013), such as persistence in STEM, is a ripe area for current and future research.

Situated Learning Theory

In situated learning theory, learning and identity development occur within Communities of Practice (COP) (Lave & Wenger, 1991; Wenger, 1998). A COP is a learning environment in which community members engage in shared, authentic learning experiences with their peers and, in many cases, with near peers (older students) and expert educators or scientists (Wenger, 1998). During these shared experiences, youth are provided opportunities to become practitioners of science; that is, to learn science while doing science, which has been found to enhance youths' learning and sustained interest (e.g., Habig et al., 2018; Winkleby et al., 2009). Research on explainer or youth docent programs have shown that in addition to stimulating awareness and interest in science careers, alumni of these programs are often motivated to become STEM educators (e.g., Gupta & Siegel, 2008; Sickler & Johnson, 2009; Siegel, 1998). Many longitudinal STEM programs have used the COP framework to situate their studies (e.g., Campbell, Lee, Kwon, & Park, 2012; Duran, Höft, Lawson, Medjahed, & Orady, 2014; Habig et al., 2018). For example, Project Exploration, a Chicago-based non-profit organization designed to make STEM accessible to historically underrepresented students (Lyon, Jafri, & St Louis, 2012), offers multi-year informal science learning experiences for youth. Program evaluators found "a domain of shared interest and inquiry, a community that nurtures relationships and helps members learn from each other, and members who share not only interests but also practices" (Chi, Snow, Goldstein, Lee, & Chung. 2010, p. 3). This COP framework has also informed research on the STEM majors and STEM career outcomes in summer and after-school programs that specifically target girls (McCreedy & Dierking, 2013; Schumacher et al., 2009), including a five-week summer program that uses alternative reality games to teach engineering concepts (Gilliam et al., 2017) and a university-based STEM summer camp for middle school students (Mohr-Schroeder et al., 2014). The COP framework has also been used in tandem with the theory of identity development (e.g., Farland-Smith, 2009; Riedinger, 2011). Promisingly, there is emerging evidence that these longitudinal informal programs employing a COP framework positively impact participants' persistence in STEM as measured by the STEM majors and STEM careers of alumni (e.g., Habig et al., 2018; McCreedy & Dierking, 2013; Winkleby et al., 2009).

Expectancy-Value Theory

Expectancy-value theory was introduced to the field of education by Eccles (1983, 1994) and further refined in subsequent years (e.g., Simpkins, Davis-Kean, & Eccles, 2006; Wigfield & Eccles, 2000; Wigfield, Eccles, Schiefele, Roeser, & Davis-Kean, 2006). Expectancy-value theory is based on the principle that STEM educational and occupational choices are a function of attainment value (personal importance to the individual), ability beliefs (an individual's belief in success), and utility (usefulness to the individual). In one of Eccles' collaborative efforts (Simpkins et al., 2006), she and her colleagues focused on OST participation of fifth-grade students in the context of expectancy-value theory. In this study, the researchers tracked OST informal science and math activities of fifth graders and their math and science self-concepts five years later. Results indicated that youths' OST math and science participation were significant predictors of both sustained interest and attainment value and, in turn, predicted participants' high school STEM course choice. In an analogous study, Blanchard et al. (2018) used mixed methods, guided by expectancy-value theory, to inform their research on the STEM outcomes of underrepresented rural youth participants of an afterschool STEM club. In interviews, students expressed that the clubs helped to build skills and content knowledge that may help them in the future, found the activities fun and different from what they do in school (subjective task value), felt a sense of belonging with other students who have similar goals and ambitions (identity), and socializing with peers was a high priority (key socializers).

Iterations of expectancy-value theory have been used to inform research on the STEM outcomes of participants of informal OST programs in several contexts, including university-based summer science enrichment programs for middle and high school youth (Weinberg, Basile, & Albright, 2011), university-based engineering and robotics camps for middle school youth (White, Crawford, Talley, Petrosino, & Bland, 2013), and a summer computing program focusing specifically on middle school girls (Denner, 2007). The use of an expectancy-value framework, generally applied using quantitative data, may offer a way to understand factors that may lead to students' choices stemming from informal program participation. Recently, the expectancy-value framework has been used to analyze qualitative data in an afterschool STEM program (Blanchard et al., 2018).

Social Cognitive Career Theory

Many studies of informal programs assess the STEM outcomes of participants through the lens of social cognitive career theory (Lent et al., 1994). Social cognitive career theory stems from social cognitive theory, which posits that interactions among personal, behavioral, and environmental factors influence an individual's academic and career choices (Bandura, 1991). Social cognitive career theory is comprised of three key elements: (1) self-efficacy (the belief individuals have in their capabilities to succeed); (2) outcome expectations (individuals' beliefs about the end results based on their behavior); and (3) career goals (Lent, Brown, & Hackett, 2002). Brown and Lent (1996) found that by helping individuals to modify their self-efficacy and career outcome expectations, clients were capable of reconsidering previously rejected career trajectories. Additionally, research on the STEM major and STEM career outcomes of participants of informal OST programs, within the framework of social cognitive career theory, have occurred in multiple contexts including: a study of high school students participating in field research internships facilitated by the Missouri Botanical Gardens and Washington University (Beyer & Flowers, 2015); a study of middle and high school participants of the 4-H Youth Development Program (Fox & Cater, 2015); research on a horseshoe crab citizen science project for middle school students (Hiller & Kitsantas, 2014); and middle school students in a university-based, intensive STEM program (Blanchard, Bedward, & McDonald, 2016). One area of future research could be to document the common programmatic design principles that help to build self-efficacy and augment the STEM career outcome expectations of informal STEM participants.

Possible Selves Theory

Possible selves theory (Markus & Nurius, 1986) provides a framework for individuals to examine future-oriented identities and to imagine possible selves, which in turn motivates students to engage in goal-directed and self-regulated behaviors essential for achieving future success. Possible selves are defined as visions of the "selves" an individual believes he or she might become in the proximal or distal future (Oyserman & James, 2009). In informal science learning contexts, the exploration of possible future science selves may prove valuable for facilitating STEM major and STEM career interest and engagement (Kelly, Dampier, & Carr, 2013). Informal programs that provide exposure to STEM careers via work experience or research internships are thought to be instrumental for youth imagining successful professional future selves (e.g., Goodyear & Carlson, 2007; Packard & Nguyen, 2003). In support of this hypothesis, one long-term informal program for middle and high school students held at a large urban museum afforded participants opportunities to "try on" possible selves each year via authentic research experiences (Habig et al., 2018). The structure of the program afforded students opportunities to engage in a research team of their choice led by a scientist or expert educator on an annual basis. Thus, in one year, participants could join a geology research team and in the subsequent year an evolutionary biology research team allowing them varied opportunities to practice science, to collaborate with scientists or expert educators, and to experience possible selves. A quantitative analysis of alumni of this program revealed that 83.2% engaged in a STEM major and 63.1% in a STEM career; the majority of alumni were females and members of historically underrepresented racial and ethnic groups. The results of these and other studies of informal science education learning communities suggest that the adoption of a possible selves theoretical framework might be instrumental for augmenting awareness, interest, and motivation to engage in a STEM trajectory.

Sociocultural theory and the five related theoretical frameworks described in this section begin to inform research in informal programs and to document some of the benefits of informal programs; however, there is still a need to bring theory and findings together in order to think more critically about how to best facilitate informal STEM learning experiences. There is great interest for informal youth programs to communicate and learn from each other, especially in terms of design principles associated with positive outcomes (Klein, Tisdal, & Hancock, 2017). We assert that attention to underlying theoretical considerations may help us to create more impactful informal STEM experiences in the future.

Conclusions

In this chapter, we reviewed the literature to describe the nature of informal STEM education, its goals, the types of programs, their benefits, and underlying theoretical constructs that drive some of the research. In Figure 12.1, we draw from these studies to propose a conceptual framework for studying informal STEM education programs. There are a number of core features of informal STEM, beginning with voluntary participation. Core features include experiences that are highly engaging, with relevant activities that stimulate curiosity and build knowledge. An ideal is that all STEM areas are represented, even if not all at the same time. Another core feature is the support of diverse students, with special attention to those who are underrepresented, often including females, first-generation students, students of color, and those who are from lower socioeconomic backgrounds. Ideally, core features of informal STEM programs include connections to career information and experiences that increase students' appreciation for STEM.

Informal STEM programs can take place in a wide range of settings. For instance, they can take the form of afterschool clubs held at schools, or they can connect schools and the community, as with STEM competitions, makerspaces, or Citizen Science. Informal STEM can take place in the community through field experiences, boys and girls clubs, museums, and other public resources. Ideally, theory guides the design of informal STEM programs and related research studies to investigate experiences related to students' identity, social learning, conceptual learning, career intentions, and personal development. To date, research indicates many positive impacts of students' involvement in a wide range of informal STEM programs and experiences.

Our review leads to a number of recommendations. Mathematics is the area of STEM that seemed least likely to be emphasized in informal, integrated STEM programs. Although there are mathematics competitions and OST programs, these tend to be mathematics only (e.g., the American Mathematics Competitions, https://www.maa.org/math-competitions) and studies were lacking in this area. Integrated STEM programs overwhelmingly focus on science, and less often include technology and engineering. This is somewhat unsurprising, given the large role that museums and other informal science institutions play in informal STEM education. In most programs, such as the STEM Clubs project (Blanchard et al., 2018), it is typical for one or two aspects of STEM to be featured in a particular activity or club meeting (Blanchard, Hoyle, & Gutierrez, 2017) rather than integration of all STEM areas. This seems appropriate, yet there may be a need to include more mathematics professionals in informal STEM efforts to increase the focus on mathematics.

There seemed to be a dearth of informal STEM education studies in countries outside of the US. Bybee (2013) found few published studies outside of the US regarding STEM educational reform with a focus on integrated STEM. Ritz and Fan (2015) examined the different approaches that countries throughout the world are taking with regard to STEM education. Unfortunately, the vast majority of international (e.g., US, England, Scotland, France, Australia, Asia [Korea, Taiwan, China, Japan, Israel], South Africa, Canada) STEM education initiatives the authors found through their literature search and interview data were focused on efforts in formal schooling. The integrated STEM described in Japan focused on informal STEM educational opportunities in museums, STEM competitions, and summer camps. Thus, we recommend a renewed focus on international work with our colleagues, to increase the presence of STEM education in informal spaces throughout the world.

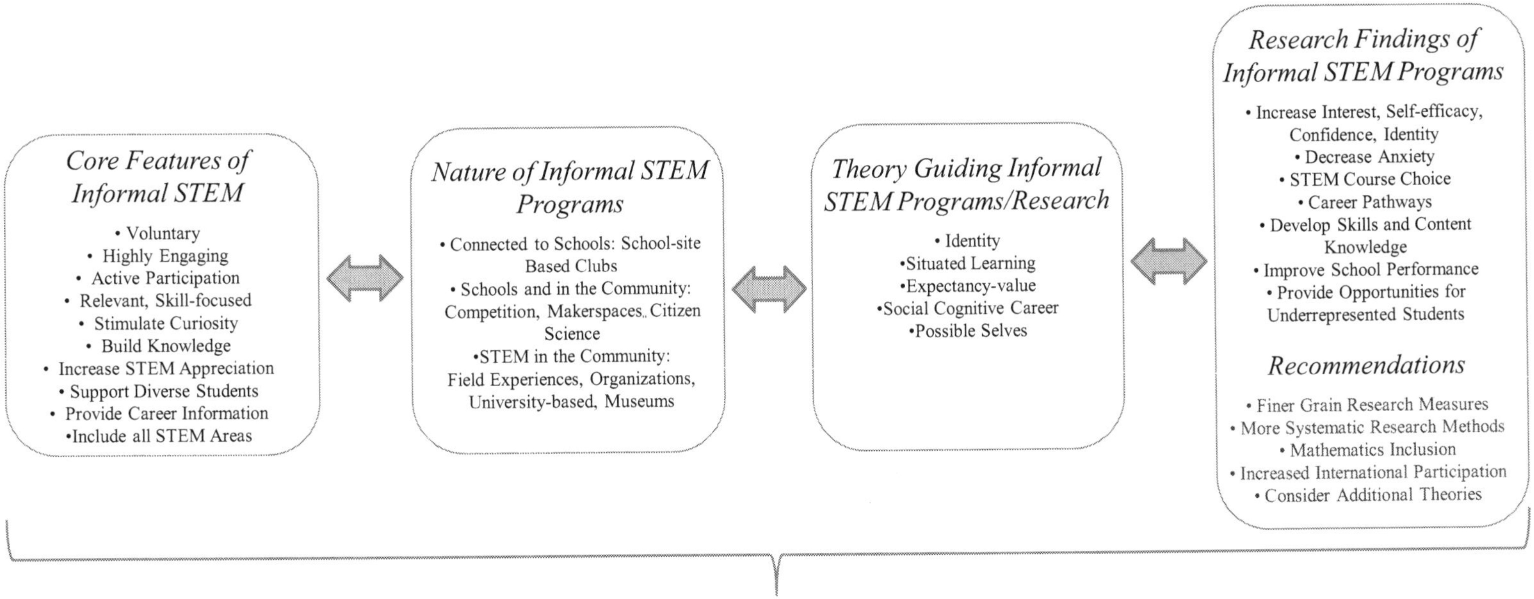

Core Features of Informal STEM

- Voluntary
- Highly Engaging
- Active Participation
- Relevant, Skill-focused
- Stimulate Curiosity
- Build Knowledge
- Increase STEM Appreciation
- Support Diverse Students
- Provide Career Information
- Include all STEM Areas

Nature of Informal STEM Programs

- Connected to Schools: School-site Based Clubs
- Schools and in the Community: Competition, Makerspaces. Citizen Science
- STEM in the Community: Field Experiences, Organizations, University-based, Museums

Theory Guiding Informal STEM Programs/Research

- Identity
- Situated Learning
- Expectancy-value
- Social Cognitive Career
- Possible Selves

Research Findings of Informal STEM Programs

- Increase Interest, Self-efficacy, Confidence, Identity
- Decrease Anxiety
- STEM Course Choice
- Career Pathways
- Develop Skills and Content Knowledge
- Improve School Performance
- Provide Opportunities for Underrepresented Students

Recommendations

- Finer Grain Research Measures
- More Systematic Research Methods
- Mathematics Inclusion
- Increased International Participation
- Consider Additional Theories

Figure 12.1 Conceptual framework for studying effects of informal STEM education programs.

Many recent studies in informal STEM education are informed by theory, and we recommend that this continue and that other theoretical perspectives are considered to help us better understand what happens though informal STEM experiences. Through the direct experience of the authors of this chapter, as well as findings in the literature, we believe there is a need for finer-grained and more theoretically driven work in order to better understand the impacts of current programs. It is possible that by using a shared conceptual model (Figure 12.1) which accommodates both empirical and conceptual studies, as done in teacher professional development by Desimone (2009), we could better understand findings from individual studies. These findings could inform future informal STEM programs and related research, thereby helping us to learn more about the students, teachers, scientists, and researchers who are involved in this work and to enhance the impact of informal STEM education experiences.

References

Adams, J. D., Gupta, P., & Cotumaccio, A. (2014). Long-term participants: A museum program enhances girls' stem interest, motivation, and persistence. *Afterschool Matters, 20*, 13–20. Retrieved from https://files.eric.ed.gov/fulltext/EJ1047233.pdf

Ballard, H. L., Robinson, L. D., Young, A. N., Pauly, G. B., Higgins, L. M., Johnson, R. F., & Twedle, J. C. (2017). Contributions to conservation outcomes of natural history museum–led citizen science: Examining evidence and next steps. *Biological Conservation, 208*, 87–97. https://doi.org/10.1016/j.biocon.2016.08.040

Banerjee, P. A. (2017). Is informal education the answer to increasing and widening participation in STEM education? *Review of Education, 5*(2), 202–224. https://doi.org/10.1002/rev3.3093

Bandura, A. (1991). Social cognitive theory of self-regulation. *Organizational Behavior and Human Decision Processes, 50*(2), 248–287.

Barker, B. S., Nugent, G., & Grandgenett, N. F. (2014). Examining fidelity of program implementation in a STEM-oriented out-of-school setting. *International Journal of Technology and Design Education, 24*(1), 39–52. https://doi.org/10.1007/s10798-013-9245-9

Barton, A. C., & Tan, E. (2018). A longitudinal study of equity-oriented STEM-rich making among youth from historically marginalized communities. *American Educational Research Journal, 55*(4), 761–800. https://doi.org/10.3102/0002831218758668

Bell, P., Lewenstein, B., Shouse, A. W., & Feder, M. A. (Eds.). (2009). *Learning science in informal environments: People, places, and pursuits.* (National Research Council, Ed.). Washington, DC: National Academies Press.

Beyer, & Flowers. (2015). *Making natural connections—an authentic field research collaboration.* Summative Evaluation Report. Retrieved from http://informalscience.org/evaluation/ic-000-000-010-806/Making_Natural_Connections

Blanchard, M. R., Bedward, J., & McDonald, S. (2016). "I get to feel like a college student": Examining the relative impacts of 8th grade STEM interventions on a college campus, in middle school classrooms, and with a comparison school. In J. Lavonen, K. Juuti, J. Lampiselkä, A. Uitto, & K. Hahl (Eds.), *Electronic Proceedings of the ESERA 2015 Conference. Science education research: Engaging learners for a sustainable future, Part 2/Strand 2* (co-ed. R. Tytler & A. Zeyer), (pp. 311–321). Helsinki, Finland: University of Helsinki.

Blanchard, M. R., Gutierrez, K. S., Hoyle, K. S., Painter, J. L., & Ragan, N. S. (2018). Rural, underrepresented students' motivation, achievement, and perceptions in afterschool STEM clubs. In Finlayson, O., McLoughlin, E., Erduran, S., & Childs, P. (Eds.), *Electronic Proceedings of the ESERA 2017 Conference. Research, practice and collaboration in science education Part 2* (co-ed. Tytler, R., & Carvalho, G. S.), (pp. 264–272). Dublin, Ireland: Dublin City University.

Blanchard, M. R., Hoyle, K. S., & Gutierrez, K. S. (2017). How to start a STEM club. *Science Scope, 41*(3), 88–94.

Bonney, R., Phillips, T. B., Ballard, H. L., & Enck, J. W. (2016). Can citizen science enhance public understanding of science? *Public Understanding of Science, 25*(1), 2–16.

Bonney, R., Shirk, J. L., Phillips, T. B., Wiggins, A., Ballard, H. L., Miller-Rushing, A. J., & Parrish, J. K. (2014). Next steps for citizen science. *Science, 343*(6178), 1436–1437. doi:10.1126/science.1251554.

Brown, S., & Lent, R. (1996). A social cognitive framework for career choice counseling. *The Career Development Quarterly, 44*, 355–367. https://doi.org/10.1002/j.2161-0045.1996.tb00451.x

Brulle, R. J., Carmichael, J., & Jenkins, J. C. (2012). Shifting public opinion on climate change: An empirical assessment of factors influencing concern over climate change in the U.S., 2002–2010. *Climatic Change, 114*(2), 169–188. https://doi.org/10.1007/s10584-012-0403-y

Brulle, R. J., & Pellow, D. N. (2006). Environmental justice: Human health and environmental inequalities. *Annual Review of Public Health, 27*, 103–124. https://doi.org/10.1146/annurev.publhealth.27.021405.102124

Burgess, H. K., Debey, L. B., Froehlich, H. E., Schmidt, N., Theobald, E. J., Ettinger, A. K., . . . Parrish, J. K. (2017). The science of citizen science: Exploring barriers to use as a primary research tool. *Biological Conservation, 208*, 113–120. https://doi.org/10.1016/j.biocon.2016.05.014

Burrows, A., Lockwood, M., Borowczak, M., Janak, E., & Barber, B. (2018). Integrated STEM: Focus on informal education and community collaboration through engineering. *Education Sciences, 8*(4), 1–15. https://doi.org/10.3390/educsci8010004

Butler, D. M., & MacGregor, I. D. (2003). GLOBE: Science and education. *Journal of Geoscience Education, 51*(1), 9–20. https://doi.org/10.5408/1089-9995-51.1.9

Bybee, R. W. (2013). *The case for STEM education: Challenges and opportunities.* Arlington: NSTA Press.

Campbell, T., Lee, H. Y., Kwon, H. S., & Park, K. S. (2012). Student motivation and interests as proxies for forming STEM identities. *Journal of the Korean Association for Science Education.* https://doi.org/10.14697/jkase.2012.32.3.532

Chi, B., Snow, J. Z., Goldstein, D., Lee, S., & Chung, J. (2010). *Project exploration: 10-year retrospective program evaluation summative report.* Berkeley: University of California.

Cole, S. (2012). *The development of science identity: An evaluation of youth development programs at the Museum of Science and Industry, Chicago* (Unpublished doctoral dissertation). Loyola University, Chicago.

Conrad, C., & Daoust, T. (2008). Community-based monitoring frameworks: Increasing the effectiveness of environmental stewardship. *Environmental Management, 41*, 356–358.

Denner, J. (2007). The girls creating games program: An innovative approach to integrating technology into middle school. *Meridian: A Middle School Computer Technologies Journal, 1*(10).

Denson, C. D. (2017). The MESA study. *Journal of Technology Education, 29*(1), 66–94. https://doi.org/10.21061/jte.v29i1.a.4

Denson, C. D., Stallworth, C. A., Hailey, C., & Householder, D. L. (2015). Benefits of informal learning environments: A focused examination of STEM-based program environments. *Journal of STEM Education: Innovations and Research, 16*(1), 11–15.

Desimone, L. M. (2009). Improving impact studies of teachers' professional development: Toward better conceptualizations and measures. *Educational Researcher, 38*(3), 181–199. https://doi.org/10.3102/0013189X08331140

Dickinson, J. L., Shirk, J., Bonter, D., Bonney, R., Crain, R. L., Martin, J., . . . Purcell, K. (2012). The current state of citizen science as a tool for ecological research and public engagement. *Frontiers in Ecology and the Environment, 10*, 291–297.

Duran, M., Höft, M., Lawson, D. B., Medjahed, B., & Orady, E. A. (2014). Urban high school students' IT/STEM learning: Findings from a collaborative inquiry- and design-based afterschool program. *Journal of Science Education and Technology, 23*(1), 116–137. https://doi.org/10.1007/s10956-013-9457-5

Eccles, J. S. (1983). Expectancies, values and academic behaviors. In J. T. Spence (Ed.), *Achievement and achievement motives: Psychological and sociological approaches* (pp. 75–146). San Francisco, CA: Freeman.

Eccles, J. S. (1994). Understanding women's educational and occupational choices. *Psychology of Women Quarterly, 18*(4), 585–609. https://doi.org/10.1111/j.1471-6402.1994.tb01049.x

Fadigan, K. A., & Hammrich, P. L. (2004). A longitudinal study of the educational and career trajectories of female participants of an urban informal science education program. *Journal of Research in Science Teaching, 41*(8), 835–860. https://doi.org/10.1002/tea.20026

Falk, J. H., Staus, N., Dierking, L. D., Penuel, W., Wyld, J., & Bailey, D. (2016). Understanding youth STEM interest pathways within a single community: The Synergies project. *International Journal of Science Education, Part B: Communication and Public Engagement, 6*(4), 369–384. https://doi.org/10.1080/21548455.2015.1093670

Farland-Smith, D. (2009). Exploring middle school girls' science identities: Examining attitudes and perceptions of scientists when working "side-by-side" with scientists. *School Science and Mathematics, 109*(7), 415–427. https://doi.org/10.1111/j.1949-8594.2009.tb17872.x

Fox, J., & Cater, M. (2015). An analysis of adolescents' Science interest and competence in programs with and without a competitive component. *Journal of Agricultural Education, 56*(4), 90–106. https://doi.org/10.5032/jae.2015.04090

Gee, J. (2000). Identity as an analytic lens for research in education. *Review of Research in Education, 25*, 99–125. https://doi.org/10.2307/1167322

Gilliam, M., Jagoda, P., Fabiyi, C., Lyman, P., Wilson, C., Hill, B., & Bouris, A. (2017). Alternate reality games as an informal learning tool for generating stem engagement among underrepresented youth: A qualitative evaluation of the source. *Journal of Science Education and Technology*, 1–14. https://doi.org/10.1007/s10956-016-9679-4

Goodyear, L., & Carlson, B. (2007). The ITEST learning resource center's online evaluation database; Examples from the collection. *International Journal of Technology in Teaching and Learning, 3*(1), 51–65.

Gottfried, M. A., & Williams, D. N. (2013). STEM club participation and STEM schooling outcomes. *Education Policy Analysis Archives, 21*(79), 1–27. https://doi.org/10.14507/epaa.v21n79.2013

Gray, S. (2013). Black students in science: More than meets the eye. *International Journal of Education and Culture, 2*(4).

Groulx, M., Brisbois, M. C., Lemieux, C. J., Winegardner, A., & Fishback, L. (2017). A role for nature-based citizen science in promoting individual and collective climate change action? A systematic review of learning outcomes. *Science Communication, 39*(1), 45–76. https://doi.org/10.1177/1075547016688324

Gupta, P., & Siegel, E. (2008). Science career ladder at the New York Hall of Science: Youth facilitators as agents of inquiry. In R. A. Yager & J. H. Falk (Eds.), *Exemplary science in informal education settings: Standards-based success stories* (pp. 71–84). Arlington, VA: National Science Teachers Association.

Gutierrez, K. S. (2016). *Investigating the climate change beliefs, knowledge, behaviors, and cultural worldviews of rural middle school students and their families during an out-of-school intervention: A mixed-methods study* (Unpublished doctoral dissertation). North Carolina State University, Raleigh, NC. Retrieved from http://www.lib.ncsu.edu/resolver/1840.16/11320

Habig, B., Gupta, P., Levine, B., & Adams, J. (2018). An informal science education program's impact on stem major and STEM career outcomes. *Research in Science Education*, 1–24. https://doi.org/10.1007/s11165-018-9722-y

Hanks, C. L., Wartes, D., Levine, R., Gonzalez, R., Fowell, S., & Owens, G. (2007). Introducing the geosciences to Alaska natives via the Rural Alaska Honors Institute (RAHI). *Journal of Geoscience Education, 55*(6), 507–513. https://doi.org/10.5408/1089-9995-55.6.507

Hartley, M. S. (2014). Science clubs: An underutilised tool for promoting science communication activities in school. In L. T. W. Hin & R. Subramaniam (Eds.), *Communicating science to the public* (pp. 21–31). Netherlands: Springer. https://doi.org/10.1177/016224399101600107

Haywood, B. K., Parrish, J. K., & Dolliver, J. (2016). Place-based and data-rich citizen science as a precursor for conservation action. *Conservation Biology, 30*(3), 476–486. https://doi.org/10.1111/cobi.12702

Heo, M., & Myrick, L. M. (2009). The girls' computing club: Making positive changes in gender inequity in computer science with an informal, female learning community. *International Journal of Information and Communication Technology Education (IJICTE), 5*(4), 44–56. https://doi.org/10.4018/jicte.2009041005

Hiller, S. E., & Kitsantas, A. (2014). The effect of a horseshoe crab citizen science program on middle school student science performance and STEM career motivation. *School Science and Mathematics, 114*(6), 302–311. https://doi.org/10.1111/ssm.12081

Hogg, M. A. (2003). Social identity. In M. R. Leary & J. P. Tangney (Eds.), *Handbook of self and identity* (pp. 462–479). New York, NY: The Guilford Press.

Jennett, C., Kloetzer, L., Schneider, D., Iacovides, I., Cox, A., Gold, M., . . . Ajani, Z. (2016). Motivations, learning and creativity in online citizen science. *Journal of Science Communication, 15*(3), 1–23. https://doi.org/10.22323/2.15030205

Kelly, K., Dampier, D. A., & Carr, K. (2013). Willing, able, and unwanted: High school girls' potential selves in computing. *Journal of Women and Minorities in Science and Engineering, 19*(1). https://doi.org/10.1615/JWomenMinorScienEng.2013004471

Klein, C., Tisdal, C., & Hancock, W. (2017). *Proceedings from association of science technology centers: Roads taken - long-term impacts of youth programs.* San Jose, CA: Association of Science Technology Centers.

Krishnamurthi, A., Ballard, M., & Noam, G. G. (2014). *Examining the impact of afterschool STEM programs,* Noyce Foundation. Retrieved from http://www.afterschoolalliance.org/ExaminingtheImpactofAfterschoolSTEMPrograms.pdf

Lakshminarayanan, S. (2007). Using citizens to do science versus citizens as scientists. *Ecology and Society, 12*(2), 1. https://doi.org/10.5751/ES-02274-1202r02

Lave, J., & Wenger, E. (1991). *Situated learning: Legitimate peripheral participation.* Cambridge, England: Cambridge University Press.

Lent, R. W., Brown, S. D., & Hackett, G. (1994). Toward a unifying social cognitive theory of career and academic interest, choice, and performance. *Journal of Vocational Behavior, 45*(1), 79–122. https://doi.org/10.1006/jvbe.1994.1027

Lent, R. W., Brown, S. D., & Hackett, G. (2002). Social cognitive career theory. *Career Choice and Development, 4,* 255–311.

Leung, M. W., Yen, I. H., & Minkler, M. (2004). Community-based participatory research: A promising approach for increasing epidemiology's relevance in the 21st century. *International Journal of Epidemiology, 33*(3), 499–506. https://doi.org/10.1093/ije/dyh010

Lyon, G. H., Jafri, J., & St Louis, K. (2012). Beyond the pipeline: STEM pathways for youth development. *Afterschool Matters, 16,* 48–57.

Maltese, A. V., & Tai, R. H. (2010). Eyeballs in the fridge: Sources of early interest in science. *International Journal of Science Education, 32,* 669–685. https://doi.org/10.1080/09500690902792385

Mannion, K., & Coldwell, M. (2008). *Afterschool science and engineering clubs evaluation.* Retrieved from http://www.dcsf.gov.uk/research/programmeofresearch/projectinformation.cfm?projectid=15385&resultspage=1

Markus, H., & Nurius, P. (1986). "Possible selves." *American Psychologist, 41*(9), 954–969. https://doi.org/10.1037/0003-066X.41.9.954

McCreedy, D., & Dierking, L. D. (2013). *Cascading influences: Long-term impacts of informal STEM experiences for girls.* Presented at 27th Annual Visitor Studies Association Conference.

McShea, W. J., Forrester, T., Costello, R., He, Z., & Kays, R. (2016). Volunteer-run cameras as distributed sensors for macrosystem mammal research. *Landscape Ecology, 31,* 55–66. https://doi.org/10.1007/s10980-015-0262-9

Mohr-Schroeder, M. J., Jackson, C., Miller, M., Walcott, B., Little, D. L., Speler, L., . . . Schroeder, D. C. (2014). Developing middle school students' interests in STEM via summer learning experiences: See Blue STEM camp. *School Science and Mathematics, 114*(6), 291–301.

NGSS Lead States. (2013). *Next generation science standards: For states, by states.* Washington, DC: National Academies Press.

Osborne, J. W., & Jones, B. D. (2011). Identification with academics and motivation to achieve in school: How the structure of the self influences academic outcomes. *Educational Psychology Review, 23*(1), 131–158. https://doi.org/10.1007/s10648-011-9151-1

Oyserman, D., & James, L. (2009). Possible selves: From content to process. In K. D. Markman, W. M. P. Klein, & J. A. Suhr (Eds.), *Handbook of imagination and mental simulation* (pp. 373–394). New York, NY: Psychology Press.

Packard, B. W.-L., & Nguyen, D. (2003). Science career-related possible selves of adolescent girls: A longitudinal study. *Journal of Career Development, 29*(4), 251–263. https://doi.org/10.1177/089484530302900403

Preddy, L. (2013). Creating school library "makerspace". *School Library Monthly, 29*(5), 41–42.

Riedinger, K. (2011). *Identity development of middle school students as learners of science at an informal science education camp* (Unpublished doctoral dissertation). University of Maryland, College Park, MD.

Ritz, J. M., & Fan, S. C. (2015). STEM and technology education: International state-of-the-art. *International Journal of Technology and Design Education, 25,* 429–451. https://doi.org/10.1007/s10798-014-9290-z

Sahin, A., Ayar, M. C., & Adiguzel, T. (2013). STEM related afterschool program activities and associated outcomes on student learning. *Educational Sciences: Theory & Practice, 14*(1), 309–323. http://doi.org/10.12738/estp.2014.1.1876

Sahin, A., Gulacar, O., & Stuessy, C. (2014). High school students' perceptions of the effects of International Science Olympiad on their STEM career aspirations and twenty-first century skill development. *Research in Science Education,* 785–805. http://doi.org/10.1007/s11165-014-9439-5.

Schnittka, C. G., Brandt, C. B., Jones, B. D., & Evans, M. A. (2012). Informal engineering education after school: Employing the studio model for motivation and identification in STEM domains. *Advances in Engineering Education, 3*(2), 1–31.

Schumacher, M. M., Stansbury, K. N., Johnson, M. N., Floyd, S. R., Reid, C. E., Noland, M. P., & Leukefeld, C. G. (2009). The young women in science program: A five-year follow-up of an intervention to change science attitudes, academic behavior, and career aspirations. *Journal of Women and Minorities in Science and Engineering, 15*(4).

Sickler, J., & Johnson, E. 2009. *Science career ladder retrospective impact study.* Edgewater, MD: Institute for Learning Innovation.

Siegel, E. (1998). The science career ladder at the New York Hall of Science. *Curator: The Museum Journal, 41*(4), 246–253.

Simpkins, S. D., Davis-Kean, P. E., & Eccles, J. S. (2006). Math and science motivation: A longitudinal examination of the links between choices and beliefs. *Developmental Psychology, 42*(1), 70. https://doi.org/10.1037/0012-1649.42.1.70

Stetsenko, A. (2008). Collaboration and cogenerativity: On bridging the gaps separating theory-practice and cognition-emotion. *Cultural Studies of Science Education, 3,* 521–533. https://doi.org/10.1007/s11422-008-9123-z

Taber, M. R., Ledley, T. S., Lynds, S., Domenico, B., & Dahlman, L. (2012). Geoscience data for educational use: Recommendations from scientific/technical and educational communities. *Journal of Geoscience Education, 60*(3), 249–256. https://doi.org/10.5408/12-297.1

Tajfel, H., & Turner, J. C. (2004). The social identity theory of intergroup behavior. In J. T. Jost & J. Sidanius (Eds.), *Political psychology: Key readings* (pp. 276–293). New York, NY: Psychology Press.

Thibaut, L., Knipprath, H., Dehaene, W., & Depaepe, F. (2018). The influence of teachers' attitudes and school context on instructional practices in integrated STEM education. *Teaching and Teacher Education, 71*, 190–205. https://doi.org/10.1016/j.tate.2017.12.01

Tulloch, A. I. T., Possingham, H. P., Joseph, L. N., Szabo, J., & Martin, T. G. (2013). Realising the full potential of citizen science monitoring programs. *Biological Conservation, 165*, 128–138. https://doi.org/10.1016/j.biocon.2013.05.025

Vygotsky, L. S. (1978). *Mind in society: The development of higher psychological processes*. Cambridge, MA: Harvard University Press.

Weinberg, A. E., Basile, C. G., & Albright, L. (2011). The effect of an experiential learning program on middle school students' motivation toward mathematics and science. *Research in Middle Level Education, 35*(3), 1–12. https://doi.org/10.1080/19404476.2011.11462086

Wenger, E. (1998). *Communities of practice: Learning, meaning and identity*. Cambridge, UK: Cambridge University Press.

White, C., Crawford, R., Talley, A., Petrosino, A., & Bland, K. (2013). *Girls go beyond blackboards towards positive attitudes about engineering*. Presented at ASEE Annual Conference, Atlanta, GA.

Wigfield, A., & Eccles, J. S. (2000). Expectancy—value theory of achievement motivation. *Contemporary Educational Psychology, 25*(1), 68–81. https://doi.org/10.1006/ceps.1999.1015

Wigfield, A., Eccles, J. S., Schiefele, U., Roeser, R. W., & Davis-Kean, P. (2006). *Development of achievement motivation*. Hoboken, NJ: Wiley.

Winkleby, M. A., Ned, J., Ahn, D., Koehler, A., & Kennedy, J. D. (2009). Increasing diversity in science and health professions: A 21-year longitudinal study documenting college and career success. *Journal of Science Education and Technology, 18*(6), 535–545. https://doi.org/10.1007/s10956-009-9168-0

Wirt, J. L. (2011). *An analysis of Science Olympiad participants' perceptions regarding their experience with the science and engineering academic competition* (Unpublished doctoral dissertation). Seton Hall University, South Orange, NJ. Retrieved from http://scholarship.shu.edu/dissertations/26

Young, J., Ortiz, N., & Young, J. (2017). STEMulating interest: A meta-analysis of the effects of out-of-school time on student STEM interest. *International Journal of Education in Mathematics, Science and Technology, 5*(1), 62–74. https://doi.org/10.18404/ijemst.61149

13

CREATING STEM LEARNING OPPORTUNITIES THROUGH PARTNERSHIPS

Danielle B. Harlow, Alexandria Hansen, Jasmine Nation,
Ron Skinner, Javier Pulgar, Alexis Spina, Mandy McLean,
Chantal Barriault and Annie Prud'homme-Généreux

Solving significant societal and environmental problems in the real world will require using and integrating knowledge, understandings, and practices from all four STEM (science, technology, engineering, and mathematics) areas. Additionally, integrating across STEM subjects has been shown to have positive effects on students' achievement (Becker & Park, 2011; Venville, Rennie, & Wallace, 2004). However, the four STEM disciplines have traditionally been taught separately (with science and mathematics the most commonly taught of those), and most students have not experienced instruction that explicitly and mindfully requires them to integrate their learning of practices and content from multiple disciplines to solve problems. Although this is changing, as STEM instruction is being reformed in countries worldwide with inquiry-based approaches focused on problem solving and creativity (Honey, Pearson, & Schweingruber, 2014; Marginson, Tytler, Freeman, & Roberts, 2013; Martins Gomes & McCauley, 2016), instruction that effectively integrates science, technology, engineering, and mathematics remains the exception.

Integrating STEM instruction requires multiple types of expertise including content knowledge in science, technology, engineering, and mathematics; an understanding of appropriate technology and materials to support learning; knowledge of state and national standards; and pedagogical strategies for engaging all learners (e.g., Harlow, Hansen, McBeath & Leak, 2018).This is difficult for classroom teachers who may have expertise in only one of the STEM disciplines and for teachers of younger grades who are often responsible for teaching all of the content areas and who may not have expertise in any of the STEM disciplines (Banilower et al., 2018). Individual teachers should not be expected to have the varied expertise required to develop and implement integrated STEM learning experiences. Other institutions, such as universities and informal science learning environments (science museums, university outreach programs, and afterschool care and enrichment programs) can share the responsibility of providing educational STEM experiences for children and support schools in engaging children in STEM learning.

The goal of this chapter is not to present research supporting integrating STEM instruction. Other chapters in this volume present arguments and research to inform decisions about whether or not to integrate STEM instruction. Instead, in this chapter, we break down the complex process of developing programs that integrate STEM content through partnerships between multiple education sectors. The term *STEM partnerships* implies that at least two STEM disciplines are included and at least two institutions are involved in program development and implementation. Thus, the partners must determine what content to include and how the disciplines will be integrated in addition to deciding how the institutions will coordinate their work together. As will be presented, there are

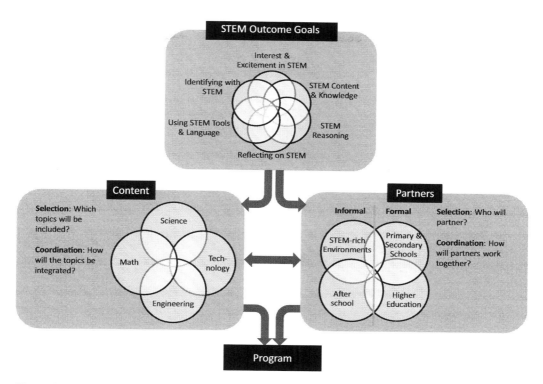

Figure 13.1   Aspects of STEM partnerships that require selection and coordination decisions.

separate models for each of these aspects. Considering these multiple types of models is useful for thinking about ways that programs might function within the resources and constraints of existing partnerships and may also serve as a framework for thinking about goals for a program and for identifying weaknesses that additional partners might be able to address. These partnerships usually take shape through an iterative process that includes making decisions, implementing decisions, assessing outcomes, and using these outcomes to iteratively improve the program.

Figure 13.1 depicts aspects of STEM partnerships that we identified as requiring choices about selection (What content will be included? Who will participate?) and coordination (How will topics be organized? How will partners work together?). These components guide the chapter organization. We begin by presenting potential STEM learning goals and then consider the STEM content and the partners separately. The first part of the chapter isolates these key decision points: outcome goals, partners, and STEM topics. We then present examples from our own work and the literature and close with a discussion about how partnerships form and evolve.

Outcome Goals and Content

The first decision we confront is the program outcome goals. Programs developed through partnerships may have learning and development outcome goals that align with the content goals of school (e.g., NGSS Lead States, 2013), or they may be designed to engage, to develop scientific identities, or to broaden participation in STEM. *Surrounded by Science* (National Research Council [NRC], 2010) describes six "strands of learning" associated with informal science institutions. Since we are considering partnerships between formal and informal learning organizations, we adapted these strands to reflect our focus on STEM, not just science.

STEM Outcome Goals

1. *Sparking Interest and Excitement in STEM*

One goal of STEM partnerships is to spark interest and excitement in the natural and designed world and the STEM disciplines. Learners who visit informal institutions have opportunities to interact with phenomena to learn about the physical and natural world. These engaging interactions, in turn, can create a motivation to learn more.

2. *Understanding STEM Content and Knowledge*

Partnerships might strive to develop learners' content knowledge across the STEM disciplines. This includes scientific explanations of the natural and designed world and understanding mathematical and engineering concepts and the interrelations among not only science concepts but the science, engineering, and math concepts and the technology that relates to these. This goal is most related to what is typically considered "content." However, it does not only include facts. In line with new vision of science and engineering education within the United States (NGSS Lead States, 2013), accomplishing this goal means learners have opportunities to engage in disciplinary-specific practices to construct their own understandings (see also goals 3 and 5). In STEM learning experiences that integrate multiple disciplines of study, students use multiple areas of learning to solve problems. Learners should have opportunities to engage in disciplinary-specific practices to learn content that allows them to make connections across individual disciplines and apply their understanding to relevant situations within their own lives.

3. *Engaging in Scientific, Technological, Engineering, and Mathematical Reasoning and Computational Thinking*

Partnerships also provide opportunities for learners to engage in STEM reasoning. Each discipline has specific ways of solving problems and constructing new knowledge, and it is critical that students learn to engage in these practices, but there are important areas of overlap. Across all the STEM disciplines, learners can observe, wonder, and make sense of the natural and designed world by constructing explanations using evidence and developing models.

4. *Reflecting on STEM*

Partnerships provide opportunities for learners to reflect on the nature of science, technology, engineering, and mathematics as ways of knowing. This includes not only how these disciplines develop new understandings and solve problems (which is related to goals 3 and 5) but also how they, as learners, construct new ideas in these disciplines and how the disciplines apply to their lived experiences. Connecting to notions of "scientific literacy" (NRC, 2012; DeBoer, 1991), all individuals should have an understanding of the types of questions science can (and cannot) answer, the types of reasoning and evidence used to justify claims, and an understanding of how science, as a discipline, can change in light of new evidence.

5. *Using the Tools and Language of STEM*

Another goal for STEM partnerships is to develop learners' ability to use tools and language characteristic of those disciplines. Students should have opportunities to observe evocative phenomena, ask questions, collect data, and construct explanations using evidence (Honey et al., 2014; NGSS Lead States, 2013; NRC, 2012). By using the tools and language of the STEM disciplines, learners are able to gain valuable experience that prepares them for future engagement with these disciplines.

6. *Identifying With the STEM Enterprise*

It is also important that learners are able to identify with the STEM enterprise. This includes developing an awareness of the possible STEM careers available and the recognition that their personal interests and values are aligned. Therefore, in addition to considering a wide variety of STEM careers, reflections should include more diverse representations within specific disciplines. For example, engineering has typically been presented as highly technical and detached from community concerns (Cech, 2013; Busch-Vishniac & Jarosz, 2004; Johnson, Leydens, Moskal, Silva, & Fantasky, 2015). Foregrounding instead the social relevance of engineering could encourage more diverse students to engage (Hill, Corbett, & St. Rose, 2010; Johnson et al., 2015). Highlighting the social relevance of STEM can be a powerful motivating factor to encourage students to pursue STEM degrees.

Traditionally, formal institutions like schools have focused more on engaging in reasoning associated with the STEM disciplines and understanding content while informal institutions like museums have focused on affective goals like interest and identity (e.g., Adams, Gupta, & Cotumaccio, 2014; Bevan, Gutwill, Petrich, & Wilkinson, 2015; Dabney, Tai, & Scott, 2016). Partnerships have the advantage of including institutions that have the affordances and norms to address both types of goals. And, while these six outcome goals are presented separately, in practice, they often overlap. Students use the tools of STEM and engage in STEM reasoning as they construct understandings of STEM content. Interest and identity guide their learning and decisions about courses and activities to pursue in and out of school (Barron, 2006).

STEM Content

Achieving the outcome goals requires decisions about the specific content that will be included and the problems that students will solve. In this section we turn to the box in Figure 13.1 labeled "content." Traditionally, most classroom teaching is *disciplinary*. This means that the concepts and skills for each discipline are taught separately. However, researchers have begun to advocate for a movement towards more *interdisciplinary* and *transdisciplinary* instruction (Wang & Knobloch, 2018; English, 2016; Vasquez, Sneider, & Comer, 2013). Interdisciplinary instruction combines closely linked concepts and skills from two or more disciplines, while transdisciplinary instruction takes this one step further to bring together knowledge and skills from multiple disciplines through projects designed to tackle real-world problems.

Many scholars have investigated the different ways that programs bring STEM content areas together. In Chapter 1 of this volume, Moore, Johnston, and Clancy (2020) describe a range of models, most which describe "a continuum of STEM integration that goes from little to no integration on one end to fully integrated, authentic project- or problem-based learning on the other" (p. 8). Here, we use Hurley's (2001) categorization of the degree of integration, or the range of temporal and sequential relationships between the content. Although these categories of integration were determined specifically for science and math, they provide a valuable lens to look at integration across all STEM disciplines. We use his categorization and adapt these to describe STEM integration. This is one of many ways we could have categorized integration (see Johnson, Peters-Burton & Moore, 2016).

1. **Sequencing topics so that one topic builds on another.** STEM topics are taught sequentially, with one preceding the other so that one topic informs the next. For example, one might teach vectors in a math class and then apply the concept to learning about forces in a science class.
2. **Teaching topics in parallel.** Different STEM subjects are taught at the same time through parallel concepts. For example, in an effort to teach about earthquakes, students might learn about seismic processes in science class and structural engineering principles in engineering class.

3. **Teaching disciplines partially together.** STEM subjects that are sometimes taught as separate content areas and sometimes taught together to show their connections to one another could help students understand their unique lens and how they fit together (Jacobs, 1989).

4. **Enhancing one discipline with the other.** One of the STEM subjects is the dominant discipline being taught, while the other discipline appears throughout the instruction.

5. **Integrating completely.** At least two of the STEM disciplines are taught together, with neither being dominant over the other (e.g., Smith, Rayfield, & McKim, 2015).

These categories work for thinking about two, three, or all four of the STEM disciplines.

While research suggests that integrating mathematics and science instruction is advantageous, studies have demonstrated larger positive impacts on science learning, as compared to math learning (Hurley, 2001; Lehrer & Schauble, 2000). These differences are attributed to the nature of mathematics and how that facilitates the modeling of natural systems. Yet, this benefit is not perceived in the opposite direction, as integrating science into mathematics may not build appropriate conceptual bridges for students to develop rich connections between math concepts and procedures (Lehrer & Schauble, 2000).

Partnerships for STEM learning

Along with determining which STEM content will be included, STEM partnerships must establish how the partners will work together to create and implement programs. In this section, we first describe informal and formal education sectors and then describe models for program implementation.

Who Are the Partners?

We consider four sectors of education: primary and secondary schools, higher education, afterschool programs, and STEM-rich environments. We define STEM-rich environments as "science centers and museums, universities and colleges, corporations and businesses, and government agencies" that work in partnership to "open up the possibility for incredibly impactful STEM learning opportunities for youth" (Alliance, 2015, p. 14).

In most countries, children enter compulsory education somewhere around age 6 and complete their compulsory schooling between ages 15 and 18. This schooling occurs largely in classrooms with a teacher leading a group of same-age children. The teachers are responsible for preparing students according to a set of standards and assigning grades before children move on to the next level of schooling. In this chapter, this type of education environment is referred to as primary and secondary schools.

The higher education sector includes colleges, universities, and vocational programs. While higher education has some overlap in affordances and structural norms with schools, students in higher education typically have more agency. They can select areas of study and can choose whether or not to attend the program. Instructors of STEM disciplines at higher education institutions also tend to have more specialized STEM expertise and less pedagogical training than their counterparts at schools for younger learners. We consider the sector that includes districts and schools for children between the ages of 6 and 18 and the sector of higher education to be "formal" education settings.

A third education sector includes community-based programs and afterschool programs for youth. These types of institutions might offer afterschool clubs, classes, summer camps, or drop-in activities. They may have regular programming, but this programming is generally not held accountable to the same curricular standards of schools, and the youth participating may not attend on as regular of a basis as schools.

The final education sector, STEM-rich environments, includes museums, science centers, zoos, and aquaria. These are sometimes called informal science institutions or science-rich environments.

Institutions from this sector serve a broad public audience and include phenomena and tools that differ from those at schools. "Informal" settings like STEM-rich environments and afterschool and community-based settings are not held to the disciplinary boundaries and expectations of classrooms, allowing them greater opportunities to build on students' interest and focus on goals like engagement and identity.

How Do Partners Work Together?

There is a wide range of ways that partners work together to implement learning opportunities. In a Center for Advancement of Informal Science Education (CAISE) report on the relationships between science education in formal and informal settings, Beven et al. (2010) describe differences in programs based on the frequency and duration of a program and the level of structure (e.g., whether activities are sequenced, the degree to which they are evaluated). They outline five types of partnerships between formal and informal education institutions.

1. **Supplementary classroom enrichment.** Supplementary classroom enrichments build on the classroom STEM goals. These include the most common ways that schools and informal institutions address student STEM learning. This category includes classroom field trips to informal institutions, visits to schools by experts from informal institutions, or opportunities for teacher professional development (e.g., Behrendt & Franklin, 2014).
2. **Integrated classroom resources.** Integrated classroom resources are typically much longer than supplementary classroom enrichment. They may be semester or year-long programs that include school-based and informal environments and pedagogies. They may take the form of multiple field trips that build on one another or kits or activities created by the informal environments that are integrated into the school curriculum or both (e.g., Stevens, Andrade, & Page, 2016).
3. **Sustained student learning communities.** Sustained student communities are programs that bring students together to focus on STEM outcomes that may not directly relate to school-based curricular goals. Typically, the informal science education institution plays a larger role in setting the goals and pedagogical direction, and which schools may provide space and recruit participants. These include afterschool, weekend, and summer programs.
4. **Sustained teacher learning communities.** Sustained teacher learning communities are longer-term professional development activities that address their classroom practice. They may focus on developing teachers' conceptual development, understanding of STEM practices, lessons, or identity as STEM learners. They do not typically depend on the teachers' curricula but instead on developing the teachers as learners. These may look like sustained workshops over multiple weeks (e.g., Heredia & Yu, 2015).
5. **District infrastructure development.** District infrastructure development includes collaborations between institutions and districts as part of long-term improvement strategies, including novice teacher training, ongoing professional development, and curriculum planning projects. These also include museum schools and other intense collaborations designed to build district capacity.

These five types of programs provide a tool to think about how institutions work together and the organization of the resulting program, but do not specify content.

What Do Integrated-STEM Partnerships Look Like?

In this section, we present examples of programs developed through partnerships to foster STEM learning that illustrate the types of programs described thus far and are generated from a range of program types with differing goals. These examples come from the literature and our own experiences working in STEM partnerships. To meet their goals, each program includes at least two of the STEM topic areas and partners from multiple education sectors. The examples were selected to demonstrate diverse ways of implementing programs through STEM partnerships. Figures 13.2–13.6 depict the STEM content included in each project and the education sectors of the institutions involved.

The City We Want. Students from over 100 schools in Brazil worked together to solve problems and design solutions. They engaged in science and engineering practices and content and link to one another through technology. The Brazilian students "chose problems to work on, evaluated design ideas and trade-offs, and determined solutions to improve their towns" (Cavallo et al., 2004, p. 1038). Students developed complex projects such as sensors that detect vacant bus seats connected to a display of available seats. Clearly, these projects involved thinking about science and technology while applying math skills and required significantly more time than typical homework. Yet, the authentic problem solving motivated students, and even students who had previously underperformed developed confidence. The teachers also developed confidence. One reported, "We may not already know all we need to know in advance, but we can learn as we go along designing and building and testing out ideas" (Cavallo et al., 2004, p. 1038). In this project the STEM disciplines were integrated. Students drew on multiple areas as they solved a real problem.

Curie–osity. "Curie-osity" brought girls from a community-based, afterschool program to the university campus to learn about women in STEM disciplines. Girls in grades 4–6 (ages 9–11) interviewed university faculty in the sciences, engineering, and mathematics and participated in hands-on activities related to the professor's area of work. The girls then wrote a book about the women STEM faculty (Arya & McBeath, 2018). The partnership provided opportunities for the young girls to learn about multiple STEM areas from geology to mathematics and chemical engineering, as well as to spend time on campus. An important goal of this project was for the girls to learn about the lives of the scientists, mathematicians, and engineers so that they could see themselves in similar roles. Meaningful experiences with role models in STEM fields have been shown to engage youth and contribute to their development of STEM identities (Buck, Clark, Leslie-Pelecky, Lu, & Cerda-Lizarraga, 2008). Role models can impact an individual's level of motivation for a particular domain, and seeing someone achieve a valued outcome through effort can instill motivating expectancies for similar outcomes in others if they put in comparable work (Bussey & Bandura, 1999). In this project, the STEM disciplines were introduced in parallel. The students drew parallels between the disciplines as they considered all of the stories together, but each discipline was introduced separately.

Fabricating Fidgets. In a third example, university education researchers, a middle school special education class, and a local museum partnered to provide students with cognitive differences with an authentic engineering design experience using new technology tools (Hansen, Hansen, Hall,

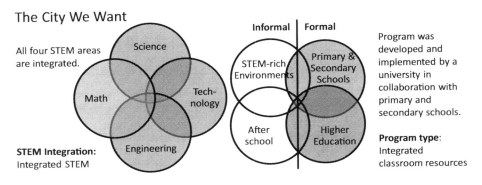

Figure 13.2 The City We Want content and partners.

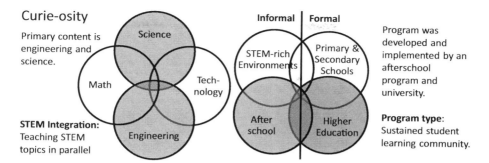

Figure 13.3   Curie–osity content and partners.

Fixler, & Harlow, 2017). The special education teacher brought expertise of his students and their needs, the education researchers brought expertise in engineering education, and the museum provided access to tools including a 3D printer and laser cutter. The students developed a set of criteria and constraints for designing a fidget tool that would help them focus in class without distracting their classmates. The students learned to use the design technology tool TinkerCad and iteratively designed a fidget tool. Through this, students practiced mathematics ideas such as measuring and proportional reasoning. Some created fidget spinners, and others created fidget tools that they could squish or otherwise manipulate. After multiple design iterations, the students took a field trip to the local interactive science museum to use their 3D printers and other tools. The museum staff helped the students fabricate their fidgets. This experience provided special education students with the opportunity to participate in an innovative and authentic problem. The STEM model here was that the two STEM topics, technology and engineering, built on one another. Students were introduced explicitly to engineering design and taught to use the relevant technology (TinkerCad, 3D printers) as a way to move their design forward.

Engineering Explorations. Engineering Explorations (e.g., Muller, Harlow, & Skinner, 2019) is a collaboration between an interactive science center, a university, elementary school teachers, and an afterschool program. The goal of the project is to develop suites of coordinated STEM activities. Each suite focuses on an engineering task completed at MOXI, The Wolf Museum of Exploration + Innovation (e.g., Harlow, Skinner & O'Brien, 2017). Activities done in classrooms prior to the field trip develop physical science and engineering ideas that the students will use in their field trip program and require students to use mathematics skills being developed in their classrooms. A final activity done in the classroom after the field trip brings all the ideas together. The suite of activities align with national standards for science (NGSS Lead States, 2013) (which includes engineering) and mathematics. In addition, the materials include resources to help teachers learn about teaching engineering. Entire suites of activities are combined to create afterschool programs for youth enrolled in Girls Inc. (Chen, Weiss, & Nicholson, 2010), an afterschool program for girls in grades kindergarten (age 6) through grade 8 (age 14). The curriculum is developed by museum and university staff with input from teachers at the participating elementary and secondary schools and leadership from the afterschool program.

21st Century Skills and Global Competencies. Science North (http://sciencenorth.ca), Canada's second largest science center, has regularly consulted and partnered with local school boards to develop relevant STEM programming. Through its strong relationship with Ontario's Ministry of Education, Science North has worked closely with curriculum policy staff to better understand the Ministry's priorities. As a result, Science North developed and continues to deliver student and teacher programs that focus on science and innovation, science literacy, and mathematics. These

Fabricating Fidgets

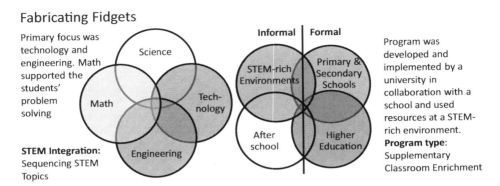

Primary focus was technology and engineering. Math supported the students' problem solving

STEM Integration: Sequencing STEM Topics

Program was developed and implemented by a university in collaboration with a school and used resources at a STEM-rich environment.
Program type: Supplementary Classroom Enrichment

Figure 13.4 Fabricating Fidgets content and partners.

Engineering Explorations

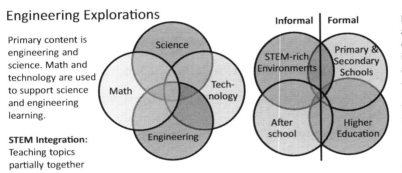

Primary content is engineering and science. Math and technology are used to support science and engineering learning.

STEM Integration: Teaching topics partially together

Program was initiated by an interactive science center and university and implemented in primary and secondary schools and afterschool program. Primary and secondary teachers provide feedback to inform program development.

Program type: Integrated classroom resource

Figure 13.5 Engineering Explorations content and partners.

experiences target and grow 21st-century skills and global competencies such as collaboration, critical thinking, problem solving, innovation, and communication. This partnership with the Ministry of Education has worked with teachers all over the province of Ontario to develop and deliver a multi-year Science North Teacher Summer Institute (Science North, 2018), and to implement a research project in partnership with Laurentian University's School of Education to build capacity for French Immersion science teachers.

Coding and Integrated STEM Learning. Science North recently received federal government support to develop and deliver coding experiences to students and teachers in Ontario, a skill that is of great importance to the Ministry of Education and to school boards. The coding workshops were designed to teach students and teachers to code, but more importantly, participants learned how to use coding as a tool to learn or teach science, mathematics, and engineering. For example, in the grade 7 program, students created a game in "Scratch" to demonstrate how invasive species can proliferate in an environment, which directly tied into the grade 7 science curriculum strand of Interactions in the Environment (Science North, n.d.).

The examples in this section all describe specific programs that evolved through partnerships between institutions and individuals from multiple education sectors. In each case, the program leveraged the diverse expertise and resources of partners from multiple sectors. The programs vary greatly in their duration (from a single activity to multi-year projects), the number of students or teachers they serve (from a small group of students to entire school districts) and their learning goals.

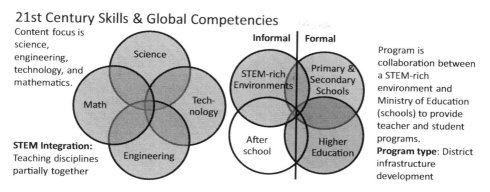

Figure 13.6 21st Century Skills and Global Competencies content and partners.

How Are Partnerships Sustained?

So far, we have outlined ways that STEM topics might be integrated and how individual programs developed through STEM partnerships might be implemented through formal-informal partnerships. However, many programs are developed and sustained through larger partnership infrastructures that develop many different programs, either simultaneously or at different times. Partnerships evolve as goals change and as evaluation and research are used to promote growth. The following frameworks describe models of partnerships that are generally larger than one particular program, but maintain a mechanism for communication and collaboration for participants in a partnership and can be applied to smaller programs to inform their development and assess outcomes.

Research–Practice Partnerships. One model for developing partnerships is that of Research–Practice Partnerships (RPPs) (e.g., Bevan, 2017; Penuel, 2017; Penuel & Gallagher, 2017). These are long-term collaborations between practitioners and researchers who work together to address problems of practice. The work of RPPs often involves iterative research and evaluation that assesses the effectiveness for multiple stakeholders and provides feedback that leads to more effective programs and dissemination of the programs. RPPs begin by identifying the needs of the educational institution and co-developing mutual problems of practice and co-designing curricular materials, contexts, or programs which lead to specific researchable questions. Henrick, Cobb, Penuel, Jackson, and Clark (2017) describe three different types of RPPs: *research alliances*, which focus on a specific school district or region; *design research partnerships*, which "design, study, improve and scale innovations in teaching and learning" (p. 2); and *Networked Improvement Communities*, which are more structured collaborations that commit to using specific tools and methods to gather data across a network. Through interviews with participants in all three types of RPPs, they developed a five-dimensional model of effectiveness. They concluded that successful RPPs (1) build trust and cultivating partnership relationships, (2) conduct rigorous research to inform action, (3) support the partner practice organization in achieving its goals, (4) produce knowledge that can inform educational improvement efforts more broadly, and (5) build the capacity of participating researchers, practitioners, practice organizations, and research organizations to engage in partnership work (Henrick et al., 2017).

Community–Based Partnerships. Other models of STEM partnerships focus on the role of the public or community partners in the research process (Belone et al., 2016; Bonney et al., 2009; Pandya, 2012). For example, collaborative and co-created citizen science projects engage the public in collecting and analyzing data, typically related to the local environment (Bonney et al., 2009). Pandya (2012) proposes a culturally relevant citizen science framework which features an alignment between research aims and community priorities, community oversight throughout the project, appreciation of local STEM knowledge, and community involvement in the dissemination of findings. Similar to citizen science, but with a focus on public health, community-based participatory research (Belone et al., 2016) engages the public as partners in research, knowledge generation, and policy implementation. Belone's framework is drawn from the health sciences and outlines the four dimensions of *contexts* (sociocultural and historical influences), *group dynamics* (individual, structural, and relational factors), *intervention* (research design and implementation), and *outcomes* (policy or practice changes). Belone and colleagues recommend using the framework for enacting change related to public health, but also as a facilitation tool for leading discussions with partners to determine best practices.

STEM Learning Ecosystems. STEM learning ecosystems are larger collaborations between many institutions usually focused on a specific geographic area. These STEM ecosystems include not only schools, afterschool settings, STEM-rich environments, and universities but may also include industry partners and other community-focused organizations. These ecosystems strive to create mutually reinforcing opportunities.

> A learning ecosystem harnesses the unique contributions of all these different settings in symbiosis to deliver STEM learning for all children. Designed pathways enable young people to become engaged, knowledgeable and skilled in the STEM disciplines as they progress through childhood into adolescence and early adulthood.
>
> *(Traphagen & Traill, 2014, p. 2)*

Recent policy documents in the United States advocate fostering STEM ecosystems as one of the primary mechanisms to advance STEM learning (Committee on STEM Education, 2018)

Research Center–Informal Science Environment (RISE). Alpert (2009) describes the Research Center–Informal Science Environment (RISE) model in which researchers at a university partner with an informal science environment (usually science museums) to implement outreach programs that meet the requirements of funding agencies funding the science research.

While there is no one right way to develop and implement programs, Hammerness, MacPherson, Macdonald, Roditi, and Curtis-Bey (2017) determined that the key components that contributed to their success at establishing and maintaining a 13-year partnership between New York schools and community cultural centers were *distributed expertise, a shared vision for teacher and student learning, turning shared vision into shared practices,* and *adapting to changing contexts.* Establishing shared vision requires institutions from different sectors to understand the affordances, constraints, and goals of the other sectors. Bevan and Dillon (2010) advocate that "Training programs for both formal and informal educators need to develop more opportunities for conversations and concrete collaborative projects, that span the goals and expertise of both formal and informal educators." Such programs would help educators understand each other's perspectives and contribute to greater alignment. The models described in this chapter all require the ongoing dialog between the individuals of the multiple institutions (Kim & Dopico, 2016).

Conclusion

Providing opportunities for youth to engage in STEM programming develops their capacity to solve complex problems that cannot be effectively addressed through any one of the STEM disciplines individually. Partnering across informal and formal institutions allows programs to leverage the expertise and resources of multiple institutions and have a collective impact that is larger than any one of the institutions would have individually (Kania & Kramer, 2011). Schools have access to consistent populations of students and teachers with classroom experience and pedagogical content knowledge in the field(s) they teach. Informal institutions such as museums, science centers, zoos, aquaria, and afterschool programs have access to phenomena, animals, and materials for youth to explore and access to experts in the STEM disciplines who may also be practicing scientists and engineers.

STEM programs developed through partnerships between informal and formal education institutions vary widely. They differ in goals, in the degree to which STEM topics are integrated, and in the roles of the partnership institutions. Partnership programs that support STEM learning require two different types of connections: (1) connections among and between the STEM subjects, *and* (2) connections among and between educational sectors. While carefully designed programs that effectively leverage the affordances and expertise of multiple institutions provide rich learning, programs created through partnerships also risk resulting in a series of disjointed activities where individual activities align with goals of individual institutions. Thoughtful attention to the ways program activities reinforce and build on one another is necessary. In closing, we note that, while this chapter has focused on institutions, those institutional partnerships are rooted in the collaborations and collective work done by individuals of those institutions such as faculty and graduate students with expertise in STEM disciplines, researchers, classroom teachers, and practitioners in out-of-school environments such as museums and afterschool programs.

References

Adams, J. D., Gupta, P., & Cotumaccio, A. (2014). Long-term participants: A museum program enhances girls' STEM interest, motivation, and persistence. *Afterschool Matters, 20*, 13–20.

Alliance, A. (2015). *Full STEM ahead: Afterschool programs step up as key partners in STEM education.* Retrieved from http://www.informalscience.org/full-stem-ahead-after-school-programs-step-key-partners-stem-education

Alpert, C. L. (2009). Broadening and deepening the impact: A theoretical framework for partnerships between science museums and STEM research centres. *Social Epistemology, 23*(3–4), 267–281.

Arya, D., & McBeath, J. (Eds.). (2018). *Steminists. The lifework of 12 woman scientists and engineers.* San Francisco, CA: Xochitl Justice Press.

Banilower, E. R., Smith, P. S., Malzahn, K. A., Plumley, C. L., Gordon, E. M., & Hayes, M. L. (2018). *Report of the 2018 National Survey of Science & Mathematics Education (NSSME).* Horizon Research Inc. Retrieved from http://horizon-research.com/NSSME/2018-nssme/research-products/reports/technical-report

Barron, B. (2006). Interest and self-sustained learning as catalysts of development: A learning ecology perspective. *Human Development, 49*(4), 193–224.

Becker, K., & Park, K. (2011). Effects of integrative approaches among science, technology, engineering, and mathematics (STEM) subjects on students' learning: A preliminary meta-analysis. *Journal of STEM Education: Innovations & Research, 12*.

Behrendt, M., & Franklin, T. (2014). A review of research on school field trips and their value in education. *International Journal of Environmental and Science Education, 9*(3), 235–245.

Belone, L., Lucero, J. E., Duran, B., Tafoya, G., Baker, E. A., Chan, D., . . . Wallerstein, N. (2016). Community-based participatory research conceptual model: Community partner consultation and face validity. *Qualitative Health Research, 26*(1), 117–135. doi:10.1177/1049732314557084

Bevan, B. (2017). Research and practice: One way, two way, no way, or new way? *Curator: The Museum Journal, 60*(2), 133–141. doi:10.1111/cura.12204

Bevan, B., & Dillon, J. (2010). Broadening views of learning: Developing educators for the 21st century through an international research partnership at the Exploratorium and King's College London. *The New Educator, 6*(3–4), 167–180. doi:10.1080/1547688X.2010.10399599

Bevan, B., Dillon, J., Hein, G. E., Macdonald, M., Michalchik, V., Miller, D., . . . Yoon, S. (2010). *Making science matter: Collaborations between informal science education organizations and schools. A CAISE inquiry group report.* Washington, DC: Center for Advancement of Informal Science Education (CAISE).

Bevan, B., Gutwill, J. P., Petrich, M., & Wilkinson, K. (2015). Learning through STEM-rich tinkering: Findings from a jointly negotiated research project taken up in practice. *Science Education, 99*(1), 98–120.

Bonney, R., Ballard, H., Jordan, R., McCallie, E., Phillips, T., Shirk, J., & Wilderman, C. C. (2009). *Public participation in scientific research: Defining the field and assessing its potential for informal science education. A CAISE Inquiry Group Report.* Washington, DC: Center for Advancement of Informal Science.

Buck, G. A., Clark, V. L. P., Leslie-Pelecky, D., Lu, Y., & Cerda-Lizarraga, P. (2008). Examining the cognitive processes used by adolescent girls and women scientists in identifying science role models: A feminist approach. *Science Education, 92*(4), 688–707. doi:10.1002/sce.20257

Busch-Vishniac, I. J., & Jarosz, J. P. (2004). Can diversity in the undergraduate engineering population be enhanced through curricular change? *Journal of Women and Minorities in Science and Engineering, 10*(3). https://doi.org/10.1615/JWomenMinorScienEng.v10.i3.50

Bussey, K., & Bandura, A. (1999). Social cognitive theory of gender development and differentiation. *Psychological Review, 106*(4), 676–713. doi:10.1037/0033–295X.106.4.676

Cavallo, D., Blikstein, P., Sipitakiat, A., Basu, A., Camargo, A., de Deus Lopes, R., & Cavallo, A. (2004). The city that we want: Generative themes, constructionist technologies and school/social change. In *IEEE International Conference on Advanced Learning Technologies, 2004. Proceedings.* Joensuu, Finland (pp. 1034–1038). doi/10.1109/ICALT.2004.1357744

Cech, E. A. (2013). Culture of disengagement in engineering education? *Science, Technology & Human Values, 39*(1), 42–72.

Chen, P., Weiss, F. L., & Nicholson, H. J. (2010). Girls study Girls Inc.: Engaging girls in evaluation through participatory action research. *American Journal of Community Psychology, 46*(1–2), 228–237.

Committee on STEM Education of the National Science and Technology Council. (2018). *Charting a course for success: America's strategy for STEM education.* Washington, DC: The White House. Retrieved from https://www.whitehouse.gov/wp-content/uploads/2018/12/STEM-Education-Strategic-Plan-2018.pdf

Dabney, K. P., Tai, R. H., & Scott, M. R. (2016). Informal science: Family education, experiences, and initial interest in science. *International Journal of Science Education, Part B, 6*(3), 263–282.

DeBoer, G. E. (1991). *A history of ideas in science education: Implications for practice.* Teachers College Press, 1234 Amsterdam Avenue, New York, NY 10027.

English, L. D. (2016). STEM education K-12: Perspectives on integration. *International Journal of STEM Education, 3*(1), 3. doi:10.1186/s40594-016-0036-1

Hammerness, K., MacPherson, A., Macdonald, M., Roditi, H., & Curtis-Bey, L. (2017). What does it take to sustain a productive partnership in education? *Phi Delta Kappan, 99*(1), 15–20. doi:10.1177/0031721717728272

Hansen, A., Hansen, E., Hall, T., Fixler, M., & Harlow, D. (2017). Fidgeting with Fabrication: Students with ADHD making tools to focus. *Proceedings of the 7th Annual Conference on Creativity and Fabrication in Education.* Stanford, CA, USA. doi:10.1145/3141798.3141812

Harlow, D., Hansen, A., McBeath, J., & Leak, A. (2018). Teacher education for maker education: Helping teachers develop appropriate PCK for engaging children in Maker education. In S. Uzzo (Ed.), *Pedagogical content knowledge in STEM.* Cham: Springer.

Harlow, D., Skinner, R., & O'Brien, S. (2017). Roll it wall: Developing a framework for evaluating practices of learning. *Proceedings of the 7th Annual Conference on Creativity and Fabrication in Education.* Stanford, CA, USA. doi:10.1145/3141798.3141813

Henrick, E. C., Cobb, P., Penuel, W. R., Jackson, K., & Clark, T. (2017). *Assessing research-practice partnerships: Five dimensions of effectiveness.* New York, NY: William T. Grant Foundation.

Heredia, S. C., & Yu, J. H. (2015). *Exploratorium teacher induction program: Results and retention.* Retrieved from https://www.exploratorium.edu/sites/default/files/pdfs/Exploratorium-TIP-Report_0.pdf

Hill, C., Corbett, C., & St. Rose, A. (2010). *Why so few? Women in science, technology, engineering, and mathematics.* Washington, DC: American Association of University Women. Retrieved from http://eric.ed.gov/?id=ED509653

Honey, M., Pearson, G., & Schweingruber, H. (Eds.). (2014). *STEM integration in K-12 education: Status, prospects, and an agenda for research.* Washington, DC: National Academies Press.

Hurley, M. M. (2001). Reviewing integrated science and mathematics: The search for evidence and definitions from new perspectives. *School Science and Mathematics, 101*(5), 259–268. doi:10.1111/j.1949-8594.2001.tb18028.x

Jacobs, H. H. (Ed.). (1989). *Interdisciplinary curriculum: Design and implementation.* Alexandria, VA: Association for Supervision and Curriculum Development.

Johnson, C. C., Peters-Burton, E. E., & Moore, T. J. (2016). *STEM road map: A framework for integrated STEM education.* New York, NY: Routledge.

Johnson, K., Leydens, J. A., Moskal, B. M., Silva, D., & Fantasky, J. S. (2015). *Social justice in control systems engineering* (pp. 1–19). American Society for Engineering Education. Retrieved from http://www.osti.gov/scitech/biblio/1225339

Kania, J., & Kramer, M. (2011). Collective impact. *Stanford Social Innovation Review.* Retrieved from https://www.everychildcq.org/wp-content/uploads/2018/06/Collective-Impact-Stanford-Social-Innovation-Review-2011.pdf

Kim, M., & Dopico, E. (2016). Science education through informal education. *Cultural Studies of Science Education, 11*(2), 439–445. doi:10.1007/s11422-014-9639-3

Lehrer, R., & L. Schauble. (2000). Modeling in mathematics and science. In R. Glaser (Ed.), *Advances in instructional psychology* (Vol. 5, pp. 101–159). Mahwah, NJ: Lawrence Erlbaum Associates.

Marginson, S., Tytler, R., Freeman, B., & Roberts, K. (2013). *STEM: Country comparisons: International comparisons of science, technology, engineering and mathematics (STEM) education.* Report for the Australian Council of Learned Academies, Melbourne, Australia.

Martins Gomes, D., & McCauley, V. (2016). Dialectical dividends: Fostering hybridity of new pedagogical practices and partnerships in science education and outreach. *International Journal of Science Education, 38*(14), 2259–2283. doi:10.1080/09500693.2016.1234729

Moore, Johnston, and Clancy. (2019). Chapter 1, this volume.

Muller, A., Harlow, D., & Skinner, R. (2019). *Engineering explorations: Integrating physics and engineering activities into classrooms.* Presented at the American Association of Physics Teachers (AAPT), Provo, UT, July 22–24, 2019.

National Research Council. (2010). *Surrounded by science: Learning science in informal environments.* Washington, DC: National Academies Press.

National Research Council. (2012). *A framework for K-12 science education: Practices, crosscutting concepts, and core ideas.* Washington, DC: The National Academies Press.

NGSS Lead States. (2013). *Next generation science standards: For states, by states.* Washington, DC: The National Academies Press.

Pandya, R. E. (2012). A framework for engaging diverse communities in citizen science in the US. *Frontiers in Ecology and the Environment, 10*(6), 314–317. doi:10.1890/120007

Penuel, W. R. (2017). Research–practice partnerships as a strategy for promoting equitable science teaching and learning through leveraging everyday science. *Science Education, 101*(4), 520–525. doi:10.1002/sce.21285

Penuel, W. R., & Gallagher, D. J. (2017). *Creating research-practice partnerships in education.* Cambridge, MA: Harvard Education Press.

Science North. (2018). *Annual report.* Retrieved from https://sciencenorth.ca/17-18-SN-AR.pdf

Science North. (n.d.). Retrieved from https://sciencenorth.ca/schools/schoolprograms/sn/

Smith, K. L., Rayfield, J., & McKim, B. R. (2015). Effective practices in STEM integration: Describing teacher perceptions and instructional method use. *Journal of Agricultural Education, 56*(4), 183–203.

Stevens, S., Andrade, R., & Page, M. (2016). Motivating young native American students to pursue STEM learning through a culturally relevant science program. *Journal of Science Education and Technology, 25*(6), 947–960.

Traphagen, K., & Traill, S. (2014). *How cross-sector collaborations are advancing STEM learning.* Los Altos, CA: Noyce Foundation.

Vasquez, J., Sneider, C., & Comer, M. (2013). *STEM lesson essentials, grades 3–8: Integrating science, technology, engineering, and mathematics.* Portsmouth, NH: Heinemann.

Venville, G., Rennie, L., & Wallace, J. (2004). Decision making and sources of knowledge: How students tackle integrated tasks in science, technology and mathematics. *Research in Science Education, 34*(2), 115–135. doi:10.1023/B:RISE.0000033762.75329.9b

Wang, H.-H., & Knobloch, N. A. (2018). Levels of STEM integration through agriculture, food, and natural resources. *Journal of Agricultural Education, 59*(3), 258–277.

SECTION 3

STEM Pedagogy, Curriculum and Assessment

14

HISTORY OF INTEGRATED STEM CURRICULUM

Christa Jackson, Kristina M. Tank, Mollie H. Appelgate,
Kari Jurgenson, Ashley Delaney and Coskun Erden

Introduction

Franklin Bobbitt in his 1918 book, *The Curriculum*, defined curriculum as "the entire range of experiences, both undirected and directed, concerned in unfolding the abilities of the individual" (1918, p. 43). While he largely accepted the more traditional definition of curriculum, John Dewey (1902), in his text *Child and the Curriculum*, noted his disagreement with the idea that you could separate the child and their experiences and asserted that "the child and the curriculum are simply two limits which define a single process" (1902, p. 11; cited in Jackson, 1992, p. 6). These differing views on curriculum from over 100 years ago highlight some of the complexities intertwined in the conceptualization of curriculum that are also present when discussing the concept of curriculum integration.

Integrated curriculum represents approximately equal attention to two or more disciplines (Huntley, 1998). Mason (1996) defines curriculum integration as "a knowledge view and curriculum approach that consciously applies methodology and language from more than one discipline to examine a central theme, issue, problem, topic, or experience" (p. 264). The integration of curriculum within STEM is not new and, as noted by several researchers, there have been a number of references to various forms of integration over the past 100 years (Beane, 1996; Berlin & White, 1994; Hurley, 1999; Lederman & Niess, 1997). Although there is not a common definition of integrated STEM curriculum, there is a consensus for organizing it around a range of experiences with some degree of connection between science, technology, engineering, and mathematics (Bybee, 2013; Czerniak & Johnson, 2014; National Academy of Engineering [NAE] and National Research Council [NRC], 2014). As we report on the history of integrated STEM curriculum, we recognize that educational goals, curriculum reforms, and curriculum development are all "influenced by changing values in the broader society" (DeBoer, 2014, p. 559). Therefore, we will report not only on some of the influential integrated curriculum projects that have shaped the development of integrated STEM curriculum, but also on periods of educational and curriculum reform that have been influential to the development of STEM curriculum. In this chapter, we provide a brief historical summary of integrated STEM curriculum in the United States and internationally (e.g., Australia, New Zealand, Japan, England/UK, Canada) from the 19th century to the present. Even though integrated STEM curriculum cannot be completely separated from the history and development of integrated STEM education (see Chapter 1), the focus of this chapter is on the history and development of STEM curriculum and the influential developments that have impacted that development from the 19th century to the present.

Early Development in Mathematics Curricula

European and American models of mathematics and science education collided during the Chicago World's Columbian Exposition of 1893 where Germany's Felix Klein, a pioneering mathematician who was interested in mathematics education, presented 12 lectures to the Congress of Mathematics and Astronomy (White, 1894). Klein encouraged the training of future teachers and development of curriculum to prepare students similarly to Germany and much of Europe (Klein, 1911). In comparison to American high schools and academies, European secondary schools implemented in-depth curricula in the humanities, mathematics, and the sciences (Servos, 1986). Teachers were highly trained in content and assessed to ensure students were adequately prepared for university across disciplines, instead of allowing the humanities to dominate (Gispert, 2009). Providing rigorous coursework in mathematics as well as applying mathematics to science fields such as physics and astronomy enriched content knowledge and extended the disciplines beyond elementary understanding (Donoghue, 2003).

During the post Antebellum period, mathematics had lost favorability at universities in the United States (Guralnick, 1975). Much of the mathematics coursework was replaced with laboratory-based sciences such as chemistry while European universities expanded courses to include both advanced mathematics and science (Servos, 1986). European devotion to elementary and secondary mathematics education was evident by the existence of multiple research journals including Britain's *The Educational Times* (1849), and the 1822 founding of the *Journal de Mathématiques Spéciales* and the 1876 founding of the *Journal de Mathématiques Élémentaires* in France. The academic journals and their governing associations held elemental roles in the growth and reform of mathematics education in Europe (Furinghetti, Matos, & Menghini, 2013). Mathematics education leaders such as Felix Klein (Germany), Charlies Émile Ernest Carlo Bourlet (France), and John Perry (Britain) led reform efforts in teacher preparation and advancing curriculum (Nabonnand, 2007). For example, Perry (1901) argued that mathematics education must consider the developmental needs and personal interests of children. "The Perry Movement" advocated a hands-on approach to doing mathematics with rules, shape manipulation, and exploration (Howson, 1982). Perry's ideas spread abroad through his publications and influenced Japanese mathematics education (Siu, 2009).

Early Curriculum Development-Committee of Ten Report

When looking at the history of curriculum, the final report of the Committee of Ten, chaired by Harvard University President Charles Elliot (National Education Association [NEA], 1894) was influential in its recommendation for the inclusion of science within the school curriculum (DeBoer, 2014). The Committee of Ten, a group of primarily college and university presidents, was charged with standardizing curriculum for secondary schools. Each of the members led a subcommittee focused on the different disciplines that may be offered by a high school, which included mathematics, chemistry, physics, and astronomy. They presented a set of educational reforms designed to make curricular recommendations for how and what subjects should be taught and how much time should be devoted to those subjects within the secondary school curriculum. The Committee of Ten 1894 report suggested approximately one-fifth of a student's time in secondary school be devoted to science with a focus on the use of a laboratory approach (NEA, 1894). With these recommendations, science was an established part of the curriculum along with mathematics and other subjects such as Latin, classical studies, modern language, and English. The mathematics subcommittee produced five reports where one was a general conclusion statement and the remaining four related to teaching arithmetic, algebra, concrete geometry, and formal geometry. One of the recommendations of the arithmetic report stated, "The study of arithmetic should be intimately associated with the study of algebra, of concrete geometry, and elementary physics," thereby explicitly recommending the integration of mathematics and science within the school curriculum.

Progressive Era and the Beginning of Integration: Early 1900s

In the 1930s and 1940s, the progressive education movement supported a new push for curriculum reform. This movement emphasized student-centered integrative approaches to education (Vars, 1991), which is often referred to as the core curriculum. Specifically, the core curriculum referred to a "problem-focused, block-time, interdisciplinary course" (Wraga, 2009, p. 93), and it focused on personal and social needs, current social problems, and democratic values (Beane, 1975; Wraga, 2009). The core curriculum identifying problems, issues, and concerns of students and the community in which they live and used the skills and content from various subjects to solve or deal with those issues. The characteristics of the core curriculum included problem-centered teaching focused on experience and student interests, and on use of group and individual work (Alberty, 1953). The purpose of the integrative nature of the core curriculum was to provide students with opportunities for collaboration in which they could apply and integrate content knowledge to analyze personal or social problems (Wraga, 2009). Several resources, including *Developing the Core Curriculum* (Fraunce & Bossing, 1951), *Developing a High School Core Program* (Lurry & Alberty, 1957), *Democratic Processes in the Secondary Classroom* (Zapf, 1959), and *Common Learnings: Core and Interdisciplinary Team Approaches* (Vars, 1969), were developed to establish interdisciplinary and problem-centered core programs.

During the Progressive Era, social and political reforms incited drastic changes in the teaching and learning of mathematics and science. The curriculum in the Progressive Era had a child-centered approach focused on exploration, problem solving, and experiential learning that prepared students to participate in democracy (Parker, 1996). The progressive curriculum, led by John Dewey, developed the social consciousness of students to ensure social progress and reform (Dewey, 1897), and required interdisciplinary knowledge, social engagement, and respect for diversity (Darling-Hammond & Ancess, 1996). Curriculum models such as the project method were common during this time (Knoll, 2012), and with roots in engineering and architecture, the project method focused on using multiple disciplines to engineer solutions to purposeful problems.

Above all else, the Progressive Era advocated for quality education for all and was a period that provided opportunity for inclusion of disenfranchised groups in the United States. For example, Black educators such as Booker T. Washington worked tirelessly to provide rich educational experiences for Black Americans. Others like W. E. B. Du Bois and Carter Woodson integrated mathematics and science curriculum within Black history. Their promotion of practical education and proficiency in art and science curriculum were central to successfully navigating White society and moving toward equality (Alridge, 2009). Progressive educators made only incremental changes in the curriculum across most of Canada and the United States despite their innovative approaches to mathematics and science education (Kilpatrick, 2014).

Progressivism was in strict contrast to the ideas of Social Darwinism (Hofstadter, 1992) that was common at this time. Led by Herbert Spencer, a British scientist, Social Darwinism applied the laws of natural selection to society, coining the phrase "survival of the fittest" to rationalize success and struggle in society (Claeys, 2000; Spencer, 1864). Social Darwinism led to justifications for eugenics, colonialism, and other forms of oppression in the United States, Japan, China, and Europe (Claeys, 2000). In fact, proponents of Social Darwinism contend knowledge could be obtained only through a scientific approach, and therefore, science curriculum required a teacher competent in science content to emphasize logic, critical thinking, and scientific investigation (DeBoer, 2000). Spencer dismissed the child-centered approach to education, advocating instead for a more discipline-specific and authoritarian approach. In his 1911 publication *Essays on Education and Kindred Subjects*, Spencer argued learning stems from experts who can tell children what to sense: see, hear, say, and believe. Spencer claimed young children were not able to comprehend many abstract concepts of upper-level science, a belief many still hold today (Sunal, Sunal, Sundberg & Wright, 2008). Although Spencer considered an interdisciplinary approach vital to a successful curriculum, he argued that scientific knowledge was most important and advocated for the laboratory approach to science curriculum as the supreme pedagogical approach to learning. The laboratory approach centered on developing children's laboratory skills: observation, description, classification, and memorization of objects to prepare them for more complex sciences (Sunal et al., 2008). Similarly, U.S. mathematician E. H. Moore, along with David Eugene Smith, "recommended a laboratory approach that used concrete materials to teach practical mathematics through the scientific method" (Donoghue, 2003, p. 168).

In contrast to a more traditionally accepted laboratory approach, the Nature Study movement was also seen during this period. Nature Study rejected formal science education as it adopted student-led lessons that emphasized biological sciences and a love of nature (Underhill, 1941). Leaders of the Nature Study, such as Anna Comstock and Louis Agassiz, combined observation with personal interaction to study nature (Kohlstedt, 2010). This evolved into curriculum integrating environmentalism, arts, problem solving, and connecting of rich interactions with nature into learning across the disciplines (e.g. Comstock, 1915). Nature Study lost its appeal around 1910 as science educators sought to emphasize the generalization, classification, and philosophical practices that bridged scientific disciplines (Underhill, 1941). Science curriculum in the early 1900s shifted to a more interdisciplinary approach as science was viewed as an application of ideas in everyday life (DeBoer, 1991).

Additionally, during this time, mathematicians, scientists, and educators established professional organizations to share ideas. In 1901, the Central Association of Physics Teachers organized by C. H. Smith and colleagues in Chicago was the first time mathematics and science educators met to collaboratively discuss an interdisciplinary approach to teaching and curriculum development. At their first meeting, the Central Association of Physics Teachers collaborated on the *Journal of School Science and Mathematics,* which disseminated and developed research and ideas about mathematics and science education. The following year, in 1902, the organization adopted a new name, the Central Association of Science and Mathematics Teachers, to better represent the goals and membership. Ultimately, the organization changed their name to School Science and Mathematics Association to match the journal (SSMA, 2018). Other early integration efforts included the first meeting of the International Commission on the Teaching of Mathematics (1911), which led to the creation, publication, and reporting of international approaches to mathematics curriculum and instruction (Donoghue, 2003). The American subcommittee of this commission identified essential curriculum elements including pure mathematics and applied mathematics (ICTM, 1911). The applied mathematics curriculum made explicit connections to science (astronomy and physics) as well as engineering (mechanics), creating fundamental links between STEM disciplines, which required elementary and secondary teachers to take mathematics and science content courses as well as methods courses to prepare them for the classroom. As a move to further solidify the connections between mathematics and engineering, the Society for the Promotion of Engineering Education adopted a comprehensive Syllabus of Mathematics in 1912 (Committee on the Teaching of Mathematics to Students of Engineering, 1912).

By the 1920s, mathematics was not perceived as practical across Canada, which led William Blatz (1936) to propose making mathematics an elective subject or completely removed from the compulsory Canadian curriculum. Numerous educators and psychologists advocated for a hands-on, interactive form of education that integrated all of the subjects (Kilpatrick, 2014). Integrating all disciplines into the academic curriculum allowed Canadian students to learn organically as they interacted with and experienced the world (Sigurdson, Kieren, Pothier, & Roulet, 2003). A similar approach to mathematics and science education was gaining support in the United States.

Sputnik Era: Curriculum Improvement Projects Focused on Integration

In the 1950s, scientists were concerned with the state of science education in the United States, however, it was the Soviet Union's successful launch of Sputnik that motivated the U.S. government to support reform efforts with money and resources (DeBoer, 1991). This came in the form of the 1958 National Defense Education Act, which had as a goal to increase science and mathematics majors and support school building projects (Klein, 2003). As a response to the need to improve science and mathematics and bridging connections between these areas, the Guidelines for Preparation Programs of Teachers of Secondary School Science and Mathematics were adopted. From 1959 to 1961 these guidelines were developed over the course of four conferences, with participants from science, mathematics, and teacher education. The eight guidelines, which focused on ensuring the secondary teacher candidates' coursework was rigorous in the content area in which they would be teaching, were quickly adopted by teacher preparation programs.

This newly heightened focus on science and mathematics led to more money for relevant curriculum. Between 1956 and 1975, over $130 million was allotted by the National Science Foundation (NSF) in the U.S. for curricular projects aimed at improving course content and developing new science curricula (Welch, 1979). However, in this era much of the curriculum development was subject-specific, which meant the curriculum projects were designed around organized bodies of knowledge (Goodlad, von Stoephasius, & Klein, 1966). In 1956, NSF awarded the first of many curriculum development grants to the Physical Science Study Committee (PSSC) to create a new high school physics curriculum (Welch, 1979). Curriculum development projects began to grow after the PSSC physics curriculum. One of the projects that followed was the Biological Science Curriculum Study (BSCS) which was established in 1959 (Welch, 1979). The activities in BSCS made connections between science, technology, and health (Bybee & Landes, 1990).

Integrated curriculum began to make a more formal appearance as many of the curriculum improvement projects emphasized integration. Berlin and Lee (2005) found the number of integrated science and mathematics curricula increased from the single digits in the early 1900s to 29 in the 1960s, and to 119 in the 1970s. Examples of integrated curriculum projects developed during this time included the Nuffield Foundation Science Teaching Project (1967), Unified Science and Mathematics for Elementary Schools (USMES) (published in 1976–77), and the Minnesota Mathematics and Science Teaching Project (MINNEMAST) (published in 1970–72).

Nation at Risk and the Standards Movement

The plethora of curriculum development and interventions produced by the Cold War Era did not produce the anticipated growth in student learning in the United States. The National Commission on Excellence in Education (NCEE) articulated a startling portrayal of the education system in their 1983 report, *A Nation at Risk*. The detailing of the dramatic gaps in the mathematics and science knowledge of U.S. students compared to students from other developed nations portrayed a doom-and-gloom failure of education in the United States. The report sparked both panic and action within the education community and provided recommendations to reform and improve mathematics and science education (NCEE, 1983). The recommendations related to standards and expectations were the impetus for forming standards that would lead to literacy in mathematics, science, and technology (NCEE, 1983). This spurred several movements toward developing rigorous standards that guided curriculum development, including *Project 2061: Science for All Americans* (American Association for the Advancement of Science [AAAS], 1989) and the *Curriculum and Evaluation Standards of School Mathematics* (National Council of Teachers of Mathematics [NCTM], 1989).

The commission envisioned an educated society, rigorous academic standards, and accountability through standardized testing (DeBoer, 2014). Similarly, *Educating Americans for the 21st Century*

(National Science Board, 1983) recommended that national goals and curricular frameworks be developed in response to the perceived neglect of the educational system. The call for a comprehensive document of what every student should know and be able to do motivated organizations in mathematics and science education to respond. For example, in 1988, the Great Educational Reform Act introduced a national curriculum in mathematics and science for children ages 5–16 in England, Northern Ireland, and Wales. The National Curriculum in Wales had three core subjects—mathematics, science, and English—and nine foundation subjects, including design and technology (Barlex, 1998). In the same year, a curriculum framework was implemented in Western Australia, and the United Kingdom organized a National Curriculum Council.

At the same time as the *Nation at Risk* report, the Commission on Precollege Education in Mathematics, Science and Technology from the National Science Board echoed a similar concern related to the need for higher expectations within mathematics and science curriculum. While it did not call for a national curriculum, the report established a need for the development of national goals and curriculum frameworks within mathematics and science. Resulting from these calls for national educational reforms was an emphasis on the need to integrate or make connections among the curriculum (NRC, 1996; NAEYC, 1987; Science for all Americans, 1989; NCTM, 1989; National Science Teachers Association [NSTA], 1996). Several curricular projects that addressed this need for a more integrated approach to curricula were developed in the 1980s and 1990s. Some of these curricular projects included: Activities Integrating Math and Science (AIMS) (published 1986–90), Lawrence Hall of Science–Great Explorations in Math and Science (GEMS) (published 1986–88), and the University of Chicago's Teaching Integrated Mathematics and Science (TIMS) (published 1991) (Czerniak & Johnson, 2014; Berlin, 1991). In England, similar reform in curriculum was also occurring. The School Mathematics Project, Midland Mathematical Experiment, and the Contemporary School Mathematics Project (CSM) were developed (Howson, 1978). During this time of curriculum development, advocates in Europe, the United States, Australia, and New Zealand began calling for "technological literacy" so individuals in society could understand the basic concepts of technology and its impact (Scarborough, 1991).

Mathematics and science policy documents and initiatives from this time included content and skills to be learned, but also emphasized the connections between mathematics, science, and technology. Although the larger focus of the 1989 AAAS publication, *Science for All Americans*, was on mathematics and science integration, there was also evidence of some of the first ideas of STEM with the integration of technology, engineering, and mathematics in science. The report identified what students should learn by 12th grade, with chapters focused on the "nature of technology," the "designed world," and the "mathematical world" as they related to science. While this document did not identify specific standards or curriculum, it highlighted a connection between STEM disciplines and laid a foundation for other documents such as the NSTA's *Scope, Sequence, and Coordination of Secondary School Science* (Aldridge, 1992), the AAAS *Benchmarks for Science Literacy* (AAAS, 1993), and the *National Science Education Standards* (NRC, 1996). The *National Science Education Standards* made explicit the importance of integrating science and mathematics. "The science program should be coordinated with the mathematics program to enhance student use and understanding of mathematics in the study of science and to improve student understanding of mathematics" (NRC, 1996, p. 214).

Following publication of *Science for All Americans*, Johnson (1989) led the release of the *Technology Panel* report from AAAS Project 2061, which defined the purpose and structure of technology education within science education (LaPorte & Sanders, 1995). In this report, Johnson (1989) described the inseparability of mathematics, science, and technology by explaining mathematics and science are vital to understanding technology and vice versa. Project 2061's *Benchmarks for Science Literacy* (as cited in Sanders, 2009) further emphasized integration by stating "The basic point is that the ideas and practices of science, mathematics, and technology are so closely intertwined that we do not see how education in any one of them can be undertaken well in isolation from the others" (p. 23). This document called for integrated curricula and instruction designed around themes that transcend the subjects of mathematics, science, technology, and social studies (AAAS, 1993). These ideas provided a foundation for integrated STEM education and a rationale for the "Science and Technology" standard within the *National Science Education Standards* (NRC, 1996), which stated that technology should be included throughout the K–12 science curriculum. This represented one of the first recommendations for integrating technology and technological design into science standards.

In 2001, AAAS published the two-volume *Atlas for Science Literacy* as another part of Project 2061 that mapped the K–12 science curriculum: topic, scope and sequence, standards and benchmarks, instructional design, teaching training, resources, and assessment (AAAS, 2001). These documents emphasized the dynamic nature of science and the interdisciplinary connections with technology and mathematics (AAAS, 2001). Around the same time, the *Standards for Technological Literacy: Content for the Study of Technology* (ITEA, 2000) was published. These standards also emphasized integration, as seen with the statement "Students will develop an understanding of the relationships among technologies and the connections between technology and other fields of study" (ITEA, 2000, p. 2), and the inclusion of text focused on connections with mathematics and science.

Support for the integration of mathematics, science, and technology was also reflected in national standards documents across science, the *National Science Education Standards* (NRC, 1996), and mathematics, *Curriculum and Evaluation Standards for School Mathematics* (NCTM, 1989). These documents emphasized the interrelatedness of mathematics and science and its implications for curriculum and instruction (Lonning & DeFranco, 1997). For example, *Science for All Americans* suggested that engineering be incorporated into science education by including discussions of "Engineering Combines Scientific Inquiry and Practical Values" and "The Essence of Engineering is Design Under Constraint" (AAAS, 1989, pp. 40–41). The *Curriculum and Evaluation Standards for School Mathematics* emphasized applications, connections of mathematics to the real world, integration of different mathematics topics, higher-order thinking, sense-making, problem solving, communication, and reasoning (Herrera & Owens, 2001). Although the *Curriculum and Evaluation Standards for School Mathematics* did not focus on or emphasize integration with technology, the language in the standards established connections between mathematics and technology, which laid the groundwork for integration between the two areas (LaPorte & Sanders, 1995). In 2000, NCTM published *The Principles and Standards for School Mathematics*, which clearly stated students should recognize and apply mathematics in contexts outside of mathematics with reference to connections between mathematics, technology, and science (NCTM, 2000).

Despite the interdisciplinary focus of these early standards documents and curricula, the acronym STEM was not used. Instead, the acronym SMET, introduced by the National Science Foundation in the late 1990s, referred to fields and curriculum that integrated science, mathematics, engineering, and technology (e.g. AAAS, 1989; NRC, 1996; NSF, 1998). In 2001, Judith Ramaley, National Science Foundation assistant director of education and human resources, rearranged the words to create the more appealing acronym STEM (Sanders, 2009). The National Science Foundation's promotion of STEM research and development led to the cultivation of a new round of standards with a greater focus on connections between the four disciplines in STEM (science, technology, engineering, and mathematics). Connections between the STEM disciplines were promoted by new standards documents including the *Common Core State Standards for Mathematics* (CCSSM) (NGA & CCSSO, 2010) and the *Next Generation Science Standards* (NGSS) (NGSS Lead States, 2013). The *Framework for K–12 Science Education* (NRC, 2012), which is a foundational document for the NGSS, emphasizes that both science and engineering practices are needed for students to engage in scientific inquiry and engineering design. Further support for the integration of STEM disciplines is seen with the inclusion of the "Model with Mathematics and Computational Thinking" practice and explicit connections to relevant standards in the CCSSM, which emphasize how mathematics and computational thinking are fundamental tools for analyzing problems and phenomena in science and engineering (NGSS Lead States, 2013). Although the CCSSM (NGA & CCSSO, 2010) do not make explicit statements about integrating the STEM disciplines, the focus on applying mathematical concepts to real-world situations and including a standard for mathematical practice to "model with mathematics" supports the integration of science and engineering with mathematics.

Mathematics and Technology Integration

As computers were becoming more common in offices, schools, and homes, *Reshaping School Mathematics: A Philosophy and Framework for Curriculum* (National Research Council, 1990) realized its potential and developed a framework for mathematics curriculum that incorporated technology and acknowledged the changing world. The report emphasized "Computing devices will decrease the value of many manual skills traditionally taught in mathematics curriculum ... [and will] focus attention as much on problem formulation as on problem solving" (pp. 18–19) and the realization that mathematics educators are still struggling with many of the issues it raises. In supporting the value of calculators, NRC states, "overemphasis on manual skills" can hinder children's learning "of how and when to use them" and "too often skill rather than meaning becomes the message" (p. 19). However, the framework included "Principle 2: Calculators and computers should be used throughout the mathematics curriculum" (p. 37). The principle is framed as being about creating active participation that increases efficiency in calculating and representation that allows students to "potentially lead to more understanding than does traditional instruction" (p. 27). As they predict, "A valuable impact of technology on the secondary curriculum will surely be the development of sophisticated software that will enable students to discover patterns rather than just manipulate symbols" (p. 45), which inevitably came to pass.

One of the first curricula developed to harness the potential of computers in mathematics was a computer-intensive algebra (CIA) curriculum developed out of the University of Maryland in 1984 by James Fey and M. Kathleen Heid. Supported by NSF, it emphasized real-world problem solving, developing conceptual understanding and using technology to solve and understand the mathematics of the problems (O'Callaghan, 1998). With a focus on the ideas of variable and function, students used computers to represent and see multiple mathematical representations (numerical, graphical, and symbolic) simultaneously (O'Callaghan, 1998). The software was a mix of commercial software developed specifically for curriculum (Lynch, Fischer, & Green, 1989). Researchers found that students who engaged in the CIA curriculum had a better understanding of both variables and functions (O'Callaghan, 1998; Boers-van Oosterum, 1990; Matras, 1988).

Mathematics and technology curriculum integration also focus on computer-assisted instruction (CAI), which provides supplemental learning support to classroom instruction (e.g., Successmaker or SRA Drill and Practice), or on integrated learning systems, which use software to assess, manage, and make decisions on what and when students should learn topics (e.g., Accelerated Math), and comprehensive models designed to use software to complete in-class learning (e.g., Cognitive Tutor) (Cheung & Slavin, 2013). Most studies found that these approaches have the ability to have a modest effect on student achievement. For example, Rakes, Valentine, McGatha, and Ronau (2010) conducted a meta-analysis of how technology was used to improve algebra instruction and found the effect size of technology-based curriculum on student achievement was +0.15, whereas using technology tools in algebra had an effect size of +0.17. Cheung and Slavin (2013) also found in their meta-analysis of K–12 mathematics classes that integrating mathematics and technology had modest effects, with CAI having the largest effect size, +0.19.

Integration of Mathematics, Science, and Technology

The ideas espoused by ITEA resounded with the National Academy of Engineering (NAE) so much so that it published *Technically Speaking: Why All Americans Need to Know More About Technology* (Pearson & Young, 2002). This document recommended that educational policymakers encourage integrating technology into subjects that are not technology-centered. LaPorte and Sanders (1993, 1995) directed the Technology, Science, and Mathematics (TSM) project which developed 15 middle school activities created for students to apply mathematics and science concepts to design, construct, and evaluate solutions to technological problems. The primary objective of the TSM Project was for students to apply mathematics and science so they can begin to understand how it can be used as problem-solving tools (LaPorte & Sanders, 1993). The activities use design–under–constraint and hands–on technology to motivate students. In the design of the activities, science content served as the foundation (LaPorte & Sanders, 1993). Then, technological problems were developed to align with the science content (LaPorte & Sanders, 1993). LaPorte and Sanders (1993) explained that since mathematical concepts naturally fit with science and technology, they were easily integrated into the activities.

Venville, Wallace, Rennie, and Malone (1998) also analyzed integrated teaching of science, mathematics, and technology in middle school classrooms in 16 Western Australian schools. Interviews with teachers and school leadership and classroom observations revealed how teachers integrated the subjects and their opinions on integrated teaching. The findings were important considering that the Western Australian Curriculum Framework (Curriculum Council, 1998) promoted integration and suggested teachers incorporate cross-curricular themes, skills, and connections in their instruction.

Curriculum Integration in the 1990s and 2000s

Curriculum integration continued to gain popularity in the 1990s. The School Science and Mathematics Association and NSF hosted a multidisciplinary group of education researchers (e.g., NSTA, NCTM, and AAAS) to discuss the new focus on the integration of mathematics and science at the Wingspread Conference Center in 1991. The conference created a network for integrated science and mathematics teaching and learning (Berlin & White, 1992). One of the products of the conference was a collection of five papers (Berger, 1994; Bransford & the Cognition and Technology Group, 1994; Dossey, 1994; Steen, 1994; Tinker, 1994) that formally outlined the rationale, vision, and significance of integrated science and mathematics. The Wingspread conference was a turning point in STEM curriculum as it aligned science and mathematics and created common goals. In other words, the Wingspread conference created common infrastructure to build integrated STEM curriculum. The National Science Teachers Association recommended a new position statement on interdisciplinary learning in grades PreK-4 in 1996. The position statement noted eight guidelines that all integrated curricula should meet. It was suggested that the integrated curricula should maintain the integrity of the content drawn from the disciplines by using meaningful connections to sustain students' inquiry between and among these disciplines (Czerniak, Weber, Sandmann & Ahern, 1999).

The integrated curriculum approach in teaching and learning received much attention in education reform documents of U.S. organizations (e.g., National Council of Teachers of English [NTCE], 1996; National Council of Teachers of Mathematics [NCTM], 1989; National Council for the Social Studies [NCSS], 1994; National Science Teachers Association [NSTA], 1996, as cited in Czerniak et al., 1999). With this growing interest in science, technology, and engineering, a small number of curricula were introduced in the mid-1990s with an overarching goal to encourage more students to pursue degrees in engineering, but these were focused mostly on engineering and technology and largely integrated into elective technology classes (Sanders, 1999). Examples of these early curricula, included "Project Lead the Way" at the secondary level, "A World in Motion" at the middle level and LEGO robotics across K-12 from Tufts (Miaoulis, 2014). Integration was advocated as a means by which students can develop deeply organized knowledge structures that are richly interconnected (Huntley, 1998).

Researchers and educators in the U.S. were also working collaboratively to align science and mathematics education. The National Science Teachers Association initiated the Project on Scope, Sequence, and Coordination (SS&C) in 1990. The project was a reform effort to restructure secondary science education. SS&C assimilated the aims of Project 2061: Science for All Americans and the National Science Education Standards to produce a well-coordinated science program ensuring all students study biology, chemistry, earth and space science, and physics in grades 6 through 12 (NSTA, 1990). In other words, SS&C recommended abandoning the traditional high school curriculum in favor of adopting an integrated approach.

In 2000, the International Technology Education Association (currently called the International Technology and Engineering Education Association, or ITEEA) published a report titled *Standards for Technological Literacy: Content for the Study of Technology*, which was developed with input from the National Academy of Engineering and the National Research Council, and which reflected a shift toward a broader understanding of technology that included engineering design (ITEA, 2000). The ITEA created curricula that helped share a broader vision of developing technologically literate students; however, the curricula was primarily for technology teachers and elective technology classes. In 2001, Massachusetts became the first state to explicitly include the term "engineering" in their state science standards, and it was not long before other states followed (Koehler, 2006). Support for the integration of technology and engineering was growing. In 2002, the NAE published the report, *Technically Speaking: Why All Americans Need to Know More About Technology,* which supported technology inclusion across the curriculum (Pearson & Young, 2002). By 2003, NSF supported more than 100 projects on teaching engineering and/or technology in science curriculum (Householder, 2007). With the increasing interest for integrating engineering, the NAE and NRC released a report in 2009 that examined the role and status of engineering in K-12 and argued that "in the real world, engineering is not performed in isolation—it inevitably involves science, technology, and mathematics. So, the question is why these subjects should be isolated in schools" (Katehi, Pearson, & Feder, 2009, pp. 164–165). Additionally, this report reviewed 34 engineering curricular materials used in K-12 science and mathematics classrooms and found the development of science and mathematics knowledge within the context of engineering and technology was a focus of many of these curricula (Katehi et al., 2009). After consideration of the K-12 education landscape, another report, *Standards for K-12 Engineering Education* (NAE, 2010), determined it was not in the best interest to create specific, separate standards for engineering, but instead emphasized the need for infusion of engineering throughout the curriculum.

Future Directions

Curricula that integrate the content across the areas within STEM have been developing for over a century; however, educators throughout the world are more likely to teach primarily within one content area. This may stem from a lack of emphasis on integrated curriculum within education policy due to a dearth of research on integrated curriculum and student learning. For example, Lederman and Niess (1997) claim limited empirical research exists supporting the use of integrated curriculum. Proponents of integrated curriculum contend separate-subject curricula lead people to believe the purpose of education is to master facts, principles, and skills instead of learning how these isolated elements might be used to inform larger, real-life purposes. Proponents also contend the integration of subject areas can help students gain critical thinking skills, deeper understanding, and knowledge required for success in the 21st century, see relevance in curriculum to their lives, make connections among central concepts, and become motivated in school in ways that lead to meaningful learning (Berlin & White, 1994; George, 1996; Mason, 1996; Lonning, DeFranco, & Weinland, 1998). Supporters of curriculum integration argue that research suggests people process information through patterns and connections rather than fragmented bits and pieces of information (Beane, 1996).

Regardless if one is a proponent of integrated STEM curriculum, it is clear more empirical research needs to be done to investigate integrated curriculum—what content it contains, how it is implemented, the effects of the implementation on student learning, how it supports students' application of knowledge in their current lives and future workplaces, and how it compares to more siloed curriculum. This research also needs to be conducted in varied locations internationally and within nations. Implementing integrated curriculum in countries that have a longer history with integrated STEM curriculum such as Australia, United Kingdom, and the United States may provide different dynamics and research findings than countries with less historical use. In addition, within countries, a better understanding of the effects of integrated STEM curriculum on students, teachers, schools, and districts is needed so policy developers and other stakeholders can see the impact of integrated STEM curriculum.

References

Alberty, H. (1953). Designing programs to meet the common needs of youth. *Adapting the secondary-school program to the needs of youth* (pp. 118–140). Chicago: University of Chicago Press.

Aldridge, B. G. (1992). Project on scope, sequence, and coordination: A new synthesis for improving science education. *Journal of Science Education and Technology, 1*(1), 13–21.

Alridge, D. P. (2009). African American educators and the Black intellectual tradition. In L. C. Tilman (Ed.)., *The Sage handbook of African American education* (pp. 23–34). University of North Carolina Chapel Hill: Sage Publications.

American Association for the Advancement of Science (AAAS). (1989). *Science for all Americans.* Washington, DC: Author.

American Association for the Advancement of Science (AAAS). (1993). *Benchmarks for scientific literacy.* New York, NY: Oxford University Press.

American Association for the Advancement of Science (AAAS). (2001). *Atlas of science literacy.* Washington, DC: Author.

Barlex, D. (1998). Design and technology–the Nuffield perspective in England and Wales. *International Journal of Technology and Design Education, 8*(2), 139–150.

Beane, J. A. (1975). The case for core in the middle school. *Middle School Journal, 6*(2), 33–38.

Beane, J. (1996). On the shoulders of giants! The case for curriculum integration. *Middle School Journal, 28*(1), 6–11.

Berger, C. F. (1994). Breaking what barriers between science and mathematics? Six myths from a technological perspective. In D. F. Berlin (Ed.), *NSF/SSMA Wingspread conference: A network for integrated science and mathematics teaching and learning* (pp. 23–27). School Science and Mathematics Association Topics for Teachers Series (No. 7). Bowling Green, OH: School Science and Mathematics Association.

Berlin, D. F. (1991). *Integrating science and mathematics in teaching and learning: A bibliography.* Columbus, OH: ERIC Clearinghouse for Science, Mathematics and Environmental Education.

Berlin, D. F., & Lee, H. (2005). Integrating science and mathematics education: Historical analysis. *School Science and Mathematics, 105*(1), 15–24.

Berlin, D. F., & White, A. L. (1992). Report from the NSF/SSMA Wingspread conference: A network for integrated science and mathematics teaching and learning. *School Science and Mathematics, 92*(6), 340–342.

Berlin, D. F., & White, A. L. (1994). The Berlin–White integrated science and mathematics model. *School Science and Mathematics, 94*(1), 2–4.

Blatz, W. E. (1936). Educational frills. *Canadian School Journal, 14*, 124.

Bobbitt, F. (1918). *The curriculum.* New York, NY: Houghton Mifflin.

Boers-Van Oosterum, M. A. M. (1990). Understanding of variables and their uses acquired by students in traditional and computer-intensive algebra (Doctoral dissertation, University of Maryland, College Park, 1990). *Dissertation Abstracts International, 51*(5), 1538A.

Bransford, J. D., & The Cognition and Technology Group at Vanderbilt. (1994). Video environments for connecting mathematics, science and other disciplines. In D. F. Berlin (Ed.), *NSF/SSMA Wingspread conference: A network for integrated science and mathematics teaching and learning* (pp. 29–48). School Science and Mathematics Association Topics for Teachers Series (No. 7). Bowling Green, OH: School Science and Mathematics Association.

Bybee, R. (2013). *The case of STEM education: Challenges and opportunities.* Arlington: NSTA Press.

Bybee, R. W., & Landes, N. M. (1990). Science for life and living: An elementary school science program from biological sciences curriculum study. *The American Biology Teacher, 52*(2), 92–98.

Cheung, A. C., & Slavin, R. E. (2013). The effectiveness of educational technology applications for enhancing mathematics achievement in K-12 classrooms: A meta-analysis. *Educational Research Review, 9,* 88–113.

Claeys, G. (2000). The "survival of the fittest" and the origins of Social Darwinism. *Journal of the History of Ideas, 61*(2), 223–240.

Committee on the Teaching of Mathematics to Students of Engineering. (1912). *Syllabus of mathematics.* Ithaca, NY: Society for the Promotion of Engineering.

Comstock, A. B. (1915). Growth and influence of nature study. *The Nature-Study Review, 11,* 5–11.

Curriculum Council. (1998). *Curriculum framework for kindergarten to year 12 education in Western Australia.* Osborne Park, WA: Author.

Czerniak, C. M., & Johnson, C. C. (2014). Interdisciplinary science teaching. In N. G. Lederman and S. K. Abell (Eds.), *Handbook of research on science education, Volume II* (pp. 409–425). London: Routledge.

Czerniak, C. M., Weber, W. B., Jr, Sandmann, A., & Ahern, J. (1999). A literature review of science and mathematics integration. *School Science and Mathematics, 99*(8), 421–430.

Darling-Hammond, L., & Ancess, J. (1996). Democracy and access to education. In R. Soder (Ed.), *Democracy, education, and the schools* (pp. 151–181). San Francisco, CA: Jossey-Bass Inc. Publishers.

DeBoer, G. E. (1991). *A history of ideas in science education: Implications for practice.* New York, NY: Teachers College Press.

DeBoer, G. E. (2000). Scientific literacy: Another look at its historical and contemporary meanings and its relationship to science education reform. *Journal of Research in Science Teaching: The Official Journal of the National Association for Research in Science Teaching, 37*(6), 582–601.

DeBoer, G. E. (2014). The history of science curriculum reform in the United States. In N. G. Lederman & S. K. Abell (Eds.), *Handbook of research on science education, Volume II* (pp. 573–592). London: Routledge.

Dewey, J. (1897). My pedagogic creed. *School Journal, 54*(3), 77–80.

Dewey, J. (1902). *The child and the curriculum.* Chicago, IL: University of Chicago Press.

Donoghue, E. (2003). The emergence of a profession: Mathematics education in the United States, 1890–1920. In G. M. A. Stanic and J. Kilpatrick (Eds.), *A history of school mathematics* (pp. 159–193). Reston, VA: National Council of Teachers of Mathematics.

Dossey, J. A. (1994). Mathematics and science education: Convergence or divergence. In D. F. Berlin (Ed.), *NSF/SSMA Wingspread conference: A network for integrated science and mathematics teaching and learning* (pp. 13–22). School Science and Mathematics Association Topics for Teachers Series (No. 7). Bowling Green, OH: School Science and Mathematics Association.

Fraunce, R. C., & Bossing, N. (1951). *Developing the core curriculum.* New York, NY: Prentice Hall.

Furinghetti, F., Matos, J. M., & Menghini, M. (2013). From mathematics and education, to mathematics education. In M. A. Clements, A. J. Bishop, C. Keitel, J. Kilpatrick, & F. K. S. Leung (Eds.), *Third international handbook of mathematics education* (pp. 273–302). New York, NY: Springer.

George, P. S. (1996). The integrated curriculum: A reality check. *Middle School Journal, 28*(1), 12–20.

Gispert, H. (2009). Two mathematics reforms in the context of twentieth century France: Similarities and differences. *International Journal for the History of Mathematics Education, 4*(1), 43–50.

Goodlad, J. I., Von Stoephasius, R., & Klein, M. F. (1966). *The changing school curriculum.* New York, NY: The Fund for the Advancement of Education.

Guralnick, S. M. (1975). *Science and the ante-bellum American college: Memoirs of the American Philosophical Society.* Philadelphia: American Philosophical Society.

Herrera, T. A., & Owens, D. T. (2001). The "new new math"? Two reform movements in mathematics education. *Theory into Practice, 40*(2), 84–92.

Hofstadter, R. (1992). *Social Darwinism in American thought, 1860–1915.* Boston: Beacon Press.

Householder, D. L. (2007). *Selected NSF project of interest to K-12 engineering and technology education.* National Science Foundation programs. Washington, DC: National Science Foundation.

Howson, A. G. (1978). Change in mathematics education since the late 1950's–ideas and realisation Great Britain. *Educational Studies in Mathematics, 9*(2), 183–223.

Howson, A. G. (1982). *A history of mathematics education in England.* Cambridge: Cambridge University Press.

Huntley, M. A. (1998). Design and implementation of a framework for defining integrated mathematics and science education. *School Science and Mathematics, 98*(6), 320–327.

Hurley, M. M. (1999). *Interdisciplinary mathematics and science: Characteristics, forms and related effect sizes for student achievement and affective outcomes* (Doctoral dissertation). University at Albany, State University of New York.

International Commission on the Teaching of Mathematics. (1911). *The training of teachers of elementary and secondary mathematics*. Committee no. 5. United States Bureau of Education Bulletin 1911, no. 12. Washington, DC: Government Printing Office.

International Technology Education Association (ITEA). (2000). *Standards for technological literacy: Content for the student of technology*. Reston, VA: Author.

Jackson, P. (1992). Conceptions of curriculum and curriculum specialists. In P. Jackson (Ed.), *Handbook of research on curriculum* (pp. 3–40). New York, NY: Macmillan.

Johnson, J. R. (1989). *Technology: Report of the Project 2061 phase I technology panel*. Washington, DC: American Association for the Advancement of Science.

Katehi, L., Pearson, G., & Feder, M. (Eds.). (2009). *Engineering in K-12 education: Understanding the status and improving the prospects*. Washington, DC: The National Academies Press.

Kilpatrick, J. (2014). Mathematics education in the United States and Canada. In A. Karp and G. Schubring (Eds.), *Handbook on the history of mathematics education*. New York, NY: Springer.

Klein, D. (2003). A brief history of American K-12 mathematics education in the 20th century. *Mathematical Cognition*, 175–259.

Klein, F. (1911). *Lectures on mathematics delivered from Aug. 28 to Sept. 9, 1893 at Northwestern University*. American Mathematical Society.

Knoll, M. (2012). "I Had Made a Mistake": William H. Kilpatrick and the project method. *Teachers College Record, 114*(2), 1–45.

Koehler, C. (2006). Are concepts of technical & engineering literacy included in state curriculum standards? A regional overview of the nexus between technical & engineering literacy and state science frameworks. In *Proceedings of the 2005 ASEE Annual Conference & Exposition*. Chicago, IL: ASEE.

Kohlstedt, S. G. (2010). *Teaching children science: Hands-on nature study in North America, 1890–1930*. Chicago: University of Chicago Press.

LaPorte, J. E., & Sanders, M. E. (1993). TSM integration project: Integrating technology, science, and mathematics in the middle school. *The Technology Teacher*, 17–21.

LaPorte, J. E., & Sanders, M. E. (1995). Integrating technology, science, and mathematics education. *Foundations of Technology Education: Forty-fourth Yearbook of the Council on Technology Teacher Education*, 179–219.

Lederman, N. G., & Niess, M. l. (1997). Integrated, interdisciplinary, or thematic Instruction? Is this a question or is it a questionable semantics? *School Science and Mathematics, 97*(2), 57–58.

Lonning, R. A., & DeFranco, T. C. (1997). Integration of science and mathematics: A theoretical model. *School Science and Mathematics, 97*(4), 212–215.

Lonning, R. A., DeFranco, T. C., & Weinland, T. P. (1998). Development of theme-based, interdisciplinary, integrated curriculum: A theoretical model. *School Science and Mathematics, 98*(6), 312–319.

Lurry, L. L., & Alberty, E. J. (1957). *Developing a high school core program*. New York, NY: Macmillan.

Lynch, J. K., Fischer, P., & Green, S. F. (1989). Teaching in a computer-intensive algebra curriculum. *The Mathematics Teacher, 82*(9), 688–694.

Mason, T. C. (1996). Integrated curricula: Potential and problems. *Journal of Teacher Education, 47*(4), 263–270.

Matras, M. A. (1988). The effects of curricula on students' ability to analyze and solve problems in algebra (Doctoral dissertation, University of Maryland, College Park, 1988). *Dissertation Abstracts International, 49*, 1726.

Miaoulis, I. (2014). K-12 engineering: The missing core discipline. In S. Purzer, J. Strobel, & M. Cardella (Eds.), *Engineering in pre-college settings: Synthesizing research, policy, and practices* (pp. 21–34). West Lafayette, IN: Purdue University Press.

Nabonnand, P. (2007). *Les réformes de l'enseignement des mathématiques au début du XXe siècle*. Une dynamique à l'échelle international.

National Academy of Engineering (NAE). (2010). Committee on standards for K-12 engineering education. In *Standards for K-12 engineering education?* Washington, DC: National Academies Press.

National Academy of Engineering and National Research Council. (2014). *STEM integration in K-12 education: Status, prospects, and an agenda for research*. Washington, DC: The National Academies Press. https://doi.org/10.17226/18612.

National Association for the Education of Young Children (NAEYC). (1987). *Developmentally appropriate practice in early childhood programs serving children from birth through age 8*. Washington, DC: NAEYC.

National Commission on Excellence in Education (NCEE). (1983). *A nation at risk: Imperative for educational reform*. Washington, DC: Government Printing Office.

National Council for the Social Studies. (1994). *Expectations of excellence: Curriculum standards for social studies* (No. 89). Washington, DC: Author.

National Council of Teachers of English. (1996). *Standards for English language arts.* Urbana, IL: Author.

National Council of Teachers of Mathematics (NCTM). (1989). *Curriculum and evaluation standards for school mathematics.* Reston, VA: Author.

National Council of Teachers of Mathematics. (2000). *Principles and standards for school mathematics.* Reston, VA: Author.

National Education Association. (1894). *Report of the committee of ten on secondary school studies with the reports of the conferences arranged by the committee.* New York, NY: American Book Company.

National Governors Association Center for Best Practices & Council of Chief State School Officers. (2010). *Common core state standards for mathematics.* Washington, DC: Author.

National Research Council. (1990). *Reshaping school mathematics: A philosophy and framework for curriculum.* National Academies Press.

National Research Council (NRC). (1996). *National science education standards.* National Committee on Science Education Standards and Assessment. Board on Science Education, Division of Behavioral and Social Science and Education. Washington, DC: National Academies Press.

National Research Council. (2012). *A framework for K–12 science education: Practices, crosscutting concepts, and core ideas.* Washington, DC: National Academies Press.

National Science Board. (1983). *Educating Americans for the 21st century: A report to the American people and the National Science Board.* Washington, DC: National Science Foundation.

National Science Foundation, Washington, DC. Directorate for Education and Human Resources. (1998). *Shaping the future. Volume II: Perspectives on undergraduate education in science, mathematics, engineering, and technology.* ERIC Clearinghouse.

National Science Teachers Association (NSTA). (1990). *Science/technology/society: A new effort for providing appropriate science for all (The NSTA Position*

National Science Teachers Association (NSTA). (1996). NSTA board endorses new position statement on interdisciplinary learning. PreK-grade 4. *NSTA Reports!* 6, 8.

NGSS Lead States. (2013). *Next generation science standards: For states, by states.* Washington: The National Academies Press.

O'Callaghan, B. R. (1998). Computer-intensive algebra and students' conceptual knowledge of functions. *Journal for Research in Mathematics Education, 29,* 21–40.

Parker, W. C. (1996). Curriculum for democracy. In R. Soder (Ed.), *Democracy, education, and the schools* (pp. 182–210). San Francisco, CA: Jossey-Bass Inc. Publishers.

Pearson, G., & Young, T. (2002). *Technically speaking: Why all Americans need to know more about technology.* Washington, DC: National Academy Press.

Perry, J. (1901). *British association: Meeting at Glasgow, 1901: Discussion on the teaching of Mathematics.* London: Macmillan.

Rakes, C. R., Valentine, J. C., McGatha, M. B., & Ronau, R. N. (2010). Methods of instructional improvement in algebra: A systematic review and meta-analysis. *Review of Educational Research, 80*(3), 372–400.

Sanders, M. E. (1999). New paradigm or old wine? The status of technology education practice within the United States. *Journal of Technology Education, 12*(2), 35–55.

Sanders, M. E. (2009). STEM, STEM education, STEMmania. *Technology Teacher, 68*(4), 20–26.

Scarborough, J. D. (1991). International perspectives on technological literacy. In M. J. Dyrenfurth & M. R. Kozak (Eds.), *Technological literacy, 40th yearbook of the council on technology teacher education* (pp. 54–79). Peoria, IL: Glencoe Division, Macmillan/McGraw-Hill.

School Science and Mathematics Association (SSMA). (2018). Retrieved from https://ssma.org/history/

Servos, J. W. (1986). Mathematics and the physical sciences in America, 1880–1930. *Isis, 77*(4), 611–629.

Sigurdson, S., Kieren, T., Pothier, Y., & Roulet, G. (2003). The mathematics education community in Canada outside Quebec before the new math era. In G. M. A. Stanic & J. Kilpatrick (Eds.), *A history of school mathematics* (pp. 195–234, 753–818). Reston, VA: National Council of Teachers of Mathematics.

Siu, M. K. (2009). Mathematics education in East Asia from antiquity to modern times. In K. Bjarnadóttir, F. Furinghetti, & G. Schubring (Eds.), *"Dig where you stand": Proceedings of the conference on "Ongoing research in the History of Mathematics Education"* (pp. 197–208). Reykjavik, Iceland: University of Iceland.

Spencer, H. (1864). *Education: Intellectual, moral, and physical.* New York, NY: D. Appleton & Co.

Spencer, H. (1911). *Essays on education and kindred subjects.* London: Dent.

Steen, L. A. (1994). Integrating school science and mathematics: Fad or folly? In Donna F. Berlin (Ed.), Appeared in *NSF/SSMA Wingspread Conference Plenary Papers* (pp. 7–12). Columbus, OH: National Center for Teaching and Learning.

Sunal, D. W., Sunal, C. S., Sundberg, & Wright, E. L. (2008). The importance of laboratory work and technology in science teaching, In D. W. Sunal, E. L. Wright, & C. S. Sundberg (Eds.), *The impact of the laboratory and technology on learning and teaching science K-16*. Charlotte, NC: Information Age Publishing, Inc.

Tinker, R. F. (1994). Integrating mathematics and science. In D. F. Berlin (Ed.), *NSF/SSMA Wingspread conference: A network for integrated science and mathematics teaching and learning* (pp. 49–52). School Science and Mathematics Association Topics for Teachers Series (No. 7). Bowling Green, OH: School Science and Mathematics Association.

Underhill, O. E. (1941). *The origins and development of elementary school science*. Chicago: Scott, Foresman and Co.

Vars, G. F. (1969). *Common learnings: Core and interdisciplinary team approaches*. Scranton, PA: International Textbook Co.

Vars, G. F. (1991). Integrated curriculum in historical perspective. *Abstracts International, 20*, 1830–1831.

Venville, G., Wallace, J., Rennie, L. J., & Malone, J. (1998). The integration of science, mathematics, and technology in a discipline–based culture. *School Science and Mathematics, 98*(6), 294–302.

Welch, W. W. (1979). Chapter 7: Twenty years of science curriculum development: A look back. *Review of Research in Education, 7*(1), 282–306.

White, E. E. (1894). Professional training in summer schools. *The Journal of Education, 40*(6), 109.

Wraga, W. G. (2009). Toward a connected core curriculum. *Educational Horizons, 87*(2), 88–96.

Zapf, R. M. (1959). *Democratic processes in the classroom*. Englewood Cliffs, NJ: Prentice Hall.

15

INFUSING EVIDENCE-BASED REASONING IN INTEGRATED STEM

Carina M. Rebello, Paul A. Asunda and Hui-Hui Wang

Introduction

As science and technology advances in the 21st century, *all* students must be prepared to be STEM-literate citizens. They should be able to utilize crosscutting concepts and core disciplinary ideas with science and engineering practices (National Academy of Engineering & National Research Council, 2014; National Research Council [NRC], 2011, 2012; NGSS Lead States, 2013). The *Next Generation Science Standards* (NGSS Lead States, 2013) outlines performance expectations based on the *Framework for K-12 Science Education* (NRC, 2012), that includes integration of eight science and engineering practices. By incorporating engineering design and practices, NGSS has inspired efforts to prepare students to think critically, collaboratively solve complex real-world problems, and apply knowledge through evidence-based reasoning. The science and engineering practices highlighted in NGSS include questioning, defining problems, interpreting evidence, constructing explanations, and engaging in evidence-based argumentation.

Evidence-based reasoning within the construct of argumentation in STEM has been studied extensively. Argumentation, used here synonymously with evidence-based reasoning, is a process of reasoning with evidence to justify and refine claims, through evaluation of data (Reiser, Berland, & Kenyon, 2012). Similar to Toulmin's (1958) model, the components of an argument are: a claim (a solution or conclusion about a problem); evidence (data supporting a claim); reasoning (justification or logic for why the evidence supports the claim); and rebuttal (claim addressing why alternatives are incorrect using additional evidence and reasoning) (McNeill & Krajcik, 2012). However, there are interdisciplinary distinctions in argumentation (Bybee, 2011). We need to consider how various disciplines or communities of practice understand and implement argumentation (Grooms, Sampson, & Enderle, 2018). We provide an overview of argumentation enacted in various STEM disciplines, a perspective on integrated STEM, and a model for using argumentation in integrated STEM.

Overview of Argumentation in STEM Education

Argumentation is a process to rationally resolve questions and solve problems. It is a critical piece of learning to think like a mathematician, scientist, or engineer (Driver, Newton, & Osborne, 2000; Jonassen & Kim, 2010). It shifts the focus from answer-oriented problem solving to the process-oriented practice of constructing and justifying claims (Berland & McNeill, 2010). Kuhn (1991) identified five argumentation skills: generating causal theories, offering supporting evidence, envisioning conditions that undermine one's theory, generating, and rebutting alternative theories. Thus, to engage in successful argumentation, learners must develop and articulate a reasonable solution, support the solution with data and evidence, identify alternative solutions, and develop theories to rebut alternative solutions (Jonassen, 2011). These skills are applicable to well- and ill-structured tasks during both construction and evaluation of arguments (Jonassen & Kim, 2010). The strength of an argument depends upon the context (Newton, Driver, & Osborne, 1999), the assessment framework (Sampson & Clark, 2008), and the nature of the task (Rebello, Sayre, & Rebello, 2012; Sampson & Clark, 2008).

To engage in argumentation, learners must participate in tasks that require constructing and/ or evaluating evidence-based claims to support their design solutions (Jonassen et al., 2009). Yet, most STEM classrooms emphasize the product of reasoning over the process of social construction through evidence-based discourse (Jin, Mehl, & Lan, 2015). The classroom should be structured to afford opportunities to engage in dialogic evidence-based reasoning (e.g., Christodoulou & Osborne, 2014; Driver et al., 2000) as well as written arguments (Chen, Park, & Hand, 2016). Student-centered learning environments must support authentic problem solving, questioning, analyzing and interpreting data, considering alternatives, and justifying choices (Berland & Hammer, 2012). Scaffolds, such as instructions emphasizing evidence, questions, sentence stems, prompts, and graphical aids can facilitate argumentation (Jonassen & Kim, 2010; Christodoulou & Osborne, 2014). Further, argumentation instruction requires a shift in the role of the instructor to frame and guide discussions, allowing students to engage in collaborative argumentative discourse (Berland & Hammer, 2012; Christodoulou & Osborne, 2014).

We provide a broad overview of policy documents concerning argumentation and how it is facilitated in the various STEM disciplines. There is a wide body of literature on argumentation, hence only a broad overview is within the scope of this chapter.

Argumentation in Science

Goals and Rationale of Practice. The *Framework* defines the practice of argumentation as "essential for clarifying strengths and weaknesses of a line of evidence and for identifying the best explanation for a natural phenomenon" (NRC, 2012, p. 71). Argumentation plays a crucial role in scientific inquiry and can facilitate an arguing-to-learn process in which students construct scientific understandings through justifying, evaluating, and confronting varying scientific views (Driver et al., 2000). To prepare our students to become scientifically literate citizens, there is a growing need to focus on argumentation, including how evidence is used in science for constructing and evaluating explanations (Osborne et al., 2004).

Argumentation activities can situate knowledge production in original contexts and afford opportunities to learn science content and practices, and understand the role of language, culture, and social interaction in the process of knowledge construction (Abi-El-Mona & Abd-El-Khalick, 2011). Embedding argumentation in science learning can enhance conceptual understanding and scientific thinking (e.g. Walker & Sampson, 2013).

The conceptualization of science as argument is based on linking the practices of scientists with those of students. Kuhn (1993) posited that learning science involved practices similar to those of scientists. Duschl and Osborne (2002) claimed that argumentation was key to learning the true nature of scientific inquiry—not a collection of facts (Driver et al., 2000) but construction of explanations and evaluation of evidence. Specifically, argumentation is considered a "core epistemic practice" of science (Bricker & Bell, 2008). Argumentation is important in both doing and communicating science. Students must be involved in reasoning that characterizes the discourse, tools, and culture of scientific communities of practice (Abi-El-Mona & Abd-El-Khalick, 2011). Identifying and assessing alternatives, weighing evidence, interpreting text, and evaluating the potential validity of scientific claims are essential components in appropriately constructing scientific arguments (Driver et al., 2000).

Curricular Implementation. Eliciting students' participation in scientific argumentation requires a carefully designed learning environment (Berland & McNeill, 2010) and explicit strategies to facilitate argumentation including highlighting the role of evidence by asking open-ended questions, prompting, comparing solutions, analyzing and interpreting data, considering alternatives, and justifying choices (Christodoulou & Osborne, 2014). Further, students must be actively engaged, attend to, and apply underlying principles of argumentation to problems (Bricker & Bell, 2008). Currently, science instruction utilizes evidence-based reasoning in written reports, worksheets or notebooks, visual representations or charts, concept cartoons, and small group or whole class debates for purposes of explaining phenomena, highlighting scientific misconceptions, or making socioscientific decisions (McNeill & Berland, 2017).

Scientific argumentation scaffolds can help students of all ages articulate the rationale underlying their problem-solving steps (Christodoulou & Osborne, 2014). Jin et al. (2015) propose a two-dimensional framework of arguing-to-learn: (1) argumentative discourse strategies to effectively interact with peers, and (2) content-base of science concepts to construct arguments. Attending to both these dimensions ensures that students are arguing to learn, not just learning to argue. Jin et al. (2015) also suggest two activities—argue first, then learn about a scientific mechanism; learn about the scientific mechanism and then apply it to argue.

Chen et al. (2016) emphasize the importance of including both oral and written argumentation due to their complementary cognitive functions to support learning. They argue that conceptual learning requires students to both co-construct and evaluate arguments. For Chen et al. (2016), argumentation is a type of inquiry that integrates learning of argumentation and science concepts. Science Writing Heuristics (SWH) facilitate construction and evaluation of evidence-based explanations in writing and discussion activities as part of the inquiry process.

Alternatively, argument-driven inquiry (ADI)—a lab-based instructional model emphasizing argumentation—is a series of steps embedded within the lab write-up to prompt students to: identify a scientific phenomenon, design experiments, collect data, and develop arguments using evidence to support claims (Sampson, Enderle, & Grooms, 2013). Activities within ADI include inquiry, oral and written argumentation, and peer critique. ADI integrates learning of science concepts and practices by emphasizing discourse in the social construction of scientific knowledge through inquiry and model-based reasoning (Walker & Sampson, 2013).

Technology-enhanced science learning environments contain tools that scaffold students to justify claims using appropriate evidence and reasoning and develop complex communication skills (Clark et al., 2009). Environments such as *BGUILE* (Reiser, Tabak, & Sandoval, 2001) actively support students' construction of arguments based on scientific data as they propose, support, evaluate, critique, and refine ideas (Yang, Lin, She, & Huang, 2015). Instructional features of such environments include synchronous or asynchronous communication and "personally seeded discussion interfaces" (Clark & Sampson, 2007) to support peer interactions for evaluation and refining of ideas through dialogic argumentation. The online environments contain integrated information systems, knowledge bases, and visualization tools that allow for co-creation, sharing, and evaluation of arguments. Embedded scripts to sequence activities and awareness heightening tools provide feedback regarding quality of interactions to support productive argumentation. Learner scaffolds such as question prompts and prototyping are also used to facilitate evidence-based argumentation (Clark, Sampson, Weinberger, & Erkens, 2007).

Argumentation in Mathematics

Goals and Rationale of Practice. In mathematics, the practice of argumentation also involves making claims, providing supporting evidence, evaluating others' reasoning, and making sense of mathematical ideas. Specifically, students are expected to "construct viable arguments and critique reasoning of others" (CCSSI, 2010, p. 6). The Common Core Standards for Mathematics emphasize the importance of argumentation in solving mathematical problems (Kelley & Knowles, 2016), and one of the five key process skills (National Council of Teachers of Mathematics (NCTM), 2009). Mathematics educators regard argumentation as a critical sense-making activity that can serve as a way for learners to build understanding by critiquing the reasoning of others (Graham & Lesseig, 2018). It can be viewed as a dynamic social discourse for enhancing ideas and convincing others. Instruction rooted in mathematical argumentation can positively affect students' mathematical understanding (Rumsey & Langrall, 2016).

Curricular Implementation. Argumentation in mathematics is more than verifying relationships (Hanna, 2000). It has been equated with the process of generating proofs—the "soul of mathematics" (Schoenfeld, 2009, p. 12; Stylianides, 2007). A proof is a deductive mathematical argument using established axioms or theorems, to support or refute a claim (Conner, 2013; Stylianides, 2007). Argumentation is a precursor to proving (Conner, 2013). Proofs are socially constructed and validated based on community criteria (Stylianou & Blanton, 2011). Purposefully designed activities emphasize that constructing arguments is not simply writing proofs but an investigation and communication of the reasoning of why something is true (Graham & Lesseig, 2018; Stylianou & Blanton, 2011).

Graham and Lesseig (2018) identify three strategies for facilitating mathematical argumentation—activities (poster presentations, peer critique, taking sides, and raking work samples), instructional practices (use of directions, sentence starters, and prompts), and structured templates (utilizing a claim, evidence, reasoning [CER] framework to scaffold more elaborate justifications and prompt discourse). Webb, Williams, and Meiring (2008) used CER-structured worksheets and visual representation such as concept cartoons to facilitate argumentation.

Classroom discourse is another approach to facilitate creating and critiquing mathematical arguments (Conner, 2013; Stylianou & Blanton, 2011). Collective argumentation, in which multiple students work as a team to arrive at a common claim, has been utilized at all grade levels (Conner, 2013; Conner, Singletary, Smith, Wagner, & Francisco, 2014; Singletary & Conner, 2015). They often may not all start with agreeing with the claim, but they work toward consensus by constructing an argument using deductive reasoning using established axioms and theorems.

Argumentation in Engineering and Technology

Goals and Rationale of Practice. Engineering and technology are closely intertwined. It is suggested that they be taught together (Barak, 2012). *Engineering in K–12 Education*, prepared by the National Academy of Engineering and the National Research Council (Katehi, Pearson, & Feder, 2009), suggested three main principles for K–12 engineering education: emphasizing engineering design; incorporating science, mathematics, and technology concepts; and aligning content with 21st-century skills—problem solving, systems thinking, creativity, collaboration, and communication to explain and justify design solutions (Katehi et al., 2009). The *Standards for Technology Literacy: Content for the Study of Technology* (International Technology and Engineering Educators Association [ITEEA], 2007) emphasize learning fundamental concepts of technology and their use in engineering design to evaluate trade-offs of technology in society (Asunda, 2012).

One of the prominent goals of integrating engineering into K–12 is to help students apply STEM content knowledge, skills, and reasoning through the engineering design process. Policy and standards emphasize argumentation as a professional skill as well as a way to support the learning of the design process, engineering thinking and communication, and application of science, mathematics, and engineering concepts to find the best solution among competing ideas through critically evaluating alternatives and communicating recommendations supported by evidence (ABET, 2016; Foutz, 2018; Mathis, Siverling, Glancy, & Moore, 2017). Arguments in engineering design are supported by scientific and mathematical principles, the criteria and constraints that the solution must meet, and external factors are related to the context in which the solution will be used (Mathis et al., 2017). Technology plays an important role in engineering design experiences to support 21st-century skills including argumentation (Asunda, 2012). Activities associated with a design process—modeling, testing, investigating, analyzing, and decision-making—are supported by technology (ITEA, 2007).

Curricular Implementation. Mathis et al. (2017) note the potential for argumentation to occur in each of the three processes of the engineering design highlighted in the *Framework for Quality K-12 Engineering Education* (Moore, Glancy, Tank, Kersten, & Smith, 2014). In the Problem and Background process, argumentation can be motivated as students identify the problem and additional information needed, including relevant evidence and/or science and mathematical content knowledge. In the Plan and Implement process, argumentation can potentially occur when students consider initial design plans and determine what materials are needed to build their design. Finally, in the Test and Evaluate process, argumentation can be facilitated as students evaluate the reasoning for success of their design using evidence from testing based on science and/or mathematics knowledge (Mathis et al., 2017).

An effective way to help students engage in argumentation in engineering design is through decision justification (Hmelo-Silver, Holton, & Kolodner, 2000; Hynes et al., 2011; Jonassen, 2011; Mathis et al., 2017). When students communicate their design solution to a client through a written letter or presentation, they are stating a claim. When students justify their solution, the justification process gives students an opportunity to present an argument to support their design solutions. Students must collect and evaluate evidence that supports the appropriateness of the design solution, applying science and mathematics content knowledge to explain design features, and argue how their final solution meets the constraints of the problem (Mathis et al., 2017).

Although argumentation may likely occur when students are required to explain and justify their design decisions to a client, argumentation can be further supported throughout the design process with the utilization of appropriate guiding questions or prompted discussions. Questions and prompts intended to scaffold the argumentation process for students can be seeded within lesson plans for productive design dialogue (Guzey & Aranda, 2017; Mathis et al., 2017), worksheets (Mathis et al., 2017) engineering notebooks, or written artifacts such as letters communicating recommendations (Gale, Koval, Ryan, Usselman, & Wind, 2018). Asking "what" and "how" questions may offer only claims with little to no justification (Mathis et al., 2017). However, asking questions that are associated with deep levels of reflection, such as "why" questions and questions that help students connect their prior experiences, and science and mathematics knowledge, with results from testing their design, could also promote students' ability to justify with evidence (Asunda & Hill, 2007; Dym, Agogino, Eris, Frey, & Leifer, 2005; Foutz, 2018; Guzey & Aranda, 2017; Katehi et al., 2009; Mathis et al., 2017). Questions targeting specific aspects of argument construction or evaluation can promote evidence-based reasoning (Jonassen et al., 2009). Reflection activities, such as giving a presentation in the analysis and evaluation stages of the design process (Schunn, 2011), students' reflective journals (Beckman & Barry, 2012), and use of content knowledge in the challenges (Asunda & Hill, 2007) also serve as effective strategies to facilitate argumentation.

Summary of Argumentation in the Disciplines

There are clear distinctions in argumentation between the disciplines (Bybee, 2011). In science, argumentation is associated with scientific inquiry to explain natural phenomena. In mathematics, argumentation is used in mathematical proofs based on established axioms and theorems. In engineering and technology, argumentation is used to search for solutions, justify design decisions, and assess tradeoffs. Mathis et al. (2017) proposes using 'scientific argumentation' in science and 'evidence-based reasoning' (EBR) in engineering. Either way, these distinctions have implications for what data are considered appropriate evidence in each discipline (Jung & McFadden, 2018) and how various disciplines or communities of practice negotiate the understanding and implementation of argumentation (Grooms et al., 2018).

A Perspective on Integrated STEM

Global challenges in the 21st century are multidisciplinary, so developing learning experiences that foster deeper consilience among STEM disciplines and utilize evidence-based reasoning to solve problems is a major goal of integrated STEM (Bryan, Moore, Johnson, & Roehrig, 2015; Bybee, 2013; Moore et al., 2014; NGSS, 2013). Integrated STEM uses engineering design challenges to model the process of solving real-world problems of personal and global relevance (Bryan et al., 2015; NRC, 2014). This approach leverages teaching STEM content alongside practices (Kelley & Knowles, 2016; Wang, Moore, Roehrig, & Park, 2011). Intentional integration scaffolds explicit connections to science and mathematics learning outcomes (Peterman, Daugherty, Custer, & Ross, 2017). Echoing NGSS's performance expectations, Bryan et al. (2015) identified five characteristics for integrated STEM lessons. (1) An "anchor" discipline determines the learning goals. (2) The "integrator" pulls in other disciplines, engineering practices, and habits of mind (Moore, Guzey, & Brown, 2014). (3) Learners *justify* their design decisions using evidence-based reasoning in science and mathematics (Llewellyn, 2014; Sampson et al., 2013). (4) Twenty-first-century workforce knowledge and skills are emphasized (Bybee, 2010). (5) The context is an authentic problem with relevance to the learners' lives, demonstrating the need for diverse, collaborative teams of learners (e.g. Dym et al., 2005).

One of the challenges of using engineering design is the tendency of learners to resort to trial-and-error strategies, rather than scientific or mathematical principles to arrive at their design solutions (Kolodner et al., 2003). The use of argumentation that requires learners to make explicit connections to science and mathematical concepts, to support or critique design decisions, can potentially facilitate deeper science learning through the process of engineering design.

Argumentation in Integrated STEM Curriculum

Argumentation has been studied within individual disciplines, yet there is limited research concerning argumentation in integrated STEM contexts involving engineering design (Mathis et al., 2017). Specific pedagogical strategies such as collaborative argumentation or case-based approaches, paired scaffolding questions to construct or evaluate arguments have been noted to improve undergraduates' conceptual understanding in engineering statistics (Foutz, 2018) and ability to further justify solutions in engineering ethics (Jonassen et al., 2009). Peterman et al. (2017) examined the extent to which engineering design practices were integrated within eighty online K–12 science lessons using the 'Engineering-Infused Lesson Rubric.' About 24% of the lessons required students to articulate their rationale of design decisions with explicit linkages to scientific or mathematical ideas. About 28% required students to articulate design decisions using general 'why' questions. Only 10% included specific questions targeting the trade-offs of design decisions or functionality of designs. Thus, there were missed opportunities to facilitate explicit connections to science and mathematical concepts to support design decisions (Peterman et al., 2017).

Carefully crafted, student-centered materials and pedagogies are needed to facilitate engagement in a meaningful practice of argumentation (Driver et al., 2000; Bybee, 2011). Curriculum must address a lack of instructional resources and difficulties with teachers' understanding of what counts as evidence (McNeill, Katsh-Singer, González-Howard, & Loper, 2016; McNeill, González-Howard, Katsh-Singer, & Loper, 2017; Sampson & Blanchard, 2012), how to critique argumentation (Sadler, 2006); how to incorporate argumentation in integrated STEM lessons (McNeill et al., 2017; Mathis et al., 2017; Sampson & Blanchard, 2012), instructional steps that facilitate argumentation (McNeill & Knight, 2013)

Model for Curriculum Design

Research has shown that most integrated STEM curricula do not explicitly attend to argumentation (Peterman et al., 2017; Mathis et al., 2017). We propose a model (Figure 15.1) of argumentation in integrated STEM that leverages the ways in which argumentation is used in various STEM disciplines as well as the five characteristics of integrated STEM lessons (Bryan et al., 2015).

Based on STEM integration frameworks (Bryan et al., 2015; Moore et al., 2014), the engineering design challenge cycle—the focus of an integrated STEM lesson—serves as the integrator, as it provides a process for addressing an authentic challenge in a personally or socially relevant real-world context. Learners bring in knowledge from other disciplines, any of which can serve as anchors, based on the learning goals. The dashed lines represent justifications, based on evidence in science, mathematics, and technology, to support design decisions. Note that the dashed lines not only connect just to engineering, but also interconnect other disciplines. Echoing Mathis et al. (2017), argumentation can occur within each stage of an engineering design cycle. This is parallel to the ADI instructional model within scientific investigations.

The model addresses an important issue in argumentation, i.e., the underspecified nature of evidence itself. Duncan, Chinn, and Barzilai (2018) point out that policy documents and standards that promote argumentation and evidence-based reasoning have not clearly specified what evidence is. Consequently, learners use a variety of evidence to support their claims, including media reports, personal experience, and empirical data. The lack of clear evidentiary standards makes it difficult for learners to engage in productive critique about the evidence let alone the collection methods, alternative interpretations, or triangulation from multiple evidences. McNeill and Berland (2017) proposed three design heuristics to guide teachers and learners to use evidence that is based on observable phenomena, is transformable to highlight patterns, and is socially constructed by students working together. Our model, too, addresses this issue by highlighting the importance of layering of evidence, in that a design justification based on evidence from one discipline may in turn need support from evidence from the other discipline(s). For instance, a claim about an engineering design decision may be based upon evidence of a relationship between two or more physical quantities

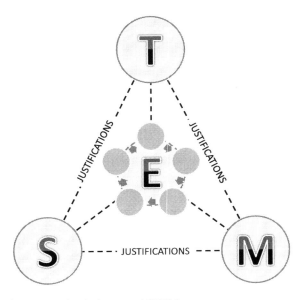

Figure 15.1　A model of argumentation in integrated STEM.

which is encapsulated in a physical law, but evidence to support this law may require support from a pattern of empirical data collected using technology, represented in a specific mathematical relationship. Thus, the model shows how a given engineering design decision may in fact be supported by an interconnected web of justifications utilizing different evidence from multiple disciplines.

Table 15.1 shows an example from a middle school integrated STEM curriculum used pre-service elementary teachers in college physics class (Uruena, Rebello, Dasgupta, Magana, & Rebello, 2017). It demonstrates how the CER framework (McNeill & Krajcik, 2012) can be used with the model in Figure 15.1. The criterion is to design a net energy-zero home that meets constraints of dimensions and cost. Students use *Energy3D* CAD software (http://energy.concord.org/energy3d) to design their home, starting with a sub-optimal design. They are required to document each change to their design and provide evidence to support their predictions and observations. Table 15.1 shows an example of discipline-specific claims, evidence, and reasoning. The overarching claim can be deconstructed into aspects related to science and mathematics. The science aspect focuses on the larger physical phenomena related to solar radiation. It uses evidence from a laboratory investigation with a solar cell under a light. The mathematical aspect of the claim is based on evidence of the quadratic relationship between the length of a side and area of a square. The technology aspect of the claim is based on evidence that a larger quantity of solar cell materials and one that uses a more sophisticated manufacturing. Thus, in an integrated STEM curriculum, learners must be encouraged to support claims about design decisions based on justifications and evidence from multiple disciplines. However, not all design decisions have ramifications in other disciplines. Furthermore, decisions might be based on aesthetic reasons or cost, rather than for scientific reasons.

Table 15.1 Claim-Evidence-Reasoning Manifests in STEM in an Engineering Design Challenge

	Science	*Mathematics*	*Engineering and Technology*
Claim	Increasing the size, location, and efficiency of the solar panels will increase the energy absorbed through radiation.	Doubling the dimensions of the solar panel from will quadruple the cost of the solar panel, but also quadruple the energy generated by the solar panel.	Using a larger and more efficient solar panel, and moving it to the north side of the roof, will make the home more energy efficient but also more expensive.
Evidence	In lab we tested different solar panels of different areas and held them at different orientations relative to a light. The larger panel that was directly facing the light generated a greater voltage.	The area of a square is proportional to the square of the length of its side.	Larger solar panels will require more material. More efficient solar panels require more expensive manufacturing processes. *Energy3D* shows that net energy consumption in the winter decreases, and building cost increases.
Reasoning	The panel that generates the greater voltage will generate greater electrical energy.	When you increase the side of a square by a factor of 2, the area increases by a factor of $2^2 = 4$. So, the area quadruples.	The larger the solar panel, the greater the material used and the greater the cost. The more sophisticated the manufacturing process, the greater the cost. But these costs are offset because it will also generate more energy.

Summary

Multiple reform documents and a vast body of literature have highlighted the importance of argumentation in STEM disciplines. There are clear differences in argumentation between the disciplines in terms of the frameworks, kinds of data used as evidence, scaffolding, and assessment strategies. These differences are relevant when considering argumentation in integrated STEM.

Integrated STEM lessons use engineering design experiences to solve authentic, real-world challenges. They present a unique opportunity to facilitate learners' argumentation skills. Design challenges require learners to make decisions based on knowledge from multiple disciplines. Our model of argumentation in integrated STEM emphasizes the use of multiple justifications using data and reasoning anchored in different disciplines to support design decisions.

There are several possibilities for research on argumentation in integrated STEM, ranging from theory to practice. These include, but are not limited to: (1) adaptation and creation of new frameworks for argumentation in integrated STEM and associated assessment strategies, (2) studying the challenges and scaffolds to facilitate learners to consider, weigh, and utilize data and evidences from different disciplines to support their design decisions, and (3) investigating the interplay of how learners use data from virtual manipulatives, e.g. CAD software with data from physical manipulatives, in constructing and evaluating arguments to support design decisions.

References

ABET. (2016). *Criteria for accrediting engineering programs, 2016–2017.* Retrieved from https://www.abet.org/accreditation/accreditation-criteria/criteria-for-accrediting-engineering-programs-2016-2017/#outcomes

Abi-El-Mona, I., & Abd-El-Khalick, F. (2011). Perceptions of nature and 'goodness' of argument among college students, science teachers, and scientists. *International Journal of Science Education, 33,* 573–605. https://www.tandfonline.com/doi/abs/10.1080/09500691003677889

Asunda, P. A. (2012). Standards for technological literacy and STEM education delivery through career and technical education programs. *Journal of Technology Education, 23,* 44–60. https://doi.org/10.21061/jte.v23i2.a.3

Asunda, P. A., & Hill, R. B. (2007). Critical features of engineering design in technology education. *Journal of Industrial Teacher Education, 44,* 25–48.

Barak, M. (2013). Teaching engineering and technology: Cognitive, knowledge and problem-solving taxonomies. *Journal of Engineering, Design and Technology, 11*(3), 316–333. https://doi.org/10.1108/JEDT-04-2012-0020

Beckman, S. L., & Barry, M. (2012). Teaching students problem framing skills with a storytelling metaphor. *International Journal of Engineering Education, 28,* 364–373.

Berland, L. K., & Hammer, D. (2012). Students' framings and their participation in scientific argumentation. In M. S. Khine (Ed.), *Perspectives on scientific argumentation* (pp. 73–93). Dordrecht, The Netherlands: Springer.

Berland, L. K., & McNeill, K. L. (2010). A learning progression for scientific argumentation: Understanding student work and designing supportive instructional contexts. *Science Education, 94,* 765–793. https://doi.org/10.1002/sce.20402

Bricker, L. A., & Bell, P. (2008). Conceptualizations of argumentation from science studies and the learning sciences and their implications for the practices of science education. *Science Education, 92,* 473–498. https://doi.org/10.1002/sce.20278

Bryan, L. A., Moore, T. J., Johnson, C. C., & Roehrig, G. H. (2015). Integrated STEM education. In C. C. Johnson, E. E. Peters-Burton, & T. J. Moore (Eds.), *STEM road map: A framework for integrated STEM education* (pp. 23–37). New York, NY: Routledge.

Bybee, R. W. (2010). Advancing STEM education: A 2020 vision. *Technology and Engineering Teacher, 70,* 30–35.

Bybee, R. W. (2011). Scientific and engineering practices in K-12 classrooms: Understanding "A Framework for K-12 Science Education." *Science Scope, 35,* 6–11.

Bybee, R. W. (2013). *The case for STEM education: Challenges and opportunities.* Arlington, VA: National Science Teachers Association.

Chen, Y., Park, S., & Hand, B. (2016). Examining the use of talk and writing for students' development of scientific conceptual knowledge through constructing and critiquing arguments. *Cognition and Instruction, 34,* 100–147. https://doi.org/10.1080/07370008.2016.1145120

Christodoulou, A., & Osborne, J. (2014). The science classroom as a site for epistemic talk: A case study of a teacher's attempts to teach science based on argument. *Journal of Research in Science Teaching, 51,* 1275–1300. https://doi.org/10.1002/tea.21166

Clark, D. B., & Sampson, V. D. (2007). Personally-seeded discussions to scaffold online argumentation. *International Journal of Science Education, 29,* 253–277. https://doi.org/10.1080/09500690600560944

Clark, D. B., Sampson, V. D., Stegmann, K., Marttunen, M., Kollar, I., Janssen, J., . . . , & Laurinen, L. (2009). *Scaffolding scientific argumentation between multiple students in online learning environments to support the development of 21st century skills.* Paper prepared for the Workshop on Exploring the Intersection of Science Education and the Development of 21st Century Skills, National Research Council. Retrieved from https://sites.national academies.org/cs/groups/dbassesite/documents/webpage/dbasse_072609.pdf

Clark, D. B., Sampson, V. D., Weinberger, A., & Erkens, G. (2007). Analytic frameworks for assessing dialogic argumentation in online learning environments. *Educational Psychology Review, 19,* 343–374. https://doi.org/10.1007/s10648-007-9050-7

Conner, A. (2013). Authentic argumentation with prospective secondary teachers. *Mathematics Teacher Educator, 1,* 172–180. https://doi:10.5951/mathteaceduc.1.2.0172

Conner, A., Singletary, L. M., Smith, R. C., Wagner, P. A., & Francisco, R. T. (2014). Teacher support for collaborative argumentation: A framework for examining how teachers support students' engagement in mathematical activities. *Educational Studies in Mathematics, 86,* 401–429. https://doi.org/10.1007/s10649-014-9532-8

Council of Chief State School Officers and the National Governors Association Center for Best Practices. (2010). *Common core state standards: Mathematics standards.* Retrieved from http://www.corestandards.org/the-standards

Driver, R., Newton, P., & Osborne, J. (2000). Establishing the norms of scientific argumentation in classrooms. *Science Education, 84,* 287–312. https://doi.org/10.1002/(SICI)1098-237X(200005)84:3<287::AID-SCE1>3.0.CO;2-A

Duncan, R. G., Chinn, C. A., & Barzilai, S. (2018). Grasp of evidence: Problematizing and expanding the next generation science standards' conceptualization of evidence. *Journal of Research in Science Teaching, 55,* 907–937. https://doi.org/10.1002/tea.21468

Duschl, R. A., & Osborne, J. (2002). Supporting and promoting argumentation discourse in science education. *Studies in Science Education, 38,* 39–72. https://doi.org/10.1080/03057260208560187

Dym, C. L.; Agogino, A. M., Eris, O., Frey, D. D., & Leifer, L. J. (2005). Engineering design thinking, teaching, and learning. *Journal of Engineering Education, 94,* 104–120.

Foutz, T. L. (2018). Using argumentation as a learning strategy to improve student performance in engineering statics. *European Journal of Engineering Education.* https://doi.org/10.1080/03043797.2018.1488818

Gale, J., Koval, J., Ryan, M., Usselman, M., & Wind, S. (2018). Implementing NGSS engineering disciplinary core ideas in middle school science classrooms: Results from the field. *Journal of Pre-College Engineering Education Research, 9,* 11–29.

Graham, M., & Lesseig, K. (2018). Back-pocket strategies for argumentation. *Mathematics Teacher, 112,* 172–178.

Grooms, J., Sampson, V., & Enderle, P. (2018). How concept familiarity and experience with scientific argumentation are related to the way groups participate in an episode of argumentation. *Journal of Research in Science Teaching, 55,* 1264–1286. https://doi.org/10.1002/tea.21451

Guzey, S. S., & Aranda, M. (2017). Student participation in engineering practices and discourse: An exploratory case study. *Journal of Engineering Education, 4,* 585–606. https://doi.org/10.1002/jee.20176

Hanna, G. (2000). Proof, explanation and exploration: an overview. *Educational Studies in Mathematics, 44*(1–2), 5–23. https://doi.org/10.1023/A:1012737223465

Hmelo-Silver, C. E., Holton, D. L., & Kolodner, J. L. (2000). Designing to learn about complex systems. *Journal of the Learning Sciences, 9,* 247–298. https://doi.org/10.1207/S15327809JLS0903_2

Hynes, M., Portsmore, M., Dare, E., Milto, E., Rogers, C., Hammer, D., & Carberry, A. (2011). Infusing engineering design into high school STEM courses. In D. Householder (Ed.), *Engineering design challenges in high school STEM course: A compilation of invited position paper.* Retrieved from http://digitalcommons.usu.edu/cgi/viewcontent.cgi?article=1020&context=ete_facpub

International Technology and Engineering Educator Association. (2007). *Standards for technological literacy: Content for the study of technology* (3rd ed.). Retrieved from https://www.iteea.org/39197.aspx

Jin, H., Mehl, C. E., & Lan, D. H. (2015). Developing an analytical framework for argumentation on energy consumption issues. *Journal of Research in Science Teaching, 52,* 1132–1162. https://doi.org/10.1002/tea.21237

Jonassen, D. H. (2011). *Learning to solve problems. A handbook for designing problem-solving learning environments.* New York, NY: Routledge.

Jonassen, D. H., & Kim, B. (2010). Arguing to learn and learning to argue: Design justifications and guidelines. *Educational Technology Research and Development, 58,* 439–457. https://doi.org/10.1007/s11423-009-9143-8

Jonassen, D. H., Shen, D., Marra, R. M., Cho, Y-H., Lo, J. L., & Lohani, V. K. (2009). Engaging and supporting problem solving in engineering ethics. *Journal of Engineering Education, 98*, 235–254. https://doi.org/10.1002/j.2168-9830.2009.tb01022.x

Jung, K. G., & McFadden, J. (2018). Student justifications in engineering design descriptions: Examining authority and legitimation. *International Journal of Education in Mathematics, Science and Technology, 6*, 398–423. doi:10.18404/ijemst.440342

Katehi, L., Pearson, G., & Feder, M. (Eds.). (2009). *Engineering in K-12 education: Understanding the status and improving the prospects.* Washington, DC: National Academies Press.

Kelley, T. R., & Knowles, J. G. (2016). A conceptual framework for integrated STEM education. *International Journal of STEM Education, 11*, 1–11. https://doi.org/10.1186/s40594-016-0046-z

Kolodner, J. L., Crismond, D., Fasse, B., Gray, J., Holbrook, J., & Puntambekar, S. (2003). Putting a student-centered learning by Designô curriculum into practice: Lessons learned. *Journal of the Learning Sciences, 12*, 485–547. https://doi.org/10.1207/S15327809JLS1204_2

Kuhn, D. (1991). *The skills of argument.* Cambridge, UK: Cambridge University Press.

Kuhn, D. (1993). Science as argument: Implications for teaching and learning scientific thinking. *Science Education, 77*, 319–337. https://doi.org/10.1002/sce.3730770306

Llewellyn, D. (2014). *Inquire within: Implementing inquiry-based science standards in grades 3–8* (3rd ed.) Thousand Oaks, CA: Corwin Press.

Mathis, C. A., Siverling, E. A., Glancy, A. W., & Moore, T. J. (2017). Teachers' incorporation of argumentation to support engineering learning in STEM integration curricula. *Journal of Pre-College Engineering Education Research, 7*, 76–89. https://doi.org/10.7771/2157-9288.1163

McNeill, K. L., & Berland, L. (2017). What is (or should be) scientific evidence use in k-12 classrooms? *Journal of Research in Science Teaching, 54*, 672–689. https://doi.org/10.1002/tea.21381

McNeill, K. L., González-Howard, M., Katsh-Singer, R., & Loper, S. (2017). Moving beyond pseudoargumentation: Teachers' enactments of an educative science curriculum focused on argumentation. *Science Education, 101*(3), 426–457. https://doi.org/10.1002/sce.21274

McNeill, K. L., Katsh-Singer, R., González-Howard, M., & Loper, S. (2016). Factors impacting teachers' argumentation instruction in their science classrooms. *International Journal of Science Education, 38*(12), 2026–2046. https://doi.org/10.1080/09500693.2016.1221547

McNeill, K. L., & Knight, A. M. (2013). Teachers' pedagogical content knowledge of scientific argumentation: The impact of professional development on K–12 teachers. *Science Education, 97*, 936–972. https://doi.org/10.1002/sce.21081

McNeill, K. L., & Krajcik, J. (2012). *Supporting grade 5–8 students in constructing explanations in science: The claim, evidence and reasoning framework for talk and writing.* New York, NY: Pearson Allyn & Bacon.

Moore, T. J., Glancy, A. W., Tank, K. M., Kersten, J. A., & Smith, K. A. (2014). A framework for quality K–12 engineering education: Research and development. *Journal of Pre-College Engineering Education Research, 4*, 1–13. https://doi.org/10.7771/2157-9288.1069

Moore, T. J., Guzey, S. S., & Brown, A. (2014). Greenhouse design: An engineering unit. *Science Scope, 37*, 51–57.

National Academy of Engineering and National Research Council. (2014). *STEM integration in K-12 education: Status, prospects, and an agenda for research.* Washington, DC: The National Academies Press.

National Council of Teachers of Mathematics (NCTM). (2009). *Focus in high school mathematics: Reasoning and sense making.* Reston, VA: NCTM.

National Research Council (NRC). (2011). *Successful K-12 STEM education: Identifying effective approaches in Science, Technology, Engineering, and Mathematics.* Washington, DC: The National Academies Press. https://doi.org/10.17226/13158

National Research Council. (2012). *A framework for K-12 science education: Practices, crosscutting concepts, and core ideas.* Washington, DC: The National Academies Press.

National Research Council (NRC). (2014). *STEM integration in K-12 education: Status, prospects, and an agenda for research.* Washington, DC: National Academies Press.

Newton, P., Driver, R., & Osborne, J. (1999). The place of argument in the pedagogy of school science. *International Journal of Science Education, 21*, 553–576. https://doi.org/10.1080/095006999290570

NGSS Lead States. (2013). *Next generation science standards: For states, by states.* Washington, DC: The National Academies Press.

Osborne, J., Erduran, S., & Simon, S. (2004). Enhancing the quality of argumentation in school science. *Journal of Research in Science Teaching, 41*, 994–1020. https://doi.org/10.1002/tea.20035

Peterman, K., Daugherty, J. L., Custer, R. L., & Ross, J. M. (2017). Analyzing the integration of engineering in science lessons with the engineering-infused lesson rubric. *International Journal of Science Education, 39*, 1913–1931. https://doi.org/10.1080/09500693.2017.1359431

Rebello, C. M., Sayre, E., & Rebello, N. S. (2012). Effects of problem representation on students' problem solution and argumentation quality in an introductory physics course. In J. V. Aalst, B. J. Reiser, C. H. Silver, & K. Thompson (Eds.), *The future of learning: Proceedings of the 10th International Conference of the Learning Sciences (ICLS 2012)—Volume 2, Short Papers, Symposia, and Abstracts*. Sydney, Australia: International Society of Learning Sciences.

Reiser, B. J., Berland, L. K., & Kenyon, L. (2012). Engaging students in the scientific practices of explanation and argumentation: Understanding "A Framework for K-12 Science Education." *Science and Children, 50*, 8–13.

Reiser, B. J., Tabak, I., & Sandoval, W. A. (2001). BGuILE: Strategic and conceptual scaffolds for scientific inquiry. In S. M. Carver & D. Klahr (Eds.), *Cognition and instruction: Twenty-five years of progress*. Mahwah, NJ: Erlbaum.

Rumsey, C., & Langrall, C. W. (2016). Promoting mathematical argumentation. *Teaching Children Mathematics, 22*, 413–419. https://www.jstor.org/stable/10.5951/teacchilmath.22.7.0412

Sadler, T. D. (2006). Promoting discourse and argumentation in science teacher education. *Journal of Science Teacher Education, 17*, 323–346. https://doi.org/10.1007/s10972-006-9025-4

Sampson, V., & Blanchard, M. R. (2012). Science teachers and scientific argumentation: Trends in views and practice. *Journal of Research in Science Teaching, 49*, 1122–1148. https://doi.org/10.1002/tea.21037

Sampson, V., & Clark, D. B. (2008). Assessment of the ways students generate arguments in science education: Current perspectives and recommendations for future directions. *Science Education, 92,* 447–472. https://doi.org/10.1002/sce.20276

Sampson, V., Enderle, P., & Grooms, J. (2013). Argumentation in science education. *Science Teacher, 80*, 30–33.

Schoenfeld, A. H. (2009). The soul of mathematics. In D. Stylianou, M. Blanton, & E. Knuth (Eds.), *Teaching and learning proof across the grades: A K–16 perspective* (pp. xii–xvi). Mahwah, NJ: Taylor and Francis Group.

Schunn, C. (2011). Design principles for high school engineering design challenges: Experiences from high school science classroom. In D. Householder (Ed.), *Engineering design challenges in high school STEM course. A compilation of invited position paper*. Retrieved from https://digitalcommons.usu.edu/cgi/viewcontent.cgi?article=1163&context=ncete_publications

Singletary, L. M., & Conner, A. (2015). Focusing on mathematical arguments. *Mathematics Teacher, 109*, 143–147. https://www.jstor.org/stable/10.5951/mathteacher.109.2.0143

Stylianides, A. (2007). Proof and proving in school mathematics. *Journal for Research in Mathematics Education, 38*, 289–321. https://www.jstor.org/stable/30034869

Stylianou, D. A., & Blanton, M. L. (2011). Developing students' capacity for constructing proofs through discourse. *Mathematics Teacher, 105*, 140–145. https://www.jstor.org/stable/10.5951/mathteacher.105.2.0140

Toulmin, S. (1958). *The uses of argument*. Cambridge, MA: Cambridge University Press.

Uruena, Y. P., Rebello, C. M., Dasgupta, C., Magana, A. J., & Rebello, N. S. (2017). Impact of contrasting designs and argumentation scaffolds on elementary pre-service teachers' use of science ideas in engineering design tasks. In D. L. Jones, L. Ding, & A. Traxler (Eds.), *2017 Physics education research conference proceedings*. Melville, NY: American Institute of Physics.

Walker, J. P., & Sampson, V. (2013). Learning to argue and arguing to learn: Argument-driven inquiry as a way to help undergraduate chemistry students learn to construct arguments and engage in argumentation during a laboratory course. *Journal of Research in Science Teaching, 50*, 561–596. https://doi.org/10.1080/09500693.2012.667581

Wang, H. H., Moore, T. J., Roehrig, G. H., & Park, M. S. (2011). STEM integration: The impact of professional development on teacher perception and practice. *Journal of Pre-College Engineering Education Research, 1*, 1–13. https://doi.org/10.5703/1288284314636

Webb, P., Williams, Y., & Meiring, L. (2008). Concept cartoons and writing frames: Developing argumentation in South African science classrooms? *African Journal of Research in Mathematics, Science, and Technology Education, 12*, 5–17. https://doi.org/10.1080/10288457.2008.10740625

Yang, W., Lin, Y., She, H., & Huang, K. (2015). The effects of prior-knowledge and online learning approaches on students' inquiry and argumentation abilities. *International Journal of Science Education, 37*, 1564–1589. https://doi.org/10.1080/09500693.2015.1045957

16

INTEGRATING COMPUTATIONAL THINKING IN STEM

Eric Wiebe, Vance Kite and Soonhye Park

Introduction

In response to the fundamental shift in how science, mathematics, engineering, and allied STEM professions conduct their work, there has been increased policy and research interest in strategies for developing computational thinking (CT) in students beginning in the elementary grades (Chen et al., 2017; Lu & Fletcher, 2009). There is growing recognition that waiting until the upper high school or undergraduate level to introduce both CT and computer science (CS) leaves students underprepared for advanced work in these areas and misses the opportunity to introduce these concepts and practices to a broad audience of students (Israel, Pearson, Tapia, Wherfel, & Reese, 2015; Qualls & Sherrell, 2010). A primary strategy being advocated for widening computational thinking exposure is the infusion of computational thinking concepts across STEM disciplinary areas, learning contexts (e.g., formal and informal), and grade levels (Yadav, Mayfield, Zhou, Hambrusch, & Korb, 2014). This chapter will provide a succinct but actionable summary of research in computational thinking integration into STEM through the lens of curriculum and assessment.

The chapter will open with a history of computer science and its evolution from an emerging occupation to an academic subject, and to the broader conception of computational thinking as a practice. A similar overview will be provided of theoretical underpinnings of learning and teaching computer science and computational thinking with an emphasis on the emergence of educational computer technologies as a vehicle for computationally rich practices within the context of STEM educational disciplines. Current and emerging frameworks of computational thinking will be used as a lens for looking at research done on the integration of computational thinking into topic areas within the individual STEM disciplines and connections between researchers' conceptualizations of computational thinking and their study designs. In addition, computational thinking as a practice will be reviewed as a strategy for integrative work across STEM. Finally, this synthesis will be used to guide a review of research done on computer science and computational thinking in informal learning settings—a historically rich source of research and innovation at the nexus of computational thinking and STEM education. Since computational thinking as an area of research has emerged in parallel across the international research community, international research efforts will be incorporated fully across the chapter.

Theoretical Framing of CT Research and Practice

This section will cover the historical basis of CT and emerging theories that inform current research and curricular strategies around CT/STEM integration, curricular development, instructional practices, and assessment. The modern use of the term computational thinking (CT) can be traced to a 2006 article by Jeannette Wing (2006). Wing articulated the need for a term, distinct from computer science (CS), that articulated a way of thinking that was integral to, but distinct from, the practices used by computer scientists and programmers. CT was a way of solving problems, designing systems, and engaging in creative design using computational tools (Shute, Sun, & Asbell-Clarke, 2017; Wing, 2006). While distinct from computer science, many of the earliest and strongest proponents of CT over the next decade were from computer science (e.g., Aho, 2012; Barr & Stephenson, 2011; Brennan & Resnick, 2012; CSTA, 2011; Shute et al., 2017). Parallel to this conversation about CT was a push to re-envision K-12 CS education (Cuny, 2011). The push for both CT and CS was emerging both out of education research circles but, perhaps, even more strongly from business-oriented policy centers who saw the evolving global economy centered around computational skills and abilities (Google & Gallup, 2015; Nager & Atkinson, 2016). Out of both of these conversations emerged a rich dialogue concerning the role of both CS and CT education in grades K-12. Perhaps most germane to this chapter is the question emerging from this discussion as to how CT might integrate into other STEM courses and content in a way that might complement stand-alone curricula in CS (cf., USDOE, 2016). While much of this work is still in its infancy, a rich body of literature has already started to emerge. This chapter will attempt to summarize its theoretical underpinnings, empirical and theoretical work to date, and identified lines of future work.

An important foundational precursor to Wing's (2006) paper is the work of Seymour Papert (1980), who conducted design-based explorations of how computers and computer programming languages could be powerful learning tools for students of all ages. Out of this work emerged the theory of Constructionism and heuristics for the design of computer-based learning environments (Harel & Papert, 1990, 1991). Papert considered Constructionism to be an extension of Piaget's (Piaget, 1970) conceptions of Constructivism. Papert agreed that children actively construct their knowledge of the world but stressed the importance of how internal knowledge construction could be supported by the production of real-world objects, especially computational artifacts (Kafai, 2006). Computer environments developed by Papert's team, such as LOGO, provided a rich interactive environment where children could interactively plan, build, test, and reflect on their ideas being put into action as they constructed understandings about ideas and principles. Educational researchers influenced directly or indirectly by Papert's work are, not surprisingly, some of the most influential voices in the CT scholarly community (e.g., Grover & Pea, 2013; Kafai & Burke, 2015; Repenning et al., 2015; Weintrop et al., 2016; Wilensky, Brady, & Horn, 2014).

An important shift in the STEM research literature took place when a much broader language around scientific inquiry shifted to a discussion of a more focused set of science practices (as distinct from disciplinary content knowledge (NRC, 2011). Among these more focused practices were computational thinking and modeling. Modeling has come to be understood as a central practice in STEM disciplines and educational practice (NGSS Lead States, 2013). In the 1990s modeling emerged as a central paradigm for the educational practice of representing mathematical or scientific concepts in a simplified form as a means of providing an explanation for the underlying mechanisms and principles for the concept (Hestenes, 1993). This concept may be highly focused and discreet, or it may represent a larger system (e.g., Chiu, DeJaegher, & Chao, 2015; Levy & Wilensky, 2011). Often models and the process of modeling involve representing the concepts in different modalities, which allows students to practice multiple forms of representation (Greeno & Hall, 1997). For example, a mathematical model might be represented as a diagram or a graph; a scientific model might be represented as an interactive simulation. Educational researchers have come to understand the myriad learning opportunities that arise through the generative process of creating the model and representing it in multiple modalities (Van Meter, Aleksic, Schwartz, & Garner, 2006). Perhaps most germane to this chapter is how Agent Based Modeling (ABM) has emerged as a key strategy for CT integration in STEM disciplinary courses through student construction of science simulations

(Basawapatna, 2016; Rates, Mulvey, & Feldon, 2016; Repenning et al., 2015; Sengupta & Clark, 2016; Weintrop et al., 2016). In the case of ABM, programming languages can be thought of as an alternative representational form for mathematical or scientific concepts. This same programming code can then also generate an interactive simulation representing the same concept, allowing students to move back and forth between the original representation (e.g., text or mathematical equations), the programming code, and the interactive graphic simulation. The generative process of creating, testing, and refining these alternative models shows considerable promise in the emerging research.

K-12 CS policy and standards documents also emphasize creative problem solving as a guiding principle in curricular design and student outcomes (CSTA, 2011; k12cs.org, 2016). A popular instantiation of this idea is problem-based learning and, in the context of engineering and technology, the engineering design process (Bertoline et al., 2013). CT can be fully embraced by engineering design process models that emphasize abstraction of the problem space and algorithmic practices to map process and procedure. Programming languages can be the representational tool to embody the design solution and carry out the actions of the functional solution—in some cases it may be mathematical manipulation taking place exclusively within a computer, or it could be electromechanical control of robotic devices. Creative problem solving, especially when carried out collaboratively, also intersects with an important line of research in CS education—pair programming (Denner, Werner, Campe, & Ortiz, 2014; Hesse, Care, Buder, Sassenberg, & Griffin, 2015; Williams, Wiebe, Yang, Ferzli, & Miller, 2002). Both collaborative problem solving and pair programming attempt to leverage the collective wisdom of a group of students while also leveraging positive affective gains that emerge from social activity. Creative problem solving when directed at intellectual challenges that are perceived as personally relevant and that result in tangible outcomes (e.g., Lee & Soep, 2016; Vakil, 2014) is another instructional strategy that taps positive motivational outcomes, as posited by Self-Determination Theory (Ryan & Deci, 2000).

Research assessing the efficacy of an intervention designed to impact a student's CT abilities requires instruments for measuring CT and a theoretical basis for what the instruments are measuring. Though CT as a construct is relatively new, there are researchers positing the relationship of CT to models of intelligence and underlying cognitive abilities (cf., Román-González, Pérez-González, & Jiménez-Fernández, 2016). This work is exploring the relationship of fluid intelligence, spatial ability, and working memory capacity to one's ability to engage in CT-related tasks. A similarly productive approach has been to use mapping processes between CS standards related to CT and abilities needed to successfully carry out curricular-driven classroom tasks (Bienkowski, Snow, Rutstein, & Grover, 2015). Both of these approaches have generated a first generation of assessment instruments and analytic methods (e.g., Wiebe et al., 2019).

Computational Thinking as a STEM Practice

As CT has been framed primarily as a practice (as opposed to disciplinary content knowledge or skill) in STEM standards documents (e.g., NGSS), this section will look at how CT has been theorized in published CT/STEM curricular frameworks as a practice in each discipline separately and then, more importantly, how it can be synthesized in integrative STEM.

Not surprisingly, programming as a CS practice is probably the most common vehicle for implementing CT as a practice in classrooms. With the current conversations about CT emerging in parallel with a deeper infusion of CS in K-12, it is perhaps no great surprise that the current K-12 CS education standards framework deeply intertwines both core CS concepts and CT practices (k12cs.org, 2016). However, one result of rethinking CS/CT education in K-12 is work around how goals of general technological literacy might align with CS/CT (Barr & Stephenson, 2011). The CSTA framework for CT articulated a view that goes beyond just programming, but that also incorporates information age competencies such as teamwork, collaborative negotiation, problem solving, and persistence. Adding another dimension are more macro-level facets such as socio-technical issues, ethics, and cybersecurity. These expanded facets then bring CS/CT practices into the realm of educational technology standards promoted by organizations such as ISTE (2018).

While the current standards for mathematics (CCSSI, 2012) do not speak directly to CT, there has been considerable discussion among CT education researchers as to points of intersection (English, 2018; Weintrop et al., 2016). Perhaps the easiest connections can be made at the programming level where algebraic tools are used frequently to both process data variables and to control functions such as looping through counters. Similarly, Boolean logic is central to control functions such as if-then statements. Finally, some CT/STEM integration standards also specifically list data (processing and visualization) as a CT practice (Weintrop et al., 2016). Perhaps more interesting is to return to the Constructionist foundations of CT and look at the parallels of mathematical inscriptional practices and the goals of CT, where one can envision carrying out CT without the need of traditional programming languages (diSessa, 2018). Similarly, instructional approaches utilizing modeling can have students use STEM concepts represented initially as mathematical inscriptions and then transformed into programming code (Cetin & Dubinsky, 2017; Weintrop et al., 2016).

The Next Generation Science Standards (NGSS; NGSS Lead States, 2013) and the precursor federal reports (i.e., NRC, 2010, 2011) were instrumental in setting the stage for current thinking on the integration of CT into STEM K-12 academics. First, NGSS established a three-dimensional framing of science learning outcomes around: (1) core disciplinary knowledge, (2) crosscutting concepts, and (3) science and engineering practices. Recognizing that both academics and future careers in science and engineering require both knowledge and practice, CT was identified as a practice through which students develop and apply scientific knowledge. While these key policy documents provided few details as to what CT as a practice would look like enacted in classrooms, it triggered considerable interest and creative thought at both the practitioner (Sneider, Stephenson, Schafer, & Flick, 2014) and researcher levels (Grover & Pea, 2013; Weintrop et al., 2016) as what CT/STEM integration might look like. NGSS also provided an entry point to thinking about how CT, as a practice, might be combined with other practices such as analyzing and interpreting data, modeling, and designing solutions to synergistically forward practice goals on multiple fronts.

Engineering education researchers have already documented the degree to which CT practices have become integral to undergraduate engineering education (Froyd, Wankat, & Smith, 2012). It is a logical next step to use tools such as the framework for K-12 engineering education (Moore et al., 2014) as a lens to see how engineering, as a practice within K-12 classrooms, can intersect with CT as a practice. The engineering process of design could describe the outer loop guiding principles for many problem-based computational challenges. The engineering design process and CT practices also both typically describe parallel activities of problem definition, decomposition, and identification of key inputs and outputs (Fraillon, Ainley, Schulz, Duckworth, & Friedman, 2019; Moore et al., 2014). The cycle of defining the problem and necessary background information, then planning, implementing, testing, and evaluating the solution, could be the primary mover for CT practices involved in constructing solutions. Clearly, more expansive definitions of CT will encompass many or all of these engineering design processes; we can imagine, for example, code debugging being an integral part of the testing and evaluation phase. It becomes an interesting research question the degree to which the application of science, engineering, and mathematics knowledge within engineering problems already encompasses the core computer science knowledge needed to move many of these computational-based engineering problems forward, or whether this becomes its own unique knowledge base within engineering education.

Moore and colleagues (2015) have noted that the most promising avenues for engineering education in K-12 education are probably not stand-alone courses and curricula, but integrative activities within science and other STEM curricula. She argues that NGSS, by embracing engineering as a core science practice, provides significant impetus and pathways for pursuing such integration work.

Others (e.g., Hansen, Iveland, Dwyer, Harlow, & Franklin, 2015) have done just that by looking at bringing engineering and science together through the aforementioned practice of modeling. CT and allied computational tools are then both explicitly and implicitly linked to many of these modeling activities. Given that automation is at the heart of computation, it may represent a vehicle for bringing engineering and technological solutions together. That is, programs provide instructions for automated activities; or, in the words of (Lee et al., 2011), computational thinking involves the process of automated abstraction. Technology as the embodiment of engineering ideas often comes in the form of automation, so it is not surprising that computational thinking can either lead or follow the goal of using engineering principles to accomplish technological automation. Finally, Lee's (Lee, Martin, & Apone, 2014; Lee et al., 2011) pedagogical strategy of "use-modify-create" provides a bridge from the typical practice in mathematics and science education of using models to understand core concepts, to investigating these concepts through modification of the models and application of these concepts through the engineering design process to create new technological artifacts. The next section will more fully explore these STEM integration strategies that link to CT.

STEM Integration Strategies

The prior section on more abstracted frameworks of CT/STEM learning and assessment is now put in the context of the emergent, published reports on integration initiatives. Reflecting both the historic and emergent trends in education, they include both discipline-specific and cross-STEM approaches. Robotics, game design, integration of arts, and modeling with big data appear to be prevalent approaches to incorporating CT as a vehicle for STEM integration.

Robotics has a long history in career technical education (CTE) and K-12 engineering education. Given that robots are driven through programmable instructions, it becomes a natural point of intersection with CT (Bers, Flannery, Kazakoff, & Sullivan, 2014; Shute et al., 2017; Witherspoon, Higashi, Schunn, Baehr, & Shoop, 2017). The historic focus of problem- or challenge-based robotics activities can be married with a more purposeful instruction and application of CT concepts. As with many technological-engineering design problems, robotics requires students to engage in algorithmic thinking whereby the component elements of sensing and motor control are decomposed and worked on both separately and in concert. This work is done through multiple cycles of iterative testing and refinement.

Game design and development as a classroom activity provides a rich space where the popularity and interest in games and gaming can be leveraged to engage students in CT activities (Repenning et al., 2015; Shute et al., 2017). Platforms such as AgentSheets and App Inventor provides the computer programming tools for students to create modally rich, interactive tools. While games have historically been thought of as non-academic distractions, the serious games movement (Mayer et al., 2014), combined with CT, has put forward the idea of programmable games which require students to apply sound STEM concepts in order to achieve their goals (Sengupta & Clark, 2016). The game-based learning paradigm can also be turned on its head, whereby students learn CT/CS concepts within a game-based learning environment (Buffum et al., 2014). Here, students need to use programming and CT knowledge to solve challenges presented to them. Ideally, students will come to understand their ability to solve problems using computational approaches that would otherwise be too difficult or time-consuming to do by other means.

Through acronyms such as STEAM, researchers and practitioners have been exploring the intersection of STEM and the arts. Through CT and CS, a number of particularly strong strategies allow students to simultaneously engage in creative expression with STEM practices and tools. Maker-inspired activities and tools have rapidly moved from niche applications among hobbyist groups to a prominent place in informal and formal STEM educational settings, and is another vehicle for bringing engineering and CT practices together (Kafai & Burke, 2015; Martin, 2015; Rode et al., 2015). There is also a long-standing interest in the intersection of music and mathematics that has, not surprisingly, been extended to CT (Edwards, 2011). Edwards makes the argument that creativity and algorithmic thinking in music go hand in hand and provide a mechanism for arts-minded students to find new venues to explore core STEM practices.

Perhaps one of the most exciting ways that CT can be used as an integrative STEM practice is through the integration of modeling with "big data" (Sneider et al., 2014). Fundamentally, computer programs are designed to process data, while K-12 STEM education has continued to struggle to meet the standards mandates around working with data (cf., West, 2012); thus, CT becomes a powerful strategy to provide tools and concepts that allow students to explore data and to solve analytic problems interactively through programmable tools. Related to this is the use of the sensor technologies, often the same used as part of, say, robotics, to collect scientific data for the purposes of testing or validating empirically synthetic programmable models (Sengupta & Clark, 2016; Sengupta, Kinnebrew, Basu, Biswas, & Clark, 2013). For example, an interactive model of a ball bouncing from various heights is created using a Newtonian mathematical model. This model can be validated against empirical data collected, cleaned, and visualized by programs controlling sensors. Robotics curricula, using systems such as LEGO Mindstorms™, has proven to be a popular method for teaching introductory programming and CT concepts (Lawhead et al., 2002; Papadakis & Orfanakis, 2016).

Computational Thinking Integration Contextualized

To more fully elaborate on the reported and conceptualized possibilities for CT/STEM instruction, representational systems used to forward CT learning and the larger policy discussions driving implementation decisions are discussed.

Central to both constructivist and constructionist theory is the understanding that learning is mediated by representational systems (Greeno & Hall, 1997). These representational systems (e.g., text, mathematical equations, flow charts, CAD drawings) are all both emergent from professional and popular culture and influence how both teaching and learning occurs (diSessa, 2000). Thus it should be no surprise that the representational tools used for CT/STEM integration represent both top-down influences of professional practice and what industry voices believe students should know, and bottom-up, pragmatic choices driven by educators in the field.

Visual, block-based programming tools such as *Scratch*™ or *Alice* stand apart as the primary approach to both stand-alone and integrated CT education. The impetus for and theoretical underpinnings of the development of these tools is the proposition that text-based programming tools (e.g., Python, Java, C++) impose unnecessary cognitive load on learners and impede the apprehension of basic programming concepts. Multiple studies comparing visual and text-based programming interventions have demonstrated that students engaged in representation via visual programming exhibit strong apprehension of fundamental CT skills (Shute, Sun, & Asbell-Clarke, 2017). The construction of simulations through ABM and block-based programming may represent one of the richest opportunities for CT/STEM integration. Through tools such as AgentSheets, Agent-Cubes, NetLogo, and CTSiM, students are afforded the opportunity to represent a scientific concept through visual coding, experience the emergent phenomena of their system through running their simulation, change model parameters and gather data, and engage in deep systems thinking (cf., Dickes, Sengupta, Farris, & Basu, 2016; Repenning et al., 2015; Sengupta & Clark, 2016).

While code-centric approaches are the predominant form of CT instruction, there are likely unexplored affordances of code-free (unplugged) approaches to integrating CT in STEM curricula (Kite, Park & Wiebe, 2019). Potential benefits of unplugged approaches to CT include lowering barriers to teaching and learning CT and CS, providing students with a view of CS that extends beyond programming, removing a reliance on technology, and leveraging the power of multiple forms of representation (Bell & Vahrenhold, 2018; Greeno & Hall, 1997). The most widely used vehicle for teaching CT without using code is the CS Unplugged curriculum, which endeavors to teach core

CS concepts through a variety of activities that do not use technology (Bell, Rosamond, & Casey, 2012). While the literature to date on the CS Unplugged approach has shown mixed results in the studied interventions, there is consensus in the literature on the potential of unplugged approaches to increase student interest in CS, teach CT concepts, reduce teacher anxiety about incorporating CT and CS, and scaffold code-centric approaches to CT (Kite et al., 2019; Bell & Vahrenhold, 2018; Peel, Sadler, & Friedrichsen, 2019). Ultimately, Bell and Vahrenhold (2018) conclude, "The 'programming vs. Unplugged' discussion should not be an 'either-or' debate, but working out how to combine the two to bring about valuable learning, where each approach is used where it is most effective" (p. 507).

K-12 CS education is truly an emerging educational experience that has been buffeted by numerous competing policy and educational factions. Computer technology curricula have been part of CTE education since personal computers first appeared in secondary education. True to its vocational roots, this curricula emerged from keyboarding courses and focused on business applications (e.g., Microsoft Word) rather than programming. However, as programming emerged as an important technical skill, both computer technology classes and specialized programming classes emerged to fill this need. Separately, organizations such as ISTE represented a parallel movement for computer literacy on the academic side of primary and secondary education (ISTE, 2007). Not surprisingly, as K-12 CS/CT education rose in prominence, so did ISTE's involvement with CS/CT standards development (ISTE, 2018). True to their broader educational technology approach, the goal was less about stand-alone courses than CT integration into existing curricula (Tran, 2018). Intersecting with the educational technology profession's push was a move to completely revamp the high school AP CS curriculum (Cuny, 2011). This effort, led by NSF and their funded partners, evolved in a larger K-12 CS/CT movement. This effort, too, has focused on CT-integration efforts in K-8 with a transition to stand-alone CS courses and curricula starting in middle grades and on into high school. Experientially, these separate efforts have meant, for example, that a current student in middle school might: (a) have a CTE-based computer technology course that has a unit on programming, (b) have an elective academic course based on the CS Discoveries™ curriculum (code.org, 2018a), (c) experience integrative CT units in their science class, (d) create programmable fashionware during a Maker unit in art class, in addition to (e) design a programmable game during a school-wide Hour of Code™ (code.org, 2018b) event.

What was just described is confined to only the formal academic educational space. In fact, CS/CT activities have had an equally robust presence in informal STEM contexts (Lye & Koh, 2014). This rapid infusion of CS/CT into STEM camps and clubs can be traced to pushes by both private foundations backed by STEM-based companies and the interrelated federal policy push providing funding for research in this area (CWCT, 2010; Google & Gallup, 2015). This work is backed by research demonstrating that informal learning opportunities contribute to young people's interest in and understanding of STEM, connect young people to adults who serve as role models, and can reduce the achievement gap between young people from low-income and high-income families (NRC, 2015). Examples of these approaches include block-based programming camps focused very specifically on developing CT- and CS-related skills (Rodger et al., 2009), K-12 mentoring through undergraduate service learning (Payton, Barnes, Buch, Rorrer, & Zuo, 2015), and broadening participation in CS through programs like Black Girls Code (Wolber, Abelson, & Friedman, 2015)

K-12 Teacher Professional Development

This section will focus on efforts to provide professional development opportunities for in-service, preservice, and alternatively certified teachers to effectively integrate CT into their classrooms. Though numerous scholars have identified systematic teacher preparation as a critical factor to successful CT/content integration (e.g., Voogt, Fisser, Good, Mishra, & Yadav, 2015; Yadav, Gretter, Good, & McLean, 2017), only a few large-scale programs have targeted in-service teachers (Sands, Yadav, &

Good, 2018). Notable examples of existing programs include Google's Computational Thinking for Educators course (Google, 2019), Repenning et al.'s (2015) Scalable Game Design initiative, and ISTE's Introduction to Computational Thinking for Every Educator (ISTE, 2019). Apart from large-scale initiatives, Bower et al. (2017) has demonstrated the effectiveness of relatively short instances of CT professional development for enhancing teachers' confidence and abilities to integrate CT in their curriculum. Beyond these programs, the majority of CT professional development opportunities for in-service teachers are situated within initiatives focusing on teaching teachers about computer science; the predominant forms being coding programs (e.g., programming boot camps), CS integration courses, and course-specific professional development for classes such as CS Principles and CS Discoveries. However, little research has been done to examine the effectiveness of the programs in terms of teacher learning and student learning outcomes. Moreover, there is no current literature dealing with CT professional development, specifically targeting alternatively certified teachers. Research has shown that alternatively certified teachers have unique challenges and needs different from those of traditionally certified teachers (Cohen-Vogel & Smith, 2007; Kee, 2012), and nearly a quarter of early career teachers entered the teaching profession through alternative teacher preparation programs (Redding & Smith, 2016). Given that, there is imperative need for CT professional development programs that address the special needs and characteristics of the alternatively certified teachers.

A future that includes CT integration across STEM disciplines is reliant on the preparation of preservice teachers for this work. Presently, CT courses for preservice teachers are not common, even though they do exist. Some examples include the computational thinking course in Michigan State's Masters in Educational Technology (MAET) program (Yadav, Hong, & Stephenson, 2016) and the University of Delaware's efforts to develop a CT course for preservice educators and infuse CT across the university's undergraduate courses (Delaware, 2019). With an eye towards wider inclusion of CT in preservice teacher education, Yadav and colleagues (2017) propose collaborations between education faculty and computer science faculty to produce programs whereby preservice teachers learn CT through their educational technology courses and learn CT integration through their subject teaching methods classes. This approach may hold promise, as it does not require the creation and implementation of stand-alone CT courses for preservice teachers. Teachers are a main mediator of any educational initiative and impact student performance greater than other variables such as class size and school finances (Hattie, 2012). Thus, in order to promote CT skills for all students, K-12 teacher professional development is an area that needs much more research efforts.

Broadening Participation in STEM Through Computational Thinking

This section will focus on an important and active area of research and policy development regarding diversity and equity issues in STEM education, and both the potential and challenges for CT/STEM to address this goal. Examples of strategies that have or might be taken are provided. K-12 CS education, and by extension CT-STEM integrative elective courses, continues to struggle with attracting a broad demographic of students (Google & Gallup, 2016). An important recent survey by Google and Gallup (2016) shows that groups underrepresented in computer science—women, African Americans, and Hispanic/Latinx—lack not interest but rather awareness of, and access to, opportunities. Findings from the survey further indicate that students who do not see people like themselves and do not have parental encouragement for "doing computer science" may struggle to imagine themselves becoming involved in computer science.

Efforts to attract student populations that are underrepresented in STEM fields need to start earlier, before many students turn away from STEM academics (Unfried, Faber, & Wiebe, 2014). There is clearly enthusiasm to engage in CS/CT activities at younger ages and from underrepresented populations (Denner, Werner, & Ortiz, 2012; Tsan, Boyer, & Lynch, 2016). However, efforts at the middle grades level have focused on elective courses and informal, out-of-school or out-of-class activities that are self-selective and that disadvantage access to students from underrepresented groups (Margolis, 2010). The degree to which CT-STEM integrative activities can be part of core STEM curricula means that the mandatory, full-access requirements of these classes assures that all students get access and exposure to these experiences. In addition, building collaboration and communication skill development into the curricular units can be a strategy for effectively bridging the gap between students having less experience with STEM and computing and students who may have both interest and strong prior experience in this area (Tsan et al., 2016).

Middle grades have been identified as a critical age range to study the potential for developing CT using block-based programming languages (Denner et al., 2012; Grover, Pea, & Cooper, 2016). Female and minority teachers, along with working professionals, can provide powerful identity and attitudinal supports for young women and minorities and thus provide social inoculation against stereotype threats (Dasgupta, 2011; Stout, Dasgupta, Hunsinger, & McManus, 2011). Strategies such as critical computational literacy, which engages students in the critique of systems of inequality through the creation of digital products (Lee & Soep, 2016), engage youth through the development of personally meaningful applications that have an impact in the real world (Tissenbaum, Sheldon, Seop, Lee, & Lao, 2017). The use of block-based programming tools such as Scratch and App Inventor represent a low-floor, high-ceiling approach to CT (Grover & Pea, 2013) that remove barriers for students with less prior experience in CT/CS to create solutions that students feel represent their ideas. Often, these creations, though using CS concepts, hinge on socio-technical issues with a strong STEM basis. An example might be tools to raise awareness among youth about global climate change.

Conclusion

The integration of CT into STEM educational contexts has emerged at a time when global economic competitiveness has zeroed in on computational literacy within STEM professions as a critical economic driving force. Computer science education has moved from a field of advanced study pursued at the undergraduate and graduate levels to a central educational policy initiative in K-12 education. CT integration in STEM has, in turn, been a primary strategy for fulfilling this policy goal. CT as a concept emerged from foundational educational theory on constructivism and constructionism. Its emergence coincided with a rethinking of STEM educational theory, more broadly, around the interplay of disciplinary content knowledge and practice. CT as a practice, thus, was able to enter into a larger discussion of reform-based instructional strategies in STEM education. The chapter has laid out curricular strategies and lines of educational research that have emerged largely in the past 10 years and show no sign of slowing down. This research reflects both the exciting possibilities of new ways of engaging students through practices such as ABM and the continued challenges of broadening participation in CS/CT. Future work is likely to begin to integrate another key emerging area of CS, artificial intelligence (Akram et al., 2018; Min et al., 2019) whereby intelligent, adaptive systems can help support student learning in CT. Similarly, AI tools deployed on scalable MOOC platforms have the potential of providing opportunities to many more individuals than in the past (Brinton et al., 2014; Wiebe, Thompson, & Behrend, 2015). As the conceptions of K-12 CS and integrated STEM education continue to evolve, the role of CT will continue to grow and mature as a key strategy to forward these goals.

References

Aho, A. V. (2012). Computation and computational thinking. *The Computer Journal, 55*(7), 832–835.

Akram, B., Mott, B., Min, W., Boyer, K. E., Wiebe, E., & Lester, J. (2018). *Improving stealth assessment in game-based learning with LSTM-based analytics.* Paper presented at the International Conference on Educational Data Mining EDM 2018, Buffalo, NY.

Barr, V., & Stephenson, C. (2011). Bringing computational thinking to k-12: What is involved and what is the role of the computer science education community? *ACM Inroads, 2*(1), 48–54.

Basawapatna, A. (2016). Alexander meets michotte: A simulation tool based on pattern programming and phenomenology. *Journal of Educational Technology & Society, 19*(1), 277.

Bell, T., Rosamond, F., & Casey, N. (2012). Computer science unplugged and related projects in math and computer science popularization. In H. L. Bodlaender, R. Downey, F. V. Fomin & D. Marx (Eds.), *The multivariate algorithmic revolution and beyond* (Vol. 7370, pp. 398–456). New York, NY: Springer.

Bell, T., & Vahrenhold, J. (2018). CS unplugged—How is it used, and does it work? In H. J. Böckenhauer, D. Komm, & W. Unger (Eds.), *Adventures between lower bounds and higher altitudes* (Vol. 11011, pp. 497–521). New York, NY: Springer.

Bers, M. U., Flannery, L., Kazakoff, E. R., & Sullivan, A. (2014). Computational thinking and tinkering: Exploration of an early childhood robotics curriculum. *Computers & Education, 72*, 145–157.

Bertoline, G. R., Wiebe, E. N., Hartman, N. W., Ross, W. A., Study, N. E., & Simmers, C. (2013). *Engineering design*. New York, NY: McGraw-Hill.

Bienkowski, M., Snow, E., Rutstein, D. W., & Grover, S. (2015). *Assessment design patterns for computational thinking practices in secondary computer science: A first look*. Menlo Park, CA. Retrieved from http://pact.sri.com/down loads/Assessment-Design-Patterns-for-Computational%20Thinking-Practices-Secondary-Computer-Sci ence.pdf

Bower, M., Wood, L. N., Lai, J. W., Howe, C., Lister, R., Mason, R., . . . Veal, J. (2017). Improving the computational thinking pedagogical capabilities of school teachers. *Australian Journal of Teacher Education, 42*(3), 4.

Brennan, K., & Resnick, M. (2012). *New frameworks for studying and assessing the development of computational thinking*. Paper presented at the Proceedings of the 2012 annual meeting of the American Educational Research Association, Vancouver, Canada.

Brinton, C. G., Mung, C., Jain, S., Lam, H., Zhenming, L., & Wong, F. M. F. (2014). Learning about social learning in moocs: From statistical analysis to generative model. *Learning Technologies, IEEE Transactions on, 7*(4), 346–359. doi:10.1109/TLT.2014.2337900

Buffum, P. S., Martinez-Arocho, A. G., Frankosky, M. H., Rodriguez, F. J., Wiebe, E. N., & Boyer, K. E. (2014). *Cs principles goes to middle school: Learning how to teach big data*. Paper presented at the Proceedings of the 45th ACM technical symposium on Computer science education.

CCSSI, Common Core State Standards Initiative. (2012). *Standards for mathematical practice*. Retrieved from http://www.corestandards.org/Math

Cetin, I., & Dubinsky, E. (2017). Reflective abstraction in computational thinking. *The Journal of Mathematical Behavior, 47*, 70–80.

Chen, G., Shen, J., Barth-Cohen, L., Jiang, S., Huang, X., & Eltoukhy, M. (2017). Assessing elementary students' computational thinking in everyday reasoning and robotics programming. *Computers & Education, 109*, 162–175.

Chiu, J. L., DeJaegher, C. J., & Chao, J. (2015). The effects of augmented virtual science laboratories on middle school students' understanding of gas properties. *Computers & Education, 85*, 59–73. http://dx.doi.org/10.1016/j.compedu.2015.02.007

code.org. (2018a). *Computer science discoveries*. Retrieved from https://code.org/educate/csd

code.org. (2018b). *Hour of code*. Retrieved from https://hourofcode.com/us

Cohen-Vogel, L., & Smith, T. M. (2007). Qualifications and assignments of alternatively certified teachers: Testing core assumptions. *American Educational Research Journal, 44*(3), 732–753.

CSTA, Computer Science Teachers Association. (2011). *K–12 computer science standards*. New York, NY: Author.

Cuny, J. (2011). Transforming computer science education in high schools. *Computer, 44*(6), 107–109. doi:10.1109/mc.2011.191

CWCT, Committee for the Workshops on Computational Thinking. (2010). *Report of a workshop on the scope and nature of computational thinking*. Washington, DC: National Research Council.

Dasgupta, N. (2011). Ingroup experts and peers as social vaccines who inoculate the self-concept: The stereotype inoculation model. *Psychological Inquiry, 22*(4), 231–246.

Denner, J., Werner, L., Campe, S., & Ortiz, E. (2014). Pair programming: Under what conditions is it advantageous for middle school students? *Journal of Research on Technology in Education, 46*(3), 277–296.

Denner, J., Werner, L., & Ortiz, E. (2012). Computer games created by middle school girls: Can they be used to measure understanding of computer science concepts? *Computers & Education, 58*(1), 240–249. http://dx.doi.org/10.1016/j.compedu.2011.08.006

Dickes, A. C., Sengupta, P., Farris, A. V., & Basu, S. (2016). Development of mechanistic reasoning and multilevel explanations of ecology in third grade using agent-based models. *Science Education, 100*(4), 734–776.

diSessa, A. A. (2000). *Changing minds: Computers, learning, and literacy*. Cambridge, MA: MIT press.

diSessa, A. A. (2018). Computational literacy and "the big picture" concerning computers in mathematics education. *Mathematical Thinking and Learning, 20*(1), 3–31. doi:10.1080/10986065.2018.1403544

Edwards, M. (2011). Algorithmic composition: Computational thinking in music. *Communications of the ACM, 54*(7), 58–67.

English, L. (2018). On MTL's second milestone: Exploring computational thinking and mathematics learning. *Mathematical Thinking and Learning, 20*(1), 1–2. doi:10.1080/10986065.2018.1405615

Fraillon, J., Ainley, J., Schulz, W., Duckworth, D., & Friedman, T. (2019). *International computer and information literacy study 2018: Assessment framework.* Amsterdam: International Association for the Evaluation of Educational Achievement (IEA).

Froyd, J. E., Wankat, P. C., & Smith, K. A. (2012). *Five major shifts in 100 years of engineering education.* Proceedings of the IEEE, 100 (Special Centennial Issue), 1344–1360. doi:10.1109/JPROC.2012.2190167

Google. (2019). *Computational thinking for educators.* Retrieved from https://computationalthinkingcourse.with-google.com/course?use_last_location=true

Google & Gallup. (2015). *Searching for computer science: Access and barriers in U.S. K-12 education.* Retrieved from https://goo.gl/oX311J

Google & Gallup. (2016). *Diversity gaps in computer science: Exploring the underrepresentation of girls, blacks and Hispanics.* Retrieved from http://goo.gl/PG34aH

Greeno, J. G., & Hall, R. (1997, January). Practicing representation: Learning with and about representational forms. *Phi Delta Kappan*, 361–367.

Grover, S., & Pea, R. (2013). Computational thinking in k–12: A review of the state of the field. *Educational Researcher, 42*(1), 38–43. doi:10.3102/0013189X12463051

Grover, S., Pea, R., & Cooper, S. (2016). *Factors influencing computer science learning in middle school.* Paper presented at the Proceedings of the 47th ACM Technical Symposium on Computer Science Education.

Hansen, A. K., Iveland, A., Dwyer, H., Harlow, D. B., & Franklin, D. (2015, November). Computer science and engineering design in the science classroom. *Science and Children*, 60–64.

Harel, I. E., & Papert, S. (1990). Software design as a learning environment. *Interactive Learning Environments, 1*(1), 1–32.

Harel, I. E., & Papert, S. (1991). *Constructionism.* Norwood, NJ: Ablex Publishing.

Hattie, J. (2012). *Visible learning for teachers: Maximizing impact on learning.* New York, NY: Routledge.

Hesse, F., Care, E., Buder, J., Sassenberg, K., & Griffin, P. (2015). A framework for teachable collaborative problem solving skills. In *Assessment and teaching of 21st century skills* (pp. 37–56). New York, NY: Springer.

Hestenes, D. (1993). *Modeling is the name of the game.* Paper presented at the A presentation at the NSF Modeling Conference, Dedham, MA.

Israel, M., Pearson, J. N., Tapia, T., Wherfel, Q. M., & Reese, G. (2015). Supporting all learners in school-wide computational thinking: A cross-case qualitative analysis. *Computers & Education, 82*, 263–279.

ISTE, International Society for Technology in Education. (2007). *The national educational technology standards and performance indicators for students.* Eugene, OR: Author.

ISTE, International Society for Technology in Education. (2018). *ISTE standards for computer science educators.* Washington, DC. Retrieved from https://www.iste.org/standards/for-computer-science-educators

ISTE, International Society for Technology in Education. (2019). *Computational thinking: Introduction to computational thinking for every educator.* Retrieved from https://www.iste.org/learn/iste-u/computational-thinking

k12cs.org. (2016). *K-12 computer science framework.* Retrieved from https://k12cs.org/

Kafai, Y. B. (2006). Playing and making games for learning: Instructionist and constructionist perspectives for game studies. *Games and Culture, 1*(1), 36–40.

Kafai, Y. B., & Burke, Q. (2015). Computer programming goes back to school. *Education Week*, 61–65.

Kee, A. N. (2012). Feelings of preparedness among alternatively certified teachers: What is the role of program features? *Journal of Teacher Education, 63*(1), 23–38.

Kite, V., Park, S., & Wiebe, E. (2019). *The code-free computational thinking framework: Teaching science and CT without writing code.* Interactive poster presentation to the National Association for Research in Science Teaching. Baltimore, MD.

Lawhead, P. B., Duncan, M. E., Bland, C. G., Goldweber, M., Schep, M., Barnes, D. J., & Hollingsworth, R. G. (2002). *A road map for teaching introductory programming using LEGO© Mindstorms robots.* Paper presented at the ACM SIGCSE Bulletin.

Lee, C. H., & Soep, E. (2016). None but ourselves can free our minds: Critical computational literacy as a pedagogy of resistance. *Equity & Excellence in Education, 49*(4), 480–492.

Lee, I., Martin, F., & Apone, K. (2014). Integrating computational thinking across the k-8 curriculum. *ACM Inroads, 5*(4), 64–71.

Lee, I., Martin, F., Denner, J., Coulter, B., Allan, W., Erickson, J., . . . Werner, L. (2011). Computational thinking for youth in practice. *ACM Inroads, 2*(1), 32–37.

Levy, S. T., & Wilensky, U. (2011). Mining students' inquiry actions for understanding of complex systems. *Computers & Education, 56*(3), 556–573.

Lu, J. J., & Fletcher, G. H. L. (2009). Thinking about computational thinking. *ACM SIGCSE Bulletin, 41*(1), 260–264.

Lye, S. Y., & Koh, J. H. L. (2014). Review on teaching and learning of computational thinking through programming: What is next for k-12? *Computers in Human Behavior, 41*, 51–61. http://dx.doi.org/10.1016/j.chb.2014.09.012

Margolis, J. (2010). *Stuck in the shallow end: Education, race, and computing.* Cambridge, MA: MIT Press.

Martin, L. (2015). The promise of the maker movement for education. *Journal of Pre-College Engineering Education Research (J-PEER), 5*(1), 4. http://dx.doi.org/10.7771/2157-9288.1099

Mayer, I., Bekebrede, G., Harteveld, C., Warmelink, H., Zhou, Q., van Ruijven, T., . . . Wenzler, I. (2014). The research and evaluation of serious games: Toward a comprehensive methodology. *British Journal of Educational Technology, 45*(3), 502–527. doi:10.1111/bjet.12067

Min, W., Frankosky, M. H., Mott, B., Rowe, J., Smith, A., Wiebe, E., Boyer, K. E., Lester, J. (2019). DeepStealth: Game-based learning stealth assessment with deep neural networks. *IEEE Transactions on Learning Technologies.* doi:10.1109/TLT.2019.2922356

Moore, T. J., Glancy, A. W., Tank, K. M., Kersten, J. A., Smith, K. A., & Stohlmann, M. S. (2014). A framework for quality k-12 engineering education: Research and development. *Journal of Pre-College Engineering Education Research (J-PEER), 4*(1), 2.

Moore, T. J., Tank, K. M., Glancy, A. W., & Kersten, J. A. (2015). NGSS and the landscape of engineering in K-12 state science standards. *Journal of Research in Science Teaching, 52*(3), 296–318. doi:10.1002/tea.21199

Nager, A., & Atkinson, R. D. (2016). *The case for improving U.S. computer science education.* Retrieved from SSRN https://ssrn.com/abstract=3066335 or http://dx.doi.org/10.2139/ssrn.3066335

NGSS Lead States. (2013). *Next generation science standards.* Washington, DC: The National Academies Press.

NRC, National Research Council. (2010). *Committee for the workshops on computational thinking: Report of a workshop on the scope and nature of computational thinking.* Washington, DC: National Academies Press.

NRC, National Research Council. (2011). *A framework for K-12 science education: Practices, crosscutting concepts, and core ideas.* Washington, DC. Retrieved from http://www.nap.edu/catalog.php?record_id=13165#

NRC, National Research Council. (2015). *Identifying and supporting productive stem programs in out-of-school settings.* Washington, DC: National Academies Press.

Papadakis, S., & Orfanakis, V. (2016). *The combined use of Lego Mindstorms NXT and app inventor for teaching novice programmers.* Paper presented at the International Conference EduRobotics 2016.

Papert, S. (1980). *Mindstorms: Children, computers, and powerful ideas.* New York, NY: Basic Books, Inc.

Payton, J., Barnes, T., Buch, K., Rorrer, A., & Zuo, H. (2015). The effects of integrating service learning into computer science: An inter-institutional longitudinal study. *Computer Science Education, 25*(3), 311–324. doi: 10.1080/08993408.2015.1086536

Peel, A., Sadler, T. D., & Friedrichsen, P. (2019). Learning natural selection through computational thinking: Unplugged design of algorithmic explanations. *Journal of Research in Science Teaching, 1–25.*

Piaget, J. (1970). *Genetic epistemology.* New York, NY: Columbia University Press.

Qualls, J. A., & Sherrell, L. B. (2010). Why computational thinking should be integrated into the curriculum. *Journal of Computing Sciences in Colleges, 25*(5), 66–71.

Rates, C. A., Mulvey, B. K., & Feldon, D. F. (2016). Promoting conceptual change for complex systems understanding: Outcomes of an agent-based participatory simulation. *Journal of Science Education and Technology, 25*(4), 610–627.

Redding, C., & Smith, T. M. (2016). Easy in, easy out: Are alternatively certified teachers turning over at increased rates? *American Educational Research Journal, 53*(4), 1086–1125.

Repenning, A., Webb, D. C., Koh, K. H., Nickerson, H., Miller, S. B., Brand, C., . . . Repenning, N. (2015). Scalable game design: A strategy to bring systemic computer science education to schools through game design and simulation creation. *Transactions on Computing Education, 15*(2), 1–31. doi:10.1145/2700517

Rode, J. A., Weibert, A., Marshall, A., Aal, K., von Rekowski, T., El Mimouni, H., & Booker, J. (2015). *From computational thinking to computational making.* Paper presented at the Proceedings of the 2015 ACM International Joint Conference on Pervasive and Ubiquitous Computing.

Rodger, S. H., Hayes, J., Lezin, G., Qin, H., Nelson, D., Tucker, R., . . . Slater, D. (2009). *Engaging middle school teachers and students with Alice in a diverse set of subjects.* Paper presented at the Proceedings of the 40th ACM technical symposium on Computer science education (SIGCSE), Chattanooga, TN, USA.

Román-González, M., Pérez-González, J.-C., & Jiménez-Fernández, C. (2016). Which cognitive abilities underlie computational thinking? Criterion validity of the computational thinking test. *Computers in Human Behavior, 72*, 678–691. http://dx.doi.org/10.1016/j.chb.2016.08.047

Ryan, R. M., & Deci, E. L. (2000). Self-determination theory and the facilitation of intrinsic motivation, social development, and well-being. *American Psychologist, 55*(1), 68–78.

Sands, P., Yadav, A., & Good, J. (2018). Computational thinking in K–12: In-service teacher perceptions of computational thinking. In M. S. Khine (Ed.), *Computational thinking in the STEM disciplines* (pp. 151–164). New York, NY: Springer.

Sengupta, P., & Clark, D. (2016). Playing modeling games in the science classroom: The case for disciplinary integration. *Educational Technology, 56*(3), 16–22.

Sengupta, P., Kinnebrew, J. S., Basu, S., Biswas, G., & Clark, D. (2013). Integrating computational thinking with k–12 science education using agent-based computation: A theoretical framework. *Education and Information Technologies, 18*(2), 351–380. doi:10.1007/s10639–012–9240-x

Shute, V. J., Sun, C., & Asbell-Clarke, J. (2017). Demystifying computational thinking. *Educational Research Review, 22*, 142–158. doi:10.1016/j.edurev.2017.09.003

Sneider, C., Stephenson, C., Schafer, B., & Flick, L. (2014). Computational thinking in high school science classrooms. *Science Teacher, 81*(5), 53.

Stout, J. G., Dasgupta, N., Hunsinger, M., & McManus, M. A. (2011). Steming the tide: Using ingroup experts to inoculate women's self-concept in science, technology, engineering, and mathematics (stem). *Journal of Personality and Social Psychology, 100*(2), 255–270.

Tissenbaum, M., Sheldon, J., Seop, L., Lee, C. H., & Lao, N. (2017). *Critical computational empowerment: Engaging youth as shapers of the digital future.* Paper presented at the Global Engineering Education Conference (EDUCON), 2017 IEEE.

Tran, Y. (2018). Computational thinking equity in elementary classrooms: What third-grade students know and can do. *Journal of Educational Computing Research*, 0735633117743918. doi:10.1177/0735633117743918

Tsan, J., Boyer, K. E., & Lynch, C. F. (2016). *How early does the CS gender gap emerge? A study of collaborative problem solving in 5th grade computer science.* Paper presented at the Proceedings of the 47th ACM Technical Symposium on Computing Science Education.

Unfried, A., Faber, M., & Wiebe, E. N. (2014). Student interest in engineering and other stem careers: An examination of school-level, gender, race/ethnicity, and urbanicity. In ASEE (Ed.), *2014 American society for engineering education annual conference & exposition.* Washington, DC: ASEE.

University of Delaware. (2019). *Educ 439/639: Computational thinking.* Retrieved from https://www1.udel.edu/edtech/ComputationalThinking/index.html

USDOE, U.S. Department of Education Office of Innovation and Improvement. (2016). *Stem 2026: A vision for innovation in stem education.* Washington, DC: Author.

Vakil, S. (2014). A critical pedagogy approach for engaging urban youth in mobile app development in an after-school program. *Equity & Excellence in Education, 47*(1), 31–45.

Van Meter, P., Aleksic, M., Schwartz, A., & Garner, J. (2006). Learner-generated drawing as a strategy for learning from content area text. *Contemporary Educational Psychology, 31*(2), 142–166.

Voogt, J., Fisser, P., Good, J., Mishra, P., & Yadav, A. (2015). Computational thinking in compulsory education: Towards an agenda for research and practice. *Education and Information Technologies, 20*(4), 715–728.

Weintrop, D., Beheshti, E., Horn, M., Orton, K., Jona, K., Trouille, L., & Wilensky, U. (2016). Defining computational thinking for mathematics and science classrooms. *Journal of Science Education and Technology, 25*(1), 127–147.

West, D. M. (2012). *Big data for education: Data mining, data analytics, and web dashboards.* Washington, DC: The Brookings Institute.

Wiebe, E., London, J., Aksit, O., Mott, B., Boyer, K. E., & Lester, J. (2019, February). *Development of a lean computational thinking abilities assessment for middle grades students.* Paper presented at the SIGCSE 2019, Minneapolis, MN. doi:10.1145/3287324.3287390

Wiebe, E., Thompson, I., & Behrend, T. (2015). MOOCs from the viewpoint of the learner: A response to Perna et al. (2014). *Educational Researcher.* doi:10.3102/0013189X15584774

Wilensky, U., Brady, C. E., & Horn, M. S. (2014). Fostering computational literacy in science classrooms. *Communications of the ACM, 57*(8), 24–28.

Williams, L., Wiebe, E. N., Yang, K., Ferzli, M., & Miller, C. (2002). In support of paired programming in the introductory computer science course. *Computer Science Education, 12*(3), 197–212.

Wing, J. M. (2006). Computational thinking. *Communications of the ACM, 49*(3), 33–35.

Witherspoon, E. B., Higashi, R. M., Schunn, C. D., Baehr, E. C., & Shoop, R. (2017). Developing computational thinking through a virtual robotics programming curriculum. *Transactions on Computing Education, 18*(1), 1–20. doi:10.1145/3104982

Wolber, D., Abelson, H., & Friedman, M. (2015). Democratizing computing with app inventor. *GetMobile: Mobile Computing and Communications, 18*(4), 53–58. doi:10.1145/2721914.2721935

Yadav, A., Gretter, S., Good, J., & McLean, T. (2017). Computational thinking in teacher education. In P. J. Rich, & C. B. Hodges (Eds.), *Emerging research, practice, and policy on computational thinking* (pp. 205–220). New York, NY: Springer.

Yadav, A., Hong, H., & Stephenson, C. (2016). Computational thinking for all: Pedagogical approaches to embedding 21st century problem solving in K–12 classrooms. *TechTrends, 60*(6), 565–568.

Yadav, A., Mayfield, C., Zhou, N., Hambrusch, S., & Korb, J. T. (2014). Computational thinking in elementary and secondary teacher education. *ACM Transactions on Computing Education (TOCE), 14*(1), 5:1–5:16.

17

SOCIO-SCIENTIFIC ISSUES AS CONTEXTS FOR THE DEVELOPMENT OF STEM LITERACY

David C. Owens and Troy D. Sadler

Introduction

STEM integration is important and has momentum across STEM disciplines, and for good reason. Real-world problems are not separated into isolated disciplines, but are interdisciplinary in nature (Beane, 1995; Czerniak, Weber, Sandmann, & Ahern, 1999; Jacobs, 1989). In fact, the most significant problems facing modern society, the world's grand challenges (e.g., energy, water, transportation, climate change), require the synthesis of vast amounts of information from varying STEM disciplines (Nadelson & Seifert, 2017). Teaching STEM disciplines in isolation serves to impede students' ability to integrate ideas in order to solve problems. While integration is expected to enhance students' ability to apply STEM knowledge for problem solving, it is not clear how to best integrate STEM disciplines or which factors increase the likelihood of positive outcomes (Pearson, 2017).

Common Conceptions of STEM Literacy

A first step toward the meaningful integration of STEM instruction is to consider how STEM literacy should look as a desired outcome. A survey of discipline-specific definitions of STEM literacy suggests that all share one commonality—the literate individual must be able to employ content knowledge and practices to solve problems or make decisions for the benefit of mankind (Table 17.1). For example, Balka (2011) defined STEM literacy as "the ability to identify, apply, and integrate concepts from science, technology, engineering, and mathematics to understand complex problems [personal, societal, economic] and to innovate to solve them" (p. 7). Nadelson and Seifert (2017) similarly characterized STEM literacy as

> the seamless amalgamation of content and concepts from multiple STEM disciplines . . . [which] takes place in ways such that knowledge and process of the specific STEM disciplines are considered simultaneously without regard to the discipline, but rather in the context of a problem, project or task.
>
> *(p. 221)*

Thus, the common thread that runs through both STEM and discipline-specific definitions of literacy is an ability to integrate understanding and practice skills so as to become more effective problem solvers.

Table 17.1 Definitions of Literacy for STEM Disciplines (Adapted From Zollman, 2012)

STEM Discipline	Definition of Literacy
Science	Ability to use scientific knowledge and processes to understand, and additionally, *to participate in decisions* that affect science in life and health, earth and environment, and technology (Organization for Economic Cooperation and Development [OECD], 2003)
Technology	Capacity to use, understand, and evaluate technology, as well as to understand technological principles and strategies needed *to develop solutions and achieve goals* (National Assessment Governing Board [NAGB], 2014)
Engineering	Knowledge of the mathematical and natural sciences gained by study, experience, and practices that is applied to develop ways to utilize economically the materials and forces of nature *for the benefit of mankind* (Accreditation Board for Engineering and Technology [ABET], 2010)
Mathematics	Ability to read, listen, think creatively, and communicate about *problem situations,* mathematical representations, *and solutions* to develop and deepen their understanding of mathematics (National Council of Teachers of Mathematics [NCTM], 2000)

Problematic Nature of the Thrust for STEM Integration

A crucial question for STEM-literate problem solving concerns whether literate individuals need to be well versed in the integration of non–STEM considerations when selecting appropriate solutions, as the definitions of STEM literacy indicated earlier, as well as those discipline-specific definitions provided by Zollman (2012) in Table 17.1, do not address such considerations. Similarly, proponents of STEM integration often support its potential to:

- Generate interest, motivation, and engagement in STEM fields where it currently lacks (Nadelson & Seifert, 2017);
- Prepare the next generation STEM workforce whereas currently a gap in core skills exists where current individuals seeking employment are not qualified (Business Roundtable, 2014; National Research Council [NRC], 2011); and
- Maintain and advance economic and technological dominance globally (NRC, 2012).

These are certainly important and valid goals that are prominent in policy documents and directly supported by standards, such as the Common Core State Standards for Mathematics and the Next Generation Science Standards in the United States, but whether they would lead to a lead to a version of STEM literacy that is functional across a global citizenry is debatable.

Critics of this perspective of STEM integration argue that these objectives are insufficient, as a rigid focus on content ideas and practices restricts the development of STEM literacy that is functional in everyday life. This view of STEM is not necessarily situated in contexts that the majority of STEM students will find meaningful. The prevailing push for STEM as workforce development may serve future STEM workers and the corporations and agencies that will employ them, but this approach is unlikely to serve the needs of the majority of individuals who do not seek STEM careers. Considering that the shortage in the STEM workforce used in support of STEM integration may be exaggerated and even inaccurate (Salzman, Kuehn, & Lowell, 2013; Teitelbaum, 2014; Xie & Killewald, 2012), such a myopic perspective is unwarranted.

Equally important, this view of STEM integration fails to provide a "global perspective of scientific literacy that entails, among other skills, the proclivity and ability to envision the role of sociocultural-political contexts in which such topics reside" (Zeidler, 2016, p. 12). In fact, the limitations of knowledge and reasoning bounded by disciplinary STEM toward resolving today's pressing issues are highlighted in the recent Next Generation Science Standards regarding the Nature of Science, which forefront non-science considerations as complementary to those of science but equally requisite to the suite of reasoning skills required to understand and resolve many STEM-informed problems. For example,

- Science knowledge can describe consequences of actions but is not responsible for society's decisions.
- Science knowledge indicates what can happen in natural systems—not what should happen. The latter involves ethics, values, and human decisions about the use of knowledge.
- Many decisions are not made using science alone, but rely on social and cultural contexts to resolve issues (see Nature of Science Standards section, NRC, 2013, p. 6).

Considering that STEM majors, as compared to non-STEM majors, lack "the proclivity to influence social values and the political structure, or be a community leader" (Nicholls, Wolfe, Besterfield-Sacre, Shuman, & Larpkiattaworn, 2007, p. 42), it is essential that STEM integration provides opportunities for students to practice making decisions that are supported with the weight of STEM understandings, but that also requires the incorporation of moral judgements that demand resolution—as occurs in everyday life. A more holistic STEM integration serves the aforementioned goals to increase membership in the STEM field and workforce, but also provides for the STEM literacy needs of all citizens and contributes to the development of the whole learner.

Socio-Scientific Issues as Meaningful Contexts for Holistic Science Education

To further clarify this idea of holistic instruction, we provide some history as to the transformation that the conception of *scientific literacy* has undergone in recent decades. The popular phrase has become an "umbrella term to represent overall educational objectives for school science programs" (Roberts & Bybee, 2014, p. 545). Roberts (2007) and later Roberts and Bybee (2014) conducted a comprehensive review of scientific literacy as a construct and suggested two visions which serve as a heuristic for distinguishing among the varying ways in which scientific literacy has been conceptualized. Vision I scientific literacy is focused on understanding concepts and principles of science and using scientific ways of thinking to solve problems with the scientific enterprise in mind. This conception of scientific literacy aligns with common definitions of STEM integration that are bounded within disciplines (thinking like a scientist or engineer) but fails to include or address the personal aspects of decision-making, such as beliefs, morals, or the tenets of citizenship. Vision II scientific literacy is focused on the application of science ideas and practices within real-world contexts. Whereas Vision I looks to the canon of science for its operationalization, Vision II looks to the situations in which science might be used to help solve problems and address challenges. Since most real-world problems and challenges are interdisciplinary, the integration of science and non-science considerations becomes a natural aspect of Vision II scientific literacy. Researchers building from the visions of scientific literacy framework (e.g., Kinslow, Sadler & Nguyen, 2018; Venville & Dawson, 2010) have argued, with evidence, that systematically embedding science instruction in learning contexts that draw from real-world issues that connect to science can promote both visions of scientific literacy.

The use of socio-scientific issues (SSI) as contexts for learning has a rich history in the sciences in terms of their potential for addressing and developing Vision II scientific literacy. SSI are "controversial social issues with conceptual, procedural, or technological ties to science" (Sadler & Donnelly, 2006, p. 1493). Though an understanding of the science that undergirds these issues is requisite to their resolution, because any number of potential resolutions exist and none equally benefit all stakeholders involved, a scientific understanding alone is unlikely to result in their successful resolution.

As a result, scientifically literate individuals must be well versed in evaluating both science and non-science considerations when considering potential resolutions to SSI that have even a modicum of chance to succeed.

SSI serve as the problems to be solved/decided upon by STEM-literate individuals or by those developing STEM literacy, as SSI situate learning in real-world contexts where the issues require familiarity with ideas and practices from both science and non-science realms (Zeidler, 2014). SSI have served as effective contexts for the development of scientific literacy, including: Science ideas and practices, such as gains in content knowledge, science practice skills, and nature of science understanding (Sadler, Romine, & Topcu, 2016; Bell, Matkins, & Gansneder, 2011), as well as non-science ideas and practices, such as empathy, morality, compassion, perspective-taking, and citizenship responsibility (Fowler, Zeidler, & Sadler, 2009; Kahn & Zeidler, 2016; Lee et al., 2013). Though little work has been done in terms of using SSI as context for learning in the other STEM disciplines and virtually zero as integrated STEM instruction, we suggest that SSI have potential for supporting functional STEM literacy across STEM subjects, especially in an integrated STEM fashion. In the sections that follow, we will:

1. Argue for the potential of SSI to serve as meaningful contexts across STEM disciplines for holistic STEM integration and the development of STEM literacy;
2. Provide an example of using SSI as contexts for holistic STEM integration (e.g., genetically modified organisms); and
3. Suggest directions for future research using SSI as contexts for STEM integration

The Potential for SSI to Serve as Meaningful Contexts for Holistic STEM Integration

In this section, we discuss the importance of non-STEM considerations in the development of literacy in the disciplines of technology, engineering, and mathematics. Borrowing from Roberts (2007), we extend the idea of Vision II scientific literacy with a focus on the applications and use of disciplinary ideas for addressing challenges and solving problems to Vision II perspectives on literacy more generally. In this section, we build a case for the use of SSI as a means of promoting Vision II perspectives of literacy across multiple STEM disciplines.

Technology. Technology is not an isolated discipline, as it informs and is informed by science, engineering, and mathematics, and thus, is integrated with the other STEM disciplines in its very nature. For example, science, engineering, and mathematics all contributed to the development of nuclear technology, including nuclear weapons and nuclear power—technologies which can be used for good and for evil. However, while STEM-specific ideas and practices were requisite to their advent, the purposes for their development and decisions concerning their usage hinge on non-STEM considerations (e.g., morality). In terms of their immense potential to be used for the good of humanity, nuclear weaponry enabled the end of World War II, and nuclear energy currently provides for 11 percent of the world's energy and one-third of the global total of low-carbon electricity (International Atomic Energy Agency, 2018). Conversely, nuclear weapons hold the potential for mass destruction and are a constant source of anxiety globally, and nuclear disasters such as Chernobyl and Fukushima have had serious repercussions. Thus, technology serves as a double-edged sword, where science, math and engineering knowledge is applied for the purpose of maintaining economic and technological dominance on one hand (Vision I technology literacy); but, as is indicated by the aforementioned examples, requires non-STEM awareness in order to be used appropriately on the other (Vision II technology literacy). For this reason, the NAGB recently defined technology literacy as "the capacity to use, understand, and evaluate technology as well as to understand technological principles and strategies needed to develop solutions and achieve goals" (2014, p. 3), where evaluation must include technology's effects on society and the natural world and "the sorts of ethical questions that arise from those effects" (NAGB, 2014, p. 5). This includes recognition of the positive and negative effects that technology has on people, as well the ability to make informed decisions that consider the perspectives of all stakeholders as to which technology is the best available for solving the problem at hand. Table 17.2 highlights practices in which technology-literate individuals engage to make decisions about the appropriateness of technological alternatives when solving problems, such as SSI.

We assert that SSI serve as ideal contexts for advancing technology literacy, especially the role of technology in society. Here is a case in point: International Atomic Energy Agency (IAEA) Director General Yukiya Amano, in his recent keynote address at the 2018 World Nuclear Exhibition event in Paris, framed the need for nuclear technology in terms of an SSI: "It will be difficult for the world to meet the challenges of securing sufficient energy, and of limiting the average global temperature increase to 2 degrees centigrade, without making more use of nuclear power" (IAEA, 2018). In fact, the decision-making process advanced by the NAGB for selecting appropriate technologies (Table 17.2) is already being used in one form or another to aid students in negotiating resolutions to SSI (e.g., Dauer & Forbes, 2016; Lee & Grace, 2012), better understanding how students' values and beliefs are to inform their decision-making (Sutter, Dauer, & Forbes, 2018), and developing sensitivity to moral and ethical aspects of technology, as well as compassion for individuals who might be negatively affected by their advancement (Lee et al., 2013).

Additionally, common definitions of technological literacy focus on the practical aspects of using technology but fail to consider media literacy (Zeidler et al., 2016). Media influences individuals' personal epistemologies and engagement in reasoning about SSI, and certain values and perspectives are embedded in different media sources. As a result, making decisions about or staking positions concerning SSI that are informed require media literacy. This ability to analyze sources of information contributes to a technological literacy for citizenship that may not be recognized or valued by technological literacies that are defined from the perspective of economic advancement (Petrina, 2000)—highlighting the need to extend the purpose of STEM integration to include the holistic development of the citizen.

Engineering. Traditionally considered a "technical field that requires the systematic application of mathematics and science knowledge to develop novel solutions to complicated problems" (Gunckel & Tolbert, 2018, p. 939), engineering may be the natural tie that binds the STEM disciplines. The National Academy of Engineering goes one step further, arguing that "In the real world, engineering is not performed in isolation—it inevitably involves science, technology, and mathematics. The question is why these subjects should be isolated in schools" (NRC, 2009, pp. 164–165). However, current definitions of engineering literacy are problematic: "Knowledge of the mathematical and natural sciences gained by study, experience, and practices that is applied to develop ways to utilize economically the materials and forces of nature for the benefit of mankind" (Accreditation Board for Engineering and Technology, 2010). Such conceptualizations of engineering literacy

Table 17.2 Practices Associated With Technology Literacy Concerning the Understanding of Technological Principles Related to Technology and Society (Adapted From NAGD, 2014, p. 12)

Decision-Making Practices
Analyze advantages and disadvantages of an existing technology
Explain costs and benefits
Compare effects of two technologies on individuals
Propose solutions and alternatives
Predict consequences of a technology
Select among alternatives

emphasize technological solutions to all problems without addressing their social or political aspects (i.e., technocracy; Danforth, 2016; Fischer, 1990). Furthermore, though engineering is often framed as an empathetic approach to solving the problems of mankind, more often than not is tied to profiteering motives (Bunge, 2003). As a result, non-STEM skills (e.g., empathy, compassion, caring) are required if engineering solutions are to be socially responsible and environmentally sustainable (Canney & Bielefeldt, 2015; Hess et al., 2012).

For these reasons, recent Frameworks for Engineering Education (e.g., Moore et al., 2014) have begun to recognize the importance of Vision II literacy and are including both STEM and non-STEM skills:

1. The problems faced by society today are complex and open ended;
2. The multidisciplinary nature of the problems requires skills and practices from all disciplines to solve the problem; and
3. The social and cultural relevance of STEM problem contexts need to be highlighted to broaden student participation and understanding of STEM disciplines (Roehrig, Moore, Wang, & Sun Park, 2012).

Additionally, criteria for accrediting engineering programs are also beginning to address the perceived dearth of ethical inclusion in engineering practice and decision-making. While engineering ideas and practices are still highlighted (e.g., the application of STEM disciplinary knowledge, experimentation, employment of engineering tools and techniques), criteria for accreditation now require recognition of non-scientific considerations, such as

> . . . the ability to design a system, component, or process to meet desired needs within realistic constraints such as economic, environmental, social, political, ethical . . .; an understanding of professional and ethical responsibility; [and] . . . the broad education necessary to understand the impact of engineering solutions in a global, economic, environmental, and societal context . . .
>
> *(ABET, 2010, p. 3)*

The importance of these social, economic, and environmental considerations are exemplified in Jonassen, Strobel, and Lee's (2006) study, where 106 practicing engineers were interviewed as to the nature of typical, everyday problem solving in their engineering careers. Typical instances of engineering complexity still included content-specific concerns, such as incomplete information (e.g., the specific heat of particular metal piping, design parameters, or adjusting designs at the last minute to accommodate hidden challenges). However, engineers in the study also indicated that ill-structured problems with multiple, conflicting goals (i.e., non-engineering considerations) that "have nothing to do with engineering outcomes" (p. 143) are often the most important problem-solving skills they employ. For example, one project required the engineers to

> find a solution that will meet the purpose and needs statement that we include in our environmental impact statement that has a level of public and community support along the corridor that is politically acceptable and ultimately that we can afford.
>
> *(Jonassen et al., 2006, p. 143)*

In this example, an ill-structured problem with ecological, political, and economic goals in conflict could be solved in different ways, each affecting the multiple goals differently. As a result, the researchers concluded that success for these engineers was rarely defined by engineering standards (the content, ideas, and practices of engineering), but rather by non-engineering considerations.

Findings, such as these have triggered calls for holistic educational approaches to engineering education (National Science Foundation, 2016) and scholarly work (Downey, 2012; Grasso & Burkins, 2010) directed at understanding how to instill in future engineers these non-engineering understandings and skills, such as perspective-taking (Hess, Strobel, & Brightman, 2017) and empathy (Hess, Strobel, Pan, & Wachter Moriss, 2017). These types of competencies and understandings align with the objectives of SSI-oriented instruction. Thus, engineering education should be rife with opportunities for students to "understand the full socio-historical-politico contexts of the problems they are trying to solve" and evaluate their engineering designs while taking those into account (Gunckel & Tolbert, 2018, p. 17). In addition to increasing the delivery of students to the STEM pipeline, framing engineering in a manner that also leads to these non-engineering skills can also contribute to a change in perception of engineering, the development of engineering identities among underrepresented students, and an increase in their participation (Mejia, Drake, & Wilson-Lopez, 2015). We suggest that contextualizing engineering instruction in SSI can accomplish this.

Mathematics. The integrated nature of mathematics with other STEM disciplines is quite apparent these days, with algorithms as the driving force behind search engines and targeted advertising. The NCTM's (2000) definition of mathematical literacy includes the ability to think about problems undergirded by mathematics (e.g., how to efficiently locate information using algorithms) and to develop solutions to those problem while deepening a mathematical understanding (e.g., development and employment of algorithms)—both a Vision I perspective of mathematics literacy. However, as non-mathematics considerations concerning problem solving appear to be absent, students are left to their own devices to reason about when and in what ways the use of mathematics, such as employing algorithms to collect user data or target users with advertising, is morally appropriate (a Vision II dimension of mathematics literacy).

In a push to rebrand and expand a traditional view of mathematics to emphasize a more practical use of numbers and statistics in real-world contexts—"a habit of mind" approach to problem solving that employs both statistics and mathematics (Steen et al., 2001, p. 5)—researchers and educators internationally have begun to refer to mathematical literacy as "quantitative literacy" or "numeracy". In fact, "the K-12 mathematics-education community is virtually united on the importance of connecting classroom mathematics to the real world" (Gainsburg, 2008, p. 199). Her claim appears to be supported by the NCTM, which asserts that students should be able to "recognize and apply mathematics in contexts outside of mathematics" (2000, p. 64). In other words, "problems embedded in real life situations that have no ready-made algorithm" that are non-routine, open-ended and include social dimensions (Cheng, 2013, p. 24). Cheng offered the Restaurant problem as an example:

> You are going out for lunch at a restaurant with your group. Use the menu to select what you want to eat. The cost of the meal must be less than and as close to $40 as possible. How can we figure out how and what to choose for lunch?
>
> *(p. 29)*

Mathematics skills were then taught, parameters for the problem were set (e.g., each person must have a drink), and students were tasked with considering solutions when different numbers of individuals were in attendance. However, not unlike the Vision I tendencies of engineering literacy, the purposeful use of mathematics in the Restaurant problem strictly serves an economic function at best, and at worst offers a superficial shell for an otherwise purely mathematical manipulation of numbers. Either way, little or no concern is payed to the role that morality, civics, or environmental ethics might play in the development of an informed solution.

Another example of a mathematics problem contextualized in the real world was offered in the *Mathematics Teacher*, the official journal of the NCTM, where the authors suggested that the ability to solve the following problem from the Program for International Student Assessment (PISA) problem would demonstrate mathematical literacy:

> Suppose that watermelons grew in cubical shapes rather than their more familiar ellipsoidal shape. What possibilities and problems would such a change of shape cause or growers, handlers, sellers, and consumers?
>
> *(Soucy McCrone, Dossey, Turner, & Lindquist, 2008, p. 34)*

To be fair, Soucy McCrone and colleagues leaned on the OECD's (2003) definition of mathematics literacy:

> an individual's capacity to identify and understand the role that mathematics plays in the world, to make well-founded judgements and to use and engage with mathematics in a ways that meet the needs of that individual's life as a constructive, concerned, and reflective citizen.
>
> *(OECD, 2003, p. 24)*

However, while there is certainly room for the engagement of students in reflective citizenship by way of the watermelon problem they provided, it does not appear that the authors, nor those behind the PISA assessment, felt that it was prudent to do so. This is evident in:

a) The items that comprise the PISA assessment of mathematical literacy, which "focus on students' mathematical ability to analyze situation in a variety of content areas involving quantity; shape and space; change and relationships; and uncertainty" (Soucy McCrone et al., 2008, p. 35); and

b) The authors' assertion that if students are able to "analyze problem situations in real-world contexts, determine what mathematics is relevant for finding a solution, solve the problems, and reflect on the solution in relation to the original problem context . . . we say they are mathematically literate" (Soucy McCrone et al., 2008, p. 38).

We argue that solving problems such as these would certainly require mathematics content knowledge and skills that align with a Vision I interpretation of mathematical literacy but clearly lack many aspects that would lead to the development of a "constructive, concerned, and reflective citizen"—those non-mathematics considerations that are generally necessary for problem solving in real life, such as empathy or compassion, or whether different perspectives exist that might influence one's decision as to which solution is more appropriate. For example, the Restaurant problem might be meaningful for individuals in affluent families but provide little context for students from families that are barely making ends meet. Could that problem be framed to be more of a real-world problem for those students, or to help students form affluent families to develop compassion or empathy? How might the choices of different items result in different ecological outcomes (in terms of energy required to produce and transport those items, waste, etc.). The Watermelon problem stated earlier might be relevant for individuals with interest in or ties to the agriculture industry, but the majority of individuals who may not work in those fields are not likely to find this interesting or meaningful to them. Additionally, the problem fails to address the moral or ethical implications of genetically modifying the watermelons, and fails to consider the stakeholders that might be disproportionately affected by the economic ramifications of the new cubical watermelons. The real-world problematized contexts of mathematics education appears to have had the least focus on non-mathematical aspects of solving problems that are undergirded by math than do the other STEM disciplines.

Similarly, such considerations also appear to have been left out of mathematics teacher preparation programs as well. For example, in an *American Educator* article titled *Knowing Mathematics for Teaching*, in which Ball, Hill, and Bass (2005) ponder what it means to know mathematics for teaching, the authors maintain a strict focus on content and procedures, with nary a mention of preparing teachers to address values, compassion, empathy, or the like in their mathematics instruction. Contextualizing mathematics instruction in SSI provides opportunities for all individuals to learn and employ mathematical skills in order to address issues that have meaning for all individuals, not just those interested in the efficient transport of watermelons. Equally important is the development of non-mathematical considerations that are requisite to informed problem solving in real-world contexts

An Example of Using SSI as a Context for Holistic STEM Integration

In the previous sections, we demonstrated the importance of non-disciplinary considerations to effective, real-world problem solving in each of the disciplines and provided rationales for how framing those discipline-specific problems in the context of SSI might allow for more robust forms of literacy (i.e., Vision II). In this section, we provide an example of using a contemporary and relevant SSI (genetic modification) for holistic STEM integration, where a growing world population and economy demands hardier, tastier, and more beautiful plants, and recent STEM developments have provided the means for genetically modifying foods to meet these demands. Table 17.3 highlights questions that can be answered through engagement in cross-disciplinary STEM instruction and practices that contribute to understanding the problem and developing plausible solutions. However,

Table 17.3 Aspects of Instruction That Address Vision II STEM Literacy in the Context of Genetically Modified Organisms (GMOs) Within each discipline, topics and questions are provided as to the types of knowledge and practices each discipline offers toward understanding and resolving the GMO issue.

Discipline	Content Addressed and Questions
Science	Genetics and inheritance
	Question: What scientific misconceptions are used to support positions regarding GMOs?
Technology	Gene editing tools; media literacy
	Question(s): How do sources of information on GMOs differentially portray them?
Engineering	Gene splicing tools, mechanisms for collecting and sorting seeds
	Question(s): What design constraints ought to be considered when selecting among potential gene editing protocols?
Mathematics	Mathematical representations for allele frequency and fitness
	Question(s): What statistical procedures would be necessary (or useful) in order to document success of the gene editing technologies?
English Language Arts	Storied history of genetic modification: traditional means (e.g., saving seeds, pollenating by hand, etc.) or employing STEM advancements (e.g., inducing mutations, splicing one organism's DNA into another.
	Question(s): As genetic modification happens in a variety of ways, what do people mean when they use the term GMO?
	Does GMO include traditional means for modifying the frequency of genes in a population?
	Is the term GMO reserved for instances when an individual's genome is modified by inserting foreign DNA with desired traits?
Non-STEM Considerations	Aspects of moral judgements that affect position-taking and decision-making regarding the regulation of GMOs
	Question(s): Is it right to insert one organism's DNA into another? At what point does genetic modification amount to playing God?

whether and how we should genetically modify plants to meet this end cannot be answered without first considering the non-STEM aspects that are requisite to informed decision-making.

Staking a position or making a decision regarding the use or potential regulation of GMOs is certainly informed and influenced by an understanding of STEM content and practices, misconceptions, and awareness of potential solutions and technologies, as well as an understanding of the spectrum of meanings that may be intended when the phrase *genetically modified organism* is uttered. However, equally important to resolving the GMO issue are non-STEM factors, such as the ability to take the perspectives of different stakeholders affected by the issue and make moral judgements concerning the appropriateness of certain solutions or technologies. A case in point is that STEM advancements are influenced by the general public's non-STEM perceptions. Consider the new Clustered Regularly Interspaced Short Palindromic Repeats (CRISPr) technology, which rearranges an individual's DNA without adding a different species' DNA. GMO vendors are hoping that CRISPr will win over a large portion of the general public, which has been anti-GMO due to their feeling that transferring other organisms' DNA is morally reprehensible. The drive, for some, behind the CRISPr technology aligns with the findings of Jonassen and colleagues (2006), where non-engineering factors provided for the most challenging and motivating aspects of problem solving—in this case, genetically modifying organisms without the (offensive, to some) insertion of a portion of another organism's genome. These examples provide support for a Vision II orientation to STEM literacy, where STEM content and practices are requisite, but non-STEM considerations must also be recognized and incorporated if individuals are to come away being STEM literate in a manner that leads to informed participation in democracy.

Implications and Future Directions for Using SSI as Contexts for STEM Integration

In this chapter, we made a case for the potential of SSI as to serve as effective learning contexts for the integration of STEM education. STEM teachers are clamoring for professional development (PD) that contributes to their ability to contextualize instruction in real-world problems (Owens, Sadler, Murakami, & Tsai, 2018). However, significant barriers must be overcome if the potential for effective integrated STEM instruction in the context of SSI is to be realized. For example, it is not clear how the outcomes of STEM instruction, integrated in the context of SSI, can be measured such that the added bonus of integration can be supported with evidence. Even with significant evidence as to the effectiveness of integrating STEM instruction in the context of SSI, many teachers still struggle to recognize the complexities and ethical aspects of SSI on their own (Owens, Herman, Oertli, & Sadler, 2019) and lack comfort with contextualizing STEM learning in SSI as a means for developing character values necessary for global citizenship, preferring to leave students to their own devices to considering the value-laden nature of issues that might stir up trouble with parents and administrators (Owens, Sadler, & Zeidler, 2017). STEM teachers who are willing to integrate STEM instruction in the context of SSI are often deficient in coursework outside the specific STEM discipline in which they were trained and have experience teaching, such that deficient STEM content knowledge and practice skills serve as a barrier to doing so (Pearson, 2017). Compounding that problem, teachers work in an educational system where segregated STEM instruction that lacks non-STEM consideration is well established (Nadelson & Seifert, 2017). Clearly, significant PD is necessary to aid STEM teachers in the development of teaching practices that will enable them to integrate STEM instruction in the context of SSI successfully (Owens, Sadler, & Friedrichsen, 2018), including opportunities for STEM teachers to negotiate SSI with individuals from across STEM disciplines, shore up deficiencies in reasoning about STEM and non-STEM aspects of SSI, and collaboratively plan integrated STEM curricula.

References

Accreditation Board for Engineering and Technology. (2010). *Criteria for accrediting engineering programs*. Baltimore, MD: Author.

Balka, D. (Summer, 2011). Standards of mathematical practice and STEM. In *Math-science connector newsletter*. Stillwater, OK: School Science and Mathematics Association.

Ball, D. L., Hill, H. C., & Bass, H. (2005). Knowing mathematics for teaching: Who knows mathematics well enough to teach third grade, and how can we decide? *American Educator*, 14–46.

Beane, J. (1995). Curriculum integration and the disciplines of knowledge. *Phi Delta Kappan, 76*, 616–622.

Bell, R. L., Matkins, J. J., & Gansneder, B. M. (2011). Impacts of contextual and explicit instruction on preservice elementary teachers' understandings of the nature of science. *Journal of Research in Science Teaching, 48*, 414–436.

Bunge, M. (2003). Philosophical inputs and outputs of technology. In R. C. Scharff & V. Dusek (Eds.), *Philosophy of technology: The technological condition* (pp. 172–181). Malden, MA: Blackwell. Originally appeared in G. Bugliarello & D. B. Doner (Eds.). (1979). *The history and philosophy of technology* (pp. 262–281). Urbana, IL: University of Illinois Press.

Business Roundtable (BRT). (2014). *Closing America's skills gap*. Retrieved February 6, 2020, from http://businessroundtable.org/resources/closing-americas-skills-gap

Canney, N., & Bielefeldt, A. (2015). A framework for the development of social responsibility in engineers. *International Journal of Engineering Education, 31*(1B), 414–424.

Cheng, L. P. (2013). The design of a mathematics problem using real-life context for young children. *Journal of Science and Mathematics Education in Southeast Asia, 36*, 23–43.

Czerniak, C. M., Weber, W. B., Sandmann, A. Jr., & Ahern, J. (1999). Literature review of science and mathematics integration. *School Science and Mathematics, 99*(8), 421–430.

Danforth, S. (2016). Social justice and technocracy: Tracing the narratives of inclusive education in the USA. *Discourse: Studies in the Cultural Politics of Education, 37*, 582–599.

Dauer, J. M., & Forbes, C. (2016). Making decisions about complex socioscientific issues: A multidisciplinary science course. *Science Education and Civic Engagement: An International Journal, 8*, 5–12.

Downey, G. L. (2012). The local engineer: Normative holism in engineering formation. In S. H. Christensen, C. Mitcham, B. Li, & Y. An (Eds.), *Engineering, development and philosophy* (Vol. 11, pp. 233–251). Dordrecht, The Netherlands: Springer.

Fischer, F. (1990). *Technocracy and the politics of expertise*. Newbury Park, CA: Sage.

Fowler, S. R., Zeidler, D. L., & Sadler, T. D. (2009). Moral sensitivity in the context of socioscientific issues in high school students. *International Journal of Science Education, 31*, 279–296.

Gainsburg, J. (2008). Real-world connections in secondary mathematics teaching. *Journal of Mathematics Teacher Education, 11*, 199–219.

Grasso, D., & Burkins, M. B. (2010). Holistic engineering education: Beyond technology. New York, NY: Springer.

Gunckel, K. L., & Tolbert, S. (2018). The imperative to move toward a dimension of care in engineering education. *Journal of Research in Science Teaching, 55*, 938–961.

Hess, J. L., Sprowl, J. E., Pan, R., Dyehouse, M., Morris, C. A. W., & Strobel, J. (2012). *Empathy and caring as conceptualized inside and outside of engineering: Extensive literature review and faculty focus group analyses*. In American Society for Engineering Education. American Society for Engineering Education, Annual Conference, San Antonio, TX.

Hess, J. L., Strobel, J., & Brightman, A. O. (2017). The development of empathic perspective-taking in an engineering ethics course. *Journal of Engineering Education, 106*(4), 534–563.

Hess, J., Strobel, J., Pan, R., & Wachter Morris, C. (2017). Insights from industry: A quantitative analysis of engineers' perceptions of empathy and care within their practice. *European Journal of Engineering Education, 42*(6), 1128–1153.

International Atomic Energy Agency. (2018, June 26). *Nuclear power can help meet developmental goals, IAEA Director General says in Paris*. Retrieved from https://www.iaea.org/newscenter/news/nuclear-power-can-help-meet-development-goals-iaea-director-general-says-in-paris

Jacobs, H. H. (1989). *Interdisciplinary curriculum: Design and implementation*. Alexandria, VA: Association for Supervision and Curriculum Development.

Jonassen, D., Strobel, J., & Lee, C. B. (2006). Everyday problem solving in engineering: Lessons for engineering educators. *Journal of Engineering Education, 95*, 139–151.

Lee, H., Yoo, J., Choi, K., Kim, S. W., Krajcik, J., Herman, B. C., & Zeidler, D. L. (2013). Socioscientific issues as a vehicle for promoting character and values for global citizens. *International Journal of Science Education, 35*(12), 2079–2113.

Lee, Y. C., & Grace, M. (2012). Students' reasoning and decision making about a socioscientific issue: A cross-context comparison. *Science Education, 96*(5), 787–807.

Kahn, S., & Zeidler, D. L. (2016). Using our heads and HARTSS★: Developing perspective-taking skills for socioscientific reasoning (★Humanities, ARTs, and Social Sciences). *Journal of Science Teacher Education, 27,* 261–281.

Kinslow, A. T., Sadler, T. D., & Nguyen, H. T. (2018). Socio-scientific reasoning and environmental literacy in a field-based ecology class. *Environmental Education Research,* 1–23.

Mejia, J. A., Drake, D., & Wilson-Lopez, A. (2015). *Changes in Latino/a adolescents' engineering self-efficacy and perceptions of engineering after addressing authentic engineering design challenges.* In Proceedings of American Society for Engineering Education Annual Conference (pp. 1–14).

Moore, T. J., Glancy, A. W., Tank, K. M., Kersten, J. A., Smith, K. A., & Stohlmann, M. S. (2014). A framework for quality K-12 engineering education: Research and development. *Journal of Pre-college Engineering Education Research (J-PEER), 4*(1), 2.

Nadelson, L. S., & Seifert, A. L. (2017). Integrated STEM defined: Contexts, challenges, and the future. *The Journal of Educational Research, 110,* 221–223.

National Assessment Governing Board. (2010). *Technology and engineering literacy assessment and item specifications for the 2014 National Assessment of Educational Progress—Pre-publication edition.* Washington, DC: Author.

National Council of Teachers of Mathematics. (2000). *Principles and standards for school mathematics.* Reston, VA: Author.

National Research Council. (2009). *Engineering in K-12 education: Understanding the status and improving the prospects.* Washington, DC: The National Academies Press.

National Research Council. (2011). *Successful K-12 STEM education: Identifying effective approaches in science, technology, engineering, and mathematics.* Washington, DC: The National Academies Press.

National Research Council. (2012). *A framework for k-12 science education: Practices, crosscutting concepts, and core ideas.* Washington, DC: The National Academies Press.

National Research Council. (2013). *Next generation science standards for states by states: Appendix H. Understanding the scientific enterprise: The nature of science in the next generation science standards.* Retrieved from: http://www.nextgenscience.org/sites/ngss/files/Appendix%20H%20-%20The%20Nature%20of%20Science%20in%20the%20Next%20Generation%20Science%20Standards%204.15.13.pdf

National Science Foundation. (2016). *Research in the Formation of Engineers.* Retrieved from https://www.nsf.gov/funding/pgm_summ.jsp?pims_id=503584

Nicholls, G. M., Wolfe, H., Besterfield-Sacre, M., Shuman, L. J., & Larpkiattaworn, S. (2007). A method for identifying variables for predicting STEM enrollment. *Journal of Engineering Education, 96,* 33–44.

Organization for Economic Cooperation and Development. (2003). *Scientific literacy: The PISA 2003 assessment framework.* Paris: Author.

Owens, D. C., Herman, B. C., Oertli, R. T., & Sadler, T. D. (in press). Secondary science and mathematics teachers' environmental issues engagement through socioscientific reasoning. *EURASIA Journal of Mathematics, Science and Technology Education, 15,* 1–27.

Owens, D. C., Sadler, T. D., & Friedrichsen, P. (2019). Teaching practices for enactment of socio-scientific issues instruction: An instrumental case study of an experienced biology teacher. *Research in Science Education,* 1–24.

Owens, D. C., Sadler, T. D., Murakami, C. D., & Tsai, C. L. (2018). Teachers' views on and preferences for meeting their professional development needs in STEM. *School Science and Mathematics, 118,* 370–384.

Owens, D. C., Sadler, T. D., & Zeidler, D. L. (2017). Controversial issues in the science classroom. *Phi Delta Kappan, 99,* 45–49.

Pearson, G. (2017). National academies piece on integrated STEM. *The Journal of Educational Research, 110,* 224–226.

Petrina, S. (2000). The politics of technological literacy. *International Journal of Technology and Design Education, 10,* 181–206.

Roberts, D. (2007). Scientific literacy/science literacy. In S. K. Abell & N. G. Lederman (Eds.), *Handbook of research on science education* (pp. 729–780). Mahwah, NJ: Lawrence Erlbaum Associates.

Roberts, D. A., & Bybee, R. W. (2014). Scientific literacy, science literacy, and science education. In N. G. Lederman & S. K. Abell (Eds.), *Handbook of research on science education, Volume II* (pp. 545–558). New York, NY: Routledge.

Roehrig, G. H., Moore, T. J., Wang, H. H., & Park, M. S. (2012). Is adding the E enough? Investigating the impact of K-12 engineering standards on the implementation of STEM integration. *School Science and Mathematics, 112,* 31–44.

Sadler, T. D., & Donnelly, L. A. (2006). Socioscientific argumentation. The effects of content knowledge and morality. *International Journal of Science Education, 28*(12), 1463–1488.

Sadler, T. D., Romine, W. L., & Topcu, M. S. (2016). Learning science content through socio-scientific issues-based instruction: A multi-level assessment study. *International Journal of Science Education, 38*, 1622–1635.

Salzman, H., Kuehn, D., & Lowell, B. L. (2013). Guestworkers in the high-skill U.S. labor market. Retrieved from http://www.epi.org/publication/bp359-guestworkers-high-skill-labor-market-analysis/

Soucy McCrone, S. M., Dossey, J. A., Turner, R., & Lindquist, M. M. (2008). Learning about Student's Mathematical Literacy from PISA 2003. *Mathematics Teacher, 102*, 34–39.

Steen, L. A., Burrill, G., Ganter, S., Goroff, D. L., Greenleaf, F. P., Grubb, W. N., . . . Wallace, D. (2001). The case for quantitative literacy. In L. A. Steen (Ed.), *Mathematics and democracy: The case for quantitative literacy* (pp. 1–22). Princeton, NJ: National Council on Education and the Disciplines.

Sutter, A. M., Dauer, J. M., & Forbes, C. T. (2018). Application of construal level and value-belief norm theories to undergraduate decision-making on a wildlife socio-scientific issue. *International Journal of Science Education*, 1–18.

Teitelbaum, M. S. (2014, March 19). *The myth of the science and engineering shortage.* Retrieved from https://www.theatlantic.com/education/archive/2014/03/the-myth-of-the-science-and-engineering-shortage/284359/

Venville, G. J., & Dawson, V. M. (2010). The impact of a classroom intervention on grade 10 students' argumentation skills, informal reasoning, and conceptual understanding of science. *Journal of Research in Science Teaching, 47*, 952–977.

Xie, Y., & Killewald, A. A. (2012). *Is American science in decline?* Cambridge, MA: Harvard University Press.

Zeidler, D. L. (2014). Socioscientific issues as a curriculum emphasis: Theory, research and practice. In N. G. Lederman & S. K. Abell (Eds.), *Handbook of research on science education, Volume II* (pp. 697–726). New York, NY: Routledge.

Zeidler, D. L. (2016). STEM education: A deficit framework for the twenty first century? A sociocultural socio-scientific response. *Cultural Studies of Science Education, 11*, 11–26.

Zollman, A. (2012). Learning for STEM literacy: STEM literacy for learning. *School Science and Mathematics, 112*, 12–19.

18

LEARNING MODELS AND MODELING ACROSS THE STEM DISCIPLINES

Margret A. Hjalmarson, Nancy Holincheck,
Courtney K. Baker and Terrie M. Galanti

> In sum, although different domains in science have their own fundamental questions, methods, and standards for "what counts" as evidence, they are all engaged in the same knowledge-building pursuit—the development of coherent and comprehensive explanations through the testing of models.
>
> *(Windschitl, Thompson, & Braaten, 2008, p. 5)*

We expand Windschitl et al's (2008) domains beyond science to include mathematics, engineering, and computational thinking. This chapter will explore how modeling is represented in each discipline in K–12 education and how models and modeling can play a unique role in integrating STEM content areas. Models and modeling as terms are used differently within and across disciplines, so it is useful to explore the disciplinary nuances. We continue with some common aspects of modeling across STEM that make it useful for integration. Modeling is inherently integrated since it is a process of applying disciplinary knowledge to describe, explain, represent, and predict real phenomena. Models are connected to the real world by a practice called "modeling" that includes some of the processes and practices in Figure 18.1.

Models in Mathematics: Mathematical Modeling and Modeling Mathematics

Models and modeling in the mathematical sense is a disciplinary practice where mathematics is used to describe or represent phenomena. Mathematical models are created to describe or represent real-world systems. Students often translate between written, verbal, physical symbolic and pictorial representations of the real world (Cramer, 2003). These can include algebraic representations but may also be models of spatial or geometric structures.

This section will focus on modeling as a practice in mathematics. When modeling is used in other disciplines, it is often mathematical modeling that is referred to as the modeling component. For instance, in engineering design or in scientific exploration, students may need to analyze data using a mathematical model. So, we focus on this aspect of mathematical modeling practice to investigate how modeling plays a role in the other disciplines. In mathematics, modeling provides a powerful platform for understanding (Lehrer & Schauble, 2007) and solving problems from the real world (Bonotto, 2007; Burkhardt, 2006) as students are able to apply mathematics in a creative and critical

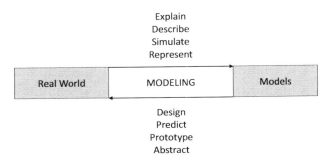

Figure 18.1   Models, the real world, and modeling.

manner that is essential to developing mathematical literacy as required by STEM fields (Carlson, Wickstrom, Burroughs, & Fulton, 2016; Lesh & Yoon, 2007; Steen, Turner, & Burkhardt, 2007). Additionally, modeling engages students and promotes productive mathematical dispositions (Lesh & Yoon, 2007) while supporting an authentic and deep integrated understanding of the involved mathematics (Lehrer & Schauble, 2007).

Since the nineteenth century, mathematics and mathematical modeling applications have played an important role in teaching and learning (Kaiser, 2016). However, since the 1960s, the international community has worked to better understand how mathematical situations are applied outside formal mathematics learning (Freudenthal, 1968; Pollak, 2016). This focus on the teaching and learning of mathematics as it is applied and modeled has been of specific interest (Kaiser, 2016; National Research Council, 2013) due to the frequent disconnect that is perceived by teachers and students (Hirsch & McDuffie, 2016). This disconnect stems from the fact that students often spend time on problems that are far removed from real-world settings (Cirillo, Bartell, & Wager, 2016; Verschaffel, Greer, & de Corte, 2000) and that word problems and applications have traditionally provided irrelevant contexts (Tran & Dougherty, 2014). Although the practice of providing nonroutine, challenging problems has increased (de Carvahlo Borba, Villarreal, & da Silva Soares, 2016), the type of problems many textbooks have identified as "modeling" are counter-productive as students are either provided a model to work with or not engaged in developing a model of their own (Meyer, 2015). Although modeling in mathematics stemmed from problem solving and its role in teaching mathematics (Lesh & Zawojewski, 2007), modeling problems differ from typical mathematics problems (Cirillo, Bartell et al., 2016). Problem solving and modeling both provide authentic contexts and engagement to students; however, modeling is unique in that the authentic problem forces the students to develop mathematical models (de Carvahlo Borba & Villarreal, 2005).

Modeling with Mathematics, Modeling Mathematics and Mathematical Modeling

A major challenge to modeling in mathematics is the limited agreement on many key aspects. Similar to how researchers have struggled to distinguish the differences between a problem-solving task and a modeling task (Lesh & Zawojewski, 2007), researchers have also struggled to consistently use the term 'modeling' similarly (Perrenet & Zwaneveld, 2012). Specifically, the distinction between modeling mathematics and mathematical modeling is not always clear in standards documents and mathematics education research (Cirillo, Pelesko, Felton-Koestler, & Rubel, 2016). For example, in 2010, the *Common Core State Standards for Mathematics* (CCSSM) (Common Core State Standards Initiative, 2010), emphasized modeling as a mathematical practice and as a high school concept (Cirillo, Pelesko et al., 2016; Zbiek & Conner, 2006). However, the CCSSM also "uses the terms *model* and *modeling* to mean both *modeling mathematics* and *mathematical modeling* without clarifying the difference in meaning" (Cirillo, Pelesko et al., 2016, p. 3). This challenge is not unique to the United States, as the international mathematics education community also recognizes that while modeling in mathematics is important to teaching and learning (Kaiser & Sriraman, 2006), the way modeling is discussed and implemented varies widely as well (Geiger, Ärlebäck, & Frejd, 2016).

In modeling mathematics, concrete objects or visual images are used to represent mathematical ideas (Cirillo, Pelesko et al., 2016; Fennema, 1972; Phillips, 2016). Specifically, the aim of modeling mathematics or creating models of mathematics is to support the facilitation and acquisition of mathematical concepts (Lesh & Zawojewski, 2007; Piaget, 1962). There are many ways an individual can create a model for a mathematical idea. However, the way in which a student creates and interacts with a model will have varying instructional implications, as students are demonstrating their understanding of the phenomenon (Sinclair, 2016). Since these models are designed to represent key mathematical ideas, they are removed from the real world (Cirillo, Pelesko et al., 2016). Modeling mathematics can be a precursory activity that students can engage in to prepare for mathematical modeling (Tam, 2011).

Mathematical modeling is different from modeling mathematics, and although it has been described in a variety of ways, there are similar characteristics or features (Germain-Williams, 2014; Gould, 2013; Lege, 2003; Niss, Blum, & Galbraith, 2007; Pollak, 2003). The CCSSM define mathematical modeling as "using mathematics or statistics to describe (i.e., model) a real-world situation and deduce additional information about the situation by mathematical or statistical computation and analysis" (Common Core Standards Writing Team, 2013, p. 5). Mathematical modeling allows students to engage in opportunities to make sense of and apply mathematical ideas in an authentic manner (Cavey & Champion, 2016; Gann, Avineri, Graves, Hernadez, & Teague, 2016; Lesh, Galbraith, Haines, & Hurford, 2010). Mathematical modeling is essential to seeing and applying mathematics in the real world (Blum & Ferri, 2009; Pollak, 2003).

Unique aspects of mathematical modeling are that it connects mathematics to real-world questions through the cyclic process of receiving a non-mathematized task, applying mathematics to better understand the phenomenon and then circling back to the real-world questions to arrive at solutions (Cirillo, Pelesko et al., 2016). Student-generated models from this iterative process provide both insight into their mathematical thinking and understanding (Lesh & Zawojewski, 2007) and an increase in student engagement (Blum & Ferri, 2009). Unlike traditionally contextualized problems, mathematical modeling problems are often considered messy real-world situations due to the multiple approaches and solutions that emerge (Bliss, Fowler, & Galluzzo, 2014; Cirillo, Bartell et al., 2016; Cirillo, Pelesko et al., 2016; Galbraith & Stillman, 2006). Generating different types of models or solutions is extremely valuable as certain models may not attend to all aspects of a problem, and an awareness of multiple approaches might demonstrate deeper student understanding of the phenomenon and new ideas to emerge for future revising (Groshong, 2016; Lesh & Zawojewski, 2007).

Models in Science—Modeling Concepts

Models in science are used to develop understanding about scientific phenomena through purposeful model construction and may serve as a tool for predicting or explaining natural systems (Berland et al., 2016). Ranging from physical models (e.g., a model of the solar system) to more abstract mental models, scientific models represent real-world phenomena and require the user to make connections between the model and the reality that is being modeled. A scientific model is "a set of representations, rules, and reasoning structures that allow one to generate predictions and explanations" (Schwarz & White, 2005, p. 166). Science makes use of mathematical models to aid in the construction of models in science, to include the use of graphs and equations to explain and predict the natural world. When used in science, models aid in the development of conceptual understanding, making predictions, and in application as the user aims to better understand the world (National Research Council, 2012).

Scientific models represent a system or phenomenon and help the user make predictions, develop explanations, and identify further questions. Models are built from data and thus are not static—rather, they are constructed, evaluated, compared, and revised in an iterative cycle (Schwarz et al., 2009). Scientific models include scale representations, idealized models (e.g., a frictionless inclined plane), diagrams, mathematical representations, analogies, and phenomenological models. Although it is tempting to classify scientific models into distinct bins, such as physical models, mathematical models, or purely conceptual models, these are false distinctions. Scientific models are sometimes physical, sometimes mathematical, but are always conceptual in nature. The construction of scientific models involves abstraction to simplify a system in order to focus on key features of the phenomena (Schwarz et al., 2009). A more useful classification system seeks to address how models are used.

Gouvea and Passmore (2017) provide a useful heuristic for differentiating between models, which examines *models of* versus *models for*. Both *models of* and *models for* involve representations of phenomena, but *models of* simply represent what is already known. In practice, this might involve users creating a physical model or drawing a diagram about something they have previously learned, to demonstrate their knowledge of the parts of the model and how it fits together. Although *models of* are widely used in education, they are not typically used by scientists, as they do not help the user develop explanations and predictions about the scientific system or phenomenon. *Models of* are focused on the model as a product; in contrast, *models for* focus on models as process.

Scientists are likely to use *models for* in their own development and testing of scientific concepts. *Models for* emphasize both the representation and what the model is for; or "the epistemic aims of the representation's intended use" (Gouvea & Passmore, 2017, p. 53). The model's purpose and structure are intertwined, so it is impossible to make sense of the model without understanding what it is for. The use of *models for* the purpose of making predictions and understanding the world, and the changeability and adaptability of models, is critical. Ultimately, the model is not the physical representation created, but the concept that incorporates the phenomenon, the questions that guided the development of the model, and the knowledge that has been developed as a result of use of the model (Gouvea & Passmore, 2017).

Scientific models enable the user to "establish, extend, and refine" their knowledge (National Research Council, 2012, p. 26), but this can happen only through the use of *models for*, or models used for the purpose of understanding the world. NGSS (2013) calls for the integration of models with other scientific practices, which calls for a shift within the science education community from *models of* to *models for* (Bybee, 2014; Gouvea & Passmore, 2017). To support this transition, it is critical to attend to the epistemological underpinnings in the application of modeling as a scientific practice. Users need to understand and consider the purpose, methods, and goals of their work while engaged in scientific practices (Schwarz, Ke, Lee, & Rosenberg, 2014). This can help students develop their epistemologies as they make use of empirical evidence in their construction, application, and revision of models (Baek & Schwarz, 2015). Models are thus epistemic tools used in explanation and prediction of scientific phenomena (Knuuttila, 2005).

Scientific models can be characterized as representations of a system that may both clarify and obscure elements of the system (NGSS Lead States, 2013). It is thus important to recognize the limitations of models when in use. The user must be challenged to engage in explicit and conscious separation of the model and the phenomenon it represents, to identify which aspects are not captured in the model (Lehrer & Schauble, 2003). Engaging in purpose-focused modeling rather than description-focused modeling can help the user address misconceptions about the science phenomenon. Further engagement in the explanation, prediction, and refinement cycle can reduce the development of further misconceptions. As understanding improves, scientific models are meant to change; as a model generates new predictions, it can be tested and refined (Schwarz et al., 2009).

Scientific modeling can play an essential role in scientific inquiry. The process of asking questions, gathering data, developing models from evidence, and then applying and refining models is a more authentic description of how scientists engage in inquiry than the scientific method (Windschitl et al., 2008). Modeling helps users organize and understand the purpose of the scientific practices in which they engage, which helps users engage in scientific sense-making (Passmore, Gouvea, & Giere, 2014). Models also typically result in the identification of new problems and new lines of inquiry (Knuuttila, 2005).

Modeling as a Design Practice in Engineering

Modeling is often part of the engineering design process (Carberry & McKenna, 2014; Lammi & Denson, 2017; Moore, Miller, Lesh, Stohlmann, & Kim, 2013). Engineering, perhaps more than the other disciplines, also uses modeling in connection with mathematics, science, technology, or computational thinking. Modeling is focused primarily on representations of the possible design, a problem or a system. As a principle for K-12 engineering education,

> The design process, the engineering approach to identifying and solving problems, is (1) highly iterative; (2) open to the idea that a problem may have many possible solutions; (3) a meaningful context for learning scientific, mathematical, and technological concepts; and (4) a stimulus to systems thinking, modeling, and analysis. In all of these ways, engineering design is a potentially useful pedagogical strategy.
>
> *(National Research Council, 2009, p. 4)*

While mathematical modeling is a part of engineering, this section will focus more on modeling as part of the design process. A significant component of the design process is iterating and considering the purposes of the design. This sense of modeling also includes creating, designing, and refining prototypes (Moore et al., 2014; Wendell & Rogers, 2013). The design process also supports students' learning of scientific models (Capobianco, Nyquist, & Tyrie, 2013; Wendell & Lee, 2010).

Engineering activities regularly include math and science applications. However, when considering integrated STEM, there are some engineering-based ways of incorporating modeling. Modeling appears in engineering in three ways related to the design processes which are essential to engineering as a discipline. The first is modeling as generating a prototype or initial design. So, students might design an initial model house (Wendell & Rogers, 2013) as part of their design and problem solving. That prototype can then be tested and revised in subsequent design cycles. This sense of prototypes is language distinctive to engineering and is not regularly seen in mathematics or science.

The second way modeling is used in engineering is to generate mathematical models (e.g., functions, equations, formulas) to describe phenomena. This mathematical modeling can be a component of model-eliciting activities (Moore et al., 2013; Tank et al., 2018). The mathematical modeling might serve an engineering goal in the design process. Related to mathematical models, engineering also relies on computational thinking for simulations, calculations, and the development of algorithms.

Third, modeling in engineering is also the application of scientific models. Engineering tasks can be used to support or elicit students' understanding of scientific constructs (e.g., heat transfer in the design of a model house; Wendell & Rogers, 2013). Another aspect of science modeling is the application of scientific models that students need to carry out their design. Throughout the design process, students need to consider science knowledge and may design artifacts that demonstrate that knowledge.

The fourth affordance of engineering to modeling is the role of context. A design activity typically includes a realistic context, including its constraints. A client may be used to set constraints like financial resources or material selection. As modeling is the connection between representations and the structure of the real world, engineering is an opportunity for the theoretical to meet the practical in terms of modeling. The context is the distinction between modeling and other types of problem solving since students need to engage with the world of the context in a meaningful and sometimes messy way (English, 2009).

The final way modeling is used for engineering is to represent students' conceptual understanding and hence a method of developing understanding of concepts (sometimes from math and science). So, the process of design creates natural opportunities to develop understanding of required concepts. For instance, designing a model house will require development of knowledge of materials science, and it presents an applied opportunity to use and develop knowledge (Wendell & Lee, 2010). Those representations (in the form of designs) are models of students' thinking. When students must express their conceptual understanding in the form of engineering design, their knowledge is tested. For instance, as they use different materials, their knowledge of the properties of those materials is tested (e.g., when selecting materials for a paper basket, they can begin to examine properties of materials) (Tank et al., 2018). Where science is modeling the real world, engineering is designing for the world using models.

Models and Simulations in Computational Thinking

Although computational thinking (CT) is often described as modeling with computers (Israel, Pearson, Tapia, Wherfel, & Reese, 2015), computer scientists define it more broadly as an analytic competency that supersedes computer programming (National Research Council, 2010). CT is a problem-solving process with specific characteristics related to problem formulation, organization and representation of data, use of abstractions such as models, procedural or algorithmic thinking, efficiency of solutions, and transferability of problem-solving processes (Grover & Pea, 2013; Weintrop et al., 2016).

Computational thinkers solve problems, design systems, and understand human behavior by drawing on computing concepts (Wing, 2008, p. 3717). Within this broader conceptualization of CT beyond programming, modeling becomes both the process and the product of abstraction (Brennan & Resnick, 2016; Wing, 2008). More specifically, instruction in CT prepares students to model the attributes of computational systems, to use computational systems and data to model problems in other STEM disciplines, and to leverage and challenge the predictive quality of models.

The consistent classification of modeling and simulation as major categories in multiple CT frameworks (Grover & Pea, 2013; Shute, Sun, & Asbell-Clarke, 2017; Weintrop et al., 2016) make it clear that CT extends far beyond computer programming because it builds the necessary problem-solving skills students need to model with computers and interpret data. Thus, we associate modeling with CT as "the conceptual foundation required to solve problems effectively and efficiently (i.e., algorithmically, with or without the assistance of computers) with solutions that are reusable in different contexts" (Shute et al., 2017, p. 142). Shute and colleagues (2017) identify six facets of CT in their exhaustive literature review (p. 153). These facets align with use of models for problem solving in K-12 mathematics and science:

a. *Decomposition:* Break problems down into smaller problems, which are then systematically solved separately.
b. *Abstraction:* Identify essential features of a problem. This includes data collection and analysis, identifying patterns within problems and solutions, and developing models to represent how a system operates.
c. *Algorithms:* Design a sequence of logical instructions to develop a solution to a problem. These instructions may be followed by a person or by a computer.
d. *Debugging:* Detect, identify, and fix errors when a system does not work as it should.

e. *Iteration:* Repetition of the design process to refine solutions.
f. *Generalization:* Transfer of CT skills to efficiently solve problems in similar and different domains.

The intentional development of CT can be made explicit in mathematics and science modeling activities beyond computer science instruction. Modeling and simulation of systems of varying complexity become exercises in CT which connect mathematical reasoning, scientific inquiry, and engineering thinking. Student processes of designing, creating, assessing, and using models as CT practices may offer a common language for connecting problem solving across STEM disciplines.

Modeling as an Integrated Practice Across the Disciplines

This section examines how modeling serves as a natural component of integrated STEM learning. The previous sections described how each discipline includes modeling (often using aspects of the other disciplines), but modeling is also an interdisciplinary, transdisciplinary, and multidisciplinary practice critical for integrated STEM learning (English, 2009). Three characteristics of modeling are themes in all of the disciplines.

1. Modeling and models as connected to real phenomenon as abstractions or representations with explanatory or descriptive relevant
2. Modeling process as cyclic or iterative (express, test, revise)
3. Modeling as an opportunity to express and to develop disciplinary knowledge and students' ways of thinking

Models and modeling are paradoxically both about real, often tangible phenomena but also about the abstract, non-tangible description of those phenomena. For prototyping in engineering, the model is not the real object but a stand-in used for testing. For mathematics and computational thinking, the model may be a program or a function that abstracts features of the real world. So, the modeling process is about both creating a representation that is as close as possible to the real phenomenon and also highlighting or emphasizing certain features and perhaps neglecting other features. For the second feature, modeling and model creation are cyclic and iterative. Students are expected to test and revise their own models when asked to design a model as part of the solution. This process includes situations where students may compare different models, similar to situations in science and engineering where new methods of measurement are regularly studied. The question is not about whether a model is "correct" or "right" but whether the model is the best one for the situation at hand.

The third feature, modeling as an opportunity for students to express and develop disciplinary knowledge and develop their own ways of thinking, refers specifically to modeling as a learning experience. Common across many of the examples is that modeling is an opportunity for students to explore phenomena and create models that reveal their current thinking and understanding. Another sense of the learning experience is that models as simulations allow students to develop understanding of possibly intangible concepts (e.g., the solar system). The other way simulation is used is for students to use a modeling environment to play with variables that cannot be quickly changed in the real world (e.g., traffic simulations, environmental populations). Modeling as a learning experience, including simulation, can bring phenomena into the classroom that might be impossible otherwise.

Discussion and Conclusions

As a product and a practice, modeling represents a method for considering learning in each discipline while simultaneously integrating content. Modeling plays a role in each disciplinary practice and is also inherently an applied practice since it is largely focused on real-world phenomena. For this reason, modeling and the creation of models are significant catalysts for integrated STEM teaching and learning. However, we have open questions. This chapter has focused on disciplinary practices and students' learning of those practices via the integration of one or more aspects of STEM. Questions of teaching and teacher knowledge were not addressed. For secondary teachers who may teach one STEM discipline, there are questions of how to coordinate integrated modeling activities across disciplines or how to meaningfully represent multiple disciplinary practices. However, there are also new areas like computational thinking or engineering that may be less familiar to many teachers at any level. By presenting the disciplinary differences in models and modeling, we wanted to clarify how the terms might be used differently, since a risk in integrated STEM activities is that subtle disciplinary differences are misinterpreted or overlooked. Teachers need to be aware of the disciplinary differences in modeling practice but also of how modeling is inherently interdisciplinary.

Modeling can provide a natural opportunity to engage students in real-world problems that are meaningful in their community contexts and are culturally sustaining. We have not explored the affective components of modeling teaching, but others have researched how modeling can support interest and engagement in STEM (Stohlmann, 2018). We have also not explored cultural relevance or meaningfulness for students, but modeling and students' development of models could be situated in contexts that are personally meaningful to them (e.g., Cirillo, Bartell et al., 2016). As experiences which prioritize students' ways of thinking and eliciting students' ideas, modeling should present opportunities for learners to express their perspectives in meaningful ways that also support learning STEM content.

References

Baek, H., & Schwarz, C. (2015). The influence of curriculum, instruction, technology, and social interactions on two fifth-grade students' epistemologies in modeling throughout a model-based curriculum unit. *Journal of Science Education & Technology, 24*(2/3), 216–233. https://doi.org/10.1007/s10956-014-9532-6

Berland, L. K., Schwarz, C. V., Krist, C., Kenyon, L., Lo, A. S., & Reiser, B. J. (2016). Epistemologies in practice: Making scientific practices meaningful for students. *Journal of Research in Science Teaching, 53*(7), 1082–1112. https://doi.org/10.1002/tea.21257

Bliss, K. M., Fowler, K. R., & Galluzzo, B. J. (2014). *Math modeling: Getting started and getting solutions.* Philadelphia, PA: Society for Industrial and Applied Mathematics.

Blum, W., & Ferri, R. B. (2009). Mathematical modelling: Can it be taught and learnt? *Journal of Mathematical Modelling and Application, 1*(1), 45–58.

Bonotto, C. (2007). How to replace word problems with activities of realistic mathematical modelling. In P. L. Galbraith, H.-W. Henn, & M. Niss (Eds.), *Modelling and applications in mathematics education: The 14th ICMI Study* (pp. 185–192). Springer US. Retrieved from https://www.springer.com/us/book/9780387298207

Brennan, K., & Resnick, M. (2016). *New frameworks for studying and assessing the development of computational thinking.* Presented at the American Educational Research Association, Vancouver, BC.

Burkhardt, H. (2006). Modelling in mathematics classrooms: Reflections on past developments and the future. *ZDM, 38*(2), 178–195. https://doi.org/10.1007/BF02655888

Bybee, R. W. (2014). NGSS and the next generation of science teachers. *Journal of Science Teacher Education, 25*(2), 211–221. https://doi.org/10.1007/s10972-014-9381-4

Capobianco, B. M., Nyquist, C., & Tyrie, N. (2013). Shedding light on engineering design. *Science and Children, 50*(5), 58–64.

Carberry, A. R., & McKenna, A. F. (2014). Exploring student conceptions of modeling and modeling uses in engineering design. *Journal of Engineering Education, 103*(1), 77–91. https://doi.org/10.1002/jee.20033

Carlson, M. A., Wickstrom, M. H., Burroughs, E. A., & Fulton, E. W. (2016). A case for mathematical modeling in the elementary school classroom. In C. R. Hirsch & A. Roth McDuffie (Eds.), *Annual perspectives in mathematics education 2016: Mathematical modeling and modeling mathematics* (pp. 121–129). Reston, VA: National Council of Teachers of Mathematics.

Cavey, L. O., & Champion, J. (2016). Learning secondary school mathematics through authentic mathematical modeling tasks. In C. R. Hirsch & A. Roth McDuffie (Eds.), *Annual perspectives in mathematics education 2016:*

Mathematical modeling and modeling mathematics (pp. 131–142). Reston, VA: National Council of Teachers of Mathematics.

Cirillo, M., Bartell, T. G., & Wager, A. A. (2016). Teaching mathematics for social justice through mathematical modeling. In C. R. Hirsch & A. Roth McDuffie (Eds.), *Annual perspectives in mathematics education 2016: Mathematical modeling and modeling mathematics* (pp. 87–96). Reston, VA: National Council of Teachers of Mathematics.

Cirillo, M., Pelesko, J. A., Felton-Koestler, M. D., & Rubel, L. (2016). Perspectives on modeling in school mathematics. In C. R. Hirsch & A. Roth McDuffie (Eds.), *Annual perspectives in mathematics education 2016: Mathematical modeling and modeling mathematics* (pp. 3–16). Reston, VA: National Council of Teachers of Mathematics.

Common Core Standards Writing Team. (2013). *Progressions for the common core standards in mathematics (draft) high school, modeling.* Tucson, AZ: Institute for Mathematics and Education, University of Arizona. Retrieved from http://ime.math.arizona.edu/ progressions

Common Core State Standards Initiative. (2010). *Common core state standards for mathematics.* Washington, DC: National Governors Association Center for Best Practices and Council of Chief State School Officers. Retrieved from http://www.corestandards.org/wp-content/uploads/Math_Standards.pdf

Cramer, K. (2003). Using a translation model for curriculum development and classroom instruction. In R. A. Lesh & H. M. Doerr (Eds.), *Beyond constructivism: Models and modeling perspectives on mathematics problem solving, learning, and teaching* (pp. 449–463). Mahwah, NJ: Lawrence Erlbaum Associates.

de Carvahlo Borba, M., & Villarreal, M. E. (2005). *Humans-with-media and the reorganization of mathematical thinking: Information and communication technologies, modeling, visualization and experimentation.* Springer US. Retrieved from //www.springer.com/us/book/9780387242637

de Carvahlo Borba, M., Villarreal, M. E., & da Silva Soares, D. (2016). Modeling using data available on the internet. In C. R. Hirsch & A. Roth McDuffie (Eds.), *Annual perspectives in mathematics education 2016: Mathematical modeling and modeling mathematics* (pp. 143–152). Reston, VA: National Council of Teachers of Mathematics.

English, L. D. (2009). Promoting interdisciplinarity through mathematical modelling. *ZDM, 41*(1), 161–181. https://doi.org/10.1007/s11858-008-0106-z

Fennema, E. (1972). Models and mathematics. *The Arithmetic Teacher, 19*(8), 635–640.

Freudenthal, H. (1968). Why to teach mathematics so as to be useful. *Educational Studies in Mathematics, 1*(1/2), 3–8.

Galbraith, P., & Stillman, G. (2006). A framework for identifying student blockages during transitions in the modelling process. *ZDM, 38*(2), 143–162. https://doi.org/10.1007/BF02655886

Gann, C., Avineri, T., Graves, J., Hernadez, M., & Teague, D. (2016). Moving students from remembering to thinking: The power of mathematical modeling. In C. R. Hirsch & A. Roth McDuffie (Eds.), *Annual perspectives in mathematics education 2016: Mathematical modeling and modeling mathematics* (pp. 97–106). Reston, VA: National Council of Teachers of Mathematics.

Geiger, V., Ärlebäck, J. B., & Frejd, P. (2016). Interpreting curricula to find opportunities for modeling: Case studies from Australia and Sweden. In C. R. Hirsch & A. Roth McDuffie (Eds.), *Annual perspectives in mathematics education 2016: Mathematical modeling and modeling mathematics* (pp. 207–216). Reston, VA: National Council of Teachers of Mathematics.

Germain-Williams, T. L. (2014). *Mathematical modeling in algebra textbooks at the onset of the common core state standards.* PhD dissertation, Columbia University, New York, NY. Retrieved from http://search.proquest.com/pqdtglobal/docview/1537949683/abstract/49662AC9BCA547F5PQ/1

Gould, H. (2013). *Teachers' conceptions of mathematical modeling.* PhD dissertation, Columbia University, New York, NY. Retrieved from http://search.proquest.com/pqdtglobal/docview/1367590532/abstract/18D205C7E6514148PQ/1

Gouvea, J., & Passmore, C. (2017). 'Models of' versus 'models for'. *Science & Education, 26*(1–2), 49–63. https://doi.org/10.1007/s11191-017-9884-4

Groshong, K. (2016). Different types of mathematical models. In C. R. Hirsch & A. Roth McDuffie (Eds.), *Annual perspectives in mathematics education 2016: Mathematical modeling and modeling mathematics* (pp. 17–23). Reston, VA: National Council of Teachers of Mathematics.

Grover, S., & Pea, R. (2013). Computational thinking in K–12: A review of the state of the field. *Educational Researcher, 42*(1), 38–43. https://doi.org/10.3102/0013189X12463051

Hirsch, C. R., & McDuffie, A. R. (2016). *Annual perspectives in mathematics education 2016: Mathematical modeling and modeling mathematics.* Reston, VA: National Council of Teachers of Mathematics.

Israel, M., Pearson, J. N., Tapia, T., Wherfel, Q. M., & Reese, G. (2015). Supporting all learners in school–wide computational thinking: A cross–case qualitative analysis. *Computers & Education, 82*, 263–279. https://doi.org/10.1016/j.compedu.2014.11.022

Kaiser, G. (2016). The teaching and learning of mathematical modeling. In J. Cai (Ed.), *Compendium for research in mathematics education* (pp. 207–291). Reston, VA: National Council of Teachers of Mathematics.

Kaiser, G., & Sriraman, B. (2006). A global survey of international perspectives on modelling in mathematics education. *ZDM, 38*(3), 302–310. https://doi.org/10.1007/BF02652813

Knuuttila, T. (2005). Models, representation, and mediation. *Philosophy of Science, 72*(5), 1260–1271. https://doi.org/10.1086/508124

Lammi, M. D., & Denson, C. D. (2017). Modeling as an engineering habit of mind and practice. *Advances in Engineering Education, 6*(1), 1–27.

Lege, G. F. (2003). *A comparative case study of contrasting instructional approaches applied to the introduction of mathematical modeling.* Ed.D. thesis, Teachers College, Columbia University, New York, NY. Retrieved from http://search.proquest.com/docview/305340621/abstract/78EC690054804A58PQ/1

Lehrer, R., & Schauble, L. (2003). Origins and evolution of model-based reasoning in mathematics and science. In R. A. Lesh & H. M. Doerr (Eds.), *Beyond constructivism: A models and modeling perspective on mathematics problem solving, learning, and teaching* (pp. 59–70). Mahwah, NJ: Lawrence Erlbaum Associates.

Lehrer, R., & Schauble, L. (2007). A developmental approach for supporting the epistemology of modeling. In W. Blum, P. L. Galbraith, H.-W. Henn, & M. Niss (Eds.), *Modelling and applications in mathematics education: The 14th ICMI study* (pp. 153–160). Boston, MA: Springer US. https://doi.org/10.1007/978-0-387-29822-1_14

Lesh, R., Galbraith, P. L., Haines, C., & Hurford, A. (Eds.). (2010). *Modeling students' mathematical modeling competencies: ICTMA 13.* Boston, MA: Springer US. Retrieved from //www.springer.com/us/book/9781441905604

Lesh, R., & Yoon, C. (2007). What is distinctive in (our views about) models & modelling perspectives on mathematics problem solving, learning, and teaching? In W. Blum, P. L. Galbraith, H.-W. Henn, & M. Niss (Eds.), *Modelling and applications in mathematics education: The 14th ICMI study* (pp. 161–170). Boston, MA: Springer US. https://doi.org/10.1007/978-0-387-29822-1_15

Lesh, R. A., & Zawojewski, J. S. (2007). Problem solving and modeling. In F. K. Lester (Ed.), *Second handbook of research on mathematics teaching and learning* (pp. 763–804). Charlotte, NC: Information Age Publishing.

Meyer, D. (2015). Missing the promise of mathematical modeling. *The Mathematics Teacher, 108*(8), 578–583. https://doi.org/10.5951/mathteacher.108.8.0578

Moore, T. J., Glancy, A. W., Tank, K. M., Kersten, J. A., Smith, K. A., & Stohlmann, M. S. (2014). A framework for quality K–12 engineering education: Research and development. *Journal of Pre-College Engineering Education Research (J-PEER), 4*(1), 1–13.

Moore, T. J., Miller, R. L., Lesh, R. A., Stohlmann, M. S., & Kim, Y. R. (2013). Modeling in engineering: The role of representational fluency in students' conceptual understanding. *Journal of Engineering Education, 102*(1), 141–178. https://doi.org/10.1002/jee.20004

National Research Council. (2009). *Engineering in K–12 education: Understanding the status and improving the prospects.* Washington, DC: National Academies Press. Retrieved from http://www.nap.edu/catalog/12635/engineering-in-k-12-education-understanding-the-status-and-improving

National Research Council. (2010). *Report of a workshop on the scope and nature of computational thinking.* Washington, DC: The National Academies Press.

National Research Council. (2012). *A framework for k-12 science education: Practices, crosscutting concepts, and core ideas.* Washington, DC: National Academies Press. Retrieved from http://www.nap.edu/catalog/13165/a-framework-for-k-12-science-education-practices-crosscutting-concepts

National Research Council. (2013). *The mathematical sciences in 2025.* Washington, DC: National Academies Press.

NGSS Lead States. (2013). *Next generation science standards: For states, by states.* Washington, DC: The National Academies Press.

Niss, M., Blum, W., & Galbraith, P. (2007). Introduction. In W. Blum, P. L. Galbraith, H.-W. Henn, & M. Niss (Eds.), *Modelling and applications in mathematics education: The 14th ICMI study* (pp. 3–32). Boston, MA: Springer US. https://doi.org/10.1007/978-0-387-29822-1_1

Passmore, C., Gouvea, J. S., & Giere, R. (2014). Models in science and in learning science: Focusing scientific practice on sense-making. In M. R. Matthews (Ed.), *International handbook of research in history, philosophy and science teaching* (pp. 1171–1202). Dordrecht, The Netherlands: Springer Netherlands. https://doi.org/10.1007/978-94-007-7654-8_36

Perrenet, J., & Zwaneveld, B. (2012). The many faces of the mathematical modeling cycle. *Journal of Mathematical Modelling and Application, 1*(6), 3–21.

Phillips, E. D. (2016). Introduction. In C. R. Hirsch & A. Roth McDuffie (Eds.), *Annual perspectives in mathematics education 2016: Mathematical modeling and modeling mathematics* (pp. 25–26). Reston, VA: National Council of Teachers of Mathematics.

Piaget, J. (1962). *Play, dreams and imitation in childhood.* New York, NY: Norton.

Pollak, H. (2003). A history of the teaching of modeling. In G. M. A. Stanic & J. Kilpatrick (Eds.), *A history of school mathematics* (pp. 647–669). Reston, VA: National Council of Teachers of Mathematics.

Pollak, H. (2016). Foreword. In C. R. Hirsch & A. Roth McDuffie (Eds.), *Annual perspectives in mathematics education 2016: Mathematical modeling and modeling mathematics* (pp. vii–viii). Reston, VA: National Council of Teachers of Mathematics.

Schwarz, C. V., Ke, L., Lee, M., & Rosenberg, J. (2014). Developing mechanistic model-based explanations of phenomena: Case studies of two fifth grade students' epistemologies in practice over time. In *Proceedings of the International Conference of the Learning Sciences*. Boulder, CO.: International Society of the Learning Sciences.

Schwarz, C. V., Reiser, B. J., Davis, E. A., Kenyon, L., Achér, A., Fortus, D., . . . Krajcik, J. (2009). Developing a learning progression for scientific modeling: Making scientific modeling accessible and meaningful for learners. *Journal of Research in Science Teaching, 46*(6), 632–654. https://doi.org/10.1002/tea.20311

Schwarz, C. V., & White, B. Y. (2005). Metamodeling knowledge: Developing students' understanding of scientific modeling. *Cognition and Instruction, 23*(2), 165–205. https://doi.org/10.1207/s1532690xci2302_1

Shute, V. J., Sun, C., & Asbell-Clarke, J. (2017). Demystifying computational thinking. *Educational Research Review, 22*, 142–158. https://doi.org/10.1016/j.edurev.2017.09.003

Sinclair, N. (2016). TouchCounts: Visual, auditory, haptic, and symbolic models for numbers and operations. In C. R. Hirsch & A. Roth McDuffie (Eds.), *Annual perspectives in mathematics education 2016: Mathematical modeling and modeling mathematics* (pp. 27–36). Reston, VA: National Council of Teachers of Mathematics.

Steen, L. A., Turner, R., & Burkhardt, H. (2007). Developing mathematical literacy. In W. Blum, P. L. Galbraith, H.-W. Henn, & M. Niss (Eds.), *Modelling and applications in mathematics education: The 14th ICMI study* (pp. 285–294). Boston, MA: Springer US. https://doi.org/10.1007/978-0-387-29822-1_30

Stohlmann, M. (2018). A vision for future work to focus on the "M" in integrated STEM. *School Science and Mathematics, 118*(7), 310–319. https://doi.org/10.1111/ssm.12301

Tam, K. C. (2011). Modeling in the common core state standards. *Journal of Mathematics Education at Teachers College, 2*(1). Retrieved from http://journals.tc-library.org/index.php/matheducation/article/view/636

Tank, K. M., Moore, T. J., Dorie, B. L., Gajdzik, E., Terri Sanger, M., Rynearson, A. M., & Mann, E. F. (2018). Engineering in early elementary classrooms through the integration of high-quality literature, design, and STEM+C content. In L. English & T. Moore (Eds.), *Early engineering learning* (pp. 175–201). Singapore: Springer Singapore. https://doi.org/10.1007/978-981-10-8621-2_9

Tran, D., & Dougherty, B. J. (2014). Authenticity of mathematical modeling. *The Mathematics Teacher, 107*(9), 672–678. https://doi.org/10.5951/mathteacher.107.9.0672

Verschaffel, L., Greer, B., & de Corte, E. (2000). *Making sense of word problems*. Exton, PA: Swets & Zeitlinger Publishers.

Weintrop, D., Beheshti, E., Horn, M., Orton, K., Jona, K., Trouille, L., & Wilensky, U. (2016). Defining computational thinking for mathematics and science classrooms. *Journal of Science Education and Technology, 25*(1), 127–147. https://doi.org/10.1007/s10956-015-9581-5

Wendell, K. B., & Lee, H.-S. (2010). Elementary students' learning of materials science practices through instruction based on engineering design tasks. *Journal of Science Education and Technology, 19*(6), 580–601. https://doi.org/10.1007/s10956-010-9225-8

Wendell, K. B., & Rogers, C. (2013). Engineering design-based science, science content performance, and science attitudes in elementary school. *Journal of Engineering Education, 102*(4), 513–540. https://doi.org/10.1002/jee.20026

Windschitl, M., Thompson, J., & Braaten, M. (2008). Beyond the scientific method: Model-based inquiry as a new paradigm of preference for school science investigations. *Science Education, 92*(5), 941–967. https://doi.org/10.1002/sce.20259

Wing, J. M. (2008). Computational thinking and thinking about computing. *Philosophical Transactions of the Royal Society of London, 366*, 3717–3725.

Zbiek, R. M., & Conner, A. (2006). Beyond motivation: Exploring mathematical modeling as a context for deepening students' understandings of curricular mathematics. *Educational Studies in Mathematics, 63*(1), 89–112. https://doi.org/10.1007/s10649-005-9002-4

19

CONTEMPORARY METHODS OF ASSESSING INTEGRATED STEM COMPETENCIES

Kerrie A. Douglas, Brian D. Gane, Knut Neumann
and James W. Pellegrino

The new vision of STEM education that has emerged from recent reform efforts across the globe envisions students developing a competence in STEM that goes well beyond simply memorizing a wide breadth of factual content. Students are expected to be able to productively engage with key disciplinary content, flexibly apply habits of minds, think critically, develop creative solutions to problems and, most importantly, to be prepared for life-long learning. In essence, competence in STEM refers to the ability to combine knowledge, skills and abilities (KSAs) from one or more disciplines to solve problems across a wide range of authentic contexts (National Governors Association Center for Best Practices & Council of Chief State School Officers, 2010; National Research Council [NRC], 2012; Ng, 2008; Pellegrino, 2014). In order to support students in developing such holistic competence, STEM education needs to engage students in STEM practices[1] to explore in depth the relationship between ideas within and across multiple STEM disciplines (NRC, 2014, 2018). Many countries have adopted policies which emphasize students' need to interact deeply with content from different disciplines, engage in STEM practices, and develop problem-solving and deeper thinking skills (Bernholt, Nentwig, & Neumann, 2012; NGSS Lead States, 2013; OECD, 2017; Roth et al., 2006).

For STEM reform to be successful, all aspects of the educational system (i.e., standards, curriculum, instruction, and assessment) must be aligned to the vision of supporting students in developing integrated competence in STEM (Pellegrino, Chudowsky, & Glaser, 2001). This is particularly important with respect to assessment of such competence, since assessment development and implementation tends to lag behind other aspects of STEM reform and is often controversial in discussions of educational policy and practice (Goldman, Lawless, Pellegrino, Braasch, Manning, & Gomez, 2012).

The purpose of this chapter is to guide researchers and practitioners who are interested in making high-quality inferences about learners' competence (or competencies) across a variety of STEM domains, including integrating KSAs across multiple STEM domains. Adopting the perspective that detailed and valid inferences about what students know and can do involves a process of evidentiary reasoning, this chapter outlines major issues in STEM assessment design and interpretation, given a variety of contexts of use and intended purposes. In the first section, we discuss various aspects of STEM assessment, including current thinking about the design and validation of assessments of integrated STEM competencies. The second section reviews frameworks for designing STEM assessments. The third section focuses on the types of STEM assessments that might be desired, while the fourth section focuses on the measurement models that can be used with these STEM assessments. This section also discusses the relationship between what is assessed, how it is to be used and what type of measurement approach is most appropriate given the intended interpretive inferences. We close by looking ahead to the future of assessment and some of the implications for assessment of integrated STEM.

Assessment in Integrated STEM

Role of Assessment in Integrated STEM Reform

In many ways, the success of integrated STEM reform hinges upon assessments being aligned to the same values and understanding of the reform that are put forward in teacher professional development, curriculum and instruction. Assessments are powerful: they clarify learning expectations for both teachers and students by providing concrete illustrations of the performances expected from students. Assessments are often used as measures of student learning outcomes, teacher effectiveness and school quality. Many decisions of educational and personal consequence are thus informed by student performance on assessments.

One significant concern is that there is a misalignment between the vision of students developing competence in integrated STEM and the traditional vision of STEM assessment, which targets isolated knowledge of STEM facts and procedures (Pellegrino, 2013). For example, several researchers have found that teachers' common practice is to assign tasks that require students to carry out prescribed activities and memorize content, rather than reason with content and develop deeper understanding (Roth et al., 2006; Weis, Pasley, Smith, & Banilower, & Heck, 2003). While there is a practical need to equip teachers with the capability to assess in ways that are aligned to the reform conceptions of competence (Tekkumru-Kisa, Stein, & Schunn, 2015), teachers are not the only ones struggling to do so for integrated STEM. Recent research found that popular integrated STEM curricular units for lower grades have very few integrated STEM assessments embedded in the curriculum (Douglas, Moore, Merzdorf, Li, & Johnston, 2017). The majority of the assessments were designed to assess memorized content and practices, with very few tasks where students must demonstrate the capacity to combine different KSAs, within or across content domains. In addition, large-scale testing programs have historically been built around multiple-choice items that cover a wide range of topics but with little depth. In response to the adoption of the U.S. Next Generation Science Standards (NGSS), Songer and Ruiz-Primo (2012) argued that assessment must be the new research priority in order to capture the learning targets set out in the standards. Innovative approaches to assessment are needed where students' reasoning and conceptual understanding are captured and in alignment with the learning objectives set out in the guiding policy documents (Gorin & Mislevy, 2013; Pellegrino, 2013). Next, we discuss design approaches that are aligned to the vision of integrated STEM competence and that should be adopted to generate innovate assessments.

Design of Assessments Aligned to Integrated STEM Competence:
Identifying the Construct(s)

All assessment design must begin with a clear definition of the construct (or constructs) of interest. Without a clear and precise definition of what is supposed to be assessed, including its scope, there can be no valid inference. In the case of integrated STEM, the construct is *competence* or *integrated competence* in STEM. Ufer and Neumann (2018) discuss in detail the origin and meaning of the term "competence". For our purposes, it should suffice to say that in the current educational environment, any STEM competency construct must go beyond the recall of isolated, factual knowledge or procedures.

More generally, *competence* in a domain is understood as the integration of all the required *KSAs* required to solve problems typical to the domain. This may also include problems primarily requiring (deep) knowledge about a particular content or the application of a (complex) procedure.

An alternate, but complementary, way to conceptualize competence in a domain is to consider different *dimensions* within the domain. This nomenclature is perhaps most prevalent in *The Framework for K-12 Science Education* (NRC, 2012) but can be also found in other documents for science or STEM education, respectively (for an overview, see Bernholt et al., 2012). The *Framework* identifies three dimensions that constitute competence in science: knowledge about *disciplinary core ideas*, knowledge about *crosscutting concepts* and the abilities and skills required to engage in practices of science and engineering (NRC, 2012). The Finnish Standards for Science Education, for example, similarly identify two dimensions: a *knowledge* dimension (including declarative, procedural and conceptual knowledge), and the *cognitive processes* dimensions (including remembering and understanding as well as applying and creating) (Krzywacki, Koistinen, & Lavonen, 2012).

At a broad level, and as discussed in earlier chapters of this book, integrated STEM refers to purposeful learning opportunities which combine aspects of science, technology, engineering and mathematics (Moore & Smith, 2014). *Integrated STEM competence* therefore refers to the ability to integrate KSAs from across different domains (e.g., mathematics and technology) in order to solve a problem.

Theoretical Framework for Assessment: Reasoning from Evidence

Assessment can be understood as a process of reasoning from evidence involving three components that comprise an "assessment triangle": cognition, observation and interpretation (Pellegrino et al., 2001). The cognition component refers to "a theory or set of beliefs about how students [. . .] develop competence in a subject domain" (Pellegrino et al., 2001, p. 44). In the assessment of integrated STEM competence, this would be a specific model of: (1) the KSAs constituting competence in the targeted domains, (2) how these develop over time given instruction and (3) the capacity to integrate the KSAs across domains as needed. The observation component specifies the type(s) of assessment tasks likely to yield performance(s) that will provide evidence that allows for drawing conclusions about the targeted competence. Tasks must provide students with the opportunity to demonstrate the integration of selected KSAs to solve problems in STEM. The interpretation component encompasses the procedures employed to reason about students' competence from the observed performance data. Task scoring rubrics, used to quantify or describe students' performance, must account for evidence of the degree to which students managed to integrate the KSAs articulated in the cognition component.

The three components of the assessment triangle are inseparably connected. For any assessment to yield reliable and valid information, each component must be consistent with the other two (Pellegrino et al., 2001; NRC, 2014). The Committee on Developing Assessments of Science Proficiency in K-12 identified two major approaches to designing assessments that can help meet this goal: the construct-modeling approach (Wilson, 2005) and the evidence-centered design approach (Mislevy, Steinberg & Almond, 2003). We review each of these approaches next.

Approaches for Designing STEM Assessments

Assessments are often designed by simply writing items based on individual interpretations of a set of standards or learning objectives. However, if items are written without a clear specification of the construct to be assessed, including relevant forms of evidence and understanding of how students master the construct, the assessment will often fail to adequately represent the construct and/or provide appropriate and sufficient evidence of the competency. This would limit the reliability and validity of the inferences that can be drawn from students' performance on the items (for details, see Messick, 1995). In order to ensure adequate coverage and representation of the construct(s) in and across a set of items, as well as reliability and validity of the inferences drawn from students' performance on those items, Wilson (2005) proposed the construct modeling approach.

The Construct Modeling Approach

The construct modeling approach envisions assessment development as a process of multiple iterations of a cycle through four building blocks: the construct map, the items design, the outcome space and the measurement model (see Figure 19.1). The first building block encompasses the specification of one or more construct maps.[2] A construct map delineates the cognitive construct (e.g., competence in integrated STEM) and its development over time into a hierarchy of qualitatively different levels based on a thorough analysis of the domain given theory, research and empirical data. The highest level defines the maximum level of competence expected from students at a certain stage of schooling, while the lower levels represent intermediate stages through which students typically progress in developing the expected level of competence. The second building block, items design, is about developing assessment tasks that can stimulate responses allowing for observations about the construct or specifying a procedure for the development of such tasks. The third building block, the outcome space, is a description of the possible responses and how they are scored. The last building block, the measurement model, relates the scored responses back to the construct. That is, the delineation of the construct and, more importantly, its specification as a construct map marks the starting point of each cycle and guides the process throughout the cycle: in the beginning, it emphasizes a developmental perspective on the construct; in the end, it provides a point of reference to determine the extent to which students have developed mastery of the construct (Wilson, 2005).

The Evidence-Centered Design Approach

The Evidence-Centered Design (ECD) approach (Mislevy et al., 2003; Mislevy & Haertel, 2006) describes assessment development as a process involving the delineation of three spaces: the claim, evidence and task space (see Figure 19.2) (Pellegrino, DiBello, & Brophy, 2014). The process begins with the delineation of the claim space; that is, specification of the claims that one wants to make about a construct such as students' competence. This involves unpacking the complexes of KSAs that constitute competence in a domain. Precise formulation of the knowledge students are expected to have and how they are expected to use it is most critical in this step. In the next step, evidence statements are formulated. These evidence statements should clearly specify the features of student performances that will be accepted as evidence that a student has met a claim. Then the types of tasks that are expected to elicit the desired performances need to be specified in terms of essential and optional task features. The entire process—from the delineation of the claims to the specification of the tasks—forms the design part of the assessment argument (Mislevy, 2007).

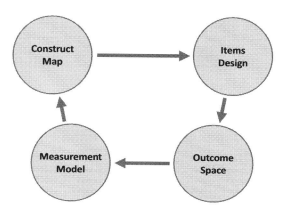

Figure 19.1   Representation of Wilson's (2005) Construct Modeling Approach.

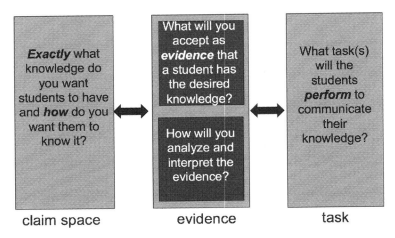

Figure 19.2   Pellegrino et al. (2014) simplified representation of evidence centered design by Mislevy et al., (2003).

Once the tasks are developed, the next step is to define an evidentiary scheme for the tasks. Based on the performances that are expected, one specifies how these performances will be evaluated in the light of the evidence statements and how these evaluations will be combined into evidence supporting (or not supporting) the claims about the construct. A scoring guide that includes a description of all possible performances, precise information on how each performance is scored and how these scores "add up" into a total score ensures that total scores are reflective of students' competency. This part is the use part of the assessment argument. Together, both the design and use parts of the assessment argument aim to ensure an optimal alignment of claims, evidence and tasks.

Combining Approaches

Both approaches to assessment development, the construct-modeling approach and the evidence-centered design approach, are construct-centered design models that help to establish coherence between the three vertices of the assessment triangle. The construct-modeling approach highlights the developmental aspect of the construct in terms of delineating how students develop competence in STEM into a hierarchy of levels, and the importance of being able to locate students on one of these levels based on their observed performances. The ECD approach highlights the importance of defining as precisely as possible what observations will be considered evidence that students have developed a given level of competence, how these observations will be obtained (by thoroughly specifying task features) and how these observations will be translated into scores reflecting different levels of competence. That is, the construct-modeling approach and the ECD approach emphasize and clarify different aspects of articulation among the vertices of the assessment triangle. The construct-modeling approach emphasizes coherence between the cognition and observation as well as between the cognition and interpretation vertices, whereas the evidence-centered design approach emphasizes coherence between the observation and the interpretation vertex. Both approaches can therefore be profitably combined in order to ensure the development of high-quality assessments of integrated STEM competence.

Unidimensional and Integrated STEM Assessments

In this section we introduce a classification scheme that applies across an array of STEM assessments. Our classification scheme will fit assessment in any of the domains, as the scheme is based on the number and type of dimensions of competency that are targeted by the assessment. Although instructors may be adopting an integrated STEM curriculum, there may be times when it is appropriate to assess, for example, knowledge of one particular content area. Thus, we review assessments of individual dimensions (of one domain) first, and then turn to assessments that target multiple, integrated dimensions of competency (across multiple domains). For each type of assessment, we review their claims about student competency and the evidence that is marshalled to support those claims.

Conceptual and Procedural Knowledge of STEM Content

The first broad class of assessments that we consider are those that focus on conceptual and/or procedural STEM knowledge. In these assessments, one is primarily interested in measuring a single dimension of a STEM domain. Consider an end-of-year course assessment that a secondary school student might take. The implicit claim is that a student has sufficient knowledge of the scientific content presented in a chemistry course. The evidence for (or against) this claim is provided by the student's performance on the end-of-year course assessment (e.g., a set of selected and constructed response items). Because the desired claimed competency is conceptual knowledge, the evidence must match this claim. The evidence may be composed of the student's response to fixed-response items, or items that require different levels of reasoning about the content (in order to ensure the item is indeed assessing conceptual knowledge over memorized factual knowledge).

One example of such assessments is that of concept inventories. A concept inventory is an assessment that is focused on measuring conceptual knowledge of a small set of key concepts, while attempting to minimize other requirements such as computation skills (e.g., Streveler et al., 2011; Jorion et al., 2015). The claims in this case are focused on conceptual knowledge and reasoning, and the evidence usually takes the form of the student's responses to multiple-choice or open-ended prompts. For example, the force concept inventory (FCI) focuses on conceptual reasoning following Newtonian principles and does not require any mathematical computations (Halloun & Hestenes, 1985; Hestenes, Wells, & Swackhamer, 1992). Likewise, the chemistry concept inventory (CCI) focuses on topics learned in a first-year chemistry sequence for post-secondary students (e.g., thermochemistry, bonding, etc.) (Pavelich, Jenkins, Birk, Bauer, & Krause, 2004; Krause, Birk, Bauer, Jenkins, & Pavelich, 2004).

Concept inventories frequently use a multiple-choice format called Distractor Driven Multiple Choice (DDMC) aimed at identifying potentially problematic thinking (e.g., alternative conceptions or misunderstandings). DDMCs have shown some success in identifying when student thinking matches normative scientific thought and/or alternate conceptions that arise from everyday observations and that reflect pre-scientific understandings. Furthermore, some have been designed to show how conceptual reasoning develops over time or experience with the domain (e.g., Herrmann-Abell, DeBoer, 2011; Sadler, 1998). Large test banks (e.g., AAAS 2061; http://assessment.aaas.org/pages/home) and adaptive testing software (e.g., Diagnoser, Thissen-Roe, Hunt, & Minstrell, 2004; http://www.diagnoser.com) have been developed to provide practitioners and researchers with access to these DDMC items. Figure 19.3 shows an example of such a DDMC, where students are reasoning about one key idea in chemistry.

In contrast to a focus on conceptual knowledge and reasoning, other assessments focus on procedural knowledge. Because the claims are different from those claims associated with conceptual knowledge, the evidence must also differ. Using DDMC items will not suffice to reveal students' procedural knowledge. For instance, if one wants to make the claim that the student has the ability to perform stochiometric calculations, then part of the evidence should be demonstrations of students' ability to balance chemical reaction equations. A student might be able to describe the law of conservation of mass but not be able to perform calculations that conform to the law. Likewise, using a student's performance on problem-solving items as evidence for his or her conceptual knowledge will invariably introduce validation problems. Because stoichiometry primarily requires procedural

A student places some baking soda and a jar of lemon juice in a plastic bag and seals the bag. She weighs the bag and everything in it. She shakes the bag so that the lemon juice spills out of the jar and mixes with the baking soda inside the bag. The student observes that bubbles form and the bag <u>expands</u>.

If the student weighs the bag and everything in it after the bubbling stops and compares the final weight to the starting weight, what will she find out?

A. The final weight will be greater than the starting weight because new atoms are produced during the experiment.

B. The final weight will be less than the starting weight because some of the atoms are destroyed during the experiment.

C. The final weight will be the same as the starting weight because the number of each kind of atom does not change during the experiment.

D. The final weight will be the same as the starting weight because some atoms are destroyed, but new ones are created during the experiment.

Figure 19.3   AAAS Item SC043005 assess the key idea: Whenever atoms interact with each other, regardless of how they are arranged or rearranged, the total mass stays the same. Distractors are linked to misconceptions: New atoms are created during chemical reactions (Distractors A and D); atoms can be destroyed during a chemical reaction (Distractors B and D).

knowledge of rules for combining molecules and balancing equations, solving those stoichiometry items might not require one to understand essential conceptual knowledge (e.g., knowledge that in an open system, it might appear that mass is not conserved).

STEM Practices and Literacy

The next broad class of assessments in integrated STEM that we consider are those that measure a student's ability to engage in a single STEM practice or a student's STEM literacy (which might involve multiple, related practices). Examples of these competencies include the ability to control variables in planning an experiment or to engage in argument (Osborne, 2010). Examples of these STEM literacies are measures of students' informational literacy in engineering contexts (Douglas, Fernandez, Purzer, Fosmire, & Van Epps, 2018), or the National Assessment of Educational Progress (NAEP) Technology and Engineering Literacy (TEL) assessment.

In these assessments, one is interested in gathering evidence to support a claim of proficiency about a single construct (e.g., the ability to design an experiment; informational literacy). Because the claim focuses on the single construct, without adding disciplinary conceptual or procedural knowledge, the evidence for the claim must likewise avoid confounding it with disciplinary conceptual or procedural knowledge. As a result, these assessments tend toward minimizing the role of content knowledge in the student's performance, since doing so is considered a control for construct-irrelevant variance. The evidence to support a claim of this type therefore places constraints on the design of assessment items because it requires that any disciplinary knowledge required to perform the task be minimized or eliminated.

Consider a prototypical inquiry task that might be used in a chemistry setting in secondary education, one that does not require deep conceptual knowledge of chemistry.[3] This task is called the mystery powders task and has multiple variants, including one implemented in the Principled Assessment Designs for Inquiry (PADI) project (e.g., Mislevy & Haertel, 2006; Seibert, Hamel, Haynie, Mislevy, & Bao, 2006). In the mystery powders task, students are presented with a scenario that can be solved through an inquiry process of investigating, analyzing data and writing an explanation/argument for their conclusions (all broadly conceived of as scientific inquiry practices). The mystery powders task is a "hypothetico–deductive reasoning problem" that requires minimal content knowledge (properties of matter and chemical reactions) (Seibert et al., 2006). Students are presented with a mystery powder that might be a mixture of several powders. Students are to conduct an investigation using standard laboratory procedures to determine which substance(s) make up the white powder. Figure 19.4 shows the first part of the mystery powders task, as implemented by the PADI project. There are multiple investigations that students can simulate (e.g., Heat, Iodine, etc.) and students need to know only about properties of matter (i.e., that there are physical properties that are characteristic of a substance and so can be used to identify the substance) to make sense of the results of some of the investigations. If the task did require deeper knowledge (e.g., *the configuration of atoms in a molecule determines the molecule's properties; an enormous variety of biological, chemical, and physical phenomena can be explained by changes in the arrangement and motion of atoms and molecules;* AAAS, 1993), it would cloud the inferences one could make relative to the intended claims. If students lack this deeper knowledge, it might interfere with their ability to demonstrate that they can conduct an investigation and engage in this hypothetical–deductive reasoning.

Integrated or Multidimensional STEM Competencies

The next broad class of assessments that we consider are those that measure the ability to engage in integrated STEM competencies. In this case, integration means the competency is conceived of multiple dimensions that are assessed simultaneously (Gane, Zaidi, & Pellegrino, 2018). Such an integration could be any combination of conceptual and/or procedural knowledge with STEM practices and/or STEM literacy. In other words, the assessment task must provide students with a chance to demonstrate their knowledge-in-use.

The arguments we make about the claims and types of evidence needed for multidimensional, integrated STEM assessments are similar, no matter which specific dimensions are being integrated. The claim itself is multidimensional (rather than unidimensional), as opposed to the types of claims we have examined in the previous sections (Harris, Krajcik, Pellegrino, & McElhaney, 2016). By saying the claimed competency is multidimensional and integrated, we emphasize that the two (or more) dimensions must be used *together* by students. The claim is integrated because for a student to engage in the performance, he or she must have KSAs that work together to allow the student to do something with their knowledge. The evidence, like the claim, needs to be multidimensional. This has strong implications for assessment task design, since any task has to be able to elicit multidimensional evidence (Gane et al., 2018; Harris, Krajcik, Pellegrino, & Debarger, 2019).

The example of multidimensional integration that we will focus on is conceptual knowledge integrated with scientific practices. In contrast to the previous section, in which we described scientific practice assessments as attempting to minimize deep conceptual knowledge, the integration does the opposite. It is through engaging in the scientific and engineering practices that one demonstrates deep conceptual knowledge. Consider the example chemistry assessment task in Figure 19.5 (College Board, 2014). This assessment task integrates two dimensions: essential disciplinary knowledge and scientific practices. Note that the learning objectives (Table 19.1) provide the claims that are

Mystery Powders

You have been given a mystery powder consisting of at least one but not more than two powder components. You can determine the components given information from the available experiments.

Current experiment: Taste

Tastes sweet.

Step one: what can you deduce so far? Indicate whether each possible component is In or Out of mixture, or whether that cannot be known yet:

In	Out	Can't tell	Can't know	
o	o	o	o	Cornstarch
o	o	o	o	Flour
o	o	o	o	Plaster
o	o	o	o	Salt
o	o	o	o	Soda
o	o	o	o	Sugar

Step two: which experiment do you want to do next?

Heat Iodine Look Taste Vinegar Water

Figure 19.4 Mystery Powder Task (Seibert et al., 2006).

being made about students, and the assessment task elicits the evidence from students. Each of the two learning objectives are multidimensional, integrating the essential knowledge with a scientific practice. The student has to develop a representation of a homogenous mixture that shows how the H_2O particles and LiCl particles are arranged, including the orientation of both particles. The science practice dimension is integrated with the essential knowledge statement to create a unified learning objective that is a multidimensional claim about students' competence. The student, in producing the response, must provide the evidence needed to support the multidimensional claim. The performance expectations in the Next Generation Science Standards are examples of three-dimensional claims that integrate disciplinary cores ideas, science and engineering practices and crosscutting concepts (NGSS, 2013).

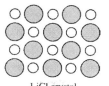

H₂O molecule   LiCl crystal

3. The structures of a water molecule and a crystal of LiCl(s) are represented above. A student prepares a 1.0 *M* solution by dissolving 4.2 g of LiCl(s) in enough water to make 100 mL of solution.

(a) In the space provided below, show the interactions of the components of LiCl(*aq*) by making a drawing that represents the different particles present in the solution. Base the particles in your drawing on the particles shown in the representations above. Include only one formula unit of LiCl and no more than 10 molecules of water. Your drawing must include the following details.

- identity of ions (symbol and charge)
- the arrangement and proper orientation of the particles in the solution

LiCl (*aq*)

(b) The student passes a direct current through the solution and observes that chlorine gas is produced at the anode. Identify the chemical species produced at the cathode and justify your answer using the information given in the table below.

Half-reaction	Standard Reduction Potential at 25°C (V)
$Li^+(aq) + e^- \rightarrow Li(s)$	− 3.05
$2 H_2O(l) + 2 e^- \rightarrow H_2(g) + 2 OH^-(aq)$	− 0.83

Figure 19.5 Example Chemistry AP task (College Board, 2014).

Table 19.1 Essential Knowledge, Science Practices, and Learning Objectives Measured by the Example Chemistry AP Task (College Board, 2014)

Essential Knowledge	2.A.3 Solutions are homogenous mixtures in which the physical properties are dependent on the concentration of the solute and the strengths of all interactions among the particles of the solutes and solvent.
	3.C.3 Electrochemistry shows the interconversion between chemical and electrical energy in galvanic and electrolytic cells.
Science Practices	1.1 The student can create representations and models of natural or man–made phenomena and systems in the domain.
	5.1 The student can analyze data to identify patterns or relationships.
Learning Objectives	2.8 The student can draw and/or interpret representations of solutions that show the interactions between the solute and solvent.
	3.13 The student can analyze data regarding galvanic or electrolytic cells to identify properties of the underlying redox reactions.

Summary

The choice of which dimension (or dimensions) of competency to assess affects the form and substance of the claims that one can make, and therefore one must be careful to consider and specify appropriate evidence for the given claim. In the current STEM education milieu, multidimensional claims are the desired targets, and therefore the type of evidence sought must be multidimensional as well. Just as these claims and evidence are multidimensional, the measurement models used to interpret the multidimensional evidence must also be able to model this multidimensional data.

Validation and Reporting: Measurement Models for STEM Assessment

Once assessment developers have clearly articulated the particular assessment purpose and intended inferences, and followed a principled approach to task design, the next step in elaborating a validity argument for the given assessment is to collect empirical data of various types (e.g., Jorion et al., 2015; Pellegrino, DiBello, & Goldman, 2016). The Standards for Educational and Psychological Testing (American Educational Research Association, American Psychological Association, & National Council of Measurement in Education, 2014) specify a variety of forms of evidence that can be used to establish the validity of an assessment given its intended interpretive use (see also Pellegrino et al., 2016). One of the most important forms of evidence regarding how the tasks function, individually and collectively, is actual student performance data. Making sense of those data relative to what was hypothesized and the intended reporting process requires application of various qualitative and quantitative interpretive procedures. The application of psychometric measurement models serves as a core element of the STEM assessment development, validation and reporting process (Wilson, 2005). Such models define the relationship between student scores on individual tasks and the construct, providing the basis for a meaningful interpretation of the scores across all tasks. More specifically, measurement models aggregate student scores across tasks in such a way that they become interpretable in terms of the construct. The choice of the measurement model defines what one can infer about the construct (i.e., competence in integrated STEM). As a consequence, one must carefully consider the intended interpretation and use of the resulting scores before choosing a measurement model. The most commonly used measurement models for integrated STEM assessment are Item Response Theory models and Diagnostic Classification Models.

Item Response Theory

Item Response Theory (IRT) locates students and assessment tasks on the same latent trait (i.e., construct) continuum. Doing so allows for deriving conclusions about: (a) the likely performance of particular students on particular tasks; (b) the progression of a student in developing competence; and (c) the distribution of a sample of students in terms of their progression in developing competence in a domain (e.g., STEM). This is under the assumption that the tasks can be arranged in a way that reflects increasing competence in the domain. IRT also provides a means to examine the extent to which a set of assessment tasks are representative of a developmental perspective about the construct (see the earlier section "Theoretical Framework for Assessment: Reasoning from Evidence"). As a consequence, IRT is often used in the process of developing and validating STEM assessments to examine the extent to which the tasks utilized define a single latent continuum reflecting development of the STEM competency in question (e.g., Jorion et al., 2015; Neumann, Schecker, & Theyßen, 2019), as well as for judging student variability with respect to those STEM competencies (e.g. Hadenfeldt, Neumann, Bernholt, Liu, & Parchmann, 2016; Harwell et al., 2015).

Item Response Theory links students' performance on a set of assessment tasks to their competence through a probabilistic model. This model describes the probability of a student performing successfully on a task as a function of the students' ability (e.g., competence in STEM) and item characteristics (e.g., task difficulty). Four typical IRT models include: (a) the Rasch Model, which, along with (b) the one-parameter logistic (1PL), includes one parameter for each item representing its difficulty; (c) the two-parameter logistic (2PL) model, which includes an additional parameter representing the item's discrimination (i.e., how well the item differentiates among students of differing ability levels); and (d) the three-parameter logistic (3PL) model, which adds a parameter to account for successful performance on forced-choice items due to the opportunity to guess the correct answer (Baker, 2001). IRT models highlight the role of the items in the assessment process. They acknowledge that although items often naturally differ in their difficulty, this variability is actually crucial for assessing different levels of competency among students (Wilson, 2005).

Both the Rasch and the 1PL models arrange persons and items (tasks) on a common continuum, with a "person ability space" on one side and a corresponding "task difficulty space" on the other side. The graphical representation mapping the distribution of students based on their ability onto the distribution of tasks based on their difficulty is commonly known as a Wright Map, an example of which is shown in Figure 19.6. The continuum is such that a person at a given point (e.g., just above 0 on the logit scale) is estimated to have a 50 percent chance of correctly answering a task also located at that given point (e.g., question 5). Tasks that range on the easier side of the continuum (lower down on the map) would be solved correctly by that same person with an increasingly higher probability, and tasks on the more difficult side (further up the map) would be solved correctly by that same person with an increasingly lower probability.

The Rasch model, like the 1PL model, differs from other IRT models in that it assumes that the items all have the same discrimination ability (i.e. all items contribute to the student ability continuum in the same way) and only differ in terms of their difficulty (i.e. their position on the latent continuum). In some cases, however, items or groups of items may differ in the extent to which they contribute to differentiating among students. In this case, we can use the 2PL IRT model, which is statistically equivalent to a confirmatory factor analysis (Wirth & Edwards, 2007). It is commonly used in order to identify items or item groups that exhibit discrimination or factor loadings that differ from the other items. The third model, the 3PL model, is simply a 2PL model with an additional term to adjust the probability of solving an item correctly. This additional term is also called the guessing parameter, as it allows for accounting for the possibility to guess the right answer in forced-choice items. The main use of the 3PL model is to account for the guessing probability or to examine the extent to which items were subject to guessing (e.g., Jorion et al., 2015).

Sometimes if whole groups of items have a similar discrimination that differs from the discrimination of the other items, this indicates that the item groups are assessing different constructs. For such cases, IRT offers multidimensional versions of the described models. These models provide one ability estimate for each dimension, plus an estimation of the correlations between the dimensions—in addition to item difficulty parameters for each item relative to each dimension. This is essentially the same as a series of independent one-dimensional models; however, the multidimensional models provide unbiased estimates of the correlations and student ability estimates because they are accounting for the correlations. Therefore, a multidimensional model is recommended over the use of multiple one-dimensional models (Wu, Adams, & Wilson, 2007).

It is important to note, however, that there are two fundamentally different types of multidimensionality. The first type, which is also known as between-item dimensionality, refers to assessments in which we have different sets of tasks measuring different constructs. For example, one set of tasks requires students to solve problems in chemistry, and one set of tasks requires them to solve mathematical problems. Sometimes, however, we are in a situation where individual tasks are measuring different aspects of a construct. This is the case, for example, when students are required to integrate their knowledge about mathematics and physics in order to solve an engineering problem, such as the egg challenge.[4] Knowledge about mathematics, physics and engineering problem-solving skills

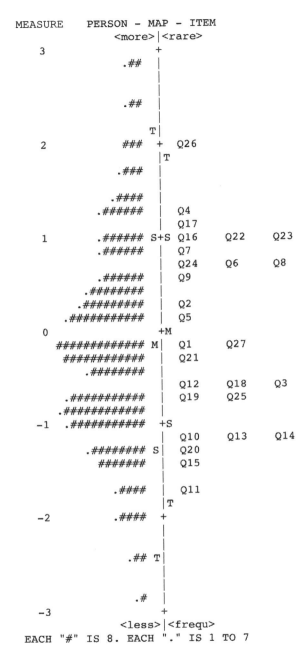

Figure 19.6 Example of a Wright Map showing the distributions of student (left side) and item (right side) performance on a concept inventory. The scale is in logit units.

would all be dimensions of their competence that students might draw on in such an assessment of their competence in engineering. This is also known as *within-item dimensionality*. Interestingly, students do not necessarily have to be competent with respect to each dimension in order to perform successfully on the described problem. It is possible that students exclusively draw on their problem-solving skills to design a solution (e.g., by trial and error), or that they draw on their physics knowledge about the forces acting on an egg upon hitting the ground and mathematics knowledge in how these forces will be spread based on the shape of the egg. That is, students' abilities in the different dimensions can to some extent compensate for each other. Such multidimensionality and the respective models are termed *compensatory models*. The multidimensional versions of Rasch, the 2PL and the 3PL model are all of this type.

Diagnostic Classification Modeling

In some assessments of students' competence, the key dimensions are non-compensatory. Imagine, for example, a task that requires students to develop and use a model of the food chain in a given ecosystem. Obviously, in order to successfully perform this task, students need to integrate their modeling skills with their knowledge about the constituents of the given ecosystem. Neither outstanding modeling skills nor extensive knowledge about the constituents of this ecosystem alone will help students solve the task. This situation requires a different approach to modeling student performance, known as Diagnostic Classification Modeling (DCM). This approach includes a family of models (for an overview, see Rupp & Templin, 2008). Amongst other uses, DCMs have been used to investigate students' responses to an assessment based on a cognitive model that delineates the specific KSAs required to solve each task of a larger task set where the tasks call upon different but overlapping assemblages. Models used in this way have also been referred to as cognitive diagnosis models or cognitive diagnostic models (Rupp & Templin, 2008).

As discussed earlier, integrated STEM competence is characterized by the capacity to integrate different knowledge, skills and abilities to identify and solve problems typical for the domain across a wide(r) range of contexts (Weinert, 2001). In assessment, we are trying to assess if or to what extent students have these KSAs and can bring them together to solve problems in the domain. Sometimes we are interested in which KSAs students do and do not possess; DCMs allow one to answer this question.

Diagnostic classification models are related to IRT models but differ in important assumptions about what governs student success on a task. In IRT models of the type discussed in the previous section, one assumes that performance on a task is predicted through a continuous latent ability (i.e., a single construct). In DCMs, students' performance is predicted by one or more dichotomous latent variables (e.g., the presence or non-presence of one or more KSAs). DCMs allow for a direct interpretation of the results in terms of the KSAs that an individual student possesses. The grain size at which these KSAs are assessed is determined (a priori) by the assessment developer and can be a key part of the assessment design process as described earlier. The heart of a DCM is the so-called Q-matrix which specifies which of the range of *n* (elements of) knowledge, skills or abilities are required for each of the *m* items in the assessment. The information carried by the Q-matrix is often also referred to as the loading structure to highlight the similarity between DCM and (confirmatory) factor analyses (CFAs).[5] In DCMs, each KSA is assumed to be required for successful task performance, and therefore, if a student does not possess a specific KSA required by the task, he or she should not perform well on the task. Thus, DCMs are often considered non-compensatory measurement models (Rupp & Templin, 2008).

One use of DCMs is in the analysis of performance on concept inventories (e.g., Jorion et al., 2015; Kuo, Chen, & de la Torre, 2018). Jorion and colleagues (2015) highlight the potential of DCMs to examine individual students' conceptual profiles; that is, which of the concepts tested by concept inventory students have mastered and which ones they have not. DCMs could also be utilized to detect if students hold a particular misconception or not (e.g., Bradshaw & Templin, 2014). Most existing DCMs can detect if students have mastered or not mastered a particular concept, or if students hold a particular misconception, but not both. However, an incorrect response to an item may be due to a student lacking mastery of a concept, possessing some misconceptions, or both

(Kuo et al., 2018, p. 180). To address this issue, Kuo et al. (2018) recently proposed a DCM that can be used to simultaneously assess mastery of a concept (or any kind of skill, for that matter) and the existence of a misconception.

In summary, while the primary purpose of IRT models is to provide a single score representing students' ability on a latent continuum, the primary purpose of a DCM approach is a more fine-grained diagnostic analysis (Rupp & Templin, 2008). As discussed in the following, the interpretive use context for applying a DCM to assessment data differs from the context of applying IRT.

STEM Assessment Along a Continuum From Classrooms to Large-Scale Interpretive Uses

Assessments can serve a range of different purposes that fall along a continuum from a fine-grained, criterion-based diagnosis to a single-value, norm-based evaluation of student learning. Teachers assess learners' competence to understand where their students are in the learning process, and to plan the next step accordingly. However, teachers also use assessments in order to *grade* student learning, so that the learners and others will know the extent to which learners have developed competence in STEM. Sometimes assessments are designed to assess the extent to which learners have the competencies to be sufficiently prepared for future learning; for example, when universities administer entry or placement tests in order to understand whether learners bring the prerequisites to successfully complete studies in medicine (Hissbach, Klusmann, & Hampe, 2011). Finally, assessment results are used to evaluate the performance of schools, districts or state or national education systems (e.g. Organisation for Economic Co-operation and Development [OECD], 2007). The one end of this continuum is marked by assessments most proximal to instruction and use in the classroom assessments. The other end of the continuum is marked by assessments rather distal to instruction, like (large-scale) assessments for accountability or normative comparison purposes (Ruiz-Primo, Shavelson, Hamilton, & Klein, 2001). Both come with their very own specific characteristics, and we review each in turn.

Classroom-Based Assessments

Assessments proximal to instruction typically aim to provide formative information to the teacher; that is, students' current competence and potential next steps in the instructional process. Classroom assessments are designed or selected by teachers and given as a part of instruction (NRC, 2014). They are given during or closely following an instructional activity or unit. Through classroom-based assessments the teacher aims to obtain information about students' learning. This information can and should be derived from multiple sources, including student verbal contributions, artifacts that students produce during learning or quizzes that the teacher administers at the end of a lesson or shorter instructional unit. Classroom assessments can be designed primarily to guide instruction (formative purposes) or to support decisions made beyond the classroom (summative purposes). Assessments for formative purposes occur during the unit, assessments for summative purposes are administered at the end of the unit. However, ideally even assessments for summative purposes such as end-of-year tests can also serve formative purposes in that they provide students and teachers with feedback about what KSAs students have mastered and what KSAs students are still struggling with and should continue to work on (or the whole class should work on if there are KSAs the whole class has failed to master). In order to provide this kind of detailed feedback to students and teachers, fine-grained information is needed beyond a single overall measure of the extent to which students have developed competence in STEM or a STEM field.

As discussed in the previous section, assessment designed to provide detailed information about students' competence in STEM at the level of the mastery of individual KSAs are well suited to the application of Cognitive Diagnostic Models. This is particularly important in the assessment of integrated STEM competence, where students are typically presented different tasks each requiring a range of KSAs. A total score across all tasks (obtained, for example, through IRT analysis) would provide only general information on where students reside on the latent continuum delineating students' development of competence or integrated competence in STEM. Information on specific ideas or skills students are struggling with would be hidden. For example, a student may be somewhat proficient in constructing explanations but lack understanding of the ideas of energy dissipation and conservation. This student will likely fail to use this idea to construct an explanation of why things stop when they are not continuously supplied with energy. CMDs can be used to provide this level of detailed information. However, it is important to note that in classroom-based assessments, we can often draw only on information from a small number of tasks (sometimes only one task, if we are counting learning activities as a task). Drawing inferences from a small number of tasks requires maximum caution in terms of the conclusions that can be drawn from students' performance on these tasks. In our example here, a student may have understood energy dissipation and conservation but have misread the task or may simply not have been motivated that day to provide an elaborate response. That is, ideally, even or better: especially in terms of more fine-grained formative assessment aiming to obtain evidence about students' mastery of a range of specific KSAs, we need a range of tasks or, more generally, a range of observations, ideally from different sources of evidence (i.e. different types of assessment). The challenge here is to integrate information from different sources. However, DCMs can also help with this. DCMs can, for example, be utilized to analyze performance on a series of different learning activities or, in fact, any kind of task administered to students, as long as these tasks can be categorized in terms of the requirement that successful performance on the task requires the KSA in question.

In summary, designing a diagnostic assessment and interpreting it via DCM is the ideal approach when the aim is to obtain detailed information about the mastery or non-mastery of specific KSAs, as is often the case in classroom-based assessments. In addition to individual student diagnostic information, a DCM-based approach can also be useful for learning about different response strategies of different groups of respondents for the same set of tasks, about different response strategies of single individuals across different tasks and about different response strategies of single individuals within the same task, if data can be collected that provide sufficient information about these cases (Rupp & Templin, 2008, p. 236; see also Pellegrino et al., 2001). The most important aspect of classroom-based assessment is to draw on multiple sources of evidence for reliable and valid inferences, since classroom-based assessments usually involve small numbers of tasks.

Large-Scale Assessments

Large-scale assessments are designed or selected by districts, states or nations to assess student achievement for various purposes including evaluation of the quality of schools and of state or national education systems. They typically test students at a particular age or grade on broad educational goals such as knowledge-in-use in a domain-like science (e.g. NGSS Lead States, 2013). The tasks used in these assessments cover a broad range of different topics across the domain (e.g., high school biology). The question is to which extent students have developed the envisioned competence in the domain. The challenge is to achieve sufficient reliability and validity in the assessment of such a more broadly defined construct given the intended interpretive use. Often large-scale assessments aim to assess the extent to which students are prepared for future learning (e.g., success in higher education). An example is the College Board's AP Chemistry Test, where scores on that test are used by colleges to judge whether students are ready to take courses beyond typical introductory college chemistry. Given such interpretive uses, not only must the assessment represent the construct domain, it also should have high reliability and minimal measurement error so that we are (a) distinguishing well between students and (b) are sufficiently confident that students who meet some scoring benchmark indeed have the knowledge-in-use envisioned as required for the judgement in question (i.e., access to or placement in a higher education program). Ideally, in such testing contexts we are less interested in what specific knowledge students have and more interested in whether students have met a certain benchmark (e.g., solved 60 percent of the questions; Hissbach et al., 2011) or how they compare to other students (e.g., when we are comparing different educational programs). In essence, we aim to obtain a single measure for each student (a) that is a function of students' competence in a domain, and (b) that reliably differentiates between students.

Given such interpretive goals, IRT models are commonly used for large-scale assessments. Such models allow test construction and administration such that different students answer different sets of items drawn from a large pool of domain-relevant tasks that have been previously calibrated in terms of difficulty relative to student ability (for an international overview over large-scale assessments of standards, see Bernholt et al., 2012). In such cases the focus is more on the extent to which a large group of students have met a particular standard than on obtaining information about how well an individual student is doing. If, for example, the Rasch Model has been demonstrated to apply to a population of students and a universe of items, the model will also apply to any sample of students or items (Bond & Fox, 2007). As a consequence, it does not make a difference which students have been administered which items as long as there is a sufficient overlap between items across sets and students having worked on the same item sets. Thus, even though students have been administered different tasks, we obtain estimates for students' ability (e.g., competence) that are all located on the same scale and can thus be easily compared. Assessments like the NAEP and PISA science assessments use such test design, analysis and reporting procedures. In addition, IRT models allow for including additional information in or through the so-called background model. A common method in large-scale assessments is to include descriptive analyses about what students abilities may depend on (see, for example, Rost, Senkbeil, Walter, Carstensen, & Prenzel, 2005). Sometimes in large-scale assessments we are interested in more differentiated analyses such as students' ability in terms of different areas or aspects of the domain. For example, in the assessment of students' competence in experimentation, we may be interested in the extent to which students can plan, carry out or analyze experiments. In this case, we can apply IRT multidimensional models, which will yield information about student competence in different yet related areas of the construct (Neumann et al., 2019).

In summary, large-scale assessments are designed to support inferences about the extent to which students have met benchmarks with respect to pre-defined educational standards that usually focus on one content domain. They typically aim to do so for large samples or entire populations of students, but sometimes they also try to reliably identify whether single students have met certain benchmarks (i.e., in entry, placement or licensure testing). IRT-based approaches provide ways to accommodate requirements of large-scale assessment such as covering a broad range of content or reliably determining students' level of competence relative to other students assessed. Through standard setting procedures, it is also possible to describe the performance continuum in terms of levels of proficiency, which allow for identifying the level of proficiency a student or group of students has achieved in terms of their progression in developing competence in the STEM disciplines.

Conclusion

In STEM education there are many different types of assessments that can be designed for different interpretive purposes and contexts of use. No one approach to assessment can evaluate everything that is important in achieving integrated STEM competence. What is common across all types and approaches is that assessment involves a process of reasoning from evidence that must follow a principled approach to design and interpretation to obtain valid and reliable inferences about competencies that are not directly observable. We have highlighted how the purpose of an assessment, the intended inferences from scores, the design of assessment tasks and the validation and psychometric measurement approaches must all be in alignment. In closing we would also note that innovations in technology are enabling the design of new types of assessments where students can virtually perform complex tasks and provide complex forms of evidence about why they might think the way they do, what they know and how they are learning (Gane et al., 2018). When applied to the assessment of integrated STEM competencies, there are numerous possibilities for innovation at both the classroom and large-scale interpretive use contexts.

In addition to the design and validation of specific assessments, coherent assessment *systems* will need to be created in order to meet the information needs of the various stakeholders in STEM education. Such systems operate across levels from the classroom to schools, districts, states and nations. Pellegrino (2014) suggests five features of a coordinated assessment system: (a) emphasis on assessment of higher-order skills more than on rote memorization; (b) high-fidelity assessment of critical abilities; (c) standards that are internationally benchmarked; (d) assessments that are instructionally sensitive and educationally valuable; and (e) assessments that show strong evidence of being valid, reliable and fair. It is our hope that the principles discussed in this chapter can be applied to inform the creation of such coordinated assessment systems for integrated STEM.

There has been a long-standing divide between the STEM teaching and learning community and the educational assessment community regarding what we assess, how we assess and what the results mean relative to gauging the progress of teaching and learning (Pellegrino, 2017). In this chapter, we have argued that in order for the new vision of integrated STEM education to be successful, all parts of the education system must align with the same goals of the reform. Considering the strong role that assessment plays in classrooms around the world, there is an opportunity for assessment and integrated STEM learning experts to work together to design assessments that help translate this vision for reform into real, authentic learning opportunities for students.

Notes

1. We define practices in the same manner as the Framework for K–12 Science Education (NRC, 2012). A practice refers to authentic "doing" in the discipline, i.e., applying deep disciplinary knowledge by engaging in the same practices that disciplinary experts engage in. Examples of practices include modeling in science, design in engineering, and reasoning abstractly and quantitively in mathematics.
2. In the case of a multidimensional construct, multiple construct maps need to be specified, one for each dimension (NRC, 2014).
3. "Deep" knowledge is relative to the experience of the learner. What is deep disciplinary knowledge for a student who is taking a chemistry class in high school might not be for a chemistry undergraduate student.
4. In the egg challenge, one has to design a device that prevents an egg that is being dropped from a given height from bursting.
5. The most prominent difference being that in factor analysis models, the latent variables are continuous.

References

AAAS. (1993). *Benchmarks for science literacy*. New York, NY: Oxford University Press.

American Educational Research Association, American Psychological Association, & National Council of Measurement in Education. (2014). *Standards for Educational and Psychological Testing*. Washington, DC. American Educational Research Association.

Baker, F. (2001). *The basics of item response theory*. In ERIC clearinghouse on assessment and evaluation. College Park, MD: University of Maryland. Retrieved from http://echo.edres. org:8080/irt/baker

Bernholt, S., Nentwig, P., & Neumann, K. (2012). *Making it tangible—learning outcomes in science education*. Münster: Waxmann.

Bond, T. G., & Fox, C. M. (2007). *Applying the Rasch model: Fundamental measurement in the human sciences* (2nd ed.). Mahwah, NJ: Lawrence Erlbaum Associates Publishers. Retrieved from http://www.worldcat.org/oclc/141188100

Bradshaw, L., & Templin, J. (2014). Combining item response theory and diagnostic classification models: A psychometric model for scaling ability and diagnosing misconceptions. *Psychometrika, 79*(3), 403–425. https://doi.org/10.1007/s11336-013-9350-4

College Board. (2014). *AP chemistry course and exam description* (Revised ed.). New York, NY: The College Board.

Douglas, K. A., Fernandez, T. M., Purzer, Ş., Fosmire, M., & Van Epps, A. S. (2018). The Critical-thinking Engineering Information Literacy Test (CELT): A validation study for fair use among diverse students. *International Journal of Engineering Education, 34*(4), 1347–1362.

Douglas, K. A, Moore, T. J., Merzdorf, H., Li, T., & Johnston, A. (2017). A content analysis of how engineering is assessed in published curricula. *Proceedings of the American Society for Engineering Education.* New Orleans, LA: ASEE – American Society for Engineering Education.

Gane, B. D., Zaidi, S. Z., & Pellegrino, J. W. (2018). Measuring what matters: Using technology to assess multidimensional learning. *European Journal of Education, 53,* 176–187. https://doi.org/10.1111/ejed.12269

Goldman, S. R., Lawless, K., Pellegrino, J., Braasch, J., Manning, F., & Gomes, K. (2012). A technology for assessing multiple source comprehension: An essential skill of the 21st Century. In M. Mayrath, J. Clarke-Midura, & D. H. Robinson (Eds), *Technology-based assessments for 21st century skills: Theoretical and practical implications from modern research* (pp. 173–210). Charlotte, NC: Information Age Publishing.

Gorin, J. S., & Mislevy, R. J. (2013). *Inherent measurement challenges in the Next Generation Science Standards for both formative and summative assessment.* Commissioned paper presented at the K-12 Center at ITS Invitational Research Symposium on Science Assessment, Washington, DC.

Hadenfeldt, J. C., Neumann, K., Bernholt, S., Liu, X., & Parchmann, I. (2016). Students' progression in understanding the matter concept: Students' progression in understanding matter. *Journal of Research in Science Teaching, 53*(5), 683–708. https://doi.org/10.1002/tea.21312

Halloun, I., & Hestenes, D. (1985). The initial knowledge state of college physics students. *American Journal of Physics, 53,* 1043–1055.

Harris, C. J., Krajcik, J. S., Pellegrino, J. W., & DeBarger, A. H. (2019). Designing knowledge-in-use assessments to promote deeper learning. *Educational Measurement: Issues and Practice.* https://doi.org/10.1111/emip.12253

Harris, C. J., Krajcik, J. S., Pellegrino, J. W., & McElhaney, K. W. (2016). *Constructing assessment tasks that blend disciplinary core ideas, crosscutting concepts, and science practices for classroom formative applications.* Menlo Park, CA: SRI International.

Harwell, M., Moreno, M., Phillips, A., Guzey, S. S., Moore, T. J., & Roehrig, G. H. (2015). A study of STEM assessments in engineering, science, and mathematics for elementary and middle school students: A measurement study of STEM assessments. *School Science and Mathematics, 115*(2), 66–74. https://doi.org/10.1111/ssm.12105

Herrmann-Abell, C. F., & DeBoer, G. E. (2011). Using distractor-driven standards-based multiple-choice assessments and Rasch modeling to investigate hierarchies of chemistry misconceptions and detect structural problems with individual items. *Chemistry Education Research and Practice, 12*(2), 184–192. doi:10.1039/C1RP90023D

Hestenes, D., Wells, M., & Swackhamer, G. (1992). Force concept inventory. *The Physics Teacher, 30,* 141–158.

Hissbach, J. C., Klusmann, D., & Hampe, W. (2011). Dimensionality and predictive validity of the HAM-Nat, a test of natural sciences for medical school admission. *BMC Medical Education, 11*(1). https://doi.org/10.1186/1472-6920-11-83

Jorion, N., Gane, B. D., James, K., Schroeder, L., DiBello, L. V., & Pellegrino, J. W. (2015). An analytic framework for evaluating the validity of concept inventory claims: Framework for evaluating validity of concept inventories. *Journal of Engineering Education, 104*(4), 454–496. https://doi.org/10.1002/jee.20104

Krause, S., Birk, J., Bauer, R., Jenkins, B., & Pavelich, M. J. (2004). *Development, testing, and application of a chemistry concept inventory.* In Proceedings of the 34th ASEE/IEEE Frontiers in Education Conference. Retrieved from http://icee.usm.edu/ICEE/conferences/FIEC2004/papers/1213.pdf 2/08/19

Krzywacki, H., Koistinen, L., & Lavonen, J. (2012). Assessment in Finnish mathematics education: Various ways, various needs. In *Proceedings of the 12th International Congress on Mathematical Education: Topic Study Group 33* (pp. 6661–6670). Seoul, Korea. Retrieved from http://www.icme12.org/upload/UpFile2/TSG/0732.pdf

Kuo, B.-C., Chen, C.-H., & de la Torre, J. (2018). A cognitive diagnosis model for identifying coexisting skills and misconceptions. *Applied Psychological Measurement, 42*(3), 179–191. https://doi.org/10.1177/0146621617722791

Messick, S. (1995). Validity of psychological assessment: Validation of inferences from persons' responses and performances as scientific inquiry into score meaning. *American Psychologist, 50*(9), 741. https://doi.org/10.1037/0003-066X.50.9.741

Mislevy, R. J. (2007). Validity by design. *Educational Researcher, 36*(8), 463–469. https://doi.org/10.3102/0013189X07311660

Mislevy, R. J., & Haertel, G. D. (2006). Implications of evidence-centered design for educational testing. *Educational Measurement: Issues and Practices, 25*(4), 6–20.

Mislevy, R. J., Steinberg, L. S., & Almond, R. G. (2003). On the structure of educational assessments. Measurement: Interdisciplinary research and perspectives, *1*, 3–67. doi:10.1207/ s15366359mea0101_02

Moore, T. J., & Smith, K. A. (2014). Advancing the state of the art of STEM integration. *Journal of STEM Education, 15*(1), 5.

National Governors Association Center for Best Practices & Council of Chief State School Officers. (2010). *Common Core State Standards*. Washington, DC: Authors. http://www.corestandards.org

National Research Council [NRC]. (2012). *A framework for K-12 science education: Practices, crosscutting concepts, and core ideas*. Washington, DC: The National Academies Press.

National Research Council [NRC]. (2014). *Developing assessments for the next generation science standards*. Washington, DC: The National Academies Press.

National Research Council [NRC]. (2018). *Science and engineering for grades 6–12: Investigation and design at the center*. Washington, DC, National Academies Press.

Neumann, K., Schecker, H., & Theyßen, H. (2019). Assessing complex patterns of student resources and behavior in the large-scale. *The ANNALS of the American Academy of Political and Social Science, 683*(1), 233–249. doi:10.1177/0002716219844963

Ng, P. G. (2008). Educational reform in Singapore: From quantity to quality. *Education Research on Policy and Practice, 7*, 5–15. https://doi.org/10.1007/s10671-007-9042-x

NGSS Lead States. (2013). *Next generation science standards: For states, by states*. Washington, DC: The National Academies Press.

OECD. (2017). *OECD skills outlook 2017: Skills and global value chains*. Paris: OECD Publishing. https://doi.org/10.1787/9789264273351–en

Organisation for Economic Co-operation and Development [OECD]. (2007). *Programme for international student assessment (PISA) 2006: Science competencies for tomorrow's world*. Paris: Organisation for Economic Co-operation and Development. Retrieved from http://public.eblib.com/EBLPublic/PublicView.do?ptiID=359823

Osborne, J. (2010). Arguing to learn in science: The role of collaborative, critical discourse. *Science, 328*, 463–466.

Pavelich, M., Jenkins, B., Birk, J., Bauer, R., & Krause, S. (2004). *Development of a chemistry concept inventory for use in chemistry, materials and other engineering courses*. In Proceedings of the 2004 American Society for Engineering Education Annual Conference & Exposition. Retrieved from https://s3.amazonaws.com/academia.edu. documents/39367909/pavelich.pdf?AWSAccessKeyId=AKIAIWOWYYGZ2Y53UL3A&Expires=15496 43009&Signature=w7Oc23%2FWL6dgYCWgd0seQVsheRI%3D&response-content-disposition=inline %3B%20filename%3DDevelopment_of_a_Chemistry_Concept_Inven.pdf 2/08/19

Pellegrino, J. W. (2013). Proficiency in science: Assessment challenges and opportunities. *Science, 340*(6130), 320–323.

Pellegrino, J. W. (2014). Assessment as a positive influence on 21st century teaching and learning: A systems approach to progress. *Psicología Educativa, 20*(2), 65–77. https://doi.org/10.1016/j.pse.2014.11.002

Pellegrino, J. W. (2017). The two disciplines problem—'it's like Déjà vu all over again!' *Assessment in Education: Principles, Policy & Practice, 24*(3), 359–368. doi:10.1080/0969594X.2017.1326876

Pellegrino, J. W., Chudowsky, N., & Glaser, R. (2001). *Knowing what students know: The science and design of educational assessment*. Washington, DC: National Academy Press.

Pellegrino, J. W., DiBello, L. V., & Brophy, S. P. (2014). The science and design of assessment in engineering education. In A. Johri & B. M. Olds (Eds.), *The Cambridge handbook of engineering education research* (pp. 571–598). https://doi.org/10.1017/cbo9781139013451.036

Pellegrino, J. W., DiBello, L. V., & Goldman, S. R. (2016). A framework for conceptualizing and evaluating the validity of instructionally relevant assessments. *Educational Psychologist, 51*(1), 59–81.

Rost, J., Senkbeil, M., Walter, O., Carstensen, C. H., & Prenzel, M. (2005). Naturwissenschaftliche Grundbildung im Ländervergleich. In P.-K. Deutschland (Ed.), *PISA 2003. Der zweite Vergleich der Länder in Deutschland - Was wissen und können Jugendliche?* (pp. 103–124). Münster: Waxmann.

Roth, K. J., Druker, S. L., Garnier, H. E., Lemmens, M., Chen, C., Kawanaka, T., & Gallimore, R. (2006). *Highlights from the TIMSS 1999 video study of eighth-grade science teaching (NCES 2006-17). U. S. Department of education, national center for education statistics*. Washington, DC: U.S. Government Printing Office.

Ruiz-Primo, M. A., Shavelson, R. J., Hamilton, L., & Klein, S. (2001). On the evaluation of systemic science education reform: Searching for instructional sensitivity. *Journal of Research in Science Teaching, 39*, 369–393.

Rupp, A. A., & Templin, J. L. (2008). Unique characteristics of diagnostic classification models: A comprehensive review of the current state-of-the-art. *Measurement: Interdisciplinary Research & Perspective, 6*(4), 219–262. https://doi.org/10.1080/15366360802490866

Sadler, P. M. (1998). Psychometric models of student conceptions in science: Reconciling qualitative studies and distractor-driven assessment instruments. *Journal of Research in Science Teaching, 35*(3), 265–296.

Seibert, G., Hamel, L., Haynie, K., Mislevy, R., & Bao, H. (2006). *Mystery powders: An application of the PADI design system using the four-process delivery system (PADI Technical Report 15)*. Menlo Park, CA: SRI International.

Songer, N. B., & Ruiz-Primo, M. A. (2012). Assessment and science education: Our essential new priority? *Journal of Research in Science Teaching, 49*(6), 683–690. https://doi.org/10.1002/tea.21033

Streveler, R. A., Miller, R. L., Santiago Román, A. I., Nelson, M. A., Geist, M. R., & Olds, B. M. (2011). Using the "assessment triangle" as a framework for developing concept inventories: A case study using the thermal and transport concept inventory. *International Journal of Engineering Education, 27*(5), 1–17.

Tekkumru-Kisa, M., Stein, M. K., & Schunn, C. (2015). A framework for analyzing cognitive demand and content-practices integration: Task analysis guide in science. *Journal of Research in Science Teaching, 52*(5), 659–685. https://doi.org/10.1002/tea.21208

Thissen-Roe, A., Hunt, E., & Minstrell, J. (2004). The DIAGNOSER project: Combining assessment and learning. *Behavior Research Methods, Instruments, & Computers, 36*(2), 234–240.

Ufer, S., & Neumann, K. (2018). Measuring competencies. In F. Fischer, C. Hmelo-Silver, S. Goldman, & P. Reimann (Eds.), *International handbook of the learning sciences* (pp. 433–443). New York, NY: Routledge.

Weinert, F. E. (2001). *Leistungsmessungen in Schulen*. Weinheim: Beltz.

Weiss, I. R., Pasley, J. D., Smith, P. S., Banilower, E. R., & Heck, D. J. (2003). *Looking inside the classroom*. Chapel Hill, NC: Horizon Research Inc. http://www.horizon-research.com/horizonresearchwp/wp-content/uploads/2013/04/complete-1.pdf

Wilson, M. (2005). *Constructing measures: An item response modeling approach 1667*. Mahwah, NJ: Lawrence Erlbaum Associates.

Wirth, R. J., & Edwards, M. C. (2007). Item factor analysis: Current approaches and future directions. *Psychological Methods, 12*(1), 58–79.

Wu, M. L., Adams, R. J., & Wilson, M. R. (2007). *Acer ConQuest: Version 2.0*. Camberwell, Victoria: Australia Council for Educational Research.

SECTION 4

Critical Issues in STEM

20

INTERSECTIONALITY IN STEM EDUCATION RESEARCH

Geraldine L. Cochran, Mildred Boveda, and Chanda Prescod-Weinstein

Introduction

On a rudimentary level, intersectionality is concerned with the power and access that is mitigated by the intersection of multiple identities. Based on social-demographic identities, some groups of individuals have either been marginalized or provided valuation and affordances that other groups have not experienced. Intersectionality, which is concerned with the experiences of individuals at the axes of intersecting identities, offers a more robust potential for accountability and responsiveness to upend inequity or disparate representation than considering one identity independent from others. As theory in research, intersectionality requires that any socio-demographic consideration is interwoven with other socio-demographic power differentials and normativities (Lykke, 2010). As an analytical framework, intersectionality involves three different forms of analyses: anti-categorical approaches, intra-categorical complexity analysis, and inter-categorial complexity analysis (see McCall, 2005). We turn to intersectionality as a lens for conceptualizing how differences are considered in interdisciplinary STEM education research to examine minoritized categories of race, gender, dis/ability, linguistic origin, age, socioeconomic status (SES), class, ethnicity, religion, sexuality, nationality, or citizenship simultaneously intersecting within the STEM education context.

In this chapter, we argue that integrated STEM education research must consider intersectionality as it relates to the intersecting identities of those conducting the research as well as the populations being studied (e.g., students, pre-service teachers, teachers, and other professionals). Two pertinent goals in STEM education include broadening participation in the STEM workforce and creating the next generation of innovators and change-makers. As researchers seek to address challenges in STEM education through research, STEM education researchers must attend to who is engaging in the research and who serve as participants. Researchers must ask: whose voices are being silenced, and whose experiences are being erased? The answers to these questions should influence the design of research, the collaborations formed, and the theories and frameworks utilized in STEM education. We forward that understanding intersectionality, in conjunction with critical race theory, is especially useful in achieving these diversifying goals. STEM education researchers who study thoughtfully executed integrated STEM could help to identify praxis and processes that mitigate oppressive forces in education and in the workforce.

Intersectionality as theory in research offers the potential for contextualized STEM inquiry. When intersectionality is used as an overarching framework, it motivates the research questions that are asked, the tools used to answer those questions, the analysis of the data, and the interpretation of findings, resulting in the potential for more nuanced understandings of individuals with multiple and intersecting minoritized identities. STEM education researchers must seek a robust understanding of intersectionality and how it influences STEM education interventions and/or the research conducted. Failing to attend to the lived experiences of individuals with multiple and intersecting minoritized identities is consequential. At best, favorable outcomes from research will not be sustainable, and at worst, the result will exacerbate the problems of inequity and injustice in STEM, resulting in a cul-de-sac of research in STEM education, either hitting a dead end or going in circles.

Historical Implications of Intersectionality and the Experiences of Minoritized People in STEM

In our collaborative chapter, we turn to intersectionality and critical race theory as analytical lenses to discuss the potential of intersectionality in STEM education research. We begin by providing a brief etymology of the term and provide historical context of its use. We explain the utility of intersectionality and critical race theory when examining STEM education. Again, we do this by anchoring our understanding of the need for intersectionality in the historical treatment and current inequities in STEM education, and the persistent disregard for the contributions of minoritized people to the STEM fields.

Mapping Out Intersectionality: Conceptual Framing

Kimberlé Crenshaw (1989) was situated in legal studies and Patricia Hill Collins (1990) in sociology when they drew from Black feminist discourse to introduce "intersectionality" in their respective fields. As Black women in the United States (e.g., hooks, 1981; Lorde, 1980) and Europe (e.g., Carby, 1982; Mirza, 1986) insisted that the experiences of being women in a patriarchal society could not be disentangled with that of being Black in a racist one, the term demonstrated how sexism and racism are entangled with one another and with other oppressive systems (e.g., classism, ableism, heteronormativity). Intersectionality, therefore, is not only about the recognition of different sociocultural identity markers (e.g., gender, ethnicity, race, nationality, sexuality, dis/ability), or even about how these markers intersect, but also about the political and oppressive forces associated with being marked as multiply different. Collins (2000) offers how intersectionality operates within a complex matrix of oppression and domination; eschewing these complexities is especially damaging to the most vulnerable people of a marginalized community. Moving away from privileging binaried thinking, Alfredo Artiles (2013) argues on behalf of the utility of intersectionality as an analytical tool for addressing complexity in education research. In this chapter, we further embrace complexity by putting the increasing dialogue about STEM identities (Cribbs, Hazari, Sonnert, & Sadler, 2015; Godwin, Potvin, Hazari, & Lock, 2016; Hazari, Cass, & Beattie, 2015) in conversation with the extant literature on intersectionality in STEM education. In our condensed genealogy of intersectionality, we begin by discussing some of the tensions that arise when examining intersectionality across disciplines and global contexts. We then discuss the potential collaborative and political implications of addressing the intersectionality of diverse students across STEM.

Since the introduction of the term, intersectionality has traveled beyond Collins and Crenshaw's respective disciplinary and geographical bounds. It is described as both a practical intervention and an academic framework, a social movement and a theoretical/analytical orientation (Lykke, 2010; McCall, 2005). Those mapping out intersectionality studies have noted that intersectionality is shaped by where and who is drawing from it; these locations may, at times, create tensions (Mügge, Montoya, Emejulu, & Weldon, 2018). Women of Color around the world have expressed concern that focusing on the North American etymology of intersectionality privileges a US-centric and Global North perspective of the term (Carastathis, 2008; Hancock, 2016). Bilge (2013) argues that the color-evasive approach by which intersectionality has been taken up in the neoliberal academy is colonial and has whitewashed race from the concept in order to be more marketable to a greater audience in the academy. In addition to geographic locations, academic disciplines also serve as a different space where the meaning of intersectionality can be forged. "Insights and nuances can be gained by attending to the institutional and field-specific ways that intersectionality is articulated" (Cho, Crenshaw, & McCall, 2013, p. 792).

Mügge et al. (2018) found that scholars' intersectional identities, geographic location, and the composition of their field play a substantive role with regard to the approach to intersectionality and how this scholarship is received. In centering its Black feminist genealogy and situating ourselves as four intersectionally diverse Black women from the United States, we argue that any analysis of intersectionality and STEM must start with the acknowledgement of the historical underrepresentation of minoritized women throughout the various disciplinary communities represented. Understanding that the positionality of a scholar influences whether and how they turn to intersectionality, we insist on the understanding of the Black feminist epistemic origins of intersectionality, not to erase or diminish other multiply-minoritized scholars' contribution to intersectionality studies, but as a reminder of the epistemic locations that initially engendered this term.

Critical Race Theory in STEM Education

Like intersectionality as framed by Crenshaw, critical race theory began within the academic discipline of legal studies and is defined by Delgado and Stefancic (2001) as "a collection of activists and scholars interested in studying and transforming the relationship among race, racism, and power" (p. 2). They go on to argue that critical race theory subverts the traditional civil rights mission by questioning the very existence of established structures of power (i.e., "the liberal order") rather than attempting to make them more equitable. Intersectionality and critical race theory respond to the need for critical legal studies to address how ascribed identities influence the application of law. Beyond legal studies, intersectionality and critical race theory teach scholars to challenge our foundational conception of who does STEM and why (Harper, 2010). Together, they provide analytic frameworks for refusing the idea that science is a race-neutral process, instead giving us a mechanism for analyzing how science is distributed to people and how power is distributed in science (Crenshaw, 1989; Ray, 2019; Peller, 1996).

The relationship between science, race, and rights has long been complex. Science has been a site of abuse for People of Color in the United States and its unfederated colonies. Here we provide examples that come from the Black American experience, acknowledging that People of Color in this country and around the world have also been exploited (e.g., Genz, 2018). Thomas Jefferson, a supposed "Founding Father," justified slavery by noting that enslaved Black people were *inherently* unhappy; instead of connecting their unhappiness with their state of enslavement, he connected their discontent with their level of *melanation* or geographic origins (Jefferson, 1787). Eugenicist ideas persisted beyond the antebellum era, and even today debates about *The Bell Curve* (Herrnstein & Murray, 1996)—that connected genetics and intelligence, thus suggesting the superiority of white people—are upheld in some academic circles. J. Marion Sims, the "father" of gynecology, infamously experimented on enslaved Black women without anesthesia. What he learned saved the lives of many white women, but his belief that Black women did not truly feel pain was effectively a form of torture (Washington, 2010). Black Americans remember the Tuskegee Experiment, where Black men who were exposed to syphilis were subjected to a study for 40 years, lied to about having the disease, and never offered the penicillin which would have cured them. The experiment came to an end only in 1972 because of a whistleblower. The fallout from broken research in the social and hard sciences loom large in the lives of Black Americans, as does the erasure of their contributions to advancements in STEM, thus shaping the community's relationship with science (Nelson, 2013).

There are tensions around how to understand the history and future of science with regard to race because of the significant history of using "race science" to *physically* harm People of Color and justify their exclusion from pursuing *intellectual* activities such as science education and research. Yet it is also evident that people of African descent were expert agriculturalists and their value as enslaved subjects was partly because of this intellectual capital (see, e.g., Carney, 1998, 2002). African peoples have, like all other peoples, their own cosmologies and astronomical systems which date back millennia. Even as 20th-century medical abuses continued, the Algebra Project reimagined math—and by extension, STEM education—as a tool in the struggle for civil rights (Moses, Kamii, Swap, & Howard, 1989; Moses & Cobb, 2002).

At the same time, science has also been reconfigured by (Black) American scholars and creatives as the stuff of revolutionary dreams in Afrofuturism (Dery, 1994; Nelson, 2002). Afrofuturism is the stuff of science fiction, for example, rooted in a recognition of the very real way that people of African descent have always been scientists and technologists. In that sense, Afrofuturism is a reclamation activity with implications for STEM pedagogy. Rather than imagining science as a space to be penetrated by barrier-breaking Black scientists, Afrofuturism recognizes Black thinkers as people who were always doing science and producing technology. To professional scientists, researchers, and STEM educators who are also Black, the implications for how this mode of thinking could transform Black children's relationship with STEM is critical.

The critical race theory movement provides a useful intervention in the effort to understand the interstices and divides between standpoints on the relationship between race, rights and STEM. Yosso (2005) importantly notes that critical race theory shifts discourse away from a deficit perspective on communities of color to one that understands traditionally minoritized peoples as intellectually and culturally rich communities. Critical race theory therefore acts, in tandem with intersectionality, as a powerful place from which to understand the social location of Black people—and more broadly, People of Color—relative to matrices of domination in science and STEM research.

Intersectionality and critical race theory urge us to consider power dynamics in the STEM classroom. What does it mean, for example, to ask a racially and ethnically diverse classroom questions in introductory physics that presume intuitive familiarity with American football and the mechanics of a car? Who has access to activities that enrich spatial intelligence? Introductory college-level physical science course evaluation structures are typically embedded with the idea that a good STEM student is one who has a "natural" spatial intuition (Hsi, Linn, & Bell, 2013). Critical race theory and intersectionality both urge us to consider the power of this underlying assumption and to make manifest how structural inequalities shape who succeeds and who fails under this paradigm. If Black girls do not have the same access to spatial intelligence building activities as white boys during their childhoods, the playing field on that physics syllabus can hardly be equal.

Intersectionality and critical race theory, in effect, demand that we see race in particular where it is usually invisibilized and that we analyze its presence as a matter of mapping where power lies. That it comes out of legal studies can hardly be surprising given that so much of civil rights activity was focused on both legislation and jurisprudence. But as a framework, it does not need to remain within discipline, even as we can draw connections between cases such as *Regents of University of California v. Bakke*, in which a white NASA engineer successfully sued to end affirmative action that used racial quotas. In his dissent to the decision, Associate Supreme Court Justice Thurgood Marshall, who had argued the *Brown v. Board* case before the court 25 years before, lamented the dearth of Black doctors, scientists, and engineers: "Although Negroes represent 11.5% of the population, they are only 1.2% of the lawyers and judges, 2% of the physicians, 2.3% of the dentists, 1.1% of the engineers and 2.6% of the college and university professors" (*Regents of the University of California v. Bakke*, 1978). Critical race theory demands that we map out and disrupt the power dynamics that continue to keep these numbers low.

Intersectionality in STEM Education Research and Discipline-Based Education Research

It is particularly important to consider the interdisciplinary nature of STEM education research. Integrated STEM pushes back against the discipline-structured ideas of science and ways of knowing. We understand that in addition to the historical abuses delineated earlier, Indigenous knowledges have been dismissed in the name of westernized definitions of fields that have in term resulted in the erasure and invalidation of the work of non-westernized people (Dei, 2000). The application of intersectionality in STEM education research in discipline-based settings can inform the use and application of this framework in integrated settings, yet that is merely a first step. For example Weinberg and Sample McMeeking (2017) describe the tradeoffs as teachers make decisions about interdisciplinary curricula and the extent to which it is a "fit" with the classroom and students. An understanding of intersectionality could have ameliorated the trade-offs the high school teachers in their study felt compelled to make. We thus examine how discipline-based education research (DBER) has addressed the needs of people with multiple marginalized identities and make connections to how intersectionality might shape integrated STEM education research. Research on integrated STEM pedagogies that factor in intersectionality, we forward, has the potential to advance agendas related to broadening participation in STEM classrooms.

DBER is a research area aimed at improving STEM education, conducted by researchers with expertise in both a disciplinary content area as well as education specializations (e.g., curriculum development, assessment, teacher preparation; NRC, 2012). The five long-term goals of DBER research are to: (1) "understand how people learn the concepts, practices, and ways of thinking of science and engineering;" (2) "understand the nature and development of expertise in a discipline;" (3) "help to identify and measure appropriate learning objectives and instructional approaches that advance students toward those objectives;" (4) "contribute to the knowledge base in a way that can guide the translation of DBER findings to classroom practice;" and (5) "identify approaches to make science and engineering education broad and inclusive" (NRC, 2012, p. 9).

If one goal of integrated STEM education is to "help students make meaning out of and gain interest in the STEM subjects and careers" (see Chapter 1), then integrated STEM education researchers do well to learn from STEM DBER that utilizes intersectionality to understand the experiences of students enrolled in STEM courses. A focus on how curriculum is developed and content delivered without a consideration of the impact of the environment and pedagogical strategies on students with multiple marginalized identities is dangerous. For example, the success of young Women of Color in physics depends on their ability to navigate environments that question their belonging and competence (Ong, 2005). Prior to the term intersectionality being coined, a conference was convened to address the dearth of literature on "minority women in science" and the reality that the needs of "minority women in science" were not being met (Malcom, Hall, & Brown, 1976). In that report, the authors spoke to a social group neglected because of their points of intersection, which McCall (2005) refers to as an *intracategorical approach* to intersectionality. Integrated STEM educators run the risk of neglecting student needs if intersectionality is not taken into account.

As a second example, one of the pedagogical strategies utilized in teaching integrated STEM is active learning. Again, using physics as an example, physics education researchers have written extensively about the benefits of using active learning (or interactive engagement) in physics classrooms to improve learning (Meltzer & Thornton, 2012). However, Nissen and Shemwell (2016) found that women's self-efficacy lowered more than men's in an introductory physics course with interactive engagement. Self-efficacy is a predictor for a student's task persistence (Cervone & Peake, 1986) as well as for a students' performance in mathematical problem solving (Pajares & Miller, 1994). Thus, it is imperative that researchers in integrated STEM education research tend toward intersectionality, and some DBER provides examples of how this can be done.

We forward that intersectionality, as discussed previously, must be considered to (1) design empirical research on how STEM teachers might identify systemic, classroom, and curricular inequities that exist and the social conditions that perpetuate these inequities; (2) conduct empirical research on how STEM teachers develop awareness and understanding of the identities of *individual* students and how these might be considered and accommodated; (3) theorize and conceptualize the intersection between culturally sustaining pedagogies, intersectionality, and integrated STEM education; and (4) engage in research on how interdisciplinary approaches might support or contribute to inclusive classrooms.

Intersectionality to Facilitate in Collaboration Across Education Equity Communities

The often-seen commitments to broadening participation are insufficient in and of themselves if there is a failure to attend to the socio-historical reasons for the exclusion, even exploitation, of minoritized people in westernized sciences and academic spaces. Classrooms, schools, and institutions must adopt inclusive pedagogies and classroom cultures that recognize and value students' and educators' intersectionalities. In this handbook, for example, there are chapters that emphasize English language learners (ELL)—with linguistic markers of identity—and Special Education—the disability markers. But as Guzman-Orth, Supalo, and King note in Chapter 25, "students from special populations are heterogeneous." Just a few years after Crenshaw (1989) first published the term, Natapoff (1995) called on intersectionality to present a legal rejoinder to a court case in which it was decided that special education should take priority over bilingual education service. Natapoff argued that intersectionality insists that both services are relevant, as bilingual special education students cannot compartmentalize these intersecting educational needs. Different equity-oriented education research communities, such as special education, urban education, bilingual education, and critical race studies in education, have turned to intersectionality to address how primary and secondary schooling are complicit in intersectional oppressions. We argue that chapters like this one can enhance conversations and collaborative opportunities for collaboration across equity communities and among STEM education researchers.

Many advocates of integrated STEM education disagree when it comes to how much emphasis should be placed on the four discrete disciplines of science, technology, engineering/engineering design, and mathematics and how they should be integrated (see Chapter 1). Discipline-based education researchers take an even more narrow perspective on the term "disciplines" and look at disciplinary content areas. Research indicates that this is important, as disciplinary identity related to content areas is an identity marker, though not considered a socio-demographic identity, and is relevant to experiences and persistence in STEM education (Hazari, Sonnert, Sadler, & Shanahan, 2010; Hazari, Sadler, & Sonnert, 2013). In this way, integrated STEM education researchers might learn from DBER that has focused on the intersection of various identity markers within specific disciplines. For example, some have focused on Women of Color in particular disciplines, such as Women of Color in physics (Ko, Kachchaf, Hodari, & Ong, 2014; Ko, Kachchaf, Ong, & Hodari, 2013), computing (Hodari, Ong, Ko, & Smith, 2016), and computer science (Ong, 2011). Still others have focused on the intersection of race and gender in specific disciplines, such as Hispanic Women in engineering (Martin, Simmons, & Yu, 2013) and Black Women in physics (Rosa & Mensah, 2016). We know that students may have wildly different experiences within a discipline based on their social-cultural identities, which may explain the variances in representation that we see within the disciplines. This is true even at the subdisciplinary level. For example, representation for women in electrical, mechanical, and aerospace engineering is 13.7%, 14.8%, and 13.5% respectively. However, in the subdisciplines of biomedical and chemical engineering, representation is much higher at 44.0% and 33.2%, respectively (Yoder, 2017).

Discipline-based STEM education researchers have also investigated the intersections of science, STEM, or disciplinary specific identity and socio-demographic identities, including, intersections of racial/gender identity and disciplinary/science identity (Hazari et al., 2015; Hazari et al., 2013; Hyater-Adams, Fracchiolla, Finkelstein, & Hinko, 2018; Lock & Hazari, 2016; Malone & Barabino, 2009). This work holds promise in integrated STEM education research as it has the potential to address recruitment and retention in STEM education for individuals with marginalized identities. The climate and culture within these narrowly defined disciplines are often exclusionary by design, as their power lies in their ability to determine what is considered study within the field and who is allowed to study these things. This often leads to the exclusion and further marginalization of people from multiply marginalized groups. Integrated STEM education may be the answer to breaking down these rigidly defined and exclusionary conceptualizations of disciplines.

More discipline-based STEM education researchers have aimed to reveal the experiences of individuals marginalized by intersecting identities by disaggregating data by multiple identities (Ohland et al., 2011) or focusing on the experiences of individuals with intersecting marginalized identities. Yet literature reviews in STEM education reveal a need for more research utilizing intersectionality as a framework and more work focused on intersections using identities related to social-class, disabilities, and sexuality (Beddoes, Borrego, & Jesiek, 2009; Eddy & Brownell, 2016; Lubienski & Bowen, 2000; Traxler, Cid, Blue, & Barthelemy, 2016).

Conclusion

Historically, science, technology, engineering, and mathematics have been used as tools to oppress marginalized people and maintain structures and hegemony. Simultaneously, science, technology, engineering, mathematics and integrated STEM education research has been used as a tool to disrupt hegemony. The traditional European and patriarchal epistemologies of what counts as science, the Cartesian way of compartmentalizing in science, and the western emphasis on rationality and reason in science has yielded Indigenous knowledge and the knowledge and ways of knowing by women and People of Color as inferior (Dei, 2000). Research on STEM education that employs intersectionality will enable researchers to understand the complexities of STEM teaching and learning, and the experiences of learners (whether they are P-12, undergraduate, or graduate students) in traditional and non-traditional educational settings.

Intersectionality pushes us to go beyond this white supremacist, patriarchal, imperialist narrow view of science and STEM. It allows researchers to interrogate dominant and mainstream notions of STEM, to give attention to intersections and connectedness, and to recognize the progenitors of STEM from marginalized backgrounds, their contributions to STEM, and the challenges students face in the current STEM education system. Intersectionality in STEM education research requires stepping outside of the confines and boundaries of what has been seen as STEM and broadening the notion of what is to be counted as STEM. It is encouraging researchers to begin decolonizing STEM and integrated STEM education.

References

Artiles, A. J. (2013). Untangling the racialization of disabilities. *Du Bois Review: Social Science Research on Race*, *10*(02), 329–347. https://doi.org/10.1017/S1742058X13000271

Beddoes, K., Borrego, M., & Jesiek, B. K. (2009, October). Mapping international perspectives on gender in engineering education research. In *2009 39th IEEE frontiers in education conference* (pp. 1–6). San Antonio, TX: IEEE.

Bilge, S. (2013). Intersectionality undone: Saving intersectionality from feminist intersectionality studies. *Du Bois Review: Social Science Research on Race, 10*(2), 405–424. https://doi.org/10.1017/S1742058X13000283

Carastathis, A. (2008). The invisibility of privilege: A critique of intersectional models of identity. *Les Ateliers de l'Éthique, 3ᵈ2ᴅ*, 23–38.

Carby, H. (1982). White woman listen: Black feminism and the boundaries of sisterhood. In Centre for Contemporary Cultural Studies (Eds.), *The empire strikes back*. London: Hutchinson. *Kerry Carrington*.

Carney, J. A. (1998). The role of African rice and slaves in the history of rice in the Americas. *Human Ecology, 26*(4), 526. https://doi.org/10.1023/A:1018716524160

Carney, J. A. (2002). *Black rice: The African origins of rice cultivation in the Americas*. Cambridge: Harvard University Press.

Cervone, D., & Peake, P. K. (1986). Anchoring, efficacy, and action: The influence of judgmental heuristics on self–efficacy judgments and behavior. *Journal of Personality and Social Psychology, 50*(3), 492.

Cho, S., Crenshaw, K. W., & McCall, L. (2013). Toward a field of intersectionality studies: Theory, applications, and praxis. *Signs: Journal of Women in Culture and Society, 38*(4), 785–810. https://doi.org/10.1086/669608

Collins, P. H. (1990). Toward an Afrocentric feminist epistemology. *Turning Points in Qualitative Research, 47*.

Collins, P. H. (2000). Gender, black feminism, and black political economy. *The Annals of the American Academy of Political and Social Science, 568*(1), 41–53. https://doi.org/10.1177/000271620056800105

Crenshaw, K. (1989). Demarginalizing the intersection of race and sex: A black feminist critique of antidiscrimination doctrine, feminist theory and antiracist politics. *University of Chicago Legal Forum, 139*.

Cribbs, J. D., Hazari, Z., Sonnert, G., & Sadler, P. M. (2015). Establishing an explanatory model for mathematics identity. *Child Development, 86*(4), 1048–1062. https://doi.org/10.1111/cdev.12363

Dei, G. J. S. (2000). Rethinking the role of indigenous knowledges in the academy. *International Journal of Inclusive Education, 4*(2), 111–132.

Delgado, R., & Stefancic, J. (2001). *Critical race theory: An introduction*. New York, NY: New York University Press.

Dery, M. (1994). Black to the future: Interviews with Samuel R. Delany, Greg Tate, and Tricia Rose. In M. Dery (Ed.), *Flame wars: The discourse of cyberculture* (pp. 179–222). Durham, NC: Duke University Press.

Eddy, S. L., & Brownell, S. E. (2016). Beneath the numbers: A review of gender disparities in undergraduate education across science, technology, engineering, and math disciplines. *Physical Review Physics Education Research, 12*(2), 020106. https://doi.org/10.1103/PhysRevPhysEducRes.12.020106

Genz, J. H. (2018). *Breaking the shell voyaging from nuclear refugees to people of the sea in the Marshall Islands*. Honolulu: University of Hawai'i Press.

Godwin, A., Potvin, G., Hazari, Z., & Lock, R. (2016). Identity, critical agency, and engineering: An affective model for predicting engineering as a career choice. *Journal of Engineering Education, 105*(2), 312–340. https://doi.org/10.1002/jee.20118

Hancock, A.-M. (2016). *Intersectionality: An intellectual history*. New York, NY: Oxford University Press. https://doi.org/10.1093/acprof:oso/9780199370368.001.0001

Harper, S. R. (2010). An anti–deficit achievement framework for research on students of color in STEM. *New Directions for Institutional Research, 148*(148), 63–74. https://doi.org/10.1002/ir.362

Hazari, Z., Cass, C., & Beattie, C. (2015). Obscuring power structures in the physics classroom: Linking teacher positioning, student engagement, and physics identity development. *Journal of Research in Science Teaching, 52*(6), 735–762. https://doi.org/10.1002/tea.21214

Hazari, Z., Sadler, P. M., & Sonnert, G. (2013). The science identity of college students: Exploring the intersection of gender, race, and ethnicity. *Journal of College Science Teaching, 42*(5), 82–91.

Hazari, Z., Sonnert, G., Sadler, P. M., & Shanahan, M. C. (2010). Connecting high school physics experiences, outcome expectations, physics identity, and physics career choice: A gender study. *Journal of Research in Science Teaching, 47*(8), 978–1003. https://doi.org/10.1002/tea.20363

Herrnstein, R. J., & Murray, C. (1996). *The bell curve: Intelligence and class structure in American life*. New York, NY: Simon & Schuster.

Hodari, A. K., Ong, M., Ko, L. T., & Smith, J. M. (2016). Enacting agency: The strategies of women of color in computing. *Computing in Science & Engineering, 18*(3), 58–68. https://doi.org/10.1109/MCSE.2016.44

hooks, b. (1981). *Ain't I a woman: Black women and feminism*. Boston, MA: South End Press.

Hsi, S., Linn, M. C., & Bell, J. E. (2013). The role of spatial reasoning in engineering and the design of spatial instruction. *Journal of Engineering Education, 86*(2), 151–158. https://doi.org/10.1002/j.2168-9830.1997.tb00278.x

Hyater-Adams, S., Fracchiolla, C., Finkelstein, N., & Hinko, K. (2018). Critical look at physics identity: An operationalized framework for examining race and physics identity. *Physical Review Physics Education Research, 14*(1), 010132. https://doi.org/10.1103/PhysRevPhysEducRes.14.010132

Jefferson, T. (1787). *Notes on the state of Virginia*. London: Printed for John Stockdale.

Ko, L. T., Kachchaf, R. R., Hodari, A. K., & Ong, M. (2014). Agency of women of color in physics and astronomy: Strategies for persistence and success. *Journal of Women and Minorities in Science and Engineering, 20*(2). https://doi.org/10.1615/JWomenMinorScienEng.2014008198

Ko, L. T., Kachchaf, R. R., Ong, M., & Hodari, A. K. (2013, January). Narratives of the double bind: Intersectionality in life stories of women of color in physics, astrophysics and astronomy. In *AIP conference proceedings* (Vol. 1513, No. 1, pp. 222–225). Philadelphia, PA: American Institute of Physics.

Lock, R. M., & Hazari, Z. (2016). Discussing underrepresentation as a means to facilitating female students' physics identity development. *Physical Review Physics Education Research, 12*(2), 020101.

Lorde, A. (1980). Age, race, class, and sex: Women redefining difference. *Women in Culture: An Intersectional Anthology for Gender and Women's Studies*, 16–22.

Lubienski, S. T., & Bowen, A. (2000). Who's counting? A survey of mathematics education research 1982–1998. *Journal for Research in Mathematics Education*, 626–633. https://doi.org/10.2307/749890

Lykke, N. (2010). *Feminist studies: A guide to intersectional theory, methodology and writing*. New York: Routledge.

Malcom, S. M., Hall, P. Q., & Brown, J. W. (1976, April). *The double bind: The price of being a minority woman in science*. Washington, DC: American Association for the Advancement of Science.

Malone, K. R., & Barabino, G. (2009). Narrations of race in STEM research settings: Identity formation and its discontents. *Science Education, 93*(3), 485–510. https://doi.org/10.1002/sce.20307

Martin, J. P., Simmons, D. R., & Yu, S. L. (2013). The role of social capital in the experiences of Hispanic women engineering majors. *Journal of Engineering Education, 102*(2), 227–243. https://doi.org/10.1002/jee.20010

McCall, L. (2005). The complexity of intersectionality. *Journal of Women in Culture and Society, 30*(3). https://doi.org/10.1086/426800

Meltzer, D. E., & Thornton, R. K. (2012). Resource letter ALIP–1: Active-learning instruction in physics. *American Journal of Physics, 80*(6), 478–496.

Mirza, H. S. (1986). The dilemma of socialist feminism: A case for black feminism. *Feminist Review, 22*(1), 102–105. https://doi.org/10.1057/fr.1986.9

Moses, R., Kamii, M., Swap, S. M., & Howard, J. (1989). The Algebra Project: Organizing in the spirit of Ella. *Harvard Educational Review, 59*(4), 423–444. https://doi:10.17763/haer.59.4.27402485mqv20582

Moses, R. P., & Cobb, C. E. (2002). *Radical equations: Civil rights from Mississippi to the algebra project*. Boston: Beacon Press.

Mügge, L., Montoya, C., Emejulu, A., & Weldon, S. L. (2018). Intersectionality and the politics of knowledge production. *European Journal of Politics and Gender, 1*(1–2), 17–36. https://doi.org/10.1332/2515108 18X15272520831166

Natapoff, A. (1995). Anatomy of a debate: Intersectionality and equality for deaf children from non-English speaking homes. *Journal of Law and Education, 24*(2), 271–278.

National Research Council. (2012). *Discipline-based education research: Understanding and improving learning in undergraduate science and engineering*. Washington, DC: The National Academies Press. https://doi.org/10.17226/13362

Nelson, A. (2002). Introduction: Future texts. In *Social text* (Vol. 71). Durham, NC: Duke University Press.

Nelson, A. (2013). *Body and soul: The Black Panther Party*. Minneapolis: University of Minnesota Press.

Nissen, J. M., & Shemwell, J. T. (2016). Gender, experience, and self-efficacy in introductory physics. *Physical Review Physics Education Research, 12*(2), 020105.

Ohland, M. W., Brawner, C. E., Camacho, M. M., Layton, R. A., Long, R. A., Lord, S. M., & Wasburn, M. H. (2011). Race, gender, and measures of success in engineering education. *Journal of Engineering Education, 100*(2), 225–252. https://doi.org/10.1002/j.2168-9830.2011.tb00012.x

Ong, M. M. (2005). Body projects of young women of color in physics: Intersections of gender, race, and science. *Social Problems, 52*(4), 593–617. https://doi.org/10.1525/sp.2005.52.4.593

Ong, M. M. (2011). The status of women of color in computer science. *Communications of the ACM, 54*(7), 32–34. https://doi.org/10.1145/1965724.1965737

Ong, M., Wright, C., Espinosa, L., & Orfield, G. (2011). Inside the double bind: A synthesis of empirical research on undergraduate and graduate women of color in science, technology, engineering, and mathematics. *Harvard Educational Review, 81*(2), 172–209. https://doi.org/10.17763/haer.81.2.t022245n7x4752v2

Pajares, F., & Miller, M. D. (1994). Role of self-efficacy and self-concept beliefs in mathematical problem solving: A path analysis. *Journal of Educational Psychology, 86*(2), 193.

Peller, G. (1996). Race-consciousness. In K. Crenshaw, N. Gotanda, G. Peller, & K. Thomas (Eds.), *Critical race theory: The key writings that formed the movement* (pp. 127–158). New York, NY: The New Press.

Ray, V. (2019). A theory of racialized organizations. *American Sociological Review*. https://doi.org/10.1177/0003 122418822335

Regents of the University of California v. Bakke, 438 U.S. 265 (1978).

Rosa, K., & Mensah, F. M. (2016). Educational pathways of Black women physicists: Stories of experiencing and overcoming obstacles in life. *Physical Review Physics Education Research, 12*(2), 020113. https://doi.org/10.1103/PhysRevPhysEducRes.12.020113

Traxler, A. L., Cid, X. C., Blue, J., & Barthelemy, R. (2016). Enriching gender in physics education research: A binary past and a complex future. *Physical Review Physics Education Research, 12*(2), 020114. https://doi.org/10.1103/PhysRevPhysEducRes.12.020114

Washington, H. A. (2010). *Medical apartheid the dark history of medical experimentation on black Americans from colonial times to the present.* New York, NY: Anchor.

Weinberg, A. E., & Sample McMeeking, L. B. (2017). Toward meaningful interdisciplinary education: High school teachers' views of mathematics and science integration. *School Science and Mathematics, 117*(5), 204–213.

Yoder, B. L. (2016). Engineering by the numbers. *American Society for Engineering Education.* https://www.asee.org/documents/papers-and-publications/publications/college-profiles/2017-Engineering-by-Numbers-Engineering-Statistics.pdf

Yosso, T. J. (2005). Whose culture has capital? A critical race theory discussion of community cultural wealth. *Race Ethnicity and Education, 8*(1), 69–91. https://doi.org/10.1080/1361332052000341006

21

PERSPECTIVES OF IDENTITY AS AN ANALYTIC FRAMEWORK IN STEM EDUCATION

Allison Godwin, Jennifer Cribbs and Shakhnoza Kayumova

Importance of Identity Research in STEM

Identity is an enduring and continuous sense of who one is (Erikson, 1956), often thought of as the answer to the questions, "Who am I?" "Who can I be?" and "Where do I belong?" Over the last two decades, research on STEM identity development has grown to include a focus on how students make sense of being a STEM professional in various levels of education and the workforce. This approach comes with both affordances and limitations for STEM education and research. This chapter will provide an overview of the ways identity has been defined, a brief summary of how it has been studied in STEM, and opportunities for future areas of research.

In STEM education, identity development has been linked to many important outcomes, including students' learning trajectories (Horn, 2008), motivation to learn (Kajfez, Matusovich, & Lee, 2016), career pathways (Godwin, Potvin, Hazari, & Lock, 2016), persistence (Patrick, Borrego, & Prybutok, 2018), and belonging in STEM communities (Darragh, 2013). These research findings make identity a powerful construct while informing researchers and educators about reasons why individuals participate in STEM activities or the STEM field. Identity is a core aspect of individuals that informs their internal states as well as actions in the world, and as a result, it has significant explanatory power in understanding multiple aspects of individual experiences in STEM.

Identity as an analytical framework allows researchers to investigate interlocking aspects of how students understand who they are within a social context, such as the psycho–social processes that students use to make meaning of themselves and the world around them (Adams, Berzonsky, & Keating, 2006). These internal processes can inform novel ways of examining the quality of teaching and learning environments of formal and informal STEM contexts. These processes can also explain why only some students feel that STEM is "for them" (Boaler & Greeno, 2000; Kayumova & Cardello, 2018). Identity also provides ways to understand how contexts inform the processes of learning and the socialization into the norms and discourse of STEM, which seeks to unearth equity issues embedded in the dominant cultural practices of STEM (Barton, 1998; Kayumova, Avraamidou, & Adams, 2018). Identity provides ways to study how participation in STEM can be broadened (Cribbs, Hazari, Sonnert, & Sadler, 2015; Godwin et al., 2016) to be inclusive of the multiple ways of being, doing, and learning that students bring with them into a learning environment (Kayumova, Karsli, Allexsaht-Snider, & Buxton, 2015).

Defining Identity

Identity theory has a broad theoretical basis rooted in disciplinary fields such as education, psychology, sociology, and anthropology. These different fields constitute a complex landscape in which identity is defined and understood. This section will highlight some common consensus about how identity is defined in the STEM education community as well as the tensions in defining and measuring identity.

In recent studies in science education, identity is defined as "relational and social, tied to how people are positioned by others, and also how they take up identities, establish agency, and build repertoires of participation" (Kelly, 2012, p. 189). A review of research on mathematics learner identity found similar ideas present when summarizing how the construct is defined by researchers in the field, stating a commonality in definitions as having a "subjective/social dimension, a representational/enacted dimension and a change/stability dimension" (Radovic, Black, Williams, & Salas, 2018, p. 26). When considering the subjective (I see myself) and social (others see me), identity has often been defined as the way individuals position themselves and are positioned by others (i.e., students, teachers, parents, community) in relation to the normative practices in a setting, or in relation to social structures (Cobb & Hodge, 2011). In addition, each individual has multiple "selves" or identities (Burke & Stets, 2009; Gee, 2000). For example, a student may identify not only as a "STEM person" but also as a soccer player, sibling, and student. The literature suggests that these multiple roles are separate identities that have different salience in particular contexts and that the accumulation of multiple identities is an inevitable outcome of life in a complex society.

Many researchers use identity as a lens for exploring connections between multiple identities, such as content or disciplinary identity (e.g., science, mathematics, engineering) and other social identities (e.g., race, ethnicity, gender; Lim, 2008a; Solomon, Lawson, & Croft, 2011). Often this body of research explores the interactions involved in an individual's STEM identity development, as well as the role of other identities, social norms, STEM practices, and other relevant factors in their identity development, which may or may not influence their current or future involvement with STEM.

Carlone and Johnson (2007) identified three interrelated dimensions of identity formation in science education, including recognition (students' recognizing and being recognized by others as science persons), performance (ability to do science), and competence (ability to understand science). More recently, Hazari, Sonnert, Sadler, and Shanahan (2010) utilized Carlone et al.'s (2007) framework to investigate girls' identity formation in physics, adding a fourth dimension (interest) to the framework. As an extension to Carlone's work, Hazari et al. (2010) showed that for minoritized students (e.g., girls), affective factors, such as interest, are important for their identification with science. Hazari et al. (2010) developed a survey instrument to explore how science identities are shaped by students' experiences in high school physics classes and by their career outcome expectations. These four dimensions (recognition, performance, competence, and interest) are important aspects of STEM identities. Other work has shown that these dimensions apply not only in science contexts but also in mathematics (Cribbs et al., 2015) and engineering (Godwin, 2016).

While these four dimensions of STEM identities are consistent across disciplines, disciplinary contexts can influence STEM identities differently. The four letters in the acronym STEM represent overlapping but distinct fields with different histories, norms, and values (Kayumova, McGuire, & Cardello, 2018). Indeed, the disciplines within a field also have different social norms and structures. For example, children's experiences with mathematics are formalized as soon as they begin school, while their experiences with engineering may be limited to non-compulsory enrichment activities. Additionally, science is often segmented into different areas such as physics, chemistry, or biology, while mathematics is often thought of as one area of study, which causes students to experience these subjects in different ways (Roehrig, Johnson, Moore, & Bryan, 2015). These differences in representation are indicators of differences within disciplines. Prior work in understanding high school students' descriptions of STEM identities showed consistent differences in how students interpret these roles (Verdín, Godwin, & Ross, 2018). In studying identity, it is important to state that there is not a universal STEM identity but rather multiple STEM identities, depending upon the individual and context in which he or she is situated.

Considerations in Identity Studies

Identity investigations must consider a number of important aspects in the understanding of this complex phenomenon. The first is the level at which identity is studied. For instance, when identity development is studied as a part of the context—that is, through interactions between individuals and social structures—the focus of investigation can be at multiple levels (Markus, 2008). At the micro, or individual, level, identity is studied on a person-centered basis, and an understanding of moment-to-moment positioning, where researchers examine discourse in a classroom or a series of actions that an individual makes (Cobb & Hodge, 2011; Lichtwarck-Aschoff, van Geert, Bosma, & Kunnen, 2008). One example of a study that follows this level of investigation uses an activity as the unit of analysis, with researchers considering moment-to-moment actions and language to be a primary source of evidence that individuals are engaging in identity-building practices (Esmonde, 2009). The meso level explores the dynamic relationship between the student and the immediate context, which provides an understanding of how the immediate context informs students' identities and how those identities shape the immediate context. A classroom environment is an example of an immediate context. Students may make bids for recognition as a "STEM person" through accepted dialogue, questioning, and engagement with peers and instructors. The individual engages in a process of positioning him/herself as a "STEM person" that may be recognized or not. Finally, the macro level examines identity related to culture or institutional structures and individuals' identities (Archer, 1995, 2000; Carlone, 2012). How particular policies at a university may shape which students engage in STEM and how those students do or do not develop identities, as a result, is one example.

Identity investigations must not only consider the level at which the study is focused but also the timescale. In the history of identity theory, scholars have taken different positions on the nature of identity and how it may (or may not) change over time (Gray, Tuchscherer, & Gray, 2018). Kuhn and McPartland (1954) argued that identity is relatively fixed and stable. A body of work on identity, especially that from a psychological perspective, has focused on identity as internal to the self, with some core aspects that are unchanging traits. Other scholars have posited that identity is dynamic and changes from moment to moment (see Vignoles, Schwartz, & Luyckx, 2011). For example, Sfard and Prusak (2005) framed identity as ongoing narratives told by the individual and by others. They emphasized that the process of telling and receiving the stories influences how the narrative is constructed, and therefore an individual's identity. This approach is opposite from identity as a trait and instead frames identity as constantly negotiated in context. Others have argued that identities are quasi-traits, relatively stable over short timescales (Wortham, 2008). The framing of identity as fluid or stable influences how it may be investigated.

Methodologically, identity has been studied more often in STEM education qualitatively. A qualitative approach allows researchers to examine the socially constructed and dynamic nature of identity work. Different approaches have been used to understand STEM student identities, often depending on the identity framework chosen. Ethnography has been used to understand how identities are developed in a particular culture, like a science classroom (Barton et al., 2013; Carlone, 2004) or engineering program (Tonso, 2006). Other work has used discourse analysis to understand identity as a discursive performance (Paretti & McNair, 2012) or an interplay between discourse and actions/positioning (Bishop, 2012). Research that frames identity as stories that an individual and others tell about themselves often use narrative inquiry (Gardner & Willey, 2018; McAlpine, Amundsen, & Turner, 2014; Sfard & Prusak, 2005). Each of these methodological ways of studying identity provides robust insights into different aspects of how individuals grapple with questions of who they are and whether they belong in STEM contexts. Qualitative approaches provide a number of affordances for identity studies, including the ability to understand identity development over time, to capture or characterize the nuanced ways in which identity is performed by individuals and recognized by others, and to understand multiple identities across different contexts in shaping who becomes a "STEM person." Qualitative approaches might also pose some challenges in terms of accurately representing students' narratives and words in ways that remain true to their experiences, and the use of these studies in large-scale reforms (Sfard & Prusak, 2005).

A few investigations have developed quantitative measures of students' physics (Hazari et al., 2010), mathematics (Cribbs et al., 2015), or engineering identities (Godwin, 2016). These investigations of identity provide quick "snapshots" of a specific disciplinary identity. These approaches are useful in understanding the ways in which students see themselves as a particular kind of person or in a specific role, especially compared to a population. However, these measures often are unable to capture small or nuanced changes in identity and instead focus on general responses of students' interest, performance, competence, and recognition within a discipline.

There are a number of ways in which the complex nature of identity is defined, theorized, and investigated. Each of these different approaches provides unique and valuable insights into how students and professionals answer questions of "Who am I?" "Who can I be?" and "Where do I belong?" within STEM contexts. In the next section, we describe what the current landscape of STEM education research tells us about the core questions of identity.

Identity in STEM Contexts

This section will provide a brief review of the current body of literature on identity in STEM education. Identity has been studied much more extensively in mathematics and science education than in engineering education, and few studies in technology education exist. For a more comprehensive discussion of science identity, see Varelas (2012); for engineering identity, see Tonso (2014) and Rodriguez, Lu, and Bartlett (2018); and for mathematics identity, see Darragh (2016) and Radovic, Black, and Salas, (2018). We split this review into two time frames: K–12 and post-secondary and beyond. We made this decision because students' experiences and disciplinary exposure in STEM differ across primary and secondary versus post-secondary contexts. We have examined the three analytic lenses of identity in these two bodies of literature: psycho–social, learning and socialization, and equity issues in STEM.

K-12 Literature

Psycho–Social Processes. The literature on engineering identity for K–12 students is much more limited than that of science and mathematics. One reason for this difference may be due in part to the fact that prior to higher education, many students do not have experience with engineering (Marra, Rodgers, Shen, & Bogue, 2012). These trends are changing with the integration of engineering into the U.S. Next Generation Science Standards, implemented in 2014, and the growing international emphasis on teaching children about engineering (Moore, Tank, Glancy, & Kersten, 2015; National Research Council, 2013). But even recent scholarship shows that students have a limited understanding of both the field and role of engineering (Francis et al., 2017; Rynearson, 2017; Verdín et al., 2018). The literature that does examine engineering identity has mostly focused on the psycho–social processes of how students decide whether engineering is a part of how they see themselves or how they position themselves in the world and equity issues. Even though these studies most often focus on gender, a growing body of work has begun to take on more intersectional approaches.

A number of studies explore students' emerging identities in STEM to understand student literacy or career pathways. Capobianco (2006) developed the engineering identity development scale (EIDS) for primary students that consists of students' self-beliefs about their academic abilities (similar to prior theorizations of performance/competence beliefs for older students and engineering career identities). The engineering aspirational scale includes statements both about what engineers do and who they are as well as students' desires to engage in engineering and engineering-related activities in the future (Capobianco, French, & Diefes-Dux, 2012). This group found that integrated science, technology, and engineering (STE) curriculum from the popular Engineering Is Elementary curriculum (Cunningham, 2017) positively influences elementary students' content knowledge acquisition in comparison to their peers who were not exposed to integrated curricula as well as higher engineering career identity than their peers. Other research explores identity through a sense of belonging, where students grapple with their sense of membership in a STEM community, which often connects to an individual's membership to other communities (i.e., gender, culture). Some researchers explore this through tensions that arise based on students' learning experiences in the classroom (Lim, 2008b), while others have explored how students sense of belonging with a STEM community changed over time (Darragh, 2013). These studies highlight the fact that learning is a social endeavor. The ways that STEM is perceived or portrayed by society, teachers, and peers inform students' perspectives on their own STEM identity and whether or not they want to be a member of that community.

Learning and Socialization. Of particular concern and interest to researchers, a variety of studies explore identity in the context of the classroom. For example, Boaler and Greeno (2000) found that students' mathematics identity is connected to the way mathematics is taught and subsequently perceived (what it means to do and know mathematics) by students in a high school setting. Other studies, across K–12, explore how students position themselves based on the interactions they have with their peers and teacher (Bishop, 2012; Black, 2009; Heyd-Metzuyanim & Sfard, 2012). Bishop (2012) found that the way that students engaged with mathematics content (e.g., the types of questions asked and the type and frequency of responses) was influenced by interactions and positioning with a peer. Kelly, Cunningham, and Ricketts (2017) described particular practices that elementary teachers employed in positioning their students as engineers, including identifying students as engineers, recognizing students' activities as engineering, and celebrating successes. The cultural norms, community practices, and experiences students bring with them into the classroom have also been connected to the ways students identify with STEM content (Anderson & Gold, 2006; Nasir & Hand, 2008). These studies underscore the complexity of identity development as a variety of factors (classroom norms, teacher actions, peer interactions, cultural perspectives, home and community experiences) that contribute to the ways students identify with the content and the identities they enact.

Equity Issues. Identity as an analytic lens is particularly useful in understanding issues of equity in STEM. Because identity examines intersections of how an individual sees him/herself and is positioned by others and by social structures, it can reveal supports and barriers for particular individuals or social groups participating in STEM. For example, Martin (2000) described the importance of connecting learning mathematics and identity development with students' cultural, historical, and community experiences and perspectives, which is supported by other research exploring issues of race and gender in the field (Berry, 2008; Wang & Hazari, 2018). Aschbacher, Li, and Roth (2010) longitudinally investigated the changing attitudes of 10th grade students towards careers in science, engineering, and medicine over a two-year period. They found that students who received positive support and messages about science, engineering, and medicine in communities of practice at home, at school, and outside of school were more likely to persist in their interest of STEM subjects; however, the number of students who received this type of support was less than half of the participants, and students from low-SES backgrounds, especially Black or Latino/a students and girls, were less likely to receive the types of support required to foster their future goals in STEM

(Kayumova et al., 2015, 2018). Their findings emphasize the importance of adults at home or in school that enthusiastically invite students to learn about science or engineering, value scientific ways of knowing, or encourage students to pursue a STEM-related career. This lack of encouragement may be explained, in part, by the results from a UK study of 132 students aged 15 and 16 and their parents' perceptions of physics and engineering careers (Francis et al., 2017). They found a consistent set of discourses that positioned physics and engineering as "quintessentially masculine," which served both as a barrier to students' interest in and development of science and engineering identities as well as an explanation for the low numbers of female participation in these fields. For students, especially those who are traditionally underrepresented, identities in STEM are informed by cultural norms and the types of people that they see and do not see in STEM roles.

Post-Secondary Education and Beyond

There is often a clear demarcation between research on K–12 students and research beyond secondary education. Reasons for this phenomenon include the funding structures of programs to support research, the access to educational institutions, and training and roles of researchers in STEM education or discipline-based education research (National Research Council, 2012). A few studies investigate the transition points between secondary and post-secondary education, often through retrospective survey work or longitudinal tracking. These studies show the importance of identity development in STEM for future career choices in pursuing a STEM degree (Cribbs, Cass, Hazari, Sadler, & Sonnert, 2016; Godwin et al., 2016; Hazari et al., 2010). Other work also emphasizes the importance of identity sustainment from K–12 to post-secondary education that supports the conceptualization that identities are not fixed and can be fostered or hindered by particular experiences (Godwin & Potvin, 2017; Tate & Linn, 2005).

Psycho–Social Processes. Similar to how identity is explored in K–12 research, the literature focusing on the psycho-social processes of identity often investigate individuals' identity development and negotiation as narratives told about themselves. In a study of how professional portfolios helped participants create narratives about themselves as engineers, Eliot and Turns's (2011) findings showed that students used both external and internal frames of reference to see themselves as engineers. The external frame of reference included students' perceptions of what potential employers and recruiters expected of them, and the internal frame included the students' own values and interests as professional engineers. The key factors for identity development from that study are similar to the ways in which Hazari et al. (2010) framed the key elements of students' disciplinary identities. For example, interest lines up with students' internal frames, and performance/competence beliefs and recognition connect with external frames of what it takes to be a professional in a particular field. Other research draws from Wenger's (1998) modes of belonging to explore undergraduate students' ways of describing themselves in context with the mathematics community (Solomon, 2007). The psycho-social process of identity development involves how an individual describes who they are as a STEM person and how that story is received in STEM education.

Learning and Socialization. Studies of identity in post-secondary education and beyond most often focus on STEM identities as a process of professional formation or association with the duties, responsibilities, and knowledge associated with a professional role (Morelock, 2017). Students continually receive messages about what it means to be a professional in the field based on what they experience as part of their education programs. Solomon (2009) discussed how many students can receive messages that leave them feeling as if they are outsiders or that their identity conflicts with membership in the mathematics community. According to Solomon (2009), "developing identities of inclusion is, therefore, a question of making the central meaning-making practices of mathematics visible, available and accessible for all learners" (p. 134). Stevens, O'Connor, Garrison, Jocuns, and Amos (2008) described a framework for understanding engineering identity development that involved the development of disciplinary knowledge, identification with the role of an engineer, and navigation of pathways through engineering degree programs. This framework focused on acquiring knowledge associated with the discipline of engineering as the key aspect in formation of an engineering identity. Other scholars have focused on the key factors that support identity development. Meyers, Ohland, Pawley, Silliman, and Smith (2012) found that most engineering students, even early in their undergraduate curricula, identified skills of making competent design decisions, working with others to share ideas, and accepting responsibility as key ways students saw themselves in the role of being an engineer. Another study of Australian students' future possible identities (i.e., possible selves; first defined in Markus & Nurius, 1986) found that students perceived gaps in their abilities to accomplish the requirements of engineering work as motivating if they felt that they could reduce the gap, but demotivating if they believed they had no control (Bennett & Male, 2017). These studies highlight the importance of disciplinary knowledge and socialization for the development of professional identities.

Equity Issues. In many ways, learning and socialization aspects of identity are intimately tied to equity issues. In engineering and other areas of STEM that are predominately White, male disciplines (Yoder, 2017), the messages conveyed about what it means to be a person in that STEM community socialize particular students into feeling like they do or do not belong. For example, Tonso (2006) described the complex cultural and social forces among students and faculty that allowed or did not allow students to form identities as engineers. Students' abilities to see themselves as part of "this whole engineering [or STEM] group" (Foor, Walden, & Trytten, 2007, p. 104) can become particularly challenging when institutional and social experiences based on gender, ethnicity, and socioeconomic differences set up roadblocks to students' efforts to develop engineering identities as a part of their academic trajectories (Du, 2006). However, other studies have noted particular experiences or support that students use to negotiate identities in STEM and succeed, despite an exclusive culture. Family support, faculty encouragement and recognition, peer mentoring, motivation tying STEM to long-term goals, and a strong academic identity as a successful student have all been found to be important for traditionally underrepresented groups in STEM (Tate & Linn, 2005). Other work in STEM professional settings has also documented the challenges faced by women as a whole (Hatmaker, 2013; Huff, 2018; Piatek-Jimenez, 2008) and women of color, in particular (Carlone & Johnson, 2007; Ross, Capobianco, & Godwin, 2017) in negotiating their social identities, or identities as a part of one's membership in a group (Tajfel, 1981) with their professional identities as engineers, mathematicians or scientists. Equity issues are persistent not only in early stages of identity development but throughout the lifetime of STEM professional formation and practice.

Opportunities for Future Research

Over the years, identity research in STEM has evolved, with researchers more clearly defining the construct and framing their work. Although there is still a need for research in this area, other gaps and opportunities for future research are evident. Hannula et al. (2016) provided some insight into these gaps, noting that much of the literature in mathematics education focuses on interviews rather than on what is happening in the classroom and has small sample sizes limiting generalizability. They also noted a need for literature to explore identity in connection with other affective measures. Part of this gap in the literature may be due to the absence of a quantitative instrument to capture short-term changes in identity. More exploration of quantitative instruments that would capture changes in students' identity over shorter periods would be useful in providing instructors and institutions with tangible ways of nurturing students' development of identity. In addition, these instruments could provide a way to explore multiple factors in conjunction.

Future work should also explore specific connections to the classroom or interventions that may promote the development of a positive STEM identity with students. These interventions should effectively support STEM identity development and sustainment across all lifetimes of identity. Most interventions appear to rely on the assumption that STEM identity construction is a natural process which develops as students have more experiences—or more professional ones—in STEM (Rahm, 2008). There are some efforts are being made in this area, connecting research findings to equity-based practice in the classroom and beyond (Aguirre, Mayfield-Ingram, & Martin, 2013), and continued efforts in this vein are needed.

Identity is a complex phenomenon with varying frameworks and definitions that guide current research efforts. There is a tension between the measurement of individual agency and structural forces that shape identity. However, researchers and educators with a deeper understanding of the literature across STEM are better positioned to have meaningful conversations across disciplinary boundaries, support students' identity development, and conduct research that will have an impact on STEM education broadly.

References

Adams, G. R., Berzonsky, M. D., & Keating, L. (2006). Psychosocial resources in first-year university students: The role of identity processes and social relationships. *Journal of Youth and Adolescence, 35*(1), 78–88.

Aguirre, J., Mayfield-Ingram, K., & Martin, D. (2013). *The impact of identity in K-8 mathematics: Rethinking equity-based practices.* Reston, VA: National Council of Teachers of Mathematics.

Anderson, D. D., & Gold, E. (2006). Home to school: Numeracy practices and mathematical identities. *Mathematical Thinking and Learning, 8*(3), 261–286. doi:10.1207/s15327833mtl0803_4

Archer, M. S. (1995). *Realist social theory: The morphogenetic approach.* Cambridge, UK: Cambridge University Press.

Archer, M. S. (2000). *Being human: The problem of agency.* Cambridge, UK: Cambridge University Press.

Aschbacher, P. R., Li, E., & Roth, E. J. (2010). Is science me? High school students' identities, participation and aspirations in science, engineering, and medicine. *Journal of Research in Science Teaching, 47*(5), 564–582. doi:10.1002/tea.20353

Barton, A. C. (1998). Teaching science with homeless children: Pedagogy, representation, and identity. *Journal of Research in Science Teaching: The Official Journal of the National Association for Research in Science Teaching, 35*(4), 379–394.

Barton, A. C., Kang, H., Tan, E., O'Neill, T. B., Bautista-Guerra, J., & Brecklin, C. (2013). Crafting a future in science: Tracing middle school girls' identity work over time and space. *American Educational Research Journal, 50*(1), 37–75. doi:10.3102/0002831212458142

Bennett, D., & Male, S. A. (2017). An Australian study of possible selves perceived by undergraduate engineering students. *European Journal of Engineering Education, 42*(6), 603–617. doi:10.1080/03043797.2016.1208149

Berry, R. Q. III. (2008). Access to upper-level mathematics: The stories of successful African American middle school boys. *Journal for Research in Mathematics Education,* 464–488.

Bishop, J. P. (2012). "She's always been the smart one. I've always been the dumb one": Identities in the mathematics classroom. *Journal for Research in Mathematics Education, 43*(1), 34–74. doi:10.5951/jresematheduc.43.1.0034

Black, L. (2009). Differential participation in whole-class discussions and the construction of marginalised identities. *The Journal of Educational Enquiry, 5*(1), 383–406.

Boaler, J., & Greeno, J. G. (2000). Identity, agency, and knowing in mathematics worlds. In J. Boaler (Ed.), *Multiple perspectives on mathematics teaching and learning* (pp. 171–200). Westport, CT: Ablex.

Burke, P. J., & Stets, J. E. (2009). *Identity theory.* Oxford, UK: Oxford University Press.

Capobianco, B. M. (2006). Undergraduate women engineering their professional identities. *Journal of Women and Minorities in Science and Engineering, 12*(2–3). doi:10.1615/JWomenMinorScienEng.v12.i2–3.10

Capobianco, B. M., French, B. F., & Diefes-dux, H. A. (2012). Engineering identity development among pre-adolescent learners. *Journal of Engineering Education, 101*(4), 698–716. doi:10.1002/j.2168–9830.2012.tb01125.x

Carlone, H. B. (2004). The cultural production of science in reform-based physics: Girls' access, participation, and resistance. *Journal of Research in Science Teaching, 41*(4), 392–414. doi:10.1002/tea.20006

Carlone, H. B. (2012). Methodological considerations for studying identities in school science. In M. Varelas (Ed.), *Identity construction and science education research* (pp. 9–25). Rotterdam, NL: Sense.

Carlone, H. B., & Johnson, A. (2007). Understanding the science experiences of successful women of color: Science identity as an analytic lens. *Journal of Research in Science Teaching, 44*(8), 1187–1218. doi:10.1002/tea.20237

Cobb, P., & Hodge, L. L. (2011). Culture, identity, and equity in the mathematics classroom. In A. J. Bishop (Managing Ed.), E. Yackel, K. Gravemeijer, & A. Sfard (Eds.), *Mathematics education library: Vol. 48. A journey in mathematics education research: Insights from the work of Paul Cobb* (pp. 179–195). New York, NY: Springer. doi:10.1007/978-90-9729-3.

Cribbs, J. D., Cass, C., Hazari, Z., Sadler, P. M., & Sonnert, G. (2016). Mathematics identity and student persistence in engineering. *International Journal of Engineering Education, 32*(1A), 163–171.

Cribbs, J. D., Hazari, Z., Sonnert, G., & Sadler, P. M. (2015). Establishing an explanatory model for mathematics identity. *Child Development, 86*(4), 1048–1062. doi:10.1111/cdev.12363

Cunningham, C. M. (2017). *Engineering in elementary STEM education: Curriculum design, instruction, learning, and assessment.* New York, NY: Teachers College Press.

Darragh, L. (2013). Constructing confidence and identities of belonging in mathematics at the transition to secondary school. *Research in Mathematics Education, 15*(3), 215–229. doi:10.1080/14794802.2013.803775

Darragh, L. (2016). Identity research in mathematics education. *Educational Studies in Mathematics, 93*(1), 19–33.

Du, X. Y. (2006). Gendered practices of constructing an engineering identity in a problem-based learning environment. *European Journal of Engineering Education, 31*(1), 35–42. doi:10.1080/03043790500430185

Eliot, M., & Turns, J. (2011). Constructing professional portfolios: Sense-making and professional identity development for engineering undergraduates. *Journal of Engineering Education, 100*(4), 630–654. doi:10.1002/j.2168–9830.2011.tb00030.x

Erikson, E. H. (1956). The problem of ego identity. *Journal of the American Psychoanalytic Association, 4*(1), 56–121. doi:10.1177/000306515600400104

Esmonde, I. (2009). Ideas and identities: Supporting equity in cooperative mathematics learning. *Review of Educational Research, 79*(2), 1008–1043. doi:10.3102/0034654309332562

Foor, C. E., Walden, S. E., & Trytten, D. A. (2007). "I wish that I belonged more in this whole engineering group": Achieving individual diversity. *Journal of Engineering Education, 96*(2), 103–115. doi:10.1002/j.2168–9830.2007.tb00921.x

Francis, B., Archer, L., Moote, J., DeWitt, J., MacLeod, E., & Yeomans, L. (2017). The construction of physics as a quintessentially masculine subject: Young people's perceptions of gender issues in access to physics. *Sex Roles, 76*(3–4), 156–174. doi:10.1007/s11199–016–0669–z

Gardner, A., & Willey, K. (2018). Academic identity reconstruction: The transition of engineering academics to engineering education researchers. *Studies in Higher Education, 43*(2), 234–250. doi:10.1080/03075079.2016.1162779

Gee, J. P. (2000). Identity as an analytic lens for research in education. *Review of Research in Education, 25*(1), 99–125. doi:10.3102/0091732X025001099

Godwin, A. (2016). *The development of a measure of engineering identity.* Paper presented at ASEE Annual Conference & Exposition, New Orleans, LA. doi:10.18260/p.26122

Godwin, A., & Potvin, G. (2017). Pushing and pulling Sara: A case study of the contrasting influences of high school and university experiences on engineering agency, identity, and participation. *Journal of Research in Science Teaching, 54*(4), 439–462. doi:10.1002/tea.21372

Godwin, A., Potvin, G., Hazari, Z., & Lock, R. (2016). Identity, critical agency, and engineering: An affective model for predicting engineering as a career choice. *Journal of Engineering Education, 105*(2), 312–340. doi:10.1002/jee.20118

Gray, C. A., Tuchscherer, R., & Gray, R. (2018, June). *The challenges and affordances of engineering identity as an analytic lens.* Paper presented at ASEE Annual Conference & Exposition, Salt Lake City, UT. https://peer.asee.org/31082

Hannula, M. S., Di Martino, P., Pantziara, M., Zhang, Q., Morselli, F., Heyd-Metzuyanim, E., ... Goldin, G. A. (2016). *Attitudes, beliefs, motivation and identity in mathematics education. ICME-13 Topical Surveys.* Cham: Springer. doi:10.1007/978-3-319-32811-9

Hatmaker, D. M. (2013). Engineering identity: Gender and professional identity negotiation among women engineers. *Gender, Work & Organization, 20*(4), 382–396. doi:10.1111/j.1468–0432.2012.00589.x

Hazari, Z., Sonnert, G., Sadler, P. M., & Shanahan, M.-C. (2010). Connecting high school physics experiences, outcome expectations, physics identity, and physics career choice: A gender study. *Journal of Research in Science Teaching, 47*(8), 978–1003. doi:10.1002/tea.20363

Heyd-Metzuyanim, E., & Sfard, A. (2012). Identity struggles in the mathematics classroom: On learning mathematics as an interplay of mathematizing and identifying. *International Journal of Educational Research, 51*, 128–145. doi:10.1016/j.ijer.2011.12.015

Horn, I. S. (2008). Turnaround students in high school mathematics: Constructing identities of competence through mathematical worlds. *Mathematical Thinking and Learning, 10*(3), 201–239. doi:10.1080/10986060802216177

Huff, J. L., Smith, J. A., Jesiek, B. K., Zoltowski, C. B., & Oakes, W. C. (2018). Identity in engineering adulthood: An interpretative phenomenological analysis of early-career engineers in the United States as they transition to the workplace. *Emerging Adulthood*, 1–18. doi:10.1177/2167696818780444

Kajfez, R. L., Matusovich, H. M., & Lee, W. C. (2016). Designing developmental experiences for graduate teaching assistants using a holistic model for motivation and identity. *International Journal of Engineering Education*, *32*(3A), 1208–1221.

Kayumova, S., Avraamidou, L., & Adams, J. D. (2018). Science education: Diversity, equity and the big picture. In *Critical issues and bold visions for science education* (pp. 285–297). Leiden, The Netherlands: Brill Sense.

Kayumova, S., & Cardello, S. (2018). *"I have an opinion about science I think part is true and part is not": Emergent bilingual/multilingual adolescents "figuring" science learning through virtual labs*. In Proceedings of 13th International Society of the Learning Sciences (Vol. 1, pp. 1751–1753).

Kayumova, S., Karsli, E., Allexsaht-Snider, M., & Buxton, C. (2015). Latina mothers and daughters: Ways of knowing, being, and becoming in the context of bilingual family science workshops. *Anthropology & Education Quarterly*, *46*(3), 260–276.

Kayumova, S., McGuire, C. J., & Cardello, S. (2019). From empowerment to response-ability: Rethinking socio-spatial, environmental justice, and nature-culture binaries in the context of STEM education. *Cultural Studies of Science Education*, *14*(1), 205–229. https://doi.org/10.1007/s11422-018-9861-5

Kelly, G. J. (2012). Developing critical conversations about identity research in science education. In M. Varelas (Ed.), *Identity construction and science education research* (pp. 189–196). Rotterdam, NL: Sense.

Kelly, G. J., Cunningham, C. M., & Ricketts, A. (2017). Engaging in identity work through engineering practices in elementary classrooms. *Linguistics and Education*, *39*, 48–59. doi:10.1016/j.linged.2017.05.003

Kuhn, M. H., & McPartland, T. S. (1954). An empirical investigation of self-attitudes. *American Sociological Review*, *19*, 68–76. doi:10.2307/2088175

Lichtwarck-Aschoff, A., van Geert, P., Bosma, H., & Kunnen, S. (2008). Time and identity: A framework for research and theory formation. *Developmental Review*, *28*(3), 370–400. doi:10.1016/j.dr.2008.04.001

Lim, J. H. (2008a). Double jeopardy: The compounding effects of class and race in school mathematics. *Equity & Excellence in Education*, *41*(1), 81–97. doi:10.1080/10665680701793360

Lim, J. H. (2008b). The road not taken: Two African-American girls' experiences with school mathematics. *Race Ethnicity and Education*, *11*(3), 303–317. doi:10.1080/13613320802291181

Markus, H., & Nurius, P. (1986). Possible selves. *American Psychologist*, *41*(9), 954–969. doi:10.1037/0003-066X.41.9.954

Markus, H. R. (2008). Identity matters: Ethnicity, race, and the American dream. In M. Minow, R. A. Shweder, & H. R. Markus (Eds.), *Just schools: Pursuing equality in societies of difference* (pp. 63–98). New York, NY: Russell Sage Foundation.

Marra, R. M., Rodgers, K. A., Shen, D., & Bogue, B. (2012). Leaving engineering: A multi-year single institution study. *Journal of Engineering Education*, *101*(1), 6–27. doi:10.1002/j.2168-9830.2012.tb00039.x

Martin, D. B. (2000). *Mathematics success and failure among African-American youth: The roles of sociohistorical context, community forces, school influence, and individual agency*. New York, NY: Routledge.

McAlpine, L., Amundsen, C., & Turner, G. (2014). Identity-trajectory: Reframing early career academic experience. *British Educational Research Journal*, *40*(6), 952–969. doi:10.1002/berj.3123

Meyers, K. L., Ohland, M. W., Pawley, A. L., Silliman, S. E., & Smith, K. A. (2012). Factors relating to engineering identity. *Global Journal of Engineering Education*, *14*(1), 119–131.

Moore, T. J., Tank, K. M., Glancy, A. W., & Kersten, J. A. (2015). NGSS and the landscape of engineering in K-12 state science standards. *Journal of Research in Science Teaching*, *52*(3), 296–318. doi:10.1002/tea.21199

Morelock, J. R. (2017). A systematic literature review of engineering identity: Definitions, factors, and interventions affecting development, and means of measurement. *European Journal of Engineering Education*, *42*(6), 1240–1262. doi:10.1080/03043797.2017.1287664

Nasir, N. S., & Hand, V. (2008). From the court to the classroom: Opportunities for engagement, learning, and identity in basketball and classroom mathematics. *The Journal of the Learning Sciences*, *17*(2), 143–179. doi:10.1080/10508400801986108

National Research Council. (2012). *Discipline-based education research: Understanding and improving learning in undergraduate science and education*. Washington, DC: National Academies Press.

National Research Council. (2013). *Next generation science standards (NGSS)*. Washington, DC: National Academies Press.

Paretti, M. C., & McNair, L. D. (2012). Analyzing the intersections of institutional and discourse identities in engineering work at the local level. *Engineering Studies*, *4*(1), 55–78. doi:10.1080/19378629.2011.652120

Patrick, A. B., Borrego, M., & Prybutok, A. N. (2018). Predicting persistence in engineering through an engineering identity scale. *International Journal of Engineering Education*, *34*(2A), 351–363.

Piatek-Jimenez, K. (2008). Images of mathematicians: A new perspective on the shortage of women in math-ematical careers. *ZDM, 40*(4), 633–646.

Radovic, D., Black, L., Williams, J., & Salas, C. E. (2018). Towards conceptual coherence in the research on mathematics learner identity: A systematic review of the literature. *Educational Studies in Mathematics, 99*(1), 21–42. doi:10.1007/s10649-018-9819-

Rahm, J. (2008). Urban youths' hybrid identity projects in science practices at the margin: A look inside a school–museum–scientist partnership project and an afterschool science program. *Cultural Studies of Science Education, 3*(1), 97–121. doi:10.1007/s11422-007-9081-x

Rodriguez, S. L., Lu, C., & Bartlett, M. (2018). Engineering identity development: A review of the higher education literature. *International Journal of Education in Mathematics, Science and Technology, 6*(3), 254–265. doi:10.18404/ijemst.428182

Roehrig, G. H., Johnson, C. C., Moore, T. J., & Bryan, L. A. (2015). Integrated STEM education. In *STEM road map* (pp. 35–50). New York, NY: Routledge.

Ross, M., Capobianco, B. M., & Godwin, A. (2017). Repositioning race, gender, and role identity formation for black women in engineering. *Journal of Women and Minorities in Science and Engineering, 23*(1), 37–52. doi:10.1615/JWomenMinorScienEng.2017016424

Rynearson, A. M. (2017). *From mechanic to designer: Evolving perceptions of elementary students over three years of engineering instruction* (Doctoral dissertation). Retrieved from ProQuest Dissertations Publishing. (10179099).

Sfard, A., & Prusak, A. (2005). Telling identities: In search of an analytic tool for investigating learning as a cul-turally shaped activity. *Educational Researcher, 34*(4), 14–22. doi:10.3102/0013189X034004014

Solomon, Y. (2007). Not belonging? What makes a functional learner identity in undergraduate mathematics? *Studies in Higher Education, 32*(1), 79–96. doi:10.1080/03075070601099473

Solomon, Y. (2009). *Mathematical literacy: Developing identities of inclusion.* New York, NY: Routledge.

Solomon, Y., Lawson, D., & Croft, T. (2011). Dealing with "fragile identities": Resistance and refiguring in women mathematics students. *Gender and Education, 23*(5), 565–583. doi:10.1080/09540253.2010.512270

Stevens, R., O'Connor, K., Garrison, L., Jocuns, A., & Amos, D. M. (2008). Becoming an engineer: Toward a three dimensional view of engineering learning. *Journal of Engineering Education, 97*(3), 355–368. doi:10.1002/j.2168-9830.2008.tb00984.x

Tajfel, H. (1981). *Human groups and social categories.* Cambridge, UK: Cambridge University Press.

Tate, E. D., & Linn, M. C. (2005). How does identity shape the experiences of women of color engineering students? *Journal of Science Education and Technology, 14*(5/6), 483–493. doi:10.1007/s10956-005-0223-1

Tonso, K. L. (2006). Student engineers and engineer identity: Campus engineer identities as figured world. *Cultural Studies of Science Education, 1*(2), 273–307. doi:10.1007/s11422-005-9009-2

Tonso, K. L. (2014). Engineering identity. In A. Johri & B. M. Olds (Eds.), *Cambridge handbook of engineering education research* (pp. 267–282). New York, NY: Cambridge University Press.

Varelas, M. (Ed.). (2012). *Identity construction and science education research: Learning, teaching, and being in multiple contexts* (Vol. 35). Rotterdam, NL: Sense.

Verdín, D., Godwin, A., & Ross, M. (2018). STEM roles: How students' ontological perspectives facilitate STEM identities. *Journal of Pre-College Engineering Education Research (J-PEER), 8*(2), 31–48. doi:10.7771/2157-9288.1167

Vignoles, V. L., Schwartz, S. J., & Luyckx, K. (2011). Introduction: Toward an integrative view of identity. In *Handbook of identity theory and research* (pp. 1–27). New York, NY: Springer.

Wang, J., & Hazari, Z. (2018). Promoting high school students' physics identity through explicit and implicit recognition. *Physical Review Physics Education Research, 14*(2), 020111.

Wenger, E. (1998). *Communities of practice: Learning, meaning, and identity.* New York, NY: Cambridge University Press.

Wortham, S. (2008). The objectification of identity across events. *Linguistics and Education, 19*(3), 294–311. doi:10.1016/j.linged.2008.05.010

Yoder, B. L. (2017). *Engineering by the numbers.* Washington, DC: ASEE. Retrieved from https://www.asee.org/documents/papers-and-publications/publications/college-profiles/2017-Engineering-by-Numbers-Engineering-Statistics.pdf

22

RACE-RELATED FACTORS IN STEM

A Review of Research on Educational Experiences and Outcomes for Racial and Ethnic Minorities

Cindy Jong, Christen Priddie, Thomas Roberts and Samuel D. Museus

Introduction

In 2009, Neil deGrasse Tyson, a world-renowned astrophysicist, commented on all the barriers he faced at every turn on his path to becoming a scientist. He shared that, after his first visit to a planetarium at age nine, he knew he wanted to be a scientist and that this choice "was *hands down* the path of most resistance through the forces of society" because he is Black. Tyson's comments underscore the harsh reality that racial and ethnic minority (REM) populations experience school differently and do not have the same opportunities as their White counterparts in science, technology, engineering, and mathematics (STEM).

In fact, while progress in efforts to increase success among these populations has been made, REMs continue to face disparities in STEM. For example, while non–White populations accounted for approximately 38% of the total U.S. population in 2015 (Anderson, 2015), they comprised 32% of the science and engineering workforce (NSF, 2017). Moreover, Blacks and Hispanics were among the most underrepresented, comprising 30% of the U.S. population (Anderson, 2015) and only 11% of the science and engineering workforce during this same year (National Science Foundation [NSF], 2017).

Within education, REMs are less likely to persist and graduate within six years of initial matriculation compared to their White peers (Whalen & Shelley, 2010). Black and Latinx students enter STEM fields and complete degrees in these areas at lower rates than White counterparts (Rincón & Lane, 2017). While Asian Americans have the highest rates of success in the aggregate, more complex analyses demonstrate that some Asian American ethnic subgroups exhibit relatively high rates of success and others face some of the most significant racial and ethnic disparities in educational attainment (Museus, 2014). However, analysis of national data on students who are U.S. citizens shows that all REMs face disparities in degree completion in engineering and biomedical/biological sciences, demonstrating that international students can skew attainment numbers (Byrd, Dika, & Ramlal, 2013). Moreover, REMs report having negative experiences in STEM that move them away from these fields. We discuss this point more thoroughly in the following sections.

There are several urgent reasons to increase success for REMs in STEM (Museus, Palmer, Davis, & Maramba, 2011). Such efforts are imperative for higher education to ensure the financial and social well-being of people of color, leverage the diverse talent pool to maintain a society that consists of diverse and global communities, and fulfill its moral and ethical obligation to help eradicate harmful inequities (p. 5). To do so requires efforts to remove economic, racial, and structural barriers to their experiences.

In this chapter, we review the most recent decade of literature on REMs in STEM education, from 2008 to 2018. For purposes of this analysis, we defined REMs in the United States as Asian Americans, Blacks, Latinx, Native Americans, and Pacific Islanders. The articles we reviewed with international perspectives primarily discuss access and equity in STEM for indigenous groups or ethnic minorities who are not part of a country's majority group, which might not necessarily be White; however, we attempt to uncover such nuances and distinctions throughout. In total, we reviewed 58 empirical studies, conceptual articles, book chapters, syntheses, or reports that examined race within STEM. While we aimed to find research on integrated STEM, we had to expand our search to disciplines across and within STEM to capture more perspectives on and from REMs.

Critical race theory (CRT) was our guiding analytical framework for the review. While different authors have proposed or delineated varying sets of "core" tenets of CRT (e.g., Delgado & Stefancic, 2017; Ladson-Billings, 1998; Solórzano, 1998), principles of CRT that are most relevant to the current analysis include the following:

- *Racism is normal*: racism is a pervasive aspect of U.S. society;
- *Race is a social construction*: race and racial categories are not biological but are socially constructed;
- *Interest convergence*: the conditions of people of color are advanced only as long as they also serve the interests of Whites;
- *Differential racialization*: different individuals and groups are racialized by the White majority for the latter's benefit;
- *Intersectionality*: systems of oppression intersect to mutually shape people's experiences in complex and unique ways;
- *Centrality of marginalized voices*: the voices of people of color can be centered through storytelling and counter narrative to challenge dominant hegemonic narratives.

We present findings from our review as factors that have the potential to influence success among REMs across both PreK-12 and higher education settings in STEM. While many barriers exist, several factors can promote success in STEM for REMs, including: (1) parents, role models, and mentors; (2) access to rigorous curricula; (3) applied content; (4) culturally relevant pedagogy; and (5) affirming experiences and environments. Among these factors that are catalysts of success, we address challenges that arise. Then, we conclude with a section of implications for research, policy, and practice based on a CRT perspective and the findings of our review.

Parents, Role Models, and Mentors

Parental support is associated with greater likelihood of REMs' success in STEM. Parents having high expectations for their children and building a strong link between school and home also promote success (Berry, Thunder, & McClain, 2011). In addition, for Black students, effective parental support in mathematics includes encouraging students to persevere through challenges, building self-efficacy in students, and serving as role models of people who successfully completed mathematics courses (McGee & Spencer, 2015).

Role models beyond parents are also important. Non-White and non-male persons are often invisible among STEM professionals, making it difficult for those who are not represented to see themselves succeeding in such careers (Morton & Smith-Mutegi, 2018). Representation also ties in to the benefits, as having more STEM women faculty can lead to better persistence of female students (Griffith, 2010). Access to diverse and relatable role models help students identify with the subjects and see themselves as able to participate as a member of the STEM community

(Coxon, Dohrman, & Nadler, 2018). The influence of role models extends to teachers. When students have a teacher of the same race, they are more likely to do well in school (Gershenson, Jacknowitz, & Brannegan, 2017).

Mentorship also tends to be a crucial factor in minority students' motivations in the STEM field (Kendricks, Nedunuri, & Arment, 2013). Faculty members who are invested in REM students' personal and academic achievements can positively shape their experience (Foltz, Gannon, & Kirschmann, 2014; Hernandez, Estrada, Woodcock, & Schultz, 2017). Rodríguez Amaya, Betancourt, Collins, Hinojosa, and Corona (2018) examined undergraduate student research experiences with mentors and found that such experiences fostered more positive attitudes toward their majors. In addition, mentoring relationships are a source of motivation for REMs. For example, Black students are motivated to get doctoral degrees to be able to reach out and provide mentorship to students of similar backgrounds who come after them (McGee et al., 2016).

Access to Rigorous Curricula

For aspirations to be nurtured, however, students must have access to advanced STEM content. Taking advanced mathematics and science courses in high school is a significant factor for students who intend to major in STEM programs in college (Wang, 2013). Hispanic students' persistence in STEM at the higher education level is impacted by their pre-college preparation, particularly by taking more advanced mathematics and science courses (Crisp, Nora, & Taggart, 2009). Access to the advanced courses is necessary but not sufficient. Achievement in advanced courses is just as critical for REMs. Twelfth-grade mathematics achievement is a significant factor in REMs' decisions to pursue STEM degrees (Wang, 2013).

Unfortunately, one pervasive and systematic means of limiting access to rigorous STEM curricula is tracking. Tracking is prominently associated with mathematics and, as such, is one reason mathematics is often described as a gatekeeper to advanced STEM study (Crisp et al., 2009; Martin, Gholson, & Leonard, 2010; McGee & Spencer, 2015; Coxon et al., 2018). The dominant discourse takes a deficit perspective with an emphasis on Black and Latinx students' failures in mathematics (McGee & Spencer, 2015), often in the forms of "discourses of deficiency and rejection" (Stinson, 2008). This perspective blames the students for not being smart or interested enough in STEM subjects instead of analyzing the systemic barriers that prevent them from participating. Moreover, students from culturally and linguistically diverse backgrounds—such as Black, Latinx, and Native American—are systematically excluded from gifted and talented programs as teachers are less likely to recommend them for these opportunities (Elhoweris, 2008; Ford, Grantham, & Whiting, 2008).

The inequitable access to rigorous STEM curricula and high-quality teachers is a global problem that contribute to the increasing opportunity gaps between dominant and minority groups not only in the United States, but in Canada, England, Singapore, China, and South Africa (Clark, 2014). Even when efforts are made to change the system, reforms are often futile. The experiments in creating inclusive STEM schools in Denver and Buffalo serve as examples (Weis et al., 2015). When these reforms were planned, the inclusive STEM schools were going to offer more advanced courses in mathematics and science. However, due to pressures to meet policy demands around accountability, graduation rates, and standardized testing, the plans failed to materialize (Weis et al., 2015). Ultimately, the schools' failures to offer the advanced mathematics and science courses served as yet another example of gatekeeping that prevents many REMs from accessing opportunities to pursue future STEM coursework (Weis et al., 2015). However, some reform efforts in STEM have been made to make mathematics and science content more accessible and relatable to students by making STEM more integrative and focusing on "complex, authentic, or real-world problems within STEM" (Moore, Johnston, & Glancy, 2020, p. 17). In Turkey, for example, curricula have been shifting to be more constructivist and student-centered by focusing on developing a variety of strategies to solve problems that are more applicable (Topcu, 2013). This is consistent with Moore et al.'s (2020) finding of the importance of implementing integrated STEM through student-centered strategies.

Applied Content and Curricula

Having the opportunity to apply STEM content to real-world issues is critical for REM success and is central to integrative STEM (Moore et al., 2020). For example, Coxon et al. (2018) used diverse characters in a narrative to set a context for an integrated STEM unit that applied mathematics to robotics. The focus of the unit was exploring fraction word problems in the context of science, while using the engineering design loop to design a variety of robots to solve the problems. This activity allowed the students to visualize the fractions and see how they could be used in real-world contexts. Students who used this unit diversified their conceptions of who can be a scientist and demonstrated significant mathematics gains. Scholars have argued that the opportunity to participate in hands-on investigations of integrated STEM content allows students to see how the content was applied in diverse contexts, from robotics to DNA extraction (Roberts et al., 2018).

Making STEM learning relevant to REM students' respective communities can also facilitate success. Calabrese and Tan (2018) highlight the importance of informal settings such as makerspaces to apply engineering design as empowering STEM learning opportunities for historically marginalized youths. Working with others in their community and collaborating in the process of making allowed for students to access knowledge their community possessed, reorganized power hierarchies, and increased the opportunity for the students to be recognized (Calabrese & Tan, 2018). Informal learning environments are one mechanism through which community-based opportunities can increase minority students' interest and future engagement in STEM (King & Pringle, 2018). For example, Morton and Smith-Mutegi (2018) describe the Girls' STEM Institute, a four-week interdisciplinary camp for girls of color, in which they prioritized community engagement to foster positive identities by integrating STEM content relevant to their lives through a focus on real-world problems in integrated STEM. They argue that such community engagement is needed for "critical systemic and long-term change to occur" (p. 32).

Meaningful community engagement can occur in specific school and classroom projects as well. Suh et al. (2018) detail an elementary school project where students investigated food insecurity in their community and used mathematical models to plan and provide meals for local families in need. This increased enjoyment of the topics leads to aspirations of pursuing the subject matter further (Riegle-Crumb, Moore, & Ramos-Wada, 2011). The nature of students' early exposure to STEM education is imperative for students (De Jarnette, 2012; Bagiati, Yoon, Evangelou, & Ngambeki, 2010). In fact, before entering eighth grade, many students develop a passion for STEM or decide that these subjects are too difficult, boring, or uninteresting (PCAST, 2010). Therefore, such early assessments can discourage these students from pursuing STEM courses and activities at the college level.

Culturally Relevant Pedagogy

Culturally relevant pedagogy is one way in which educators make teaching relevant to students' lives, while taking societal power dynamics into account. Teachers who use culturally relevant teaching practice are cognizant of the ways in which mainstream pedagogy and curricula often excludes and discourages REMs, and construct curricula in ways that are intended to center their cultures, communities, and voices to empower these students. Such practices have a positive impact on REM students' success in STEM (King & Pringle, 2018; Savage et al., 2011; Vincent-Ruz & Schunn, 2018). One example of culturally relevant pedagogy and its impact is the Northwest Indian College's use of Native and Tribal knowledge in the mathematics courses (Bunton, Cook, & Tamburini, 2018). The college integrates algebraic patterns related to beading and geometric concepts from natural resources into curricula to rehumanize mathematics and "combats the notion that only topics that have emerged from a colonialist society are inherently mathematical or worthy of inclusion in a mathematics classroom" (p. 111). When culturally relevant teaching is effectively integrated, students feel more valued in the classroom and perform better academically (Savage et al., 2011).

A major barrier to culturally relevant teaching practices are deficit perspectives, which center the perceived inadequacy of the cultures, abilities, and traits of non-White children and de-emphasize the powerful role of context in explaining racial disparities in educational outcomes (Stinson, 2008; Basile & Lopez, 2015). Such perspectives perpetuate a *blame the victim* way of thinking about students of color (Valencia & Solórzano, 1997). Deficit perspectives exist in and are communicated through various contexts. For example, there are times when students face "unproductive beliefs" (National Council of Teachers of Mathematics, 2014; Sandholtz & Ringstaff, 2014) about their abilities to fully engage in STEM disciplines. Unproductive beliefs are evident when teachers do not take students' culture and native language into consideration. Zavala (2014) suggested recent Latinx immigrants to the United States could have greater access to the academic language of mathematics when taught in Spanish. Similarly, Māori children in New Zealand are often classified as underachieving while being expected to participate in a European New Zealand education system (Savage et al., 2011). In this system, the Māori children sometimes face racism, such as when teachers are more likely to call on European students instead of Māori students and when schools implement rules that forbid Māori cultural artifacts (Savage et al., 2011).

Affirming Environments and Identities

Research has shown that affirming environments promote REMs' success in STEM. Positive and influential peer networks was a common theme in why minority students persevere through adversity in their STEM experiences (Espinosa, 2011; Palmer, Maramba, & Dancy, 2011). REM students rely on each other to maintain interest in pursuing a STEM education, whether it be with the larger STEM academic community or with peers who share similar racial and ethnic identities (Espinosa, 2011; Hurtado, Newman, Tran, & Chang, 2010; Meador, 2018). Similarly, scholars have noted that international students feel that peers are more helpful than faculty when it comes to their STEM success (Burrell, Fleming, Fredericks, & Moore, 2015). The significance of maintaining healthy relationships with others does not stop at PreK-12 or undergraduate education, as STEM graduate students also benefit from positive peer pressure and peer modeling through cohort-type departmental structures (Charleston & Leon, 2016).

Counterspaces are critical spaces within which students connect with people who share their experiences and construct supportive environments. King and Pringle (2018) argue that counterspaces, where teachers can create affirming learning experiences by listening to students' stories and validating their narratives, can provide a buffer from the larger, more hostile environment of educational institutions.

Hostile environments can hinder REM students' ability to see themselves as mathematicians or scientists, impair their sense of belonging and empowerment, and contribute to their experiencing lower achievement and persistence rates (Coxon et al., 2018; Hurtado et al., 2010; Vincent-Ruz & Schunn, 2018). This hostility can be compounded by the competitive nature of the culture of siloed STEM fields. Integrative STEM often emphasizes collaboration and teamwork (Moore et al., 2020), which has potential to alleviate the negative effects of the competitive culture.

A major challenge to constructing more affirming environments for REMs is the pervasiveness of colorblind ideologies, which are racial belief systems that perpetuate perspectives that the best way to eradicate racism and racial inequities is to view and treat people as individuals without regard to their race, culture, and identity (Bonilla-Silva, 2006). Colorblind ideologies can be used by the White majority to absolve themselves of responsibility for systemic inequities and avoid focusing on race-conscious solutions to racial inequities in STEM education. For example, Basile and Lopez (2015) reviewed 17 policy documents related to STEM education. They found that most STEM policies discuss race in broad terms, minimize shared racialized experiences, and focus primarily on economic arguments for broadening participation in STEM to benefit the "owners and operators of the STEM enterprise" (Basile & Lopez, 2015, p. 540). Similarly, Gutstein (2009) argued that, while many mathematics education policies are written to serve all students, only wealthy students benefit while the needs of urban schools (i.e., those predominantly attended by Latinx and Black students) remain unaddressed.

People often adopt systemic racialized beliefs and internalize colorblind ideologies simultaneously. For example, Zavala (2014) noted that many Latinx high school students adopted the pervasive model minority stereotype and racialized Asian Americans as exceptionally hard-working, studious pupils who are good at math to explain their relative success in mathematics. However, when describing their own success, many of the same students took a colorblind approach and attributed their achievements to their individual motivation and commitment to education. The ways in which colorblind ideologies induce a focus on individual determinants of student outcomes can contribute to deficit perspectives, which can lead to people blaming students of color for the disparities that they face.

Another important component in minority student persistence in STEM majors is their psychological processes as they relate to their development of STEM identities. Motivation played a role in maintained interest in the STEM major, as well as sustained efforts to obtain graduate degrees (Hurtado et al., 2010; McGee et al., 2016). Confidence, or self-efficacy, in academic ability was influential in research production and peer comparison (Charleston & Leon, 2016; Grineski et al., 2018; Litzler, Samuelson, & Lorah, 2014). There are some disparities in STEM confidence between racial and ethnic groups. Similar to PreK–12 students, all racial and ethnic groups had lower STEM confidence than White men; Hispanic women, in particular, struggled to develop science identities (Hazari, Sadler, & Sonnert, 2013; Litzler et al., 2014). When controlling for concepts such as peer comparison, good professors, and prior experience, Black and Hispanic men have higher STEM confidence, while Black and Hispanic women have similar STEM confidence to White men. In addition, there is some evidence that students with multiple intersecting minority identities—such as people of color who are also from low socioeconomic status backgrounds or who are women—had lower academic performance than their counterparts with a single minority identity (MacPhee, Farro, & Canetto, 2013). For example, STEM majors continue to be dominated by men, which further negatively impacts women of color (Charleston & Leon, 2016), as women of color often feel isolated and ignored by peers in their field (Johnson et al., 2017) and perceive themselves as academically inferior compared to men in these fields (MacPhee et al., 2013).

Implications for Research, Policy, and Practice in STEM Education

There are several implications for research based on the literature we reviewed and the gaps that exist, such as the voices of REMs that were missing. There needs to be more counter narratives and intersectional work that center on the experiences of REMs. A comparative framework was often used when the experiences of REMs are explored. This comparison continues to use White students' experiences as normalized and REMs as "others." Implicit and sometimes explicit in this work is that the REM experience should be equivalent to the White student experience, and if it is not, then action needs to be taken to fix this. Tying this back to endemic racism, REMs are not receiving the equitable resources that White students receive, meaning that there is an equivalency measure that REMs may never reach. Researchers addressing this in their work on REMs in STEM can catalyze different conversations on how to improve their participation while recognizing the systemic inequities that are always present. More recent literature, especially in mathematics education, has become more inclusive of REMs' experiences and voices (cf. Goffney, Gutierrez, & Boston, 2018). As a whole, unfortunately, STEM education and its related fields need greater emphasis on the experiences, stories, and voices of REMs, especially at the PreK-12 levels.

We also suggest that quantitative research use disaggregated data in an effort to examine the experiences of REM groups. Twelve of the higher education articles specifically focused on REMs' experiences in STEM fields, while other articles examined how race and ethnic identity influenced specific experiences. Of the 12 articles, seven used disaggregated information to report on the experiences of REMs in STEM, and six of those articles used an intersectional approach by combining respondent identities, such as race/ethnicity, gender, and socioeconomic status, to analyze their results. Both the disaggregated and intersectional approaches researchers used were crucial to examine the specific groups and their very different experiences. This practice ensures that efforts are being made to not treat racial and ethnic groups as a monolith. In addition to the use of disaggregated information and intersectional approaches, nine articles used either a qualitative or mixed-methods approach to discuss REMs' experiences in STEM fields. The use of qualitative methods ties into the CRT notion of counterstorytelling and why it is important to center the voices of REMs when examining factors that promote and inhibit their success in the STEM fields.

A myriad of policy implications can be gleaned from the literature to promote systematic factors that have an influence on the success of REMs. These policies include: anti-tracking, honoring the use of native languages, increased funding for programs that support and supplement STEM learning, and a more transparent use of high-stakes test scores. In the PreK-12 literature examined, only the more recent pieces critically discussed the systemic racism REMs face in STEM education. Most often, this appeared in discussions of how the systemic practice of tracking disproportionately limits opportunities for REMs to take advanced mathematics courses, which often serve as the gatekeeper to more advanced STEM courses. Only four of the articles specifically addressed this issue in terms of race, which speaks to the dominance of researchers using economic preparedness arguments as a reason to diversify the STEM community. This reifies the interest convergence tenet in CRT as the needs and desires of REMs are overwhelmingly ignored in the interest of maintaining policies that benefit and serve interests of the dominant group.

This was similar to the higher education literature, where the majority of the researchers examined how providing more adequate resources and minority faculty representation can play a vital role in increasing the participation of REMs in STEM. However, only five articles mentioned how systemic inequities can contribute to the lack of participation. The failure to mention the endemic nature of racism ties into the interest convergence tenet of CRT and the tendency of researchers to name national and global competitiveness as a primary reason for diversifying the STEM fields while disregarding other reasons why REMs participate in STEM fields, some of which involve giving back to their own communities. Discussions related to resources rarely included analyses on funding disparities that exist at a global level, which only exacerbate the disparities related to rigorous curricula and high-quality teachers.

In regard to practice, several implications are interrelated to policies and research findings in which more integrative approaches to STEM are effective. Teaching with culturally relevant pedagogy and making meaningful connections with communities are practices that can have a lasting impression on REMs. Earlier exposure of students to integrated STEM practices, where the content is applied to their lives through complex, authentic, or real-world problems (Moore et al., 2020), will aid in the development of interest in STEM. Anti-deficit perspectives, where REMs' backgrounds are valued and drawn upon to enhance the learning experiences, are important to students as well. It is also clear that relationships are critical to the success of REMs in STEM. Thus, engaging parents in

STEM initiatives, increasing representation of educators and allies to serve as mentors, and creating counterspaces for REMs will provide more opportunities for them to thrive.

Racial and ethnic minorities face many barriers to success in STEM education. Many of these barriers are the result of a system that dehumanizes and marginalizes non-White students (Gholson, 2016; Gutierrez, 2018; Joseph, 2017; Morton & Smith-Mutegi, 2018). Until recently, this marginalization has occurred in the research literature, too, as the dominant discourses are those of "deficiency and rejection" (Stinson, 2008), with voices of people of color having little to no presence. Many of the strategies for success rely on systemic disruptions (Morton & Smith-Mutegi, 2018). Increasing opportunities for racial and ethnic minorities to access integrative STEM experiences to have a more diverse workforce requires less tracking and greater access to advanced STEM courses. A more diverse workforce could lead to the availability of a more diverse set of role models. Co-curricular and informal learning opportunities that allow students to explore integrated applications of STEM content through authentic problems require funding and staff that are not provided to most schools in the current system. Even when districts have attempted to create STEM academies with the goals of offering more advanced courses in mathematics and science courses, they have failed due to policy constraints that maintain the status quo (Weis et al., 2015) and often ignore issues relevant to students of diverse racial and ethnic backgrounds (Berry, Pinter, & McClain, 2013). Valuing diverse forms of community knowledge, such as how students participate in making in their community (Calabrese & Tan, 2018), and connecting that knowledge to the classroom require teachers who do not marginalize differences but embrace students' backgrounds. In short, students need good teaching, but, as Ladson-Billings (1995) noted nearly a quarter century ago, all students do not consistently receive good teaching. Without significant disruptions to the current system, the same inequities will persist.

References

Anderson, M. (2015). *The race gap in science knowledge*. Pew Research Center. Retrieved from https://www. pewresearch.org/fact-tank/2015/09/15/the-race-gap-in-science-knowledge/

Bagiati, A., Yoon, S. Y., Evangelou, D., & Ngambeki, I. (2010). Engineering curricula in early education: Describing the landscape of open resources. *Early Childhood Research & Practice, 12*(2), n2.

Basile, V., & Lopez, E. (2015). And still I see no changes: Enduring views of students of color in science and mathematics education policy reports. *Science Education, 99*(3), 519–548. https://doi.org/10.1002/sce.21156

Berry, R. Q. III, Pinter, H. H., & McClain, O. L. (2013). A critical review of American K-12 mathematics education, 1900-present: Implications for the experiences and achievement of Black children. In J. Leonard & D. B. Martin (Eds.), *The brilliance of black children in mathematics: Beyond the numbers and toward new discourse* (pp. 22–53). Charlotte, NC: Information Age Publishing.

Berry, R. Q. III, Thunder, K., & McClain, O. L. (2011). Counter narratives: Examining the mathematics and racial identities of black boys who are successful with school mathematics. *Journal of African American Males in Education, 2*, 10–23.

Bonilla-Silva, E. (2006). The central frames of color-blind racism. *Racism Without Racists*, 25–52.

Bunton, Z., Cook, C., & Tamburini, M. (2018). Centering students' mathematical agency at Northwest Indian College. In I. Goffney., R. Gutierrez, & M. Boston (Eds.), *Annual perspectives in mathematics education 2018: Rehumanizing mathematics for black, indigenous, and Latinx students* (pp. 107–120). Reston, VA: NCTM.

Burrell, J. O., Fleming, L., Fredericks, A. C., & Moore, I. (2015). Domestic and international student matters: The college experiences of black males majoring in engineering at an HBCU. *The Journal of Negro Education, 84*(1), 40–55. https://doi.org/10.7709/jnegroeducation.84.1.040

Byrd, W. C., Dika, S. L., & Ramlal, L. T. (2013). Who's in STEM? An exploration of race, ethnicity, and citizenship reporting in a federal education dataset. *Equity & Excellence in Education, 46*(4), 484–501. https://doi.org/10.1080/10665684.2013.838485

Calabrese, B. A., & Tan, E. (2018). A longitudinal study of equity-oriented STEM-rich making among youth from historically marginalized communities. *American Educational Research Journal, 55*(4), 761–800. https://doi.org/10.3102/0002831218758668

Charleston, L., & Leon, R. (2016). Constructing self-efficacy in STEM graduate education. *Journal for Multicultural Education, 10*(2), 152–166. https://doi.org/10.1108/JME-12-2015-0048

Clark, J. V. (Ed.). (2014). *Closing the achievement gap from an international perspective: Transforming STEM for effective education.* Dordrecht, The Netherlands: Springer.

Coxon, S. V., Dohrman, R. L., & Nadler, D. R. (2018). Children using robotics for engineering, science, technology, and math (CREST-M): The development and evaluation of an engaging math curriculum. *Roeper Review, 40*(2), 86. https://doi.org/10.1080/02783193.2018.1434711

Crisp, G., Nora, A., & Taggart, A. (2009). Student characteristics, pre-college, college, and environmental factors as predictors of majoring in and earning a STEM degree: An analysis of students attending a Hispanic serving institution. *American Educational Research Journal, 46*(4), 924–942. https://doi.org/10.3102/0002831209349460

De Jarnette, N. (2012). America's children: Providing early exposure to STEM (science, technology, engineering and math) initiatives. *Education, 133*(1), 77–84.

Delgado, R., & Stefancic, J. (2017). *Critical race theory: An introduction.* NYU Press. https://doi.org/10.2307/j.ctt1ggjjn3

Elhoweris, H. (2008). Teacher judgment in identifying gifted/talented students. *Multicultural Education, 15*(3), 35–38.

Espinosa, L. (2011). Pipelines and pathways: Women of color in undergraduate STEM majors and the college experiences that contribute to persistence. *Harvard Educational Review, 81*(2), 209–241. https://doi.org/10.17763/haer.81.2.92315ww157656k3u

Foltz, L. G., Gannon, S., & Kirschmann, S. L. (2014). Factors that contribute to the persistence of minority students in STEM Fields. *Planning for Higher Education, 42*(4), 1–13.

Ford, D. Y., Grantham, T. C., & Whiting, G. W. (2008). Culturally and linguistically diverse students in gifted education: Recruitment and retention issues. *Exceptional Children, 74*(3), 289–306. https://doi.org/10.1177/001440290807400302

Gershenson, S., Jacknowitz, A., & Brannegan, A. (2017). Are student absences worth the worry in US primary schools? *Education Finance and Policy, 12*(2), 137–165. https://doi.org/10.1162/EDFP_a_00207

Gholson, M. L. (2016). Clean corners and algebra: A critical examination of the constructed invisibility of black girls and women in mathematics. *The Journal of Negro Education, 85*(3), 290–301. https://doi.org/10.7709/jnegroeducation.85.3.0290

Goffney, I., Gutierrez, R., & Boston, M. (Eds.). (2018). *Annual perspectives in mathematics education 2018: Rehumanizing mathematics for black, indigenous, and latinx students.* Reston, VA: NCTM.

Griffith, A. L. (2010). Persistence of women and minorities in STEM field majors: Is it the school that matters? *Economics of Education Review, 29*(6), 911–922. https://doi.org/10.1016/j.econedurev.2010.06.010

Grineski, S., Daniels, H., Collins, T., Morales, D. X., Frederick, A., & Garcia, M. (2018). The conundrum of social class: Disparities in publishing among STEM students in undergraduate research programs at a Hispanic majority institution. *Science Education, 102*(2), 283–303. https://doi.org/10.1002/sce.21330

Gutierrez, R. (2018). Introduction: The need to rehumanize mathematics. In I. Goffney, R. Gutierrez, & M. Boston (Eds.), *Annual perspectives in mathematics education 2018: Rehumanizing mathematics for black, indigenous, and latinx students* (pp. 1–12). Reston, VA: NCTM.

Gutstein, E. (2009). The politics of mathematics education in the US: Dominant and counter agendas. In B. Greer, S. Mukhopadhyay, A. Powell, & S. Nelson-Barber (Eds.), *Culturally responsive mathematics education* (pp. 137–164). New York, NY: Routledge.

Hazari, Z., Sadler, P. M., & Sonnert, G. (2013). The science identity of college students: Exploring the intersection of gender, race, and ethnicity. *Journal of College Science Teaching, 42*(5), 82–91.

Hernandez, P. R., Estrada, M., Woodcock, A., & Schultz, P. W. (2017). Protégé perceptions of high mentorship quality depend on shared values more than on demographic match. *The Journal of Experimental Education, 85*(3), 450–468. https://doi.org/10.1080/00220973.2016.1246405

Hurtado, S., Newman, C. B., Tran, M. C., & Chang, M. J. (2010). Improving the rate of success for underrepresented racial minorities in STEM fields: Insights from a national project. *New Directions for Institutional Research, 2010*(148), 5–15. https://doi.org/10.1002/ir.357

Johnson, A., Ong, M., Ko, L. T., Smith, J., & Hodari, A. (2017). Common challenges faced by women of color in physics, and actions faculty can take to minimize those challenges. *The Physics Teacher, 55*(6), 356–360. https://doi.org/10.1119/1.4999731

Joseph, N. M., Hailu, M., & Boston, D. (2017). Black women's and girls' persistence in the P–20 mathematics pipeline: Two decades of children, youth, and adult education research. *Review of Research in Education, 41*(1), 203–227. https://doi.org/10.3102/0091732X16689045

Kendricks, K. D., Nedunuri, K. V., & Arment, A. R. (2013). Minority student perceptions of the impact of mentoring to enhance academic performance in STEM disciplines. *Journal of STEM Education: Innovations and Research, 14*(2), 38.

King, N. S., & Pringle, R. M. (2018). Black girls speak STEM: Counterstories of informal and formal learning experiences. *Journal of Research in Science Teaching.* https://doi.org/10.1002/tea.21513

Ladson–Billings, G. (1998). Just what is critical race theory and what's it doing in a nice field like education? *International Journal of Qualitative Studies in Education, 11*(1), 7–24. https://doi.org/10.1080/095183998236863

Ladson–Billings, G., & Tate, W. F. (1995). Toward a critical race theory of education. *Teachers College Record, 97*(1), 47–68.

Litzler, E., Samuelson, C. C., & Lorah, J. A. (2014). Breaking it down: Engineering student STEM confidence at the intersection of race/ethnicity and gender. *Research in Higher Education, 55*(8), 810–832. https://doi.org/10.1007/s11162-014-9333-z

MacPhee, D., Farro, S., & Canetto, S. S. (2013). Academic self-efficacy and performance of underrepresented STEM majors: Gender, ethnic, and social class patterns. *Analyses of Social Issues and Public Policy, 13*(1), 347–369. https://doi.org/10.1111/asap.12033

Martin, D. B., Gholson, M. L., & Leonard, J. (2010). Mathematics as gatekeeper: Power and privilege in the production of knowledge. *Journal of Urban Mathematics Education, 3*(2), 12–24.

McGee, E., & Spencer, M. B. (2015). Black parents as advocates, motivators, and teachers of mathematics. *The Journal of Negro Education, 84*(3), 473–490. https://doi.org/10.7709/jnegroeducation.84.3.0473

McGee, E. O., White, D. T., Jenkins, A. T., Houston, S., Bentley, L. C., Smith, W. J., & Robinson, W. H. (2016). Black engineering students' motivation for PhD attainment: Passion plus purpose. *Journal for Multicultural Education, 10*(2), 167–193. https://doi.org/10.1108/JME-01-2016-0007

Meador, A. (2018). Examining recruitment and retention factors for minority STEM majors through a stereotype threat lens. *School Science and Mathematics, 118*(1–2), 61–69. https://doi.org/10.1111/ssm.12260

Moore, T. J., Johnston, A. C., & Glancy, A. W. (2020). STEM integration: A synthesis of conceptual frameworks and definitions. In C. C. Johnson, M. Mohr-Schroeder, T. J. Moore, & English (Eds.), *Handbook of research on STEM education.* London: Routledge.

Morton, C. H., & Smith–Mutegi, D. (2018). Girls STEM institute: Transforming and empowering black girls in mathematics through STEM. In I. Goffney, R. Gutierrez, & M. Boston (Eds.), *Annual perspectives in mathematics education 2018: Rehumanizing mathematics for black, indigenous, and latinx students* (pp. 23–38). Reston, VA: NCTM.

Museus, S. D. (2014). *Asian American students in higher education.* New York, NY: Routledge.

Museus, S. D., Palmer, R. T., Davis, R. J., & Maramba, D. C. (2011). Special issue: Racial and ethnic minority students' success in STEM education. *ASHE Higher Education Report, 36*(6), 1–140. https://doi.org/10.1002/aehe.v36.6

National Council of Teachers of Mathematics. (2014). *Principles to actions: Ensuring mathematical success for all.* Reston, VA: NCTM.

National Science Foundation. (2017). *Women, minorities, and persons with disabilities in science and engineering.* Retrieved from https://www.nsf.gov/statistics/2017/nsf17310/static/downloads/nsf17310-digest.pdf

Palmer, R. T., Maramba, D. C., & Dancy, T. E. (2011). A qualitative investigation of factors promoting the retention and persistence of students of color in STEM. *The Journal of Negro Education,* 491–504.

The President's Council of Advisors on Science and Technology (PCAST). (2010). *Prepare and inspire: K-12 education in science, technology, engineering, and math (STEM) for America's future.* Executive Office of the President of the U.S.A. Retrieved from https://nsf.gov/attachments/117803/public/2a—Prepare_and_Inspire—PCAST.pdf

Riegle-Crumb, C., Moore, C., & Ramos-Wada, A. (2011). Who wants to have a career in science or math? Exploring adolescents' future aspirations by gender and race/ethnicity. *Science Education, 95*(3), 458–476. https://doi.org/10.1002/sce.20431

Rincón, B. E., & Lane, T. B. (2017). Latin@ s in science, technology, engineering, and mathematics (STEM) at the intersections. *Equity & Excellence in Education, 50*(2), 182–195. https://doi.org/10.1080/10665684.2017.1301838

Roberts, T., Jackson, C., Mohr–Schroeder, M. J., Bush, S. B., Maiorca, C., Cavalcanti, M., . . . Cremeans, C. (2018). Students' perceptions of STEM learning after participating in a summer informal learning experience. *International Journal of STEM Education, 5*(1), 35. https://doi.org/10.1186/s40594-018-0133-4

Rodríguez Amaya, L., Betancourt, T., Collins, K. H., Hinojosa, O., & Corona, C. (2018). Undergraduate research experiences: Mentoring, awareness, and perceptions—a case study at a Hispanic-serving institution. *International Journal of STEM Education, 5*(1), 1–13. https://doi.org/10.1186/s40594-018-0105-8

Sandholtz, J. H., & Ringstaff, C. (2014). Inspiring instructional change in elementary school science: The relationship between enhanced self-efficacy and teacher practices. *Journal of Science Teacher Education, 25*(6), 729–751. https://doi.org/10.1007/s10972-014-9393-0

Savage, C., Hindle, R., Meyer, L. H., Hynds, A., Penetito, W., & Sleeter, C. E. (2011). Culturally responsive pedagogies in the classroom: Indigenous student experiences across the curriculum. *Asia-Pacific Journal of Teacher Education, 39*(3), 183–198. https://doi.org/10.1080/1359866X.2011.588311

Solórzano, D. G. (1998). Critical race theory, race and gender microaggressions, and the experience of Chicana and Chicano scholars. *International Journal of Qualitative Studies in Education, 11*(1), 121–136. https://doi.org/10.1080/095183998236926

Stinson, D. W. (2008). Negotiating sociocultural discourses: The counter-storytelling of academically (and mathematically) successful African American male students. *American Educational Research Journal, 45*(4), 975–1010. https://doi.org/10.3102/0002831208319723

Suh, J., Britton, L., Burke, K., Matson, K., Ferguson, L., Jamieson, S., & Seshaiyer, P. (2018). Every penny counts: Promoting community engagement to engage students in mathematical modeling. In I. Goffney, R. Gutierrez, & M. Boston (Eds.), *Annual perspectives in mathematics education 2018: Rehumanizing mathematics for black, indigenous, and Latinx students* (pp. 63–78). Reston, VA: NCTM.

Topcu, M. S. (2013). The achievement gap in science and mathematics: A Turkish perspective. In J. V. Clark (Ed.), *Closing the achievement gap from an international perspective: Transforming STEM for effective education* (pp. 193–213). Dordrecht, The Netherlands: Springer. https://doi.org/10.1007/978-94-007-4357-1_9

Valencia, R. R., & Solórzano, D. G. (1997). Contemporary deficit thinking. *The Evolution of Deficit Thinking: Educational Thought and Practice,* 160–210.

Vincent-Ruz, P., & Schunn, C. D. (2018). The nature of science identity and its role as the driver of student choices. *International Journal of STEM Education, 5*(1), 48. https://doi.org/10.1186/s40594-018-0140-5

Wang, X. (2013). Why students choose STEM majors: Motivation, high school learning, and postsecondary context of support. *American Educational Research Journal, 50*(5), 1081–1121. https://doi.org/10.3102/0002831213488622

Weis, L., Eisenhart, M., Cipollone, K., Stich, A. E., Nikischer, A. B., Hanson, J., . . . Dominguez, R. (2015). In the guise of STEM education reform: Opportunity structures and outcomes in inclusive STEM-focused high schools. *American Educational Research Journal, 52*(6), 1024–1059. https://doi.org/10.3102/0002831215604045

Whalen, D. F., & Shelley, M. C. II. (2010). Academic success for STEM and non–STEM majors. *Journal of STEM Education: Innovations and Research, 11*(1/2), 45.

Zavala, M. D. R. (2014). Latina/o youth's perspectives on race, language, and learning mathematics. *Journal of Urban Mathematics Education, 7*(1), 55–87.

23

RESEARCH ON GENDER EQUITY IN STEM EDUCATION

Gayle A. Buck, Dionne Cross Francis and Kerrie G. Wilkins-Yel

Although the gender gap between men and women is shrinking in several STEM professional fields, women continue to constitute disproportionately smaller percentages (National Science Foundation, 2017). Researchers seek to explore and address the gaps for a variety of reasons. For example, broadening participation increases the pool of potential employees. Similarly, higher pay rates in certain STEM professions hold promise to address gender-based income inequities. Furthermore, the inclusion of diverse voices and perspectives into the design and development process results in solutions that are applicable to a wider cross-section of individuals. Irrespective of the rationale underlying discussions on addressing the underrepresentation of women, these efforts are realizing positive changes—for some STEM fields. Women account for the majority (70%) of the workforce in health-related STEM professions (National Science Foundation, 2018). They also account for 48% of the positions in professions where the main focus lies within the life sciences. The impact of these efforts, however, have not been as successful in all STEM professions. Currently, women make up only 15% of engineers and hold only 24% of the computer-related jobs (Funk & Parker, 2018), the latter reflecting a 7% increase in the gender gap (National Science Foundation, 2018).

Although still heavily focused on women, gender-related research discussions are increasingly considering men, as well as the differences found within the male/female gaps. As noted, gender parity has been achieved in some fields and men are underrepresented in others. In addition, societal challenges to the binary classification of gender are expanding our understandings even further. For example, an increasing amount of research is focused on the underrepresentation of transgender individuals (Yoder & Mattheis, 2016) as well as on challenges to the practice of ignoring race/ethnicity and socioeconomic status in this social construction of gender (Ong, Wright, Espinosa, & Orfield, 2011). Consequently, although the gender and STEM research-related discussions are still overwhelmingly focused on women in STEM, they are evolving.

The purpose of this chapter is to provide an overview of the contemporary research efforts related to gender equity and integrative STEM education. The parameters for our search of empirical literature included: (1) an explicit link to gender (as defined in the next section), and (2) explicit reference to integrated STEM education or crosscutting discussions of STEM professions.

Defining Gender

In coming together to identify the body of research we would review for this chapter, we found ourselves necessarily articulating our construct of gender. First, we understand that gender is not synonymous with women. Although research in this area is overwhelmingly guided by an interest in the underrepresentation of women, we questioned if this approach to gender could ever be inclusive if we do not explore the conversation in regard to men as well. Thus, our definition also acknowledges men in STEM. Second, we acknowledge that gender research is often constructed around understandings of the biological notion of sex and not the dominant modes of social organizations that characterize heterosexist structures and assumptions about gender (O'Malley, 2013). Our definition aligns with the latter perspective, although admittingly still very limited in this regard. Although we don't seek to totally reject the biological boundary of gender in this discussion, we do seek to use a broader definition that would somehow encompass a more inclusive approach to gender. Thus, we also sought to deliberately capture gender work considering transgender (gender identity and expression that does not conform to what is associated with biological sex), cisgender (gender identity and expression that aligns with what is associated with biological sex), and pangender (gender identity and expression as fluid) individuals. Third, we share an understanding that a person's construction of self is influenced not only by gender, but also by their race and socioeconomics (Collins, 1991; Crenshaw, 1994). We seek to challenge what many have come to portray as the universal understanding of gender in STEM; noting that although early discussions sought to address the political and social inequalities that affect women, White, middle-class women were often the focus (Lather, 2007; Ong et al., 2011).

In sum, although we understand that discussions of underrepresentation in STEM do reveal very real inequities for women, our definition of gender in STEM includes cisgender, transgender, and pangender individuals from multiple races and socioeconomic situations. In doing so, we foreground intersectionality, a critical element in understanding the nuanced ways in which STEM participation is gendered, classed, and raced differently (Collins, 1991; Crenshaw, 1994).

STEM College and Career Paths

Despite more than 50 decades of sustained efforts to diversify the STEM participation, many STEM professions remain overwhelmingly comprised of White cisgender men. Women constitute 50.8% of the U.S. population and earn 57% of the bachelor's degrees (U.S. Census Bureau, 2017). A look at the commonalities and differences in the representation across STEM fields reveals that despite this nearly equal representation, women's participation is well below men's in all fields of engineering, computer sciences, and physics. For some STEM fields, this trend was not always the case. In the early 1980s, women comprised more than 36% of bachelor's computer-based science degree recipients. In 2014, however, this number dropped to 18.1%. Additionally, the nearly equal representation of women does not hold true for women of color, who make up less than 12% of STEM bachelor's degree recipients. The gap is even greater for men of color, who make up less than 9%. Counter to this trend of favoring the White male, the gender gap favors women in the fields of biosciences, where they represent 58% of bachelor's degree recipients (National Science Foundation, 2017).

For these reasons, many scholars have begun to discuss and explore gender issues in STEM in an integrative manner. For example, various disciplines within STEM are often grouped into math-intensive fields (e.g., mathematics, physics, engineering) or caring-related fields of STEM (e.g., medicine, biology) (Wang & Degol, 2017). Unfortunately, although survey developers/sponsors (e.g., the National Science Foundation) are increasingly piloting LGBTQ+ questions on their surveys, such quantitative information is not yet available for those in the LGBTQ+ community. The American Physical Society (APS, 2015), however, stated that over one-third of those who responded to their *LGBT Climate in Physics* survey noted they considered leaving their workplace or school after experiencing or observing harassment or discrimination, suggesting that a pipeline problem does exist for LGBTQ+ individuals. Similar experiences were noted by Haverkamp et al. (2019) in an autoethnography of transgender students in engineering. This departure from STEM spaces was regarded by these individuals as a 'positive change' given the toxicity they would have endured had they continued in their STEM fields.

At the undergraduate level, despite possessing comparable qualifications to their male counterparts, women are far less likely to declare a STEM major. In fact, only 15% of all women in their first year planned to pursue a STEM major (compared to 29% of freshman male students). This disparity becomes more evident within the physical sciences, technology, engineering, and mathematics specifically. Of the women who do declare a STEM major in the beginning, many discontinue these majors shortly after entering college. Although men and women show similar retention in programs such as engineering, women make up a smaller percentage of STEM students to begin with, so any loss throughout the collegiate years is cause for concern.

Reasons for Gender Discrepancies in College and Career Pathways

Given the distinct differences in the rates at which men, women, and those who identify as non-binary pursue STEM professions, more attention has been placed on understanding contributing factors towards a leaky pipeline. Essentially, this leaking creates a gender-based filter that privileges one gender while severely marginalizing others, thereby removing them from the stream (Blickenstaff, 2005). The belief that this biased system was not purposely created, along with evidence that the attrition rates for men and women at the postsecondary level are similar (Leslie, McClure, & Oaxaca, 1998), supports the notion that this imbalance is the result of the cumulative effect of a multiplicity of related factors that act on students throughout their lives, especially during the pre-college years. The research on gender and STEM provides insight into these factors. Taken together, this research highlights the factors associated with differences in: (1) achievement and choice, (2) levels of self-efficacy, (3) stereotypes and their influences on STEM identity, (4) sociocultural marginalization within the professional communities, and (5) family support and resources.

Achievement and Choice

The research literature on the gender gap(s) in the STEM pipeline reveals a strong interest in the relationship between the achievement in prerequisite subjects and academic/career interests of students. Because of the rigorous and sequential nature of how the content develops in these disciplines, to choose to major in certain STEM fields in college requires the appropriate academic achievement in science and mathematics in P-12 education. The research is showing, however, that achievement in these areas does not always lead individuals to pursue STEM majors (Wang & Degol, 2017).

Although data show a persistent gender gap in regard to achievement on NAEP and ACT exams in prerequisite subjects, research shows that girls and boys perform similarly in the classrooms (O'Dea, Lagisz, Jennions, & Nakagawa, 2018; Reardon, Fahle, Kalogrides, Podolsky, & Zárate, 2018). These findings contrast with common perceptions of math gender achievement gaps (Lee, Moon, & Hegar, 2011; Robinson & Lubienski, 2011). Researchers are questioning why, if school-level achievement in prerequisite subjects is not preventing members of various gender populations from entering the STEM pipeline, many are choosing not to pursue STEM at the postsecondary level. There is equity in the number of men and women who initially expressed (those who indicated a STEM major on the ACT) and measured (identified on a research-validated interest inventory) interest in STEM. Looking more closely within the broader category of STEM, however, gender differences exist, with men showing greater interest in engineering and women being more interested in health fields and medicine (Sadler, Sonnert, Hazari, & Tai, 2012). In addition, Seymour (1997) found that interest was the most cited reason women provided for why they left the science pipeline, with the second most cited reason being a greater interest in non-STEM fields. There is also a disparity in STEM interest when we consider intersectionality and integrate race and gender. The proportion of students planning to major in STEM were higher for men than for women in every racial and ethnic group (National Science Board, 2014).

Self-Efficacy

Results of studies (e.g., PISA) show that women tend to have lower confidence in their abilities in mathematics and science even when their achievement is on par with men. These lower feelings of competence begin as early as first grade and tend to persist into college. Tellhed, Bäckström, and Björklund (2017) found that only college women had gender-stereotypical self-efficacy, while men believed that they would be able to excel at tasks that were aligned with all STEM occupations, including the more caring-related professions. They posit that women's varied self-efficacy may mediate interest in STEM. Research also notes that women are more likely to undervalue their performance and achievement, while men may overvalue theirs despite similar performance. These self-beliefs are important as they shape behavior (Bandura, 1997), determine the level of motivation and perseverance an individual will apply to completing a task, and influence the choices the individual makes (Wigfield & Eccles, 2000). Bench et al. (2015) found that this overestimation of performance by males accounted for their more focused and intentional pursuit of mathematically based STEM careers compared to women. They suggest that gender gaps in the higher-paying STEM fields may be more related to men overvaluing their abilities than women underestimating theirs.

PISA results in 2006 and 2012 showed that girls have lower self-efficacy than boys in general, but the gap was wider in math than in science. Closer examination of the responses show that gender differences aligned with the type of questions, with girls feeling more confident in answering questions related to issues within the context of health. Similar patterns were observed in math tasks with gender-stereotypical content (Eccles, Jacobs, & Harold, 1990). Overall across genders, low-efficacy positively correlates with performance in math and science. These trends tend to persist through college, showing that compared to men, women tend to have lower self-efficacy for STEM occupations like engineering (Hackett, 1995). Given that self-efficacy mediates interest, it follows that women tend to be less attracted to STEM careers than men (Tellhed et al., 2017).

Stereotypes and STEM Identity

Stereotypes about STEM professionals and STEM identity are among the factors influencing, and being influenced by, students' self-efficacy and interest in STEM. For the percentage of females that do express an interest in STEM, research shows this interest does not always translate into career choice (e.g., Modi, Schoenberg, & Salmond, 2012). The disconnect between ability, interest, and career choice is often explained by issues of identity that develop as a result of the internalization of society's portrayal of the various genders. While these gender stereotypes serve as a significant influence on children's identification with STEM education and their career choice, it is the psychological residue from internalizing these images and perspectives through early childhood and adolescence that seems to be greatly impactful.

One cannot go far into the gender research with encountering a connection to Chambers' work on the stereotypical image of the scientist. Over 50 years after this research was published, which initially collected data of children's images of scientists, students at various levels still consider the stereotypical White male when they think of "scientist" and "STEM" professional often drawing White men when representing scientists (Mason, Kahle, & Gardner, 1991) and mathematicians (Berry & Picker, 2000). Research shows children's gender-based stereotypes of scientists have changed over five decades (Miller, Nolla, Eagly, & Uttal, 2018) as the drawings of scientists now show female scientists more often. Although not overwhelmingly so, children's thoughts and depictions of scientists have become more diverse with respect to gender over time, although children still seem to associate the sciences with men as they develop. Stienke (2013) suggested that more recent portrayals of female scientists in the media have shifted to provide more substantial representations of the varied professional roles of women that "challenge traditional gender stereotypes that formerly relegated them to secondary roles subordinate to male scientists" (p. 2). While showing the brilliance, creativity, intelligence and power of females in high-profile STEM positions, however, the media also displays the challenges females experience, which may serve as a barrier to girls identifying with the character, thereby potentially undermining any STEM aspirations (Steinke, 2005, 2013). Despite these more positive media depictions of females in STEM, it is clear we have not completely left behind stereotypical and negative images of people in STEM. In particular, professionals in computer science and information technology are often represented as deficient in interpersonal skills, as nerdy, geeky, or hackers with no meaningful personal lives (Cheryan, Plaut, Davies, & Steele, 2009).

Gender stereotypes embody beliefs about particular roles, expected behavior assigned to these roles, and particular academic strengths that are innate to males and females. Stereotypes still remain prevalent in the United States despite cultural and ideological shifts in women's roles (Haines, Deaux, & Lofaro, 2016). Some of these include men are assertive while women are meek and modest, and men are highly competent (Fiske, Cuddy, Glick, & Xu, 2002) with talents in math and science while women exude warmth and are innately talented with verbal and associated skills. Because these are widely accepted in society, they are often perpetuated in the classrooms and by parents and females who are respected (Modi, Schoenberg, & Salmond, 2012). The stereotypes then tend to shape the beliefs, interests, or actions of boys and girls as they grow and develop. Similarly, these stereotypes may influence students' beliefs, and subsequently their academic performance.

Findings from research studies suggest that female students often experience stereotype threat during math testing, adversely affecting their performance to some degree (Tomasetto, Alparone, & Cadinu, 2011). Stereotype threat is thought to account for as much as a 20-point difference on the math portion of the SAT (Walton & Spencer, 2009) which becomes significant considering an average of a 30-point difference between males and females. With respect to STEM, stereotype threat has been shown to impact high-achieving women pursuing STEM majors. Women tended to score equally with men under threat-induced conditions and performed significantly better in threat-free conditions (Good, Aronson, & Harder, 2008). Beyond test-taking, researchers suggest that stereotype threat can influence students' aspirations and areas of interest through dis-identification (Aronson, Blanton, & Cooper, 1995). So, given the view that girls are not good at math and science, a female may express disinterest in STEM and try to avoid it completely. However, research (Cromley et al., 2013) shows women score significantly higher than men on sex stereotype bias, suggesting that stereotype threat may only affect a small subset within a group and that constructs other than stereotype threat may better explain gaps in STEM achievement and retention.

Support and Resources

Although not emphasized as much as other themes across the research, the theme of family/community support and resources is regarded as an influential factor. As it pertains to differences between minority male/female students' interests or abilities in STEM, researchers have noted that students situated at the intersection of race and gender tend to have less access to high-quality teaching and rigorous courses (Lee, 2004). In contrast, a survey of minority male undergraduate STEM students revealed that the majority of them were exposed to a rigorous curriculum (Gasman, Nguyen, Conrad, Lundberg, & Commodore, 2017). However, the schools K–12 students who fall within this demographic often attend, vary widely in regard to the availability of such curricula.

Research findings (e.g., Hao & Yeung, 2015) also suggest that socioeconomic status and education manifested through parental spending on their children. It is not necessarily the amount parents spend; rather, data show that parents allocate resources to their children in gendered ways (Raley & Bianchi, 2006). For example, parents tend to engage with girls in more reading and verbal activities (Baker & Milligan, 2016) while holding and enacting the belief that their sons are more talented in STEM (Raley & Bianchi, 2006). These gendered interactions tend to perpetuate existing stereotypes which may lead children to develop gendered interests. For example, research from the Minority Male STEM Initiative (Toldson & Esters, 2012) revealed that support from family was a key theme for minority males who entered STEM fields in college. Also, research on African American women in the STEM education pipeline (Perna et al., 2009) revealed that an institutional atmosphere that conveys an assumption that all African American women at the institution can succeed in STEM fields encouraged persistence.

Sociocultural Marginalization Within the Professional Communities

Many professionals in the STEM disciplines that emphasize neutrality of practices often assume tolerance (Yoder & Mattheis, 2016). Research has revealed, however, that both females and members of the LGBTQ+ community can often feel like outsiders and are often treated as such (Dasgupta, 2015). Individuals tend to have in groups favoritism (Rudman & Glick, 2008). Combined, this suggests that individuals are going to seek out spaces that are dominated by people they consider to be within their group. Given that gender tends to be the first social group children identify and learn (Mehta & Strough, 2009), the dominance of the cisgender male in STEM fields tend to minimize the feelings of belongingness for females and LGBTQ+ people as STEM professionals. Tellhed, Bäckström, and Björklund (2017) found that both university men and women anticipated much stronger social belongingness in gender ingroup-dominated majors. They posited that this may explain why males were less interested in helping professions and why both male and female high school students tended to align themselves with majors that were dominated by the same gender.

Gasman et al. (2017) reported on the effectiveness of a program designed to support persistence in STEM for Black males. The three pillars of participation that contributed to learning and persistence were (a) peers and brotherhood, (b) faculty investment in students, and (c) research opportunities. Research also supports these findings with respect to women (Young, Rudman, Buettner, & McLean, 2013). Results reveal that when female professors are perceived as positive role models, women more closely identified with science, considered science as more of a feminine than a masculine field, and had more pro-science career aspirations and attitudes. Unfortunately, by virtue of being female in an environment of overrepresentation of males in most STEM fields, women often do not have access to such connections and supports.

STEM Educational Programming

Taking into consideration the noted factors that research shows discourages interest and participation in STEM for students from underrepresented genders, a range of stakeholders have designed educational experiences to directly counteract these effects. Most of these programs are grounded in research and involve a combination of the following activities: active learning of STEM content embedded in collaborative projects or activities that are personally meaningful (Liston, Peterson, & Ragan, 2008); engagement with STEM mentors and role models (Mosatche, Matloff-Nieves, Kekelis, & Lawner, 2013); and open discussions and activities to promote resilience, STEM-related efficacy, and STEM identities (Kim, Wei, Xu, Ko, & Ilieva, 2007).

Involvement of girls in programs designed around these principles have yielded positive student outcomes, although there were surprisingly negative results in some cases that serve as cautionary tales. Perhaps one of the most accessible outreach programs aimed at increasing girls' engagement in STEM is *SciGirls* (http://www.scigirlsconnect.org/scigirls)—a National Science Foundation-funded (NSF) PBS television series, website, and outreach that draws from existing research and utilizes strategies designed to improve STEM engagement for tweens. Similar to many such programs, the range of activities and resources target middle school-aged girls. With respect to programming in formal and informal settings that aligns with the aforementioned principles, Girls in Science

(GIS) (Koenig & Hanson, 2008) serves as an example of comprehensive programming designed for middle grade girls, at no cost, to address the perceived barriers of disinterest, underachievement, and misidentification in STEM subjects and careers. GIS aimed to provide positive mastery experiences for girls in science and math to encourage STEM persistence through high school, and increased exposure to real-world applications of math and science through exploration of STEM careers. The program also educates parents with strategies to bolster their daughters' interest in STEM. Implementation involved monthly afterschool meetings with female scientists, a field trip to a local university, and an end-of-year presentation where the girls showcased their knowledge of one STEM career of interest. Similarly, the Black Girls Code program (2018) seeks to become innovators in STEM fields by exposure to computer science and technology. This program offers workshops and afterschool programs free of charge to African American girls. The programs have seven established institutions in seven U.S. states, as well as one in Johannesburg, South Africa. While in the programs, the girls code and design mobile apps that help solve problems in their communities.

There are also several programs seeking to increase the involvement of young Black men in STEM (Rucker, 2013). The Summer Engineering Experience for Kids, sponsored by the National Society of Black Engineers, consists of camps designed to expose students to hands-on projects, African American college students working on degrees in STEM, and minority images in science. This is one of the programs addressing the recommendations from the final report for the African American Males in STEM 2010 workshop. The recommendations included: (a) summer camps in math and science for middle and high school African American males, (b) increasing/encouraging the involvement of African American males in extracurricular activities such as science clubs/fairs, (c) identify mentors for African American boys at an early age, (d) more K-12 activities that have strong motivational and learning components such as making science relevant to the students' everyday lives, and (e) increasing the involvement of parents/families (The Quality Education for Minorities Network, 2010).

Across these initiatives, core elements to which success is attributed are: (a) accessibility to program activities, (b) affordability of participation, (c) flexibility to allow for greater participation, (d) engaging activities that motivated participation, and (e) the incorporation of underrepresented genders in STEM professionals. Role models and mentors help broaden various students' perspectives of who can work in the STEM field, and most importantly expands their vision of their own potential. Many studies report the positive impact of interaction with these professions in a range of capacities promote STEM interest, efficacy, and identity (Breda, Grenet, Monnett, & Van Effenterre, 2018; Holmes, Redmond, Thomas, & High, 2012; Mosatche et al., 2013). In fact, Kesar (2018) showed that on average across math, physics, biology, chemistry, and computer science, opportunities to have a STEM role model resulted in a 12% increase in interest. Moreover, even if the role model was in only one content area, there was a corresponding positive effect across other STEM subjects. However, there seems to be a cultural component that results in different trends outside of North America. For example, Breda et al. (2018) showed that girls with role models in the Czech Republic are only 2% more interested in STEM subjects. Additionally, decrease in interest was observed when girls had role models in some subjects such as computer science, math, and physics. This latter finding aligns with Bamberger (2014), who found Israeli ninth-grade girls' engagement and interaction with female scientists decreased the girls' confidence in their ability to pursue a STEM career.

Challenges and Future Directions in Gender Equity and Integrative STEM Education

As highlighted in other chapters throughout this book, integrative STEM education has many benefits. Specifically, STEM integration calls for engaging students in authentic problem solving, using crosscutting STEM ideas, and student-centered teaching and classroom strategies (Moore,

Johnston, & Glancy, 2020). It is likely that such an integrative approach to STEM education could contribute to decreasing the gender disparity. Research has shown that engagement in activities that demonstrate the real-world applicability of STEM concepts can increase STEM interest and motivation among women, women of color, and men of color. However, given the relatively new call for an integrative STEM approach, much of the extant literature has focused on identifying effective teaching strategies to convey such an approach (e.g., Smith, Rayfield, & McKim, 2015). Little research has directly examined the effect of an integrated STEM curriculum on reducing the gender gaps. Future research is needed to better examine this relation.

Nonetheless, research with participants in STEM has shown that a number of barriers contribute to the widening gender disparity in STEM. Several themes cut across this research. First, research reveals that gender does make a difference in regard to the STEM pipeline. This is supported by both large quantitative studies (e.g., National Science Foundation, 2017) and qualitative studies (e.g., Seymour, 1997). Second, the empirical evidence suggests that this gap is due to individuals from marginalized genders *choosing* to leave the pipeline as opposed to innate or immutable differences that prevent them from continuing. A third common theme across all the research is that the gender disparity in STEM is detrimental to all of us. These gaps prevent marginalized gender groups from gaining equal access to professional fields and benefiting from the higher pay rates. The gaps also prevent the professional communities from realizing an adequate pool of potential employees and benefiting from a diverse pool of perspectives (Hegewisch, Liepmann, Hayes, & Hartmann, 2010).

Overall, the extant research base is heavily focused on the underrepresentation of women in STEM. However, a woman's construction of self is not only influenced by their gender, but also by their race and socioeconomic status (Lather, 2007). It follows then that an intersectional approach is necessary. Consequently, research has expanded to include explorations that focus on the intersection of gender and race (e.g., Perna et al., 2009). Research has also shed light on men in STEM (e.g., Dill, Price-Glynn, & Rakovski, 2016) as well as the intersectional experience of Black men in STEM (e.g., Strayhorn, 2015). Further work is needed to understand the STEM experiences of individuals who identify as transgender. Allowing this evolution of our understanding of gender equity in STEM facilitates a critical examination of our own perspectives and biases (Crawford & Unger, 2000).

Several formal and informal efforts have been developed to combat the gender gap in STEM. These are often summer camps or afterschool programs that engage gendered groups in experiential STEM activities and provide access to professionals who serve as mentors or role models. These programs have largely been effective in engendering STEM interest and motivation. Future efforts can expand on these approaches to include a more integrated STEM curriculum versus a focus on one STEM area (e.g., coding). In keeping with our expanded focus on gender, these formal and informal efforts can be expanded to focus on trans youth as well.

Concluding Remarks

Our review suggests that research on gender equity in STEM education is important and still necessary. The future direction of this body of research, however, needs to change considering the insights gained from gender-equity interventions, our own understandings of gender, and natural evolution of the social structure. Given the nuanced nature of gender and STEM, this is a wonderfully complex and dynamic task that must be taken on if STEM is going to truly be a viable and desirable option for all.

References

American Physical Society. (2015). *LGBT climate in physics.* Retrieved from: https://www-aps-org.proxyiub.uits. iu.edu/programs/lgbt/

Aronson, J., Blanton, H., & Cooper, J. (1995). From dissonance to disidentification: Selectivity in the self-affirmation process. *Journal of Personality and Social Psychology, 68*(6), 986–996.

Baker, M., & Milligan, K. (2016). Boy-girl differences in parental time investments: Evidence from three countries. *Journal of Human Capital, 10*(4), 399–441.

Bamberger, Y. (2014). Encouraging girls into science and technology with feminine role model: Does this work? *Journal of Science Education and Technology, 23*(4), 549–561.

Bandura, A. (1997). *Self-efficacy: The exercise of control.* New York, NY: Freeman.

Bench, S. W., Lench, H. C., Miner, K., Flores, S. A., & Liew, J. (2015). Gender gaps in overestimation of math performance. *Sex Roles, 72,* 536–546.

Berry, J., & Picker, S. H. (2000). Your pupils' images of mathematicians and mathematics. *Mathematics in School, 29*(2), 24–26.

Black Girls Code. (2018). Retrieved from http://www.blackgirlscode.com/what-we-do.html

Blickenstaff, J. C. (2005). Women and science careers: Leaky pipeline or gender filter? *Gender and Education, 17,* 369–386.

Breda, T., Grenet, J., Monnet, M., & Van Effenterre, C. (2018). Can female role models reduce the gender gap in science? *Evidence* from classroom interventions in French high schools. halshs-01713068.

Cheryan, S., Plaut, V. C., Davies, P. G., & Steele, C. M. (2009). Ambient belonging: How stereotypical cues impact gender participation in computer science. *Journal of Personality and Social Psychology, 97*(6), 1045–1060. https://doi.org/10.1037/a0016239

Collins, P. (1991). *Black feminist thought: Knowledge, consciousness and the politics of empowerment.* London: Routledge.

Crawford, M., & Unger, R. (2000). *Women and gender: A feminist psychology* (4th ed.). New York, NY: McGraw-Hill.

Crenshaw, K. W. (1994/2005). Mapping the margins: Intersectionality, identity politics, and violence against women of color. In M. A. Fineman & R. Mykitiuk (Eds.), *The public nature of private violence* (pp. 93–118). New York, NY: Routledge.

Cromley, J. G., Perez, T., Wills, T. W., Tanaka, J. C., Horvat, E. M. N., & Agbenyega, E. T. B. (2013). Changes in race and sex stereotype threat among diverse STEM students: Relation to grades and retention in the majors. *Contemporary Educational Psychology, 38*(3), 247–258. doi:10.1016/j.cedpsych.2013.04.003

Dasgupta, N. (2015). Role models and peers as a social vaccine to enhance women's self-concept in STEM. *The American Society for Cell Biology.* Retrieved from https://www.iwitts.org/proven-practices/retention-sub-topics/lab-team-work/893-role-models-and-peers-as-a-social-vaccine-to-enhance-women-s-self-concept-in-stem2

Dill, J. S., Price-Glynn, K., & Rakovski, C. (2016). Does the "glass escalator" compensate for the devaluation of care work occupations? The careers of men in low-and middle-skill health care jobs. *Gender & Society, 30*(2), 334–360.

Eccles, J. S., Jacobs, J. E., & Harold, R. D. (1990). Gender role stereotypes, expectancy effects, and parents' socialization of gender differences. *Journal of Social Issues, 46,* 183–201. doi:10.1111/j.1540-4560.1990.tb01929.x

Fiske, S. T., Cuddy, A. J. C., Glick, P., & Xu, J. (2002). A model of (often mixed) stereotype content: Competence and warmth respectively follow from perceived status and competition. *Journal of Personality and Social Psychology, 82*(6), 878–902.

Funk, C., & Parker, K. (2018). Diversity in the STEM workforce varies widely across jobs. In *Report: Women and minorities in STEM often at odds over workplace equity.* Retrieved from: http://www.pewsocialtrends.org/2018/01/09/diversity-in-the-stem-workforce-varies-widely-across-jobs/

Gasman, M., Nguyen, T. H., Conrad, C. F., Lundberg, T., & Commodore, F. (2017). Black male success in STEM: A case study of Morehouse College. *Journal of Diversity in Higher Education, 10*(2), 181–200. doi:10.1037/dhe0000013

Good, C., Aronson, J., & Harder, J. A. (2008). Problems in the pipeline: Stereotype threat and achievement in high-level math courses. *Journal of Applied Developmental Psychology, 29*(1), 17–28.

Hackett, G. (1995). Self-efficacy in career choice and development. In A. Bandura (Ed.), *Self-efficacy in changing societies* (pp. 232–258). New York, NY: Cambridge University Press.

Haines, E. L., Deaux, K., & Lofaro, N. (2016). The times they are a-changing … or are they not? A comparison of gender stereotypes, 1983–2014. *Psychology of Women Quarterly, 40*(3), 353–363.

Hao, L., & Yeung, W. -J. J. (2015). Parental spending on school-age children: Structural stratification and parental expectation. *Demography, 52*(3), 835–860.

Haverkamp, A., Butler, A., Pelzl, N., Bothwell, M., Montfort, D., & Driskill, Q. (2019). *Exploring transgender and gender nonconforming engineering undergraduate experiences through autoethnography.* Paper presentation American Society for Engineering Education, Tampa, FL.

Hegewisch, A., Liepmann, H., Hayes, J., & Hartmann, H. (2010). *Separate and not equal? Gender segregation in the labor market and the gender wage gap.* IWPR Briefing Paper 377.

Holmes, S., Redmond, A., Thomas, J., & High, K. (2012). Girls helping girls: Assessing the influence of college student mentors in an afterschool engineering program. *Mentoring and Teaching: Partnership in Learning, 20*(1), 137–150.

Kesar, S. (2018). *Closing the STEM gap: Why STEM classes and careers still lack girls and what we can do about it.* Microsoft. Retrieved from https://query.prod.cms.rt.microsoft.com/cms/api/am/binary/RE1UMWz

Kim, Y., Wei, Q., Xu, B., Ko, Y., & Ilieva, V. (2007). MathGirls: Toward developing girls' positive attitude and self-efficacy through pedagogical agents. In R. Luckin, K. R. Koedinger, & J. Greer (Eds.), *Artificial intelligence in education: Building technology rich learning contexts that work* (pp. 119–126). Los Angeles, CA: IOS Press.

Koenig, K., & Hanson, M. (2008). Fueling interest in science: An after-school program model that works! *Science Scope, 32*(4), 48.

Lather, P. (2007). *Getting lost: Feminist efforts toward a double(d) science.* Albany: SUNY Press.

Lee, C. (2004). *Racial segregation and educational outcomes in metropolitan Boston.* Cambridge, MA: The Civil Rights Project at Harvard University.

Lee, J., Moon, S., & Hegar, R. (2011). Mathematics skills in early childhood: Exploring gender and ethnic patterns. *Child Indicators Research, 4*(3), 353–368. doi:10.1007/s12187-010-9088-9

Leslie, L. L., McClure, G. T., & Oaxaca, R. L. (1998). Women and minorities in science and engineering. A life sequence analysis. *Journal of Higher Education, 69*(3), 239.

Liston, C., Peterson, K., & Ragan, V. (2008). *Evaluating promising practices in informal science, technology, engineering, and mathematics (STEM) education for girls.* New York, NY: Girl Scouts of the USA.

Mason, C. L., Kahle, J. B., & Gardner, A. L. (1991). Draw-A-Scientist test: Future implications. *School Science and Mathematics, 91*(5), 193–198.

Mehta, C. M., & Strough, J. (2009). Sex segregation in friendships and normative contexts across the life span. *Developmental Review, 29*(3), 201–220. doi:10.1016/j.dr.2009.06.001

Miller, D. I., Nolla, K. M., Eagly, A. H., & Uttal, D. H. (2018). The development of children's gender-science stereotypes: A meta-analysis of 5 decades of U.S. Draw-A-Scientist studies. *Child Development, 89*(6), 1943–1955. doi:10.1111/cdev.13039

Modi, K., Schoenberg, J., & Salmond, K. (2012). *Generation STEM: What girls say about science, technology, engineering and math.* New York City, NY: The Girl Scout Research Institute.

Moore, T., Johnston, A., & Glancy, A. (2020). STEM integration: A synthesis of conceptual frameworks and definitions. In C. Johnson, M. Mohr-Schroeder, T. Moore, & L. English (Eds.), *Handbook of research on STEM education.* New York, NY: Routledge.

Mosatche, H. S., Matloff-Nieves, S., Kekelis, L., & Lawner, E. K. (2013, Spring). Effective STEM programs for adolescent girls: Three approaches and many lessons learned. *Afterschool Matters, 17*, 17–25.

National Science Board. (2014). *Science and engineering indicators 2014.* Arlington, VA: Author.

National Science Foundation. (2017). *Report: Women, minorities, and persons with disabilities in science and engineering.* Washington, DC: Author. Retrieved from https://www.nsf.gov/statistics/2017/nsf17310/static/downloads/nsf17310-digest.pdf

National Science Foundation. (2018). *Report: Science and engineering indicators 2018.* Alexandria, VA: Author. Retrieved from https://www.nsf.gov/statistics/2018/nsb20181/report/sections/science-and-engineering-labor-force/women-and-minorities-in-the-s-e-workforce

O'Dea, R. E., Lagisz, M., Jennions, M. D., & Nakagawa, S. (2018). Gender differences in individual variation in academic grades fail to fit expected patterns for STEM. *Nature Communications, 9.* doi:10.1038/s41467-018-06292-0

O'Malley, M. P. (2013). Creating inclusive schools for LGBTIQ youth, staff, and families. In L. Tillman & J. Scheurich (Eds.), *Handbook of research on educational leadership for equity and diversity* (pp. 355–379). doi:10.4324/9780203076934

Ong, M., Wright, C., Espinosa, L., & Orfield, G. (2011). Inside the double bind: A synthesis of empirical research on undergraduate and graduate women of color in science, technology, engineering, and mathematics. *Harvard Educational Review, 81*(2), 172–209. doi:10.17763/haer.81.2.t022245n7x4752v2

Perna, L., Lundy-Wagner, V., Drezner, N. D., Gasman, M., Yoon, S., Bose, E., & Gary, S. (2009). The contribution of HBCUS to the preparation of African American women for STEM careers: A case study. *Research in Higher Education, 50,* 1–23. doi:10.1007/s11162–008–9110-y

The Quality Education for Minorities Network. (2010, September). *Spring 2010 workshop on the recruitment and retention of African American male students in science, technology, engineering and mathematics (STEM).* Washington, DC: Author. Retrieved from https://static1.squarespace.com/static/57b5ee7d440243ac78571d0a/t/57bda47fff7c5054037a92ce/1472046207690/African+American+Males+Report%5B5%5D.pdf

Raley, S., & Bianchi, S. (2006). Sons, daughters, and family processes: Does gender of children matter? *Annual Review of Sociology, 32*(1), 401–421. doi:10.1146/annurev.soc.32.061604.123106

Reardon, S. F., Fahle, E. M., Kalogrides, D., Podolsky, A., & Zárate, R. C. (2018). *Gender achievement gaps in U.S. school districts.* (CEPA Working Paper No.18–13). Retrieved from Stanford Center for Education Policy Analysis: http://cepa.stanford.edu/wp18-13

Robinson, J. P., & Lubienski, S. T. (2011). The development of gender achievement gaps in mathematics and reading during elementary and middle school: Examining direct cognitive assessments and teacher ratings. *American Educational Research Journal, 48*(2), 268–302. doi:10.3102/0002831210372249

Rucker. (2013, June). *Education to innovation: 5 STEM programs for young Black men.* Retrieved from https://www.blackenterprise.com/stem-science-engineering-programs-for-young-black-men/

Rudman, L. A., & Glick, P. (2008). *Texts in social psychology. The social psychology of gender: How power and intimacy shape gender relations.* New York, NY, US: Guilford Press.

Sadler, P. M., Sonnert, G., Hazari, Z., & Tai, R. H. (2012). Stability and volatility of STEM career interest in high school: A gender study. *Science Education, 96*(3), 411–427. doi:10.1002/ sce.21007

Seymour, E. (1997). *Talking about leaving: Why undergraduates leave the sciences.* Boulder, CO: Westview Press.

Smith, K. L., Rayfield, J., & McKim, B. R. (2015). Effective practices in STEM integration: Describing teacher perceptions and instructional method use. *Journal of Agricultural Education, 56*(4), 183–203.

Steinke, J. (2005). Cultural representations of gender and science: Portrayals of female scientists and engineers in popular films. *Science Communication, 27*(1), 27–63.

Steinke, J. (2013). Portrayals of female scientists in the mass media. In A. Valdivia & S. R. Mazzarella (Eds.), *The international encyclopedia of media studies* (pp. 1–18). Oxford, UK: Blackwell.

Strayhorn, T. L. (2015). Factors influencing Black males' preparation for college and success in STEM majors: A mixed methods study. *Western Journal of Black Studies, 39*(1), 45–63.

Tellhed, U., Bäckström, M., & Björklund, F. (2017). Will I fit in and do well? The importance of social belongingness and self-efficacy for explaining gender differences in interest in STEM and HEED majors. *Sex Roles, 77*(1–2), 86–96. doi:10.1007/s11199–016–0694-y

Toldson, I. A., & Esters, L. L. (2012). *The quest for excellence: Supporting the academic success of minority males in science, technology, engineering and mathematics (STEM).* Washington, DC: Association of Public and Land-grant Universities.

Tomasetto, C., Alparone, F. R., & Cadinu, M. (2011). Girls' math performance under stereotype threat: The moderating role of mothers' gender stereotypes. *Developmental Psychology, 47*(4), 943–949. doi:10.1037/ a0024047

U.S. Census Bureau. (2017). *Educational attainment in the United States.* Retrieved from https://www.census.gov/data/tables/2017/demo/education-attainment/cps-detailed-tables.html

Walton, G. M., & Spencer, S. J. (2009). Latent ability: Grades and test scores systematically underestimate the intellectual ability of negatively stereotyped students. *Psychological Science, 20*, 1132–1139. doi:10.1111/ j.1467–9280.2009.02417.x

Wang, M., & Degol, J. (2017). Gender gap in science, technology, engineering, and mathematics (STEM): Current knowledge, implications for practice, policy, and future directions. *Educational Psychology Review, 29*(1), 119–140. doi:10.1007/s10648–015–9355-x

Wigfield, A., & Eccles, J. S. (2000). Expectancy-value theory of achievement motivation. *Contemporary Educational Psychology, 25*, 68–81. doi:10.1006/ceps.1999.1015

Yoder, J. B., & Mattheis, A. (2016). Queer in STEM: Workplace experiences reported in a national survey of LGBTQA individuals in science, technology, engineering, and mathematics careers. *Journal of Homosexuality, 63*(1), 1–27. doi:10.1080/00918369.2015.1078632

Young, D. M., Rudman, L. A., Buettner, H. M., & McLean, M. C. (2013). The influence of female role models on women's implicit science cognitions. *Psychology of Women Quarterly, 37*(3), 283–292.

24

THE AFFORDANCES AND CHALLENGES OF ENACTING CULTURALLY RELEVANT STEM PEDAGOGY

*Paula A. Magee, Craig Willey, Esra Ceran, Jeremy Price
and Javier Barrera Cervantes*

Around the world, nations have struggled to provide culturally relevant curriculum and pedagogy for all children, particularly those from non-dominant economic, social and cultural status backgrounds. That is, schooling structures and processes have tended to be designed by, and for, those in power positions—the affluent and those from high-status social, racial and cultural backgrounds (e.g., Spring, 2014; Watkins, 2001). Only through persistent efforts have considerations been made for underrepresented cultural traditions in educating youth (Walker, 2013), and for the values and ways of being of underrepresented groups (González, Moll, & Amanti, 2006). This is even more evident in science, mathematics, engineering and technology (STEM) disciplines, which have come to be defined in a certain way by those in power who put forth particular ideological narratives about what it means to do STEM (Gee, 2007). Given the inherent power relations that serve to include some and exclude others, access to, and success within, STEM teaching and learning spaces is a clear social justice issue.

STEM teaching and learning must be connected to critical, social issues that respond to the happenings in students' lives. Over the past 15 years, researchers have documented how and when STEM can be used as a way to teach and promote social justice (Barton, 2003; Gutstein, 2006). For example, in her book *Teaching Science for Social Justice*, Barton (2003) challenges conventional notions of what science looks like and implores teachers to hear and see the work of youth—specifically youth of color and those living in poverty—as valuable, important and scientific. With this vision, STEM can be used as a tool for improving the world and making it a more equitable place for children and their communities.

Centralized governments around the world address complaints of inequitable schooling arrangements, opportunities, and outcomes for children based on particular markers (e.g., race, class, ability, physical location). Glewwe and Kremer (2006), for example, stressed that in many developing countries, students are taught in a language that is not their native tongue. Since almost all developing countries were at one time colonies, school systems were developed under colonial rule where the language of the colonizer was used. In addition, students do not have equal opportunities compared to their peers, due to the different socioeconomic backgrounds present in most developing countries (OECD, 2016). This socioeconomic difference results in significant gaps in educational outcomes (Balestra, Llena-Nozal, Murtin, Tosetto, & Arnoud, 2018). For instance, Alacacı and Erbaş (2010) analyzed data obtained from PISA 2006 (the Program for International Student Assessment), a system of international assessment focused on the capabilities of students' reading, mathematics and science literacy among 57 countries. Since PISA collects data about students' performances as well as students' family background, researchers were able to correlate students' background profiles to their performance in these disciplines. It is clear that, across nations, the socioeconomic backgrounds of students adversely affects students' academic achievement.

Considering heterogeneity in educational background, school quality and students' race, ethnicity and language, it is challenging to design a single curriculum appropriate for all students. Yet, most developing countries have a single, centrally set curriculum, and this limits the ability of schools to adjust to local needs (Glewwe & Kremer, 2006; Lockheed & Verspoor, 1991). Such materials, overwhelmingly focusing on dominant cultural narratives (Griffin & James, 2018; Le & Matias, 2019) and presenting limited views of historical oppression and contributions from non-dominant STEM researchers and practitioners, fail to address the educational needs of all students.

Scripted curricula, lack of teacher autonomy and historical socioeconomic disparities ensure that educational inequities persist (So & Kang, 2014). Culturally relevant STEM pedagogy (CRSP) represents a promising avenue not only to help children make meaning of academic concepts, but also to develop cultural competence and a sense of justice and agency in pluralistic communities around the globe (Leonard, Brooks, Barnes-Johnson, & Berry III, 2010; Mensah, 2011). The tenets of CRP represent many of the values and aspirations that are being fought for across international contexts: justice, dignity and access to critical resources (Gutstein, Lipman, Hernandez, & de los Reyes, 1997; Tate, 1995).

Research has demonstrated that CRP promotes high achievement and effective learning opportunities in schools (Howard, 2010; Ladson-Billings, 2009; Richards, Brown & Forde, 2004), but better understanding of how to implement CRP in integrated STEM education remains underexplored (Johnson, 2011; Johnson, Bolshakova, & Waldron, 2016). As discussed in the next section, examples of variations of CRSP can be found worldwide (George, 2013; Nichol & Robinson, 2010; Abrams, Taylor, & Guo, 2013). By analyzing research and disseminating current and potentially new ways to enact CRSP, STEM education can become even more connected to the original ideas of culturally relevant pedagogy.

Preparing socially just and critically conscious elementary STEM teachers is complex. Teacher educators contend with teachers' fear of STEM as well as the ingrained, and often invisible, structurally racist practices that exist in elementary classrooms, where children's STEM identities are forming (Boutte, Kelly-Jackson, & Johnson, 2010; Mensah & Jackson, 2018). Identifying resources, activities and theoretical frameworks that are accessible to teachers and preservice teachers, and that support their development in these key areas, remains difficult (Ladson-Billings, 2014; Willey & Magee, 2015, 2018). Often, considerations of race, equity and oppression are far removed from the expectations elementary teachers have when they teach science and mathematics or engage in professional development. One approach to connecting theory to practice is to help teachers understand and use the tenets of CRP (Ladson-Billings, 1995). While teacher educators have engaged and used CRP for decades, with mixed success, some published work in this area falls short of complex enactments, and sometimes misinterprets Ladson-Billings's intentions (Ladson-Billings, 2014; Young, 2010). As is to be expected, researchers and teachers enact and understand CRP based on their lived experiences, and these enactments are not always in line with the researcher's original intent (Ladson-Billings, 2014). One way this is addressed is through the development of alternatively named pedagogies (for an example, see Paris, 2012) that work to recapture and redefine the tenets. Another way is to analyze the current literature and make suggestions for how to move toward a more comprehensive enactment of CRP.

This chapter begins with a brief overview of the central tenets of CRP and culturally responsive teaching. We then examine the existing international literature on CRSP, delineating research studies into three categories: (1) student engagement and outcomes, (2) instructional practices, dispositions and teacher training and (3) curricular materials. Finally, the chapter summarizes the inherent difficulties found in enacting CRSP and offer suggestions for how to incorporate a CRSP agenda into classrooms.

Literature Review

Culturally relevant pedagogy has emerged as a way to challenge the White, Eurocentric curricula and teaching found in many schools worldwide (Ladson-Billings, 1995; Blanchet-Cohen & Reilly, 2017; Milner, 2011). While definitions of culturally relevant/responsive education/pedagogy vary (Banks, 2004; Gay, 2010; Ladson-Billings, 1995), generally agreed-upon tenants include: explicit valuing of students' language, home life and family and the incorporation of these into educative experiences; for all students, a commitment to academic success that breaks down existing educational barriers (e.g., tracking); and the development of education as a critical activity that actively seeks to make the world a more just and equitable place. Issues of (in)equity pertaining to first language, race and culture are systemic within countries and local communities worldwide. In fact, many cultural groups experience continued or exacerbated levels of oppression and marginalization, despite ongoing struggles for liberation. For example, in her seminal article "But That's Just Good Teaching," Ladson-Billings (1995) describes how teachers' interactions with, and expectations of, students of color—particularly African American males—can result in unintentional power struggles, microaggressions toward students and student failure (Gay, 2010). In her book *Dreamkeepers*, Ladson-Billings (2009) outlines how teachers, both white and of color, are successful with African American children by holding deep-rooted, anti-racist perceptions about people of color. Teachers who truly succeed with all students are aware of their own racial biases and work intentionally to dismantle them (Obidah & Teel, 2001; Milner, Cunningham, Delale-O'Connor, & Kestenberg, 2019). In addition to a personal commitment to a critical consciousness, successful teachers acknowledge the systemic racism and oppression that exists and causes significant burdens to people of color (Milner et al., 2019). While always reluctant to describe *what* culturally relevant pedagogy *is* (for fear of reducing it to a checklist of easy-to-follow steps), Ladson-Billings does include examples such as including families in the curriculum, collaborating with students to create a classroom community and *always* looking below the surface for how CRP is enacted.

In their review of the literature on culturally relevant education (CRE), Aaronson and Laughter (2016) discuss the subtle differences between culturally relevant pedagogy (Ladson-Billings, 1995, 2014), culturally responsive teaching (Gay, 2002, 2013) and multicultural education as they respond to the call to document CRP/CRE to student learning outcomes (Sleeter, 2012). Their findings suggest that the culturally relevant/responsive frameworks are more similar than different and that framework foci shift between teachers' dispositions (Ladson-Billings, 2014) and/or teacher practice (Gay, 2002). In response to this they use the term "culturally relevant education" to capture a more complete view of these pedagogies.

As will be described more fully, all enactments of culturally relevant teaching exist on a *continuum of criticality*. We use the idea of a continuum of criticality to both accept where beginning and pre-service teachers are with respect to understanding CRP, and as a tool to encourage a deeper, more sophisticated understanding of the enactment of CRSP. For example, teachers may recognize that authentic word problems are necessary in mathematics, but they may still struggle to use relevant examples despite this recognition. The development of actual real-world problems, as opposed to contrived ones, would be farther along the continuum. Or, as described by Hernandez and colleagues (2013), teachers may enact some tenets (cultural competence) but not others (critical consciousness). Many researchers identify which culturally relevant tenet(s) their studies connect to, and this is a critical piece in developing a theory to practice trajectory. To better understand this trajectory, we have mined the studies discussed here and our own experiences with teachers and preservice teachers to document pedagogical specificities of CRSP.

Despite a generally agreed-upon need for CRP, there remains a lack of CRSP in practice (Ladson-Billings, 2006; Milner, 2011; Howard & Rodriguez-Scheel, 2017). The reasons are complicated but can be generalized into several categories: teachers' difficulty developing complex understandings of CRP and the unconscious retention of teacher-centered pedagogies (Ladson-Billings, 2014); pressure from administrators to use teacher-centered and direct instruction pedagogies (Rivera Maulucci, Brown, Grey, & Sullivan, 2014) and teachers' unrevealed but present racist/biased beliefs (Milner, 2011; Ladson-Billings, 2014).

Culturally Relevant STEM Pedagogy Across International Contexts

A goal of this chapter is to offer readers a way to conceptualize CRSP in practice. Understanding the theoretical underpinnings is crucial, but if a teacher's understanding cannot be translated to productive classroom practice, the theories do little good. As a means to this end we have conducted a thorough reading and analysis of the international articles in our database. This analysis revealed three categories to which specific CRSP practices could be assigned. From the articles it is clear that these practices are globally relevant as well. What "works" in one locale may not in another. This does not mean that a practice is wrong. Instead it reminds us that we must always be mindful of our context and of local practices and norms.

The categories emerged as we looked at the components that constitute CRP (Ladson-Billings, 1995; Aronson & Laughter, 2016; Vazquez Dominguez, Allexsaht-Snider, & Buxton, 2018) and teaching for social justice (Villegas & Lucas, 2002; Barton, 2003). The three categories identified are: student engagement and outcomes (SEO), instructional practices and dispositions (IPD) and curricular materials (CM). Table 24.1 summarizes the overall coding process we arrived at after reading and analyzing the articles.

CRP Influence on Student Engagement and Outcomes

How has CRSP influenced student engagement and academic learning outcomes? While it can be tempting to reduce student outcomes to test scores, scholars have cautioned against such a reductionist approach (Boutte et al., 2010). Specifically, Ladson-Billings (2014) regrets her own use of the term "academic achievement" because it is often misconstrued as test scores. Milner (2011) follows this by expanding the idea of science outcomes to include student empowerment, culture-rich curriculum and complex classroom dynamics (curricula are challenging and innovative; focus on student learning; build cultural competence and link curriculum and instruction to sociopolitical realities). Many of the researchers included in this review (e.g., Johnson et al., 2016; Mensah, 2011; Varelas, Martin, & Kane, 2012) tend to measure learning through participation, engagement and the formation of positive STEM identities. Given the systemic inequities in science education, researchers call for more careful examinations of these measures and their correspondences to long-term success.

For example, in the United States people of African descent are more likely to drop out/be forced out of high school and to be disciplined with expulsion (Artiles, Kozleski, Trent, Osher, & Ortiz, 2010; Harry & Klingner, 2014; US DOE OCR, 2014). In Jamaica, Lodge (2017) revealed the marginalization of Jamaican Creole and the subsequent injurious effects this has on Jamaican students and their science education. In New Zealand, Averill and colleagues (Averill, Anderson, Easton, Maro, Smith, & Hynds, 2009) explored the complexities of the continued ineffectiveness of math education despite years of policies aimed at supporting bicultural mathematics education.

In response to this, CRSP encourages teachers to authentically incorporate culturally relevant practices as a way to enhance learning. One way to do this is for teachers to consider how cultural practices (e.g., music genres) can be used as a way to increase student engagement and subsequent

Table 24.1 Results From Analysis of Literature on Culturally Relevant STEM Pedagogy

Key Theme	Big Ideas	Practice Example
Student Engagement and Outcomes	CRSP increases student engagement Student empowerment, culture-rich curriculum and complex classroom dynamics CRSP supports a deeper more critical learning of STEM	Broadening notions of academic success beyond test scores Helping students feel included within STEM learning community Students see themselves as STEM professionals Students' use their own music and popular culture preferences
Instructional Practices, Dispositions and Teacher Training	Connections to community Authenticity in STEM Inquiry-based instruction Building relationships Awareness of, and attention to, race/ethnicity	Inclusion of elders in instructional spaces Prioritizing students' needs Students voice and choice were always included in teaching Giving students a second chance/not holding a grudge Working through difficult situations with commitment and care Honor students' perceptions of reality/recognize importance of children Include history and contributions of diverse STEM professionals whenever possible "[A]n understanding that people's way of thinking, behaving, and being are deeply influenced by such factors as race/ethnicity, social class, and language" (Villegas & Lucas, 2002, p. 22)
Curricular Materials	Ethnocentric curriculum Curriculum that makes explicit connections to sociopolitical realities	Software to analyze cultural practices such as hair braiding Use of texts that resonate with students Use of culturally relevant music and media (i.e., hip-hop call and response) Honoring cultural assets Supports understanding of relationship to each other and to the earth

learning. For example, Adjapong and Emdin (2015) list several ways for middle school science teachers, "These include but are not limited to graffiti art, MCing, Bboying (break dancing), DJing and knowledge of self" (p. 67). In this study the authors share how both call and response and student/teacher co-teaching "allows them [students] to move from memorization to active participation through the use of culturally rooted approaches to teaching" (p. 75).

Another potential strategy for increasing student engagement and hence opportunities for learning is for educators to be open-minded about how and when students' interests are incorporated into the curriculum. When students' suggestions fall in line with teachers' expectations, incorporating them into the curriculum is low risk. However, researchers stress that being open-minded and creative about how to hear and build off of students' ideas is a critical skill. For example, in her book *Teaching Science for Social Justice*, Barton (2003) described that when researchers recognized and valued students' interests in creating an outdoor tunnel, students saw themselves as scientists and re-envisioned what school science could look like.

With regard to mathematics classrooms, Aronson and Laughter (2016) conclude, "Despite differing grade levels, Tate (1995), Ensign (2003), and Civil and Khan's (2001) studies demonstrated through the legitimization of the students' culture and everyday lives that an interest in mathematics could occur and in turn improve academic achievement and engagement" (p. 180). With regard to culturally relevant science education, similar trends are noted. For example, in their work on authentic scientific inquiry, Rivera Maulucci and colleagues (2014) explain, "Authentic science inquiry requires that students actively produce authentic scientific knowledge—knowledge driven by their own questions with/in the world—and distribute their knowledge through written and oral forms of communication, rather than simply consuming and regurgitating pre-packaged knowledge sets" (p. 1145). These ideas of agency and student voice were common themes in the articles we found (e.g., Johnson, 2011) and serve as evidence of the continued commitment, in the STEM education community, to CRSP. While the specific activities and projects varied according to discipline (science, technology, engineering and mathematics), all connected to the fundamental ideas of connecting teaching to students' lives and honoring who they are as people (e.g., critical social justice issues such as poverty, racism and valuing communities' funds of knowledge). As a bridge to increased student engagement and enhanced learning outcomes, a focus on non-trivial experiences was stressed and consistently challenged as a necessary component to CRSP in practice.

Instructional Practices, Dispositions and Teacher Training

The choices that teachers make are fundamentally tied to their pedagogical practice. Understanding how both in-service and preservice teachers use curricular materials and respond to students are critical components to CRSP. As observed by Morrison, Robbins and Rose (2008), "simply providing challenging curricula does not ensure culturally relevant pedagogy is occurring" (p. 435). In their examination of empirical research, they found that teachers' instructional practices were key to increasing the efficacy of the students' experiences; when teachers incorporated specific instructional practices that supported their work as culturally relevant teachers, students were much more successful academically. In one example, Johnson et al. (2016) chronicled a three-year professional development initiative and describes how teachers were able to master inquiry-based teaching and to leverage cooperative learning and the integration of culture and language into their science lessons. Not only did the teachers describe a higher level of instructional practices, but their students' performance on assessments improved as well. In another example, Ensign (2003) describes how teachers were able to incorporate real-life mathematical examples into their curriculum. In this instance teachers demonstrated a willingness, even an eagerness, to draw on experiences shared by their students.

CRSP can begin during teacher preparation programs. As a leader in this area, Mensah (2011) in her work with preservice teachers describes how the PSTs enacted culturally relevant pedagogy in science by intentionally choosing activities that were in the best interest of their students. An additional finding from this study was the importance of teachers sharing their own personal experiences with science (STEM) and to connect the content to real-world applications. In this example the real-world connections are not contrived or trivial, but rather they focus on social justice and equity. Importantly, teachers who viewed students as capable and able were more likely to engage students in authentic science.

How a teacher acts towards his students reveals many hidden teacher beliefs. When these beliefs are unexamined. they often contain biases that render students of color and others traditionally marginalized in STEM, unsuccessful in school STEM experiences. How can teachers learn to interrogate their own actions? Two big ideas emerged from this analysis: (1) building relationships and (2) awareness and attention to race. Milner's article (2011) is an excellent example of what these can look like in action. The main character in the study is a White male teacher, Mr. Hall. In this study,

Mr. Hall's dispositions are described in great detail and offer specific dispositional traits that one can use to conceptualize CRSP. Essentially, Mr. Hall commits to: giving students a second chance/ not holding a grudge; working through difficult situations with commitment and care; and honoring students' perceptions of reality/recognizing the importance of children. While these may seem "obvious" dispositional traits, they are not, given the overwhelming number of students of color who receive disproportionate disciplinary actions when compared to their White counterparts. If teachers remain unaware of their unconscious biases towards children of color, and other marginalized groups, they are destined to maintain the inequitable practices found in schools. What we are calling dispositions connects closely to what Villegas and Lucas (2002) refer to as "an affirming attitude toward students from culturally diverse backgrounds" (p. 23). Specifically this asset-based view of students recognizes that culturally relevant teachers "are convinced that all students, not just those from the dominant group, are capable learners who bring a wealth of knowledge and experiences to school" (p. 23). If teachers do not see all their students as potentially brilliant with STEM, the students are unlikely to be successful.

To varying degrees, researchers and teachers have discussed the time it takes for practitioners to become culturally relevant educators. Most of the results suggest that PSTs are emergent in their ability to incorporate culturally relevant teaching practices with sophistication and complexity. This is not surprising given the time it takes for anyone to develop a critical consciousness and a subsequent ability to apply that to educative experiences. Several studies focused on long-term professional development initiatives and/or multiyear work with individual teachers (Aguirre & del Rosario Zavala, 2013; Johnson, 2011; Rivera Maulucci et al., 2014). All of these speak to the necessity of significant time and practice for educators to understand and eventually practice CRSP.

Other studies focused on work with preservice teachers and expressed the challenges associated with working with those new to critically conscious ideas (Johnson, 2011; Mensah, 2011; Hernandez, Morales, & Shroyer, 2013). Hernandez and colleagues (2013) point out, however, that "based on the data collected as part of this study, the teacher candidates did not illustrate or model the development of socio-political consciousness during science and math instruction." Instead of viewing this as a failure, we can see this as a recognition of the difficulty of developing a critical consciousness, specifically within STEM disciplines historically characterized as culturally neutral and free of biases. As discussed in the article, this finding can help STEM teacher educators understand how to better prepare preservice teachers to be culturally relevant STEM educators by explicitly highlighting ways in which social justice intersects with STEM teaching, learning and professional membership.

Curricular Materials

For decades, scholars have criticized the way in which STEM pedagogy and curriculum represent White values and experiences (Battey & Leyva, 2016; Martin, 2010). Tate (1995) recollects that Woodson (1933/1990) "posited that education built strictly on the thinking, experiences, and desires of Whites was inappropriate for African Americans" (p. 166). Yet, due to the prevalence of white supremacy and the schooling structures designed by White architects (Watkins, 2001), the public school apparatus in general, and STEM curriculum in particular, still remains "foreign" (Martin, 2015; Mensah & Jackson, 2018; Tate, 1995) and, for students of color, overwhelmingly focused on memorization and skills (Ladson-Billings, 2008; Gutierrez, Willey, & Khisty, 2011).

Curricular materials are often the first and most accessible way to approach CRSP. Collecting and organizing concrete materials that visually represent a commitment to culturally relevant teaching inherently makes sense to teachers. For example, Laughter and Adams (2012) chronicle a middle school teacher's use of Derrick Bell's (1992) *The Space Traders*, a science fiction text, in a discussion lab associated with a lesson on scientific bias in order to extend their thinking on biases in the larger social contexts and in their lives. *The Space Traders* contains important sociological themes about racism and immigration and positions Black characters prominently.

Similarly, Lipka, Sharp, Brenner, Yanez, and Sharp (2005) showcase how one experienced Yup'ik teacher modified a commercial curriculum to bring together core mathematical concepts and Yup'ik traditions. Specifically, this case study focuses on a module called "Parkas and Patterns" to connect the art of creating Yup'ik border patterns and basic geometrical concepts. The authors note that this module "developed slowly over many years and multiple iterations" (p. 34), which underscores the sophistication required to innovate, or even modify, curriculum that centers the cultural heritage of non-dominant youth and communities.

Another example is that of the curricular materials developed as part of the Flathead Geoscience Education Project (FGEP; Johnson et al., 2014). FGEP was a collaboration between tribal teachers, community members and science educators in Montana. Curricular materials were developed that were inclusive and honored native tribal knowledge and customs about the mountain geology. Specific curricula included: tribal guest instructors and mentor–apprentice observational learning; traditional stories, native languages and indigenous science knowledge; and language and visual arts activities. Another example is software developed to analyze the mathematics of African American hair braiding (Lachney, 2017). In this example, ethnocomputing research was undertaken to develop Cornrow Curves. According to the authors,

> researchers first interviewed cornrow hair braiders and learned how to make braids. Data from this collaboration helped them see the underlying mathematical and computational thinking involved in cornrow braiding from the perspective of a professional rather than imposing an outsider's view on the material practice.

Finally, curricular materials can also include mild modifications that represent visual representation of a more diverse and relevant student body. Such examples include word problems with students' names and favorite activities and a classroom library that includes books and media with diverse characters.

Conclusions and Recommendations for Future Research

Certain disciplines have been exploring culturally relevant pedagogy for at least a decade but work remains to be done in this area for STEM overall (Barton, 2003; Martin, 2010; Johnson, 2011; Willey & Magee, 2018; Vazquez Dominguez et al., 2018). Indeed the literature on CRSP is limited, as it is not too common that CRP is used as a conceptual framework to present, analyze and discuss equitable STEM teaching across all disciplines. Still, we find the tenets to be useful in delineating what exactly makes CRSP promising as well as making explicit how meaningful STEM education is connected to larger issues of (in)equity and (in)justice worldwide. Our review of the literature shows how CRSP expands notions of what counts as engagements and learning outcomes, highlights instructional practices and dispositions that center students' racial and cultural backgrounds, and reveals how educators committed to CRSP modify and innovate curriculum to reflect students' knowledge bases and experiences.

The literature also presents a range of practices that, to greater or lesser degrees, constitute CRSP and led to variable outcomes. For example, in Miller and Roehrig (2018), we see an excellent example of how both the culture and participation of the Anishinaabeg/Anishinaabe people of the Ojibwe Tribe elders can be infused into productive STEM teaching. On the other hand, Lachney (2017) addresses the complexity of making cultural connections in classrooms: "In its trivial forms, it merely changes the skin color of media characters or dresses up standard word problems in ethnic garb" (p. 2); it does not address students' academic success directly, including the formation and development of identities as STEM knowers and doers. Like other analyses of teacher learning, we know that movement towards equitable opportunities to learn and thrive within STEM communities depends on a commitment to long-term professional development, one that includes a focus on racial justice and equity (Johnson, 2011) as well as inquiry pedagogy.

When we keep in mind that schools, writ large, have been designed to serve the interests of White people (Watkins, 2001), as well as the fact that all (White) institutional spaces serve to perpetuate whiteness (Martin, 2010), it becomes apparent that the factors inhibiting the realization of CRSP are much more robust and complex, and the implications for social justice are brought into sharper relief. This analysis serves to celebrate the movement towards justice and equity but also lays bare the work of educators and teacher educators to work creatively and urgently within and outside of the current system to dramatically alter the landscape of STEM teaching and learning to be more inclusive, relevant and engaging.

References

Abrams, E., Taylor, P., & Guo, C. (2013). *International Journal of Science & Mathematics Education, 11*(1), 1–21. doi:10.1007/s10763-012-9388-2

Adjapong, E. S., & Emdin, C. (2015). Rethinking pedagogy in urban spaces: Implementing hip-hop pedagogy in the urban science classroom. *Journal of Urban Learning, Teaching, and Research, 11*, 66–77.

Aguirre, J. M., & del Rosario Zavala, M. (2013). Making culturally responsive mathematics teaching explicit: A lesson analysis tool. *Pedagogies: An International Journal, 8*(2), 163–190.

Alacacı, C., & Erbaş, A. K. (2010). Unpacking the inequality among Turkish schools: Findings from PISA 2006. *International Journal of Educational Development, 30*(2), 182–192.

Aronson, B., & Laughter, J. (2016). The theory and practice of culturally relevant education: A synthesis of research across content areas. *Review of Educational Research, 86*(1), 163–206.

Artiles, A. J., Kozleski, E. B., Trent, S. C., Osher, D., & Ortiz, A. (2010). Justifying and explaining disproportionality, 1968–2008: A critique of underlying views of culture. *Exceptional Children, 76*(3), 279–299.

Averill, R., Anderson, D., Easton, H., Maro, P. T., Smith, D., & Hynds, A. (2009). Culturally responsive teaching of mathematics: Three models from linked studies. *Journal for Research in Mathematics Education*, 157–186.

Balestra, C., Llena-Nozal, A., Murtin, F., Tosetto, E., & Arnoud, B. (2018). *Inequalities in emerging economies: Informing the policy dialogue on inclusive growth.* Paris: OECD Publishing.

Banks, J. A. (2004). Multicultural education: Historical development, dimensions and practice. In J. A. Banks & C. A. M. Banks (Eds.), *Handbook of research on multicultural education* (2nd ed., pp. 3–29). San Francisco, CA: Jossey-Bass.

Barton, A. C. (2003). *Teaching science for social justice.* New York, NY: Teachers College Press.

Battey, D., & Leyva, L. A. (2016). A framework for understanding whiteness in mathematics education. *Journal of Urban Mathematics Education, 9*(2), 49–80.

Bell, D. (1992). The space traders. *Faces at the Bottom of the Well*, 158–194.

Blanchet-Cohen, N., & Reilly, R. C. (2017). Immigrant children promoting environmental care: Enhancing learning, agency and integration through culturally-responsive environmental education. *Environmental Education Research, 23*(4), 553–572.

Boutte, G., Kelly-Jackson, C., & Johnson, G. L. (2010). Culturally relevant teaching in science classrooms: Addressing academic achievement, cultural competence, and critical consciousness. *International Journal of Multicultural Education, 12*(2).

Civil, M., & Khan, L. H. (2001). Mathematics instruction developed from a garden theme. *Teaching Children Mathematics, 7*(7), 400.

Ensign, J. (2003). Including culturally relevant math in an urban school. *Educational Studies, 34*(4), 414–423.

Gay, G. (2002). Preparing for culturally responsive teaching. *Journal of Teacher Education, 53*(2), 106–116.

Gay, G. (2010). *Culturally responsive teaching: Theory, research, and practice.* New York, NY: Teachers College Press.

Gay, G. (2013). Teaching to and through cultural diversity. *Curriculum Inquiry, 43*(1), 48–70.

Gee, J. P. (2007). *Social linguistics and literacies: Ideology in discourses.* London: Routledge.

George, J. M. (2013). "Do You Have to Pack?"—Preparing for culturally relevant science teaching in the Caribbean. *International Journal of Science Education, 35*(12), 2114–2131.

Glewwe, P., & Kremer, M. (2006). Schools, teachers, and education outcomes in developing countries. In E. A. Hanushek, S. Machin, & L. Woessmann (Eds.), *Handbook of the economics of education* (Vol. 2, pp. 945–1017). Amsterdam, The Netherlands: Elsevier B. V. doi:10.1016/S1574-0692(06)02016-2

González, N., Moll, L. C., & Amanti, C. (Eds.). (2006). *Funds of knowledge: Theorizing practices in households, communities, and classrooms.* New York, NY: Routledge.

Griffin, A., & James, A. (2018). Humanities curricula as white property: Toward a reclamation of black creative thought in social studies & literary curricula. *Multicultural Education, 25*(3/4), 10–17.

Gutierrez, M. V., Willey, C., & Khisty, L. L. (2011). (In) equitable schooling and mathematics of marginalized students: Through the voices of urban Latinas/os. *Journal of Urban Mathematics Education, 4*(2), 26–43.

Gutstein, E. (2006). *Reading and writing the world with mathematics: Toward a pedagogy for social justice.* New York, NY: Taylor & Francis.

Gutstein, E., Lipman, P., Hernandez, P., & De los Reyes, R. (1997). Culturally relevant mathematics teaching in a Mexican American context. *Journal for Research in Mathematics Education, 28,* 709–737.

Harry, B., & Klingner, J. (2014). *Why are so many minority students in special education?* New York, NY: Teachers College Press.

Hernandez, C. M., Morales, A. R., & Shroyer, M. G. (2013). The development of a model of culturally responsive science and mathematics teaching. *Cultural Studies of Science Education, 8*(4), 803–820.

Howard, T. C. (2010). *Why race and culture matter in schools: Closing the achievement gap in America's classrooms.* New York, NY: Teachers College Press.

Howard, T. C., & Rodriguez-Scheel, A. C. (2017). *Culturally relevant pedagogy 20 years later: Progress or pontificating? What have we learned, and where do we go?* Teachers College Record. https://www.tcrecord.org/content.asp?contentid=21718

Johnson, A. N., Sievert, R., Durglo, M. Sr, Finley, V., Adams, L., & Hofmann, M. H. (2014). Indigenous knowledge and geoscience on the Flathead Indian Reservation, northwest Montana: Implications for place-based and culturally congruent education. *Journal of Geoscience Education, 62*(2), 187–202.

Johnson, C. C. (2011). The road to culturally relevant science: Exploring how teachers navigate change in pedagogy. *Journal of Research in Science Teaching, 48*(2), 170–198.

Johnson, C. C., Bolshakova, V. L. J., & Waldron, T. (2016). When good intentions and reality meet: Large-scale reform of science teaching in urban schools with predominantly Hispanic ELL Students. *Urban Education, 49,* 1–38.

Lachney, M. (2017). Culturally responsive computing as brokerage: Toward asset building with education-based social movements. *Learning, Media and Technology.* doi:10.1080/17439884.2016.1211679

Ladson-Billings, G. (1995). But that's just good teaching! The case for culturally relevant pedagogy. *Theory into Practice, 34*(3), 159–165.

Ladson-Billings, G. (2006). Yes, but how do we do it? Practicing culturally relevant pedagogy. In J. Landsman & C. W. Lewis (Eds.), *White teachers/diverse classrooms: A guide to building inclusive schools, promoting high expectations and eliminating racism* (pp. 29–42). Sterling, VA: Stylus Publishers.

Ladson-Billings, G. (2008). "Yes, but how do we do it?": Practicing culturally relevant pedagogy. In W. Ayers, G. Ladson-Billings, G. Michie, & P. Noguera (Eds.), *City kids, city schools: More reports from the front row* (pp. 162–177). New York, NY: The New Press.

Ladson-Billings, G. (2009). *The dreamkeepers: Successful teachers of African American children.* Hoboken, NJ: John Wiley & Sons.

Ladson-Billings, G. (2014). Culturally relevant pedagogy 2.0: Aka the remix. *Harvard Educational Review, 84*(1), 74–84.

Laughter, J. C., & Adams, A. D. (2012). Culturally relevant science teaching in middle school. *Urban Education, 47*(6), 1106–1134.

Le, P. T., & Matias, C. E. (2019). Towards a truer multicultural science education: How whiteness impacts science education. *Cultural Studies of Science Education, 14*(1), 15–31.

Leonard, J., Brooks, W., Barnes-Johnson, J., & Berry, R. Q. III. (2010). The nuances and complexities of teaching mathematics for cultural relevance and social justice. *Journal of Teacher Education, 61*(3), 261–270.

Lipka, J., Sharp, N., Brenner, B., Yanez, E., & Sharp, F. (2005). The relevance of culturally based curriculum and instruction: The case of Nancy Sharp. *Journal of American Indian Education, 44*(3), 31–54.

Lockheed, M. E., & Verspoor, A. M. (1991). *Improving primary education in developing countries.* New York, NY: Oxford University Press for World Bank.

Lodge, W. (2017). Science learning and teaching in a Creole-speaking environment. *Cultural Studies of Science Education, 12*(3), 661–675.

Martin, D. B. (2010). What does quality mean in the context of white institutional space? In *Mapping equity and quality in mathematics education* (pp. 437–450). Dordrecht, The Netherlands: Springer.

Martin, D. B. (2015). The collective Black and principles to actions. *Journal of Urban Mathematics Education, 8*(1), 17–23.

Mensah, F. M. (2011). A case for culturally relevant teaching in science education and lessons learned for teacher education. *The Journal of Negro Education,* 296–309.

Mensah, F. M., & Jackson, I. (2018). Whiteness as property in science teacher education. *Teachers College Record, 120*(1), n1.

Miller, B. G., & Roehrig, G. (2018). Indigenous cultural contexts for STEM experiences: Snow snakes' impact on students and the community. *Cultural Studies of Science Education, 13*(1), 31–58.

Milner, H. R. IV. (2011). Culturally relevant pedagogy in a diverse urban classroom. *The Urban Review, 43*(1), 66–89.

Milner, H. E. IV., Cunningham, H. B., Delale-O'Connor, L., & Kestenberg, E. G. (2019). *"These kids are out of control": Why we must reimagine "classroom management" for equity*. Thousand Oaks, CA: Corwin Press.

Morrison, K. A., Robbins, H. H., & Rose, D. G. (2008). Operationalizing culturally relevant pedagogy: A synthesis of classroom-based research. *Equity & Excellence in Education, 41*(4), 433–452.

Nichol, R., & Robinson, J. (2010). Pedagogical challenges in making mathematics relevant for indigenous Australians. *International Journal of Mathematical Education in Science and Technology, 31*(4), 495–504.

Obidah, J. E., & Teel, K. M. (2001). *Because of the kids: Facing racial and cultural differences in schools* (Vol. 18). New York, NY: Teachers College Press.

OECD. (2016). *PISA 2015 results (Volume I): Excellence and equity in education*. PISA. Paris: OECD Publishing. Retrieved from https://doi.org/10.1787/9789264266490-en

Paris, D. (2012). Culturally sustaining pedagogy: A needed change in stance, terminology, and practice. *Educational Researcher, 41*(3), 93–97.

Richards, H., Brown, A., & Forde, T. (2004). Practitioner brief: Addressing diversity in schools: Culturally responsive pedagogy. Retrieved from www.nccrest.org/Briefs/Diversity_Brief. pdf

Rivera Maulucci, M. S., Brown, B. A., Grey, S. T., & Sullivan, S. (2014). Urban middle school students' reflections on authentic science inquiry. *Journal of Research in Science Teaching, 51*(9), 1119–1149.

Sleeter, C. (2012). Confronting the marginalization of culturally responsive pedagogy. *Urban Education, 47*, 562–584. doi:10.1177/0042085911431472

So, K., & Kang, J. (2014, December). Curriculum reform in Korea: Issues and challenges for twenty-first century learning. *The Asia-Pacific Education Researcher, 23*(4), 795–803. https://doi.org/10.1007/s40299-013-0161-2

Spring, J. (2014). *Globalization of education: An introduction*. New York, NY: Routledge.

Tate, W. F. (1995). Returning to the root: A culturally relevant approach to mathematics pedagogy. *Theory into Practice, 34*(3), 166–173.

U.S. Department of Education Office for Civil Rights. (2014). *Civil rights data collection data snapshot: School discipline*. Issue brief no. 1.

Varelas, M., Martin, D. B., & Kane, J. M. (2012). Content learning and identity construction: A framework to strengthen African American students' mathematics and science learning in urban elementary schools. *Human Development, 55*(5–6), 319–339.

Vazquez Dominguez, M., Allexsaht-Snider, M., & Buxton, C. (2018). Connecting soccer to middle school science: Latino students' passion in learning. *Journal of Latinos and Education, 17*(3), 225–237.

Villegas, A. M., & Lucas, T. (2002). Preparing culturally responsive teachers: Rethinking the curriculum. *Journal of Teacher Education, 53*(1), 20–32.

Walker, V. S. (2013). Ninth annual Brown lecture in education research: Black educators as educational advocates in the decades before Brown V. Board of Education. *Educational Researcher, 42*(4), 207–222.

Watkins, W. H. (2001). *The white architects of black education: Ideology and power in America, 1865–1954*. New York, NY: Teachers College Press.

Willey, C., & Magee, P. A. (2015). Teacher educators and preservice teachers working through the complexities of whiteness and race in mathematics and science. In N. M. Joseph, C. N. Haynes, & F. Cobb (Eds.), *Interrogating whiteness and relinquishing power: White faculty's commitment to racial consciousness in STEM classrooms* (pp. 131–149). New York, NY: Peter Lang.

Willey, C., & Magee, P. A. (2018). Whiteness as a barrier to becoming a culturally relevant teacher: Clinical experiences and the role of supervision. *Journal of Educational Supervision, 1*(2), 33–51.

Woodson, C. G. (1990). *The mis-education of the Negro. 1933*. Trenton: Africa World Press.

Young, E. (2010). Challenges to conceptualizing and actualizing culturally relevant pedagogy: How viable is the theory in classroom practice? *Journal of Teacher Education, 61*(3), 248–260.

25

STEM INCLUSION RESEARCH FOR ENGLISH LANGUAGE LEARNERS (ELLS)

Making STEM Accessible to All

Emily K. Suh, Lisa Hoffman and Alan Zollman

Learning environments in many global educational contexts are becoming increasingly linguistically and culturally diverse. STEM educators often are not trained to work with students whose home language is not the dominant language of instruction (Hart & Lee, 2003). These educators would benefit from increased understanding of language development (Henry, Baltes, & Nistor, 2014; Janzen, 2008). According to the National Academies of Science, Engineering, and Medicine (2018), attention to culturally and linguistically diverse STEM students' educational needs is particularly important considering the historical inequities and lack of diversity among STEM professions and professionals.

After introducing some relevant terminology from the field of second language acquisition (SLA), this chapter addresses the following areas of STEM education research related to English language learners (ELLs): (1) emergent areas of collaboration between STEM educators and applied linguistics researchers, (2) overlap between STEM and language acquisition standards, (3) research-based practices for language development and content mastery, (4) professional development for STEM educators' understanding of SLA, literacy instruction, and assessment, and (5) areas for future research.

Rationale for Considering Language and Culture in STEM Education Research

As multilinguals come to represent an increasing proportion of students, emergent multilingualism in the content areas has received increasing attention (Buxton & Lee, 2014; Barwell, 2009). Discipline-specific academic vocabulary and language functions can differ markedly from conversational language use (Cummins, 2005). *Registers* are features within a language used to vary formality, tone or meaning (Halliday, 1988). Although students often acquire basic interpersonal communication skills in two or fewer years, their academic content knowledge and registers develop in interrelated and lengthier processes (Collier & Thomas, 2009). Research suggests it takes a minimum of five to seven years of continuous linguistic support for students to develop an academic register (Cummins, 2005). Educators often assume that students must have advanced language proficiency before they can understand grade-level content, but research documents how the two types of learning can be successfully integrated (Stoddart, Pinal, Latzke, & Canaday, 2002). Furthermore, research consistently identifies the importance of personal relationships and mutual respect between teachers and learners of all backgrounds. STEM educators need training to develop personal and cultural connections with students from diverse backgrounds (Oliveira, Weinburgh, McBride, Bobowski, & Shea, 2019; Hudley & Mallinson, 2017). Future research could address issues of inequitable curriculum access and assessment practices in STEM (Mallinson & Charity Hudley, 2014).

Emergent multilinguals face challenges related to the language registers required for STEM learning. Multilingual students utilize their knowledge of multiple languages and registers and additional meaning-making modalities to participate in STEM contexts and activities (National Academies of Science, Engineering, and Medicine, 2018). STEM content is inseparable from the language through which it is presented, and research indicates that proficiency in English is a strong predictor of success in STEM disciplines (Howie, 2003). Additionally, individual disciplines present their own unique challenges and opportunities for language development. For example, students must develop multi-semiotic reasoning within complex mathematical discourse (de Oliveira & Cheng, 2011; Ellerton & Clarkson, 1996; Hansen-Thomas & Bright, 2019), but research indicates that when ELLs receive continued literacy support, they can increase their mathematical reasoning (Henry et al., 2014). Science registers focused on interpretation and use of evidence can present additional linguistic challenges, particularly because of written disciplinary expectations (Rosenthal, 1996), yet science instruction is often de-emphasized in favor of basic literacy and numeracy skills (Lee & Avalos, 2002). The open-endedness of authentic engineering tasks allows ELLs to demonstrate understanding by exploring and producing a material product. Less research is available on technology and engineering education among ELLs, suggesting future research potential for examining language acquisition within these disciplines, particularly related to issues of access to technology and hands-on experiences. Available research investigates both the linguistic challenges within the STEM disciplines and the unique knowledge and abilities ELLs bring to the classroom (Dos Santos, 2019; Esquinca, de la Piedra, & Herrera-Rocha, 2018).

Language and STEM Standards

In many countries there is overlap between standards for acquiring the dominant language (i.e., the PreK-12 English Language Proficiency Standards Framework released by the international organization; Teachers of English to Speakers of Other Languages, 2006) and STEM area proficiencies (see Cheuk, 2013; Lee, Quinn, & Valdés, 2013). These standards provide recommendations for student proficiency, teacher professional development and practices, and assessment. Both language and STEM standards emphasize developing all students' ability to communicate and apply their knowledge, such as by using academic language to analyze or make evidence-based arguments (Lin & Zhang, 2014; National Academies of Science, Engineering, and Medicine, 2018; ITEEA, 2007; TESOL, 2006; WIDA, 2012). The U.S. Common Core standards identify practices for mathematics, science and engineering, and English language acquisition (Common Core, n.d.) and include using evidence to support complex textual analysis, and to construct, critique, and enhance arguments (Cheuk, 2013). The Principles and Standards for School Mathematics similarly call for students to be able to make sense of and apply critical information to real-world situations (NCTM, 2000).

Recommendations for teaching include teacher training and classroom practices emphasizing English language learners' ability to communicate in the content areas, including mathematics and science (TESOL, 2006). The Committee on Supporting English Learners in STEM Subjects recommends teacher learning opportunities to introduce and develop curriculum, research-based practices, and assessments that support ELLs (National Academies of Science, Engineering, and Medicine, 2018). The committee further recommends that schools and teachers collaborate with families and community organizations to directly engage ELLs and understand their assets and growth areas. Other disciplines (e.g., technology and engineering; see ITEEA, 2007) and language development standards (Lin & Zhang, 2014; WIDA, 2012) share this emphasis on local contexts.

Related to classroom practice, language development and STEM standards emphasize creating language-rich classroom environments with opportunities for practical application. Language learners benefit from context-rich language environments in which they can demonstrate comprehension through application (WIDA, 2012). The National Research Council's (2012) "Framework for K–12 Science Education" similarly embeds language instruction in science and engineering education practices (Lee et al., 2013), and the Next Generation Science Standards include providing rich language learning environments (NGSS Lead States, 2013).

Finally, STEM and language acquisition standards both provide assessment recommendations. The Committee on Supporting English Learners in STEM Subjects advocates for increasing the representativeness of sample populations for large-scale STEM assessments, reviewing accommodations policies, and developing accessibility resources or new STEM assessments (National Academies of Science, Engineering, and Medicine, 2018). In addition to issues of equitable access, English language acquisition standards emphasize assessing language use for specific communicative purposes (TESOL, 2006; WIDA, 2012). International assessments of STEM proficiencies similarly focus on communication for daily living. The Program for International Student Assessment (PISA) measures broad knowledge and skills in science, mathematics and reading literacy as they are relevant to students' real-world preparation (Carr, 2016).

Research-Based Practices for STEM Content Mastery and Language Development

This section introduces research-based practices including respecting students' cultural and community assets, building off students' first language knowledge, introducing STEM-related academic discourses, and prioritizing vocabulary acquisition. The section also includes high-impact teaching strategies for STEM learners developing English proficiency.

Cultural norms and community knowledge play a significant role in students' sense-making of their educational environments (Esmonde & Caswell, 2010). Cultural norms affect forms of reasoning, inquiry, and argumentation valued in STEM fields (Johnson & Bolshakova, 2015). Effective STEM education with emergent multilinguals considers students' "funds of knowledge"—that is, their wealth of background knowledge from family and community resources—and incorporates cultural knowledge and beliefs into STEM learning (Moll, Amanti, Neff, & Gonzalez, 1992). Even when ELLs are not literate or academically proficient in their first language, making connections to communities' funds of knowledge can positively impact students' STEM learning (Buxton, Allexsaht-Snider, & Rivera, 2013). One aspect of accessing funds of knowledge is explicit family involvement in STEM education. Family involvement can be particularly significant for culturally and linguistically diverse students, families, and communities (Wassell, Hawrylak, & Scantlebury, 2017) and is identified as an essential practice by STEM education organizations, such as ITEEA (2007) and the National Research Council (2013).

Whether or not STEM educators speak a student's first language, they can leverage students' existing linguistic strengths to develop target language skills while acquiring STEM content knowledge (Hansen-Thomas & Bright, 2019; Oliveira et al., 2019). Learning about students' first language(s) can help STEM educators access vocabulary learning opportunities. For example, Reed, Medina, Martinez, and Veleta (2013) found that over 85% of terms in biology textbooks and standards had Spanish-English cognates. Explicitly teaching students about cognates and word roots allows students proficient in languages with Latin and Greek roots to access STEM content vocabulary by connecting new terminology to home language (Echevarria, Vogt, & Short, 2012). Even if students have not previously learned STEM content vocabulary in their first language, explicit word root connections allow students to make associations among known words with similar roots. Understanding difficult aspects of language development can also help educators recognize assets and pinpoint challenges students from all language backgrounds are likely to face (Wong Fillmore & Snow, 2002). Teachers also need to recognize additional challenges faced by preliterate students, students from cultures without written forms of language, students with interrupted formal education, and students who have learning disabilities (Helman, Calhoon, & Kern, 2015). These students—indeed, all students—benefit greatly from multimodal forms of teaching that provide multiple types of input and avenues for expressing STEM content (McVee, Silvestri, Shanahan, & English, 2017; Takeuchi, 2015; Manavathu & Zhou, 2012).

In discussing STEM topics with students, educators bring learners into the academic discourse of a particular community of knowledge (Willey, Gatza, & Flessner, 2017; Yerrick & Gilbert, 2011). Understanding content area discourses is essential for learning and engagement with complex STEM topics (Reyes, 2008). For example, DiGisi and Fleming (2005) documented how students' scores improved on high-stakes assessments after explicit instruction in reading and interpreting math questions. Limited empirical research is available on science reading comprehension among language learners (Taboada, Bianco, & Bowerman, 2012), but existing research highlights benefits of attending to print literacy to increase content mastery (Gomez, Lozano, Rodela, & Mancevice, 2013). Moschkovich (2015) proposes that academic literacy in mathematics includes proficiency, practices, and discourse of the field—and that instruction for ELLs must address each of these components simultaneously.

Academic discourse becomes most accessible when connected to social language (Ryoo, 2015). Among the key points STEM educators need to understand about working with language learners is the difference between social and academic language and that a student's use of social English does not indicate comparable academic language proficiency (Cummins, 2005). Beck, McKeown, and Kucan (2013) review research into vocabulary learning and identify multiple tiers of vocabulary students need in particular academic fields. For STEM fields, this includes Tier 1 vocabulary (i.e., common words used in conversation) and Tier 3 vocabulary (i.e., content-specific words all students learn over the course of a lesson). STEM teachers must also help emergent multilingual students access Tier 2 vocabulary words which are used across STEM fields but which language learners may have never explicitly learned, such as "investigate" and "analyze." This general academic vocabulary is just as crucial for academic success as specific academic vocabulary (Haag, Heppt, Stanat, Kuhl, & Pant, 2013). Yet privileging more abstract vocabulary as more "academic" belies the complexity with which students learn about and understand the world (Warren, Ogonowski, & Pothier, 2005).

Vocabulary instruction may be extended or embedded, and research supports a variety of approaches for teaching both Tier 2 and Tier 3 vocabulary—that is, both general academic and discipline-specific language (Echevarria et al., 2012). Multiple studies demonstrate the benefits of embedded vocabulary in STEM fields (August et al., 2014; Tong, Irby, Lara-Alecio, & Koch, 2014). Science notebooks are one STEM-specific example shown to increase student learning of both disciplinary vocabulary and concepts (Huerta, Tong, Irby, & Lara-Alecio, 2016). Contextualized vocabulary instruction can include other high-impact instructional strategies, including explicit instruction in reading comprehension strategies embedded within implicit instruction of academic science vocabulary to support student motivation and self-direction (Hagena, Leiss, & Schwippert, 2017).

Teaching strategies supported by research include a number of models integrating STEM content and intentional focus on literacy development (Silva, Weinburgh, Malloy, Smith, & Marshall, 2012; Tong et al., 2014). Gomez et al. (2015) engaged community college mathematics instructors in a successful curriculum redesign process to embed literacy support into mathematics while removing unintended language barriers. Literacy activities are most effective when they include explicit attention to language acquisition and forms, as Kasmer (2013) studied among language learners in Tanzania. The focus on literacy development can follow an apprenticeship model of academic literacy exposure in the STEM discipline (Greenleaf, Schoenbach, Cziko, & Mueller, 2001). Educators should encourage students to use their first language in literacy activities; relevant research addressing biliteracy and binumeracy development includes Takeuchi's (2015) ethnography of classroom mathematics practice and Rubinstein-Ávila, Sox, Kaplan, and McGraw's (2015) study of collaborative multilingual mathematical problem solving. Effective reading strategies for language learners include text-based questioning activities in science (Taboada et al., 2012) and structured feedback (i.e., Dynamic Strategic Math) for mathematical word problem solving (Orosco, Lee Swanson, O'Connor, & Lussier, 2013). Students also benefit from reading and writing in different genres related to science (Lee & Buxton, 2013).

Inquiry-based STEM instruction has been a successful approach with ELLs in a number of research studies (Mercuri & Mercuri, 2019; Lee, & Buxton, 2013; Stoddart et al., 2002). August et al. (2014) and Johnson (2011) both showed that ELLs showed increased learning of academic language when using a science curriculum with experiments and materials usually used with gifted and talented students. Technology also can be a powerful tool for language learners accessing STEM content. Ryoo and Bedell (2017) used visualizations in web-based inquiry instruction in middle school science, and Terrazas-Arellanes, Gallard, Strycker, and Walden (2018) showed that interactive online learning units helped close gaps in science knowledge between English-learner and English-only middle school students. Alegria (2014) took a critical pedagogy approach to support ELLs in the science classroom. Driver and Powell (2017) combined culturally and linguistically responsive instruction with explicit schema instruction to teach elementary ELLs how to solve mathematics word problems. Students in the intervention increased word problem-solving skills and reported satisfaction with the intervention.

Many other research-supported instructional practices which support ELLs also benefit English-proficient students (Hoffman & Zollman, 2016). Using visual aids such as pictures, graphic organizers, and sentence frames supports content knowledge and academic language development (Llosa et al., 2016; August et al., 2014; Silverman & Hines, 2009; National Academies of Sciences, Engineering, and Medicine, 2017). Providing multimedia and hands-on classroom opportunities and expressing concepts in multiple ways are positively associated with ELL learning (Hoffman & Zollman, 2016) but are also recommended practices for mainstream classrooms regardless of students' language proficiency. Peer collaboration and interaction opportunities in both first language and target language are also positively associated with increased student learning (August et al., 2014; Echevarria et al., 2012). The importance of peer interaction and the advantages of first language support bear mentioning in particular because of educators' common misconception that students should always use English rather than incorporate first-language knowledge and check comprehension using students' strengths in other languages (August, 2018).

Promising strategies include explicit literacy instruction and matching linguistic features of the domain and the assessment to measure achievement (Avenia-Tapper & Llosa, 2015; Hussain, 2017). ELLs perform significantly higher on linguistically modified items (Sato, Rabinowitz, Gallagher, & Huang, 2010). In assessing learning through tasks that involve student language production (such as written or oral performance), educators must focus on students' STEM reasoning processes rather than language errors (Moschkovich, 2012). Improving classroom-based and school- and state-level assessments of English learners' STEM content knowledge is a key research opportunity. The following section discusses assessment in greater detail.

STEM Teacher Professional Development and Multilingual Student Assessment

Several STEM organizations include professional development for pre-service and in-service teachers as an essential component of quality STEM education (ITEEA, 2007; National Research Council, 2012; NCTM, 2000; NGSS Lead States, 2013). These organizations identify teacher professional development as particularly necessary for meeting STEM equity goals regarding ELL access to academically and linguistically rich content (National Research Council, 2012). Wong Fillmore and

Snow (2002) recommend that professional development includes foundational information about the complexities of language and language learning. Researchers suggests the effectiveness of teacher training which pairs developing content knowledge with acquiring academic discourses in English. For example, Garza et al. (2018) found significant gains in both science content and language when fifth-grade teachers were trained to promote verbal and written interaction. The Sheltered Instruction Observation Protocol (SIOP) is highly popular within the United States' K-12 system and focuses professional development on supporting ELLs, although the model is intended to help all students increase language and content proficiency (Short, 2017). Research documents both greater consistency of best practices for ELLs and greater student English language gains when teachers implement the SIOP model after a three-day staff development institute (Echevarria, Short, & Powers, 2006). Professional development on culturally relevant pedagogy has also been linked to assessment gains for culturally and linguistically diverse students' science achievement (Johnson & Fargo, 2014). Currently, however, only a limited amount of research exists on STEM teacher professional development efficacy (Chval, Pinnow, & Thomas, 2015; Desimone, 2009; Prediger & Schüler-Meyer, 2017); instead, available research examines the effectiveness of various in-class interventions after providing teacher training to support implementation.

Research on the effectiveness of STEM teacher training and professional development suggests that trainings for supporting ELLs are most effective when trainers consistently implement standards-based, inquiry-oriented, and language-focused interventions (Llosa et al., 2016; Johnson, Sondergeld, & Walton, 2017). In their work with U.S. urban elementary school teachers in science classes, Santau, Secada, Maerten-Rivera, Cone, and Lee (2010) found that after a year-long professional development intervention, teachers effectively used language support strategies for emergent multilingual students. Additional research is necessary to determine the effectiveness of different professional development trainings, which vary in length and focus.

Even when teacher professional development is most effective, standardized assessments may not show immediate or significant achievement gains as teachers become familiar with new curriculum and adjust their practices (Maerten-Rivera, Ahn, Lanier, Diaz, & Lee, 2016). Assessing STEM learning among ELLs presents challenges in large part because of the common reliance on literacy-based performances and evaluations (Newkirk-Turner & Johnson, 2018). Both linguistic complexity and cultural assumptions of many assessments pose a threat to assessment validity (Solano-Flores & Trumbull, 2003).

Furthermore, the research is extremely limited on how ELLs are represented in classroom assessment data (National Academies of Science, Engineering, and Medicine, 2018). In fact, recognition of problematic assessments and assessment practices have led some STEM organizations, including the National Academies of Science, Engineering, and Medicine, to call for improved assessment practices as a part of wider STEM education reform to support ELLs (National Academies of Science, Engineering, and Medicine, 2018). Regarding assessments of ELLs in the United States, the National Academy recommend (1) using multiple measures to accurately measure ELLs' academic achievement, (2) providing individualized accommodations during large-scale STEM assessments, (3) incorporating into classroom summative assessment visuals, multiple smaller parts to divide larger tasks, and collaboration. In terms of analyzing assessment data, the group recommends disaggregating data by students' level of English proficiency and including students who began school receiving English language services but who are no longer classified as ELLs. By collecting data on these "Ever ELLs," data users can better understand how programs, schools, districts, and states are serving emergent multilingual students at various stages of their language acquisition.

Future Research Directions

Much research has applied a deficit approach to students. For example, students increasingly are referred to as "emergent multilinguals" rather than "English language learners" as a way of signaling existing linguistic assets. Research should progress from identifying barriers for ELLs to seeking ways to utilize their unique attributes and breadth of experience in order to further STEM learning for all students in computational proficiencies, conceptual understandings, and real-world applications. Likewise, research related to instruction and assessment must go beyond deficit-focused observations and attitudinal studies.

"Too often schools operate under the incorrect assumption that proficiency in English is a prerequisite to meaningful engagement with STEM learning and fail to leverage [ELL]s' meaningful engagement with content and disciplinary practices as a route to language proficiency" (Mitchell, 2019). In the Proceedings of the National Academy of Sciences, Rangel and Shi (2018) found that immigrant children in the United States with languages dissimilar to English tend to study more mathematics and science in high school and college than their peers.

Problem-Based Learning, Math Circles, TechnoCode, Project Lead the Way, and other programs are being investigated currently (Van Overschelde, 2013). These projects can be expanded to guide implementation studies of STEM for ELLs. A new direction for research is the connections of content and process standards to ELLs' academic achievement in STEM (Moschkovich, 2012, 2015). Further structured research is needed on increasing ELLs' STEM content achievement in the context of an integrated curriculum.

Understudied areas also include the economic and social impact of ELLs' STEM learning. While there are studies in the STEM areas of science and mathematics (Johnson et al., 2017), more research is needed on increasing achievement of language learners in technology and engineering, and going beyond vocabulary and syntax to ways of using academic discourse. Several organizations call for integrating teacher preparation, curriculum, instruction, and assessment to support all students' STEM learning (see National Academies of Science, Engineering, and Medicine, 2018; National Research Council, 2012). Although these professional organizations advocate for an integrated approach to supporting multilingual students' developing language and content proficiencies, additional research is needed on the efficacy of different instructional and assessment methods. Researchers must examine the effectiveness of initiatives that create language-rich environments and align assessments with teaching practical application over abstract knowledge.

"There is a general consensus that everyone needs to be STEM literate, but there is a difference between literacy and being literate. . . . Literacy in STEM goes beyond understanding, communicating and applying . . . from learning for STEM literacy to using STEM literacy for learning" (Zollman, 2012, p. 12). Engaging, real-world problem-solving activities that incorporate mathematical vocabulary, concepts, and applications are important critically for students learning English—as well as monolingual English-speaking students. "Good instruction for learning is good for every student" (Hoffman & Zollman, 2016, p. 92)—it makes STEM accessible to all.

References

Alegria, A. (2014). Supporting English language learners in the science classroom through critical pedagogy. *International Journal of Science and Mathematics Education, 12*(1), 99–121.

August, D. (2018). Educating English language learners: A review of the latest research. *American Educator, 42*(3). Retrieved from https://www.aft.org/sites/default/files/aefall2018.pdf

August, D., Branum-Martin, L., Cardenas-Hagan, E., Francis, D. J., Powell, J., Moore, S., & Haynes, E. F. (2014). Helping ELLs meet the common core state standards for literacy in science: The impact of an instructional intervention focused on academic language. *Journal of Research on Educational Effectiveness, 7*(1), 54–82. doi: 10.1080/19345747.2013.836763

Avenia-Tapper, B., & Llosa, L. (2015). Construct relevant or irrelevant? The role of linguistic complexity in the assessment of English language learners' science knowledge. *Educational Assessment, 20*(2), 95–111. doi:10.10 80/10627197.2015.1028622

Barwell, R. (2009). Multilingualism in mathematics classrooms: An introductory discussion. In R. Barwell (Ed.), *Multilingualism in mathematics classrooms: Global perspectives* (pp. 1–13). Bristol, United Kingdom: Multilingual Matters.

Beck, I. L., McKeown, M. G., & Kucan, L. (2013). *Bringing words to life: Robust vocabulary instruction* (2nd ed.). New York, NY: Guilford Press.

Buxton, C. A., Allexsaht-Snider, M., & Rivera, C. (2013). Science, language, and families: Constructing a model of steps to college through language-rich science inquiry. In *Moving the equity agenda forward* (pp. 241–259). Dordrecht, The Netherlands: Springer.

Buxton, C. A., & Lee, O. (2014). English language learners in science education. In N. G. Lederman & S. K. Abell (Eds.), *Handbook of research on science education* (pp. 204–222). New York, NY: Routledge.

Carr, P. G. (2016). *NCES statement on PISA 2015 results*. National Center for Education Statistics. Retrieved from https://nces.ed.gov/whatsnew/commissioner/remarks2016/12_06_2016.asp

Cheuk, T. (2013). *Relationships and convergences among the mathematics, science, and ELA practices*. Refined version of diagram created by the Understanding Language Initiative for ELP Standards. Palo Alto, CA: Stanford University.

Chval, K. B., Pinnow, R. J., & Thomas, A. (2015). Learning how to focus on language while teaching mathematics to English language learners: A case study of Courtney. *Mathematics Education Research Journal, 27*(1), 103–127. doi:10.1007/s13394-013-0101-8

Collier, V. P., & Thomas, W. P. (2009). *Educating English learners for a transformed world*. Albuquerque, NM: Dual Language Education of New Mexico/Fuente Press.

Common Core State Standards Initiative. (n.d.). *Mathematics standards*. Retrieved from http://www.corestandards.org/Math/

Cummins, J. (2005). Teaching the language of academic success: A framework for school-based language policies. In *California state department of education, schooling and language minority students: A theoretical-practical framework* (3rd ed., pp. 3–32). Los Angeles, CA: California State University Evaluation, Dissemination, and Assessment Center.

de Oliveira, L. C., & Cheng, D. (2011). Language and the multisemiotic nature of mathematics. *Reading Matrix: An International Online Journal, 11*(3), 255–268. Retrieved from http://www.readingmatrix.com/articles/september_2011/oliveira_cheng.pdf

Desimone, L. M. (2009). Improving impact studies of teachers' professional development: Toward better conceptualizations and measures. *Educational Researcher, 38*(3), 181–199.

DiGisi, L. L., & Fleming, D. (2005). Literacy specialists in math class! Closing the achievement gap on state math assessments. *Voices from the Middle, 13*(10), 48–52.

Dos Santos, L. M. (2019). English language learning for engineering students: Application of a visual-only video teaching strategy. *Global Journal of Engineering Education, 21*(1).

Driver, M. K., & Powell, S. R. (2017). Culturally and linguistically responsive schema intervention: Improving word problem solving for English language learners with mathematics difficulty. *Learning Disability Quarterly, 40*, 41–53. doi:10.1177/0731948716646730

Echevarria, J., Short, D., & Powers, K. (2006). School reform and standards-based education: A model for English-language learners. *The Journal of Educational Research, 99*(4), 195–211. Retrieved from https://journals.uic.edu/ojs/index.php/IURJ/article/viewFile/6668/5462

Echevarria, J., Vogt, M., & Short, D. J. (2012). *Making content comprehensible for English learners: The SIOP model* (4th ed.). Boston: Pearson.

Ellerton, N., & Clarkson, P. (1996). Language factors in mathematics teaching and learning. In A. Bishop, M. A. K. Clements, C. Keitel-Kreidt, J. Kilpatrick, & C. Laborde (Eds.), *International handbook of mathematics education* (pp. 987–1033). Dordrecht, The Netherlands: Kluwer.

Esmonde, I., & Caswell, B. (2010). Teaching mathematics for social justice in multicultural, multilingual elementary classrooms. *Canadian Journal of Science, Mathematics and Technology Education, 10*(3), 244–254. doi:10.1080/14926156.2010.504485

Esquinca, A., de la Piedra, M. T., & Herrera-Rocha, L. (2018). Hegemonic language practices in engineering design and dual language education. *Association of Mexican American Educators Journal, 12*(2), 44–68.

Garza, T., Huerta, M., Spies, T. G., Lara-Alecio, R., Irby, B. J., & Tong, F. (2018). Science classroom interactions and academic language use with English learners. *International Journal of Science and Mathematics Education, 16*(8), 1499–1519. doi:10.1007/s10763-017-9855-x

Gomez, K., Gomez, L. M., Rodela, K. C., Horton, E. S., Cunningham, J., & Ambrocio, R. (2015). Embedding language support in developmental mathematics lessons: Exploring the value of design as professional development for community college mathematics instructors. *Journal of Teacher Education, 66*(5), 450–465. doi:10.1177/0022487115602127

Gomez, K., Lozano, M., Rodela, K., & Mancevice, N. (2013). Designing embedded language and literacy supports for developmental mathematics teaching and learning. *MathAMATYC Educator, 5*(1), 43–56.

Greenleaf, C., Schoenbach, R., Cziko, C., & Mueller, F. (2001). Apprenticing adolescent readers to academic literacy. *Harvard Educational Review, 71*(1), 79–130. doi:10.17763/haer.71.1.q811712577334038

Haag, N., Heppt, B., Stanat, P., Kuhl, P., & Pant, H. A. (2013). Second language learners' performance in mathematics: Disentangling the effects of academic language features. *Learning and Instruction, 28*, 24–34.

Hagena, M., Leiss, D., & Schwippert, K. (2017). Using reading strategy training to foster students' mathematical modelling competencies: Results of a quasi-experimental control trial. *Eurasia Journal of Mathematics, Science and Technology Education, 13*(7), 4058–4085. doi:10.12973/eurasia.2017.00803a

Halliday, M. A. (1988). On the language of physical science. In M. Ghadessy (Ed.), *Registers of written English: Situational factors and linguistic features* (pp. 162–178). London: Pinter.

Hansen-Thomas, H., & Bright, A. (2019). Teaching mathematics to emergent bilinguals. *The Handbook of TESOL in K-12*, 265–276.

Hart, J. E., & Lee, O. (2003). Teacher professional development to improve the science and literacy achievement of English language learners. *Bilingual Research Journal, 27*(3), 475–501.

Helman, A. L., Calhoon, M. B., & Kern, L. (2015). Improving science vocabulary of high school English language learners with reading disabilities. *Learning Disability Quarterly, 38*(1), 40–52. doi:10.1177/0731948714539769

Henry, D. L., Baltes, B., & Nistor, N. (2014). Examining the relationship between math scores and English language proficiency. *Journal of Educational Research and Practice, 4*(1), 11–29. doi:10.5590/JERAP.2014.04.1.02

Hoffman, L., & Zollman, A. (2016). What STEM teachers need to know and do for English language learners (ELLs): Using literacy to learn. *Journal of STEM Teacher Education, 51*(1), 83–94. doi:10.30707/JSTE51.1Hoffman

Howie, S. J. (2003). Language and other background factors affecting secondary pupils' performance in mathematics in South Africa. *African Journal of Research in Mathematics, Science and Technology Education, 7*(1), 1–20. doi:10.1080/10288457.2003.10740545

Hudley, A. H. C., & Mallinson, C. (2017). "It's worth our time": A model of culturally and linguistically supportive professional development for K-12 STEM educators. *Cultural Studies of Science Education, 12*(3), 637–660. doi:10.1007/s11422-016-9743-7

Huerta, M., Tong, F., Irby, B. J., & Lara-Alecio, R. (2016). Measuring and comparing academic language development and conceptual understanding via science notebooks. *The Journal of Educational Research, 109*(5), 503–517. doi:10.1080/00220671.2014.992582

Hussain, S. S. (2017). Teaching writing to second language learners: Bench-marking strategies for classroom. *Arab World English Journal, 8*(2). doi:10.24093/awej/vol8no2.15

International Technology and Engineering Education Association (ITEEA). (2007). *Standards for technology literacy (STL): Content for the study of technology.* (3rd ed.). Reston, VA: Author.

Janzen, J. (2008). Teaching English language learners in the content areas. *Review of Educational Research, 78*(4), 1010–1038. doi:10.3102/0034654308325580

Johnson, C. C. (2011). The road to culturally relevant science: Exploring how teachers navigate change in pedagogy. *Journal of Research in Science Teaching, 48*(2), 170–198.

Johnson, C. C., & Bolshakova, V. L. J. (2015). Moving beyond "those kids": Addressing teacher beliefs regarding the role of culture within effective science pedagogy for diverse learners. *School Science and Mathematics Journal, 115*(4), 179–185. doi:10.1111/ssm.12120

Johnson, C. C., & Fargo, J. D. (2014). A study of the impact of transformative professional development on Hispanic student performance on state mandated assessments of science in elementary school. *Journal of Science Teacher Education, 25*(7), 845–859. doi:10.1007/s10972-014-9396-x

Johnson, C., Sondergeld, T., & Walton, J. B. (2017). A statewide implementation of the critical features of professional development: Impact on teacher outcomes. *School Science and Mathematics, 117*, 341–349. doi:10.1111/ssm.12251

Kasmer, L. (2013). Pre-service teachers' experiences teaching secondary mathematics in English-medium schools in Tanzania. *Mathematics Education Research Journal, 25*, 399–413. doi:10.1007/s13394-013-0078-3

Lee, O., & Avalos, M. (2002). Promoting science instruction and assessment for English language learners. *Electronic Journal of Science Education, 7*(2). Retrieved from http://ejse.southwestern.edu/article/view/7704

Lee, O., & Buxton, C. A. (2013). Teacher professional development to improve science and literacy achievement of English language learners. *Theory into Practice, 52*(2), 110–117. doi:10.1080/00405841.2013.770328

Lee, O., Quinn, H., & Valdés, G. (2013). Science and language for English language learners in relation to next generation science standards and with implications for common core state standards for English language arts and mathematics. *Educational Researcher, 42*(4), 223–233. doi:10.3102/0013189X13480524

Lin, C. K., & Zhang, J. (2014). Investigating correspondence between language proficiency standards and academic content standards: A generalizability theory study. *Language Testing, 31*(4), 413–431.

Llosa, L., Lee, O., Jiang, F., Haas, A., O'Connor, C., Van Booven, C. D., & Kieffer, M. J. (2016). Impact of a large-scale science intervention focused on English language learners. *American Educational Research Journal, 53*(2), 395–424. doi:10.3102/0002831216637348

Maerten-Rivera, J., Ahn, S., Lanier, K., Diaz, J., & Lee, O. (2016). Effect of a multiyear intervention on science achievement of all students including English language learners. *The Elementary School Journal, 116*(4), 600–624. doi:10.1086/686250

Mallinson, C., & Charity Hudley, A. H. (2014). Partnering through science: Developing linguistic insight to address educational inequality for culturally and linguistically diverse students in US STEM education. *Language and Linguistics Compass, 8*(1), 11–23. doi:10.1111/lnc3.12060

Manavathu, M., & Zhou, G. (2012). The impact of differentiated instructional materials on English language learner (ELL) students' comprehension of science laboratory tasks. *Canadian Journal of Science, Mathematics and Technology Education, 12*(4), 334–349. doi:10.1080/14926156.2012.732255

McVee, M., Silvestri, K., Shanahan, L., & English, K. (2017). Productive communication in an afterschool engineering club with girls who are English language learners. *Theory into Practice, 56*(4), 246–254. doi:10.1080/00405841.2017.1350490

Mercuri, S., & Mercuri, N. (2019). Scaffolding English language learners' literacy development through a science inquiry approach. In L. de Oliveira, K. Obenchain, R. Kenney, & A. Oliveira (Eds.), *Teaching the content areas to English language learners in secondary schools* (Vol. 17, pp. 231–245). English Language Education. Cham, Switzerland: Springer.

Mitchell, C. (2019). Study: Language barriers can steer immigrant students to STEM Courses. *Blog Post*, January 10. Retrieved from https://blogs.edweek.org/edweek/learning-the-language/2019/01/language_bar riers_immigrants_STEM.html

Moll, L. C., Amanti, C., Neff, D., & Gonzalez, N. E. (1992). Funds of knowledge for teaching: Using a qualitative approach to connect homes and classrooms. *Theory into Practice, 31*(2), 132–141. doi:10.1080/004058492095 43534

Moschkovich, J. (2012). Mathematics, the common core, and language: Recommendations for mathematics instruction for ELs aligned with the common core. In *Commissioned papers on language and literacy issues in the common core state standards and next generation science standards* (pp. 17–31). Palo Alto, CA: Stanford University.

Moschkovich, J. (2015). Academic literacy in mathematics for English learners. *The Journal of Mathematical Behavior, 40*, 43–62. doi:10.1016/j.jmathb.2015.01.005

National Academies of Sciences, Engineering, and Medicine. (2017). *Promoting the educational success of children and youth learning English: Promising futures*. Washington, DC: The National Academies Press. doi:10.17226/24677

National Academies of Sciences, Engineering, and Medicine. (2018). *English learners in STEM subjects: Transforming classrooms, schools, and lives*. Washington, DC: The National Academies Press. doi:10.17226/25182

National Council of Teachers of Mathematics (NCTM). (2000). *Principles and standards for school mathematics*. Reston, VA: Author.

National Research Council. (2012). *A framework for K–12 science education: Practices, crosscutting concepts, and core ideas*. Washington, DC: The National Academies Press.

Newkirk-Turner, B. L., & Johnson, V. E. (2018). Curriculum-based language assessment with culturally and linguistically diverse students in the context of mathematics. *Language, Speech, and Hearing Services in Schools, 49*(2), 189–196. doi:10.1044/2017_LSHSS-17-0050

NGSS Lead States. (2013). *Next generation science standards: For states, by states*. Washington, DC: The National Academies Press.

Oliveira, A. W., Weinburgh, M., McBride, E., Bobowski, T., & Shea, R. (2019). Teaching science to English language learners: Current research and practices in the field of science education. *The Handbook of TESOL in K-12*, 277–290.

Orosco, M. J., Lee Swanson, H., O'Connor, R., & Lussier, C. (2013). The effects of dynamic strategic math on English language learners' word problem solving. *The Journal of Special Education, 47*(2), 96–107. doi:10.1177/0022466911416248

Prediger, S., & Schüler-Meyer, A. (2017). Fostering the mathematics learning of language learners: Introduction to trends and issues in research and professional development. *Eurasia Journal of Mathematics, Science and Technology Education, 13*(7b), 4049–4056. https://doi.org/10.12973/eurasia.2017.00801a

Rangel, M. A., & Shi, Y. (2018). Early patterns of skill acquisition and immigrants' specialization in STEM careers. *Proceedings of the National Academy of Sciences, 116*(2), 484–489. doi:10.1073/pnas.1812041116

Reed, D. K., Medina, L. A., Martinez, N. A., & Veleta, L. G. (2013). The accessibility of academic vocabulary to Spanish speaking high school biology students. *The High School Journal, 97*(2), 80–91. doi:10.1353/hsj.2013.0025

Reyes, I. (2008). English language learners' discourse strategies in science instruction. *Bilingual Research Journal, 31*, 95–114. doi:10.1080/15235880802640631

Rosenthal, J. W. (1996). *Teaching science to language minority students: Theory and practice* (Vol. 3). Bristol, UK: Multilingual Matters.

Rubinstein-Ávila, E., Sox, A. A., Kaplan, S., & McGraw, R. (2015). Does biliteracy + mathematical discourse = binumerate development? Language use in a middle school dual-language mathematics classroom. *Urban Education, 50*(8), 899–937. doi:10.1177/0042085914536997

Ryoo, K. (2015). Teaching science through the language of students in technology-enhanced instruction. *Journal of Science Education and Technology, 24*(1), 29–42. doi:10.1007/s10956-014-9518-4

Ryoo, K., & Bedell, K. (2017). The effects of visualizations on linguistically diverse students' understanding of energy and matter in life science. *Journal of Research in Science Teaching, 54*(10), 1274–1301. doi:10.1002/tea.21405

Santau, A. O., Secada, W., Maerten-Rivera, J., Cone, N., & Lee, O. (2010). US urban elementary teachers' knowledge and practices in teaching science to English language learners: Results from the first year of a professional development intervention. *International Journal of Science Education, 32*(15), 2007–2032. doi:10.1080/09500690903280588

Sato, E., Rabinowitz, S., Gallagher, C., & Huang, C.-W. (2010). *Accommodations for English language learner students: The effect of linguistic modification of math test item sets.* Washington, DC: Institute of Education Sciences.

Short, D. (2017). How to integrate content and language learning effectively for English language learners. *Eurasia Journal of Mathematics, Science and Technology Education, 13*(7), 4237–4260. doi:10.12973/eurasia.2017.00806a

Silva, C., Weinburgh, M., Malloy, R., Smith, K. H., & Marshall, J. N. (2012). Toward integration: An instructional model of science and academic language. *Childhood Education, 88*(2), 91–95. doi:10.1080/00094056.2012.662119

Silverman, R., & Hines, S. (2009). The effects of multimedia-enhanced instruction on the vocabulary of English-language learners and non-English-language learners in pre-kindergarten through second grade. *Journal of Educational Psychology, 101,* 305–314. doi:10.1037/a0014217

Solano-Flores, G., & Trumbull, E. (2003). Examining language in context: The need for new research and practice paradigms in the testing of English-language learners. *Educational Researcher, 32*(2), 3–13. doi:10.3102/0013189X032002003

Stoddart, T., Pinal, A., Latzke, M., & Canaday, D. (2002). Integrating inquiry science and language development for English Language Learners. *Journal of Research in Science Teaching, 39,* 664–687. doi:10.1002/tea.10040

Taboada, A., Bianco, S., & Bowerman, V. (2012). Text-based questioning: A comprehension strategy to build English language learners' content knowledge, literacy research and instruction. *Literacy Research and Instruction, 51*(2), 87–109. doi:10.1080/19388071.2010.522884

Takeuchi, M. A. (2015). The situated multiliteracies approach to classroom participation: English language learners' participation in classroom mathematics practices. *Journal of Language, Identity & Education, 14,* 159–178. doi:10.1080/15348458.2015.1041341

Teachers of English to Speakers of Other Languages (TESOL). (2006). *Pre-k–12 English language proficiency standards.* Annapolis Junction, MD: TESOL Press.

Terrazas-Arellanes, F. E., Gallard, M. A. J., Strycker, L. A., & Walden, E. D. (2018). Impact of interactive online units on learning science among students with learning disabilities and English learners. *International Journal of Science Education, 40*(5), 498–518. doi:10.1080/09500693.2018.1432915

Tong, F., Irby, B. J., Lara-Alecio, R., & Koch, J. (2014). Integrating literacy and science for English language learners: From learning-to-read to reading-to-learn. *The Journal of Educational Research, 107*(5), 410–426. doi:10.1080/00220671.2013.833072

Van Overschelde, J. P. (2013). Project Lead the Way students more prepared for higher education. *American Journal of Engineering Education, 4*(1), 1–12.

Warren, B., Ogonowski, M., & Pothier, S. (2005). "Everyday" and "Scientific": Rethinking dichotomies in modes of thinking in science learning. In R. Nemirovsky, A. Rosebery, J. Solomon, & B. Warren (Eds.), *Everyday matters in science and mathematics* (pp. 119–151). New York, NY: Routledge. doi:10.4324/9781410611666

Wassell, B. A., Hawrylak, M. F., & Scantlebury, K. (2017). Barriers, resources, frustrations, and empathy: Teachers' expectations for family involvement for Latino/a ELL students in urban STEM classrooms. *Urban Education, 52*(10), 1233–1254. doi:10.1177/0042085915602539

WIDA Consortium. (2012). *Amplification of the English language development standards, kindergarten–grade 12.* Madison, WI: Board of Regents of the University of Wisconsin System.

Willey, C., Gatza, A., & Flessner, C. (2017). Mathematics discourse communities: Language ideologies and urban mathematics teaching with Latinas/os. *Journal of Cases in Educational Leadership, 20*(1), 34–48. doi:10.1177/1555458916687600

Wong Fillmore, L., & Snow, C. (2002). What teachers need to know about language. In C. T. Adger, C. E. Snow, & D. Christian (Eds.), *What teachers need to know about language*. (pp. 10–46). McHenry, IL: The Center for Applied Linguistics.

Yerrick, R. K., & Gilbert, A. (2011). Constraining the discourse community: How science discourse perpetuates marginalization of underrepresented students. *Journal of Multicultural Discourses, 6*(1), 67–91. doi:10.1080/174 47143.2010.510909

Zollman, A. (2012). Learning for STEM literacy: STEM literacy for learning. *School Science and Mathematics, 112*(1), 12–19. doi:10.1111/j.1949-8594.2012.00101.x

26

PARENT INVOLVEMENT AND ITS INFLUENCE ON CHILDREN'S STEM LEARNING

A Review of the Research

Julie Thomas, Juliana Utley, Soo-Young Hong,
Hunkar Korkmaz and Gwen Nugent

A growing understanding that parents and teachers can effectively collaborate to help children succeed in school has led worldwide policymakers and school leaders to begin deliberate actions to increase parents' participation in school life (e.g., Epstein, 2018; Raikes & Love, 2002). For example, the Chilean Education Minister recently encouraged contracts between parents, schools, and the state to increase parental involvement (Borgonovi & Montt, 2012). The Australian government has formed a Research Alliance for Children and Youth (Australian Government Department of Education and Training, 2018) to develop and promote understanding of parent involvement (i.e. what it is, why it matters, how it influences learning) and to build evidence about what works. From a sociological perspective, a school's organizational boundaries are permeable (Ballantine & Spade, 2008), thus the outside environment (which includes parental culture, values, and knowledge) can mediate student achievement. Therefore, a considerable body of research demonstrates the cultural capital parents wield as they (intentionally or unintentionally) hand down familial norms, skills, and habits (Ceglie & Setlage, 2016).

The purpose of this chapter is to discern the international scope of research that describes parent involvement as it relates to children's STEM learning. However, this noble intent was offset somewhat by (a) the limited research on parent involvement in STEM (though considerable research has been done on parent involvement in science and mathematics independently) and (b) the limited international research on parent involvement in STEM as an integrated focus. Authors identified these limitations as a chance to broadly recognize cultural context as both a U.S. and an international concern and to generate recommendations for future opportunities in the burgeoning field of research on parent involvement. While seeking to develop an international perspective, this international team of authors continuously generated a list of search terms, online databases, and references that came to include more than 300 articles, reports, books, and dissertations relevant to this research review. Through a system of independent reading and team discussions, authors distilled current research findings within three broad categories: (1) academic advantages related to parent involvement, (2) culture as a context for parent involvement, and (3) teacher/school perspectives on parent involvement. In closing, authors pointed to gaps in the knowledge of parent involvement in STEM education and opportunities for future research.

Academic Advantages of Parent Involvement

Parent involvement in education is widely believed to influence student outcomes. A plethora of research shows that children demonstrate a variety of achievement-related outcomes when parents are actively involved with their child's education. In the case of general socialization benefits, research has shown parent involvement impacts children's:

- *social, emotional, and character development* (e.g., Green, Walker, Hoover-Dempsey, & Sandler, 2007; Lewin & Luckin, 2010; Selwyn, Banaji, Hadjithoma-Garstka, & Clark, 2011; Schnee & Bose, 2010); and
- *increased attendance, reduced suspensions, and reduced high school dropouts* (e.g., Christenson & Sheridan, 2001; Epstein & Sheldon, 2002; Sheldon, 2007).

With regard to general, school achievement, research has shown parent involvement positively influences children's:

- *attitude toward school* (Aunola, Stattin, & Nurmi, 2000; Christenson & Sheridan, 2001; Eccles, 2007; Epstein & Sheldon, 2002; Frome & Eccles, 1998; Gonzalez-DeHass, Willems, & Holbein, 2005; Grolnick, Friendly, & Bellas, 2009; Sheldon, 2007; Vauras, Salonen, Lehtinen, & Lepola, 2001);
- *academic motivation* (Eccles, 2007; Fan & Williams, 2010; Grolnick, Kurowski, Dunlap, & Hevey, 2000; Häfner et al., 2018; Hoover-Dempsey et al., 2001; West, 2000);
- *pursuit of difficult tasks* (Gonzales-DeHass, Willems, & Holbein, 2005);
- *self-efficacy* (Fan & Williams, 2010; McGrath & Repetti, 2000); and
- *academic performance* (Domina, 2005; Epstein & Sheldon, 2002; Galindo & Sheldon, 2012; Häfner et al., 2018; Jeynes, 2010; Kim & Sheridan, 2015; Ma, Siu, & Tse, 2018; McNeal, 1999; Organization for Economic Cooperation and Development, 2017; Park & Holloway, 2017; Wilder, 2014).

Considering the specific skills in STEM content areas, research has shown parent involvement positively affects children's:

- *quantitative skills* (Evans, 2004; Yan & Lin, 2005); and
- *problem-solving skills* (Cai, 2003; Evans, 2004).

Though few studies have analyzed the impact of parent involvement in a cross-national context (Borgonovi & Montt, 2012), some international comparisons of the impact of parent involvement are included in the Program for International Student Assessment (PISA) results. PISA, the highest-profile international comparative study of 15-year-olds, has assessed parental involvement in selected Organization for Economic Cooperation and Development (OECD) countries since 2006. PISA's 2012 assessment (distributed across 13 countries and economies to include Croatia, China [Hong Kong and Macao], Denmark, Germany, Hungary, Italy, New Zealand, Portugal, Panama, and Qatar) focused on mathematics literacy. Some of the parent survey questions explored parent involvement as it related to student success, variations across school systems, and variations across different culture/socioeconomic groups. These results showed parents' expectations were strongly and positively associated with students' mathematics performance and positive dispositions towards learning (OECD, 2014). Borgonovi and Montt (2012) linked these data to student achievement and demographics and reasoned that, though the rates of parent involvement varied greatly in socioeconomically disadvantaged households, some (more successful students) were better equipped to benefit from parent involvement.

PISA's 2015 assessment focused on students' proficiency in science. In this year, the parent and student survey queried parents' participation in science-related activities with their child at age 10 (e.g., reading books on scientific discoveries, watching science programs on TV, and experimenting with a science kit). While this review of parents' early support of science activities did not determine any causal link, the data did reveal a close relationship between parents' early engagement in science activities and students' attitudes towards science (i.e., science enjoyment and science self-efficacy) at age 15 (OCED, 2017). Thus, it is possible these early learning experiences were the result of an early interest to begin with, it is also possible these parent-led activities led to a deeper enjoyment of science and helped these students become more confident about learning science.

In addition to student outcomes, researchers have examined parent and student perceptions of parent involvement in at-home or out-of-school activities. For example, when parents perceive that academic achievement is correlated to homework completion, they are more likely to get involved in children's homework (Mora & Escardibul, 2018). Some researchers have found children feel that they do better at school when parents assist them with their homework (Balli, 1998; Dumont et al., 2012) and teenagers explained parents' emotional support was valued and important to their perception of the future (Irwin, 2009). In this case, the data determined parents' direct involvement in students' science education (e.g., helping with science homework or gathering science-related materials) was negatively related to students' science achievement (OECD, 2017). Given that PISA students are early adolescents, these results are consistent with others' findings about parents' support with homework (Hill & Tyson, 2009; Hoover-Dempsey et al., 2001; Sibley & Dearing, 2014; Xu, Benson, Mudrey-Camino, & Steiner, 2010). However, this PISA 2015 data may also reflect causal differences in parental involvement with children who are performing well and those who are performing poorly in science (OCED, 2017).

Lastly, as parents become more involved in their children's education, research has shown parent involvement positively influences teachers and the school at large:

- *teachers gain confidence in teaching children* (Epstein, 1987; Hoover-Dempsey, Bassler, & Brissie, 1987);
- *student-teacher relationships are enhanced* (Hill & Craft, 2003; Stevenson & Baker, 1987);
- *administrators strengthen community relations* (Henderson, Marburger, & Ooms, 1986; Heystek, 2003);
- *curricula is transformed* as teachers build on community funds of knowledge (Moll, 1992; Peressini, 1997); and
- *schools become more collaborative and caring* when they work with the community at large (Feuerstein, 2000; Henry, 1996; Zhao & Akiba, 2009).

Culture as a Macrosystemic Context for Parent Involvement in a Child's STEM Learning

Learning involves socially and culturally mediated processes (Vygotsky, 1978). Thus, to understand how interactions between parents and schools influence children's achievement in any country, the cultural variations in how parents define and express their expectations for children's learning need to be examined (McKenna & Millen, 2013). Understanding how parents see their role in a child's STEM-related learning can help schools engage parents effectively and meaningfully. To this end, researchers have begun to notice variations within and between cultures in terms of how the parents' role is understood and manifested. Thus, this section reports on recent research related to (a) the ways cultural beliefs are embedded in parents' beliefs about involvement in their child's education and (b) how the association between parental involvement and children's STEM-related performance differ across social and cultural groups.

Culture and Parental Beliefs

Culture is a macrosystemic context of human development frequently considered to play an indirect role in an individual's learning and development (Bronfenbrenner & Morris, 2006). Given that cultural expectations are embedded consistently in children's everyday interactions and activities, culture has been regarded as one of the most important factors in children's development (Velez-Agosto, Soto-Crespo, Vizcarrondo-Oppenheimer, Vega-Molina, & Coll, 2017). Cultural context situates the way parents form expectations about their child's achievement in STEM-related areas. Importantly, these parental expectations help to form children's self-efficacy and achievement across all ages. By way of example, parents' educational expectations and aspirations have been highly associated with elementary achievement in science (Thomas & Strunk, 2017) and high school achievement in mathematics (Yan & Lin, 2005). As well, parents' beliefs and expectations have been shown to predict elementary science achievement (Thomas & Strunk, 2017) as well as elementary and middle school mathematics achievement (Entwisle & Alexander, 1996; Gill & Reynolds, 1999; Halle, Kurtz-Costes, & Mahoney, 1997; Holloway, 1986).

Parents' communication of the value of education, linking education to future success, and providing support for their child's academic and career expectations are important (Hill & Tyson, 2009; Jeynes, 2005). However, a child's ethnicity is associated with different kinds of parent involvement in their STEM-related achievement. For example, in the case of older children, social capital has been an important predictor of achievement for White children, whereas parent-teen relationships are a more critical factor influencing the learning of children from minority groups (Yan & Lin, 2005). Parental beliefs about their own, personal ability to help their child be successful in STEM-related activities is another key variable in parent involvement. In fact, parents tend to avoid contact with schools when they believe they lack the ability to help their child be successful at school (Hoover-Dempsey & Sandler, 1997). Furthermore, when parents believe they lack the necessary content knowledge to help their child learn mathematics or science, a condition that becomes more prevalent as the child moves into secondary school, parents avoid supporting STEM experiences outside of school (Eccles & Harold, 1993; Knapp, Landers, Lian, & Jefferson, 2017). Parents' beliefs about their child's intelligence also influences parental involvement (Hoover-Dempsey & Sandler, 1997). For instance, a mother's beliefs about her elementary child's capability in mathematics positively influences her involvement with the child's education and has been shown to predict the child's perceptions of his or her own abilities (Simpkins, Fredricks, & Eccles, 2012).

Culture and Socioeconomic Status

Research has shown that the family's socioeconomic status (SES) is related to children's learning outcomes. Even within the same cultural group, parents with high SES seem to provide direct support for a more extended period as compared with those with low SES (Liang, 2013). When controlling for SES, parents' motivational beliefs and other perceived contextual variables explained a significant amount of variance in parents' involvement in their child's education (Davis-Kean, 2005; Green et al., 2007). Prior research has shown that parents of certain ethnic backgrounds are more likely to be involved in children's education. For example, how parents are connected to their own culture of origin and whether parents and teachers share the same ethnic backgrounds are both associated with their level of engagement (Calzada et al., 2015). Importantly, incongruence in U.S. and Latino parents' cultural beliefs and expectations about parent involvement seems to provide potential explanation for the low academic performance of Latino children (Hill & Torres, 2010). On the other hand, schools in both the United States and Japan value the concept of 'parents as partners of teachers and other parents' (Jabar, 2010). Chinese American culture also emphasizes parents' important role in their child's education (Chen & Luster, 2010). In this culture, parents' high aspirations for their child's education is evident in the ways these parents make careful decisions about which school districts their children attend (Liang, 2013).

PISA 2015 parent survey data from Latin American countries (i.e., Chile, the Dominican Republic, and Mexico) suggested inflexible work schedules, childcare services, and problems with transportation hindered parents' participation in school activities (OCED, 2017). In addition, parents largely reported that they did not know how they could participate in school activities, nor did they expect their participation was relevant to their child's development/school success. These data, about barriers to parents' participation in their child's school activities, help illuminate the various ways parent-school communications are constrained.

Teacher/School Perspective on Parent Involvement

Research shows the importance of schools and families working together to ensure student success. Parents' and teachers' interactional experiences, across home and school, form the foundation for educational pathways lasting through adulthood. Together, parents and teachers arrange the large contextual influence regulating children's learning and development. The perceptions of parents, teachers, and principals towards family-school partnerships are instrumental in developing a family-friendly school culture that supports a partnership approach. Gordon and Louis (2009) found teachers' perception of the level of parents' involvement in their child's learning, as well as their own beliefs in shared partnerships, were related to a child's school achievement. In addition, principals' perceptions and support of family-school partnerships have been linked to the successful development and sustainability of parental involvement (e.g., Payne, 2008; Payne & Eckert, 2010). At an even higher level, district structures and policies substantially influence school-based implementation of family-school programs and activities. For example, Sheldon (2016) found that schools reporting greater support from the district office tended to have stronger, more sustainable partnership programs. Importantly, national educational policy can influence collaboration between schools and parents. In Sweden, for example, the democratic mission of the school system leads to inclusion of parents in formal school decision-making (Dahlstedt, 2009). The following sections include research related to the features of impactful partnership practices and teachers' limited opportunities to learn about how to initiate and manage parent involvement.

Impactful Parent Involvement

Not all parent involvement seems to influence children's learning. For example, research on classroom volunteerism, school event attendance, and parent-teacher conference attendance (e.g., Hill & Tyson, 2009; McWayne, Hampton, Fantuzzo, Cohen, & Sekino, 2004) has not determined a positive relationship between children's academic achievement and parents' involvement. Some research, however, has determined that parent involvement in school activities can lead to positive social benefits. For example, Bouffard and Weiss (2008) discovered that the engagement of parents in learning in the home has a large effect on children's learning. These parent engagement activities include supporting in-school learning, fostering children's expectancy of success in school and their future, and providing needed resources to support both in-school and out-of-school learning (Epstein, Sanders, Sheldon, Simon, & Salinas, 2009). Research has shown that learning activities and parent-teen discussions conducted at home specifically predict higher student mathematics achievement in middle and high schools (Ho & Willms, 1996; Keith et al., 1993). Other research, on the relationship of partnership practices and the percentage of children scoring satisfactorily on mathematics achievement tests, showed significant correlations related to homework that required parent-child interactions or use of take-home mathematics materials (Sheldon & Epstein, 2005). This research determined that the *use* of the activity was not enough; it was the *quality* of implementation that was associated with student mathematics achievement. Similar findings have been linked to science outcomes; providing parents with specific guidance (on how to be involved in science homework) improved their children's homework accuracy and led to improved science classroom performance (Van Voorhis, 2003).

Researchers have found that beneficial parental involvement may also take the form of supporting children's informal STEM activities (Hill & Tyson, 2009; McWayne et al., 2004) that include after-school STEM-focused programs (Dearing, Sibley, & Nguyen, 2015; Nugent, Barker, Grandgenett, & Welch, 2016). In addition to influencing both STEM learning and STEM attitudes, these opportunities encourage children to seek out additional opportunities and to further explore STEM topics. One parent intervention, which helped parents encourage their children to take STEM courses in high school, showed a significant effect on high school STEM preparation and predicted subsequent STEM career pursuit (Rozek, Svoboda, Harackiewica, Hulleman, & Hyde, 2016). Successful implementation of this strategy required parental knowledge of relevant school and community resources and STEM career and college pathways. Some researchers have explored the relative differences of parents' funds of knowledge (related to education pathways beyond high school) as they varied across ethnic and socioeconomic differences (Hill et al., 2004; Lareau, 2003; Lareau & Horvat, 1999). Hill (2015) found middle-class parents held advanced knowledge about how schools function and about the pathway from high school to college (Hill, 2015).

Teacher Preparation

Despite research demonstrating that family-school partnerships are critical to student behavioral and academic success, many teachers do not receive training in ways to effectively engage parents—either internationally (e.g., Guo & Wu, 2018) or in the United States (e.g., Stormshak, Dishion, Light, & Yasui, 2005; Stormshak, Connell, & Véronneau, 2011). It seems that novice and experienced teachers alike need to learn how to engage families from different cultures (LaRocque, Kleima, & Darling, 2011). Gottfredson and Gottfredson (2002) argued that teachers need encouragement, scaffolding, and feedback about their interactions with parents. One successful intervention for U.S. preservice mathematics teachers involved school-family nights, showing positive effects on preservice teachers' comfort level and perceptions in working with parents (Boefferding, Kastberg, & Hoffman, 2016). Successful programs in other countries have involved co-teaching between parents, teachers, and preservice teachers in Australia (Willis, 2018) and a participatory approach by preservice teachers in Canada using ongoing dialogue with parents of ELL learners (Shin & Robertson, 2018).

Conclusion and Opportunities for Future Research

Importantly, we set out to review international research defining how parent involvement influences children's STEM learning. Instead, the available research led us to focus this research review on parent involvement and its impact on children's success in science and mathematics. In this, we chose to explore the importance of cultural context (as both a U.S. and an international concern) and to generate research recommendations on parent involvement in STEM learning environments. Similar to Hoover-Dempsey and Sandler's (1997) earlier landmark review of parent involvement, further research on the evolution of parents' role construction related to school success can aid the design and measurement of school efforts to create an affirmative construct for parent involvement. This literature review revealed several areas for future research related to parent involvement in STEM classrooms.

To begin, researchers might help advance understanding about parent experiences (e.g., direct experience, vicarious experience, persuasion, and emotional arousal) that contribute to self-efficacy (Bandura, Barbaranelli, Caprara, & Pastoreli, 1996) relative to parents' involvement in school. In the case of STEM classrooms, a researcher could explore alignment between parents' and children's STEM efficacies: how and when are children's aspirations related to parents' attitudes and self-concepts? More research on parent involvement in STEM classrooms can help us to understand the complex interplay between the classroom context and varying levels of parents' self-efficacy across the STEM content areas as it is related to children's STEM achievement and STEM career aspirations.

Researchers might also consider the ways in which a STEM learning environment offers affordances that increase parent involvement. Here, researchers might explore programs designed to help parents overcome challenges posed by contextual variables (e.g., time, work schedules) and work with families to discern innovative involvement practices. Future research might examine how socioeconomic variables moderate the relationship between STEM learning environments and parents' involvement decisions. What research model could help delineate the differences between those parents who do participate in their child's school life and those parents who do not? How and when does a STEM learning environment constrain or expand parent involvement? What communication strategies enable parents' sense of efficacy for helping children succeed and lead to increasing effective parent involvement? What policies and practices enhance parental engagement across race, culture, and socioeconomic background?

Given the corpus of research displaying the critical balance between the family-school relationship and student achievement, teacher education programs might increase teachers' (preservice and in-service) opportunity to learn how to maximize parent involvement in schools. How might teachers learn to take an active role in enhancing parents' positive engagement at home and in school (e.g., exploring take-home activities or communication tools)? Research focused on this proposition would enhance our understanding about how to prepare teachers to build and maintain family relationships and guide development of school policies as well.

Lastly, researchers might explore responsive family communications that extend beyond the traditional activities (e.g., newsletters). How might schools strategically plan activities to promote purposeful, curriculum-related STEM interactions between student and family members? As Harris and Goodall (2008) explained, parental engagement cannot be a bolt on extra—it must be a central priority. In this, parents need to be seen as an integral part of children's learning. How do school policies define parents' roles? How might unique options (e.g., teacher-release time, a parent-community liaison to facilitate increased parent-school interactions, or an editor to help create and distribute regular communications from teachers to parents) improve school-home communications about learning goals, activities, and focused suggestions for parental help?

References

Aunola, K., Stattin, H., & Nurmi, J. E. (2000). Parenting styles and adolescents' achievement strategies. *Journal of Adolescence, 23*(2), 205–222. doi:10.1006/jado.2000.0308

Australian Government Department of Education and Training. (2018). *Parent engagement in children's learning.* Retrieved from https://www.education.gov.au/parent-engagement-children-s-learning/

Ballantine, J. Z., & Spade, J. H. (2008). *Schools and society: A sociological approach to education.* Los Angeles, CA: Pine Forge Press.

Balli, S. J. (1998). When mom and dad help: Student reflections on student involvement with homework. *Journal of Research and Development in Education, 31*, 142–146.

Bandura, A., Barbaranelli, C., Caprara, G. V., & Pastoreli, C. (1996). Multifaceted impact of self-efficacy beliefs on academic functioning. *Child Development, 67*, 1206–1222.

Boefferding, L., Kastberg, S., & Hoffman, A. (2016). Family mathematics nights: An opportunity to improve preservice teachers' understating of parents' roles and expectations. *School Science and Mathematics, 118*, 17–28. https://doi.org/10.1111/ssm.12109

Borgonovi, F., & Montt, G. (2012). *Parental involvement in selected PISA countries and economies.* OECD Education Working Papers, No. 73, OECD Publishing, Paris. http://dx.doi.org/10.1787/5k990rk0jsjj-en

Bouffard, S. M., & Weiss, H. (2008). Thinking big: A new framework for family involvement, policy, practice, and research. *Evaluation Exchange, 14*(1 & 2), 2–5.

Bronfenbrenner, U., & Morris, S. (2006). The bioecological model of human development. In W. Damon & R. M. Lerner (Eds.), *Handbook of child psychology: Theoretical models of human development* (Vol. 1, 6th ed., pp. 793–823). New York, NY: Wiley.

Cai, J. (2003). Investigating parental roles in students' learning of mathematics from across-national perspective. *Mathematics Education Research Journal, 15*(2), 87–106.

Calzada, E. J., Huang, K., Hernandez, M., Soriano, E., Acra, C. F., Dawson-McClure, S., Kamboukos, D., & Brotman, L. (2015). Family and teacher characteristics as predictors of parent involvement in education during early childhood among Afro-Caribbean and Latino immigrant families. *Urban Education, 50*, 870–896. https://doi.org/10.1177/0042085914534862

Ceglie, R. J., & Setlage, J. (2016). College student persistence in scientific disciplines: Cultural and social capital as contributing factors. *International Journal of Science and Mathematics Education, 14*(1), 169–186. doi:10.1007/s10763-014-9592-3

Chen, F., & Luster, T. (2010). Factors related to parenting practices in Taiwan. *Early Childhood Development and Care, 172*, 413–430. https://doi.org/10.1080/03004430214549

Christenson, S., & Sheridan, S. (2001). *Schools and families.* New York, NY: The Guilford Press.

Dahlstedt, M. (2009). Governing by partnerships. *Journal of Education Policy, 24*(6), 787–801. https://doi.org/10.1080/02680930903301548

Davis-Kean, P. E. (2005). The influence of parent education and family income on child achievement: The indirect role of parental expectations and the home environment. *Journal of Family Psychology, 19*, 294–304. doi:10.1037/0893-3200.19.2.294

Dearing, E., Sibley, E., & Nguyen, H. N. (2015). Achievement mediators of family engagement in children's education: A family–school–community systems model. In S. M. Sheridan & E. M. Kim (Eds.), *Processes and pathways of family–school partnerships across development* (pp. 17–39). New York, NY: Springer.

Domina, T. (2005). Leveling the home advantage: Assessing the effectiveness of parental involvement in elementary school. *Sociology of Education, 78*, 233–249. https://doi.org/10.1177/003804070507800303

Dumont, H., Trautwein, U., Lüdtke, O., Neumann, M., Niggli, A., & Schnyder, I. (2012). Does parental homework involvement mediate the relationship between family background and educational outcomes? *Contemporary Educational Psychology, 37*(1), 55–69. http://dx.doi.org/10.1016/j.cedpsych.2011.09.004

Eccles, J. S. (2007). Families, schools, and developing of achievement-related motivations and engagement. In J. E. Grusec & P. D. Hastings (Eds.), *Handbook of socialization: Theory and research* (pp. 665–691). New York, NY: The Guilford Press.

Eccles, J. S., & Harold, R. D. (1993). Parent–school involvement during the early adolescent years. *Teachers College Record, 94*(3), 568–587.

Entwisle, D. R., & Alexander, K. L. (1996). Family type and children's growth in reading and math over the primary grades. *Journal of Marriage and Family, 58*, 341–355.

Epstein, J. L. (1987). Teacher practices of parent involvement: What research says to teachers and administrators. *Education in Urban Society, 19,* 119–136.

Epstein, J. L. (2018). *School, family, and community partnerships.* Thousand Oaks, CA: Corwin Press.

Epstein, J. L., Sanders, M. G., Sheldon, S., Simon, B. S., & Salinas, K. C. (2009). *School, family, and community partnerships: Your handbook for action* (3rd ed.). Thousand Oaks, CA: Corwin Press.

Epstein, J. L., & Sheldon, S. B. (2002). Present and accounted for: Improving student attendance through family and community involvement. *Journal of Educational Research, 95*, 308–318. http://dx.doi.org/10.1080/00220670209596604

Evans, R. (2004). Talking with parents today. *Independent School, 63*, 96–100.

Fan, W., & Williams, C. M. (2010). The effects of parental involvement on students' academic self-efficacy, engagement and intrinsic motivation. *Educational Psychology, 30*(1), 53–74. doi:10.1080/01443410903353302

Feuerstein, A. (2000). School characteristics and parent involvement: Influences on participation in children's schools. *The Journal of Educational Research, 94*, 29–39.

Frome, P. M., & Eccles, J. S. (1998). Parents' influence on children's achievement- related perceptions. *Journal of Personality and Social Psychology, 74*(2), 435–452. doi:10.1037/ 0022-3514.74.2.435

Galindo, C., & Sheldon, S. B. (2012). School and home connections and children's kindergarten achievement gains: The mediating role of family involvement. *Early Childhood Research Quarterly, 27*, 90–103. http://dx.doi.org/10.1016/j.ecresq.2011.05.004

Gill, S., & Reynolds, A. J. (1999). Educational expectations and school achievement of urban African American children. *Journal of School Psychology, 37*, 403–424.

Gonzalez-DeHass, A., Willems, P., & Holbein, M. (2005). Examining the relationship between parental involvement and student motivation. *Educational Psychology Review, 17*(2), 99–123. https://doi.org/10.1007/s10648-005-3949-7

Gordon, M., & Louis, K. (2009). Linking parent and community involvement with student achievement: Comparing principal and teacher perceptions of stakeholder influence. *American Journal of Education, 116*, 1–31. https://doi.org/10.1086/605098

Gottfredson, D., & Gottfredson, G. (2002). Quality of school-based prevention programs: Results from a national survey. *Journal of Research in Crime and Delinquency, 39*, 3–35. https://doi.org/10.1177/002242780203900101

Green, C., Walker, J. M. T., Hoover-Dempsey, K. V., & Sandler, H. M. (2007). Parents' motivations for involvement in children's education: An empirical test of a theoretical model of parental involvement. *Journal of Educational Psychology, 99*, 532–544. doi:10.1037/0022-0663.99.3.532

Grolnick, W. S., Friendly, R. W., & Bellas, V. M. (2009). Parenting and children's motivation at school. In K. R. Wentzel & A. Wigfield (Eds.), *Handbook of motivation at school* (pp. 279–300). New York, NY: Routledge/ Tylor & Francis.

Grolnick, W. S., Kurowski, C. O., Dunlap, K. G., & Hevey, C. (2000). Parental resources and the transition to junior high. *Journal of Research on Adolescence, 10*(4), 465–488.

Guo, Y., & Wu, X. (2018). Home-school relations: An introduction. In Y. Guo (Ed.), *Home-school relations: International perspectives* (pp. 8–10). Singapore: Springer.

Häfner, I., Flunger, B., Dicke, A. L, Gaspard, H., Brisson, B. M., Nagengast, B., Trautwein, U. (2018). The role of family characteristics for students' academic outcomes: A person-centered approach. *Child Development, 89*(4), 1405–14222. doi:10.1111/cdev.12809

Halle, T. G., Kurtz–Costes, B., & Mahoney, J. L. (1997). Family influences on school achievement in low-income, African-American children. *Journal of Educational Psychology, 89*, 527–537.

Harris, A., & Goodall, J. (2008). Do parents know they matter? Engaging all parents in learning. *Educational Research, 50*(3), 277–289. https://doi.org/10.1080/00131880802309424

Henderson, A. T., Marburger, C. L., & Ooms, T. (1986). *Beyond the bake sale: An educator's guide to working with parents*. Columbia, MD: The National Committee for Citizens in Education.

Henry, M. (1996). *Parent-school collaboration: Feminist organizational structures and school leadership*. Albany, NY: State University of New York Press.

Heystek, J. (2003). Parents as governors and partners in schools. *Education and Urban Society, 35*, 328–315. https://doi.org/10.1177/0013124503035003005

Hill, N. E. (2015). Family–school relationships during adolescence: Clarifying goals, broadening conceptualizations, and deepening impact. In S. M. Sheridan & E. M. Kim (Eds.), *Processes and pathways of family–school partnerships across development* (pp. 41–59). New York, NY: Springer.

Hill, N. E, Castellino, D., Lansford, J., Nowlin, P., Dodge, K., Bates, J., & Pettit, G. (2004). Parent academic involvement as related to school behavior, achievement, and aspirations: Demographic variations across adolescence. *Child Development, 79*, 1491–1509. https://doi.org/10.1111/j.1467-8624.2004.00753.x

Hill, N. E., & Craft, S. A. (2003). Parent-school involvement and school performance: Mediated pathways among socioeconomically comparable African American and Euro American families. *Journal of Educational Psychology, 95*, 74–83. http://dx.doi.org/10.1037/0022-0663.95.1.74

Hill, N. E., & Torres, K. (2010). Negotiating the American dream: The paradox of aspirations and achievement among Latino students and engagement between their families and schools. *Journal of Social Issues, 66*, 95–112. https://doi.org/10.1111/j.1540-4560.2009.01635.x

Hill, N. E., & Tyson, D. F. (2009). Parental involvement in middle school: A meta-analytic assessment of the strategies that promote achievement. *Developmental Psychology, 45*, 740–763. doi:10.1037/a0015362

Ho, E. S, & Willms, J. D. (1996). Effects of parental involvement on eighth-grade achievement. *Sociology of Education, 69*, 126–141.

Holloway, S. (1986). The relationship of mothers' beliefs to children's mathematics achievement: Some effects of sex differences. *Merrill-Palmer Quarterly, 32*, 231–250.

Hoover-Dempsey, K. V., Bassler, O. C., & Brissie, J. S. (1987). Parent involvement: Contributions of teacher efficacy, school socioeconomic status, and other school characteristics. *American Educational Research Journal, 24*, 417–435.

Hoover-Dempsey, K. V., Battiato, A. C., Walker, J. M. T., Reed, R. P., DeJong, J. M., & Jones, K. P. (2001). Parental involvement in home-work. *Educational Psychologist, 36*, 195–210. https://doi.org/10.1207/S1532 6985EP3603_5

Hoover-Dempsey, K. V., & Sandler, H. M. (1997). Why do parents become involved in their children's education? *Review of Educational Research, 67*(1), 3–42.

Irwin, S. (2009). Family contexts, norms and young people's orientations: Researching diversity. *Journal of Youth Studies, 12*(4), 337–354. https://doi.org/10.1080/13676260902807235

Jabar, M. A. (2010). How do Japanese schools promote parental involvement? *International Journal of Social Sciences and Humanity Studies, 2*(1), 91–98.

Jeynes, W. (2005). A meta-analysis of the relation of parental involvement to urban elementary school student academic achievement. *Urban Education, 40*, 237–269. https://doi.org/10.1177/0042085905274540

Jeynes, W. (2010). The salience of the subtle aspects of parental involvement and encouraging that involvement: Implications for school-based programs. *Teachers College Record, 112*, 747–774.

Keith, T. Z., Keith, P. B., Troutman, G. C., Bickley, P. G., Trivette, P. S., & Singh, K. (1993). Does parental involvement affect eighth-grade student achievement? Structural analysis of national data. *School Psychology Review, 22*, 474–496.

Kim, E. M., & Sheridan, S. M. (2015). Foundational aspects of family–school connections: Definitions, conceptual frameworks, and research needs. In S. M. Sheridan and E. M. Kim (Eds.), *Foundational aspects of family school partnership research* (pp. 1–14). Switzerland: Springer International Publishing.

Knapp, A., Landers, R., Lian, S., & Jefferson, V. (2017). We all as a family are graduating tonight: A case for mathematical knowledge for parental involvement. *Educational Studies in Mathematics, 95*, 79–95. doi:10.1008/s10649-016-9741-4

Lareau, A. (2003). *Unequal childhoods: Class, race and family life.* Berkeley, CA: University of California.

Lareau, A., & Horvat, E. M. (1999). Moments of social inclusion and exclusion: Race, class, and cultural capital in family–school relationships. *Sociology of Education, 72*, 37–53.

LaRocque, M., Kleima, I., & Darling, S. M. (2011). Parental involvement: The missing link in school achievement. *Preventing School Failure, 55*(3), 115–122. https://doi.org/10.1080/10459880903472876

Lewin, C., & Luckin, R. (2010). Technology to support parental engagement in elementary education: Lessons learned from the UK. *Computers & Education, 54*, 749–758. https://doi.org/10.1016/j.compedu.2009.08.010

Liang, S. (2013). *Family involvement in children's mathematical education experiences: Voices of immigrant Chinese American students and their parents* (Unpublished doctoral dissertation). University of Maryland, College Park, MD.

Ma, Y., Siu, A., & Tse, W. S. (2018). The role of high parental expectations in adolescents' academic performance and depression in Hong Kong. *Journal of Family Issues, 39*(9), 2505–2522. https://doi.org/10.1177/0192513X18755194

McGrath, E. P., & Repetti, R. L. (2000). Mothers' and fathers' attitudes toward their children's academic performance and children's perceptions of their academic competence. *Journal of Youth and Adolescence, 29*(6), 713–723. http://dx.doi.org/10.1023/A:1026460007421

McKenna, M. K., & Millen, J. (2013). Look! Listen! Learn! Parent narratives and grounded theory models of parent voice, presence, and engagement in K–12 education. *School Community Journal, 23*, 9–48.

McNeal, R. Jr. (1999). Parent involvement as social capital: Differential effectiveness on science achievement, truancy and dropping out. *Social Forces, 78*(1), 117–144.

McWayne, C., Hampton, V., Fantuzzo, J., Cohen, H. L., & Sekino, Y. (2004). A multivariate examination of parent involvement and the social and academic competencies of urban kindergarten children. *Psychology in the Schools, 41*, 363–377. https://doi.org/10.1002/pits.10163

Moll, L. C. (1992). Bilingual classroom studies and community analysis: Some recent trends. *Educational Researcher, 20*, 20–24.

Mora, T., & Escardíbul, J. O. (2018). Home environment and parental involvement in homework during adolescence in Catalonia (Spain). *Youth & Society, 50*(2), 183–203. doi:10.1177/0044118X15626050

Nugent, G., Barker, B., Grandgenett, N., & Welch, G. (2016). Robotics camps, clubs, and competitions: Results from a US robotics project. *Robotics and Autonomous Systems, 75*, 686–691. https://doi.org/10.1016/j.robot.2015.07.011

Organization for Economic Cooperation and Development (OCED). (2014, February). *PISA 2012 results: What students know and can do student performance in mathematics, reading and science* (Vol. I, Revised ed.). PISA, OECD Publishing. http://dx.doi.org/10.1787/9789264201118-en

Organization for Economic Cooperation and Development (OCED). (2017). *PISA 2015 results (Volume III): Students' well-being.* PISA. Paris: OECD Publishing. http://dx.doi.org/10.1787/9789264273856-en

Park, S., & Holloway, S. D. (2017). The effects of school-based parental involvement on academic achievement at the child and elementary school level: A longitudinal study. *The Journal of Educational Research, 110*, 1–16. doi:10.1080/00220671.2015.1016600

Payne, A. A. (2008). A multilevel analysis of the relationships among communal school organization, student bonding, and delinquency. *Journal of Research in Crime and Delinquency, 45*, 429–455. https://doi.org/10.1177/0022427808322621

Payne, A. A., & Eckert, R. (2010). The relative importance of provider, program, school, and community predictors of the implementation quality of school-based prevention programs. *Prevention Science, 11*, 126–141.

Peressini, D. (1997, March). *The role of parents in the reform of high school mathematics.* Paper presented at the annual meeting of the American Educational Research Association, Chicago, IL.

Raikes, H., & Love, J. M. (2002). Early head start: A dynamic new program for infants and toddlers and their families. *Infant Mental Health Journal: Early Head Start Special Issue, 23*(1–2), 1–13.

Rozek, C., Svoboda, R., Harackiewica, J., Hulleman, C., & Hyde, J. (2016). Utility-value intervention with parents increases students' STEM preparation and career pursuit. *PNAS, 114*, 909–915. https://doi.org/10.1073/pnas.1607386114

Schnee, E., & Bose, E. (2010). Parents don't do nothing: Reconceptualizing parental null actions as agency. *The School Community Journal, 20*(2), 91–114.

Selwyn, N., Banaji, S., Hadjithoma-Garstka, C., & Clark, W. (2011). Providing a platform for parents? Exploring the nature of parental engagement with school learning platforms. *Journal of Computer Assisted Learning, 27*(4), 314–323. http://dx.doi.org/10.1111/j.1365-2729.2011.00428.x

Sheldon, S. B. (2007). Improving student attendance with school, family, and community partnerships. *The Journal of Educational Research, 100*(5), 267–275. https://doi.org/10.3200/JOER.100.5.267-275

Sheldon, S. B. (2016). Moving beyond monitoring: A district leadership approach to school, family, and community partnerships. In S. M. Sheridan & E. M. Kim (Eds.), *Family–school partnerships in context* (pp. 45–63). New York, NY: Springer.

Sheldon, S. B., & Epstein, J. L. (2005). Involvement counts: Family and community partnerships and mathematics achievement. *Journal of Educational Research, 98*, 196–206. https://doi.org/10.3200/JOER.98.4.196-207

Shin, H., & Robertson, H. (2018). Immigrant and minority parent engagement: A participatory approach in pre-service teacher education programme. In Y. Guo (Ed.), *Home-School relations: International perspectives* (pp. 267–284). Singapore: Springer.

Sibley, E., & Dearing, E. (2014). Family educational involvement and child achievement in early elementary school for American-born and immigrant families. *Psychology in the Schools, 51*(8), 814–831. doi:10.1002/pits.21784

Simpkins, S. D., Fredricks, J. A., & Eccles, J. S. (2012). Charting the Eccles' expectancy-value model from mothers' beliefs in childhood to youths' activities in adolescence. *Developmental Psychology, 48*, 1019–1032. doi:10.1037/a0027468

Stevenson, D. L., & Baker, D. P. (1987). The family-school relation and the child's school performance. *Child Development, 58*, 1348–1357.

Stormshak, E. A., Connell, A. M., & Véronneau, M. H. (2011). An ecological approach to promoting early adolescent mental health and social adaptation: Family-centered intervention in public middle schools. *Child Development, 82*, 209–225. https://doi.org/10.1111/j.1467-8624.2010.01551.x

Stormshak, E. A., Dishion, T., Light, J., & Yasui, M. (2005). Implementing family-centered interventions within the public middle school: Linking service delivery to change in student problem behavior. *Journal of Abnormal Child Psychology, 33*, 723–733. https://doi.org/10.1007/s10802-005-7650-6

Thomas, J. A., & Strunk, K. K. (2017). Expectancy-value and children's science achievement: Parents matter. *Journal of Research in Science Teaching, 54*, 693–712. https://doi.org/10.1002/tea.21382

Van Voorhis, F. L. (2003). Interactive homework in middle school: Effects on family involvement and science achievement. *Journal of Educational Research, 96*, 323–338. https://doi.org/10.1080/00220670309596616

Vauras, M., Salonen, P., Lehtinen, E., & Lepola, J. (2001). Long-term development of motivation and cognition in family and school contexts. In S. Volet & S. Jarvela (Eds.), *Motivation in learning contexts: Theoretical advances and methodological implications* (pp. 295–315). Oxford, UK: Pergamon.

Velez-Agosto, N. M., Soto-Crespo, J. G., Vizcarrondo-Oppenheimer, M., Vega-Molina, S., & Coll, C. G. (2017). Bronfenbrenner's bioecological theory revision: Moving culture from the macro into the micro. *Perspectives on Psychological Science, 12*, 900–910. https://doi.org/10.1177/1745691617704397

Vygostky, L. S. (1978). *Mind in society: The development of higher psychological processes.* Cambridge, MA: Harvard University Press.

West, J. M. (2000). *Increasing parent involvement for student motivation.* Retrieved from ERIC database. (ED448411)

Wilder, S. (2014). Effects of parental involvement on academic achievement: A meta-synthesis. *Educational Review, 66*(3), 377–397. doi:10.1080/00131911.2013.780009

Willis, L. D. (2018). Creating new spaces for pre-service teachers to engage with parents: An Australian coteaching and cogenerative dialoguing project. In Y. Guo (Ed.), *Home-School relations: International perspectives* (pp. 207–226). Singapore: Springer.

Xu, M., Benson, S. N. K., Mudrey-Camino, R., & Steiner, R. P. (2010). The relationship between parental involvement, self-regulated learning, and reading achievement of fifth graders: A path analysis using the ECLS-K database. *Social Psychology of Education: An International Journal, 13*(2), 237–269. http://dx.doi.org/10.1007/s11218-009-9104-4

Yan, W., & Lin, Q. (2005). Parent involvement and mathematics achievement: Contrast across racial and ethnic groups. *The Journal of Educational Research, 99*, 116–127. https://doi.org/10.3200/JOER.99.2.116

Zhao, H., & Akiba, M. (2009). School expectations for parental involvement and student mathematics achievement: A comparative study of middle schools in the US and South Korea. *A Journal of Comparative and International Education, 39*(3), 411–428. https://doi.org/10.1080/03057920701603347

SECTION 5

STEM Teacher Education

27

ELEMENTARY STEM TEACHER EDUCATION

Recent Practices to Prepare General Elementary Teachers for STEM

Amy Corp, Melanie Fields and Gilbert Naizer

Science, technology, engineering, and mathematics (STEM) content and skills are highly valued in the 21st century. As more and more jobs utilize these skills and knowledge, education has the responsibility of teaching these content areas and skills. In the United States, the federal government has allocated billions of dollars to STEM education efforts (e.g., professional development, curriculum, and partnerships with institutes of higher learning) in hopes of producing this workforce (Breiner, Harkness, Johnson, & Koehler, 2012). Internationally, funding for STEM and STEM education remains a priority in many countries (e.g., Granovskiy, 2018; Marginson, Tytler, Freeman, & Roberts, 2013; Ritz & Fan, 2015). Science teachers (K–12) are now encouraged and required by some states to include the engineering design process and engineering standards as one method for presenting science content based on the Next Generation Science Standards (NGSS; NGSS Lead States, 2013).

Interest in STEM fields starts with an interest in science and mathematics at a young age. Conversely, elementary is also the time when students could become disengaged in these subjects and choose not to pursue these fields as they grow older. This has become especially true for mathematics and science teaching and for low-income students (Epstein & Miller, 2011).

Since integrated STEM curriculum starts in elementary/primary school (Moomaw & Davis, 2010; Sullivan & Bers, 2018), these teachers must be equipped to teach integrated STEM. Recent studies show a connection between early experiences with STEM subjects and later success in those subjects or in school generally (McClure et al., 2017).

The typical elementary teacher is trained in all subjects with minimal depth in science or mathematics and little, if any, in engineering and technology. In a science report for the Center for American Progress, Epstein and Miller (2011) discussed how the current path for elementary teachers does not ensure the appropriate knowledge of or disposition toward science or mathematics because the course requirements do not include upper mathematics or science courses such as chemistry or calculus. They suggested strengthening these two areas in particular as a more targeted approach to improving elementary teacher preparation for STEM in the United States. Moore's research (2014) described how K–12 curriculum is being developed toward STEM integration. She iterated that undergraduate programs need to adopt collaboration of STEM faculty in preparing teachers to understand and teach integrated STEM. In Singapore, Teo and Ke (2014) noted the lack of elementary STEM training despite the increase in STEM elementary specialized schools in their country. They concluded that even the one-year post-graduate diploma for elementary teacher training is not enough and recommended more training in STEM subjects and specific pedagogies such as scientific inquiry and information and communication technologies.

Shernoff, Sinha, Bressler, and Ginsburg (2017) conducted survey research and found that current elementary teachers were interested in teaching integrated STEM but felt unprepared in content and pedagogy. Some teachers told how they knew only their subject and did not really understand integration with the other STEM subjects. In their list of obstacles to teaching STEM, poor (teacher) preparation was listed first, and they later noted a lack not just of content but of constructivist pedagogical knowledge. Their data on teacher responses demonstrated that teachers recognized their own inability to envision what integrated STEM really looks like. They also concluded that integration from the teachers' responses would best be addressed in elementary teacher preparation courses and workshops, or in service workshops, both with demonstrations of how to integrate across multiple disciplines by collaboration and connections to real-world problem solving.

Clearly, if integrated STEM is to be successful in elementary schools, there is a need for changes to occur in elementary teacher preparation regarding STEM and STEM integration. In this chapter, research on current practices of integrated STEM in Elementary Teacher preparation are described.

Methodology

Finding Articles for Integrated STEM in Elementary Teacher Preparation

In order to describe the research of integrated STEM in elementary teacher preparation, a large-scale article search was conducted. Utilizing a university library system, including listings outside the university collection, the lead researcher typed in key words to perform multiple searches for articles from 2000 to 2018: preservice teachers (and) STEM, teacher preparation (and) pre-service teacher experiences in STEM, STEM (and) elementary teacher preparation, alternative teacher certification (and) STEM, teacher certification (and) STEM, STEM (and) elementary teacher certification

Then the lead researcher used tools within the system to refine the search, which reduced thousands of articles, which mentioned elementary teachers or elementary schools to several hundred indicating teacher preparation. This was repeated with each search using every set of keywords. The articles titles were saved in a web-based bibliography and database manager by search, and duplicates were eliminated. When searches began to yield only repeated articles, the process stopped. One last search was conducted a month later to harvest research published for fall 2018 (null). The research team noted that this search was limited to published articles and did not include presented studies not yet published.

The article titles and abstracts were then entered into a spreadsheet for analysis of meeting core criteria of this study: Were the participants preparing to become elementary teachers? Was integrated STEM the main topic of the article? These articles ($N = 60$) were member checked by the three-person research team and coded into three separately filled categories: articles that met criteria in abstract ($N = 20$); articles that were unclear if they meet criteria but showed indications ($N = 16$); and articles with abstracts that did not meet criteria for elementary teacher preparation but gave strong evidence of the need for integrated STEM and of frameworks to explore integrated STEM ($N = 10$). The articles were divided amongst the researchers for a closer read.

As the research team read the articles, they completed columns in the spreadsheet for evidence of: meeting criteria, descriptions of content or pedagogy, and results. They also scanned the references of each article for other criteria matching articles missed in the database searches ($N = 4$). The team met and discussed in greater detail how articles in the showed *evidence of STEM integration* category met or did not meet criteria. For example, several articles stated working with P-12 teachers in the abstract, but in reading the article we uncovered that the participants were middle and high school student teachers. Other articles mentioned integrated STEM, but a closer read revealed only one

Table 27.1 Changes in Elementary Teacher Preparation Program for STEM Integration

Type of change to teacher preparation	# of studies
Program changes	7
Pedagogical changes	5
STEM component added to course	7

STEM subject or one subject in combination with language arts, or social studies (not another STEM content area). Based on the integrated STEM framework developed in Chapter 1, we were able to analyze and eliminate studies that were not describing integrated STEM.

Refining the List of Articles

The team then examined the titles and abstracts in the *evidence of possibly meeting criteria* category and eliminated those that did not meet the common themes defined for integrated STEM from Chapter 1. The rest of the articles in this category were given a closer read by the researchers and the data for evidence of criteria, descriptions of content or pedagogy, and results were entered in the spreadsheet. The researchers came to consensus about eliminating those that did not meet the definition for integrated STEM in Chapter 1 and those found to have participants that were not in elementary teacher preparation. The articles that remained were merged into the category of *demonstrates evidence of integrated STEM*.

Analyzing Articles

Remaining articles were further examined for content about integrating STEM within an elementary teacher preparation program. Two clear categories emerged: *program change*, and *pedagogical change within a course*. The articles were separated into these categories. Data in each column (descriptions of content or pedagogy, and results) were scrutinized to provide overall descriptions of the research in integrated STEM for elementary teacher preparation for this study (see findings).

Working within the framework for integrated STEM with an emphasis on common STEM practices (described in Chapter 1) allowed us to more closely examine the articles within pedagogical change. Examining the articles in this manner led to separating these articles into two categories: one remaining *pedagogical changes in a course* and the addition of another, *STEM component added*, for a total of three categories (see Table 27.1).

Results

As the United States adopts the Next Generation Science Standards (NGSS), and national and state entities such as the National Research Council (NRC) and the President's Council of Advisors on Science and Technology (PCAST) call for reform in STEM education, teacher education preparation programs are being tasked to include STEM pedagogy and content knowledge (Counsell, Jacobs, & Gatewood, 2017; Radloff & Guzey, 2017; Rinke, Gladstone-Brown, Kinlaw, & Cappiello, 2016). In answer to the need for STEM education, universities across the United States are implementing various versions of their understanding of STEM preparation. Similarly, Korea has placed an educational focus on STEAM (science, technology, engineering, arts, mathematics); therefore their teacher preparation programs have added STEAM to the curriculum (Kim & Bolger, 2017). Other countries (France, Australia, Japan, China, South Africa, and the UK) are focusing on STEM in schools, but in this global research review the response of elementary teacher preparation programs in these countries is unsupported (Ritz & Fan, 2015). Many teacher preparation programs in the United States have responded to this task by revising their programs (e.g., Rose, Carter, Brown, & Shumway, 2017).

Rose et al. (2017) undertook a mixed-methods study to identify and characterize the models of teacher preparation programs that prepared preservice elementary teachers to deliver TE experiences in elementary classrooms. Their research examined 44 programs that now offer technology and engineering (TE) as part of their teacher preparation program in the United States. Their search specifically looked for technology and engineering components; they also identified programs that were STEM, or that included technology and engineering in their teacher preparation (particularly in science methods).

They found that of the 44 institutions, 14 indicated that they included technology and engineering experiences for elementary teachers to deliver such experiences in the elementary classrooms. The study identified six different models in elementary teacher preparation: specific courses, a concentration, a certificate, a minor, a bachelor's degree, and a combined bachelor's and master's certificate specific to TE or STEM integration. Although this study was specifically looking for TE education, they also identified models that current elementary teacher preparation programs are using to address the need for integrated STEM preparation. While this article provided useful information, details on specific programs and research on those programs were not included.

After culling various articles on STEM in elementary education, the researchers determined that only 19 published studies discussed implementation and outcomes of changes to incorporate integrated STEM in their elementary teacher preparation programs. Table 27.1 highlights the findings of program implementation.

Program changes were defined as elementary teacher preparation programs that described changes in the courses offered or by combining methods courses to focus on integrated STEM. *Pedagogical changes* described additions of STEM activities to an existing course or changes in pedagogy toward integrated STEM. *STEM component added to course* designated strategies for included STEM components into preservice teachers' activities designed for elementary students.

Research Findings of Program Changes in Elementary Teacher Preparation

The following articles highlight examples of program changes for better STEM preparation for elementary teachers. These include the creation of a STEM certificate specifically for elementary teachers, designing STEM as a choice of majors for elementary teachers, and combining traditional science and mathematics methods courses into a STEM block. We also include evidence of program changes to include STEM in elementary preparation programs in Turkey. For clarity, the name of each article examined is also the title of that section.

Graduating STEM Competent and Confident Teachers: The Creation of a STEM Certificate for Elementary Education Majors. Murphy and Mancini-Samuelson (2012) described how they created a STEM certificate for elementary teachers. The certificate was created with collaboration between education and STEM faculty and consists of three interdisciplinary, team taught, lab-based classes: Chemistry of Life (chemistry integrated with physics, mathematics, and technology), Environmental Biology (biology integrated with Earth Science, mathematics, and technology) and Engineering in Your World (engineering integrated with physics, mathematics, and technology). This article suggested that collaborating with STEM faculty to include integrated science courses within the elementary teacher preparation program increases students' confidence in teaching integrated science and knowledge of science content. Based on these initial findings, the courses are now part of the elementary education curriculum and continue to be taught in partnership with the STEM faculty. These students are also required to complete student teaching in local schools and to use their understanding from these courses to teach science.

Characterization of a Unique Undergraduate Multidisciplinary STEM K–5 Teacher Preparation Program. O'Brien (2010) described program changes at the College of New Jersey to increase the number of STEM-trained elementary teachers by specifically including technology and engineering education. The Multidisciplinary major for elementary education students was approved in 1998 (formally called the Math–Science–Technology program, MST) and has requirements in all STEM areas. The purpose of this research was to investigate the depth of content knowledge in the MST program and is intended to inspire ideas for preparing elementary teachers for providing STEM experiences in their teaching. The research indicated that changes in this program to include a major in integrated Math–Science–Technology increased graduates' scores in mathematics and science, while still remaining on par with TE (Technology Education) students. He also concluded that since these (STEM) courses focused on education, not just S, T, E, and M in isolation, this process better prepares them for providing integrated STEM experiences to their elementary students.

Characterizing STEM Teacher Education: Affordances and Constraints of Explicit STEM Preparation for Elementary Teachers: Characterizing STEM Teacher Education. Rinke et al. (2016) explored the outcomes of redesigning the mathematics and science methods courses in their current elementary teacher preparation program into a combined STEM block with integrated engineering and technology themes (six hours). The combined STEM block courses stressed the same development of pedagogical content knowledge goals, learning opportunities around instruction, curriculum development, reflection, and assessment as the separate math and science methods courses. In the STEM block the STEM literacies of technology, engineering, content integration, the 21st-century skills and the arts were introduced by providing personal experiences with the fundamentals of computer coding and the engineering design process. The final assignment in the STEM block was modified to reflect this focus: an integrated curricular unit that relates to a real–world problem.

The researchers analyzed student work and surveys of efficacy from the two groups and found that everyone developed in general strategies and mathematics and science efficacy. They also noted that those in the STEM block had greater gains in confidence after the course than those in the separated courses. From analysis of the lesson plan artifacts for pedagogical skills for teaching mathematics and science they concluded that in content integration and STEM literacies, 75% of the STEM preservice teachers adopted an interdisciplinary approach with interdependence between the subjects. They found that the traditional students adopted a more multidisciplinary approach that typically included one STEM subject and literacy (reading or writing). When artifacts were analyzed for evidence of STEM literacies, they discovered that 87.5% of STEM preservice teachers included two literacies and that 21st-century skills were found in 100% of STEM student lesson plans compared to 77.7% of students in the traditional methods courses. This was a single–institution study of self-reported data, suggesting that combining traditional mathematics and science methods courses into one STEM (six-hour) block is more effective in increasing students' self-efficacy in teaching mathematics and science, creating integrated lessons, and employing 21st-century skills as pedagogies in their lessons for students.

Examining Elementary Pre–Service Teachers' Science, Technology, Engineering, and Mathematics (STEM) Teaching Intention. Very little published research is available from the international community about preparing elementary teachers for STEM. This article, although not directly about program change, implies that changes occurred recently in Turkey. Hacıömeroğlu (2018) wrote about the resulting intentions of preservice teachers from two Turkish universities to teach integrated STEM. The author translated the Pre-Service Teachers' Integrative STEM Teaching Intention Questionnaire into Turkish and administered it to 401 preservice teachers majoring in elementary teaching (306 females and 95 males). The questionnaire examined five sub-dimensions (knowledge, value, attitude, subjective norm, perceived behavioral control, and behavioral intention) with a 7-point Likert scale.

Results indicated positive results overall for intentions. Hacıömeroğlu concludes that these positive results are natural since they will be qualified to teach these subjects (plus the Turkish language). He suggested longitudinal studies with these preservice teachers in their classroom environments with integrated STEM activities. Only a portion of this article is translated to English, and some of the details are vague. The article does point to programs in Turkish universities that are specifically training preservice elementary teachers for integrated STEM.

Where Is the 'E' in STEM for Young Children? DiFrancesca, Lee, and McIntyre (2014) examined and discussed their implementation of an elementary STEM program that intentionally focuses on engineering and technology. The program has implemented a complete set of courses for pedagogy and content in mathematics and science, with a dedicated series for engineering. Within the series of courses, the course instructors focus on connections between the STEM fields, highlighting math and science in the engineering courses explicitly. Partnering with various colleges at their university, the program consists of 27 credit hours of courses in science, mathematics, and engineering methods. Teacher candidates select one of two introductory engineering-based courses intended to provide a basic understanding of engineering and an introduction to the engineering design process.

The preservice teachers take a second engineering course in their junior year designed to build on their introductory concepts of engineering and the pedagogy of teaching through engineering. Within all courses, the focus is on pedagogy and content demonstrated through inquiry-based approaches, cognitively guided instruction, field-based experiences, and self-made lessons. The courses are layered throughout all semesters until their final student teaching experience.

The anecdotal data demonstrated that students enjoyed the courses but did not always see the connections to STEM. Additionally, the authors reported on planned longitudinal research on the program and the relationships with the other colleges with respect to preparing STEM teachers. One student published her own narrative, a summary of which follows.

Growing Strong STEMs Reflections of a Beginning Teacher's Preservice Program. Glavich (2016) wrote a personal narrative on her experiences in the elementary STEM preparation program discussed in the previous subsection. Through the use of several pedagogies including inquiry-based instruction, PBL, practical experiences, and reflective opportunities, the preservice teacher was encouraged to use engineering to teach mathematics and science in her field experiences. Overall, the author felt highly prepared and more confident in her daily practices to integrate engineering into concepts of mathematics and science.

Findings on Pedagogical Changes in Elementary Teacher Preparation

In this section we report on pedagogical changes made within courses of elementary teacher preparation. All the articles found for elementary teacher education were university-based programs, although a search was conducted to include alternative programs. Changes included the use of videos as engineering cases, providing digital media instruction for lesson planning and integration, hands–on training designed specifically for science-focused STEM lessons, specific focus on STEAM integration, and the evaluation and creation of STEM kits.

Investigating Changes in Preservice Teachers' Conceptions of STEM Education Following Video Analysis and Reflection. In a typical elementary preparation program, Radloff and Guzey (2017) reported on the changes in PSTs from viewing exemplary cases of teachers utilizing integration lessons throughout their student teaching semester. The goal of the intervention was to determine if the PSTs could identify STEM integration, methods, interactions with students/teachers, and concepts. They conducted a case study by interviewing two PSTs about STEM integration before and after the intervention. In their findings, both preservice teachers' concept of STEM changed; they were able to define and explain in depth about STEM, differing from the beginning, as initially neither had a good definition of integration. Additionally, both PSTs reported they could see themselves using integration in their future classes with greater confidence, and they appeared to gain appreciation for intentional and purposeful use of STEM lessons in a classroom.

Assessment of Creativity in Arts and STEM Integrated Pedagogy by Pre-Service Elementary Teachers. Tillman, An, and Boren (2015) reported on findings from a pedagogical strategy of having elementary preservice teachers design lesson plans to specifically teach integrated STEM and the arts in creative ways utilizing digital media production. The purpose of this study was to analyze the differences in bilingual (Spanish), regular, and undecided generalists' peer evaluation and assessment of these STEAM lessons regarding opportunities for students to engage in creativity. One hundred twenty-four Hispanic female preservice elementary students participated (61 regular generalists, 43 bilingual, and 20 undecided). As students in an educational technology course, they received instruction and assignments on how to utilize digital media productions to create lesson plans. Students worked in groups of three or four (with a combination of bilingual generalist, regular generalist, and undecided generalist in each group) to create STEAM lessons using technology and presented them to their peers. Then immediately after each group's lesson, they completed a peer evaluation survey, and after all the presentations were completed, they answered two open-ended questions regarding their perceptions of the peer evaluation experience.

Participants were given a survey created by the researchers, based on STEM content and creativity in interdisciplinary STEM pedagogy. Analysis of the survey and questions given after presentations yielded data for the three groups: bilingual, regular, and undecided generalist. The authors concluded that all preservice elementary teachers utilized what they learned by combining technology skills with lesson planning to design more creative integrated STEAM lesson plans. They believe this change in pedagogy helps address the lack of integrated STEM and the lack of arts education for elementary teachers.

What's in Our Soil? A University–Nonprofit–School Partnership Aims to Raise Environmental Awareness. Counsell et al. (2017) reported on a change toward integrated STEM in their early childhood teacher preparation program. In partnership with a local non-profit organization and local elementary school, preservice elementary teachers investigated, designed, and implemented STEM lessons in K–2 classes over one semester. The authors discussed how the PSTs created the 'three phase lesson'; a lesson cycle provided by the instructors. The three-phase cycle included: productive questions, engineering designing, and thinking maps to support math/science reasoning. The PSTs utilized resources such as National Science Teachers Association Teacher Resources, PBS Kids, and others for assistance in creating engaging STEM lessons for young children. Although they reported more about the lessons developed, we conclude that the partnerships and lesson development during this field based time were to encourage PSTs to plan and integrate STEM lessons in their own teaching.

Analysis of Korean Elementary Pre-Service Teachers' Changing Attitudes About Integrated STEAM Pedagogy Through Developing Lesson Plans. Kim and Bolger (2017) researched a science methods course in a Korean elementary teacher preparation program which focused on training PSTs to create integrated STEAM lessons. The study involved 119 elementary preservice teachers with no prior exposure to STEAM. Throughout the course the PSTs were introduced to theory on STEAM, inquiry-based instruction, and lesson planning. The PSTs were assigned to generate integrated lessons and then improve them based on feedback. Their findings from survey data and review of lesson plans included a lack of integrated lessons, a lack of focus on science, and a struggle to improve throughout the lessons. However, they also noted increases in positive attitudes, perceived ability, and confidence and awareness towards STEAM.

Creating STEM Kits for the Classroom. Carroll and Scott (2017) described a pedagogical change to their methods courses for early childhood preservice teachers. As part of their science, mathematics, and social studies methods course, the instructors dedicated two classes to integrated

STEM learning. Although not research-based, they described how students could identify the STEM subjects before the intervention but could not describe what an integrated STEM activity looked like for early childhood. Initially students learned about integrating STEM with literacy and examined ready-made STEM kits. Students then completed a kit of their choice and reflected on the experience. Later they created their own STEM kits with a focus on science and the engineering design process. They also learned about lesson planning for integrating a Next Generation Science Standard core idea, with a science and engineering practice by creating learning objectives, student tasks, and assessments. Students tested out their plans and kits in small groups and reflected on the experience. Candidates indicated that they were more confident in STEM, felt more motivated when doing the STEM kits, and their pedagogical skills for STEM improved.

STEM Component Added

Similar to the studies outlined previously, we report on other published efforts to add STEM integration knowledge and/or experiences within the elementary preparation courses. These articles report on the experiences of small additions to the course instead of pedagogical changes. They provide a sample of revised units, or added projects and activities to encourage STEM integration. Since the articles provided details of the experiences and little research data, we provide a brief summary of these added components and their reported impacts on elementary teacher preparedness for STEM teaching.

One added activity to integrate STEM was the inclusion of experiences with robotics through the use of LEGO robotics sets. Jaipal-Jamani and Angeli (2017) reported on their experiences of a three-week LEGO robotics unit at a university within the United States. They concluded that pre-service teachers reported inclinations to implement robotics in teaching science and mathematics topics in their future elementary classes. In a Canadian study, Kaya, Newley, Deniz, Yesilyurt, and Newley (2017) highlighted how one program used two weeks in a 12-week methods course to teach engineering through LEGO robotics. In each study, courses allowed class time for the PSTs to build the robots. PSTs commented about the potential robotics has for integrating all core subjects, reduced anxiety for teaching the complex sciences such as physics, and reported significant gains in content knowledge of science topics such as gears. In general, these cases suggest that robotics can demonstrate integration experiences for technology and engineering with science and potentially mathematical concepts (Jaipal-Jamani & Angeli, 2017; Kaya et al., 2017).

Following Bybee's (2010) recommendation to introduce changes toward integrated STEM from the bottom up through introductory and exemplary units, Schmidt and Fulton (2017) transformed an inquiry-based traditional unit on the moon into a richly integrated inquiry-based unit with technology. PSTs in a STEM undergraduate elementary methods course were actively participating in inquiry with technology while learning science content. Schmidt and Fulton found evidence that students gained scientific knowledge, but more importantly concluded that they practiced integrated technology and 21st-century skills. Although not seen as a quick fix, the authors find power to change elementary teacher preparation from within the classroom by designing exemplary units for students to work through.

Two articles described another way to create experiences in STEM integration from within the university curriculum. Both partnered with field teaching experiences to add a STEM event in which PSTs had to learn about integrated STEM and work together to plan lessons and activities. The first includes planning STEM events and the second includes planning projects at a museum. Although they were not program changes or pedagogical changes, these additions to the courses explained in this section provided valuable experiences for PSTs learning about planning and implementing integrated STEM.

Dani, Hartman, and Helfrich (2017) led their students (50 participants in the P-3 science methods course) to plan and implement informal STEM events at their field placement school, outside of school hours. They conducted this study to determine how planning and preparing for these events would affect PSTs' learning about STEM teaching. After analysis of PSTs' reflections and plans/preparations for the event, they concluded several themes had emerged: PSTs understood that telling students is not enough, and they identified a need to shift control to the students to explore. PSTs noticed how much a child knows before the event makes a big difference in their understanding during the lesson, and they also determined that choosing examples is important and can be complex based on the scope of learning. The authors also noted how this added component gave PSTs opportunities to develop their 21st-century skills while learning about teaching STEM in their community.

Counsell, Peat, Vaughan, and Johnson (2015) described four integrated STEM units developed by their early childhood preservice teachers for implementation in their field placements or the local science museum. The introduction to their article described how these students increase their STEM learning as they utilize the learning cycle approach, the inquiry approach, and the engineering design approach. The authors felt that working beyond the field was even more valuable, as students not only increased STEM skills and knowledge as they implemented lessons with children, but also that they were part of building a STEM partnership in the community.

Stein and Muzzin (2018) described how elementary PSTs learned from failure with STEM lessons in their STEM camp. The authors focused on PSTs' learning from failure with STEM lessons, particularly in executing an experiment. Students developed STEM lessons, practiced them with peers, and then presented them 14 times with elementary campers, providing multiple opportunities to capitalize on failures and redesign the lesson. The authors concluded that when PSTs see failure through the lens of an opportunity (instead of failure as defeat), they learned even more. PSTs learned to ask open-ended questions, how to better scaffold activities for learning, and how to better engage students for the 'testing' phase of their experiment. The authors concluded that although the focus was on STEM learning for students, the PSTs were learning that discussion and activities in STEM are often based on failure or problematic situations, and that questions about how to solve these problems or failures motivate students' thinking and get them ready to do the STEM learning.

Conclusions

It is clear that preparation programs are attempting to create changes toward integrated STEM, and many universities across the world are working toward better preparing elementary teachers for integrated STEM; however, the research is not conclusive about best practices or the impact of so many of these changes since little has been reported. Also many of the articles published are not research-based. We encourage our colleagues to make a concerted effort to publish based on their research of practices that best prepare our future elementary teachers in STEM education.

As a result of our article search and review, we found fewer than ten articles that described program changes (including course changes). These changes varied and measured different outcomes. Murphy and Mancini-Samuelson (2012) and O'Brien (2010) reported increase confidence and knowledge. Rinke, Gladstone-Brown, Kinlaw, and Cappiello (2016) described students in the changed program increased efficacy and lesson planning for integrating STEM. Glavich (2016) described her experience in a newly created program as giving her confidence and preparation to integrate STEM in her classroom.

Only five articles described pedagogical changes and gave limited results of their effectiveness on students' ability to create integrated STEM lessons. Several of these studies included students learning how to create STEM lessons/activities. But the results were conflicting. Radloff and Guzey (2017) found that the PSTs could explain integration of STEM along with perception changes on how to use STEM with intent. But Kim and Bolger (2017) of Korea found that despite more positive attitudes, confidence, and awareness of STEM, lessons lacked integration or a science focus. Tillman et al. (2015) looked at different types of PSTs (general education, bilingual, and undecided) to determine if this impacted their view of creativity in designing integrated STEM lessons and found that all students improved and felt more confident about planning integrated STEM.

Self–efficacy was also noted as a positive change when PSTs were asked to integrate content as an added component to the class in both Canadian and American elementary teacher preparation courses (Jaipal-Jamani & Angeli, 2017; Kaya et al., 2017). Schmidt and Fulton (2017) reported on gains in content knowledge and increases in desire to implement technology after modeling a creative integrated STEM unit with PSTs. Conversely, Kim et al. (2015) found little difference in change in content knowledge from the addition of their STEM unit to the single course despite an increase in their aspiration to expose students to STEM. We conclude the results are too scant and varied for clear recommendations of what is happening to prepare elementary teachers for integrated STEM.

Implications

Clearly, the lack of published research regarding elementary teacher STEM preparation provides a concern. Given the growing focus on STEM in elementary schools, it is clear that preparation programs are attempting to create changes toward integrated STEM; however, the research is not conclusive about best practices or the impact of these changes due to the scarce amount published. We join with others such as PCAST (Holdren, Lander, & Varmus, 2010) in recommending greater focus on preparation of STEM teachers (NCTM, 2019; NSF, 2018; NRC, 2013), particularly elementary teachers who will teach STEM (Epstein & Miller, 2011; Honey, Pearson, & Schweingruber, 2014; Radloff & Guzey, 2017). O'Brien, Karsnitz, Sandt, Bottomley, and Parry (2014) reported the lack of intentional practices on the part of preparation programs, and their assertions cannot be refuted by evidence from the review conducted for this chapter.

Future Research Directions

Within the few studies reviewed in this chapter, it appears that changes to preservice elementary teacher programs that focus on STEM content and/or pedagogy tend to produce increased knowledge in STEM content, growth in attitude and confidence towards STEM and STEM teaching, and slight improvement in the ability to develop integrated STEM lesson plans. However, research is needed on every aspect of elementary STEM teacher preparation. There were no published data supporting the number and type of content or pedagogy courses needed for elementary teachers to effectively teach integrated STEM. What programs are offered in STEM within elementary teacher preparation? What courses or certificates are offered for elementary preservice teachers? We described some of these changes, but there needs to be much more evidence of what is being done and more research into what is effective in producing PSTs with STEM-literate skills.

What courses have been changed to integrated STEM, and how effective is this in preparing them to teach integrated STEM? We reported on just a few activities and specific field experiences. But what types of field experiences and in-class activities are most proficient in preparing elementary teachers to effectively teach integrated STEM?

Perhaps the most telling data lie just beyond the teacher preparation program. How are these students doing as teachers? We suggest research that follows teachers into their first years of teaching to determine what skills were gained through preservice STEM experiences in their preparation that have transferred to in-service practice.

While models of elementary teacher STEM preparation exist, our review of current research found extremely limited data on effectiveness of program changes, course changes, pedagogical changes within courses, and addition of STEM or TE activities to current courses for elementary teacher preparation. The potential impact of teachers who are better prepared to teach integrated

STEM is desperately needed. Describing their review of the literature of integrated STEM curriculum, Honey et al. (2014) found two areas most impacted by teaching integrated STEM: conceptual learning and interest and identity. They found the potential for increased learning in all STEM areas, but particularly science. Noting that the practices and research for how students interest and identify with STEM varied, they still concluded that the strongest positive impacts of integrated STEM practices were on students who have been historically underrepresented in STEM fields.

We have anecdotal/personal evidence that some research is being presented at conferences, but it has not yet reached the published literature. If we continue developing programs without research support, how are we adequately meeting the need of elementary students and schools? Could preparation programs inadvertently be contributing to the lack of quality students for the STEM pipeline?

References

Breiner, J. M., Harkness, S. S., Johnson, C. C., & Koehler, C. M. (2012). What is STEM? A discussion about conceptions of STEM in education and partnerships. *School Science and Mathematics, 112*(1), 3–11. https://doi.org/10.1111/j.1949-8594.2011.00109.x

Bybee, R. W. (2010). Advancing STEM education: A 2020 vision. *Technology and Engineering Teacher, 70*(1), 30–35.

Carroll, K., & Scott, C. (2017). Creating STEM kits for the classroom. *Science and Children, 55*(1), 36–41. https://doi.org/10.2505/4/sc17_055_01_36

Counsell, S., Jacobs, K., & Gatewood, S. (2017). What's in our soil? *Science and Children, 55*(1), 58. https://doi.org/10.2505/4/sc17_055_01_58

Counsell, S., Peat, F., Vaughan, R., & Johnson, T. (2015). Inventing mystery machines: Collaborating to improve teacher STEM preparation. *Science and Children, 52*(7), 64. https://doi.org/10.2505/4/sc15_052_07_64

Dani, D. E., Hartman, S. L., & Helfrich, S. R. (2017). Learning to teach science: Elementary teacher candidates facilitate informal STEM events. *The New Educator*, 1–18. https://doi.org/10.1080/1547688X.2017.1356413

DiFrancesca, D., Lee, C., & McIntyre, E. (2014). Where is the "E" in STEM for young children? engineering design education in an elementary teacher preparation program. *Issues in Teacher Education, 23*(1), 49.

Epstein, D., & Miller, R. T. (2011). Slow off the mark: Elementary school teachers and the crisis in STEM education. *Education Digest: Essential Readings Condensed for Quick Review, 77*(1), 4.

Glavich, C. (2016). Growing strong STEMs reflections of a beginning teacher's preservice program. *Issues in Teacher Education, 25*(2), 89.

Granovskiy, B. (2018). *Science, technology, engineering, and mathematics (STEM) education: An overview.* (CRS Report no. R45223). Retrieved from Congressional Research Service Website https://fas.org/sgp/crs/misc/R45223.pdf

Hacıömeroğlu, G. (2018). Examining elementary pre-service teachers' science, technology, engineering, and mathematics (STEM) teaching intention. *International Online Journal of Educational Sciences, 10*(1), 2–12. https://doi.org/10.15345/iojes.2018.01.014

Holdren, J. P., Lander, E. S., & Varmus, H. (2010). *Prepare and inspire: K-12 education in science, technology, engineering, and math (STEM) for America's future. Executive Report).* Washington, DC: President's Council of Advisors on Science and Technology.

Honey, M., Pearson, G., & Schweingruber, H. (Eds.). (2014). *STEM integration in K-12 education: Status, prospects, and an agenda for research.* Washington, DC: National Academies Press.

Jaipal-Jamani, K., & Angeli, C. (2017). Effect of robotics on elementary preservice teachers' self-efficacy, science learning, and computational thinking. *Journal of Science Education and Technology, 26*(2), 175–192. https://doi.org/10.1007/s10956-016-9663-z

Kaya, E., Newley, A., Deniz, H., Yesilyurt, E., & Newley, P. (2017). Introducing engineering design to a science teaching methods course through educational robotics and exploring changes in views of preservice elementary teachers. *Journal of College Science Teaching, 47*(2), 66–75. https://doi.org/10.2505/4/jcst17_047_02_66

Kim, C., Kim, D., Yuan, J., Hill, R. B., Doshi, P., & Thai, C. N. (2015). Robotics to promote elementary education pre-service teachers' STEM engagement, learning, and teaching. *Computers & Education, 91*(15), 14–31. https://doi.org/10.1016/j.compedu.2015.08.005

Kim, D., & Bolger, M. (2017). Analysis of Korean elementary pre-service teachers' changing attitudes about integrated STEAM pedagogy through developing lesson plans. *International Journal of Science and Mathematics Education, 15*(4), 587–605. https://doi.org/10.1007/s10763-015-9709-3

Marginson, S., Tytler, R., Freeman, B., & Roberts, K. (2013). *STEM: Country comparisons: International comparisons of science, technology, engineering and mathematics (STEM) education.* Final report.

McClure, E. R., Guernsey, L., Clements, D. H., Bales, S. N., Nichols, J., Kendall-Taylor, N., & Levine, M. H. (2017). STEM starts early: Grounding science, technology, engineering, and math education in early childhood. In *Joan Ganz Cooney center at sesame workshop*. New York, NY: Joan Ganz Cooney Center at Sesame Workshop.

Moomaw, S., & Davis, J. A. (2010). STEM comes to preschool. *YC Young Children, 65*(5), 12.

Moore, T. J., & Smith, K. A. (2014). Advancing the state of the art of STEM integration. *Journal of STEM Education: Innovations and Research, 15*(1), 5.

Murphy, T. P., & Mancini-Samuelson, G. J. (2012). Graduating STEM competent and confident teachers: The creation of a STEM certificate for elementary education majors. *Journal of College Science Teaching, 42*(2), 18–23.

National Council of Teachers of Mathematics. (2019). *NCTM Legislative Platform for the 115th Congress.* Retrieved from https://www.nctm.org/uploadedFiles/2019-NCTM-Legislative-Platform-Final%20.pdf

National Research Council. (2013). *Developing assessments for the next generation science standards*. Washington, DC: The National Academies Press.

National Science Foundation. (2018). *Science & engineering indicators*. Retrieved from https://www.nsf.gov/statistics/2018/nsb20181/

NGSS Lead States. (2013). *Next generation science standards: For states, by states*. Washington, DC: The National Academies Press.

O'Brien, S. (2010). Characterization of a unique undergraduate multidisciplinary STEM K-5 teacher preparation program. *Journal of Technology Education, 21*(2), 35–51.

O'Brien, S., Karsnitz, J., Sandt, S., Bottomley, L., & Parry, E. (2014). Engineering in preservice teacher education. In S. Purzer, J. Strobel, & M. Cardella (Eds.), *Engineering in Pre-college Settings: Synthesizing research, policy, and practices* (pp. 277–300). West Lafayette, IN: Purdue University Press.

Radloff, J., & Guzey, S. (2017). Investigating changes in preservice teachers' conceptions of STEM education following video analysis and reflection. *School Science and Mathematics, 117*(3–4), 158–167. https://doi.org/10.1111/ssm.12218

Rinke, C. R., Gladstone-Brown, W., Kinlaw, C. R., & Cappiello, J. (2016). Characterizing STEM teacher education: Affordances and constraints of explicit STEM preparation for elementary teachers: Characterizing STEM teacher education. *School Science and Mathematics, 116*(6), 300–309. https://doi.org/10.1111/ssm.12185

Ritz, J. M., & Fan, S. C. (2015). STEM and technology education: International state-of-the-art. *International Journal of Technology and Design Education, 25*(4), 429–451. https://doi.org/10.1007/s10798-014-9290-z

Rose, M. A., Carter, V., Brown, J., & Shumway, S. (2017). Status of elementary teacher development: Preparing elementary teachers to deliver technology and engineering experiences. *Journal of Technology Education, 28*(2), 2–18. https://doi.org/10.21061/jte.v28i2.a.1

Schmidt, M., & Fulton, L. (2017). Lessons learned from creation of an exemplary STEM unit for elementary pre-service teachers: A case study. *Journal of Computers in Mathematics and Science Teaching, 36*(2), 189.

Shernoff, D. J., Sinha, S., Bressler, D. M., & Ginsburg, L. (2017). Assessing teacher education and professional development needs for the implementation of integrated approaches to STEM education. *International Journal of STEM Education, 4*(1), 1–16. https://doi.org/10.1186/s40594-017-0068-1

Stein, M., & Muzzin, M. (2018). Learning from failure. *Science and Children, 55*(8), 62–65. https://doi.org/10.2505/4/sc18_055_08_62

Sullivan, A., & Bers, M. U. (2018). Dancing robots: Integrating art, music, and robotics in Singapore's early childhood centers. *International Journal of Technology and Design Education, 28*(2), 325–346.

Teo, T. W., & Ke, K. J. (2014). Challenges in STEM teaching: Implication for preservice and inservice teacher education program. *Theory into Practice, 53*(1), 18–24. https://doi.org/10.1080/00405841.2014.862116

Tillman, D. A., An, S. A., & Boren, R. L. (2015). Assessment of creativity in arts and STEM integrated pedagogy by pre-service elementary teachers. *Journal of Technology and Teacher Education, 23*(3), 301.

28

SECONDARY STEM TEACHER EDUCATION

Mary C. Enderson, Philip A. Reed and Melva R. Grant

Growing Need for STEM Teachers Across the World

Teacher preparation has always been a field of questions on how best to groom novice teachers for the demands of the profession. This is especially true for the sciences with debates on teachers needing more content, more pedagogy, or greater insight into applications involving multiple disciplines. These challenges get magnified when one looks at what is involved in training a science, technology, engineering, and mathematics (STEM) teacher and coming to some type of consensus on what it means and how universities should support this endeavor.

Globally, countries perceive economic dominance is tied to developing a STEM workforce (Blackley & Howell, 2015; Marginson, Tytler, Freeman, & Roberts, 2013) Growing the STEM workforce requires STEM teacher preparation and effective teaching that is emerging as yet another educational challenge without including teacher training and support or ensuring equitable access for all. Even so, STEM teacher preparation is emerging but with little uniformity, which is unsurprising considering STEM education was once described as ambiguous (Sanders, 2009). It was even proposed to rename STEM education to integrative STEM or iSTEM as a way to press for disciplinary framing (Sanders, 2012). Moore, Johnston, and Glancy address the widespread interpretations of STEM integration (see Chapter 1) but acknowledge the importance of uniformity in describing STEM as a field itself. A research-based constructed definition of integrated STEM is using technology and engineering design approaches for learning one or more concepts and practices of science and/or mathematics (Corlu, Capraro, & Capraro, 2014; Sanders, 2012). Given this definition, STEM requires a reformed approach for teacher preparation. The traditional approach to STEM education typically manifests as teaching that maintains disciplinary purity, an approach that is well supported by traditional preparation programs, but is not integrative (Burrows & Slater, 2015). Unlike the current STEM approach, many countries, with the exception of those known for their high-quality vocational education, give little attention to technology education in relation to STEM policy or public discourse (Marginson et al., 2013).

Countries globally anticipate insufficient numbers of people being prepared to meet the STEM workforce need. There is also unanimity that the solution to meet the need will require an equitably inclusive approach that broadens participation in STEM by including more women and minoritized people. Internationally, women represent 35% of the population enrolled in post-secondary STEM education and only 28% of STEM researchers (UNESCO, 2017). This study also reported gender stereotypes and bias diminish learning experiences and school choices for girls and women as well as their being less likely to enter STEM careers and more likely to leave. In the United States, STEM teacher demographics have shifted between 1988 and 2012—64% are women and most are White. Further, more affluent schools with larger White populations have more qualified STEM teachers, and this gap by race/ethnicity mediated by class persists for preparation and teaching (Nguyen & Redding, 2018). This race/ethnicity and class gap supports the argument for broadening STEM participation that is equitable and inclusive if the goal is to increase the STEM workforce for all people, including those who are minoritized and less affluent. While race/ethnicity are prominent identity characteristics in the United States, if this class argument were situated in another country where race and ethnicity are more homogeneous, a comparable identity characteristic might be indigenous, clan, or religious affiliation.

This chapter addresses the challenge set before STEM teacher preparation programs in confronting the methods of preparing secondary STEM teachers for future classrooms. While the international community has continued to espouse the importance of STEM, it has become increasingly clear that educational paths are not all the same and how entities define STEM varies greatly. This chapter addresses some perspectives as well as providing evidence that STEM integration, as presented in Chapter 1, should be rooted in project- and problem-based learning, student–centered pedagogy, and 21st-century transferrable skills (Shernoff, Sinha, Bressler, & Ginsburgh, 2017). Training teachers who are well versed in multiple content fields and are able to engage students in such active learning environments is the task set before teacher education.

STEM Movement Presents New Challenges for Educating Teachers Globally

The concept of STEM education has been around for almost three decades (LaPorte & Sanders, 1993; Sanders, 2009), but there are still significant issues that maintain the silo approach in secondary education. Historically, each STEM discipline has focused on the three cornerstones that define their academic discipline: content, an epistemological basis, and a history of practice, inclusive of curriculum, teaching, and research (Reed, 2018). Has the educational community broken from tradition to effectively create secondary STEM education programs? There has been significant progress, but three prominent obstacles remain in the form of teacher content specialization, teacher education models, and the existing secondary school structure.

Secondary programs are still very content specific, with each field providing great detail regarding the content expertise teachers should possess (McREL International, 2014). Many of these standards have made cross–disciplinary connections, but there is a lack of consensus across disciplines as well as a lack of teacher content knowledge across STEM. For example, the American Association for the Advancement of Science (AAAS, 1993), the National Council of Teachers of Mathematics (NCTM, 1989, 2000), the National Research Council (NRC, 1996), and the International Technology and Engineering Educators Association (ITEA/ITEEA, 2007) make strong connections between science, mathematics, and technology; but only ITEA/ITEEA (2007) and Next Generation Science Standards (NGSS) Lead States (2013) make a strong connection to engineering. Confounding the STEM content picture is the fact that the "T" and the "E" are often misunderstood and not as prominent at the secondary level (NRC, 2011). This confusion is mainly due to the four T's in STEM education: technology education, technical education, information technology, and instructional technology. Additionally, many feel the T in STEM is "covered" through the most prominent T in STEM education, instructional/educational technology (Reed, 2018). Instructional/educational technology by nature is implemented across all disciplines and is therefore highly visible within schools (ISTE, 2017). With regard to the E in STEM, the National Academies in the United States have given considerable effort in detailing the lack of engineering in K–12 schools due primarily to insufficient teacher content knowledge (Katehi, Pearson, & Feder, 2009; National Academy of Engineering, 2010).

A second obstacle of STEM integration lies with the teacher preparation models adopted internationally by colleges and universities. Teacher education programs often do not have faculty trained in STEM or in more than one content (i.e. STEM) area. Because STEM teachers are often credentialed in a specific field of study, they tend to focus on what they know best. It is well established that many European and Asian countries have a high regard of teaching in science and mathematics and would be challenged to change this structure, whether it is adding more content or a greater focus on developing pedagogies around inquiry and design (Marginson et al., 2013). In the United States, regional accreditation for colleges and universities perpetuates the model of one-discipline expertise. For example, university faculty must have 18 graduate hours in a discipline to teach undergraduate courses and a terminal degree (i.e. PhD, EdD) in a specific STEM discipline for graduate instruction (Southern Association of Colleges and Schools, 2018). To compensate for these requirements, the common approach for teacher educators is to train teachers for integrative STEM by using contextual learning lessons and units (LaPorte & Sanders, 1993; Crawford, 1999a, 1999b, 2001). An additional approach is to use design-based learning with convergent and divergent questioning (Wells, 2016a). These approaches are detailed later in the chapter.

A third obstacle of STEM integration is the structure of schools. School administrators are faced with obstacles to integrative STEM instruction due to license regulations for school personnel and standardized testing for students. Teacher preparation programs must prepare teachers for the classroom by making sure teachers have discipline-specific content expertise (Honey, Pearson, & Schweingruber, 2014). This is due in large part to the pressure state and local education agencies in the United States are under to meet the definition of a highly qualified teacher as defined in the Every Child Succeeds Act (U.S. DOE, 2018). In order to meet this legislation and receive federal education funds, state license regulations require teachers to have documented content knowledge, usually in the form of an assessment such as Praxis (Educational Testing Service, 2018) or edTPA (Pearson Education, 2018), where teachers typically sit for one content area test.

Internationally, teacher content specialization, teacher education models, and the existing secondary school structure have been obstacles of varying degrees. The Organisation for Economic Co-operation and Development (OECD) Teaching and Learning International Survey (TALIS) of 23 member nations indicated that ongoing teacher professional development had not been widely incorporated as a standard practice in many nations (OECD, 2009). A second TALIS survey five years later reinforced that most teachers still receive professional development but also feel isolated (OECD, 2013). As of this writing, we await findings from the third TALIS administration. Jensen, Sonnemann, Roberts-Hull, and Hunter (2016) compared school systems that had high student scores on the 2012 PISA (Program for International Student Assessment) assessments in reading, mathematics, and science against school systems in the United States, Australia, and the European Union. With regard to content knowledge, the researchers found that teachers in Hong Kong, Singapore, British Columbia in Canada, and most notably Shanghai, had considerably less teaching time and more time devoted to professional development. More importantly, the systems with high student test scores on PISA created a detailed structure of sustained professional development and accountability for school personnel.

Program Elements That Promote STEM Teacher Preparation and Teaching

Secondary teacher preparation programs centered on STEM education adopt a variety of models that differ from traditional content degree programs promoting a STEM agenda in one or two courses with multidisciplinary projects to programs that promote a more integrated STEM curriculum. Teachers are faced with the reality of an overly packed curriculum (Blackley & Howell, 2015) and the dilemma of how to work another topic or concept into mathematics or science classes when they hardly have sufficient time to cover mandatory topics. This section concentrates on three avenues that can contribute to teacher training in STEM education, including: (1) integrated STEM (see Chapter 1), (2) STEM specialists or leaders, and (3) programs that focus on more than one field/ discipline in educational coursework.

Recent reports by the National Research Council and National Academy of Engineering have addressed current teaching practices of STEM, emphasizing the need for explicit and intentional integration of STEM subjects (NAE & NRC, 2014; NRC, 2012, 2013). Integrated STEM education programs include approaches that explore teaching and learning between/among any two or more of the STEM disciplines, and/or between a STEM subject and one or more other school subjects (Sanders, 2009). While this has been a fairly accepted definition, there is wide variation in how this translates into preparing STEM teachers. There is often a mismatch in preparation programs that focus specifically on one or two disciplines that overlook ways to integrate the four disciplines of STEM.

Burrows and Slater (2015) attribute some of these challenges to the fact that the teacher preparation community lacks a clear conceptual framework on training STEM teachers. In their research on science pre-service teachers (Burrows & Slater, 2015), they propose a five-tier hierarchical STEM teaching trajectory framework on teacher engagement. This framework ranges from level zero, where a teacher focuses only on a single discipline (science in this case), to level four, which involves total STEM integration. Levels one, two, and three exist between the two extremes and consist of (1) discipline (science in this case) plus mathematics, (2) multiple disciplines, and (3) engineering projects. They identify what each level can achieve and how important it is for teacher preparation programs to develop a theoretical model such as the one described in this study. The framework is presented in a manner that supports the standards movements in science (Next Generation Science Standards—NGSS) and mathematics (Common Core State Standards—CCSSM), which have strong ties to integration of engineering and technology. "A vision of iSTEM requires teacher candidates to be skilled in constructivist teaching approaches where student exploration and novel applications are valued and emphasized" (Burrows & Slater, 2015, p. 328). Teacher preparation programs need to groom teachers in ways that help them develop instructional strategies to energize students in STEM and, in turn, consider the pursuit of careers in STEM fields.

Over the course of the past 10 to 20 years, the coaching/specialist model has taken root in many classrooms across the United States (McGatha, Davis, & Stokes, 2015) and has a slightly different look internationally with programs like Lesson Study (Huang & Li, 2009). There has been growing interest in a variety of curriculum specialists in the classroom, including mathematics specialist, reading/literacy specialist, science specialist, and library media specialist. The mathematics specialist movement has gained strength in looking at ways to educate and support specialists/coaches to work with teachers, which in turn helps student learning. The characteristics and support for such practices include boards of education and professional organizations such as the National Council of Teachers of Mathematics, Association of Mathematics Teacher Educators, Advisory Committee on Mathematics Education (Britain), and the Australian Association of Mathematics Teachers. Such organizations, along with movements like lesson study (Huang & Li, 2009; Huang, Li, Zhang, & Li, 2011), identify the importance of training and supporting teachers in and near their classrooms to develop expertise in teaching steeped in strong content and pedagogical knowledge.

Building on this concept, the professional community is witnessing development of STEM specialists who work with STEM teachers. One university in the United States, McDaniel College (Maryland), is taking small steps in its development of a STEM instructional leadership program for elementary placements. While this is an important start, there still remain questions on what a STEM specialist looks like and what he/she does to support teachers in today's classrooms. Until more schools adopt the notion of STEM teachers, it is questionable what exactly this person would do to support teachers of science, technology, engineering, and mathematics.

Lastly, programs where more than one field may be addressed throughout coursework are another means for colleges and universities to invest in STEM teacher preparation. For example, programs like UTeach (see http://uteach.utexas.edu) group STEM pre-service teachers together in educational coursework. The UTeach model eliminates traditional barriers to teacher certification, warranting that students obtain a degree in a STEM discipline and teaching credentials in four years so they have a dual career path—one in the discipline and one in education (Pérez & Romero, 2014). The program provides early field-based experiences where pre-service teachers go into schools to teach lessons in one or more of the STEM areas with the support of university and school mentor-teachers. These field experiences, sometimes referred to as clinical practices, occur throughout a program of study and provide novices the opportunity to develop skills to teach effectively. Burn and Mutton (2015) describe this process of learning to teach

> within an established community of practice, with access to the practical wisdom of experts, "clinical practice" allows them [pre-service teachers] to engage in a process of enquiry: seeking to interpret and make sense of the specific needs of particular students, to formulate and implement particular pedagogical actions and to evaluate the outcomes.
>
> *(p. 219)*

One of the most significant challenges for STEM teacher preparation programs replicating UTeach is implementing the course sequence, a streamlined and tightly articulated set of courses that integrates STEM content and pedagogy (Beth, Hughes, Romero, Walker, & Dodson, 2011). This integration depends on how lessons and concepts might be presented in UTeach courses and how pre-service teachers are positioned to think about concepts that blend ideas across STEM disciplines. Again, this is an important aspect for studying more deeply about STEM teacher preparation, but there is still more work to be done. Otero and colleagues (2006) recommended that the colleges of science support the interest of education by becoming more involved in teacher recruitment and preparation. Programs like UTeach provide a good starting place where sciences and education faculty and staff work together to prepare STEM teachers.

The notion of STEM teachers has not been widely embraced by secondary schools, and as a result, STEM teacher preparation programs have not done an adequate job grooming teachers for classrooms. There may be programs where one may declare two areas of science—a math/science combination, a technology/engineering combination—but one is hard-pressed to find a program that focuses solely on STEM teacher education and where such a teacher "fits" into a school. One teacher described the dilemma he faced in trying to teach from a STEM viewpoint (O'Neill, Yamagata, Yamagata, & Togioka, 2012):

> Initially, I believed that teaching STEM just meant integrating science, technology, engineering, and mathematics. I've since learned that STEM is about more than that; STEM is a shift in thinking. STEM is the integration of these four content areas in ways that are inquiry-based, project-based, and set in real-world applications. Much of the learning is discovery. Students are active participants in building new content understanding. STEM pedagogy uses the integration of these disciplines to empower students with a sense of control, appealing to their innate desire to learn.
>
> *(p. 38)*

This perspective is often promoted in teaching focused on technology and engineering or project-based learning (PBL) practices. Such instruction requires students to study and research problems from multiple lenses as well as learn how to work through real problems with several components.

While these practices are important to develop in teacher education programs, they often are not clearly defined in traditional preparation programs.

Bybee (2010) presents an interpretation of STEM literacy adopted from the PISA 2006 science framework (OECD, 2006). Of the four themes, two stand out in addressing teacher interactions with STEM and the information they need to teach from a STEM viewpoint:

- Acquiring scientific, technological, engineering, and mathematical knowledge and using this understanding to identify issues, acquire new knowledge, and apply the expertise to STEM topics.
- Understanding the characteristic features of STEM disciplines as forms of human endeavors that include the processes of inquiry, design, and analysis.

Helping pre-service teachers develop these areas of STEM literacy and comprehension is no small task. In order for STEM teacher preparation programs to be STEM-focused or possess multiple content areas of STEM, experts in science, technology, engineering, mathematics, and education must work together to support this endeavor.

The traditional model of secondary teacher preparation has long existed in a format where teachers earn a degree in a specific content area with a minor in the field of teaching. What often occurs is content faculty focus only on content and discipline education faculty (e.g., science education, mathematics education) focus only on pedagogy—instances where never the two shall meet. In such programs, pre-service teachers often see little connection of Shulman's content knowledge and pedagogical content knowledge (1986), which offers little support for growth and understanding of STEM education.

Challenges and questions arise when generic or content-specific teacher preparation programs attempt to prepare STEM teachers to enter specialized classrooms or schools (Teo & Ke, 2014). Designated specialty schools across the world may require more focused training for STEM teachers to be prepared to work with students who are in learning environments that promote STEM in integrative ways rather than in separate courses. Coming to a consensus on ways to accomplish this may be yet another hurdle in teacher preparation programs of today.

With a renewed focus on STEM, the international teacher preparation community needs to address key concepts or practices that could be embraced to educate secondary STEM teachers. As was presented earlier in this chapter, integrated STEM programs exist and do a suitable job of integrating the disciplines together in learning experiences. The problem is that the educational community does not typically have an approved curriculum for STEM teachers to teach, or knowledge of where such classrooms exist in traditional school environments. Generally speaking, teachers develop expertise in one or two of the STEM disciplines and incorporate projects or PBL approaches into classroom instruction (e.g., Enderson & Grant, 2013; Fantz & Grant, 2013). Research has shown that PBL that integrates concepts in STEM disciplines has supported students to transfer their knowledge and skills to solving real-world problems (Fortus, Krajcik, Dershimer, Marx, & Mamlok-Naaman, 2005), which in some instances lead to improved scores in higher-level mathematical problem solving and scientific process skills (Satchwell & Loepp, 2002). Such evidence of higher-level thinking is a victory for teachers working with students in the classroom and the global workforce for future STEM careers.

While there may be various methods of preparing teachers to carry out project-based learning, engineering design projects, or STEM tasks, it is clear that traditional single-disciplinary preparation is not sufficient (Shernoff et al., 2017). Teacher candidates need to be able to learn for themselves and then teach STEM through integrative approaches (Corlu et al., 2014; Stubbs & Myers, 2016) rather than stand-alone concepts that might fit together after the fact. In Ryu and colleagues' (2018) research with pre-service teachers, evidence indicated that collaboration, support, and knowledge of real problems solved by interdisciplinary teams were all critical factors to growth and understanding of STEM integration in class instruction. With this knowledge, STEM teacher preparation programs need to ask themselves, "How do we get there?"

Equity and Inclusion in STEM Teacher Preparation

Internationally, issues of equity in teacher preparation are complex, and in spite of many initiatives, educational inequity persists for teachers, their initial training, and for learners (Cochran-Smith et al., 2016). According to Cochran and colleagues, as income disparities grow within countries, so do systemic educational inequalities and outcomes with the least favorable for children from families living in poverty. Additionally, in many countries there are additional discrepancies that fuel differences in educational opportunities, such as gender, language, religion, able-ness, or one's immigration status and the time in status. To mitigate these systemic inequities that diminish teaching and learning in STEM and other classrooms, it is incumbent upon educators to develop and research teacher preparation that centers on equity as proposed by Cochran-Smith and others.

An equity-centered teacher preparation is not a new idea. Nieto (2000) articulated the perspective, "take a stand on social justice and diversity, make social justice ubiquitous in teacher education, and promote teaching as a life-long journey of transformation" (p. 180). This equity-centered approach requires one to consider questions of access and inclusion for teacher educators, teachers, and students. Florian and Rouse (2009) described an inclusive preparation approach that focuses teacher preparation around the variability of humanistic ways of learning and knowing. They posit the need for ending student deficit categorization and training teachers to support a wider spectrum of learners and the diverse ways they learn. Some might conclude that both Nieto's and Florian and Rouse's perspectives are captured by a policy to educate *all* learners, and many countries have adopted initiatives governed by this type of mandate. However, these well-intentioned initiatives continue to leave many students educationally underserved by pushing methods and practices that research has shown do not improve outcomes—antiquated organizational structures, homogeneous ability grouping, and ineffective teaching methods, like remediation (Florian & Rouse, 2009).

Broadening participation in STEM teacher education is vitally important if we are to achieve equity-centered inclusive preparation and teaching. In order to attract more diverse STEM teacher candidates, teacher preparation programs must increase access and be more receptive to different people, ideas, and approaches that are more diverse and inclusive. There are innumerable ways to take incremental steps toward improving traditional preparation programs, Teo and Ke (2014) suggest adding supplemental training as needed for ensuring maximum career flexibility for secondary science, technology, engineering, and mathematics content-trained teachers who may transition between traditional siloed content teaching and STEM teaching using integrated content during their careers. Supplemental STEM credentialing could potentially increase secondary teachers' access to myriad STEM teaching opportunities, especially for experienced teachers who may possess greater disciplinary and teaching knowledge. Independent of the preparation approach adopted, traditional, extended STEM instruction worked into science, mathematics, or technology courses, or STEM (see Chapter 1), the Florian and Rouse (2009) inclusive preparation approach might enhance STEM preparation and ensure maximum inclusion, which may render greater equity for both teacher candidates and learners in the long run.

Steps to Shape STEM Teacher Preparation

The three decades of promoting STEM education has clearly shaped perceptions on need and produced some secondary education exemplars, but overall STEM education implementation is still lacking in key areas. A national poll by Phi Delta Kapan (2017) reported that 37% of respondents thought technology and engineering offerings were extremely important indicators for quality of schools, yet the National Research Council's (2011) report *Successful K-12 STEM Education: Identifying Effective Approaches in Science, Technology, Engineering and Mathematics* limited recommendations to science and mathematics because technology and engineering "are not as commonly taught in K12 education" (p. 2). Additionally, the STEM focus in many parts of the world tends to be on the outcome of STEM jobs, not on the context of PreK-12 integrative STEM education or teacher preparation (see Office of Science and Technology Policy, 2018; Rothwell, 2013; Symonds, Schwartz, & Ferguson, 2011; Williams, 2011). Despite the continued murkiness of STEM education, there are key lessons learned that have proven successful in the preparation of secondary STEM teachers.

A first step is to prepare teachers for true integrated STEM (see Chapter 1) teaching. Unfortunately, many current teachers do not have the content knowledge, confidence, or pedagogical skills for STEM integration (Ejiwale, 2013). Training secondary teachers how to confidently implement contextual learning lessons and units has proven successful in technology, science, and mathematics education (LaPorte & Sanders, 1993; Crawford, 1999a, 1999b, 2001; Hacker, Crismond, Hecht, & Lomask, 2017; Wells, 2016a, 2016b). Despite these successful initiatives, many other STEM education initiatives merely mean more mathematics and science and little to no technology and engineering (Reed, 2018). Teachers need base content across all STEM disciplines, especially since areas with minimal footprints in secondary education such as career and technical education (CTE) have been shown to be an integral part of STEM education (Rothwell, 2013; Symonds et al., 2011). Interestingly, 82% of Americans in one national survey said they support career and technical education classes even if that means students might spend less time in their core classes (Phi Delta Kappan, 2017). Having all secondary STEM teachers take content courses in each STEM area is one strategy that may increase secondary teacher STEM content and pedagogical knowledge as well as confidence.

Secondary students are already being tested on STEM content through contextual items on large-scale assessments such as the National Assessment of Educational Progress, Technology and Engineering Literacy (NAEP TEL) in the United States (NAGB, 2014) and the Program for International Student Assessment (PISA) that contains scenarios to assess collaborative problem solving (OECD, 2018). To keep up with these assessments, training in STEM teacher preparation programs and professional development for current secondary teachers must include more contextual learning like those in the NAEP and PISA assessments.

Design-based learning is a proven strategy for professionally preparing STEM teachers to use contextual learning. Wells (2016a, 2016b) provides an example of design-based learning using a unit on bioprocessing and the conceptual/pedagogical PIRPOSAL model of STEM. Two additional examples of contextual learning units have been developed, tested, and implemented for food and water by Hacker et al. (2017). Professional organizations have also developed contextual learning materials that use design-based learning. The Engineering by Design (EbD) program by the International Technology and Engineering Educators Association (ITEEA) is a PreK-12 curriculum developed by cross-walking the Common Core State Standards, STEM discipline content standards, and the National Academy of Engineering's Grand Challenges for Engineering (ITEEA, 2019). The National Center for Technological Literacy (2019) at the Boston Museum of Science has also created a PreK-12 STEM standards-based curriculum that, like EbD, contains a professional development component. Both of these curricula have been implemented widely in the United States, and EbD has been implemented internationally. Additional international materials and professional development are offered by the Design and Technology Association based in Britain (see https://www.data.org.uk).

Informal learning environments such as school makerspaces and museums (i.e. Boston Museum of Science), as well as afterschool programs (i.e. robotics) and co-curricular programs such as the Technology Student Association (TSA), can aid with learning to teach STEM. Teachers can use these environments and programs to increase STEM knowledge because they are often developed and organized by professional groups and educators who have a primary goal of partnering with classroom teachers. These efforts may help ease some of the apprehension teachers have about their knowledge of STEM. The National Research Council (2014) also recommended learning networks (including online) and STEM-focused schools as two keys to successful STEM education. All of these STEM initiatives take time for teacher professional development. As mentioned previously, the amount of time provided for teacher professional development has been shown as a significant factor in student achievement (Jensen et al., 2016). Developing a culture of professional development, therefore, must be a priority for secondary teacher education programs. The successful curriculum, pedagogy, organizations, and other STEM integration initiatives mentioned here, among other best practices not mentioned here, are successful due in large part to the amount of time devoted to professional development. Adequate pre-service and in-service professional development must be a cornerstone for the success of secondary STEM education.

Closing Thoughts

There is a perception that current teacher education is inadequate and needs to be redesigned for STEM to succeed in schools (Shernoff et al., 2017). It has also been claimed that on some levels, attention to the various STEM disciplines is not impartial when it comes to integrative STEM (English, 2016). Much of this has to do with the lack of a globally accepted definition of STEM education and the different perspectives and approaches one takes to implement integrative STEM programs (English, 2016). In order to make progress in the STEM movement, several changes need to occur, including curricula development, teacher and administrator training initiatives, and school and policy changes (Moore & Smith, 2014). Teachers need learning experiences to help them develop STEM knowledge so they can in turn develop STEM learning environments. This will come about only with new models of STEM teacher training and support so that meaningful STEM learning—with connections of subjects—can occur (Moore & Smith, 2014).

STEM teacher education programs must make the integration piece front and center (Honey et al., 2014) by demonstrating connections between STEM disciplines in solving real-world problems (Shernoff et al., 2017). By broadening opportunities for more diverse people to have access in becoming STEM teachers, the potential exists to relate to and influence more secondary students to pursue STEM education as well as future careers. It is time to help educate the world's students to think in interdisciplinary ways *and* time for the future scientists, technologists, engineers, and mathematicians to work together in solving life's real problems. Who better to do this than a secondary STEM teacher?

References

American Association for the Advancement of Science. (1993). *Benchmarks for science literacy.* New York, NY: Oxford University Press.

Beth, A. D., Hughes, K. K., Romero, P., Walker, M. H., & Dodson, M. M. (2011). *Replication as a strategy for expanding educational programs that work: The UTeach Institute's approach to program replication.* Paper presented at the annual meeting of the American Association of Colleges for Teacher Education, San Diego, CA.

Blackley, S., & Howell, J. (2015). A STEM narrative: 15 years in the making. *Australian Journal of Teacher Education, 40*(7), 102–112.

Burn, K., & Mutton, T. (2015). A review of "research-informed clinical practice" in initial teacher education. *Oxford Review of Education, 41*(2), 217–233.

Burrows, A., & Slater, T. (2015). A proposed integrated STEM framework for contemporary teacher preparation. *Teacher Education and Practice, 28*(2/3), 318–330.

Bybee, R. W. (2010). Advancing STEM education: A 2020 vision. *Technology and Engineering Teacher, 70*(1), 30–35.

Cochran-Smith, M., Ell, F., Grudnoff, L., Haigh, M., Hill, M., & Ludlow, L. (2016). Initial teacher education: What does it take to put equity at the center? *Teaching and Teacher Education, 57,* 67–78.

Corlu, M. S., Capraro, R. M., & Capraro, M. M. (2014). Introducing STEM education: Implications for educating our teachers for the age of innovation. *Education and Science, 39*(171), 74–85.

Crawford, M. L. (1999a). *Teaching mathematics contextually: The cornerstone of tech prep.* Waco, TX: CCI Publishing, Inc.

Crawford, M. L. (1999b). *Teaching science contextually: The cornerstone of tech prep.* Waco, TX: CCI Publishing, Inc.

Crawford, M. L. (2001). *Teaching contextually: Research, rationale, and techniques for improving student motivation and achievement in mathematics and science.* Waco, TX: CCI Publishing, Inc.

Educational Testing Service. (2018). *The praxis tests.* Retrieved from: https://www.ets.org/praxis

Ejiwale, J. (2013). Barriers to successful implementation of STEM education. *Journal of Education and Learning, 7*(2), 63–74.

Enderson, M., & Grant, M. (2013). Emerging engineers in middle school mathematics classes. *Mathematics Teaching in the Middle School, 18*(6), 362–369.

English, L. D. (2016). STEM education K-12: Perspectives on integration. *International Journal of STEM Education, 3*(3). doi:10.1186/s40594-016-0036-1

Fantz, T., & Grant, M. (2013). An engineering design STEM project: T-shirt launcher. *The Technology and Engineering Teacher, 72*(8), 14–20.

Florian, L., & Rouse, M. (2009). The inclusive practice project in Scotland: Teacher education for inclusive education. *Teaching and Teacher Education, 25*(4), 594–601.

Fortus, D., Krajcik, J., Dershimer, R. C., Marx, R. W., & Mamlok-Naaman, R. (2005). Design-based science and real-world problem solving. *International Journal of Science Education, 27*(7), 855–879.

Hacker, M., Crismond, D., Hecht, D., & Lomask, M. (2017). Engineering for all: A middle school program to introduce students to engineering as a potential social good. *Technology and Teacher, 77*(3), 8–14.

Honey, M., Pearson, G., & Schweingruber, H. (Eds.). (2014). *STEM integration in K-12 education: Status, prospects, and an agenda for research.* Washington, DC: National Academies Press.

Huang, R., & Li, Y. (2009). Pursuing excellence in mathematics classroom instruction through exemplary lesson development in China: A case study. *ZDM—The International Journal on Mathematics Education, 41,* 297–309.

Huang, R., Li, Y., Zhang, J., & Li, X. (2011). Developing teachers' expertise in teaching through exemplary lesson development and collaboration. *ZDM—The International Journal on Mathematics Education, 43*(6–7), 805–817.

International Society for Technology in Education (ISTE). (2017). *ISTE standards.* Retrieved from www.iste.org/standards

International Technology and Engineering Educators Association (ITEA/ITEEA). (2007). *Standards for technological literacy: Content for the study of technology* (3rd ed.). Reston, VA: Author.

International Technology and Engineering Educators Association (ITEEA). (2019). *Engineering by design.* Retrieved from https://www.iteea.org/STEMCenter/EbD.aspx

Jensen, B., Sonnemann, J., Roberts-Hull, K., & Hunter, A. (2016). *Beyond PD: Teacher professional learning in high-performing systems.* Washington, DC: National Center on Education and the Economy.

Katehi, L., Pearson, G., & Feder, M. (Eds.). (2009). *Engineering in K-12 education: Understanding the status and improving the prospects.* Washington, DC: National Academies Press.

LaPorte, J. E., & Sanders, M. E. (1993). The TSM integration project: Integrating technology, science, and mathematics in the middle school. *The Technology Teacher, 52*(6), 17–21.

Marginson, S., Tytler, R., Freeman, B., & Roberts, K. (2013). *STEM: Country comparisons: International comparisons of science, technology, engineering and mathematics (STEM) education.* Final report. Australian Council of Learned Academies, Melbourne, Vic.

McGatha, M. B., Davis, R., & Stokes, A. (2015). *The impact of mathematics coaching on teachers and students. Professional development, research brief.* Reston, VA: NCTM.

Mid-continent Research for Education and Learning (McREL), International. (2014). *Content knowledge (online edition): A compendium of content standards and benchmarks for K-12 education in both searchable and browsable formats.* Retrieved from: http://www2.mcrel.org/compendium/

Moore, T., & Smith, K. (2014). Advancing the state of the art of STEM integration. *Journal of STEM Education, 15*(1), 5–9.

National Academy of Engineering. (2010). *Standards for K-12 engineering education?* Washington, DC: National Academies Press

National Academy of Engineering and National Research Council. (2014). *STEM integration in K-12 education: Status, prospects, and an agenda for research.* Washington, DC: National Academies Press.

National Assessment Governing Board. (2014). *Technology and engineering literacy framework for the 2014 national assessment of educational progress.* Washington, DC. Retrieved from www.nagb.org/content/nagb/assets/documents/publications/frameworks/technology/2014-technology-framework.pdf

National Center for Technological Literacy. (2019). *Engineering curriculum.* Retrieved from https://www.mos.org/engineering-curriculum

National Council of Teachers of Mathematics. (1989). *Curriculum and evaluation standards for school mathematics.* Reston: Author.

National Council of Teachers of Mathematics. (2000). *Principles and standards for school mathematics.* Reston: Author.

National Research Council. (1996). *National science education standards.* Washington, DC: The National Academies Press.

National Research Council. (2011). *Successful K-12 STEM education: Identifying effective approaches in science, technology, engineering, and mathematics.* Committee on Highly Successful Science Programs for K-12 Science Education. Board on Science Education and Board on Testing and Assessment, Division of Behavioral and Social Sciences and education. The National Academies Press, Washington, DC.

National Research Council. (2012). *A framework for K-12 science education: Practices, crosscutting concepts, and core ideas.* Washington, DC: National Academies Press.

National Research Council. (2013). *Monitoring progress toward successful K-12 STEM education: A nation advancing?* Washington, DC: National Academies Press.

National Research Council. (2014). *STEM learning is everywhere: Summary of a convocation on building learning systems.* Washington, DC: The National Academies Press.

NGSS Lead States. (2013). *Next generation science standards: For states, by states.* Washington, DC: National Academies Press. doi:10.17226/18290

Nguyen, T. D., & Redding, C. (2018). Changes in the demographics, qualifications, and turnover of American STEM teachers, 1988–2012. *AERA Open.* https://doi.org/10.1177/2332858418802790

Nieto, S. (2000). Placing equity front and center: Some thoughts on transforming teacher education for a new century. *Journal of Teacher Education, 51*(3), 180–187.

Office of Science and Technology Policy. (2018). *Charting a course for success: America's strategy for STEM education.* Washington, DC: Author.

O'Neill, T., Yamagata, L., Yamagata, J., & Togioka, S. (2012). Teaching STEM means teacher learning. *Phi Delta Kappan, 94*(1), 36–40.

Organisation for Economic Co-operation and Development (OECD). (2006). *Assessing scientific, reading and mathematical literacy: A framework for PISA 2006.* Paris: OECD.

Organisation for Economic Co-operation and Development (OECD). (2009). *Creating effective teaching and learning environments: First results from TALIS.* Retrieved from: http://www.oecd.org/education/school/creatingeffectiveteachingandlearningenvironmentsfirstresultsfromtalis.htm

Organisation for Economic Co-operation and Development (OECD). (2013). *Teaching and learning international survey (TALIS) - 2013 results.* Retrieved from http://www.oecd.org/education/school/talis-2013-results.htm

Organisation for Economic Co-operation and Development (OECD). (2018). About PISA. Retrieved from http://www.oecd.org/pisa/aboutpisa/

Otero, V., Finkelstein, N., McCray, R., & Pollock, S. (2006). Who is responsible for preparing science teachers? *Science, 313*(28), 445–446.

Pearson Education. (2018). *edTPA assessment areas.* Retrieved from: http://www.edtpa.com/PageView.aspx?f=GEN_AssessmentAreas.html

Pérez, M., & Romero, P. (2014). Secondary STEM teacher preparation as a top priority for the university of the future: National UTeach replication as a strategic initiative. *Journal of the World Universities Forum, 6*(4), 21–36.

Phi Delta Kappan. (2017). The 49th annual PDK poll of the public's attitudes toward the public schools. A supplement to *Kappan, 99*(2), Magazine.

Reed, P. A. (2018). Reflections on STEM, standards, and disciplinary focus. *The Technology Teacher, 77*(7), 16–20.

Rothwell, J. (2013). *The hidden STEM economy.* Washington, DC: The Brookings Institute.

Ryu, M., Mentzer, N., & Knobloch, N. (2018). Preservice teachers' experiences of STEM integration: Challenges and implications for integrated STEM teacher preparation. *International Journal of Technology and Design Education.* https://doi.org/10.1007/s10798-018-9440-9

Sanders, M. E. (2009). Integrative STEM education: A primer. *The Technology Teacher, 68*(4), 20–26.

Sanders, M. E. (2012). *Integrative STEM education as "best practice".* Queensland, Australia: Griffith Institute for Educational Research.

Satchwell, R. E., & Loepp, F. L. (2002). Designing and implementing an integrated mathematics, science and technology curriculum for the middle school. *Journal of Industrial Teacher Education, 39*(3), Retrieved from http://scholar.lib.vt.edu/ejournals/JITE/v39n3/satchwell.html

Shernoff, D. J., Sinha, S., Bressler, D. M., & Ginsburg, L. (2017). Assessing teacher education and professional development needs for the implementation of integrated approaches to STEM education. *International Journal of STEM Education, 4,* 13. doi:10.1186/s40594-017-0068-1

Shulman, L. S. (1986). Those who understand: Knowledge growth in teaching. *Educational Researcher, 15*(2), 4–14.

Southern Association of Colleges and Schools. (2018). *Faculty credentials.* Retrieved from: http://www.sacscoc.org/policies.asp

Stubbs, E. A., & Myers, B. E. (2016). Part of what we do: Teacher perceptions of STEM integration. *Journal of Agricultural Education, 57*(3), 87–100.

Symonds, W. C., Schwartz, R. B., & Ferguson, R. (2011). *Pathways to prosperity: Meeting the challenge of preparing young Americans for the 21st century.* Cambridge, MA: Harvard Graduate School of Education.

Teo, T. W., & Ke, K. J. (2014). Challenges in STEM teaching: Implication for preservice and inservice teacher education program. *Theory into Practice, 53*, 18–24.

United Nations Educational, Scientific and Cultural Organization (UNESCO). (2017). *Cracking the code: Girls' and women's education in science, technology, engineering and mathematics (STEM).* Paris, France: Author.

U.S. Department of Education. (2018). *Highly qualified teachers revised state plans.* Retrieved from https://www2.ed.gov/programs/teacherqual/hqtplans/index.html

Wells, J. G. (2016a). PIRPOSAL model of integrative STEM education: Conceptual and pedagogical framework for classroom implementation. *The Technology and Engineering Teacher, 75*(6), 12–19.

Wells, J. G. (2016b). I-STEM Ed exemplar: Implementation of the PIRPOSAL model. *The Technology and Engineering Teacher, 76*(2), 16–23.

Williams, P. J. (2011). STEM education: Proceed with caution. *Design and Technology Education, 16*(1), 26–35.

29

RESEARCH ON K-12 STEM PROFESSIONAL DEVELOPMENT PROGRAMS

An Examination of Program Design and Teacher Knowledge and Practice

Julie A. Luft, Jaime M. Diamond, Chunlei Zhang and Dorothy Y. White

Typical professional development (PD) programs in the separate science, technology, engineering, and mathematics (STEM) disciplines have the goal of enhancing teacher knowledge and practice to improve student knowledge (Borko, 2004; Darling-Hammond, Hyler, & Gardner, 2017; Desimone, 2009; Luft & Hewson, 2014). These PD programs support teacher learning by incorporating features that allow teachers to work collectively, in an active setting, in the context of their classrooms, and with a focus on a disciplinary area (see Carney, Brendefur, Thiede, Hughes, & Sutton, 2016; Garet, Porter, Desimone, Birman, & Yoon, 2001; Guzey, Tank, Wang, Roehrig, & Moore, 2014). PD programs adopting these design features indeed have been shown to improve teachers' instruction and student knowledge (e.g., Heller, Daehler, Wong, Shinohara, & Miratrix, 2012; Johnson & Fargo, 2010; Johnson, Sondergeld, & Walton, 2017; Polly et al., 2015).

Recent standards and international priorities in STEM areas challenge the single discipline model of PD programs. For instance, in the United States (US), both the *Next Generation Science Standards* (National Research Council, 2013) and the *Common Core State Standards for Mathematics* (National Governors Association Center for Best Practices & Council of Chief State School Officers, 2010) have stressed a connection between mathematics and science in the K-12 classroom. Alongside these standards is a call for increasing the STEM literacy of citizens to ensure they are prepared to engage in today's advanced technological and scientific global society (e.g., Morgan & Kirby, 2016; Office of the Chief Scientist, 2013; Teacher Advisory Council & National Research Council, 2014). These initiatives require that K-12 teachers advance their knowledge in ways that demonstrate the connections between the STEM disciplines and in ways that can help their students connect STEM learning to their daily lives. PD programs are essential in supporting K-12 teachers in their use of integrated STEM content.

Unfortunately, few evidence-based roadmaps exist for creating and studying well-conceptualized STEM PD programs. Honey, Pearson, and Schweingruber (2014) noted a need to articulate how the STEM areas are integrated, how important outcomes associated with an integrated program are studied, and how to configure STEM PD programs. They specifically reported that "many well-meaning efforts to develop STEM integrated programs are unclear about goals or do not collect outcome data" (p. 150). They also noted that those who are responsible for designing educational initiatives need to be purposeful in their integration of STEM. Clearly, more direction should be offered to those who work with and study the professional learning of STEM teachers.

This review of research was conducted with the goal of assisting those who design, implement, and study STEM PD programs. In order to be a purposeful review, it examines the configuration of current STEM PD programs. Guiding this analysis are the design features associated with high-quality PD programs. This review also explores how STEM PD programs support the development of teacher knowledge and practices. Framing this examination is the concept of transfer, which pertains to the influence of one's learning on one's engagement in a novel situation. These frameworks provide insights into the integrated nature of STEM PD programs that can be used by those who develop and study PD programs.

Review Methodology

Articles included in this review focused on full-time K-12 teachers who participated in a STEM PD program that aimed to improve their knowledge or instructional practice. Identified articles had an empirical (qualitative, quantitative, or mixed methods) orientation toward understanding the knowledge or change of teachers and included data associated with at least two STEM areas. For instance, articles that explored how teachers learned about technological applications to support their mathematics instruction were included in the pool, while articles focused on climatology and geology (both are earth sciences), descriptions of online PD programs, or studies focused on using technology in teaching were not included. Additionally, reviews of research were not included in the pool of studies, but their conclusions contributed to the discussion of the findings.

This review of research spans 13 years, 2005–2017. This period captures the increased attention to STEM initiatives for teachers by educational researchers. The articles that comprise this review were found using three different approaches to locate articles in the area of STEM PD programming in an effort to capture the different approaches to K-12 STEM PD programs. First, the top 100 journals from an eigenfactor and Scimago ranking system were compared to one another. Journals that appeared in both lists and were relevant to STEM education comprised the first search. This initial list consisted of 22 journals, such as the *Journal of Research in Science Teaching, American Educational Research Journal,* and *Learning and Instruction.* Each issue in each year of the journal was searched to identify articles that aligned with the inclusion criteria. This review identified approximately 36 articles. Second, seven databases in ERIC were searched using the following criteria: Abstract: STEM or math★ or science or tech★ or engineering; Subject: "professional development"; Text: qualitative or quantitative or "mixed method★". This search was limited to peer-reviewed and scholarly journal publications in English. Over 500 articles were initially listed in this search. A review of these articles against the inclusion criteria resulted in 27 articles. Finally, a Google Scholar search was conducted using the terms *STEM teacher professional development, STEM professional development,* and *STEM in service.* In each search, the top 30 articles were examined to identify empirical articles pertaining to the professional development of STEM teachers. Of the 90 articles that surfaced during this review, 22 articles were focused on teachers participating in STEM PD programs. Most of the identified articles were from the US, with other studies coming from the United Kingdom, Belgium, Australia, and Asia.

The resulting 85 articles were reviewed more closely to determine their alignment with the study area and their research quality. To gauge the research quality of each publication, a scoring rubric was used that was developed by Luft, Dubois, Nixon, and Campbell (2015), which drew upon the guidelines by the American Educational Research Association (AERA, 2006), and the work of Bybee (1982) and Clarke, Triggs, and Nielsen (2013) (see Table 29.1). Articles that scored a 0 in the area of Design and Procedures or Results and Discussion were eliminated immediately. Articles not excluded needed a score of at least 1.5 to be included in this review. One person who was familiar

Table 29.1 Rubric to Review Research Articles

Criteria	Score = 1.0	Score = 0.5	Score = 0.0	Comment
Research Question or Research Focus	Clearly stated question or focus and relates to theory and/or literature.	Loosely stated and somewhat connects to theory and/or literature.	Absent or poorly grounded in literature and/or theory.	Early studies may not have a clear connection to theory.
Design and Procedures	Detailed information about an appropriate design, and appropriate data collection and analysis process based on a question.	Adequate information is presented, but more information could be provided about the design, data collection, or data analysis, or a better design, data collection, and analysis process could be used.	Limited or no information provided regarding the design, data collection, and analysis.	Limitations in this area may be a result of the page limits of the journal, and/or the expectations within the field.
Results and Discussion	Claims are well supported by the analysis.	Claims made but may lack thorough substantiation, or important claims are not made.	Claims step beyond the data, are unsupported, or are not made.	There may be adequate data, but the description is limited.
Contribution to the Field	Well-reasoned and justified commentary about the contribution to the field. Clear contribution to the field. Not overstated.	Reasonable contribution to the field, but may lack clear justification, reasoning, or significance.	Limited or no clear contribution to the field specified.	Contributions are often situated within specific contexts, which change over time.

Source: Luft, Dubois, Nixon, & Campbell, Supporting newly hired teachers of science: Attaining teacher professional standards, *Studies in Science Education*, 51, p. 6, 2015, Taylor & Francis as publisher, reprinted and adapted with permission.

with this type of rubric reviewed the articles. If questions arose about the quality of the article, other coauthors were consulted. This process resulted in 41 articles.

Framing

Two areas were important in examining the articles in this review. The first area pertained to the design of PD programs for STEM teachers. Drawing upon the PD literature in the individual STEM areas, general guidelines can be suggested for the design of STEM PD programs. The second area of literature pertained to transfer, which should be a vital consideration when contemplating the impact of PD programs on the knowledge and practices of teachers.

Designing PD Programs for Teachers

Much has been written about the features of PD programs in the separate STEM areas (e.g., Darling-Hammond et al., 2017; Desimone, 2009; Garet et al., 2001; Heck, Banilower, Weiss, & Rosenberg, 2008; Johnson, Sondergeld, & Walton, 2017; National Academies of Sciences,

Engineering, & Medicine, 2015). Some of these studies are the result of an analysis of data from teachers involved in PD programs, while other studies reviewed the research on teacher PD programming. From these studies a consensus emerged regarding the design features of PD programs for teachers in the separate STEM areas, which include the following:

Collaboration With Other Teachers. Opportunities for teachers to work with one another are essential when they are learning new knowledge and instructional approaches. Collaborative opportunities, for example, may arise for teachers to share their challenges and accomplishments in teaching the new material and to contemplate ways they may modify the instructional approach to be used in their classrooms. Exceptional collaborative environments provide teachers with opportunities to work together in school or district teams. Additionally, experts associated with the PD program should work directly with the teachers to help them develop, reflect upon, or evaluate their new knowledge and/or instructional approach.

Coherence of the PD Program With the School Programming. The content of the PD program needs to be coherent with the programs and standards of the schools in which the teachers work. Administrators often play an important role in terms of supporting school programs and are essential as teachers carry out the work of the PD program. When coherence exists between the program and the school, the material in the PD program can be enacted in the classroom by the teacher.

Coherence is exceptional when teachers have the opportunity to develop curricula or instructional materials connected directly to their standards and aligned with the district or region standards, especially when their development work includes multiple individuals associated with the school. In addition, teachers experience ongoing opportunities to use and reflect on their curriculum or instructional materials, often in the form of PD program follow-up. This follow-up ensures that the developed materials are indeed coherent with the school/district/region standards.

Subject Matter Knowledge (SMK) and How the Students Learn SMK. PD programs need to specifically address SMK. In STEM, this SMK often includes the conceptual and exploratory content in the STEM disciplines. For instance, when scientists investigate particles (SMK), they draw upon specific exploratory methods (doing science). Teachers should learn both the conceptual and exploratory SMK, and they should also examine how their K–12 students learn conceptual and exploratory SMK. Simply put, when teachers understand how students learn SMK, they are able to modify the instructional environment to better support student learning.

Exceptional STEM PD programs tailor the SMK instruction to the teacher. Assessing the SMK of the teachers and providing specific instruction ensures that teachers develop their understanding of the integration of SMK. Some disciplinary instruction may be included, but the program should emphasize how the disciplines are integrated. Along with learning tailored SMK, teachers also learn how STEM areas progress. Similar to SMK, this content area is also tailored to the knowledge of the teacher. Within this instruction are also opportunities for the teachers to examine how students learn integrated SMK.

Adequate Time and Resources. When teachers are improving their knowledge and instruction, adequate time and resources are essential in supporting their learning. An understanding of the teachers' prior knowledge and current level of implementation of the PD program topic is needed to make decisions about the necessary time and resources. The timing can vary by length and intensity, which should include time to try the instructional approaches in a classroom. Resources should exist during and after the PD program.

Exceptional PD programs are structured to provide teachers adequate time to practice using their new knowledge and instructional approaches. This structure should extend to their classrooms when they have ample time to implement and refine their new knowledge and instruction. Exceptional PD programs also ensure that teachers have enough resources for their classroom instruction as well as for their interested peers.

Ongoing Evaluation Pertaining to the Outcomes of the PD Program. The learning of teachers should be constantly monitored during a PD program. An ongoing evaluation of the PD program provides data to the designers and instructors, which allows them to modify the PD program.

Exceptional evaluation in a PD program is ongoing, along with providing formative and summative data about the program. Evaluation should occur during the individual days of PD programming and over time. These data can come from many sources and can be used to modify the program to meet the participating teachers' and students' learning needs.

In summary, many of the same design features found in a single-discipline PD program are useful for a STEM PD program. One area that is notably different from single-disciplinary PD programs is the way the program approaches the instruction of the content. In a STEM PD program the content should be integrated, which will bring new challenges to those who are designing and instructing this type of PD program.

Transfer

Traditionally, *transfer* has been characterized as "how knowledge acquired from one task or situation can be applied to a different one" (Nokes, 2009, p. 2). In this way, transfer is said to occur when a learner correctly applies a particular principle or procedure to a new task situation (e.g., Bassok & Holyoak, 1989; Singley & Anderson, 1989). Some contemporary researchers conceive of transfer more broadly by characterizing it in terms of the influence of individuals' learning on their activity in a novel situation. In this case, transfer is said to occur any time individuals generalize their learning in a novel situation, even when that generalization results in what a teacher or other expert considers the incorrect or unproductive use of learning (e.g., Lobato, 2012; Wagner, 2006). We use the term *transfer* here to refer to the phenomenon (rather than a particular conceptualization of the phenomenon) wherein one generalizes, extends, applies, or in some way makes use of prior learning while engaging in a novel situation.

In the context of PD programming specifically designed to support teachers' teaching of two or more of the STEM disciplines, transfer becomes an issue of critical concern. For example, the designers of PD experiences must support teachers in accessing, leveraging, and transferring their prior learning (which most likely was developed in very different and separate classrooms) so that they are enabled to engage productively with and teach integrated content. Within the transfer framework, it is important to consider the design of the PD experience that will ultimately support teachers in their different interdisciplinary approaches.

STEM PD Program Design and Transfer

Area 1: Design of STEM PD Programs

To determine the adequacy of the design of the STEM PD programs in this collection of studies, the programs were compared to the previously identified consensus features associated with PD programing. Initially, we worked collectively to evaluate each study regarding the consensus features. When we achieved 90% agreement in terms of our assessment of a PD program, we worked independently to evaluate the remaining PD program studies. The scores were compiled to depict the presence or absence of the different consensus features.

While determining the consensus features in the PD programs, salient areas emerged between the papers that were pertinent to STEM PD programming. For instance, when determining if the content was siloed or integrated, it was evident that different types of integration occurred in the PD programs. These areas were noted and examined after all of the papers were reviewed. Specific areas essential to the design of STEM PD programs are shared in the following sections, in addition to the features in the STEM PD programs.

Most STEM PD Programs Contained Several of the Consensus Features Associated With Sound PD Design. A few important trends are noted in Table 29.2, which is a descriptive analysis of the different features in the PD programs. In terms of the content, an important design feature is that most STEM programs had integrated content. Additionally, most STEM PD programs had features of collaboration, adequate time, and resources. More than half of the STEM PD programs created opportunities for coherence between the program and the school, but PD program designers could be more attentive to this area. Finally, the descriptions of the STEM PD programs did not always include discussions of the evaluation or how the programs were revised in light of teacher and student learning. This area is another in which those who design and implement STEM PD programs can improve.

Integrated STEM PD Programs Were Oriented in One of Three Ways. These ways were: (a) one driving STEM area that then included one or more other areas, (b) an instructional approach that supported the inclusion of multiple STEM areas, or (c) a combination of STEM areas. Among the studies noted as having a level of integration among the STEM areas, the most prominent integrated orientation of PD programs consisted of a driving disciplinary area that included another disciplinary area and was referred to as "disciplinary" integration by Vasquez, Sneider, and Comer (2013). Among these articles, technology and engineering were often the conduits for the integration of either science or mathematics (e.g., De Smet, Valcke, Schellens, De Wever, & Vanderlinde, 2016; Mouza, 2011). The study by Mouza (2011) highlighted this orientation. Science and mathematics teachers participated in a PD program that supported the use of technology in their content courses. The facilitators of the program provided different technological tools that could be used to support content instruction in order to improve teacher and student learning.

A number of the PD programs focused on providing a framework for the inclusion of STEM (e.g., Asghar, Ellington, Rice, Johnson, & Prime, 2012), often problem- or project-based learning (PBL). This transdisciplinary approach (Vasquez et al., 2013) allowed teachers to learn how to draw in the different STEM areas to address a societal or contextual problem. PBL was often selected because it mirrors the process used by scientists and engineers and deliberately breaks down siloed disciplines. Ashgar et al. (2012), for example, reported that PBL was useful in advancing the interdisciplinary knowledge of teachers, and in assisting teachers in facing challenges associated with an integrated curriculum. However, the teachers in the PD program still indicated that they experienced barriers in implementing PBL in their classrooms. Some of these barriers were the teachers' own discomfort in using integrated instruction or the institution's local standards that were not well suited for integrated instruction.

Table 29.2 Summary of the Different Studies and Their Inclusion of PD Program Features (*N* = 38)

	Not Present	*Not Explicitly Present*	*Present*	*Exceptional*
Collaboration	10% (4)	18% (7)	50% (19)	22% (8)
Coherence	5% (2)	29% (11)	42% (16)	24% (9)
Content-Siloed	77% (29)	10% (4)	13% (5)	
Content-Integrated	13% (5)	13% (5)	69% (26)	5% (2)
Adequate time and resources	13% (5)	13% (5)	50% (19)	24% (9)
Ongoing evaluation and/or potential for adjustment	42% (16)	13% (5)	37% (14)	8% (3)

Note: Papers that used the same PD program were counted only once.

Another orientation evident in the integration of STEM disciplines, but not described by Vasquez et al. (2013), was a combination of disciplines that advance knowledge. These combined disciplines exist as their own field and advance understanding or investigate phenomena. Borgerding, Sadler, and Koroly (2013), for instance, reported that teachers used their technological knowledge in the discipline of biology to promote a better understanding of genetic information in organisms. Additional examples are PD programs focused on physics (including mathematics and science), environmental science (including chemistry, biology, and mathematics), or a distinct form of mathematics instruction that relied upon technological applications (e.g., Mualem & Eylon, 2009; Roschelle et al., 2010). Without one of the STEM disciplines, this type of integrated discipline would not exist.

The Technological Component Was the Most Varied in the STEM PD Programs. Among the reviewed studies, the inclusion of technology varied significantly, as well as the ways the technology was accessed by the teachers for classroom use. In some settings, technology was a mechanism to improve the instruction of teachers as they taught science, mathematics, or engineering. De Smet et al. (2016), for example, explored how biology teachers changed their instruction as they embedded technology into their classroom practice. Some of these systems involved wikis that could be used to encourage collaboration or explanation and, thus, learning among students. In other settings, technology was essential in representing a scientific or mathematical idea. Gonczi, Chiu, Maeng, and Bell (2016) focused on having teachers use simulations in their instruction. These simulations were models regarding important science phenomena, and they allowed students to manipulate them to better understand the phenomena.

Along with the varied use of technology was variation in the outcome of using technology. In Roschelle et al. (2010), the teachers' use of technology was varied but resulted in students learning both basic and advanced concepts. Roschelle et al. (2010) suggested that PD programs using technology should focus on a learning activity and not only a lesson or assessment. Longhurst, Jones, and Campbell (2017) noted an uneven accessing of technology among science teachers, which resulted in varied pedagogical considerations among the teachers. They also suggested that PD program designers need to tailor their use of technology to the participating teachers. Teachers who are not as familiar with different forms of technology may need additional support in using technology in their classrooms.

Equity and Diversity Were Notably Absent in the Design and Implementation of STEM PD Programs. An important goal of STEM PD programs is to improve the learning of all students. Enacting this goal requires that STEM PD programs acknowledge and prepare teachers to work with all students. Without a purposeful discussion of equity or diversity, STEM PD programs may not be enacted in a way that supports all students. Only two studies directly addressed how teachers would learn about diversity or equity as they enacted the content associated with the STEM PD program (see Leonard et al., 2017; Zozakiewicz & Rodriguez, 2007). Other studies reported that their programs resulted in gains for students who identified as female, Black, or Hispanic (e.g., Blanchard, LeProvost, Tolin, & Gutierrez, 2016; Capraro et al., 2016)—groups that are historically not well represented in STEM fields. For instance, Blanchard et al. (2016) implemented a PD program that allowed teachers to learn about new technologies to enhance their teaching of mathematics and science. Black students who had teachers who participated in this PD program showed notable gains over time. Similarly, Capraro et al. (2016) studied the enactment of PBL in a diverse, rural school district. They found a positive effect on student learning when teachers implemented PBL, as was intended by those providing the PD program. The students of the teachers who deviated from the intended program did not have any positive gains.

Summary. Most STEM PD programs we reviewed included features associated with effective PD programs. The prevalence of the consensus features in PD programs suggests that those who designed and studied PD programming were aware of these features, although inclusion of the features was uneven. Those who design and implement PD programs should continue to consider how they create coherent programs and adjust programs to meet the instructional needs of teachers. These two areas are essential in ensuring that programmatic content is embedded in the classrooms of teachers.

The STEM PD programs often emphasized a connection or integration of the different STEM areas. Given that STEM education should represent the integration of disciplines, this finding is important. Different ways exist, however, for integrating the STEM disciplines. This review and other chapters in this handbook (for example, see Moore, Johnston, & Glancy, Chapter 1) note this variation. With the different approaches to STEM integration, continuing to discuss both the how and the why of STEM integration is important. These types of discussions can help elucidate different approaches to STEM education and potentially influence the development of local and national standards that are conducive to STEM instruction.

STEM PD program design should also consider how participating teachers are supported in working with diverse student populations. Ways the advocated approaches can address issues of equity and diversity must be clearly articulated in STEM PD program design. After all, building a knowledgeable workforce and citizenry in the STEM fields requires that all students are supported to learn STEM content. Integrated instruction that attends to the content and issues of equity and diversity is a long-standing challenge among those involved in STEM PD programs (Battey, Kafai, Nixon, & Kao, 2007).

Area 2: Knowledge and Practices of Teachers

In contemplating how the knowledge and practices of STEM teachers were impacted by the PD programs, we considered how transfer was addressed (e.g., consideration of prior knowledge) in the reviewed studies. To characterize how transfer occurred between the STEM PD programs and the teachers, we constructed a matrix to document the different emergent areas associated with transfer (guided by Miles, Huberman, & Saldaña, 2014).

As each article was reviewed, a memo was written pertaining to the potential representation of transfer in the paper. The salient areas associated with the memos were then consolidated into headings of rows. Columns were added that noted the abstractions pertaining to the area. Four themes emerged from the rows and the columns that highlight how transfer was supported in the different STEM PD programs:

Teachers Have Different Learning Thresholds, Which Requires Nimble STEM PD Programs. Many discipline-specific teachers have experienced opportunities to learn about different STEM areas. Several of the studies revealed that teachers learned the presented content differently (e.g., Annetta et al., 2013; Longhurst et al., 2017; Xie, Kim, Cheng, & Luthy, 2017). This finding is not unexpected, as science teachers often have different levels of understanding of different content areas. Depending upon their disciplinary expertise, some content areas may be easier for teachers to learn than others.

In the studies we reviewed, teachers differed in how they learned the new content. Some teachers found their prior knowledge to be important when learning new content. Haag and Megowan (2015), for instance, found that teachers with prior experiences in modeling felt better positioned to tackle different subjects and could better draw upon the content presented in the STEM PD program. In other programs, teachers needed different durations of programming to understand the program content (Schuchardt, Tekkumru-Kisa, Schunn, Stein, & Reynolds, 2017). Content that was familiar, yet novel to the teachers, required additional time for learning. When teachers did not have an adequate knowledge base, they could not even access the provided support in the PD program in ways that would ensure the development of their knowledge or instruction (Baker-Doyle & Yoon, 2011).

Anchoring Experiences in PD Programs May Support Teacher Learning. Preplanned anchoring experiences may influence how teachers engage in the content and PD program support structures, which may influence their instruction in STEM areas. The different types of anchoring experiences were often conceptual. For instance, Seraphin et al. (2017) found that anchoring the PD program in inquiry promoted teacher learning. Their teachers were able to make linkages to the different content areas within the inquiry approach. Similarly, Leonard et al. (2017) focused on computational thinking to frame the learning experience in the PD program. While the teachers were more receptive to this focus, Leonard et al. (2017) found that some of the activities were more useful than other activities in supporting the learning of the teachers. In a different approach to anchoring, Maeng, Whitworth, Gonczi, Navy, and Wheeler (2017) concluded that elementary teachers may need specific examples to support their use of engineering practices. These examples should connect to the engineering content (which was the anchoring experience) and demonstrate how to teach in areas unfamiliar to the teachers.

Working in Communities is Essential to Promoting Transfer. Collaborative learning environments are a staple of sound PD programs. In collaborative settings, teachers have opportunities to contemplate, challenge, revise, and construct their knowledge and instructional practices. Collaboration is essential as teachers plan to enact their new knowledge in their classrooms. Hardré et al. (2013) concluded that teachers want opportunities to work with their peers, which gives them an opportunity to revisit their understanding of the content. Outside of the peer-to-peer learning model, Miller, Curwen, White-Smith, and Calfee (2015) explored the benefits of teachers working with experts in the different fields. They found that these types of collaborations resulted in the teachers thinking of new ways to integrate the content in their classrooms.

As the teachers work in communities, their learning of the PD program content should be monitored. For instance, as teachers in Lehman, George, Buchanan, and Rush (2006) worked together, they could not clearly understand how the disciplines were integrated with one another. The facilitator in the program was important in addressing their construction of knowledge. Similarly, Jones and Dexter (2014) concluded that different communities impacted how teachers learned the content. Formal and informal settings provided different supports for learning, which resulted in different levels of enhanced understanding of the teachers.

The PD Program, Schools, and Colleagues Can Constrain the Transfer of Knowledge and Instructional Practices. These factors are important in supporting the learning of teachers, but they can equally constrain the transfer of new knowledge and instructional practices to a classroom. Supporting the transfer of knowledge or practices needs to be built into a PD program, which can include opportunities to develop knowledge and practice. Ermeling and Yarbo (2016) and Capraro et al. (2016) developed programs that were focused on building knowledge and implementation. Yet, they provided few opportunities for teachers to engage in the content in ways that could result in new or revised knowledge or instructional approaches.

Within a school, several factors can limit the transfer of the content to the classroom (see De Smet et al., 2016; Fore, Feldhaus, Sorge, Agarwal, & Varahramyan, 2015). For example, colleagues may not be supportive or receptive to the new instructional practices advocated by a teacher who participated in the STEM PD program. Additionally, a focus on siloed instruction at the school can negate the instruction learned by the teacher in the STEM PD program. The final constraint can be as simple as not having adequate materials to support the envisioned instruction. Gonczi et al. (2016) found that a lack of resources and human support limited the actual implementation of the PD program content in the teachers' classrooms. Resources can be the physical materials that are used during STEM instruction, while human support often consists of colleagues and administrators who encourage the instructional approach.

Summary. STEM PD designers often do not consider the complexity of transfer. Transfer certainly occurs at the individual level, and it can be supported or constrained in different ways. Within the PD program, transfer can be supported by designing programs that are responsive to the prior knowledge and learning of participating teachers. Collecting data on teacher knowledge and learning can guide the adjustment of a PD program. The change in the PD program may involve modifying the duration of the program, altering the instructional approaches in the program, or ensuring that teachers have access to other individuals who can support their instruction.

In addition, learning about different disciplines and their connections to one another is certainly more complex than the learning associated with a single-discipline PD program. Using well-conceptualized anchoring experiences in a PD program may enable teachers to enact their new knowledge and practices in their classrooms. Anchoring experiences can be a focal or supportive experience for teachers.

Finally, the communities in which the teachers work can either support or constrain their transfer of the knowledge and instructional practices advocated in the PD program—and sometimes they do both. On one hand, the communities can help teachers build and refine their knowledge and instructional practices. On the other hand, communities may knowingly or unknowingly limit or constrain the use of emerging knowledge and instructional practices, whether through an emphasis on single-discipline instruction or a lack of support at the school site. Navigating the learning community entails monitoring how the teacher's knowledge and instructional practices are changing over time, ensuring the PD program aligns with the school's instructional approach, and having adequate supports in the PD program.

Summary

This review was completed to contribute to the knowledge base about the design of STEM PD programs and how they can be configured to better support transfer. The knowledge and instructional practices of the teachers were an important consideration in contemplating the design of STEM PD programs and transfer.

This review revealed that the development and enactment of STEM PD programs is an emerging and challenging area. The following recommendations based on the reviewed literature may guide those who design and implement STEM PD programming for K-12 teachers.

1. STEM PD programs transcend the traditional design assumptions found in single-discipline PD programs. The integration of different disciplines brings new challenges to those who design and implement these types of programs. Determining how to represent the integrated disciplines is essential to consider when designing a PD program. Different integrative approaches may require different PD program configurations.
2. The design of such programs should account for issues associated with equity and diversity. All students can and must develop their STEM knowledge, which requires well-prepared teachers who can work in diverse settings.
3. Supporting the development of teacher knowledge and practices in STEM areas will also bring new challenges to those who work with teachers. Monitoring the development of teachers engaged in STEM PD programs is essential, as well as modifying the STEM PD program to best meet the learning needs of the teachers.

In the area of future research, many areas can provide additional insights into STEM PD program design and teacher learning. Two of the most pressing areas are as follows:

*   How do STEM PD programs (in their different configurations) cultivate the disciplinary and interconnected knowledge and practices of teachers? This question focuses on the role of the PD program in supporting teacher learning and ways to adjust interdisciplinary PD programs to better support the learning needs of teachers who are entering the field of STEM education. Transfer, equity, and diversity will be essential in this line of work.

- How do teachers represent their newly learned integrated knowledge in the classroom? This question focuses on how teachers actually represent their new knowledge in their classrooms and how it impacts the learning of *all* students. These studies can be certainly structured in different ways.

Along with the research, STEM researchers need to be more comprehensive in the ways they report their findings. Supplemental files or expanded descriptions of PD programs will be important to include in research reports.

If anything, this review highlights the pressing need for STEM PD research that informs PD program design. Teachers who engage in programming based upon empirical work will ultimately cultivate STEM-literate citizens and a diverse STEM workforce.

References

(★Designates studies used in the review but not cited.)

American Educational Research Association. (2006). Standards for reporting on empirical social science research in AERA publications. *Educational Researcher, 35*(6), 33–40. https://doi.org/10.3102/0013189X035006033

Annetta, L. A., Frazier, W. M., Folta, E., Holmes, S., Lamb, R., & Cheng, M. T. (2013). Science teacher efficacy and extrinsic factors toward professional development using video games in a design-based research model: The next generation of STEM learning. *Journal of Science Education and Technology, 22*(1), 47–61. https://doi.org/10.1007/s10956-012-9375-y

Asghar, A., Ellington, R., Rice, E., Johnson, F., & Prime, G. M. (2012). Supporting STEM education in secondary science contexts. *Interdisciplinary Journal of Problem-Based Learning, 6*(2), 4. https://doi.org/10.7771/1541-5015.1349

Baker-Doyle, K. J., & Yoon, S. A. (2011). In search of practitioner-based social capital: A social network analysis tool for understanding and facilitating teacher collaboration in a US-based STEM professional development program. *Professional Development in Education, 37*(1), 75–93. https://doi.org/10.1080/19415257.2010.494450

Bassok, M., & Holyoak, K. J. (1989). Interdomain transfer between isomorphic topics in algebra and physics. *Journal of Experimental Psychology: Learning, Memory, and Cognition, 15*, 153–166. doi:10.1037/0278-7393.15.1.153

Battey, D., Kafai, Y., Nixon, A. S., & Kao, L. (2007). Professional development for teachers on gender equity in the sciences: Initiating the conversation. *Teachers College Record, 109*, 221–243.

★Beaudoin, C., Johnston, P., Jones, L., & Waggett, R. (2013). University support of secondary STEM teachers through professional development. *Education, 133*(3), 330–339.

★Bers, M., Seddighin, S., & Sullivan, A. (2013). Ready for robotics: Bringing together the T and E of STEM in early childhood teacher education. *Journal of Technology and Teacher Education, 21*(3), 355–377.

Blanchard, M., LeProvost, C. E., Tolin, D. E., & Gutierrez, K. S. (2016). Investigating technology-enhance professional development in rural, high-poverty, middle schools. *Educational Researcher, 45*, 207–220. https://doi.org/10.3102/0013189X16644602

Borgerding, L. A., Sadler, T. D., & Koroly, M. J. (2013). Teachers' concerns about biotechnology education. *Journal of Science Education and Technology, 22*(2), 133–147. https://doi.org/10.1007/s10956-012-9382-z

Borko, H. (2004). Professional development and teacher learning: Mapping the terrain. *Educational Researcher, 33*(8), 3–15. https://doi.org/10.3102/0013189X033008003

★Burns, M., Pierson, E., & Reddy, S. (2014). Working together: How teachers teacher and students learn in collaborative learning environments. *International Journal of Instruction, 7*(1), 1308–1470.

Bybee, R. W. (1982). Historical research in science education. *Journal of Research in Science Teaching, 19*, 1–13. https://doi.org/10.1002/tea.3660190102

Capraro, R. M., Capraro, M. M., Scheurich, J. J., Jones, M., Morgan, J., Huggins, K. S., . . . Han S. (2016). Impact of sustained professional development in STEM on outcome measures in a diverse urban district. *The Journal of Educational Research, 109*, 181–196. https://doi.org/10.1080/00220671.2014.936997

Carney, M. B., Brendefur, J. L., Thiede, K., Hughes, G., & Sutton, J. (2016). Statewide mathematics professional development: Teacher knowledge, self-efficacy, and beliefs. *Educational Policy, 30*(4), 539–572. https://doi.org/10.1177/0895904814550075

Clarke, A., Triggs, V., & Nielsen, W. (2013). Cooperating teacher participation in teacher education. *Review of Educational Research, 84*(2), 163–202. doi:10.3102/003465431349961

Darling-Hammond, L., Hyler, M. E., & Gardner, M. (2017). *Effective teacher professional development.* Retrieved from the Learning Policy Institute website https://learningpolicyinstitute.org/sites/default/files/product-files/Effective_Teacher_Professional_Development_REPORT.pdf

★Daugherty, J. L. (2009). Engineering professional development design for secondary school teachers: A multiple case study. *Journal of Technology Education, 21*(1), 10–24. https://doi.org/10.21061/jte.v21i1.a.1

Desimone, L. M. (2009). Improving impact studies of teachers' professional development: Toward better conceptualizations and measures. *Educational Researcher, 38*(3), 181–199. https://doi.org/10.3102/0013189X08331140

De Smet, C., Valcke, M., Schellens, T., De Wever, B., & Vanderlinde, R. (2016). A qualitative study on learning and teaching with learning paths in a learning management system. *Journal of Social Science Education, 15*(1), 27–37.

Ermeling, B. A., & Yarbo, J. (2016). Expanding instructional horizons: A case study of teacher team–outside expert partnerships. *Teachers College Record, 118*(2), 1–43.

Fore, G. A., Feldhaus, C. R., Sorge, B. H., Agarwal, M., & Varahramyan, K. (2015). Learning at the nanolevel: Accounting for complexity in the internalization of secondary STEM teacher professional development. *Teaching and Teacher Education, 51*, 101–112.

Garet, M. S., Porter, A. C., Desimone, L., Birman, B. F., & Yoon, K. S. (2001). What makes professional development effective? Results from a national sample of teachers. *American Educational Research Journal, 38*(4), 915–945. https://doi.org/10.3102/00028312038004915

Gonczi, A. L., Chiu, J. L., Maeng, J. L., & Bell, R. L. (2016). Instructional support and implementation structure during elementary teachers' science education simulation use. *International Journal of Science Education, 38*(11), 1800–1824. https://doi.org/10.1080/09500693.2016.1217363

Guzey, S. S., Tank, K., Wang, H. H., Roehrig, G., & Moore, T. (2014). A high-quality professional development for teachers of grades 3–6 for implementing engineering into classrooms. *School Science and Mathematics, 114*(3), 139–149. https://doi.org/10.1111/ssm.12061

Haag, S., & Megowan, C. (2015). Next generation science standards: A national mixed-methods study on teacher readiness. *School Science and Mathematics, 15*(8), 416–426. https://doi.org/10.1111/ssm.12145

★Han, S., Yalvac, B., Capraro, M. M., & Capraro, R. M. (2015). In-service teachers' implementation and understanding of STEM project based learning. *Eurasia Journal of Mathematics, Science & Technology Education, 11*(1), 63–76.

Hardré, P. L., Ling, C., Shehab, R. L., Nanny, M. A., Nollert, M. U., Refai, H., . . . Wollega, E. D. (2013). Teachers in an interdisciplinary learning community: Engaging, integrating, and strengthening K-12 education. *Journal of Teacher Education, 64*(5), 409–425. https://doi.org/10.1177/0022487113496640

Heck, D. J., Banilower, E. R., Weiss, I. R., & Rosenberg, S. L. (2008). Studying the effects of professional development: The case of the NSF's local systemic change through teacher enhancement initiative. *Journal for Research in Mathematics Education, 39*(2), 113–152.

Heller, J. I., Daehler, K. R., Wong, N., Shinohara, M., & Miratrix, L. W. (2012). Differential effects of three professional development models on teacher knowledge and student achievement in elementary science. *Journal of Research in Science Teaching, 49*(3), 333–362. https://doi.org/10.1002/tea.21004

Honey, M., Pearson, G., & Schweingruber, H. (Eds.). (2014). *STEM integration in K-12 education: Status, prospects, and an agenda for research*. Washington, DC: National Academies Press.

Johnson, C. C., & Fargo, J. D. (2010). Urban school reform enabled by transformative professional development: Impact on teacher change and student learning of science. *Urban Education, 45*(1), 4–29. https://doi.org/10.1177/0042085909352073

Johnson, C. C., Sondergeld, T. A., & Walton, J. (2017). A statewide implementation of the critical features of professional development: Impact on teacher outcomes. *School Science and Mathematics, 117*(8), 341–349. https://doi.org/10.1111/ssm.12251

Jones, W. M., & Dexter, S. (2014). How teachers learn: The roles of formal, informal, and independent learning. *Educational Technology Research and Development, 62*(3), 367–384. https://doi.org/10.1007/s11423-014-9337-6

★Lee, H., Longhurst, M., & Campbell, T. (2017). Teacher learning in technology professional development and its impact on student achievement in science. *International Journal of Science Education, 39*(10), 1282–1303. https://doi.org/10.1080/09500693.2017.1327733

Lehman, J. D., George, M., Buchanan, P., & Rush, M. (2006). Preparing teachers to use problem-centered, inquiry-based science: Lessons from a four-year professional development project. *Interdisciplinary Journal of Problem-Based Learning, 1*(1), 7. https://doi.org/10.7771/1541-5015.1007

Leonard, J., Mitchell, M., Barnes-Johnson, J., Unertl, A., Outka-Hill, J., Robinson, R., & Hester-Croff, C. (2017). Preparing teachers to engage rural students in computational thinking through robotics, game design, and culturally responsive teaching. *Journal of Teacher Education, 69*(4), 386–407. https://doi.org/10.1177/0022487117732317

Lobato, J. (2012). The actor-oriented transfer perspective and its contributions to educational research and practice. *Educational Psychologist, 47*, 1–16. https://doi.org/10.1080/00461520.2012.693353

Longhurst, M. L., Jones, S. H., & Campbell, T. (2017). Factors influencing teacher appropriation of professional learning focused on the use of technology in science classrooms. *Teacher Development, 21*(3), 365–387. https://doi.org/10.1080/13664530.2016.1273848

Luft, J. A., Dubois, S. L., Nixon, R. S., & Campbell, B. K. (2015). Supporting newly hired teachers of science: Attaining professional standards. *Studies in Science Education, 41*, 1–48. https://doi.org/10.1080/03057267.2014.980559

Luft, J. A, & Hewson, P. W. (2014). Research on teacher professional development programs in science. In S. K. Abell & N. Lederman (Eds.), *Handbook of research in science education* (2nd ed., pp. 889–909). New York, NY: Routledge.

Maeng, J. L., Whitworth, B. A., Gonczi, A. L., Navy, S. L., & Wheeler, L. B. (2017). Elementary science teachers' integration of engineering design into science instruction: Results from a randomized controlled trial. *International Journal of Science Education, 39*(11), 1529–1548. https://doi.org/10.1080/09500693.2017.1340688

Miles, M. B., Huberman, A. M., & Saldaña, J. (2014). *Qualitative data analysis*. Thousand Oaks, CA: Sage.

Miller, R. G., Curwen, M. S., White-Smith, K. A., & Calfee, R. C. (2015). Cultivating primary students' scientific thinking through sustained teacher professional development. *Journal of Early Childhood Education, 43*, 317–326. https://doi.org/10.1007/s10643-014-0656-3

Moore, T. J., Johnston, A. C., & Glancy, A. W. (in press). STEM integration: A synthesis of conceptual frameworks and definitions. In C. C. Johnson, M. Mohr-Schroeder, T. J. Moore, & L. English (Eds.), *Handbook of research on STEM education*. London: Routledge.

Morgan, R., & Kirby, C. (2016). *The UK STEM education landscape*. Retrieved from the Royal Academy of Engineering website: https://www.raeng.org.uk/publications/reports/uk-stem-education-landscape

Mouza, C. (2011). Promoting urban teachers' understanding of technology, content, and pedagogy in the context of case development. *Journal of Research on Technology in Education, 44*(1), 1–29. https://doi.org/10.1080/15391523.2011.10782577

Mualem, R., & Eylon, B.-S. (2009). Teaching physics in junior high school: Crossing the boarders of fear. *European Journal of Teacher Education, 32*(2), 135–150. https://doi.org/10.1080/02619760902779014

★Nadelson, L. S., Callahan, J., Pyke, P., Hay, A., Dance, M., & Pfiester, J. (2013). Teacher STEM perception and preparation: Inquiry-based STEM professional development for elementary teachers. *The Journal of Educational Research, 106*(2), 157–168. https://doi.org/10.1080/00220671.2012.667014

★Nadelson, L. S., Seifert, A., Moll, A. J., & Coats, B. (2012). i-STEM summer institute: An integrated approach to teacher professional development in STEM. *Journal of STEM Education: Innovation and Outreach, 13*(2), 60–83.

National Academies of Sciences, Engineering, and Medicine. (2015). *Science teachers' learning: Enhancing opportunities, creating supportive contexts*. Washington, DC: The National Academies Press. doi:10.17226/2183

National Governors Association Center for Best Practices & Council of Chief State School Officers. (2010). *Common core state standards for mathematics*. Washington, DC: Authors.

National Research Council. (2013). *Next generation science standards: For states, by states*. Washington, DC: The National Academies Press. doi:10.17226/18290

★Nelson, T. H. (2009). Teachers' collaborative inquiry and professional growth: Should we be optimistic? *Science Education, 93*(3), 548–580. https://doi.org/10.1002/sce.20302

Nokes, T. J. (2009). Mechanisms of knowledge transfer. *Thinking and Reasoning, 15*, 1–36. doi:10.1080/13546780802490186

Office of the Chief Scientist. (2013). *Science, technology, engineering and mathematics in the national interest: A strategic approach*. Retrieved from the Australian Government website https://www.chiefscientist.gov.au/wp-content/uploads/STEMstrategy290713FINALweb.pdf

★Owston, R., Wideman, H., Murphy, J., & Lupshenyuk, D. (2008). Blended teacher professional development: A synthesis of three program evaluations. *The Internet and Higher Education, 11*(3–4), 201–210. https://doi.org/10.1016/j.iheduc.2008.07.003

Polly, D., McGee, J., Wang, C., Martin, C., Lambert, R., & Pugalee, D. K. (2015). Linking professional development, teacher outcomes, and student achievement: The case of a learner-centered mathematics program for elementary school teachers. *International Journal of Educational Research, 72*, 26–37. https://doi.org/10.1016/j.ijer.2015.04.002

Roschelle, J., Shechtman, N., Tatar, D., Hegedus, S., Hopkins, B., Empson, S., . . . Gallagher, L. P. (2010). Integration of technology, curriculum, and professional development for advancing middle school mathematics: Three large-scale studies. *American Educational Research Journal, 47*(4), 833–878. https://doi.org/10.3102/0002831210367426

Schuchardt, A. M., Tekkumru-Kisa, M., Schunn, C. D., Stein, M. K., & Reynolds, B. (2017). How much professional development is needed with educative curriculum materials? It depends upon the intended student learning outcomes. *Science Education, 101*(6), 1015–1033. https://doi.org/10.1002/sce.21302

Seraphin, K. D., Harrison, G. M., Philippoff, J., Brandon, P. R., Nguyen, T. T. T., Lawton, B. E., & Vallin, L. M. (2017). Teaching aquatic science as inquiry through professional development: Teacher characteristics and student outcomes. *Journal of Research in Science Teaching, 54*(9), 1219–1245. https://doi.org/10.1002/tea.21403

★Siew, N. M., Amir, N., & Chong, C. L. (2015). The perceptions of pre-service and in-service teachers regarding a project-based STEM approach to teaching science. *SpringerPlus, 4*(1), 8. https://doi.org/10.1186/2193-1801-4-8

Singley, M. K., & Anderson, J. R. (1989). *The transfer of cognitive skill* (No. 9). Boston, MA: Harvard University Press.

★Smith, J., & Nadelson, L. (2016). Learning for you and learning for me: Mentoring as professional development for mentor teachers. *Mentoring & Tutoring: Partnership in Learning, 24*(1), 59–72. https://doi.org/10.1080/13611267.2016.1165489

★Stohlmann, M., Moore, T. J., & Roehrig, G. H. (2012). Considerations for teaching integrated STEM education. *Journal of Pre-College Engineering Education Research, 2*(1), 4. https://doi.org/10.5703/1288284314653

Teacher Advisory Council & National Research Council. (2014). *STEM learning is everywhere: Summary of a convocation on building learning systems.* Washington, DC: National Academies Press.

Vasquez, J., Sneider, C., & Comer, M. (2013). *STEM lesson essentials, grades 3–8: Integrating science, technology, engineering, and mathematics.* Portsmouth, NH: Heinemann.

Wagner, J. F. (2006). Transfer in pieces. *Cognition and Instruction, 24,* 1–71. doi:10.1207/s1532690xci2401_1

★Wang, H. H., Moore, T. J., Roehrig, G. H., & Park, M. S. (2011). STEM integration: Teacher perceptions and practice. *Journal of Pre-College Engineering Education Research, 1*(2), 2.

Xie, K., Kim, M. K., Cheng, S. L., & Luthy, N. C. (2017). Teacher professional development through digital content evaluation. *Educational Technology Research and Development, 65*(4), 1067–1103. https://doi.org/10.1007/s11423-017-9519-0

★Yoon, S. A., Anderson, E., Koehler-Yom, J., Evans, C., Park, M., Sheldon, J., . . . Klopfer, E. (2017). Teaching about complex systems is no simple matter: Building effective professional development for computer-supported complex systems instruction. *Instructional Science, 45*(1), 99–121. https://doi.org/10.1007/s11251-016-9388-7

Zozakiewicz, C., & Rodriguez, A. J. (2007). Using sociotransformative constructivism to create multicultural and gender-inclusive classrooms: An intervention project for teacher professional development. *Educational Policy, 21*(2), 397–425. https://doi.org/10.1177/0895904806290126

30

TEACHER LEADERSHIP FOR STEM PROGRAMMING

Elizabeth A. Crotty and Gillian H. Roehrig

Conceptualization of Teacher Leadership

STEM reforms are directed through various leadership approaches ranging from more top-down and traditional leadership practices to bottom-up and distributed practices driven through teacher collectives. For this chapter, we posit our conceptualization of teacher leadership while noting that this is only one of many ways to define this role. According to Wenner and Campbell (2017), teacher leaders are "Teachers who maintain K-12 teaching responsibilities while also taking on leadership responsibilities outside of the classroom" (p. 7). This definition inherently assumes a degree of proximity to the classroom space, while also extending beyond the walls of one's individual classroom. York-Barr and Duke (2004) describe multiple definitions of teacher leadership, which can be summarized as a set of attributes and experiences that result in a teacher's ability to share their expertise with others. This definition places emphasis on the attributes and experiences that teachers have, while acknowledging that certain attributes and experiences foster a greater degree of influence within schools and beyond. This definition of teacher leadership implies that teacher leadership can be developed through appropriate experiences with individuals who possess the attributes for leadership.

Theoretical Framework

The theoretical grounding for this work comes from a perspective on learning from a situated cognition framework (Brown, Collins, & Duguid, 1989). The framework requires consideration for how social, cultural, and contextual factors influence the learning that occurs in a space. Learning and cognition are fundamentally situated and cannot be separate from the way the learner experiences the learning environment (Brown et al., 1989). This theoretical approach asserts that learning occurs when the content is applied and practiced in authentic contexts.

The work is further supported by the work of Lave and Wenger (1991) with regard to *situated learning* occurring through an exploration of *legitimate peripheral participation* within the communities of practice. Legitimate peripheral participation is a way to describe the process by which newcomers become part of a community of practice. A community of practice is developed through the work of individuals sharing in pursuit of a common goal over time. In our work, the shared practice is centered on building STEM capacity in emerging STEM schools through teacher leadership teams.

Putnam and Borko (2000) extended this theory to apply to teacher learning to consider cognition as situated and social in nature. In their application of the theory, teacher learning should be situated within authentic activities to teachers' practice. Furthermore, taking a sociocentric view on teacher learning informs how interactions with people determine what is learned and how the learning ultimately takes place. Putnam and Borko (2000) account for the ways that cultural components and ways of thinking can influence how learning proceeds.

Need for Teacher Leadership to Drive STEM Reforms

Teacher leadership has been defined in three general ways within the research literature (Silva, Gimbert, & Nolan, 2000). In earlier approaches to teacher leadership, administrators would select teachers to participate in formal leadership roles such as department heads and grade level leads. Following this initial movement, teachers were then called upon to lead through their instructional and pedagogical expertise. Teachers were encouraged to take on roles furthering the development of effective classroom instruction through roles such as mentoring other teachers and designing curriculum/assessments. Current approaches for developing teacher leadership recognize that teachers should serve as the primary actors for driving school culture and reforms and incorporate school leadership as an integral part of each teacher's day-to-day work. Our work described in this chapter explored the ways in which teacher leaders can support STEM reforms in schools within this third approach to teacher leadership. Teachers need to be engaged in the leadership process to sustain comprehensive and meaningful school changes around STEM development, as greater involvement in the process yields greater ownership of the reforms (York-Barr & Duke, 2004). Furthermore, allowing for teacher leaders to drive the process of developing STEM in their schools ensures a grow-your-own approach that is tailored to the needs of an individual school's context and community.

There is a need for teachers with STEM content expertise to be involved in the process of implementing STEM reforms, as school administrators often have more experience and interest in mathematics and reading, as those subjects are prioritized (Wenner & Campbell, 2017). Teacher leadership is contextualized in subjects and specific knowledge domains, and often science is facilitated through more informal leadership in schools due to mathematics and reading being prioritized (Wenner & Campbell, 2017). There is a need to build collective efficacy around STEM by leveraging teachers' content expertise in interdisciplinary collaborative teams to foster integrated STEM reforms.

Facets of Teacher Leadership for STEM Reforms

Teachers are an incredible resource for driving school changes that are appropriate for the unique contexts of their own schools (Lieberman & Friedrich, 2010). Lieberman and Friedrich (2010) extensively examined the research literature regarding teacher leadership and developed four key dimensions that inform teachers learning leadership: identity, community, productive use of conflict, and practice. In our work, we further explore these initial four dimensions while synthesizing additional resources on teacher leadership from the research literature to develop our interpretation of these dimensions for STEM reforms. The framework presented in Figure 30.1 synthesizes the research on teacher professional learning and leadership across these four dimensions outlined by Lieberman and Friedrich (2010). They organize their ideas around these four dimensions and explore the ways in which teacher leadership capacity can develop and influence work in schools. The framework provided in Figure 30.1 allows for the analysis of the component features of teacher

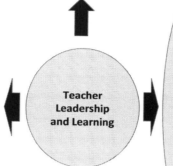

Identity
Teacher identity is informed by two things: (1) teachers' sense of positive professional identity (not fixed), and (2) their professional life phases (Day & Gu, 2007). How teachers identify their roles, place, contributions, and action in their schools is significant to the leadership potential they might exert on their school's culture (Lieberman & Freidrich, 2010). Enacted practical leadership is the result of teachers' daily actions (Sato & Rogers, 2016). Teachers' mindsets about their work influence their leadership potential (Berry, Byrd, & Weider, 2013)

Practice
Teacher learning should be situated in aspects of one's own teaching practice (Putnam & Borko, 2000; Ball & Cohen, 1999). Learning and leadership occur through teachers addressing unique and local problems of practice (Lieberman & Friedrich, 2010). Teacher learning happens gradually over an extended period of time through changes in practice and teacher beliefs and attitudes (Guzkey, 2002).

Teacher Leadership and Learning

Community
Distributed cognition—teachers must be equipped to collaborate in meaningful ways and share what they know to produce original thought (Grossman et al., 2001). Distributing cognition across people and tools increases capacity for innovation (Putnam & Borko, 2000).

Use of Conflict
Perspective transformation occurs in phases—disorienting dilemmas can lead to self-examination and ultimately result in changes in thought or action with the appropriate communities and structures in place (Mezirow, 1995; Taylor, n.d.). Teachers engaging in productive disequilibrium through self-reflection, dialogue, and analysis of practice aides in teacher learning (Van Es et al., 2014).

Figure 30.1 Framework for analyzing teacher learning and leadership development in teacher leader teams. Adapted from *How teachers become leaders: Learning from practice and research* by A. Lieberman, 2010, New York, NY: Teachers College Press.

learning and leadership development through teacher collaboration to better understand how the teacher teams could influence STEM reforms in their respective schools. Each of the four dimensions of the conceptual framework are presented in Figure 30.1, and each dimension will be further detailed in the sections that follow.

Teacher Leader Identity Development

Lieberman and Friedrich (2010) developed three key ideas that inform their understanding of teacher leadership identity: (1) identity is not fixed, but rather it is constantly being negotiated with individuals reconciling multiple conceptions of self, (2) identity is social, informed and constrained by preexisting cultural expectations, and (3) individuals make sense of their cultural worlds in what Holland, Lachicotte, Skinner, and Cain (1998) deem "the space of authoring" (p. 169). In our work it was useful to consider how teacher identity shapes the work that teacher leaders do. Holland et al. (1998) extend the notion of individual identity to include how cultural norms interact with one's identity development and influence how a member of the community will act. They put forward the notion of "identities in practice" (p. 271), in which identities are constantly constructed and negotiated through interaction with one's community and cultural norms. The ways in which teacher leadership is understood within our culture and within the teachers' individual schools will likely influence the work they do. Day and Gu (2007) argue that teacher identity is informed by their sense of positive professional identity and their professional life phases. Day and Gu (2007) further assert that teachers' personal learning needs are connected to their professional life phase. Understanding the professional life phase within which a teacher might be operating could further inform their professional learning and leadership needs.

How teachers identify their roles, place, contributions, and action in their schools is significant to the leadership potential they might exert on their school's culture (Lieberman & Friedrich, 2010). Sato and Rogers (2017) expand this notion of teacher leadership and identity by making a case that teachers do not need to be consciously engaging in formalized leadership roles to be effective leaders and influence outcomes for students. Instead, they hold that "enactment of leadership is bound up in the practical actions of teachers and leadership is the result of action, not the cause" (p. 10). They make a case that teacher leadership is happening in schools every day through practical enactment of leadership by teachers—in finding solutions to everyday problems and driving initiatives that they personally find significant that gradually influence the culture of the schools in which the work is performed (Sato and Rogers, 2017). In their work, the teachers' leadership enactments influenced school cultures, even though teachers were not necessarily identifying as leaders. This definition of practical leadership expands the current approach to teacher leadership in less traditional and hierarchical terms. Thus, teacher leadership is seen as the product of teachers who strongly believe in the changes they hope to see in their schools and have passion for the implementing the changes they promote (Sato and Rogers, 2017). Teachers' mindsets influence their leadership potential as well, in that they can see leadership roles and agendas as an opportunity to learn something new, or they can see these roles as more work or an added responsibility on their already taxing work (Berry, Byrd, & Wieder, 2013). Thus, the mindsets that teachers have about enacting STEM can be a significant part of their identity, which has the potential to drive or limit STEM reforms.

Teacher Leadership and Community

Feiman-Nemser (2001) presented a new paradigm of professional development for practicing teachers in which professional communities of practice were at the center and leveraged for ongoing teacher growth and development. Grossman, Wineburg, and Woolworth (2001) developed a related theory toward building teacher community. They asserted that effective teacher communities can facilitate teacher learning and leadership development. Within these communities, intellectual work needs to be distributed across the group by developing conditions for teachers to participate in sharing what they know with each other and learning from each other's ways of knowing. Teacher communities should foster teachers in the collective to think about problems of practice in novel ways and cultivate new leadership (Grossman et al., 2001).

Putnam and Borko (2000) emphasize this notion of distributed cognition across the teachers and tools in the community to foster innovation. According to Putnam and Borko (2000), the use of performance and pedagogical tools change how a task can be accomplished. Thus, curriculum, lesson plans, design projects, and inquiry demonstrations can all influence the ways teachers think about teaching STEM—and these tools will be important to consider in the analysis of how teachers work through understanding and enacting STEM in their schools

There are some generally agreed-upon attributes of effective communities and also obstacles toward building such professional communities. Grossman et al. (2001) discuss common obstacles to effective community building, which include: time, resources, context, location, the social organization and leadership functions, and when teachers in the collectives lack common experiences. Desimone (2009) outlined five critical features for improving teacher professional learning: having a content focus, active learning, coherence (consistent with teachers' knowledge and beliefs as well as reforms and policies), duration (at least 20 hours over an extended period), and collective participation among teachers—teacher leadership teams provide an additional structure for collective participation among the teachers in the team toward ongoing professional learning.

Teacher Leadership and Conflict

Teachers with strong leadership capacities find ways to make conflict productive for themselves and others (Lieberman & Friedrich, 2010). Connecting back to the theoretical framework for this work and acknowledging the social nature of this work, we can inherently expect conflicting ideas. Taylor (n.d.) provides additional resources for understanding conflict as a site for teacher learning based on the notion of perspective transformation that was originally outlined by Mezirow (1991). Perspective transformation leads people to develop a frame of understanding that is more inclusive, differentiating, permeable, critically reflective, and integrative of the experiences of others. Mezirow (1991) identified phases for perspective transformation: initiating with a disorienting dilemma, followed by a critical assessment of assumptions, recognition of discontent, exploration of options for new roles, relationships, and actions, acquisition of knowledge and skills, provisionally trying out new roles, building of competence and self-confidence in new roles and relationships, and a reintegration into one's life on the basis of conditions dictated by one's new perspective. Examination of conflict in these terms provides a lens for interpreting conflict in ways that could be instructive and productive to the teacher or teacher leadership teams. Van Es, Tunney, Goldsmith, and Seago (2014) suggest that when teachers engage in the analysis of their practice, they are encouraged to be self-reflective through productive disequilibrium and dialogue with one another in ways that can result in professional growth and learning.

Teacher Leadership and Practice

Teacher learning should be situated in one's own teaching practice (Putnam & Borko, 2000; Ball & Cohen, 1999). Teachers learn to become better teachers by working within the contexts of their classroom practices in social and collaborative ways. Thus, teacher leadership teams are an excellent context for teachers working together to examine elements of their teaching practice and engage in ongoing, informal professional learning. One measure of teacher learning is through implemented changes in one's classroom practices (Guskey, 2002).

School Cases of Teacher Leader STEM Teams

In this chapter, we highlight two case vignettes of teacher leader STEM teams to show how the framework played out differently in varied school contexts and leadership approaches. This work comes out of a study from the 2016–2017 school year of a larger grant-funded project exploring the development of STEM capacity in five schools in an urban Midwestern district. This work draws on and contrasts two of the five schools in the project with very different opportunity structures for teacher leadership. The goal of the grant was to support reform efforts toward building STEM schools in these five schools in a large Midwestern district. A local university team partnered with school leaders in the five schools to develop teacher leader STEM teams at each school site.

One public middle school and one ninth-grade academy are described here. Both schools were from a Midwestern, metropolitan urban district. The two schools were identified with pseudonyms—Noddack Middle School and Noether Ninth Grade Academy—to ensure anonymity for the schools involved in this research. The schools presented here are high-poverty, diverse, urban schools.

STEM Teacher Leadership Contexts

Noether Academy—Traditional Leadership Approach. Noether Academy is a ninth-grade academy with a rich STEM history. The school previously had a SciTech Academy in operation about 20 years ago in which Dr. Robinson (Assistant Principal) and Ms. Lee (STEM Coordinator) were formerly teachers together for many years. Dr. Robinson's leadership, STEM vision, and standing in this community were an essential part of this school's success in developing STEM in this context. This school was nearly closed due to dwindling enrollment and proficiency trends on the state test in recent years. The community protested this school's closing and called for a reinvestment in the former STEM program.

This school was comprised of the ninth-grade teacher team within the STEM Academy. All content areas were represented on the team for the ninth-grade academy. Dr. Robinson developed the STEM Academy and selected Ms. Lee to serve as the STEM Coordinator for the school's program.

Noether was classified as a traditional leadership approach, as there were clearly defined roles on the STEM team that were aligned with traditional hierarchies in school. Dr. Robinson was the primary leader of the STEM team and set the vision for the team's work. In examination of this traditional leadership approach through the conceptual framework, Dr. Robinson had a strong *identity* as a leader in catalyzing the focus around developing a STEM Academy. She was also an administrator in the school who was responsible for the formal observations of the science and mathematics teachers. Ms. Lee was previously a biology teacher and was transitioning out of full-time classroom teaching to occupying a more formal leadership position with the school as the STEM Coordinator. She continued to teach two sections of biology, and the rest of her professional duties focused on facilitation of the STEM team and building the STEM Academy. Ms. Lee was not an evaluator for the other teachers, but the teachers on the team were starting to see her in more of a formalized leadership role than when she was primarily a ninth-grade biology teacher in the school, with her new position. Ms. Lee's *identity* was strongly oriented as a teacher more than as a leader, as she had been a teacher for 12 years and was just beginning her transition to a more formal leadership role.

The conceptual framework dimensions of *community* and *practice* at Noether were integral to the work of the STEM teacher leadership team. The support for STEM came in large part from the larger community members and families of students in the area who wanted to see a reinvigorated effort around the former SciTech Academy through a community rally and response to the district presenting a plan that would have closed the school at that time. Dr. Robinson and Ms. Lee had strong connections to students, teachers in the building, and the larger community after having taught in the school for a combined 30 years between the two of them, which was essential in developing STEM for this community of learners. Dr. Robinson and Ms. Lee were respected as educators in this community as a result of their deep commitment to effective teaching practice in STEM, and people trusted them to drive a vision for the STEM Academy that would work well for the people in this school community as a result of their extensive teaching practice. The other teachers on the STEM team, however, were all in their first or second year of teaching and less connected to the community of learners. Ms. Lee's commitment to continue teaching two sections of biology in the STEM Academy in addition to her new role as STEM Coordinator situated her leadership on the team strongly within an instructional *practice* lens while also carving out a more formalized leadership space for her work.

The dimension of *conflict* was influential to this team's work in many ways. The primary conflict the team experienced in development of the STEM Academy was teacher resistance to changes in practice. The teachers who were the most adept at transitioning their teaching to a more project-oriented approach based around a STEM theme or cross-disciplinary problem were the English language arts (ELA) teacher and social studies teacher. The social studies teacher brought his experience with history day and large-scale projects to bear in challenging the science teacher and mathematics teacher to structure learning in a more problem-based and student-centered way. The ELA teacher was the teacher on the team who was utilizing technology in her classroom in the most innovative ways, and she was consistently pushing her colleagues to do the same. She was instrumental in setting up organizational mechanisms for ongoing collaboration with curriculum integration across the STEM team. Dr. Robinson was able to leverage the content expertise of the science and mathematics teachers in ways that helped them identify with the work the team was doing in framing these reforms around inquiry, problem solving, and design in support of their content.

Noddack Middle School—Distributed Leadership Approach. Noddack Middle School is a large middle school located in an urban district, a historically diverse neighborhood that, in recent years, has attracted a large number of aspiring artists and young professionals. According to administration, the continued diversity at Noddack stems from the large number of students who enroll in the school from nearby areas due to parents choosing to send their children to different neighborhood schools. Noddack is an International Baccalaureate (IB) school.

There is a focus on the whole child and in helping students to develop emotionally and intellectually to be prepared for the 21st-century world and workforce. As such, students and staff at Noddack use common language to describe and identify behaviors of successful learners. Additionally, there is a strong emphasis on cultural relevance and inclusiveness at this school. The administration and teachers at Noddack are committed to growing the school's reputation in these areas, as is evidenced by the school's mission statement including a focus on valuing difference and emphasizing the importance of respecting culture.

The STEM team at Noddack was comprised of teachers across sixth, seventh, and eighth grades and represented various subject areas. Teachers on this team self-selected due to their interest in STEM teaching and learning. This self-selection method for the team posed unforeseen problems with implementing STEM curriculum when not all teachers working on the STEM team shared the same students. Mr. Rush, the sixth-grade science teacher, was the original contact person for the University team and the primary teacher leader on this team; however, the leadership approach on this team was much more distributed across all members of the team making decisions to drive STEM reforms.

Noddack Middle School was classified as a distributed leadership approach because the teachers were functioning as an interdisciplinary PLC with a strong focus on developing STEM curriculum in their classrooms. There was no school-wide commitment to STEM, and the leadership team did not see the school vision aligning with STEM. Teachers were given the agency to work together on driving STEM learning opportunities but only within the context of their classrooms, as opposed to having a school-wide systemic effect.

Examining the work of Noddack's teacher leadership STEM team through the conceptual framework posed many distinctions from the approach to leadership in place described at Noether Academy. *Identity* played out differently on this team, as Mr. Rush was the primary facilitator of organizing the team's work, yet he didn't see himself as a leader. His approach to leadership was in bringing together good people and providing them a space and time to collaborate to develop innovative STEM reforms. As such, his leadership style fostered a more evenly distributed representation of teacher voice, agency, and decision-making across the teachers on the team for developing STEM reforms. With this distributed nature of leadership identity across the team, the team focused more on developing STEM curriculum, as curriculum development was the area they felt they could exercise the most agency in creating STEM experiences for students in a school with a leadership team that wasn't interested in adopting a STEM vision. This lack of formal commitment to STEM was the primary *conflict* the team faced, and they resolved this by focusing on the locus of control they were able to exercise in their instruction and teaching *practice*. This STEM leadership around curriculum and developing meaningful content integration with other disciplines was strongly situated in teachers' practices. The teachers on the team were all personally invested in creating STEM opportunities for their students and were experienced teachers who were teaching in student-centered and reform-based ways. The comfort and expertise these teachers demonstrated in their practice, as well as the experience these teachers had in working together, established a strong *community* for the teachers on the STEM team with pre-established trust and open dialogue, which was in contrast to the mostly new teachers at Noether who were in the first or second year of teaching.

Overview of the STEM Teams Within the Leadership Approaches

The cases illustrate varying commitments to STEM by the STEM teams both in terms of individual and school-wide systematic efforts towards STEM reforms. Noether Academy (traditional leadership) had significantly more supports in place that were systematic for developing STEM than Noddack. This was due to several factors that existed at Noether, which were absent in the other school: (a) the leadership team's vision for a STEM Academy aligned with the work of the STEM team, (b) Dr. Robinson's extensive science teaching background at Noether and her role as an administrator in the school drove a clear STEM vision for the STEM academy, as she was trusted by the staff to lead this process, (c) the creation of the STEM Coordinator position (Ms. Lee's role) formally supported developing STEM, (d) Ms. Lee's background as a science teacher for many years in the former SciTech program teaching alongside Dr. Robinson created an aligned vision for STEM between Ms. Lee and Dr. Robinson, and (e) the additional funding for STEM through grants and partnerships supported the STEM vision.

The majority of the Noddack (distributed leadership) team's acts of STEM resulted in developing the STEM curriculum units, which were individual in nature and unsustainable if the teachers left their school. This team produced many interdisciplinary units through their collaboration on the team to "STEMify" their teaching practice; however, there were no structural changes to allow for this interdisciplinary collaboration that would sustain these STEM reforms in a teacher's or this grant's absence. The teachers on the STEM team reported valuing the interdisciplinary collaboration they found on the STEM team and felt this collaboration pushed their instruction and allowed for them to exercise greater innovation in their work.

Findings on Teacher Leadership for STEM Reforms

Identity and Community: Teachers Need Leadership Skills and STEM Understandings to Support STEM Development Through Teacher Leadership Teams

In examining the ways STEM reforms were developed across the two STEM teams within the different school contexts, there was evidence that teacher leaders needed to have a vision for STEM *and* be able to articulate how that vision looked in practice. Teacher leaders needed to be equipped with both *leadership skills* and a *vision and goals for STEM* to collaboratively move STEM reforms forward.

STEM Understandings and Vision. The teacher leaders across the two schools had an understanding of and a vision for STEM. Mr. Rush at Noddack (distributed leadership) had prior professional development experiences around understanding STEM and implementing STEM curricula. Dr. Robinson and Ms. Lee at Noether (traditional leadership) held a project-based vision for STEM. This vision was developed through personal research on STEM pedagogies and effective STEM schools and was deeply rooted in their practice as science teachers. The result was that the teacher leaders across both schools had strong visions for and understandings of STEM that were rooted in their experiences. However, their approaches to building a STEM vision and asserting their own ideas varied among the teacher leaders.

Leadership Identities. While the individual teacher leaders had clear visions for how they saw STEM in each context, they had different approaches to leadership and possessed different leadership identities. This influenced the work they were able to do. Mr. Rush and Ms. Lee both saw their roles as building a collaborative effort and supporting teachers on their STEM teams. Mr. Rush perceived his leadership role to be one of bringing good people together and letting them come up with ideas and goals collaboratively. Mr. Rush was willing to contribute to shaping a vision for the team to focus on the development of STEM curriculum during the team's work. He was also modestly inclined to rely on his previous experiences (professional development activity with STEM) to assert objectives around writing STEM curriculum, and he modeled many of the same activities for his STEM team that he had previously experienced as a participant in STEM professional development through the University on a different grant. Ms. Lee saw herself more as a facilitator and supporter for teachers to drive the STEM team's work. She wanted to provide teachers with the resources they needed and then "get out of their way" to let them work. However, her position as a STEM coordinator was a more formalized leadership role, and the teachers on the team understood that she was in an administrative position that necessitated a more formal leadership position, which she adopted gradually over time.

Collectively Establishing Clear Goals. These varied leadership approaches resulted in different levels of clarity regarding team goals. The ways in which those goals were established varied across the different cases. Dr. Robinson set the vision for STEM initially in the STEM Academy and coached Ms. Lee toward meeting these established outcomes. This was more of a traditional leadership approach, as the goals were predetermined by the leaders. Mr. Rush shared his STEM curriculum-writing experiences with the teachers on the team, and as a result the teachers responded by collectively identifying STEM curriculum as a goal for their work. Establishing goals for their work, either collectively or through more traditional leadership hierarchies, seemed to be a driving factor for the STEM outcomes the teams developed.

Many leadership approaches call for building collective efficacy through distributed leadership that flattens traditional hierarchies in school structure (Peters-Burton, Lynch, Behrend, & Means, 2014; Schmoker, 2011). But this approach also entails fostering collaboration around clearly articulated goals. Kouzes and Posner (2017) identified, "The most important ingredient in every collective achievement is a common goal." The authors extend this idea, "If you want individuals or groups to work cooperatively, you have to give them a good reason to do so, such as a goal that can be accomplished only by working together" (Kouzes & Posner, 2017, p. 208).

Identity and Practice: Instructional Leadership for Driving Reform-Based Practices Is Important to STEM Teaching

Reform-Based Instruction Is a Precondition for STEM. Reform-based instructional strategies were identified as critical to the successful implementation of STEM teaching across both teams.

Dr. Robinson and Ms. Lee identified this need for reform-based teaching practices as an area for improvement on the team after reflecting on several less successful attempts by the teacher team at designing STEM curriculum. Teachers at Noether demonstrated success with implementing STEM instruction after targeted professional development was provided around reform-based pedagogies. The teachers who were most comfortable teaching in reform-based ways had the most success in developing STEM curriculum. This was consistent with the research literature as effective inclusive STEM schools examined previously utilized reform-based instructional strategies in which learning experiences required students to apply their learning across different content areas using a project-based or problem-based approach (LaForce et al., 2016; Peters-Burton et al., 2014).

Developing Instruction Around Engineering Design. Leveraging reform-based teaching strategies within the context of the engineering design process to promote critical thinking and collaboration was a logical next step for teachers who were already comfortable employing reform-based instructional pedagogies at Noddack and Noether. Mr. Rush heavily emphasized engineering design within the work of the STEM team at Noddack. Dr. Robinson and Ms. Lee emphasized the iterative nature of engineering design as a theme for the team's STEM work at Noether throughout the year. This notion of multiple iterations and revisions was emphasized in thinking about student work, students learning from feedback, fostering a degree of failure tolerance in students to persist through their initial struggles, developing a productive growth mindset around revisions and learning for students and teachers (Dweck, 2010), and STEM team projects in general.

Implications

Teachers in both of these schools were able to do work to support additional STEM reforms for students in some capacity. This work varied in scope and influence across the teacher STEM teams. Several implications that can be gleaned from the work presented here.

Support for STEM From All Stakeholders

The first implication is that teachers need to feel fully supported by their administration in this work of integrating STEM in order to comprehensively develop STEM schools using a teacher leadership approach. Flattening traditional leadership hierarchies to allow for teacher leadership and autonomy was only as effective as the individual leadership that existed on the teacher STEM teams. In order to invest in teachers working to integrate STEM reforms well, teachers need to be equipped with leadership skills and training, STEM professional development, opportunities to share their teaching practices, time to meaningfully engage in interdisciplinary planning and collaboration with their colleagues that is consistent and adequate in duration, have clearly established goals that align to the mission and vision for STEM in the school, and be able to focus of their collective work around student learning within STEM.

Selecting Teacher Leaders for STEM Development

Identifying teacher leaders for STEM reforms who are flexible and willing to try new things with their instructional approaches is key to initiating this work. Next, teacher leaders were more success-ful when they had a strong understanding of what STEM meant in ways that were strongly rooted in their teaching practices and inclusive of all learners. Teachers who were already comfortable employing reform-based pedagogies in a design-based approach could model STEM pedagogies for other teachers on the team in the classroom context. However, developing an understanding of STEM alone is not sufficient. Teachers need to have opportunities for professional development on leadership strategies for guiding STEM integration efforts with a team. Identifying the teacher leaders who will drive STEM reforms will require intentionally identifying teachers with strong STEM backgrounds and investing in the development of their leadership capacity to support this process for other teachers.

Developing STEM PLCs Could Support This Process in a Systematic Way

Based on our work, once the STEM teacher leaders who will drive this work are appropriately selected, there is potential in exploring how systematic STEM Interdisciplinary Professional Learning Communities (STEM PLCs) could be utilized for teacher leadership efforts in emerging STEM schools. The general PLC structures as outlined by DuFour (2004) could provide a framework for envisioning how STEM PLCs might operate within a school to drive STEM integration efforts and reforms. This would be a more systematic way that teachers could experience STEM professional development through professional communities of practice that leverage collective efficacy around STEM in ways that are situated in their teaching practice. The teachers in this research all reported that job-embedded interdisciplinary collaboration was necessary in order to meaningfully integrate the disciplines and drive STEM approaches to teaching.

Develop Mentoring Systems That Honor and Share Teacher Practices

Intentionally building collaboration between teachers from varied content areas through STEM PLCs could further promote opportunities for teachers to observe classroom teaching in different content areas and learn from each other's collective teaching efficacy. Building expectations for peer collaboration and sharing of teaching practices among teachers on the STEM team facilitated more intentional and aligned integration between the content areas within STEM curriculum, while systematically breaking down traditional notions of teaching being an isolating and solitary act. Coupling opportunities for teachers to learn from each other through collaboration with leaders who have strong STEM understandings can drive changes in teacher practices. STEM teacher teams need to promote avenues for teachers to learn from the collective efficacy within the group and create opportunities for teachers to share, discuss, reflect, and try pedagogies that support mutually determined, desired learning outcomes around STEM through peer observation, co-planning, and co-teaching opportunities with different content area teachers.

Teacher leaders on collaborative STEM teams were able to find success implementing STEM reforms when the school systematically structured opportunities for interdisciplinary collaboration and prioritized STEM as a vision. Teacher leadership was more effective when there were established opportunities to develop collective efficacy through sharing of best practices, content expertise, and ideas on the teams. Providing professional development for teacher leaders that supports both teachers' STEM understandings as well as their leadership capacity supports teachers in this work to effectively drive STEM reforms in our public schools.

References

Ball, D., & Cohen, D. (1999). Developing practice, developing practitioners: Toward a practice-based theory of professional education. In L. Darling-Hammond & G. Sykes (Eds.), *Teaching as the learning profession: Handbook of policy and practice* (pp. 3–32). San Francisco, CA: Jossey-Bass Publishers.

Berry, B., Byrd, A., & Wieder, A. (2013). *Teacherpreneurs: Innovative teachers who lead but don't leave.* San Francisco, CA: John Wiley & Sons.

Brown, J. S., Collins, A., & Duguid, P. (1989). Situated cognition and the culture of learning. *Educational Researcher, 18*(1), 32–42.

Day, C., & Gu, Q. (2007). Variation in the conditions for teachers' professional learning and development: Sustaining commitment and effectiveness over a career. *Oxford Review of Education, 33*(4), 423–443.

Desimone, L. M. (2009). Improving impact studies of teachers' professional development: Toward better conceptualizations and measures. *Educational Researcher, 38*(3), 181–199.

DuFour, R. (2004). What is a "professional learning community?" *Educational Leadership, 61*(8), 6–11.

Dweck, C. S. (2010). Mind-sets. *Principal Leadership, 10*(5), 26–29.

Feiman-Nemser, S. (2001). From preparation to practice: Designing a continuum to strengthen and sustain teaching. *Teachers College Record, 103,* 1013–1055.

Grossman, P., Wineburg, S., & Woolworth, S. (2001). Toward a theory of teacher community. *Teachers College Record, 103*(6), 942–1012.

Guskey, T. R. (2002). Professional development and teacher change. *Teachers and Teaching: Theory and Practice, 8*(3/4), 381–391.

Holland, D., Lachicotte, W. Jr., Skinner, D., & Cain, C. (1998). *Identity and agency in cultural worlds.* Cambridge, MA: Harvard University Press.

Kouzes, J. M., & Posner, B. Z. (2017). *The leadership challenge: How to make extraordinary things happen in organizations* (6th ed.). Hoboken, NJ: Wiley.

LaForce, M., Noble, E., King, H., Century, J., Blackwell, C., Holt, S., . . . Loo, S. (2016). The eight essential elements of inclusive STEM high schools. *International Journal of STEM Education, 3*(1). doi:10.1186/s40594-016-0054-z

Lave, J., & Wenger, E. (1991). *Situated learning: Legitimate peripheral participation.* New York, NY: Cambridge University Press.

Lieberman, A., & Friedrich, L. D. (2010). *How teachers become leaders: Learning from practice and research.* New York, NY: Teaches College Press.

Mezirow, J. (1991). *Transformative dimensions of adult learning.* San Francisco, CA: Jossey-Bass.

Peters-Burton, E. E., Lynch, S. J., Behrend, T. S., & Means, B. B. (2014). Inclusive STEM high school design: 10 critical components. *Theory into Practice, 53*(1), 64–71.

Putnam, R. T., & Borko, H. (2000). What do new views of knowledge and thinking have to say about research on teacher learning? *Educational Researcher, 29*(1), 4–15.

Sato, M., & Rogers, C. B. (2017). Practical leadership: How teachers enact leadership to re-culture their schools. In C. Rogers, K. Lomotey & A. Hilton (Eds.), *Innovative approaches to educational leadership* (pp. 27–41). Frankfurt: Die Deutsche Nationalbibliothek.

Schmoker, M. (2011). *Focus: Elevating the essentials to radically improve student learning.* Alexandria, VA: ASCD.

Silva, D. Y., Gimbert, B., & Nolan, J. (2000). Sliding the doors: Locking and unlocking possibilities for teacher leadership. *Teachers College Record, 102*(4), 779–804.

Taylor, E. W. (n.d.). *Transformative learning: An overview.* Retrieved from http://www.calpro-online.org/eric/docs/taylor/taylor_02.pdf

van Es, E. A., Tunney, J., Goldsmith, L. T., & Seago, N. (2014). A framework for the facilitation of teachers' analysis of video. *Journal of Teacher Education, 65*(4). 340–356.

Wenner, J. A., & Campbell, T. (2017). The theoretical and empirical basis of teacher leadership: A review of the literature. *Review of Educational Research, 87*(1), 134–171.

York-Barr, J., & Duke, K. (2004). What do we know about teacher leadership? Findings from two decades of scholarship. *Review of Educational Research, 74*(3), 255–316.

SECTION 6

STEM Policy and Reform

31

STEM-FOCUSED SCHOOL MODELS

Erin E. Peters-Burton, Ann House, Vanessa Peters,
Julie Remold and Lynn Goldsmith

The Emergence of STEM Schools

The concept of schools that have a focused theme is not new. In the 1960s, the United States opened magnet schools as a protest against racially segregated schools (Waltrip, 2000). The former Soviet Union offered schools that specialized in physics and mathematics, sports, or foreign languages. The United Kingdom has offered specialized school programs for nearly 3,000 secondary schools. Schools specializing in science, technology, engineering, and mathematics (STEM) are not new either. One of the first specialized schools focusing on STEM subjects, now known as Stuyvesant High School located in New York City, was established in 1904 as a boy's trade school, and in the 1930s shifted to an emphasis on mathematics and science (Hanford, 1997). Specialized STEM schools have been in existence for some time; however, these early STEM schools were small in number and had competitive standards for admission, allowing only elite students to attend (Kaser, 2006). More recently, there has been a worldwide marked trend to broaden rigorous STEM offerings to all students. This movement has produced more STEM schools, often fueled by dwindling performance on global comparative exams or economic standing (Bybee, 2013).

The Need for STEM Education

The purpose of education offered at a specialized STEM school, whether it is selective or inclusive, takes two forms: (a) attract students to STEM subjects in secondary and higher education, with the aim of encouraging them to move to STEM professions, and (b) promote STEM literacy among all students (Johnson et al., 2015). The first goal, to attract students to a STEM career, was developed to address the global shortage of STEM graduates. According to the European Schoolnet (EUN), there is a need for one million additional STEM researchers by 2020 in order to keep Europe economically sound. In the United States, national concern about STEM education has motivated financial support for diverse STEM education activities. Over 200 distinct federally funded STEM education programs awarded a total of nearly three billion dollars for STEM education in 2004, with most of the funds coming from the National Institutes of Health and the National Science Foundation (Kuenzi, 2008). Globally, there are efforts directed toward the development of a technically competent workforce that includes a variety of educational levels from skilled labor to terminal degree.

Not only is there is there a need for people to participate directly in STEM careers, but there is a need for STEM literacy worldwide. As stated in the recent Report of the European Commission

(EC), Science Education for Responsible Citizenship (Hazelkorn et al. 2015), knowledge of and about STEM are integral to preparing people to be actively engaged and responsible citizens. STEM education has the potential to teach people to be creative and innovative, able to interpret data and think computationally, able to evaluate the reliability of data sources, and able to work collaboratively no matter their field of choice. With the complex challenges facing our global society, people must be fully aware of and conversant with ways of knowing in STEM, such backing claims with evidence, improving ideas with feedback and healthy skepticism (Peters-Burton, 2014). Roehrig, Moore, Wang, and Park (2012) argued that our daily challenges are "multidisciplinary, and many require integration of multiple STEM concepts to solve them" (p. 31). In response to the recognition of the need for STEM education, specialized STEM schools have begun to proliferate worldwide. In the next sections, we present a summary of specialized STEM schools organized into two categories: selective and inclusive.

Selective STEM Schools

The goal of selective STEM schools is to bring together the most academically talented and STEM-focused students (Hugo, 2006). Often these schools attract high-quality teachers and are viewed as the top schools in their region (Subotnik, Tai, Rickoff, & Almarode, 2010). However, selective STEM schools were not always focused on serving gifted and talented students. When these schools were first established in the early 1900s, they focused on the practical need to develop a specialized technical workforce. For example, Stuyvesant High School and Brooklyn Technical High School, which opened in 1922, offered enhanced curriculum in mathematics, science, and drafting (Thomas & Williams, 2010). In response to sudden advances in science and technology in the mid-20th century, specialized STEM schools shifted to focusing on talent development of highly abled students in mathematics and science (Gallagher & Gallagher, 1994). Bolstered by the success of these stand-alone selective STEM schools, advocates of gifted students and scientists concerned with broadening access to science education encouraged the establishment of residential STEM schools, particularly in rural and impoverished areas (Lederman, 1992; Stanley, 1987).

Teachers at specialized STEM schools are highly prepared and certified in STEM subjects, which has been linked to greater gains in student learning (Goldhaber & Brewer, 2000; Hill, 2007). Students who attend selective STEM schools are more likely to pursue STEM in postsecondary environments when provided with challenging curricula, expert instruction, and peer stimulation (Bloom, 1985; Pyryt, 2000; Subotnik, Duschl, & Selmon, 1993; Tai, Liu, Maltese, & Fan, 2006). Comparisons of graduates from specialized STEM high schools in the United States to a national sample demonstrates that these schools do motivate students to pursue STEM careers. Ten percent of specialized STEM school graduates majored in mathematics and/or computation science, whereas only 3% of college graduates majored in math/computer science nationally. In addition, 51% of specialized high-school students reported majoring in the sciences, whereas 23% of the national sample graduated with such majors (Thomas, 2000).

Specialized STEM schools have been successful in providing gifted and talented students a high-quality educational experience, yet there are a few drawbacks. Specialized STEM schools are expensive to operate due to the need for the newest technologies and equipment to engage students and high-level teacher professional development in STEM subjects (Atkinson, Hugo, Lundgren, Shapiro, & Thomas, 2007). Additionally, concerns have been raised that offering a rigorous STEM curriculum to only those who can achieve high entrance exam scores is restrictive. Demographic trends demonstrate this concern, as participation in STEM careers tends to skew toward White males (Summers & Hrabowski, 2006). In response to the need for greater diversity in STEM fields, a new school concept has emerged, the inclusive STEM school, which offers a college-preparatory STEM curriculum to students from groups historically underrepresented in STEM fields (Means, Confrey, House, & Bhanot, 2008).

Inclusive STEM Schools

Unlike selective STEM-focused schools, the goal of inclusive STEM schools is to identify new sources of STEM talent among underrepresented minority students and provide them with the means to succeed in school, college majors, and careers (Means et al., 2008; Peters-Burton, Behrend, Lynch, & Means, 2014). They do so by making explicit connections between experiences in K–12 schooling, higher education, and STEM careers through innovative education programs that expand the boundaries of the normal school day and year and reconfigure relationships among teachers, students, and knowledge (Lynch et al., 2018). Inclusive STEM school designs engage students with their communities, STEM business and industry, and early opportunities for higher education experiences (Means et al., 2008).

Aside from admission standards and instructional support, there are many similarities between selective STEM schools and inclusive STEM schools. Course requirements and program offerings in selective and inclusive schools are similar, as both offer rigorous STEM instruction, although selective STEM schools offer a broader range of Advanced Placement courses (Means et al., 2008). Inclusive STEM schools are equally likely as selective STEM schools to provide opportunities for students to take college-level courses while in high school. Teachers at both types of STEM schools report using similar instructional approaches, with teachers at inclusive STEM schools being more likely to offer students intact cohort groups and contact with mentors in STEM from diverse backgrounds (Means et al., 2008). The missions of both selective and inclusive STEM schools have the potential to reduce the global shortage of STEM graduates by motivating and engaging students from diverse backgrounds

The proliferation of STEM schools occurred without an overarching governing body. As a result, a definitive standard for what makes a STEM school does not exist. Simply, a STEM school is one that focuses on STEM education (Tofel-Grehl & Callahan, 2014). The organizational design of STEM schools come in many forms, such as school-within-a-school, residential school, stand-alone school, university-based school, or a school that offers an extracurricular pull-out program (Tofel-Grehl & Callahan, 2014). STEM school curriculum and instruction has many forms as well; one extreme being STEM disciplines offered as advanced discipline-specific classes, such as college-level science or mathematics classes, to the other extreme of the fully integrated STEM curriculum, where student groups engage in authentic projects that combine the learning objectives of all of the STEM disciplines (Bybee, 2013). STEM school models come in a variety of designs based on admission, organizational structure, and curricular offerings. In the next sections, we present a composite understanding of elementary and secondary STEM school models, and then examine what is common across the models as well as what is unique in the model components.

Elementary STEM School Models

Limited research exists on the growing number of STEM-focused schools serving elementary grade students and the investment in expanding and improving STEM learning experiences at the elementary grades (DeJarnette, 2012). These schools are valuable because "they can serve as exemplars for districts across the nation that are attempting to elevate the quality of STEM education" (NRC, 2011, p.7). Identification of the effective components found at successful STEM-focused elementary schools can give direction to approaches to increase young students' experiences with STEM topics and skills.

In a 2013 follow-up volume, the National Research Council gave specific indicators for success for quality STEM experiences in schools, including increased instructional time for science in kindergarten through fifth grade. Researchers have pointed to the strategy of integrating science content with other areas as a means for increasing efficiency of school time and making room for science in the school day (Knowles, 2014). Barriers to integrating science and STEM into other content areas persist in traditional elementary schools (Dorph et al., 2011; Merritt, Chiu, Peters-Burton, & Bell, 2017). However, STEM-focused elementary schools, which ordinarily work within the same schedules and are accountable to the same standards as other schools in their districts, tend to have frequent use of instructional units that integrate science or engineering content with mathematics and English language arts (Peters-Burton, House, Peters, & Remold, 2019). The teachers at a STEM-focused elementary school typically author these integrated instructional units, which increases STEM content expertise and buy-in for implementation. Students not only gain STEM content knowledge when engaged in these integrated units, but they also learn workplace and life skills, such as collaboration, communication, creativity, and a growth mindset (Peters-Burton, House, Peters-Hinton, & Remold, 2019).

Another driver for recommendations of increased STEM instructional time in elementary grades is development of positive attitudes and interest in STEM. Alexander, Johnson, and Kelley (2012) found that STEM interests in children emerge as early as preschool. Early exposure to science experiences and positive attitudes toward science prior to high school has long-term impacts, including increased likelihood of choosing STEM college majors (Tai et al., 2006; Maltese & Tai, 2011). STEM-focused elementary schools articulate and carry out the mission to provide opportunities that develop interest and STEM competencies for all students (Peters-Burton et al., 2019). As an added bonus, providing opportunities for developing STEM interests before secondary school may improve the diversity of students seeking STEM careers.

Self-efficacy of elementary teachers is a frequently cited cause for teachers spending little class time on STEM (Madden, 2016). Teachers have reported low confidence with content included in the science content standards, and teachers in STEM positions are often teaching outside of their credential area (Appleton, 2003; NRC, 2011). Elementary schools are typically unable to hire STEM specialists, as most elementary education programs focus on teachers as generalists. In response, administrators at STEM-focused elementary schools hire teachers who understand the STEM-focused mission and are open to innovation, even if they do not have content expertise. These schools develop new teacher capacity through a combination of STEM-focused professional development offered outside of the school and a community of practice populated by veteran teachers who have STEM education expertise (Peters-Burton et al., 2019). Administrators and teachers at the STEM-focused elementary schools value and protect the time that is spent improving instructional practices, using an engineering design approach to plan, test, and improve curriculum.

In addition to providing additional STEM instruction and having a community of teachers that embrace STEM knowledge and skills, STEM-focused elementary schools have school-wide components that improve their STEM programming. Successful STEM-focused elementary schools share a common focus on developing student interest in STEM and identities as STEM-capable learners and students, parents, teachers, community partners, and administrators all understand and value the STEM-focused mission (Peters-Burton et al., 2019). For example, many STEM school design leaders take time to adapt their physical spaces to support engagement with science and to inspire students (Martin, 2016; Knowles, 2014; Peters-Burton et al., 2019) and successful STEM elementary schools often incorporate opportunity for student choice in approaching large projects (Peters-Burton, House, Peters-Hinton, & Remold, 2019).

The literature on STEM-focused elementary schools continues to emerge, and future research will provide even more insight into the ways elementary schools design and implement STEM-focused learning opportunities for students. Unfortunately, little information is known about intermediate and middle school STEM school models at this time. Therefore, the following section will focus on high school STEM models.

High School STEM Models

Since high school is typically the last stage of schooling prior to entering college or university, it is not surprising that much of the emphasis on STEM teaching and learning occurs here. In all parts of the world, in order to study STEM at the tertiary level, colleges and universities will require evidence of academic achievement. Yet, the duration of high school STEM preparation that students receive varies drastically between countries. Secondary students in the United States, for example, generally experience four years of high school, while students from some European countries, such as Germany, begin high school immediately after completing primary school, which is typically at ten years of age. For countries without middle schools, this would equate to students beginning high school preparation in the fourth grade.

The length of high school STEM preparation is only one of many factors that impact students' STEM achievement in postsecondary school and beyond. The design and quality of STEM curriculum and assessments, the provision of real-world experiences, and teacher preparation all contribute to students' overall STEM experience. With this in mind, many high schools have adopted a STEM focus to bolster students' interest and achievement in STEM subjects. Overall, STEM-focused high schools provide students with advanced coursework in the physical and life sciences as well as engineering and computer science. In the United States, high school STEM models have been established by Batelle's STEMx program (www.stemx.us), the Arizona STEM Network (http://stem.sfaz. org), and by the Texas Education Agency (www.tea.texas.gov/T-STEM). Collectively, these agencies strive to enhance students' STEM learning in high schools through rigorous curriculum taught by well-qualified STEM teachers, project-based learning experiences, and opportunities for mentoring by STEM experts (Means, Wang, Young, Peters, & Lynch, 2016).

Enhancing high-school STEM experiences has also been made possible by partnerships between schools and business or industry. In the United States, these partnerships are managed at the state level and emerge largely out a need to fill high-demand occupations in STEM fields (Rothwell, 2013). The Iowa STEM Businesses Engaging Students and Teachers (STEM BEST) program (www. iowastem.gov/STEMBEST), for example, is an innovative high school program built out of partnerships between businesses, public schools, and higher education institutions. In this program, students solve real-world problems by using industry standards and are mentored by employers of participating businesses (Carnavale, 2011). In Turkey, the Ministry of National Education, Ford Foundation, International Development Agency, and two universities began establishing "Science High Schools" starting in 1963 (Colakoglu, 2016). To develop these schools, an advisory board of STEM academics chose 30 teachers from existing Turkish high schools that taught mathematics, chemistry, physics, and biology and assessed them through rigorous oral and written exams. Selected science teachers received special training on the instruction and assessments of these disciplines and provided some teachers with opportunities to study the curriculum at universities in the United States. Between 1964 and 2014, this initiative helped establish over 200 science high schools in Turkey, and many private high schools have started to use the same curriculum (Colakoglu, 2016).

Although all STEM high schools aim to provide students with more STEM opportunities and higher-quality STEM instruction, until recently the specific design elements of these schools were still largely unknown. Peters-Burton et al. (2014) have conducted in-depth descriptive studies on the design features of inclusive STEM high schools (ISHSs) in the United States. Of the many design elements, a hallmark of successful STEM-focused high schools is the inclusion of an integrated STEM curriculum that blends different STEM subjects with engineering, computer science, and, importantly, non-STEM subjects. Teaching staff employ research-based instructional approaches that emphasize practices and strategies for active teaching and immersing students in STEM content, processes, habits of mind, and skills.

Students' STEM experiences also extend beyond the classroom and include connections with industry and the world of work in addition to internship and mentoring by STEM professionals (Peters-Burton et al., 2014). Europe is just beginning to define the design characteristics of high school STEM models through the "STEM School Label" project (www.eun.org/projects/stem). The objective of the project is to guide European schools in increasing young Europeans' interest and skills in STEM and to provide schools with the necessary tools to engage their students, teachers, and other stakeholders in related activities. Funded by the Erasmus+ Programme of the European Union, project activities include the development of a transnational set of criteria for defining STEM schools along with supports to foster a network and community of STEM schools that engage in peer-to-peer learning.

Key Characteristics of STEM-Focused Schools

Having described the features in STEM-focused elementary and secondary schools, we will now turn to the key features in these school designs, the similarities and differences across these designs, and the potential for vertical articulation in K–12 STEM-focused schools. Certainly, the STEM focus designs at the elementary and secondary STEM levels have in common the structures, practices, and resources that allow them to provide more and deeper opportunities to learn integrated STEM content for the purpose of supporting student sense making, creative thinking, and problem solving in multiple domains. Yet, the parallel between STEM-focused elementary and high schools is limited by the different structures, practices, and resources at the two different levels. Issues such as course selection, career connections, college preparation, and internships and/or mentorship are not driving concerns for elementary-aged educators. Most high school courses are taught in a departmentalized setting, resulting in siloed subject areas, whereas the flexibility accorded many elementary school teachers can offer the opportunity for integration across content areas. High school teachers are specialists in their content areas and generally have high confidence with their subject matter knowledge. Elementary teachers are typically generalists and often lack the background and confidence in STEM subjects (Appleton, 2003; Bleicher, 2006; Hanuscin, Lee, & Akerson, 2010; Metz, 1995). It is important to examine, then, the influential aspects of STEM-focused elementary and secondary schools, and to identify the points where these features overlap.

Most Influential Aspects of Elementary and High Schools

At the primary level, Peters-Burton et al. (2019) have identified 26 design components common to exemplar STEM-focused elementary schools. These components are clustered into six categories. The first category, STEM-focused learning opportunities, describes the features of lesson design and content (e.g., STEM is integrated with other content areas, presented through project-based lessons, and provides greater exposure to STEM content than in traditional elementary curricula). A second category is school staff, in which school leadership is distributed, staff are supported with professional development to strengthen STEM pedagogical content knowledge and lesson design, and teachers have an orientation toward innovation and continual learning. Additional categories include practices of data-driven decision-making, use of technology to support teaching and learning, leveraging the school's physical support STEM-learning opportunities, outreach to families and local community, as well as external partners to support STEM resources and student STEM learning. Finally, additional components include a school culture of intellectual safety and interpersonal trust, as well as future orientations of school sustainability and continued engagement in STEM for students in future studies. Some of these components are more clearly STEM-focused than others—elementary schools of many designs and focus areas employ things such as project-based lessons and data–driven decision-making practices. When harnessed in combination with a STEM focus, features such as these become channels for that STEM focus to be put into practice. Data-driven decision-making practices are not unique to STEM-focused schools. Nevertheless, it is a natural practice of a school staff that daily emphasizes the engineering design cycle of design-build-test-improve for problem solving with students.

At the secondary level, most inclusive STEM-focused high schools offer a greater number of STEM courses than is required by state and or/college admissions, and these courses have greater depth than the minimal state graduation and college admission requirements (Peters-Burton, House, Han, & Lynch, 2018). In these STEM-focused high schools, STEM topics are integrated throughout the curriculum, including representation in the core humanities and language arts. In addition, the number and scope of STEM courses, and the courses that include STEM integration, are curricular requirements for all students attending the school—there cannot be an opportunity to "opt out." Other components found to be common among STEM-focused high schools include a project-based learning approach, research experiences for students, technology integration with teaching and learning approaches, career exploration, early college, and internship and/or mentorship opportunities (Lynch et al., 2015, 2018; Means, Lynch, Young, House, & Wang, 2015; Century et al., 2015).

Similarities and Differences Across Schools

In examining the specific design components among STEM-focused elementary and secondary schools, these schools might on their face appear quite distinct. Three common aspects, however, create strong similarities. First, some similarities grow out of their common mission of providing an inclusive opportunity to ensure all students with interest in STEM, no matter their prior achievement, can successfully participate in STEM education. These schools also emphasize student agency and choice in learning, and work to foster a school climate of intellectual safety and growth mindset. Second, similarities in design between elementary and secondary STEM-focused schools also have common approaches to instruction, including a focus on STEM content learning and providing STEM learning opportunities outside of class, such as afterschool experiences. STEM-focused schools also typically have a school-wide use of project-based learning and hands-on experiences, allowing for the integration of interdisciplinary STEM content. Third, at both the elementary and secondary school levels, these STEM-focused schools are often a unique model within a district. This often means the ability to offer specialized teacher professional development to strengthen STEM pedagogical content knowledge and lesson design. School leadership has greater autonomy to operate in ways different from other schools in the district, the schools engage external partners to support and expand the school's STEM resources and offerings, and the schools providing opportunities for families to engage with and support STEM learning. While there is strong alignment between the STEM-focused school design at the elementary and high school levels, there are also several significant distinctions: (a) the process of STEM integration, (b) approaches to teacher STEM expertise, and (c) the target outcomes for students.

STEM Integration

First, STEM integration is accomplished in distinct ways between elementary and high schools. In elementary school, STEM instruction is provided by a single classroom teacher, who is responsible for STEM subjects as well as nearly all other subjects (depending on whether there is an art teacher, a PE teacher, or perhaps a technology teacher). As described by Peters-Burton, House, Peters, and Remold (2019), integration at one STEM-focused elementary school happened lesson by lesson, for example, asking students to build rockets from straws in a lesson combining mathematics and science. Also, at this school, art, music and physical education (PE) instruction routinely integrated STEM topics such as geometry and fractions to help make STEM part of a student's daily schedule. This type of daily integration allowed teachers in elementary schools to break down the silos between STEM subjects, as well as include non-STEM subjects within a single lesson. This type of integration helps build student interest and engagement for subjects over the isolated and disjointed teaching of math and science, and provides greater real-world engagement by including crosscutting concepts and real-world applications (Kelley & Knowles, 2016).

At the high school level, there is greater specialization in STEM subject areas. These schools require rigorous STEM curriculum for all students, typically exceeding state- or district-level course requirements, and are aimed at preparing all students for STEM college majors. Because high school courses and teachers are organized into departments, students typically study STEM subjects in separate periods over the course of a school day and have course designs that provide deep explorations of individual STEM disciplines such as algebra, geometry, physics, life sciences, computer science, and engineering. STEM-focused high schools typically provide cross–disciplinary experiences, but these tend to be a single course or a single project or capstone experience each year. In a high school setting, then, integration happens not at the lesson level, but in capstone experiences, unique courses, or events such as an annual design challenge

Teacher STEM Expertise

Second, the balance between teacher STEM expertise is viewed differently between elementary and high school STEM-focused schools. The high school and elementary school components both call out STEM expertise among the teaching staff as critical components of the STEM-focused school design. At the high school level, this expertise is in service of their core mission to prepare students to succeed in STEM college majors, making disciplinary knowledge essential. At the elementary level, most teachers had taken a college-level science course and a college-level mathematics course, but teachers did not have college degrees in STEM fields. A stronger priority over content knowledge was, instead, a disposition toward learning and development. Certainly, teachers must have sufficient pedagogical content knowledge, but at the elementary level, the depth of this knowledge requires less training and experience. Instead, the expertise required to design and lead engaging lessons on integrated STEM subjects is most significant at the primary level.

Goals for Students

Third, the goals are quite distinct for students in elementary and secondary STEM-focused schools. The impetus for inclusive STEM-focused high schools is to provide students with opportunities to prepare for and participate in STEM careers (Lynch et al., 2017; Lynch et al., 2018; President's Council of Advisors on Science and Technology, 2010). In fact, Means et al. (2016) examined inclusive STEM-focused high schools across three states for evidence that graduates from these schools are more fully prepared for and interested in STEM majors and careers, finding evidence that graduates from this type of high school had taken more courses that prepare them for STEM college majors, participated in more STEM-related activities, and expressed interest in STEM-related careers. ISHS were born of a motivation to reduce the barriers experienced by students from groups underrepresented in STEM majors and careers in STEM college majors and careers (Means et al., 2008), in order to open opportunities in the STEM career pipeline.

At the elementary level, however, the goals for students are quite different. Many certainly see STEM-focused elementary schools as an early, yet important, component in the trajectory of students to enter, persist, and complete the STEM pipeline. In particular, by providing a STEM focus for younger learners, these elementary STEM-focused schools can help students build STEM learner identities through STEM performance, recognition, and competence (Carlone & Johnson, 2007), as well as interest (Hazari et al., 2010). They also provide settings for connecting STEM to students' lives and the world beyond the classroom, providing opportunities to participate in inquiry-based study and collaborating with peers, both of which are associated with later persistence in STEM majors and careers (Tai, Sadler, & Mintzes, 2006).

Yet college and career are distant goals for elementary-age students. When exploring the goals staff have for their students in our eSTEM case studies, informants emphasized to us that they want to help students develop interest in STEM learning as well as 21st-century skills. The staff at STEM-focused elementary schools describe a mission of preparing children not to specialize in STEM, but to help children use STEM as a way of learning and engaging with the world around them, perhaps sparking an interest in future STEM studies.

Potential for Vertical Articulation in STEM Schools

Given the extent of similarities across the elementary and secondary STEM-focused school designs, there is strong potential for a model of vertical articulation in STEM schools. While the comparison of models described here shows that STEM school design features may vary in their implementation for different grade ranges, there remain sufficient components that are fundamental across STEM school designs to build an integrated model.

Early research on STEM-focused high schools were, for a number of years, the only models available of STEM-focused schools. The more recent research into STEM-focused elementary schools extends this work and has identified important differences between the goals, logistics, human resources, and expectations in how elementary school programs integrate and emphasize STEM. Elementary schools have opportunities to integrate STEM in ways that would be more difficult at the high school level, such as through extensive use of interdisciplinary approaches. Likewise, they face challenges that are less of a concern at high schools, such as human resources prepared to work in a STEM-rich environment. Articulating these distinctions opens the opportunity to advance the conceptualization and definition of STEM-focused schools, at both the elementary and high school levels, by identifying and distinguishing common underlying principles from adaptations in implementation. This will ultimately lead toward an articulated description of STEM-focused school pipeline for grades K-12.

References

Alexander, J. M., Johnson, K. E., & Kelley, K. (2012). Longitudinal analysis of the relations between opportunities to learn about science and the development of interests related to science. *Science Education, 96*(5), 763–786.

Appleton, K. (2003). How do beginning primary school teachers cope with science? Toward an understanding of science teaching practices. *Research in Science Education, 33*, 1–25.

Atkinson, R. D., Hugo, J., Lundgren, D., Shapiro, M. J., & Thomas, J. (2007). Addressing the STEM challenge by expanding specialty math and science high schools. *NCSSSMST Journal, 12*(2), 14–23.

Bleicher, R. E. (2006). Nurturing confidence in preservice elementary science teachers. *Journal of Science Teacher Education, 17*, 165–187.

Bloom, B. S. (Ed.). (1985). *Developing talent in young people*. New York, NY: Ballantine Books.

Bybee, R. W. (2013). *The case for STEM education: Challenges and opportunities*. Arlington, Virginia: NSTA press.

Carlone, H. B., & Johnson, A. (2007). Understanding the science experiences of women of color: Science identity as an analytic lens. *Journal of Research in Science Teaching, 44*(8), 1187–1218.

Carnavale, A., Smith, N., & Melton, M. (2011). *STEM workforce study*. Georgetown University Center on Education and the Workforce. Retrieved from http://cew.georgetown.edu/STEM/

Century et al. (2015). *What is STEM?* Paper presented at A Forum on STEM Learning for All sponsored by the National Science Foundation, Washington, DC.

Colakoglu, M. H. (2016). STEM applications in Turkish science high schools. *Journal of Education in Science, Environment and Health (JESEH), 2*(2), 176–187.

DeJarnette, N. (2012). *America's children: Providing early exposure to STEM (science, technology, engineering and math) initiatives.* Retrieved from https://www.ingentaconnect.com/content/prin/ed/2012/00000133/00000001/art00008

Dorph, R., Shields, P., Tiffany-Morales, J., Hartry, A., & McCaffrey, T. (2011). High hopes--few opportunities: The status of elementary science education in California. *Strengthening Science Education in California.* Retrieved from https://www.wested.org/resources/high-hopes-mdash-few-opportunities-full-report-the-status-of-elementary-science-education-in-california/

Gallagher, J. J., & Gallagher, S. A. (1994). *Teaching the gifted child.* Boston: Allyn & Bacon.

Goldhaber, D. D., & Brewer, D. (2000). Does teacher certification matter? High school certification status and student achievement. *Educational Evaluation and Policy Analysis, 22,* 122–145.

Hanford, S. (1997). *An examination of specialized schools as agents of educational change.* New York, NY: Columbia University.

Hanuscin, D. L., Lee, M. H., & Akerson, V. L. (2010). Elementary teachers' pedagogical content knowledge for teaching the nature of science. *Science Education, 95,* 145–167.

Hazari, Z., Sonnert, G., Sadler, P. M., & Shanahan, M.-C. (2010). Connecting high school physics experiences, outcome expectations, physics identity, and physics career choice: A gender study. *Journal of Research in Science Teaching, 47*(8), 978–1003. doi:10.1002/tea.20363

Hazelkorn, E., Ryan, C., Beernaers, Y., Constantinou, C. P., Deca, L., Grangeat, M., Karikorpi, M., Lazoudis, A., Casulleras, R. P., & Weizel-Breuer, M. (2015). *Science education for responsible citizenship.* Directorate-General for Research and Innovation: Science with and for Society.

House, A., Peters-Hinton, V., Peters-Burton, E., & Remold, J. (2019). Understanding STEM-focused elementary schools: Case study of Walter Bracken STEAM Academy. *School Science and Mathematics, 119,* 446–456.

Hugo, J. (2006). Inside a consortium school. *NCSSSMST Journal, 12*(1), 6–7.

Johnson, C. C., Peters-Burton E. E. & Moore, T. J. (Eds.). (2015). *STEM road map: A framework for integrated STEM education.* New York: Routledge.

Kaser, J. S. (2006). *Mathematics and science specialty high schools service a diverse student body: What's different?* Pittsburgh, PA: Learning Research and Development Center, University of Pittsburgh.

Kelley, T. R., & Knowles, J. G. (2016). A conceptual framework for integrated STEM education. *International Journal of STEM Education, 3*(1), 11.

Knowles, B. (2014). Planning a whole-school approach to STEM. *School Science Review, 96*(355), 27–35.

Kuenzi, J. J. (2008). *Science, technology, engineering and mathematics (STEM) education: Background, federal policy and legislative action.* Washington, DC: Congressional Research Service.

Lederman, L. (1992). Of scientists and school systems. *Physics Today, 45*(5), 9–10.

Lynch, S. J., House, A., Peters-Burton, E., Behrend, T., Means, B., Ford, M., Spillane, N., Matray, S., Moore, I., Coyne, C., Williams, C., & Corn, J. (2015). *A logic model that describes and explains eight exemplary STEM-focused high schools with diverse student populations.* Washington, DC: George Washington University OSPrI Project.

Lynch, S. J., Peters-Burton, E. E., Behrend, T., House, A., Ford, M., Spillane, N., Matray, S., Han, E., & Means, B. (2018). Understanding inclusive STEM high schools as opportunity structures for underrepresented students: Critical components. *Journal of Research in Science Teaching.* doi:10.1002/tea.21437

Lynch, S. J., Spillane, N., House, A., Peters-Burton, E., Behrend, T., Ross, K. M., & Han, E. M. (2017). A policy-relevant instrumental case study of an inclusive STEM-Focused high school: Manor new tech high. *International Journal of Education in Mathematics, Science and Technology, 5*(1), 1–20.

Madden, M. R. (2016). *Systemic changes occurring in elementary schools that pursue a STEM focus.* (Dissertation.) University of West Georgia.

Maltese, A. V., & Tai, R. H. (2010). Eyeballs in the fridge: Sources of early interest in science. *International Journal of Science Education, 32*(5), 669–685.

Martin, B. J. (2016). *A case study investigation of practices and beliefs of teachers at a STEM-focused elementary school* (Dissertation), San Francisco State University.

Means, B., Confrey, J., House, A., & Bhanot, R. (2008). *STEM high schools: Specialized science technology engineering and mathematics secondary schools in the U.S.* (Bill and Melinda Gates Foundation Report). Retrieved from http://www.hsalliance.org/stem/index.asp

Means, B., Lynch, S., Young, V., House, A., & Wang, H. (2015). *Envisioning STEM schools.* Paper presented at A Forum on STEM Learning for All sponsored by the National Science Foundation, Washington, DC.

Means, B., Wang, H., Young, V., Peters, V., & Lynch, S. J. (2016). STEM-focused high schools as a strategy for enhancing readiness for postsecondary STEM programs. *Journal of Research in Science Teaching, 53*(5), 709–736.

Merritt, E., Chiu, J. L., Peters-Burton, E. E., & Bell, R. (2017). Teachers' integration of scientific and engineering practices in primary classrooms. *Research in Science Education.* doi:10.1007/s11165-016-9604-0

Metz, K. E. (1995). Reassessment of developmental constraints on children's science instruction. *Review of Educational Research, 65,* 93–127.

National Research Council. (2011). *Successful K-12 STEM education: Identifying effective approaches in science, technology, engineering, and mathematics.* Washington, DC: The National Academies Press. https://doi.org/10.17226/13158

National Research Council. (2013). *Monitoring progress toward successful K-12 STEM education: A nation advancing?* Washington, DC: National Academies Press.

Peters–Burton, E. E. (2014). Is there a nature of STEM? *School Science and Mathematics, 114,* 99–101.

Peters–Burton, E. E., Behrend, T., Lynch, S. J., & Means, B. (2014). Inclusive STEM high school design: 10 critical components. *Theory into Practice, 53,* 1–8.

Peters–Burton, E. E., House, A., Han, E., & Lynch, S. (2018). Curriculum and instruction at inclusive STEM high schools. *Journal of Research in STEM Education, 4*(2), 193–212.

Peters–Burton, E. E., House, A., Peters-Hinton, V., & Remold, J., (2019, April). *Models of exemplary stem-focused elementary schools: What are the critical components?* Paper presented at the annual meeting of the National Association of Research on Science Teaching, Baltimore, MD.

Peters–Burton, E., House, A., Peters, V., & Remold, J. (2019). Understanding STEM-focused elementary schools: Case study of Walter Bracken STEAM Academy. *School Science and Mathematics, 119,* 446–456.

President's Council of Advisors on Science and Technology (PCAST). (2010). *Prepare and inspire: K-12 education in science, technology, engineering, and math (stem) for America's future.* Washington, DC: Author.

Pyryt, M. C. (2000). Talent development in science and technology. In K. A. Heller, F. J. Monks, R. J. Sternberg, & R. F. Subotnik (Eds.), *International handbook of giftedness and talent* (2nd ed., pp. 427–437). Oxford, England: Elsevier.

Roehrig, G. H., Moore, T. J., Wang, H. H., & Park, M. S. (2012). Is adding the E enough? Investigating the impact of K-12 engineering standards on the implementation of STEM integration. *School Science and Mathematics, 112*(1), 31–44.

Rothwell, J. (2013, June). *The hidden economy.* Metropolitan Policy Program, Brookings Institution. Retrieved from https://www.brookings.edu/wp-content/uploads/2016/06/TheHiddenSTEMEconomy610.pdf

Stanley, J. C. (1987). State residential high schools for mathematically talented youth. *Phi Delta Kappan, 68*(10), 770.

Subotnik, R. F., Duschl, R., & Selmon, E. (1993). Retention and attrition of science talent: A longitudinal study of Westinghouse science talent search winners. *International Journal of Science Education, 15*(1), 61–72.

Subotnik, R. F., Tai, R. H., Rickoff, R., & Almarode, J. (2010). Specialized public high schools of science, mathematics, and technology and the STEM pipeline: What do we know now and what will we know in 5 years? *Roeper Review, 32,* 7–16.

Summers, M. F., & Hrabowski, F. A. III. (2006). Diversity enhanced: Preparing minority scientists and engineers. *Science, 311,* 1870–1871.

Tai, R. H., Liu, C. Q., Maltese, A. V., & Fan, X. (2006). Planning early for careers in science. *Science, 312*(5777), 1143–1144.

Thomas, J. (2000). First year findings: NCSSSMST longitudinal study of gifted students. *NCSSSMST Journal, 5*(2), 4–6.

Thomas, J., & Williams, C. (2010). The history of specialized STEM schools and the formation and role of the NCSSSMST. *Roeper Review, 32,* 17–24.

Tofel-Grehl, C., & Callahan, C. M. (2014). STEM high school communities: Common and differing features. *Journal of Advanced Academics, 25,* 237–271. doi:10.1177/1932202x14539156

Waltrip, D. (2000). *A brief history of magnet schools.* Magnet Schools of America. Retrieved from http://magnet.edu/brief-history-of-magnets

32

STEM POLICY IN THE UNITED STATES AND CANADA

Carla C. Johnson, Janet B. Walton and Jonathan M. Breiner

This chapter examines the nature of STEM federal and state policies that have been enacted within the United States (U.S.) and Canada across the past two decades. Arguably, the U.S. sparked what we consider now the era of STEM education in the early 1990s with the National Science Foundation's (NSF) use of the acronym SMET to refer to science, mathematics, engineering, and technology, an acronym that was changed to STEM in 2001 by the same agency (e.g., Breiner, Harkness, Johnson, & Koehler, 2012; Sanders, 2009). In the nearly three decades that have passed since the NSF started using an acronym to represent the various STEM disciplines, the meaning of STEM has transformed into a way to describe curriculum, programs, schools, and training in the U.S. and beyond. The focus of this chapter will be to examine the historical context of STEM policy and research on impact of investments, and future directions for STEM education in the U.S. and Canada.

STEM Education Policy in the U.S.

In spite of the burgeoning federal interest in STEM education and workforce development, the question *What is STEM?* has largely defied policymakers and federal agencies—mostly due to the manner in which the acronym STEM was put into use and the meanings which have evolved over time (e.g. Breiner et al., 2012; Johnson, 2013a, 2019). STEM has been defined quite broadly by agencies such as the National Science Foundation (NSF), which includes psychology and social sciences in addition to physical and life sciences within the scope of STEM (America COMPETES Act of 2010) and more narrowly by others, such as the Department of Homeland Security (DHS) and U.S. Immigration and Customs Enforcement (ICE), agencies that exclude most social sciences in their definitions of STEM (Granovskiy, 2018). Some attempts have been made to standardize the definition of STEM across federal agencies, including the 2012 recommendation by the Standard Occupational Classification (SOC) Policy Committee to categorize STEM occupations into two broad domains: Science, Engineering, Mathematics, and Information Technology; and Science and Engineering-related occupations (Granovskiy, 2018). Furthermore, the STEM Education Act of 2015 included a specific provision to add computer science to the definition of STEM used by selected federal agencies. It is noteworthy that this lack of focus on a STEM definition is not unique to the federal government, and debates continue among analysts and educators on issues such as whether STEM should be defined vocationally or in broader conceptual terms (e.g., Breiner et al., 2012; Johnson, 2013b, 2019).

With 50 distinct state educational systems within the U.S., it is not surprising that there are substantial variations in STEM policy across the nation. Differing conceptualizations of STEM education across the nation mirror the multiple definitions of STEM among federal agencies. Carmichael (2017) investigated STEM policy across all 50 states, identified four categories of STEM definitions in states' policy materials, and found that most states (72%) included definitions of STEM that reflected its integrative nature across disciplines, while only 10% identified STEM by its constituent disciplines alone. The most commonly identified focus of STEM in policy statements (78% of states) related STEM to workforce or economic development, and most also emphasized equity (68% included statements that STEM is for all students, and 56% identified broadening minority representation in STEM as a priority) (Carmichael, 2017). Mechanisms for instituting programs to align with these goals were less often articulated in STEM policy statements, with just under a third (30%) identifying CTE programs as vehicles for STEM education, 18% identifying afterschool programs as opportunities for STEM learning, and 16% stipulating that more advanced high school coursework was a means to improve STEM education in the state (Carmichael, 2017). This tapestry of state-by-state variations in STEM definition and focus illustrate that one of the major challenges in effecting and assessing STEM education reform efforts nationally lies in the structure of U.S. education, in which states maintain primary control of and authority over K–12 education.

In 2018, the Education Commission of the States (ECS) published a profile of state level STEM initiatives across the U.S. Data collected by the ECS included policy information related to teacher recruitment and professional development as well as various student-level policies. The ECS (2018) found that 38 states had policies to provide some sort of financial incentives in their STEM teacher recruitment efforts and that 23 provided targeted STEM professional development for high school teachers. There was less consensus regarding student-level policies. For example, only eight states had policies to support student STEM mentoring and internship or other work-based learning programs, and only 12 had policies to support afterschool STEM programs. ECS determined that 18 states had rigorous graduation requirements for science and mathematics (defined as three credits of laboratory science and three mathematics credits including Algebra II). Twelve states had policies to support programs targeting groups underrepresented in STEM.

Early 21st-century claims about impending shortages of American workers in science, technology, engineering, and mathematics (STEM) fields, most notably the 2005 *Rising Above the Gathering Storm* report published by the National Academies Press, fueled federal interest in K–12 STEM education. Bolstered by the unprecedented federal foray into K–12 education represented by the No Child Left Behind Act (NCLB) in 2002, members of Congress took a new interest in STEM education in the nation's K–12 and postsecondary institutions, resulting in a flurry of legislative and policy efforts in the ensuing years. These efforts included the formation of a new federal-level oversight committee charged with monitoring federal STEM investments as well as various non-legislative policy initiatives emanating from the White House, the U.S. Department of Education (ED), and other federal agencies. Considerable investments of taxpayer dollars were directed toward these efforts, with federal spending on STEM over the seven-year period from 2010 to 2016 estimated at around $3 billion. Less clear, however, is what the results of these investments have been.

Summary of U.S. Federal STEM Policy, 2002 to Present

NCLB launched an unprecedented level of federal involvement in education, a function heretofore left largely to states. Although this legislation was not targeted specifically at STEM, acting instead as a reauthorization of the 1965 Elementary and Secondary Education Act (ESEA), it is worth noting because of its pivotal role in laying the groundwork for future federal STEM policy initiatives. Additionally, there is evidence that the associated implementation of mandatory assessments in NCLB may have had unintended consequences for the S, T, and E components of STEM at the school level, decreasing the use of inquiry-based learning and cutting time from science instruction in schools (e.g., Griffith & Scharmann, 2008; Johnson, Bolshakova, & Waldron, 2014; Johnson, 2013a, 2013b; Milner et al., 2012).

In 2007, in the aftermath of the 2005 *Rising Above the Gathering Storm* report, Congress passed the America Creating Opportunities to Meaningfully Promote Excellence in Technology, Education, and Science Act of 2007 (America COMPETES). This legislation was intended to spur innovation through research and development in federal agencies and contained several provisions directly targeting K-12 education. The legislation charged the National Academy of Sciences (NAS) with developing a research-based best-practice inventory for STEM in K-12. In addition, the act included provisions to increase the number of STEM teachers, enrollment and number of teachers for Advanced Placement and International Baccalaureate courses, and established Mathematics and Science Partnership grants for high-needs schools. In 2010 the act was reauthorized, and several of the K-12 STEM education provisions were repealed in favor of a more targeted focus on postsecondary education. The 2010 reauthorization of America COMPETES included the formation of CoSTEM, a federal-level committee with oversight for STEM. A review of outcomes from America COMPETES revealed that the act was never fully funded, nor were all the provisions implemented (Congressional Research Service, 2015). Furthermore, the Congressional Research Service (CRS) report noted that most funding authorizations associated with the act had expired and concluded that while STEM programs that pre-existed the act have fared relatively well, most of the new STEM education programs associated with the act were either "partially implemented or not implemented at all" (CRS, 2015, p. 8).

In the wake of the Great Recession from 2007 to 2009, Congress passed the American Recovery and Reinvestment Act (ARRA) in 2009, which included several educational provisions. Among these was the Race to the Top (RTTT) competitive grant program that earmarked $4.35 billion to spur innovation and reform in state and local education. The RTTT grants included six competitive preference priority areas, one of which was STEM. Eighteen states and the District of Columbia were ultimately awarded grants in three rounds of funding. RTTT outcomes for students that were reported by USDOE did not include specific findings regarding STEM, but did demonstrate improved graduation rates, higher standards for student achievement, growth in participation and success in Advanced Placement (AP) courses, and increased focus on effective instruction and use of data to inform instruction (U.S. Department of Education, 2015). However, research studies examining the impact of RTTT investments in selected states in STEM specifically revealed more effective STEM teaching practice for teachers who were engaged in research-based professional development programs (e.g., Johnson, Sondergeld, & Walton, 2017), growth in community stakeholder understanding of importance of STEM (e.g., Sondergeld, Johnson, & Walton, 2016), and increased college readiness outcomes for STEM schools (e.g., Johnson & Sondergeld, in press).

In 2009, President Barack Obama launched the Educate to Innovate initiative with the goal of improving student performance in STEM. While this initiative was not connected to any legislation or funding source, it represented a novel approach to educational improvement by focusing on public-private partnerships as a means to K-12 educational improvement. In 2013, the White House announced that Educate to Innovate had resulted in over $700 million in public-private partnerships, including the establishment of a CEO-led coalition to leverage private sector capacities for education, expanded STEM education programs across the country, and development of a blueprint for business creation of and investment in STEM programs (White House, 2013).

The ESEA was again reauthorized in 2015 under the auspices of the Every Student Succeeds Act (ESSA). The ESSA legislation had provisions that aimed to reverse portions of NCLB by shifting the responsibility for educational accountability to the states. STEM-related provisions included replacing formula grants for the Mathematics and Science Partnership (MSP) program with block grants called Student Support and Academic Enrichment Grants. The ESSA also authorized the STEM Master Teacher Corps program that would create a network of exceptional STEM educators to disseminate best practices and serve as representatives for educational policy. In addition, the act included general education provisions that would encompass STEM teaching and learning, including measures for improving assessment practices in K-12 schools, providing professional development, increasing the use of technology in the nation's schools, and establishing local-level 21st Century Community Learning Centers. Although funding was approved for some provisions of ESSA, no funding was approved for the Master Teacher Corps in either 2017 or 2018 federal appropriations, and funding for the 21st Century Community Learning Centers was eliminated in the 2018 federal budget proposal (Peterson, 2018). Thus, the impact of ESSA legislation, especially for STEM, was limited.

During the 114th Congress, legislators approved the STEM Education Act of 2015 that included computer science in the definition of STEM education and continued existing STEM education programs at the National Science Foundation (NSF). This piece of legislation was a policy bill with no spending authorizations included with it. The act specified that the NSF should continue to award grants for research and development into innovative out-of-school STEM programs and research into informal STEM education. The act also amended the NSF's Noyce Master Teacher Fellowship program to allow teachers pursuing master's degrees to participate in the program.

In 2017, Congress reauthorized portions of the America COMPETES act by passage of the American Innovation and Competitiveness Act (AICA). The act charged the NSF, the National Oceanic and Atmospheric Administration (NOAA), and the National Aeronautics and Space Administration (NASA) to form an advisory panel to advise CoSTEM. In addition, the act supported research into apprenticeship programs and the coordination of citizen science. The AICA also amended the STEM Education Act of 2015 to allow the use of funding to foster partnerships between organizations involved in informal STEM learning, postsecondary education, and education research centers. Like the STEM Education Act of 2015, the AICA was a policy bill with no authorized funding attached to its provisions.

The 115th Congress also marked the passage of the Inspiring the Next Space Pioneers, Innovators, Researchers, and Explorers (INSPIRE) Women Act, which directed NASA to encourage female participation in STEM and in careers in aerospace. The act had no funding attached to it, but established (a) NASA Girls and Boys, a virtual mentoring program; (b) the Aspire to Inspire program that encourages girls to explore STEM careers by making connections with women in NASA careers; and (c) the Summer Institute in Science, Technology, Engineering, and Research for middle school students at Goddard Space Center. NASA was also charged to submit plans to Congress about ways to encourage and involve scientists, astronauts, engineers, and innovators in engaging with female K-12 students and inspiring them to pursue STEM fields and aerospace careers. Also in 2017, the USDOE released a document entitled "Resources for STEM Education." Although not connected with any legislation, this document is noteworthy for its focus on assisting state and local educational agencies better understand how they can leverage federal STEM funds to support STEM education by providing examples of the use of funds such as those associated with ESEA and the Carl D. Perkins Career and Technical Education Act to support PK-12 STEM instruction and student outcomes (U.S. Department of Education, 2017). A range of examples are provided, such as utilizing ESSA funds for professional development activities, hiring STEM coaches, to develop statewide STEM Master Teacher Corps, providing students with mobile learning devices, to create and enhance STEM-focused schools, and integrating arts, history, and writing into STEM instruction (U.S. Department of Education, 2017).

Career and technical education has been a subject of legislation and federal investment via the Carl D. Perkins Vocational and Technical Education Act (Perkins Act). First passed in 1984, the act was reauthorized in 1998 and 2006. In 2018, the Perkins Act was reauthorized as the Strengthening Career and Technical Education for the 21st Century Act with the aim of improving career and technical education (CTE) to support the U.S. economy by investing in secondary and postsecondary CTE programs, and it grants states the authority to set goals for their own CTE programs. This act, in addition to the 2006 reauthorization, is notable because of the increased academic emphasis. This is significant since many CTE fields have significant STEM linkages, and the "T" and "E" of STEM in secondary schools frequently are highly represented within CTE programs. Perkins funds have traditionally been used for equipment, curricular materials, professional development, career counseling and guidance, and expansion of programs. The 2018 reauthorization specifies that instructional content must align with ESSA state-identified academic standards (Advance CTE, 2018). The USDOE recognized the applicability of the Perkins Act to state and local STEM initiatives in its "Resources for STEM Education" document, citing Perkins funds as useful to support career-based experiential learning opportunities and to develop STEM pathway programs.

U.S. policymakers continue to delve into the area of STEM education with the objectives of developing a STEM-literate citizenry and STEM-competent workforce to ensure the longevity of the nation's democracy and the ongoing health of the U.S. economy. These concerns mean that STEM policy will likely continue to influence and be influenced by policy areas such as immigration and civil rights. Policymakers are concerned about issues such as the participation of traditionally underrepresented groups in STEM, the quality and number of STEM teachers, U.S. students' performance on assessments relative to their international peers, the proportion of foreign students enrolled in postsecondary STEM programs, and the U.S. STEM labor supply (Granovskiy, 2018). These concerns, along with the increasing ideological divides in the U.S. two-party system, mean that federal policy, as well as STEM policy specifically, will likely continue to rise and fall with presidential administrations and therefore defy most attempts at longevity and consistency.

Infrastructure and Funding for STEM Education in the U.S.

The profusion of federal policy initiatives around STEM, coupled with the fact that resulting policies are enacted by potentially up to 13 federal agencies, promulgates the need for an organizational structure for STEM education at the federal level. The infrastructure of federal STEM policy administration has existed since prior to 1980 but has evolved over the past several decades. The Office of Science and Technology Policy (OSTP) was established in 1976 to advise the President and other executive branch officers on scientific and technical issues related to the U.S. economy. In 1993, an executive order by President Clinton established the National Science and Technology Council (NSTC), a Cabinet-level council led by the President with the aim of coordinating science and technology policy across federal agencies. In 2011, a subcommittee of the NSTC, the Committee on STEM Education (CoSTEM), was established to coordinate STEM education programs across federal agencies. CoSTEM is co-chaired by the director of the NSF and the associate director of the OSTP, and it includes members from 10 federal agencies, including, among others, the USDOE, NASA, the Department of Defense (DoD), the Department of Energy (DOE), and the Environmental Protection Agency (EPA). CoSTEM is charged with the following three functions (NSTC, 2011):

1. Review STEM education activities and programs, and the respective assessments of each, throughout Federal agencies to ensure effectiveness;
2. Coordinate, with the Office of Management and Budget, STEM education activities and programs throughout Federal agencies; and
3. Develop and implement through the participating agencies a five-year STEM education strategic plan, to be updated every five years.

In recognition of the confusing array of STEM educational policy and the possibility of overlap in programs, CoSTEM, in accordance with the requirements set in place by the legislation that established the committee, conducted an inventory of federal STEM efforts published in 2011 as *The Federal Science Technology, Engineering, and Mathematics (STEM) Education Portfolio*, referred to as NSTC-11 for the purposes of this discussion. Using the findings from this inventory, CoSTEM created the *Federal Science Technology, Engineering, and Mathematics (STEM) Education 5-Year Strategic*

Plan in 2013 to reduce overlap between programs and duplication of efforts and funding among agencies.

Federal STEM investments can be placed in two broad categories. The first is programs with a general focus on education that may include STEM as an optional element, such as Title IA of the Elementary and Secondary Education Act and federal financial aid for postsecondary students in the form of Pell Grants and loans. The second is programs conceived with the primary goal of improving STEM education outcomes, including initiatives to improve K-12 STEM teaching and learning, to improve access to STEM fields for underrepresented students, and to provide direct support for students pursuing STEM degrees and careers. Although substantial, federal investments in STEM education represent less than 1% of the approximately $1.1 trillion spent on education in the U.S. annually (NSTC, 2011).

The NSTC-11 reported that as of 2011, U.S. agencies were making 252 investments (defined as a STEM education activity with staff and a dedicated budget of at least $300,000) totaling $3.4 billion (NSTC, 2011). The largest areas of investment were programs with the following primary focus areas: increasing postsecondary STEM degree attainment (34%), STEM career preparation (25%), and STEM education research and development (15%) (NSTC, 2011). It is not surprising, therefore, that the bulk of the funding, a total of 235 investments, was directed toward undergraduate and graduate learners. The NSF is the federal agency with the largest proportion (22%) of its research and development budget directed toward STEM education, followed by the Nuclear Regulatory Agency (NRC) (20%), and the Department of Transportation (DOT) (10%). Interestingly, only 1% of the USDOE's total budget was directed to programs with a primary STEM focus.

Based upon these findings, CoSTEM formulated its five-year strategic plan for STEM education. The plan designated five priority areas for investment with overarching goals for each area (NSTC, 2013):

1. Improve STEM instruction.
2. Increase and sustain youth and public engagement in STEM.
3. Enhance STEM experiences of undergraduate students.
4. Better serve groups historically underrepresented in STEM fields.
5. Design graduate education for tomorrow's STEM workforce.

The National Science and Technology Council (NSTC) issued a new U.S. Federal STEM Strategic Plan in December 2018 entitled *Charting a Course for Success: America's Strategy for STEM Education*. The new plan is driven by a vision for the future "where all Americans will have lifelong access to high-quality STEM education and the United States will be the global leader in STEM literacy, innovation, and employment" (NSTC, 2018, p. v.). The plan was developed with collaborative engagement from all federal agencies including the Department of Commerce, Department of Defense, Department of Labor, Department of Interior, Department of Education, Department of State, Department of Energy, Department of Transportation, Environmental Protection Agency, Health and Human Services, NASA, NSF, and Department of Agriculture. The goals of the 2018 STEM plan (NSTC, 2018, p.v.) were to:

1. Build strong foundations for STEM literacy;
2. Increase diversity, equity, and inclusion in STEM; and
3. Prepare the STEM workforce for the future.

The goals for the 2018 federal strategy are guided by four pathways that include focus on strategic partnerships, interdisciplinary learning, computational literacy, and transparency and accountability (NSTC, 2018). This plan marked a new effort to purposefully examine the outcomes of STEM policy investments to determine impact on student and other outcomes. The implementation of this plan commenced in 2019.

President Obama's 2009 Educate to Innovate initiative, with its focus on the use of partnerships between education and private sector stakeholders, set the stage for a new emphasis on collaborative engagement as a vehicle for improving STEM education nationwide. These ideas came to fruition in CoSTEM's 2018 strategic plan where STEM ecosystems were proposed as a key mechanism for achieving its vision. The report maintains that "the innovation capacity of the United States—and its prosperity and security—depends on an effective and inclusive STEM education ecosystem" (NSTC, 2018, p. v) and ties this idea to its strategic goals. For example, CoSTEM advocated for the use of local STEM ecosystems to engage adult professionals to act as mentors for students and teachers in support of the goal of increasing diversity, equity, and inclusion in STEM (NSTC, 2018). The emergence of STEM education networks at the national, state, regional, and local levels may be examples of such ecosystems. There are a growing number of STEM networks and partnerships across the U.S., ranging from national, macro-level networks that engage state and local networks, to local STEM networks that bring together specific schools with community partners. Magliaro and Ernst (2018) identified, in their inventory of statewide and regional networks, 31 national, 187 statewide or regional, and 24 metro-level STEM networks. Network leadership is situated variously within universities, state departments of education, for-profit entities, and non-profit entities, with the structure of leadership largely dependent on the source of the network's funding; and networks are often nested within one another, creating various levels of leadership and organizational structure (Maglioro & Ernst, 2018).

STEMx is one example of a STEM network at the national level with leadership based in the non-profit sector. STEMx was established by Battelle Memorial Institute in 2012 with the goal of connecting state STEM networks and other partners. It aims to "accelerate the growth of policies, practices and partnerships that are needed to expand the number of STEM teachers, increase student achievement in STEM education and, ultimately, grow tomorrow's innovators" (STEMx, n.d.). Another example of such a macro-level network that seeks to initiate or engage state and local level networks is the STEM Funders Network STEM Learning Ecosystems Initiative (STEM Ecosystems). This organization aims to provide "expert coaching and support from leaders such as superintendents, scientists, industry and others" (STEM Ecosystems, n.d.).

Various states across the nation have convened statewide learning networks. The Ohio STEM Learning Network (OSLN), initiated in 2008, was the first of the statewide networks. Established by the Ohio Business Roundtable, Battelle, and a $17 million donation from the Bill & Melinda Gates Foundation, the OSLN conducts its work through seven regional hubs throughout the state and, as of this writing, listed 59 STEM platform schools on its website (OSLN Schools n.d.). Among its practices, OSLN cites "engaging the public and private sector to design, start-up and operate STEM teaching and learning systems" and "pushing the envelope of education systems design to solve the complex problems in education" (OSLN Promises, Principles, Practices, n.d.). Leadership of the OSLN is based within the education arm of Battelle, a non-profit research and development organization. Notably, the OSLN served as a model for the Tennessee STEM Innovation Network (TSIN), established in 2010 with funds from the Race to the Top grant program. The TSIN modeled the OSLN's structure, with leadership based within Battelle and the state department of education and its work conducted through a series of regional hubs throughout the state.

Impact of STEM Education Policy in the U.S.

In 2018, the Government Accountability Office (GAO) recommended that CoSTEM review and document assessments of federal STEM investments, noting that while identifying evidence-based practices across the federal investment portfolio is a key goal of STEM education policy, the committee needed to focus on evaluation of the programs (GAO, 2018, Highlights). Meanwhile, surveys were conducted by the NSTC of agencies administering federal STEM funds in which agencies were asked to respond to items about their evaluation activities. In spite of the GAO's findings, agencies reported on surveys that 86% of the 139 "broader STEM investments" (NSTC, 2013, p. xiii) had been evaluated between 2005 and 2011 with the aim of improving programs or evaluating their impact, although only 40% of agency-specific investments had been evaluated. While the NSTC inventory collected information about evaluation activities generally, no information about the findings from those evaluations was collected.

The 2018 U.S. Federal STEM Strategic Plan has included accountability as one of the focus areas for scope of work, and this shift should produce data that will inform policy regarding the impact of federal STEM investments. Some agencies, including the Department of Defense (DoD) Army's Education Outreach Program (AEOP), have been engaged in assessing the impact of their STEM education outreach investments across the past decade. The AEOP evaluation includes pre and post assessment of participants' growth in 21st-century skills using the 21st Century Skills Assessment (Sondergeld & Johnson, 2019). Findings from the 2017 Summative Evaluation Report indicated participation in AEOP initiatives resulted in significant growth in mentor assessed 21st-century skills for high school and college participants (AEOP, 2017).

In regard to U.S. student outcomes, the Program for International Student Assessment (PISA) has been a long-standing means for comparing U.S. student STEM performance to other countries around the globe. This assessment is coordinated by the Organization for Economic Cooperation and Development (OECD). The U.S. average score for science literacy in 2015 was 496, just above the OECD average of 493 (National Center for Education Statistics, 2017). Singapore ranked highest at 556 and the Dominican Republic scored the lowest at 332. In mathematics, the U.S. scored 470, lower than the OECD average of 490 (National Center for Education Statistics, 2017). Again, Singapore scored highest at 564 and the Dominican Republic came in lowest at 328. Science scores for the U.S. were similar to the previous three assessments in 2006, 2009, and 2012. The U.S. score in mathematics, however, is on a downward trend, and was lower than for the years 2009 and 2012 for the U.S. (National Center for Education Statistics, 2017).

In sum, there are growing efforts to assess the impact of U.S. STEM education policy investments. These calls, along with the identification of accountability through the use of evidence-based practices in the 2018 strategic plan, may refocus legislators' attention on the need for outcomes data. The 2018 plan calls for federal agencies to develop processes for "data collection and reporting mechanisms" (NSTC, 2018, p. 31) and to use these data for evaluating program performance. To this end, the strategic plan calls for disseminating "examples and templates" (NSTC, 2018, p. 32) of best practices for sharing data about program performance and outcomes, and for a publicly available resource to visually display common performance metrics across programs. Given the limited pool of federal dollars available for STEM education programs, however, it is unclear how assessment and evaluation activities will be supported at a scale that permits a broad expansion of these activities in a cohesive and rigorous manner.

STEM Education Policy in Canada

Canada's STEM policies focus on all students and not just the creation of a STEM elite; however, it faces the same challenges as do the 36 member countries of the OECD. Less than half of Canadian high school students graduate with senior STEM courses, although 70% of Canada's top jobs require expertise in science, technology, engineering, and mathematics (Let's Talk Science, 2018).

Canada experiences similar underrepresentation issues as some other countries in terms of STEM majors and STEM jobs. Even when graduating with a bachelor's degree in STEM, women are less likely than men to work in a STEM occupation (Baird, Bozick, & Harris, 2017). Further, Canadian students from low-income families are underrepresented in STEM (Duodu, Noble, Yusuf, Garay, & Bean, 2017). Brown, Tam, and Marmureanu (2015) highlight a strong relationship between low socioeconomic status of youth and their underachievement in STEM-related areas based on standardized tests at the elementary school level. Other barriers to entering STEM, such as a lack of finances, access, and awareness for STEM programs and a lack of mentors and understanding of future career opportunities, further marginalize students who are already underrepresented (Grossman & Porche, 2014). Additionally, indigenous populations are greatly underrepresented in STEM. According to research from the Environics Institute (2015), while the proportion of First Nations, Métis, and Inuit people in the country between ages 25 and 54 with a university degree increased from 8% to 10% from 2006 to 2011, the degree attainment of non-aboriginal Canadians grew at a faster rate (23% to 27%), Further, non-aboriginal populations were more likely to be enrolled in a STEM degree program.

Like the rest of the world, Canada also has a strong and rising demand for STEM workers. In addition to new areas of growth in sustainability, biomedical engineering, and waste management, 20% of engineers are over the age of 55, resulting in an increased demand for engineers in the short term due to retirements. International Data Corporation (IDC, 2018) predicts spending on informational technology (IT) professional services to reach CA$8.7 billion by 2019, an increase of CA$1.1 billion in only the last four years accompanied by a need to fill thousands of positions.

Canada has developed a strong government, industry, and private (charitable) approach to STEM policy and engagement. Partnerships and collaborations focus strongly on literacy and technology skill development as their foundation. The largest efforts to improve STEM education are led by private charitable stakeholders, often in partnership with both the federal and provincial governments and also with private industry. The federal government's main roles are in educational support and oversight and in job creation and retainment.

Due to the structure of Canada's federated system of education and constitutional requirements, the federal government is not directly involved in policy related to education of school-age students. Several of their federal research councils encompass STEM disciplines however, including the Canadian Institutes of Health Research (CIHR) and National Sciences and Engineering Research Council (NSERC). In addition, Canadian Networks of Centres of Excellence (NCE) support research-driven university, industry, and government partnerships, including several that are STEM discipline based. However, outside of research, most of the federal government's STEM investment takes the form of financially supporting STEM networks, career tool development, and science fairs and STEM competitions.

Since each Canadian province controls its own curricula and overall education system, the Council of Ministers of Education, Canada (CMEC) acts as the central figure in setting national policies and goals related to education, including STEM. The CMEC is an intergovernmental body formed in 1967 that includes the Minister of Education from each province and territory. It provides a means of national oversight and the ability to better share ideas and best practices among all 13 provinces and territories. The CMEC has led most national governmental efforts related to STEM education, albeit with an emphasis on science and mathematics.

The Science Council of Canada (SCC) published a report entitled *Science for Every Student: Educating Canadians for Tomorrow's World* (Science Council of Canada, 1984) with recommendations organized around three general areas: science education for all, redirecting science education, and monitoring science education. After the release of Science for Every Student, science curriculum development began to emphasize the importance of developing a scientifically literate population. The CMEC was the first to attempt to use assessments at the national level. In 1989 the CMEC initiated the School Achievement Indicators Program (SAIP), the first-ever attempt to arrive at a consensus on the elements of a national assessment (Fournier, 2001). The SAIP Mathematics I for

13- and 16-year-old students was the first pan-Canadian assessment to be administered in 1993. SAIP Mathematics II and III were administered in 1997 and 2001, respectively.

Though the Canadian constitution forbids a required national curriculum, in 1997 the CMEC published the *Common Framework of Science Learning Outcomes, K to 12: Pan-Canadian Protocol for Collaboration on School Curriculum* (CMEC, 1997) with the intent to provide direction for curriculum developers across Canada and to harmonize science learning when revising science curricula. Even though SAIP was not the sole determinant in the decision to set pan-Canadian standards of achievement in science, it did play a role in convincing jurisdictions of the advantages of participating in such a project. Many jurisdictions adopted these learning outcomes (Fournier, 2001).

Infrastructure and Funding for STEM Education in Canada

Canada's Innovation and Skills Plan, outlined in the 2017 budget, provides a five-year $950 million investment that focuses on how best to support Canadians impacted by the dramatic changes to the world of work and the subsequent impact to the Canadian economy. Its emphasis is on innovation to create STEM jobs with a focus on six key areas—advanced manufacturing, agriculture and food, clean technology, digital industries, health and bio-sciences, and clean resources. The plan also invested in science, research, and development as a way of retaining Canadian professionals in these fields.

The 2018 Canadian budget included the government's largest ever investment in STEM with a clear emphasis on diversity and innovation. Overall, almost $4 billion was committed to Canada's research system through 2023. The budget included $1.7 billion over the next five years to support the next generation of researchers, $925 million to fund research through Canada's three granting agencies of which as much as $700 million could be STEM-related, and $700 million over five years through the Industrial Research Assistance Program for business innovation (Canada, 2018). Multiple initiatives in this budget are attempting to create a more diverse workforce which will have a direct impact on STEM—$1.4 billion in financing is earmarked for female-led small businesses; $210 million over five years for the Canada Research Chairs Program that aims to attract younger scientists and retain them in Canada, and to increase diversity among the chairs; $15 million to improve equality and diversity in academia; and $3.8 million to create a strategic plan to build better partnerships and methods of research with indigenous cultures (Canada, 2018).

The 2019 Canadian budget approached STEM with funding that complemented what the government began with the 2018 budget. Major STEM funding included $2.05 billion over the next 24 years to keep Canada as a leader in space robotics, including $150 million in the first five years for small and medium-sized companies to develop technologies for the Lunar Exploration Accelerator Program (Canada, 2019).

The remaining STEM emphasis within the 2019 budget was on funding items that had a more direct impact on the population, such as employee retraining, diversity and inclusion, and support for various projects. The budget introduced a training benefit program that will cost $1.7 billion through 2025, and $586.5 million a year thereafter, and will allow workers ages 25 to 64 to retrain for jobs of the future by giving individuals up to $1,000 every four years toward tuition and up to four weeks of paid leave from their current jobs to complete educational programs (Canada, 2019). The 2019 budget addressed diversity through multiple initiatives that will impact STEM and illustrates the federal government's policy of supporting K-12 STEM education through charitable STEM organizations. A program was created to increase access and provide support for postsecondary studies for indigenous students; $60 million in funding was provided for CanCode, which teaches coding with a focus on underrepresented groups in STEM, and $10 million for Let's Talk Science, which focuses on hands-on STEM activities and learning programs, with an emphasis on girls taking a greater an interest in STEM (Canada, 2019). Additionally, the budget supports other STEM programs, including an initiative to increase work–study experiences to connect with STEM course-work and better develop STEM skills, and \$114 million over five years for graduate scholarships for STEM students to increase STEM master's and doctoral students by 500 and 167, respectively, per year (Canada, 2019).

Canada has established both infrastructure and resources to support STEM education efforts in the country. For example, Canada has STEM network support for both local education agencies such as museums, science centers, zoos, and aquariums. Additionally, Canada has invested in national initiatives including financial support to increase the quality of education and opportunities in STEM and to increase public awareness of the importance of STEM education. One example of this is the PromoScience Program, which was founded by the Natural Sciences and Engineering Research Council (NSERC) of Canada. This program provides grants to organizations working to promote STEM opportunities for school-age children. The grants are designed to support hands-on learning experiences, improvements to program content or delivery, and new STEM programs and activities.

Canada's Science and Technology Awareness Network (STAN) was created to provide a common voice for government and industry. It aims to raise the profile of STEM, increase general public awareness, provide a forum for collaborations and partnerships, and develop common standards of measuring STEM improvements. STAN is attempting to strengthen the national culture related to STEM while supporting collaborations among stakeholders to focus this capacity on increasing Canada's global competitiveness.

Canada also has invested in tools for STEM careers via support for non-profits such as Mitacs and through their own Employment and Social Development Canada (ESDC, 2019). Mitacs is a national non-profit that is focused on establishing partnerships across higher education, business/industry, and other global entities with the goal of making Canada more innovative. Founded in 1999, Mitacs partners with 60 universities, 4,000 companies, and both federal and provincial governments. Mitacs-funded research has helped to strengthen collaborations, improve economic performance, and create jobs (Mitacs, n.d.).

The ESDC's goal is to provide tools that improve the quality of Canadian life by promoting a highly skilled workforce that is both efficient and inclusive, and to help Canada's youth transition into careers, including STEM. In the 2013 and 2014 federal budgets, \$110 million was provided for ESDC to help youth transition from school to career, and included up to 3,000 full-time internships for postsecondary graduates in high-demand STEM fields. An additional \$15 million was reallocated annually within the Youth Employment Strategy (YES) to support up to 1,000 internships (Duclos, 2015). In 2017–2018, the ESDC's new Student Work Placement (SWP) program created co-op placement for students in STEM and related business programs in partnership with employers and postsecondary education institutions. The program supported the creation of over 1,100 new student work placements with employers in eight key economic sectors. Almost half of placements were filled by students from underrepresented groups, including women, indigenous students, persons with disabilities, newcomers, and first-year students. The SWP was particularly successful in supporting women in STEM, with 367 placements being filled by women (ESDC, 2019).

Canada's largest and perhaps most effective STEM organizations are charities that create partnerships beetween stakeholders. These private organizations reach PK-20 students and are mostly funded by industry and government grants. While these organizations have similar policies and end goals to those of many other countries, such as increasing the number of students taking STEM coursework and entering STEM careers, there is a marked emphasis on inclusion and creation of opportunities for underrepresented populations. Canada's private organizations are mostly collaborations between universities and colleges, local education, government, cultural agencies, industry, and media outlets, and STEM initiatives are designed to offer experiential and innovative learning and job opportunities. Mostly the goals are to increase the number and type of STEM learning opportunities for students and educators, promote the overall public profile of science knowledge and careers, and grow interest in STEM among students with the aim of creating a larger and more supportive environment for STEM education.

Let's Talk Science is one of Canada's leading STEM outreach organizations. Recently celebrating its 25th anniversary, Let's Talk Science offers professional learning opportunities for educators and online resources for both students and educators. Let's Talk Science was formed as a grass roots outreach operation in 1993 and, as of the 2016–2017 school year, had 45 postsecondary partners and 54,000 hours of outreach volunteers with 285,000 interactions with children and youth, had partnered with more than 2,800 educators, and had delivered over 6,800 hands-on/minds-on activities. Additionally, their programs were used in 43% of schools, reaching 916,000 of the five million school-age children in Canada (Let's Talk Science, n.d.).

In 2017, Let's Talk Science launched the national action plan and vision for youth science learning, Canada 2067. Co-founded by Amgen, 3M, Hill + Knowlton Strategies and the Trottier Foundation, Canada 2067 has the goal of creating an action plan and national vision for STEM learning to ensure that all youth benefit from strengthened education systems designed for the 21st century—a system that will ensure Canadian youth graduate as critical thinkers and informed citizens (Canada 2067, n.d.). The initial Canada 2067 National Leadership Conference included youth, educators, industry, policymakers, and community partners. In addition to the goals previously outlined, they also developed a focus on inequities in STEM. They noted that a successful learning framework places the student at the center and emphasizes the need to include and support students from all backgrounds. Canada 2067 highlights three recurrent inequities in terms of participation and achievement in STEM education and careers: inequities between girls and boys, socioeconomic inequities, and inequities between students from majority and minority cultures.

Impact of STEM Education Policy in Canada

Canada's efforts to improve STEM education are producing some early signs of impact. Overall, postsecondary participation is increasing. In 2016, 54% of Canadians ages 25 to 64 had either college or university qualifications, up from 48% in 2006 (Wall, Zhao, Ferguson, & Rodriguez, 2018). Statistics Canada reported that 532,158 students received a credential, such as a certificate, diploma, or degree, from a public postsecondary institution in 2016 (Statistics Canada, 2018). This represented the eighth consecutive annual increase for Canada. Canada continues to rank first among the OECD countries in the proportion of college and university graduates.

Between 2006 and 2016, the number of Canadians ages 25 to 64 with a master's degree or an earned doctorate increased by more than 40%, to nearly 1.3 million (representing 7% of the population in this age group), and more than one-half (58%) of earned doctorates were in STEM fields (Wall, Zhao, Ferguson, & Rodriguez, 2018). Canada's 2016 census revealed STEM fields provided the highest salaries and that STEM graduates are more likely to find jobs, but Canada is still unable to fill all of its STEM positions, particularly in engineering, IT, and computer science (Katam, 2017). Investment in start-ups and high-tech innovation is being supported by unprecedented venture capital funding and by the government's Innovation and Skills Plan from the 2017 budget (Randstad Canada, n.d.). The Canadian government recently approved expedited work-permit and shortened approval visa processes and is acquiring the same foreign STEM talent that the U.S. recently barred from entering (Randstad Canada, n.d.).

In Canada, STEM remains a male-dominated area. University-educated women are still less likely to choose a STEM major over other fields such as social science or business. Twenty percent of women who attended a postsecondary program opted for a STEM degree, compared to over 40% of postsecondary men; women continue to be underrepresented at 22% of the total workforce in STEM fields (Turcotte, 2011).

The most recent results from PISA 2015 show that Canada remains in the group of top-performing countries and achieves its standing with relatively equitable outcomes (CMEC, 2016). In regard to performance on the science component of the PISA, Canada scored 528, much higher than the U.S. and the OECD average. In mathematics, Canada scored 516 compared to 470 for the U.S. and 490 for the OECD average (CMEC, 2016).

Future Directions for STEM Education in Canada

Currently Canada has a shortage of workers in many STEM-related occupations, with expectations of shortages to increase over the next decade due to retirements. In addition to previously discussed programs aimed at filling STEM employment needs, one of Canada's biggest ongoing efforts is recruiting foreign nationals to attend institutions of higher education and pursue careers in Canada. These international students will provide a short-term fix for the Canadian workforce until more Canadian citizens are prepared and willing to enter STEM degree fields. Canada has seen extreme growth in international students, with study permits during the past two decades growing from less than 50,000 in the late 1990s to 572,000 in 2018, with 250,000 of them in postsecondary programs (Immigration, Refugees and Citizenship Canada, 2018; Usher, 2019). One in seven postsecondary students in Canada are foreign nationals and provide the Canadian higher education system with additional revenue by paying higher tuition, resulting in additional opportunities for Canadian students (Usher, 2019). *Building Through Success*, Canada's international education strategy through 2024, will direct near-term future efforts. This program will provide $148 million per year to increase diversification, boost innovation, increase global ties, and support a strong economy, allowing for Canadians to travel abroad to study and also to allow for additional recruitment of foreign nationals (Canadian Bureau for International Education [CBIE], 2019).

Chapter Summary

STEM education policy efforts that emerged nearly two decades ago in the U.S. have gained momentum in recent years. Federal strategic plans have been coupled with funding that has given rise to state-level STEM planning, networks, programs, standards, assessments, and growth—all driven by the desire for improved access, equity, opportunities, performance, and STEM-literate citizenry in the U.S. Increased attention, resources, and advocacy have resulted in early impacts including the transformation of K-20 education in various pockets across the country. Moving forward, it is anticipated that policy will continue to support STEM education investments and accountability for positive outcomes, along with growth of the pipeline of STEM talent and competitiveness in the global innovation marketplace.

While Canadian regional governments will continue to control K-12 STEM education in their curricula, Canada's federal STEM policy is designed to provide support at the K-12 level and present opportunities for postsecondary education and careers in STEM. Data seem to suggest that some gains are being made in graduating students in STEM fields, although gaps remain for underrepresented groups. Moreover, Canada has a growing need for more students to graduate and enter STEM fields, especially in engineering, and has policies in place to meet the needs in the short term by adding international talent to the STEM pool. Long-term plans include increasing the number of Canadian students entering and graduating from STEM degree programs and then entering STEM careers by increasing STEM opportunities for youth, including underrepresented groups.

References

Advance CTE. (2018). *Strengthening career and technical education for the 21st century act*. Retrieved from https://careertech.org/Perkins

American Innovation and Competitiveness Act. Pub. L. No. 114–329. U.S.C. § 3084 (2016).

Army Educational Outreach Program. (2017). *2017 Summative evaluation report: Part 2: Findings*. Retrieved from https://www.usaeop.com/wp-content/uploads/2018/06/FY17-AEOP-Summative-Evaluation-Report-Findings.pdf

Baird, M. D., Bozick, R., & Harris, M. (2017). *The uphill climb: Women and some minorities encounter disparities in STEM occupations, Even with post-secondary education*. Santa Monica, CA: RAND Corporation. Retrieved from https://www.rand.org/pubs/research_briefs/RB9978.html

Breiner, J., Harkness, M., Johnson, C. C., & Koehler, C. (2012). What is STEM? A discussion about conceptions of STEM in education and partnerships. *School Science and Mathematics, 112*(1), 3–11.

Brown, R. S., Tam, G., & Marmureanu, C. (2015). Toronto district school board maps representing demographics and achievement by geographic area. (Research Report no. 14/15–11). Toronto: Toronto District School Board.

Canada 2067. (n.d.). Retrieved from https://canada2067.ca/

Canada 2067. (2017). *Canada 2067 National Leadership Conference*. Retrieved from https://canada2067.ca/en/conference/national-leadership-conference/

Canadian Bureau for International Education. (2019). *Building on success: Canada's International Education Strategy (2019–2024)*. Retrieved from https://www.international.gc.ca/education/strategy-2019-2024-strategie.aspx?lang=eng

Carl D. Perkins Vocational and Technical Education Act. Pub. L. No. 98–524 (1984).

Carl D. Perkins Vocational and Technical Education Act. Pub. L. No. 105–220 (1998).

Carl D. Perkins Vocational and Technical Education Act. Pub. L. No. 109–270 (2006).

Carmichael, C. C. (2017). *A state-by-state policy analysis of STEM education for K-12 public schools* (Doctoral dissertation). Retrieved from https://scholarship.shu.edu/cgi/viewcontent.cgi?article=3342&context=dissertations

Congressional Research Service. (2015). *The America COMPETES act: An overview*. CRS Publication R43880. Retrieved from https://www.everycrsreport.com/reports/R43880.html.

Council of Ministers of Education, Canada (CMEC). (1997). *Common framework of science learning outcomes, K to 12: Pan-Canadian protocol for collaboration on school curriculum*. Toronto: CMEC.

Council of Ministers of Education, Canada (CMEC). (2016). *Measuring up: Canadian results of the OECD PISA study: The performance of Canada's youth in science, reading and mathematics 2015; first results for Canadians aged 15*. Retrieved from https://www.cmec.ca/Publications/Lists/Publications/Attachments/365/PISA2015-CdnReport-EN.pdf

Duclos, J. Y. (2015). *Employment and social development Canada 2014–15 departmental performance report*. Retrieved from http://publications.gc.ca/collections/collection_2016/edsc-esdc/Em1-4-2015-eng.pdf.

Duodu, E., Noble, J., Yusuf, Y., Garay, C., & Bean, C. (2017). Understanding the delivery of a Canadian-based after-school STEM program: A case study. *International Journal of STEM Education, 4*(1), 20.

Education Commission of the States. (2018). *High school level STEM initiatives—All state profiles* [Database]. Retrieved from http://ecs.force.com/mbdata/mbprofall?rep=stema

Employment and Social Development Canada. (2019). Retrieved from https://www.canada.ca/en/employment-social-development/corporate/reports/departmental-results/2017-2018/results.html

Every Student Succeeds Act, P.L. 114–95, U.S.C. § 1177 (2015).

Fournier, G. (2001). School Achievement Indicators Program (SAIP): Bridging the gap to jurisdictional assessments. Empirical Issues in Canadian Education Conference, Queens College. November 23, 2001. Retrieved from http://qed.econ.queensu.ca/pub/jdi/deutsch/edu_conf/Fournier.pdf

Granovskiy, B. (2018). *Science, technology, engineering, and mathematics (STEM) education: An overview*. CRS Publication R45223. Retrieved from https://eric.ed.gov/?id=ED593605.

Griffith, G., & Scharmann, L. (2008). Initial impacts of No Child Left Behind on elementary science education. *Journal of Elementary Science Education, 20*(3), 35–48. doi:10.1007/BF03174707

Grossman, J. M., & Porche, M. V. (2014). Perceived gender and racial/ethnic barriers to STEM success. *Urban Education, 49*(6), 698–727.

Immigration, Refugees and Citizenship Canada (IRCC) data. (2018). Retrieved from https://cbie.ca/infographic/

Inspiring the Next Space Pioneers, Innovators, Researchers, and Explorers (INSPIRE) Women Act. Pub. L. No. 115–7. 51 U.S.C. § 51 USC 40901 (2017).

International Data Corporation. (2018). Retrieved from https://www.brighttalk.com/webcast/15593/336993/idc-canada-predictions-2019

Johnson, C. C. (2013a). Conceptualizing integrated STEM education—Editorial. *School Science and Mathematics, 113*(8), 367–368.

Johnson, C. C. (2013b). Educational turbulence: The influence of macro and micro policy on science education reform. *Journal of Science Teacher Education, 24*(4), 693–715.

Johnson, C. C. (2019). Understanding what is STEM a decade later—Editorial. *School Science and Mathematics, 119*(7), 367–368.

Johnson, C. C., Bolshakova, V. L. J., & Waldron, T. (2014). When good intentions and reality meet: Large-scale reform of science teaching in urban schools with predominantly Hispanic ELL students. *Urban Education, 49,* 1–38.

Johnson, C. C., & Sondergeld, T. A. (in press). Outcomes of an integrated STEM high school: Enabling access and achievement for all students. *Urban Education.*

Johnson, C. C., Sondergeld, T. A., & Walton, J. (2017). A statewide implementation of the critical features of professional development: Impact on teacher outcomes. *School Science and Mathematics, 117*(8).

Katam, E. (2017, November 30). *STEM graduates earn more and find employment, Statistics Canada reveals.* Retrieved from https://www.canadastudynews.com/2017/11/30/stem-graduates-earn-more-and-find-employ ment-statistics-canada-reveals/

Let's Talk Science. (2018). *Canada 2067 Youth Insights Overview Imagining the future of STEM education.* Retrieved from https://canada2067.ca/app/uploads/2018/09/Canada-2067-Youth-Insights-Overview_EN-1.pdf.

Let's Talk Science (n.d.). *Let's Talk Science annual report 2016–17.* Retrieved from https://letstalkscience.ca/sites/ default/files/2019-08/2016-2017%20Annual%20Report%20EN_0.pdf

Magliaro, S. G., & Ernst, J. V. (2018). *Inventory of statewide STEM education networks.* Blacksburg, VA: Center for Research in SEAD Education, Virginia Tech. Retrieved from https://drive.google.com/drive/u/0/folders/ 1OdVxPvbl7Wwbm3KYsWLzMpFSa-nxCtEM

Milner, A., Sondergeld, T., Demir, K., Czerniak, C. M., & Johnson, C. C. (2012). Elementary teachers' beliefs about teaching science and classroom practice: An examination of pre/post NCLB testing in science. *Journal of Science Teacher Education, 23* 111–132.

Mitacs. (n.d.). Retrieved from https://www.mitacs.ca/en

National Academy of Sciences, National Academy of Engineering, and Institute of Medicine. (2007). *Rising above the gathering storm: Energizing and employing America for a brighter economic future.* Washington, DC: The National Academies Press. https://doi.org/10.17226/11463.

National Center for Education Statistics. (2017). *Select findings from PISA 2015.* Retrieved from https://nces. ed.gov/surveys/pisa/pisa2015/pisa2015highlights_1.asp

National Science and Technology Council. (2011). *The federal science, technology, engineering, and mathematics (STEM) education portfolio.* NSTC Publication L. No. 111–358. Retrieved from https://obamawhitehouse. archives.gov/sites/default/files/microsites/ostp/stem_stratplan_2013.pdf.

National Science and Technology Council Committee on STEM Education. (2011). *Charter of the committee on science, technology, engineering, and mathematics (STEM) education.* Retrieved from https://obamawhitehouse. archives.gov/sites/default/files/microsites/ostp/costem_charter_signed_01-31-11.pdf

National Science and Technology Council Committee on STEM Education. (2013). *Federal science, technology, engineering, and mathematics (STEM) education: 5-year strategic plan.* National Science and Technology Coun-cil. Retrieved from https://obamawhitehouse.archives.gov/sites/default/files/microsites/ostp/stem_strat plan_2013.pdf.

National Science and Technology Council Committee on STEM Education. (2018). *Charting a course for success: America's strategy for STEM education.* National Science and Technology Council. Retrieved from https:// www.whitehouse.gov/wp-content/uploads/2018/12/STEM-Education-Strategic-Plan-2018.pdf.

Ohio STEM Learning Network. (n.d. a). *Promises, principles, practice.* Retrieve from https://www.osln.org/about/ promise-principles-practice/

Ohio STEM Learning Network. (n.d. b). *Schools.* Retrieved from https://www.osln.org/schools/

Peterson, E. (2018, February 12). Administration slashes federal afterschool funding. Retrieved from http://www. afterschoolalliance.org/afterschoolSnack/Administration-slashes-federal-afterschool-funding_02-12-2018.cfm

Randstad Canada. (n.d.). *STEM jobs: The good, the bad and the ugly.* Retrieved from https://www.randstad.ca/ job-seeker/career-resources/tech-jobs/stem-jobs-the-good-the-bad-and-the-ugly/

Sanders, M. (2009). STEM, STEM education, STEMmania. *The Technology Teacher, 68*(4), 20–26.

Science Council of Canada. (1984). *Science for every student: Educating Canadians for tomorrow's world* (Vol. 36). Ottawa, Canada: Supply and Services Canada.

Sondergeld, T. A., & Johnson, C. C. (2019). Development and validation of a 21st Century Skills Assessment: Using an iterative multimethod approach. *School Science and Mathematics, 119*(6), 312–326.

Sondergeld, T. A., Johnson, C. C., & Walton, J. (2016). The impact of a statewide investment on K-12, higher education, and business/community stakeholder STEM awareness. *School Science and Mathematics, 116*(2), 104–110.

Statistics Canada. (2018). *Canadian postsecondary enrolments and graduates, 2016/2017.* Retrieved from https:// www150.statcan.gc.ca/n1/daily-quotidien/181128/dq181128c-eng.htm

STEM Ecosystems. (n.d.). *STEM learning ecosystems overview.* Retrieved from https://stemecosystems.org/ ecosystem/indiana-stem-ecosystem-initiative/

STEM Education Act of 2015. Pub. L. No. 114–59. 42 U.S.C. §§ 1861–1862. (2015).

STEMx (n.d.). *STEMx: Educate. Engage. Exchange.* Retrieved from http://www.stemx.us/wp-content/uploads/2013/01/STEMx-8.5X11.pdf

Strengthening Career and Technical Education for the 21st Century Act. Pub. L. No. 115–224. 20 U.S.C. § 2301. (2018).

Turcotte, M. (2011). Women in Canada: A gender-based statistical report. Statistics Canada. Component of Statistics Canada Catalogue no. 89-503-X. Retrieved from https://www150.statcan.gc.ca/n1/pub/89-503-x/2010001/article/11542-eng.pdf

U.S. Department of Education. (2015). *Fundamental change: Innovation in America's schools under Race To The Top.* Retrieved from https://www2.ed.gov/programs/racetothetop/rttfinalrptfull.pdf.

U.S. Department of Education. (2017). *Resources for STEM education.* Retrieved from https://innovation.ed.gov/files/2017/04/Resources_for_STEM_Education.pdf.

U.S. Government Accountability Office. (2018). *Science, technology, engineering, and mathematics Education: Actions needed to better assess the federal investment.* GAO Publication GAO-18-290. Retrieved from https://www.gao.gov/products/GAO-18-290.

U.S. Immigration and Customs Enforcement. (2016). *STEM designated degree program list.* Retrieved from https://www.ice.gov/sites/default/files/documents/Document/2016/stem-list.pdf.

Usher, A. (2019). *The state of postsecondary education in Canada, 2019.* Toronto: Higher Education Strategy Associates.

Wall, K., Zhao, J., Ferguson, S. J., & Rodriguez, C. (2018). Results from the 2016 Census: Is field of study a factor in the payoff of a graduate degree? Statistics Canada. Catalogue no. 75-006-X. Retrieved from https://www150.statcan.gc.ca/n1/pub/75-006-x/2018001/article/54978-eng.htm

White House (2013). Educate to innovate [webpage]. Retrieved from https://obamawhitehouse.archives.gov/issues/education/k-12/educate-innovate.

33

STEM POLICY IN ASIA

Jia Li, Jian-Xin Yao, Tian Luo and Winnie Wing Mui So

Introduction

A growing number of countries in the world are aware of the significance of STEM (science, technology, engineering and mathematics) education to the development of the country. STEM has also been introduced into Asia and is an initiative with a view to becoming a practice in the education arena (NIES, P. R. of China, 2017; Korean Ministry of Education, Science and Technology, 2011), as it has great potential for cultivating innovative talents for the 21st century. Therefore, it is important to reveal the development of STEM policies in Asia and their influences on school/extracurricular courses, which are the normal ways for Asian students to participate in STEM education.

In this chapter, STEM policies in China, Japan, South Korea and Singapore are examined as these countries are Asia's major economies, with GDP totaling more than $18 trillion, accounting for about 110% of the European Union's GDP and 20% of global GDP (World Bank, 2018). These four nations, influenced by Confucianism, mostly have an examination-oriented education system. Furthermore, all four nations rank high according to international assessments in science and mathematics, such as PISA (OECD, 2016) and TIMSS (Mullis, Martin, Foy, & Hooper, 2016).

The Concept of STEM

The concept of "STEM" has been expanding since the day it was first conceived, and some derived concepts have appeared, such as STEAM by adding Arts, or STREAM by adding Robotics or Reading and so on. China and Singapore officially use "STEM" instead of other derived terms, and "STEM" is considered as a superordinate concept, including other extended concepts (NIES, P. R. of China, 2017). The most representative organization in Japan for promoting STEM education is the Japan Society for STEM Education (JSTEM), and coding education is emphasized as being included in STEM education (JSTEM, 2018a). The use of "STEAM" is more popular in Korea. As Korean students showed high performance but very low interest in science and mathematics (Korea Institute of Curriculum and Evaluation, 2014a, 2014b), the integration of art and other disciplines was expected to raise students' interest in and understanding of science and problem-solving ability (Kim, Hong, Cho, & Im, 2013).

In the past, STEM education researchers in Asia have defined "STEM" as disciplines related to science, technology, engineering or mathematics, for instance, life and health sciences, computing and information sciences (Ishikawa, Fujii, & Moehle, 2013; Gao, 2013). In this study, "STEM" refers to integrated STEM, which is defined as "an effort to combine some or all of the four disciplines of science, technology, engineering, and mathematics into one class, unit, or lesson that is based on connections between the subjects and real-world problems" (Moore et al., 2014). What's more, in this study, the domain of STEM education is considered to include not only the four disciplines but also other disciplines such as arts, coding, computing and so on. "STEM" is therefore the equivalent of the other derived concepts such as "STEAM".

Conceptual Framework of the Chapter

This study uses the tripartite curriculum framework (including policy, programmatic and classroom levels) derived by Doyle (1992) and Westbury (2003, 2008) to examine the impact of national investment on STEM education in Asia. The policy curriculum is a "public" construction of what school and education should be and can build connections between the society's ideal expectations for future generations and schools' realistic practices with contemporary students. The programmatic curriculum defines the subject structure, the priority and weight, and the compulsory and optional content and is normally embodied through curriculum schemes and curriculum standards. The classroom curriculum, which is the final translation of the policy and programmatic curriculum, refers to the educational events that teachers and students implement together (Yao & Guo, 2018).

This study mainly utilizes a literature review to analyze the STEM education policies and practices in Asia. Information from the websites of government and semi-government institutions and from research articles is used.

Overview of Historical STEM Policy and Context for Asia

The Asian countries have realized the essential role of science, technology and mathematics in keeping pace with technological/engineering developments and to eliminate the threat of national defense (Ritz & Fan, 2015). After stepping into the 21st century, the continuous improvement of technology has been promoting the development of human society. New technologies are setting off a profound change affecting all aspects of human life and pushing human society forward into a new era. In order to maintain national competitiveness, some Asian countries have adopted different STEM development strategies.

China

The Chinese were known for their innovation and inventiveness in empirical technologies up until the 16th century. Afterwards, China experienced a stage of declining innovation capacity and stagnant technology development (Ministry of Science and Technology of the People's Republic of China, 2018). In recent decades, the Chinese government has made great endeavors to modernize and has become the world's second largest economy. According to the urgent need to build a well-to-do society and to develop internationally competitive manufacturing, the Chinese government has clearly seen the challenges and implemented a series of policies to improve science and technology (S&T) innovation (The State Council, P. R. of China, 2015).

The National Medium- and Long-Term Program for Science and Technology Development (2006–2020) (The State Council, P. R. of China, 2006) was formulated to call for China to develop into an innovative country, and to cope with a series of problems concerning the nation's economic growth, economic structure, employment, distribution, health care and national security. This program aims to enhance China's S&T and innovation capabilities, restructure Chinese industry through innovation, shift economic growth from investment-driven to innovation-driven, build a conservation-minded and environmentally friendly society and enhance independent innovation capabilities as a national priority. In 2016, the *Outline of the National Strategy on Innovation-Driven Development* (Ministry of Science and Technology, P.R. China, 2016) was issued. This is a top-level design and systemic plan for the implementation of the innovation–driven strategy. The Outline established the goals, direction and priorities for China's innovation-driven development in the next 30 years, and takes scientific and technological innovation as the core to promote innovation, which is considered as the first driving force for development.

Japan

In the 19th century, Japan began to assimilate technologies from abroad for modernization and industrialization. In 1995, the promulgation of the Science and Technology Basic Law gave the government legal competence in S&T (Yuko, 2001). Based on this law, the Japanese Cabinet formulated the first S&T Basic Plan in 1996 and aimed to upgrade the S&T throughout Japan by promoting research and development (R&D) activities with its resources (Government of Japan, 1996). New basic plans were then promulgated every five years.

After the promulgation of the First S&T Basic Plan, the Japanese government increased investment in R&D, and the number of researchers and scientific papers increased as well. In addition, Japan has the world's second highest number of Nobel Prize laureates in natural sciences in the 21st century (Government of Japan, 2016). This shows Japan's scientific and technological strength and international status. However, in recent years, Japan's ranking in S&T has been falling (Government of Japan, 2016). For example, the quality and quantity of scientific and technological papers in Japan have declined in international rankings. What's more, with the rapid development of information and communication technology, social and economic structure will experience great changes in the future. Japan realizes that scientific and technological innovation will play an increasingly prominent role in solving the future challenges.

To cope with these challenges, besides the promulgation of the long-term strategic guidelines "Innovation 25" in 2007, which aims at creating innovation in medicine, engineering, information technology and other fields before the year 2025, the latest promulgated policies were the Comprehensive Strategy on Science, Technology and Innovation (OECD Publishing, 2014) and the 5th S&T Basic Plan in 2016 (Government of Japan, 2016), which states that in the next 10 years, Japan will promote and implement the S&T innovation policy to become "the most innovation-friendly country in the world."

South Korea

South Korea's "rags-to-riches" development in the last century is considered as a miracle because it became the 12th largest economy in 1995 from one of the world's poorest countries in the 1960s (Campbell, 2012). In the 1960s, in order to change the backward development situation, South Korea chose the strategy of promoting economic development with the development of S&T and formulated a series of policies and measures (Campbell, 2012). After the 1990s, Korea entered the stage of improving innovation, and S&T innovation was developing at a high speed. South Korea has constantly readjusted its strategic plan and management system to adapt to the S&T development (Chung, 2011). The Framework Act on Science and Technology was enacted in 2001 and is the basis for guiding the development and innovation of S&T. According to this law, the Basic Plan for National Science and Technology was determined to be promulgated every five years.

In 2018, the 4th Basic Plan for National Science and Technology (2018–2022) was formally launched to change the lives of citizens through S&T. The specific tasks were pointed out as strengthening basic research to cope with the Fourth Industrial Revolution, revitalizing scientific exploration, and strengthening challenging research. What's more, the use of 120 kinds of technologies was emphasized to draw the blueprint of South Korea in 2040.

Singapore

Since Singapore's independence in 1965, it took only about 50 years to transform itself from a developing country with scarce natural resources to a thriving global economy. Singapore owes its success to many factors, research and innovation in S&T is one of the critical elements, because it is the best way to overcome the constraints of the country size and natural resources.

Before 1990, the development of indigenous R&D capabilities did not come to the Singapore government's attention. Singapore's technological upgrading mainly relied on technology transferred from foreign multinational corporations (Wong, 2003). After the 1990s, Singapore began to change the structure of its innovation system and S&T policies to meet the needs of global competition. In 1991, Singapore launched the first five-year S&T plan (National Technology Plan), and invested $2 billion to drive the development of S&T by cultivating the research ecosystem and culture, increasing research funding, training researchers and building infrastructure (Reuben, Lim, & Wong, 2018). The latest five-year S&T plan is the Research, Innovation and Enterprise 2020 Plan issued in 2016, which aimed "to develop a knowledge-based innovation-driven economy and society" (National Research Foundation, 2016), and $19 billion was committed to investment in four strategic technology domains, underpinned by three crosscutting programs. This plan is also a response to Singapore's Smart Nation Initiative launched in 2014, aiming at making Singapore the world's first Smart Nation by 2025 (Smart Nation and Digital Government Office, 2018).

To sum up, although there are different national problems to deal with in these four Asian countries, in this increasingly competitive world, they have reached a consensus that invention, development 'and profusion of new technologies through S&T are the fundamental source of economic progress, national security and future problems. The needs of national development in Asia are inevitably leading to changes in education.

The Impact of STEM Investment at the National Level in Asia

The investment in STEM fields is valued in Asia and brings a profound change to the demand for future labor; hence traditional education in Asia faces an unprecedented challenge. Based on investment in STEM fields, Asian countries have begun to adopt different STEM education policies and practices (see Table 33.1). However, due to historical and cultural reasons, school education in the four Asian countries has been focusing on single-discipline curricula. Although STEM practices have been explored and implemented progressively by a large number of educators, Asian countries

Table 33.1 National-Level Programs for STEM Education in Asia

Nation	Institutions Promoting STEM Education	Actions Promoting STEM Education
China	National Institute of Education Sciences (NIES)	China STEM Education 2029 Innovation Action Plan
Japan	Japan Society for STEM Education (JSTEM)	STEM activities
South Korea	Korean Ministry of Education, Science and Technology (MEST)	STEM education framework
	Korea Foundation for the Advancement of Science and Creativity (KOFAC)	Cultivating creative talents in S&T with integrated minds
Singapore	STEM Inc	STEM Applied Learning Programmes (ALP) STEM Industrial Partnership Programmes (IPP)

are still conservative when it comes to formulating and promulgating STEM education policies at a national level. In this section, we will introduce the STEM education at the policy, programmatic and classroom levels.

STEM Education at the Policy Level

China. In China, the Hong Kong SAR Government took the lead in implementing STEM education with the objective of nurturing diverse talents in relevant fields and enhancing Hong Kong's international competitiveness (Education Bureau, 2016). In mainland China, integrated STEM education has just entered the vision of the national curriculum.

In the national curriculum system, STEM education as an expanded form of science education needs further improvement. In primary schools, the promulgation of the newly revised *Science Curriculum Standards for Primary Schools* (Ministry of Education, P. R. of China, 2017) was viewed as a big move for STEM education (Yao & Guo, 2017; Liu, 2017), because "technology and engineering" were added into the science courses in primary schools as a main theme for the first time (Ministry of Education, P. R. of China, 2017a). In secondary and high schools, though STEM education has been divided into several disciplines (physics, chemistry, biology, geography, information technology, etc.), STEM education was mentioned and is explored in some of the disciplines. For example, exploring "interdisciplinary learning" was first proposed by the Ministry of Education in 2016 (Ministry of Education, P. R. of China, 2016), and then further requests for STEM education were made in the *13th Five-Year Plan for Education Informatization* (Center for Educational Information Management, Ministry of Education, 2016). It was advocated that information technology be applied to new educational modes such as interdisciplinary learning and innovative education. Moreover, in 2017 the *Ordinary High School Biology Curriculum Standard* proposed for the first time that students should participate in engineering tasks in biology learning (Ministry of Education, P. R. of China, 2017b).

Furthermore, China's national STEM education plan has just emerged and is still in its infancy. The National Institute of Education Sciences (NIES), the think tank of the Ministry of Education, is the most representative institution in promoting STEM education development in China. The NIES announced the *White Paper on STEM Education in China* (National Institute of Educational Sciences, P. R. of China, 2017), which analyzed the background and current situation of China's STEM education, and put forward the *China STEM Education 2029 Innovation Action Plan*. This plan was officially launched in 2018, aiming at serving the national innovation-driven development strategy, establishing a STEM education ecosystem in China through integrating social resources including government departments, scientific research institutes, high-tech enterprises, communities and schools. According to this plan, China will build a number of STEM education model schools and will cultivate innovative talents that are urgently needed for China's development. There are mainly six objectives for this plan: promoting the design of national STEM education policy; implementing a STEM personnel training plan; building a platform for resource integration and teacher training; constructing STEM education standards and an evaluation system; building an integrated STEM Innovation Ecosystem; and exploring the strategies of education and talent cultivation for economic development.

Japan. Although Japan has not enacted specific STEM education policies, STEM education has been valued and implemented in different ways. First, the "Integrated Studies" (IS) program was implemented by the MEXT (Ministry of Education, Culture, Sports, Science, and Technology) and has been gradually introduced in all schools from elementary to high schools since 1998 (Ogawa, 2001, 2008). The IS curriculum gave schools great flexibility to determine the lesson length, theme, materials and so on; students were encouraged to do their own unique investigations, and technology was incorporated into learning activities. Second, the MEXT launched the program of super science high school (SSH) as part of the "Science Literacy Enhancement Initiatives" in 2002. Schools prioritize science, technology and mathematics and can be awarded SSH status and aided by Japan Science and Technology Agency (MEXT, 2003). Third, computer programming will be a compulsory subject in Japanese primary schools from 2020 (MEXT, 2016). Last, STEM education was stated and discussed at many meetings of the MEXT since 2011 (MEXT, 2019), which also shows Japan's determination in developing STEM education.

Japanese researchers have made many efforts to explore integrated STEM education. Most noteworthy, the JSTEM was established to promote educational practices of the STEM field, including coding education, defining the next generation of STEM education and contributing to the development of 21st-century competencies by collaborating with academic societies overseas (JSTEM, 2018a). The JSTEM has conducted many activities to achieve these objectives. However, the government may need more evidence to prove that integrated STEM learning will become a fruitful way to improve students' knowledge, skills or abilities to survive in this complicated world and its future (Saito, Gunji, & Kumano, 2015). Japan still needs time to promulgate STEM policies at the national level.

South Korea. The first policy that emphasized STEM education in South Korea was *The Second Basic Plan to Foster and Support Human Resources in S&T (2011–2015)*, issued by the Korean Ministry of Education, Science and Technology (MEST) (Korean Ministry of Education, Science and Technology, 2011), which was formulated based on the Special Support Act for Science and Engineering for Improving National Competitiveness in 2004. The basic plans were stipulated to be initiated every five years. The second basic plan aimed at educating talents for a creativity-based economy by promoting STEM education. The STEM education strategies mainly include promoting STEM education in primary and secondary schools, as well as providing a research-friendly environment.

In 2011, MEST launched STEM education as a main policy for reorganizing the national curriculum and proposed a STEM education framework by working with the Korea Foundation for the Advancement of Science and Creativity (KOFAC), which is a government-affiliated organization and belongs to the Korean Ministry of Science and ICT. As the most representative national institution for promoting STEM education, KOFAC has managed systematic STEM education programs at the national level.

Singapore. In Singapore's education system, STEM-related disciplines, especially science and mathematics, are highly valued. Considering the performance of Singapore in both PISA and TIMSS in recent years, Singapore is one of the top-scoring countries in the world in both mathematics and science (Idris, Daud, Meng, & Eu, 2013). However, national policies for integrated STEM education have only recently been put on the government's agenda.

Singapore's Prime Minister has emphasized the importance of STEM education because the skills are crucial to Singapore for the next 50 years (Straits Times, 2015). To promote STEM education, the Ministry of Education (MOE) partnered with the Singapore Science Centre and established STEM Inc (Innovation and creativity, or Incorporation) in 2014. In order to ignite students' passion for STEM courses, raise students' aspirations in pursuing STEM careers, and uplift students' professional STEM career images, STEM Inc has launched two sets of programs, the STEM Applied Learning Programmes (ALP) and the STEM Industrial Partnership Programmes (IPP).

STEM Education at the Programmatic Curriculum Level

Although there are no specialized or comprehensive STEM curriculum standards at the national level in Asian countries, some local governments, semi-official institutions, universities and schools have been working on STEM curriculum standards. Of these four Asian countries, China and Korea have attempted in exploring such standards.

The Hong Kong SAR Government in China has proposed two STEM learning models, as well as suggestions and strategies to develop STEM education. However, the details of curriculum standards are still missing. After that, the NIES is taking actions in developing STEM curriculum standards with the help of Tsinghua University High School. In South Korea, the KOFAC proposed much more specific STEM curriculum standards (KOFAC, 2016), including the learning standards framework of the STEM lessons and a detailed STEM lesson checklist, which are recommended as a base to design and conduct STEM lessons. STEM education at the programmatic curriculum level in China and Korea is listed in Table 33.2.

STEM Education at the Classroom Curriculum Level

STEM education in Asia which emerges as school or extracurricular practices has gradually become a typical bottom-up paradigm of educational integration. In general, the gap between policy and practice still exists in most Asian countries. Compared to the conservative progress in making policies, STEM education research and practice in Asia in recent years has attracted the attention of the government and promoted the formulation of STEM education policy. STEM practices are mainly conducted by national institutions, local institutions, universities and schools as well as by education companies. This section mainly introduces the STEM practices conducted by national institutions depending on national investment in STEM education.

Most of the predominant national institutes in developing STEM education have developed kinds of STEM curricula. Firstly, NIES offered STEM courses to schools in several provinces of China. The STEM courses mainly include four types focusing on innovation, manufacturing, inquiry and verification. The themes of these courses are diverse, with some courses closely related to daily life, such as healthcare, environmental protection and transportation. Some courses involve the latest advanced technologies, such as 3D printing and simulation technology. In addition, these courses are designed based on STEM learning ecosystems, because government institutions, research institutions, industries, companies, schools and communities are involved in implementing these STEM courses. For example, the satellite course implemented in middle school invites professors from research institutions to give students lectures, and the satellite launch center will eventually launch the satellite designed by students into space (Shenzhen Press Group, 2018).

Secondly, as an important member of the JSTEM, the Children's Institute for the Future of Gakugei University has implemented three programs in promoting STEM education (JSTEM, 2018b). These included the promotion of STEM education in the Technology Department of junior high school with a new series of courses, "Technology Future", which have been launched in nearly 100 schools; the cooperation with private educational institutions in developing STEM teaching materials and curricula; and the workshop "STEM Quest Stadium" which aims to improve children's interest in STEM.

Thirdly, KOFAC researchers are exploring effective approaches and suitable content for STEM education in Korea. They offer four types of STEM projects to schools: integration-based programs for each theme of STEM, programs utilizing up-to-date products, programs with science and art integration and design-based programs connected to future careers. KOFAC also provides out-of-school STEM programs for students with the help of field experts from enterprises, laboratories and local governments. Vocational opportunities are provided for students in those programs. (Hong, 2017).

Fourthly, STEM Inc provides STEM curricula for schools through ALP and IPP. ALP usually targets students of year one and two in secondary schools and provides 12 types of courses (Asin & Alejandro, 2014). MOE and STEM Inc work closely with schools on deciding which specific domains they would choose as a focus to best suit students' needs in that school. IPP emphasizes the role played by industry and other social sectors in providing STEM career-related information to students. STEM Inc works together with industrial partners and provides career talks, organizes workshops where students can work to solve an industrial problem, provides STEMchat (web chat with STEM professionals), offers job shadowing and so on.

Table 33.2 Comparison of STEM Education in Asia

	China	Korea
Objective	Nurturing diverse talents in STEM-relevant fields and enhancing international competitiveness (Education Bureau, 2016).	Nurturing talents for integration (KOFAC, 2016).
Curriculum Form	STEM education is promoted mainly through current school courses, school-based curricula and extracurricular courses (Education Bureau, 2016; NIES, P. R. of China, 2017).	Integration-based programs for each theme of STEM; Programs to utilize up-to-date products; Integration-based programs in science and art; Design-based programs connected to promising future jobs (Hong, 2017).
Concept of STEM Education	1. Part of the national strategy of cultivating innovative talents; 2. National lifelong learning activities; 3. Interdisciplinary and coherent curriculum group from kindergarten to university; 4. Cultivating the comprehensive ability of all students; 5. An educational innovation practice participated in by the whole society (NIES, P. R. of China, 2017)	1. Increasing students' interest; 2. Connection to the real world; 3. Cultivation of integrated thinking abilities (KOFAC, 2016).
STEM Learning Framework	Model 1 Model 2 *Source:* Education Bureau, 2016 (p. 6)	 *Source:* KOFAC, 2016 (p. 25)

To conclude, STEM practices are developing extensively in the four Asian countries. The main features of STEM practice can be concluded as follows. First, a STEM learning ecosystem is emerging. In the four countries, useful STEM curricula are being designed and implemented with the integration of various social resources from governments, research institutions, universities, schools, museums, science centers, private companies and industries. Second, the themes of the STEM practices are related to the realities of the nations. Third, there is a lack of standardization and quality control of STEM courses.

Future Directions for STEM Education for Asia

According to the study of the impact of national investment on STEM education based on the three curriculum levels, the policy curriculum, programmatic curriculum and classroom curriculum, the potential future directions for STEM education for Asia can be speculated in the following aspects.

Initially, for the policy curriculum, in order to promote sustainable and healthy development of STEM education, the policy orientation should first be defined. Future research should further clarify the goal of STEM education, especially its complementary relationship with the national curriculum.

Further, for the programmatic curriculum, STEM curriculum standards should be promulgated as soon as possible to guide and evaluate the development of STEM curricula which meet the needs of Asian countries. The curriculum is expected to be carefully designed based on educational research to comply with students' progression in learning science, technology, engineering and mathematics.

Moreover, for the classroom curriculum, although national institutions conducted some STEM practices, currently the STEM curricula in schools are mainly explored and designed by teachers and STEM education companies. Teachers are reported to have difficulties in implementing and assessing STEM education (Ramli, Talib, Abdul Manaf, & Hassan, 2017). STEM learning resources for schools should be developed, national STEM curriculum should be published as a model and the STEM education market needs to be better regulated. Systematic teacher education programs is in need for equipping teachers with the necessary concept, skill for designing, conducting and evaluating STEM curricula.

Finally, a STEM learning ecosystem needs to be built, because the development of STEM education has to integrate multiple social resources, provide students with richer and more personalized learning resources, help students gain comprehensive understandings of STEM industries and professions and provide students with career-related experiences. A STEM learning ecosystem can also enhance the communication and cooperation of different nations, thus promoting the development of STEM education in Asia.

Conclusions

With importance and urgency of STEM education being gradually realized, the four countries in Asia have increased investments in STEM education over the past few decades. In the four Asian countries, actions have been undertaken to make and modify policies related to STEM education, and national programs have been launched to develop STEM education. Some semi-official institutions have started to explore STEM education practices, and the STEM curricula shows a tendency to establish STEM learning ecosystems. Future efforts should be made especially on detailing STEM education policies, promulgating STEM curriculum standards and creating STEM learning ecosystems.

References

Asin & Alejandro. (2014, November 17 Published). *Teaching STEM with real-world relevance in Singapore.* Retrieved from https://www.astc.org/astc-dimensions/teaching-stem-real-world-relevance-singapore/

Campbell, J. (2012). Building an IT economy: South Korean science and technology policy. *Issues in Technology and Innovation, 19.*

Center for Educational Information Management, Ministry of Education. (2016). *The 13th five-year plan for educational informatization.* Beijing. Retrieved from http://www.moe.gov.cn/srcsite/A16/s3342/201606/t20160622_269367.html

Chung, S. (2011). Innovation, competitiveness, and growth: Korean experiences. ABCDE, 333.

Doyle, W. (1992). Curriculum and pedagogy. In P. W. Jackson (Ed.), *Handbook of research on curriculum* (pp. 486–516). New York, NY: Macmillan.

Education Bureau, Hong Kong. (2016). *Driving STEM education - developing creative potential.* Retrieved from http://www.edb.gov.hk/attachment/tc/curriculum-development/renewal/STEM/STEM%20Overview_c.pdf

Gao, Y. (2013). *Report on China's STEM system.* Retrieved from http://www.acola.org.au/PDF/SAF02Consultants/Consultant%20Report%20- %20China.pdf

Government of Japan. (1996). *The first science and technology basic plan.* Tokyo. Retrieved from https://www8.cao.go.jp/cstp/english/basic/1st-BasicPlan_96-00.pdf

Government of Japan. (2016). *The 5th science and technology basic plan.* Tokyo. Retrieved from http://www8.cao.go.jp/cstp/english/basic/5thbasicplan.pdf

Hong, O. (2017). STEAM education in Korea: Current policies and future directions. *Policy Trajectories and Initiatives in STEM Education.* Retrieved from http://www.arpjournal.org/download/usr_downloadFile.do?requestedFile=2017122091496550.pdf&path=journal&tp=isdwn&seq=154

Idris, N., Daud, M., Meng, C., Eu, L. & Ariffin, A. (2013). *Country report Singapore STEM Consultant report: securing Australia's future: STEM: Country comparisons.* Melbourne: Australian Council of Learned Academies. Retrieved from http://www.acola.org.au/ACOLA/PDF/SAF02Consultants/Consultant%20Report%20-%20Singapore.pdf

Ishikawa, M., Fujii, S., & Moehle, A. (2013). *STEM country comparisons: Japan.* NCVER's international tertiary education research database.

Japan Society for STEM Education. (2018a). *About JSTEM.* Retrieved October 27, 2018, from, https://www.j-stem.jp/about/

Japan Society for STEM Education. (2018b). *Practice cases: Education for children to solve creative problems.* Retrieved January 11, 2019, from, https://www.j-stem.jp/features/interview_201809/

Kim, H. J., Hong, O., Cho, H., & Im, S. (2013). An analysis of change on science interest and self- directed learning through STEAM educational period. *Journal of Learner-Centered Curriculum and Instruction, 13*(3), 269–289.

Korea Foundation for the Advancement of Science and Creativity. (2015). *STEAM for future talent.* Seoul: KOFAC.

Korea Foundation for the Advancement of Science and Creativity. (2016). *Introduction to STEAM education.* Seoul: KOFAC.

Korea Institute of Curriculum and Evaluation. (2014a). *PISA 2012 main outcomes: Mathematics, reading, science and problem solving* (Vol. PIM 2014–12). Seoul: KICE.

Korea Institute of Curriculum and Evaluation. (2014b). *The trends in international mathematics and science study (TIMSS 2015): A technical report of the TIMSS 2015 field survey and the results* (Vol. RRE 2014–3-1). Seoul: KICE.

Korean Ministry of Education, Science and Technology. (2011). *The second basic plan to foster and support the human resources in science and technology (2011–2015).* Seoul: MEST.

Liu, E. S. (2017). The change and influence of the curriculum standards for primary school science. *People's Education,* (7), 46–49.

MEXT. (2003). *White paper on science and technology.* Retrieved January 17, 2019, from http://www.mext.go.jp/b_menu/hakusho/html/hpag200301/hpag200301_2_019.html

MEXT. (2016). *Programming education in the primary school stage.* Retrieved January 17, 2019, from http://www.mext.go.jp/b_menu/shingi/chousa/shotou/122/attach/1372525.htm

MEXT. (2019). *Council information.* Retrieved January 21, 2019, from http://www.mext.go.jp/b_menu/shingi/main_b5.htm

Ministry of Education, P. R. of China. (2016). *The 13th five-year plan for educational informatization.* Beijing. Retrieved from http://www.czimt.edu.cn/s/18/t/24/6d/96/info93590.htm

Ministry of Education, P. R. of China (2017a). *Science curriculum standards for primary school.* Beijing. Retrieved from http://www.moe.edu.cn/srcsite/A26/s8001/201702/W020170215542129302110.pdf

Ministry of Education, P. R. of China (2017b). *Ordinary high school biology curriculum standard.* Beijing. Retrieved from https://wenku.baidu.com/view/b8be582acbaedd3383c4bb4cf7ec4afe04a1b1d0.html

Ministry of Information and Communication, South Korea. (2018). *The fourth science and technology master plan.* Sejong City: Ministry of Information and Communication, Korea Science and Technology Corporation. Retrieved from http://www.ibric.org/myboard/read.php?Board=report&id=2984

Ministry of Science and Technology, P. R. of China. (2016). *Outline of the national strategy of innovation-driven development.* Beijing. Retrieved from http://www.moe.gov.cn/srcsite/A16/s3342/201606/t20160622_269367.html

Ministry of Science and Technology of the People's Republic of China. (2018). *Ancient China—brilliant achievements in science and technology.* Retrieved October 23, 2018, from http://www.most.gov.cn/kjfz/kjlc/

Moore, T. J., Stohlmann, M. S., Wang, H. H., Tank, K. M., Glancy, A. W., & Roehrig, G. H. (2014). Implementation and integration of engineering in K–12 STEM education. In *Engineering in pre-college settings: Synthesizing research, policy, and practices* (pp. 35–60). West Lafayette, IN: Purdue University Press.

Mullis, I. V. S., Martin, M. O., Foy, P., & Hooper, M. (2016). *TIMSS 2015 international results in mathematics.* Retrieved from Boston College, TIMSS & PIRLS International Study Center website: http://timssandpirls.bc.edu/timss2015/international-results/

National Institute of Educational Sciences, P. R. of China. (2017). *White paper on STEM education in China.* Beijing: Unpublished report from National Institute of Educational Sciences. Retrieved from http://beed.Asia/wpcontent/uploads/2017/06/%E4%B8%AD%E5%9B%BDSTEM%E6%95%99%E8%82%B2%E7%99%BD%E7%9A%AE%E4%B9%A6%EF%BC%88%E7%B2%BE%E5%8D%8E%E7%89%88%EF%BC%89.pdf

National Research Foundation. (2016). *Research, innovation and enterprise 2020 plan (RIE2020 Plan).* Prime Minister's Office, Singapore. Retrieved from http://www.nrf.gov.sg/research/rie2020

OECD. (2016). *PISA 2015 results (volume I): Excellence and equity in education.* Paris: PISA, OECD Publishing. Retrieved from https://doi.org/10.1787/9789264266490-en.

OECD. (2014). *OECD science, technology and industry outlook 2014.* Paris: OECD Publishing.

Ogawa, M. (2001). Reform Japanese style: Voyage into an unknown and chaotic future. *Science Education, 85*(5), 586–606.

Ogawa, M. (2008). *Science education Japanized and education of Japanese indigenous science.* Retrieved from https://www.researchgate.net/publication/279534945_Science_Education_Japanized_and_Education_of_Japanese_Indigenous_Science

Ramli, N. F., Talib, O., Abdul Manaf, U. K., & Hassan, S. A. (2017). Instructional approaches and challenges of STEM instructional implementation: A Systematic review. In *Graduate research in education seminar (GREduc 17)* Universiti Putra Malaysia.

Reuben, Ng, Lim, S. Q., & Wong, P. (2018). Singapore: 50 years of science and technology. Retrieved December 21, 2018, from, https://lkyspp.nus.edu.sg/gia/article/singapore-50-years-of-science-and-technology

Ritz, J. M., & Fan, S. C. (2015). Stem and technology education: International state-of-the-art. *International Journal of Technology & Design Education, 25*(4), 429–451.

Saito, T., Gunji, Y., & Kumano, Y. (2015). The problem about technology in STEM education: Some findings from action research on the professional development & integrated STEM lessons in informal fields. *K-12 STEM Education, 1*(2), 85–100.

Shenzhen Press Group. (2018). *Advanced science and technology was used in STEM courses in Futian Science and Technology Middle School.* Retrieved January 21, 2019, from, http://wb.sznews.com/MB/content/201807/10/content_412671.html

Smart Nation and Digital Government Office. (2018). *Smart nation progress.* Retrieved December 21, 2018, from, https://www.smartnation.sg/why-Smart-Nation/smart-nation-progress

STEM Inc. (2019). *About STEM Inc.* Retrieved January 2, 2019, from https://www.science.edu.sg/stem-inc/

Straits Times. (2015). *Science, technology, engineering, math skills crucial to Singapore for next 50 years: PM Lee.* Retrieved December 30, 2018, from, https://www.straitstimes.com/singapore/education/science-technology-engineering-math-skills-crucial-to-singapore-for-next-50

The State Council, P. R. of China. (2006). *The national medium- and long-term program for science and technology development (2006–2020).* Beijing. Retrieved from https://www.itu.int/en/ITU-D/Cybersecurity/Documents/National_Strategies_Repository/China_2006.pdf

The State Council, P. R. of China. (2015). *Made in China 2025.* Beijing. Retrieved from http://www.cittadellascienza.it/cina/wp-content/uploads/2017/02/IoT-ONE-Made-in-China-2025.pdf

Westbury, I. (2003). Curriculum, school: Overview. In J. W. Guthrie (Ed.), *The encyclopedia of education* (2nd ed., pp. 529–535). New York, NY: Macmillan.

Westbury, I. (2008). Making curricula: Why do states make curricula, and how? In F. M. Connelly, M. F. He, & J. Phillion (Eds.), *The sage handbook of curriculum and instruction* (pp. 45–65). Thousand Oaks, CA: Sage.

Wong, P. K. (2003). From using to creating technology: The evolution of Singapore's national innovation system and the changing role of public policy. *Competitiveness, FDI and Technological Activity in East Asia,* 191–238.

World Bank. (2018). *World Bank open data.* Retrieved October 27, 2018, from https://data.worldbank.org/

Yao, J. X., & Guo, Y. Y. (2017). The curriculum development and practical challenge of science education in primary school. *Curriculum, Teaching Material and Method, 37*(9), 98–102.

Yao, J. X., & Guo, Y. Y. (2018). Core competences and scientific literacy: The recent reform of the school science curriculum in China. *International Journal of Science Education, 40*(15), 1913–1933.

Yuko, H. (2001). *Japanese technology policy: History and a new perspective.* Tokyo: Research Institute of Economy, Trade and Industry.

34

STEM POLICY IN AUSTRALIA

David Ellis and P. John Williams

Political Warming Towards STEM

Australian educational researchers and practitioners of science, mathematics and technology education were initially introduced to the concept of STEM education through our engagement with international colleagues and publications. Arguably, prior to 2012, the explicit labelling of STEM as an educational concept didn't exist in Australia. However, as this section of the chapter will elaborate, motivated by international testing results, political postulating, economic goals and a protean future, politicians, and in turn educators, are beginning to develop an appetite for STEM. As a result, over a relatively short period of time, STEM as a foreign concept has become part of an Australian future economic solution. However, what this chapter reveals about STEM education in Australia, is that, not unlike other countries around the world, STEM in Australia is ill-defined, and neither interpreted nor implemented uniformly.

A political interest in STEM education in Australia didn't appear until the Chief Scientist, Professor Ian Chubb, produced the 'MES' report titled, 'Mathematics, Engineering & Science in the National Interest' (Australian Government, 2012), exhibiting a bias towards science, and to a lesser extent mathematics. According to Barlow and Ellis (2016), this was the foundation STEM document addressing the economic agenda that touted the need for an increased engagement in STEM in order for Australia to compete in a future economy (Carter, 2017). As "an adequate supply of people highly skilled in mathematics and science is critical for our future success" (Australian Government, 2012, p. 26), the document primarily focussed on addressing the trend of declining numbers of students enrolling in science and mathematics courses without any suggestion of an integrated STEM approach.

The following year, the Office of the Chief Scientist published a position paper titled, 'Science, Technology, Engineering and Mathematics in the National Interest: A Strategic Approach' (Australian Government, 2013). Similar to the previous document, the position paper presented the case for a need to increase enrolments and graduates in STEM; however, from a pedagogical perspective, the document proposed an "inquiry-based learning" (Australian Government, 2013, p. 13) approach with no suggestion of any integration of the STEM disciplines, but arguably, an elaboration that they are "distinct and complementary" (p. 24).

The following year, the Chief Scientist's 2014 paper was published, to build upon the developing case for STEM in the 2013 position paper, stating that "Australia is now the only country in the OECD not to have a current national strategy that bears on science and/ or technology and/ or innovation" (Australian Government, 2014, p. 10). It continued to state the importance for STEM to "build a stronger Australia with a competitive economy" (Australian Government, 2014, p. 6) by developing the capacity of Australians to participate in 'free market' activities, however with an appetite for students to engage in STEM from childhood. Outside a continued push for trained teachers, more graduates and better mathematics and science results, the concept of 'STEM skills' was introduced to replicate was also can be labelled as 'Soft' or '21st Century skills' that demonstrate creativity, critical thinking and communication, to name a few (van Laar, van Deursen, van Dijk, & de Haan, 2017; Hirsch, 2017). In what appears to be a consideration of other traditional 'disciplinary' pedagogies, as well as the inquiry-based approaches offered in science, the paper also mentioned the implementation of problem-based pedagogies and the application of knowledge in different contexts. Even though there were references to different contexts and 'real-world' topics, the political understanding of STEM at this point was that it was 'just an acronym' for distinct but complementary disciplines (Australian Government, 2014).

Endorsed by the Australian Education Ministers from the eight states and territories of Australia in 2015 was the anticipated 'National STEM School Education Strategy, 2016–2026'. This collaborative document published educational goals in an effort to develop Australian students (and their teachers) who are "more STEM capable" (Education Services Australia, 2015, p. 5) exhibiting the desirable 21st-century skills, and an improved mathematical and scientific literacy.

To achieve these educational goals, the strategy suggested that in order to encourage students to enrol in the STEM subjects at senior secondary and tertiary levels, exposure to STEM from early childhood will assist in developing students' 'foundational knowledge' to build upon, and to inspire their curiosity in STEM using "cross-disciplinary curriculum" (Education Services Australia, 2015, p. 5). This strategy presented a shift in the political discourse, from the use of the acronym of STEM to capture and label disciplinary knowledge and skills under a broad mathematical and scientific banner, to the consideration that STEM education could include a process that involves cross-disciplinary content and alternative, engaging pedagogies. These pedagogical comments indicated a change in focus from spruiking the need for STEM to the consideration of how these strategic goals may be achieved.

The endorsement of governmental STEM initiatives through a national plan became a mechanism for delivering on 'STEM goals' at both state and national levels as state and territory ministers began to provide support to coincide with national STEM initiatives. As Australia is a federation in which certain powers, such as education, are administered by the individual states (Birch, 1975), this was an expected pathway of implementation. As a result, resources aligned to STEM initiatives such as grants provided the opportunity for STEM initiatives to be implemented at not only a national level, but at a more localised state and territory level. We shall now discuss the realisation of these STEM initiatives.

Enabling STEM in Australia

Noted Tensions

In reference to the curriculum offered in Australia and the implementation of STEM programs, some tensions need to be addressed. Of these tensions discussed in this chapter, the first is the development of the Australian Curriculum, and the absence of STEM in that development.

To be fully implemented by January 2019, the national Australian Curriculum is the product of curriculum development that has been in progress since the Australian Education Ministers met in Hobart back in 1989 and produced the 'Hobart Declaration' outlining the goals of education (MYCEETA, 1998). With these educational goals in mind, STEM education being 'foreign' to the Australian Educational landscape was not a part of the political or education discourse. As the timing would have it, just when the development of the Australian Curriculum was being packaged into 'traditional' disciplinary Learning Areas, the Chief Scientist was spruiking his case for the increased engagement of students in STEM. This dichotomous inconsistency then developed so that STEM was, and still is, absent from the Australian Curriculum.

In terms of formal Learning Areas implicated in Australian STEM, Mathematics, Science and Technologies were three distinct Learning Areas, with Engineering content being included within these disciplines, and in some states, an Engineering subject with the Technologies Learning Area. However, a STEM curriculum has not been included in the development of the national Australian Curriculum.

Another noted tension is the attitude towards STEM by teachers, varying from concern as teachers feeling threatened by the inequity of STEM, or as an alternative to replace disciplinary subjects, to enthusiasm over the potential skills and knowledge that engagement in STEM can develop. As a result of this, both the tensions and the STEM initiatives that have been implemented will be discussed.

One would think that any STEM program, particularly an integrated STEM program, would be welcomed by technology educators due to the increased visibility of the discipline and recognition of the importance of engagement in technology education to develop student capacity. Unfortunately this is not the case, as some educators working within technology education have indicated that they feel threatened by STEM education. Exactly what seems to be a threat to concerned technology educators has not been adequately captured in the literature; however, the labelling of STEM programs that focus specifically on science and to a lesser degree mathematics concepts had not gone unnoticed by technology educators. This concern has also been perpetuated by the government documentation that uses the STEM acronym; however, its focus had not been specifically on an integrated approach to STEM education and tends to preference science. Research by Barlow and Ellis (2016) demonstrated that within the Australian Government's STEM publication, there was not an equitable focus on all of the disciplines.

Thirdly, another concern of STEM perceived by teachers are the limitations, or the narrowing effect in the Australian political discourse in STEM. Some concern has been the identified narrowing of science education to represent economic agendas, such as an increase in science graduates, or an improvement in PISA Scientific Rankings (Carter, 2017; Sharma, 2016), or based around a notion of innovative workforce competitiveness (Williams, 2011). Technology educators have also indicated that within STEM there has been a narrowing of what is understood as technology to the digital technologies process of coding, digital literacy and ICTs. Unlike the Standards for Technological Literacy (ITEA, 2007), this narrowing has also been reinforced with the only measure of technology education being ICT literacy, and the investment in digital technologies resources such as the 'Digital Technologies Hub' (Education Services Australia, 2017). Whilst this investment is good for student learning outcomes in digital technologies, it failed to invest in other aspects of technology education, such as the technological knowledge, and practice that incorporates 'design thinking' and making activities.

Some technology educators have stated that they are concerned that STEM has the potential to replace the discipline of technology education, and that a STEM focus is a vehicle for operating within leaner budgets, as the need for technology education's expensive machinery resources can be bypassed with makerspaces that are more suited for interdisciplinary STEM projects, compared to skills-focussed, project-based learning. Whilst there is no evidence of any truth to this concern, Australian educators had witnessed a decline in technology education in the United States (Brown, 2012), and in England (Barlex, 2015), which have both had an historic influence on Australian education. Also the steering committee who reviewed the 1999 Australian educational goals suggested that rather than exist as a separate discipline, that technology should be applied across other learning areas (Council for Australian Federation, 2007), however the reality is that the continued development of the Australian Curriculum ensured that Technologies was an independent learning area.

A final concern about the implementation of STEM in Australia is the lack of qualified teachers to teach STEM (Targeted News Service, 2018). As STEM is relatively new in Australian schools, it is not just qualified teachers who have been formally educated in the interdisciplinary concept of STEM, where the shortage exists, but also across the disciplines that make up STEM (Beanland, 2007). Educators are also concerned about the quality of STEM programs and whether these STEM programs are able to meet educational and enrolment objectives with teachers teaching out of field (Herbert & Hobbs, 2018). From a supply perspective, qualified teacher shortages are also a concern in other countries, such as the United States and the UK, where demand exceeds supply and issues such as gender bias and retention contribute to these shortages (Diekman & Benson-Greenwald, 2018; Kelley, 2010; Waite & McDonald, 2018).

Enthusiastic Uptake

Whilst some of the concerns regarding STEM in an Australian context have been noted, the discourse and activity is not all negative. The push for and implementation of STEM in schools continues to gain momentum, and many teachers have been enthusiastic to utilise the opportunities to implement STEM programs in schools. To support this Kennedy, Quinn and Lyons (2018) reported that in the year following the implementation of the National STEM School Education in 2015, there were reported to be over 250 extra-curricular school STEM programs across Australia in 2016. This uptake is in stark contrast to the tensions discussed, as this enthusiasm has been enabled by both public and private funding for STEM programs that have enabled various initiatives to be implemented in schools across the country. The various sources of funding have influenced the level of 'coordination' between these programs varies, with the degree of variation being attributable to the criteria (or focus) attached to the funding, the interpretation of STEM and implementation of STEM based on what is deemed appropriate for that particular educational setting. As a result, this diversity of STEM programs in Australia varies from early childhood through to higher education settings, as well as programs still labelled as a STEM program whether they are integrated or focus on a specific discipline. Due to this diversity, a broader discussion on the implementation of STEM in Australia will follow; however, it has been noted that the concept of integrated STEM is becoming more popular (Kennedy, Quinn, & Lyons, 2018). The discussion will now look at the how the funding was focussed and allocated to address specific STEM objectives.

In 2015, as STEM was still an acronym used by policymakers to reference the need for science and mathematics graduates, the National Education STEM strategy was supported by the Australian government's 'National Innovation and Science Agenda' (2015). The agenda publicly announced its financial commitment to STEM through the funding of two major initiatives such as the 'Early Learning STEM initiatives' ($14 million), and the 'Embracing the Digital Age' school initiative ($51 million) (Australian Government, 2019). This funding supported the message touted in the public press and presented by the Chief Scientist that students needed to engage in STEM from early childhood, and to provide students with an opportunity to develop 21st-century skills such as coding (Australian Government, 2009). The new Australian Curriculum Technologies structure for students from F (Foundation) to Year 10 introduced the subject of Digital Technologies. This new subject mandated all primary (elementary) school teachers and secondary technology teachers to teach content incorporating concepts such as computational thinking, and to develop student skills in coding, data representation and developing algorithms to name a few (ACARA 2015). As teacher capacity was an identified area of concern (Sharma & Yarlagadda, 2018; Education Services Australia, 2015), along with primary teachers tending to be educated as generalist teachers (Cordova, Eaton, & Taylor, 2011), it was anticipated that they would be challenged by the new content. As a result, a significant amount of federal funding was allocated to digital technologies support, such as the Digital Technologies Hub website and the Digital Technologies MOOCs offer free teacher professional development in this area (Vivian, Falkner, & Falkner, 2014). This investment in teacher professional development was an attempt to address the concerns previously discussed in terms of teacher knowledge and teachers teaching out of field (Du Plessis, 2018).

Published on the Office of the Chief Scientist's website, the STARportal is "Australia's first centralised national portal for exciting and engaging STEM activities from around the country" (Australian Government, 2019). In the period between its establishment in 2017 and March 2018, more than 500 STEM activities were registered on the site. The STARportal site was developed not only to inform parents and support teachers and their students with a centralised repository to access STEM activities, but also a way of connecting schools and teachers with STEM-related industries. From a neoliberal viewpoint, this link between industry and education has been seen as an effective way for education to be contextualised so students develop not only disciplinary knowledge, but enterprise skills (Education Council, 2018).

The focus of funding initiatives for STEM in Australia revolve around strategies that develop and maintain a sustainable 'pipeline' of young Australians who are prepared to enter into the various STEM-related fields (Timms, Moyle, Weldon, & Mitchell, 2018) as they progress through schooling and into higher education. It is from the perspective of 'supply' that governments at all levels are either developing or supporting the implementation of STEM initiatives in an effort to stop any 'leaks' in the pipeline from individuals shying away from STEM fields (Feeney, 2018).

The Gender Gap in Australian STEM

One focus on Australian STEM funding has been on the inspiration, encouragement and objective to address the 'leak' in the number of students engaging in STEM including addressing the 'gender gap'. A similar problem faced around the world is that research has shown that girls are as capable as boys in maths and science (National Science Board, 2018); however, women are not equitably represented in STEM fields in Australia. In an effort to support gender equity in the STEM fields the government has invested in programs that celebrated women in STEM to inspire and encourage girls to develop both confidence and reduce gender bias due to stereotyping.

Allocated in the 2018–19 federal budget was $4.5 million to develop a plan to encourage more women to pursue STEM education (Australian Government, 2019). The development of this plan was a collaborative project undertaken by the Australian Academy of Science and the Australian Academy of Technology and Engineering, who collaborated to develop a Women in Science, Technology, Engineering and Mathematics (STEM) Decadal Plan. The consultation part of this plan began in September 2018, with the aim to not only increase women's participation in STEM, but to sustain it (Australian Academy of Science, 2019).

The Science in Australia Gender Equity (SAGE) initiative was developed to improve the equity outcomes for women in science and research fields (Australian Academy of Science, 2015). As a result, the SAGE network is currently trialling the adoption of the Athena SWAN Charter Accreditation Framework based on the process developed in the UK (SAGE, 2019). The overall aim is creating an impact within the higher education sector to ensure that there are action plans in place that encourage gender equity. The charter has reportedly grown since its introduction in the UK in 2005, and it is hoped that the framework will also replicate this impact in Australia (Australian Academy of Science, 2015; Keenihan, 2018).

Other gender-based initiatives include the showcasing of inspirational women who are excelling in STEM fields. This strategy is undertaken across Australia at both national and state levels. Examples of these showcases include the 'Superstars of STEM' showcase. This initiative by the organisation Science & Technology Australia chooses to celebrate inspirational Australian women in an attempt to break down gender biases (Science & Technology Australia, 2019). Another federal strategy was the appointment of astrophysicist Professor Lisa Harvey-Smith in October 2018 as Australia's first

'Women in STEM Ambassador'. In her two-year tenure, Professor Harvey-Smith has been an inspirational and visible advocate for social and cultural change towards gender equity in STEM (Australian Government, 2018). At a more localised state and territory level, to inspire girls in choosing to STEM subjects at school and at university, some states aim to inspire girls and young women using strategies that push back at STEM gender stereotypes. Examples of these types of strategies is the Queensland Women in STEM Prize. The Queensland government provides three cash prizes of $5000 to showcase inspiring women in STEM.

Indigenous Students and STEM

Another identified 'leak' in the STEM pipeline is the engagement of indigenous Australians in STEM. According the 2018 report by the Education Council, indigenous students are "underrepresented in the STEM workforce" (p. 21). Similar to the gender gap, there is an identified gap between indigenous and non-indigenous students when it comes to science and mathematics achievement outcomes taken from international testing (Education Council, 2018). Currently, initiatives to close this gap have come from digital technologies content strategies that either improve teacher and student knowledge, such as the federally funded CSER MOOCs delivered by the University of Adelaide (University of Adelaide, 2019), or from other online resources such as the STARportal or the Digital Technologies Hub. Not just specific to indigenous students, these professional learning courses and digital resources are also aimed to assist other students in need, such as students from remote or low socioeconomic backgrounds (Timms et al., 2018).

It has been suggested that a student's geography (for example, living 'remote') and their financial situation are contributing factors that may discourage indigenous students from engaging in STEM programs, and that Australia should look to other countries such as New Zealand for examples of bicultural curriculum (TKI, 2012), and to Canada for solutions to engage indigenous students in STEM (McKinley, 2016). STEM programs that aim to be 'culturally responsive' rather than culturally competitive may assist teachers to develop positive teacher, student, parent and community relationships. From this perspective, student-centred pedagogies that are inclusive of cultural knowledge or prior experiences, or mitigate the "discontinuity between the home cultures of the students" (Boon & Lewthwaite, 2016, p. 456) and the school, may be beneficial.

A program that has been culturally responsive in its use of role models in STEM, and its strategy to develop the 'pipeline', was the Indigenous STEM Education project that was privately funded by the BHP Billiton Foundation in 2014. Whilst still ongoing, the first evaluation report indicates that from the perspective of culturally responsive pedagogies, the enquiry-based pedagogies common to science are more consistent with indigenous ways of learning, and that there is a closing of the gap between indigenous and non-indigenous students due to indigenous students' contextualised interest in science (Tynan & Noon, 2017). One exemplary pedagogical practice is that of 'two-way science', described by David Broun from the Commonwealth Scientific and Industrial Research Organisation (CSIRO) as "an approach that connects the traditional ecological knowledge of Aboriginal people—that is the cultural understanding of people, animals and the environment—with western science inquiry, and links that to the Australian Curriculum in a learning program" (ACARA, 2019, p. 1). Similar to the strategies used to close the gender gap, in an effort to inspire indigenous students, the Indigenous STEM Awards were implemented in 2016 to profile high-achieving primary and secondary school students.

The access to funding has encouraged Australia's appetite for STEM. As discussed previously, due to the criteria attached to funding, the types of STEM education programs have been determined by the documented educational and political goals. The broader goals of teacher expertise contributing to student achievement and securing the supply of STEM graduates have been the major focus of funding initiatives since 2014. Exactly how these funded initiatives are translated at the coalface will be discussed in the next section. As there are a vast number of STEM education programs (over 500) on the STARportal repository alone, the uptake of STEM is continuing to expand. In the next section, specific examples of STEM education programs will be elaborated on.

Examples of How STEM Is Being Realised in Australian Educational Settings

STEM education in Australia is not confined to a particular level or education such as Primary (Elementary) or secondary classroom, nor is it constrained to school hours. Whilst Australia was slow to warm to STEM, compared to the USA and the UK, to develop and maintain a 'pipeline' of STEM graduates, STEM education programs are currently found in all levels of education. However, its implementation has manifested in the dyads of either curricular or extra-curricular approaches, or that of integrated STEM, or a program from one or more of the STEM disciplines. This next section will discuss a dyad that has emerged as STEM is being implemented as either a curricular approach or an extra-curricular approach to STEM. The chapter will elaborate on this dyad of STEM implementation using examples from early childhood (EC) through to higher education STEM programs.

Curricular Approaches

In this discussion on curricular approaches, the interpretation taken by the authors aligns with the work of Schwab (1969) and Grundy (1987) in that the curriculum is process or action between the four commonplaces of the teachers, students, environment and subject matter. In this chapter the subject matter from a curricular perspective is the formal documented content or learning outcomes that guide teaching and learning activities. As a result of this position, the dyads of discipline-specific and integrated STEM will be discussed from a 'curricular' perspective of the mandatory, or formal subject matter that teachers are required to teach.

It has been recognised that a challenge to the implementation of STEM and the depth of student learning outcomes is the expertise of the teacher (Prinsley & Johnston, 2015; Hattie, 2003). It has also been recognised that Australian primary (elementary) school teachers tend to be 'generalist' in their formal education as they are expected to teach all subjects across the curriculum (Cordova et al., 2011). To improve student STEM learning outcomes, there has been a call to introduce STEM specialist teachers in primary schools in order to "introduce the foundational ideas and practices early" (Call for specialist STEM teachers from primary up, 2019). Whilst these reports indicate that 'generalist' primary school teachers who teach across the curriculum was a limitation to realising STEM educational goals (Prinsley & Johnston, 2015), the versatility that having one teacher teaching across the curriculum provides makes integrated STEM much easier to implement in primary schools (Cafarella, McCulloch, & Bell, 2017). Compared to secondary schools, primary school settings don't have the added complexity of organising specialist teachers, or the rotation of classes around the availability of specialist teachers. As a result, support is available for enthusiastic primary teachers who are keen to deliver STEM from both a disciplinary and integrated perspective. Whilst the argument for an integrated approach to STEM seeks to address 21st-century skills and enables students to understand the 'real-world' significance of STEM (ACARA, 2016), there are also arguments for any approach that seeks to develop "foundational numeracy and scientific proficiency" (PwC, 2016, p. 8) as the antecedent to integrated STEM.

Based on a disciplinary focus of science in STEM, the primary schools resource titled 'Primary Connections' is an online program with a focus on the teaching of science (Australian Academy of Science, n.d.). The resource, developed by the Australian Academy of Science back in 2005, was supported through an injection of funding from the 2015 National Innovation and Science Agenda. Directly aligned to all of the science strands in the Australian Curriculum, the program can be categorised as a curricular approach focussed on the science within STEM. The program incorporates an inquiry-based approach using the 5Es constructivist model to develop identified 21st-century skills (Bybee, 2009). Whilst not an integrated approach from a STEM perspective or aligned to a design process framework, the phases of the 5E model do incorporate a social-cultural constructivist perspective (Skamp & Peers, 2012) which aligns with the desired 'soft' or 21st-century skills. Whilst the use of the 5E pedagogical approach is said to reform science pedagogical practices, evaluations of the program have been positive; however, teachers should expect to invest the time to understand the theoretical underpinnings of the approach (Skamp & Peers, 2012).

In Australia, the secondary school curriculum is segregated along the traditional disciplinary divisions. The subjects that the students engage in is often dependent on factors such as the student's year or grade from 7 to 12, and the state or territory, as well as the system of education (i.e. Catholic, Independent or Government). In most secondary contexts, students attend multiple lessons a day depending on their individualised timetable. Each timetable consists of a number of lessons that are specific to the individual disciplines that they are required to study.

In Australia, the curriculum is implemented and administered by each state or territory. 'What' students are required to learn is specified in the curriculum document called a syllabus, developed externally to schools by either the national (ACARA) or state or territory curriculum authority. Like many other countries around the world (Molstad & Kareseth, 2016), the contemporary curriculum in Australia consists of prescribed content and learning outcomes that are packaged into individual disciplinary courses. This level of specificity constrains the role of Australian teachers to that of workers that deliver rather than develop the curriculum. A consequence of having a prescribed curriculum is the increased level of accountability placed on teachers to cover the specified disciplinary content by the end of a course. As a result, this accountability, the constraints of prescribed curriculum and a finite amount of time contribute can impede teachers looking to extend student learning beyond the traditional secondary disciplinary boundaries, in an effort to contextualise abstract scientific and mathematics concepts. Unfortunately, in the busy world of a full-time teacher, these perceived impediments may discourage some teachers from engaging in secondary STEM programs.

Fortunately, regardless of the challenges, some teachers do still have an appetite for STEM and have both planned for and implemented STEM programs in their schools. As there is no mandated secondary STEM curriculum in Australia, and with a degree of uncertainty regarding what STEM is or should be, STEM programs continue to be offered in secondary schools. It is how these programs are realised that is of interest in this chapter. We will view an authentic STEM experience as an integrated approach that incorporates the three disciplines of science, mathematics and technology, using project- or problem-based learning approaches that 'engineer' solutions to address identified needs. To elaborate on whether STEM in Australian secondary schools is authentic, we will discuss what has been happening in schools using examples of actual STEM programs.

In an observation of the University of Sydney's STEM Teacher Enrichment Program, the author had observed that of the secondary schools who participated in the integrated STEM program, fewer schools chose to adopt a curricular approach to STEM instead offering an extra-curricular STEM program. The teachers involved in these approaches indicated that within the period of the program, the additional work required to identify disciplinary outcomes, align these to STEM activities, and generate time for STEM in the daily timetable was quite a challenge. To facilitate the 'space' for STEM within the timetable, some teachers reported that a 'donation' of lessons from the science, maths and technology classes enabled the room for STEM in the timetable. And to ensure that there weren't gaps in prescribed disciplinary content, or that specific outcomes were not repeated, the planning activities in these approaches required the additional administrative activities to track or 'map' which disciplines the outcomes were addressing. From an accountability perspective, this approach ensured that the prescribed discipline content was still being addressed.

As the non-elective curricular approach requires each discipline to donate lessons to the STEM program, the observed realities of this approach tended towards the lesson being taught by the teacher from the discipline who 'was' timetabled on at that time. As students move from class to class in their normal school day, there are some maths, science and technology lessons that are pitched as STEM classes, and at other times they are their 'normal' disciplinary classes. From an accountability perspective, this STEM implementation strategy ensured that students continue to engage deeply in discipline-specific content, using traditional pedagogies as well as the problem and project-based pedagogies common to engineering processes. What has been noted as beneficial with this approach to STEM is that the contextualised disciplinary content is taught by the subject-matter experts who possess the depth of knowledge required to support students in their engagement in the STEM program.

In the most populous state of Australia, New South Wales, an example of a curricular and integrated STEM program is offered as an elective course in the form of a 'Board Endorsed' (curriculum authority approved) course called iSTEM, meaning integrated STEM (Regional Development Australia's Hunter region, 2013). As a Board Endorsed course, the course syllabus, originally developed by Maitland Grossmann High School in conjunction with Regional Development Australia's Hunter Valley region in 2013 to showcase the employment opportunities in the defence industry through experience in the Defence Industry Skilling Program (DISP) (Regional Develop Australia's Hunter region, 2019). Since its inception in 2013, there are 135 schools offering the iSTEM program, indicating that the program is appealing to schools across the state of New South Wales.

Tertiary STEM is generally reported on in terms of student enrolments at Australian universities. In the 'Broad Fields of Education', such as engineering and related technologies, agriculture, IT and the natural and physical Sciences to name a few. In an analysis of the data from the period 2002 to 2015, the number of enrolments in the STEM fields had grown by 32%; however, this growth was not as much as the other non-STEM fields (Dobson, 2018). Beyond compulsory secondary education, there is also a gender gap in STEM. In non-STEM fields, 61% of higher education enrolments are women; however, in the STEM fields their enrolments are just 32% (Dobson, 2018). Rather than this discussion being limited to the enrolment patterns of students at Australian universities, it will take an alternative route to focus on tertiary programs that will have the greatest impact on Australian STEM—the development of STEM educators. Therefore, this chapter will discuss the formal education of STEM in teacher education programs in Australia.

Prior to STEM being part of the educational discourse in Australia, it had already been noted that there was an undersupply of qualified mathematics and science teachers both in Australia and abroad (OECD, 2012). This lack of qualified teachers has also contributed to the concept of 'out-of-field teaching' as a 'band-aid' solution to teacher shortages (Du Plessis, 2018; Weldon, 2016) where teachers have no qualification or background (Hobbs & Torner, 2019). Emanating from the Chief Scientists papers in 2012–14, the growing impetus for STEM education in Australia demanded an adequate number of qualified and capable STEM teachers (Prinsley & Johnston, 2015). Different from the disciplinary under- and post-graduate programs that are commonly delivered at universities, to meet these demands, tertiary education providers have begun to offer formal STEM teacher education around the country. Examples include postgraduate Graduate Certificate of STEM Education courses, and Master of Education in STEM Education.

A final point in the discussion of curricular implementation of STEM education is the planning and implementation of programs that focus on the provision of STEM professional learning to in-service teachers. Teaching standards, and teacher registration and accreditation requirements linked to the 'professionalisation of teaching', have resulted in 'endorsed' professional learning programs that are linked to specific curriculum outcomes. In order for the STEM professional learning programs to be endorsed, they may focus on particular formal curriculum content. As an example using the Australian Professional Teaching Standard 2, 'Know the content and how to teach it' (AITSL, 2011), teacher professional learning providers (such as teacher associations or private businesses) will target professional learning to address specific outcomes from a syllabus. Over the last few year, a focus on digital technologies has witnessed providers address digital technologies concepts such as algorithms and processes such as programming. From an integrated STEM perspective, the STEM Teacher Enrichment Academy run by the University of Sydney hosts STEM-specific professional learning courses for both primary and secondary educators. Whilst the STEM programs developed by the schools could be curricular or extra-curricular to suit the needs of the students at their school, the professional learning itself by this provider adopted a philosophy of integrated STEM (University of Sydney, 2017).

Extra-Curricular Approaches

In this chapter, the interpretation of extra-curricular STEM programs align with Clegg, Stevenson, & Willott's (2010) notion of activities that 'value-add' or are in addition to the formal curriculum. It is common for schools and other educational organisations (inclusive of private businesses hosting STEM courses/workshops) to offer STEM enrichment activities that are offered 'in addition' to students' normal courses of study. Extra-curricular approaches to STEM in Australia are common, as these programs are easily catered for outside of 'normal' school hours, not constrained by resource availability and timetabling issues. Being an extra-curricular activity, they enable opportunities for students to deepen their knowledge beyond what is normally offered during school hours, or to encourage participation by providing opportunities for engagement. In some instances, these programs are voluntary; however, there are instances where participation of the whole cohort is expected. The discussion will begin with voluntary extra-curricular STEM education.

Play-based learning as well as hands-on learning experiences are common to, and encouraged in, Australian early childhood education settings where play is seen to provide a "supportive environment where children can ask questions, solve problems and engage in critical thinking" (Australian Government, 2009, p. 17). These pedagogical approaches align with those traditionally used in technology and engineering education which make up the T and the E in the STEM acronym as students create knowledge 'by doing' (Tang & Williams, in press).

Even though there is no explicit STEM in the national Early Years Learning Framework that prescribes national learning outcomes, some of these outcomes align with those typical to STEM education. This is not surprising considering the framework was first published in 2009; however, the document was recently modified in March 2019, with no mention of STEM. Examples of these outcomes include the development of skills and processes such as problem solving, experimentation, researching and hypothesizing as well as the engagement in activities that promote the use of ICTs and explore ideas and the purpose of tools (Australian Government, 2009). After 2013, when STEM was starting to gain traction in political discourse, early childhood education was identified as part of the Australian government's National Innovation and Science Agenda and endeavoured to motivate educational environments to "inspire curiosity and engagement in STEM concepts" (Lowrie, Leonard, & Fitzgerald, 2018, p. 3; Australian Government, 2015).

To encourage this, the Australian government tendered the pilot Early Learning STEM Australia (ELSA) project in 2017 (Simoncini & Lasen, 2018). This voluntary project, run by the University of Canberra, has been influenced by the 2017 Tasmanian STEM Framework that emphasises an interdisciplinary approach to teaching and learning (Tasmanian Government, 2017). Considering this, a paper published on the ELSA pilot by Lowrie et al. (2018) concluded that the framework used was based on the conclusion that integrated STEM was "not particularly useful for early learning design" (p. 2), and as a result, modified a design process to suit early learning environments to that of an "experience, represent, apply" heuristic (Janssen, Westbroek, & Doyle, 2014). Related research into the use of digital tools among early learners supported this result as it did not lead to significant learning gains (Mattoon, Bates, Shifflet, Lathan, & Ennis, 2015; Miller, 2018). The 2018 pilot project included 100 Early Childhood centres which provided an opportunity for over 1700 children to engage in the STEM program involving four "highly engaging early learning apps" (Lowrie et al., 2018, p. 3). The pilot program was extended and continued in 2019 (ELSA, 2019).

Research has suggested that girls' interests in STEM decrease during adolescence (Stoeger et al., 2016). Two unrelated examples are non-integrated STEM programs that encourage girls to get involved in STEM and are labelled as the 'Girl Power' camps. The 'STEM Girl Power Camp' was supported by funding from the Queensland government (Queensland Government, 2016) in March 2018. It targeted 58 Year 10 girls and incorporated activities to build upon their existing experiences in STEM, such as the opportunity to undertake activities in research laboratories and networking with leading experts and role models (Queensland Government, 2019). Using a strategy to ensure that the pathway from school to university is visible, the University of Melbourne's School of Engineering also offers a 'Girl Power' program; however, this program hosted at the university offers 'staged' programs targeting girls in Year 9, Year 10 and Years 11 and 12.

Inspired by the 2015 Education Council's National STEM School Education Strategy to "facilitate effective partnerships" (Education Services Australia, 2015, p. 6) between education providers and industry, a direct pipeline between school students and industry employers, the New South Wales Department of Education funded the STEM Industry School Partnerships Program (SISP) focusing on the transition years from Year 5 to Year 8. In this program, participating schools are matched with industry partners to collaborate in providing activities that are contextualised and 'age-appropriate' (NSW Department of Education, 2017).

Observed by one of the authors since 2014, were some examples of secondary integrated STEM programs developed with the assistance of the University of Sydney's privately funded STEM Teacher Enrichment Academy that provides professional learning to teachers from the STEM disciplines. As there is no formal separate engineering Learning Area in secondary education, school teams of teachers from the three disciplines of science, technology and mathematics apply to be a part of the program each year. To assist schools in the planning and implementing a successful integrated STEM program, school teams attend formal workshops to "develop a draft plan for implementation of STEM strategies within and across disciplines" (The University of Sydney, 2019); then with the guidance of a mentor assigned to each school, they implement their STEM program, and complete their program with the presentation of their evaluation. Evaluation comments collected by the author indicated that some schools identified that the task of mapping, and reallocating specific disciplinary curriculum outcomes to embed them in a dedicated STEM program would be unachievable at this stage of their engagement in STEM. As a result, school teams with this mindset chose to implement their school STEM program as an extra-curricular activity implemented at a one-off STEM event, or as a program that ran over a number of days. Another example of this approach is the 'STEM in Schools' Event hosted by the CSIRO during National Science Week since 2017 (CSIRO, n.d.). Through the planning and implementation of STEM programs that sits outside the standard disciplinary curriculum, schools with an appetite to introduce integrated STEM, or enrichment activities in the various disciplines of STEM, use these events to 'trial' STEM education.

This discussion of extra-curricular STEM implementation will conclude with teacher professional learning. Whilst some professional development programs target teacher expertise in the curriculum, other programs sit outside the curriculum and exist based on deepening subject matter, or disciplinary expertise. The differing definitions of STEM (Timms et al., 2018), appear to provide 'degrees of freedom' for teachers to engage in STEM teacher education. One approach enables teachers to engage with disciplinary teacher professional associations, attending annual conferences or teacher professional learning events such as the 2018 Design and Technology Teachers' Association Australia (DATTA) Conference (DATTA Australia, 2018). Whilst considered important 'STEM-related' knowledge that would benefit technology educators, the presentations are not chosen to specifically align with particular technology education curriculum outcomes. As a result conference participants exercise a degree of autonomy in their selection and attendance of presentations. From this perspective, autonomy can enable teachers to exercise their individual STEM interests. One could argue that this may be a solution to keeping them engaged in Australian STEM (Scheicher, 2018).

Conclusion

Compared to other countries around the world, uptake in the implementation of STEM education programs in Australia has been relatively slow. The original impetus for STEM education programs in Australia has been a political one, grounded in economic values of competitiveness dated as late as 2012. It was not until 2014, until the political discourse had begun to transform into educational policy. Following this, potential STEM initiatives, which were reliant on funding, had to wait for Australian governments to attached financial resources to STEM initiatives. The majority of these initiatives have resulted in STEM funding to address Australian STEM issues such as gender gaps, indigenous gaps and poor student outcomes in maths and science. Outside of the school education, other initiatives have aimed to focus in improving teacher expertise in STEM and boosting the number of graduates in the STEM fields.

The discussion has noted the timing of the implementation of a national Australian Curriculum (AC). Twenty-five years in the making, the AC was designed around specific (disciplinary) learning areas. As a result, the thoughts around an interdisciplinary approach to education and increasing educational accountability have initially constrained STEM, but it is starting to gain momentum in Australian schools. The observed examples of STEM programs implemented in Australian schools tend to be manifested around two specific dyads: the integrated verses the discipline focused models of STEM, and the curricular verses the extra-curricular modes of implementation. Given the timeframe, it is too early to tell whether these initiatives will satisfy Australia's educational goals; however from a STEM educator's perspective, it is pleasing to see STEM education being visible in both educational as well as political discourse.

References

ACARA. (2015). *Australian curriculum: Technologies key ideas*. Sydney: Australian Curriculum and Reporting Authority. Retrieved from Australian Curriculum: https://www.australiancurriculum.edu.au/f-10-curriculum/technologies/key-ideas/

ACARA. (2016). *ACARA STEM connections project report*. Australian Curriculum Assessment and Reporting Authority.

ACARA. (2019, March 19). *Two-way science*. Retrieved from Australian Curriculum: https://www.acara.edu.au/docs/default-source/Media-Releases/20190318-two-way-science-media-release.pdf?sfvrsn=2

AITSL. (2011). *Australian professional standards for teachers*. Retrieved from https://www.aitsl.edu.au/docs/default-source/apst-resources/australian_professional_standard_for_teachers_final.pdf

Australian Academy of Science. (2015). *Science in Australia gender equity forum gender equity in science workshop - November 2014 Summary of workshop findings*. Canberra. Retrieved from https://www.sciencegenderequity.org.au/wp-content/uploads/2015/10/SAGE-Forum-Workshop-2014-Summary_Report.pdf

Australian Academy of Science. (2019, March 28). *Scope*. Retrieved from Women in STEM Decadal Plan: https://aas.eventsair.com/women-in-stem/scope

Australian Academy of Science. (n.d.). *About primary connections*. Retrieved March 27, 2019, from, Primary Connections: https://www.primaryconnections.org.au/about

Australian Government. (2009). *Belonging, being & becoming the early years learning framework for Australia*. Canberra: Department of Education and Training.

Australian Government. (2012). *Mathematics, engineering & science in the national interest*. Office of the Chief Scientist, Canberra. Retrieved from https://www.chiefscientist.gov.au/wp-content/uploads/Office-of-the-Chief-Scientist-MES-Report-8-May-2012.pdf

Australian Government. (2013). *Science, technology, engineering and mathematics in the national interest: A strategic approach*. Office of the Chief Scientist. Canberra: Author.

Australian Government. (2014). *Science, technology, engineering and mathematics: Australia's future*. Canberra: Office of the Chief Scientist.

Australian Government. (2015). *National innovation and science agenda report*. Department of the Prime Minister and Cabinet. Canberra: Commonwealth of Australia. Retrieved from National Innovation and Science Agenda: https://www.innovation.gov.au/page/national-innovation-and-science-agenda-report

Australian Government. (2018, October 19). *Australia's first women in STEM ambassador*. Retrieved from Department of Industry, Innovation and Science: https://www.industry.gov.au/news-media/science-news/australias-first-women-in-stem-ambassador

Australian Government. (2019, February 28). *Support for science, technology, engineering and mathematics (STEM)*. Retrieved from Department of Education and Training: https://www.education.gov.au/support-science-technology-engineering-and-mathematics

Australian Government. (2019, March 15). *About us*. (Office of the Chief Scientist) Retrieved from STARportal: https://www.starportal.edu.au/about-star-portal

Australian Government. (2019, March 28). *A 10-year plan for women in STEM*. Retrieved from Ministers for the Department of Industry, Innovation and Science: https://www.minister.industry.gov.au/ministers/karenandrews/media-releases/10-year-plan-women-stem

Barlex, D. (2015). Design & Technology in England: Currently we are in difficult times but there is a light at the end of the tunnel. *Institute of Industrial Arts Technology Education Journal, 5*(1), 12–26.

Barlow, J., & Ellis, D. (2016). Are the T and the E dimensions being recognised in the Australian STEM education discourse? In H. Middleton (Ed.), *Creating contexts for learning in technology education* (pp. 8–14). Adelaide: The Design and Technology Association of Australia.

Beanland, D. (2007, December). The future of schooling from a STEM perspective. *ASTE Focus* (147), 12–13. Retrieved from https://www.atse.org.au/wp-content/uploads/2019/02/Focus-issue-147.pdf

Birch, I. K. (1975). *Constitutional responsibility for education in Australia*. Canberra: Australian National University Press.

Boon, H. J., & Lewthwaite, B. E. (2016). Signatures of quality teaching for Indigenous students. *Australian Educational Researcher, 43*, 453–471. doi:10.1007/s13384-016-0209-4

Brown, T. T. (2012, May 30). *The death of shop class and America's skilled workforce*. Retrieved from Forbes: https://www.forbes.com/sites/tarabrown/2012/05/30/the-death-of-shop-class-and-americas-high-skilled-workforce/#5e9c3ffb541f

Bybee, R. W. (2009). *The BSCS 5E instructional model and 21st century skills*. National Academies Board on Science Education.

Cafarella, J., McCulloch, A., & Bell, P. (2017, 1). *Why do we need to teach science in elementary school?* Retrieved from STEM teaching tools: http://stemteachingtools.org/brief/43

Call for specialist STEM teachers from primary up. (2019, 3 28). Retrieved from Engineers Australia: https://www.engineersaustralia.org.au/News/call-specialist-stem-teachers-primary

Carter, L. (2017). Neoliberalism and STEM education: Some Australian policy discourse. *Canadian Journal of Science Mathematics and Technology Education, 17*(4), 247–257. doi:10.1080/14926156.2017.1380868

Clegg, S., Stevenson, J., & Willott, J. (2010). Staff conceptions of curricular and extracurricular activities in higher education. *Higher Education, 59*, 615–626. doi:10.1007/s10734-009-9269-y

Cordova, J., Eaton, V., & Taylor, K. (2011). Experiences in computer science wonderland: A success story with Alice. *Journal of Computing Sciences in Colleges, 26*(5), 16–22.

Council for Australian Federation. (2007). *Federalism paper 2: The future of schooling in Australia. A report by the states and territories*. Retrieved from http://education.qld.gov.au/publication/production/reports/pdfs/2007/federalist-paper.pdf

CSIRO. (n.d.). *STEM in schools 2018*. Retrieved April 1, 2019, from Commonwealth Scientific and Industrial Research Organisation: https://www.csiro.au/en/Education/Community-engagement/National-Science-Week-2018/STEM-in-schools-2018

DATTA Australia. (2018, December 6). *2018 conference*. Retrieved from Design & Technology Teachers Association Australia: http://dattaaustralia.com/2018conference

Diekman, A. B., & Benson-Greenwald, T. M. (2018). Fixing STEM workforce and teacher shortages: How goal congruity can inform individuals and institutions. *Policy Insights from the Behavioral and Brain Sciences, 5*(1), 11–18. doi:10.1177/2372732217747889

Dobson, I. R. (2018). *STEM in Australia: The statistical patterns of university science and technology in the twenty-first century*. Ballarat West: Australian XCouncil of Deans of Science 2018.

Du Plessis, A. E. (2018). The lived experience of out-of-field STEM teachers: A quandary for strategising quality teaching in STEM? *Research in Science Education*, 1–35. doi:10.1007%2Fs11165-018-9740-9

Education Council. (2018). *Optimising STEM industry-school partnerships: Inspiring Australia's next generation final report*. Carlton South: Education Services Australia.

Education Services Australia. (2015). *National STEM school education strategy, 2016–2026*. Education Council.

Education Services Australia. (2017, March 10). *Digital Technologies Hub media release*. Retrieved from Education Services Australia: https://www.esa.edu.au/solutions/our-solutions/digital-technologies-hub/digital-technologies-hub-media-release

ELSA. (2019, March 28). *2019 ELSA pilot*. Retrieved from Early Learning STEM Australia: https://elsa.edu.au/2019-pilot/

Feeney, M. K. (2018, October 6). *Why more women don't win science nobles*. Retrieved from The Conversation: https://theconversation.com/why-more-women-dont-win-science-nobels-104370

Grundy, S. (1987). *Curriculum: Product or praxis?* London: Falmer Press.

Hattie, J. A. (2003). *Teachers make a difference: What is the research evidence?* Melbourne: ACER. Retrieved from https://research.acer.edu.au/research_conference_2003/4

Herbert, S., & Hobbs, L. (2018). Pre-service teachers' views of school-based approaches to pre-service primary science teacher education. *Research in Science Education, 48*(4), 777–809. doi:10.1007/s11165-016-9587-x

Hirsch, B. J. (2017). Wanted: Soft skills for today's jobs. *Phi Delta Kappan, 98*(5), 12–17. doi:10.1177/0031721717690359

Hobbs, L., & Torner, G. (2019). *Examining the phenomenon of "teaching out-of-field"*. Singapore: Springer.

ITEA. (2007). *Standards for technological literacy: Content for the study of technology*. Retrieved from https://www.iteea.org/File.aspx?id=67767&v=b26b7852

Janssen, F., Westbroek, H., & Doyle, W. (2014). Practicality studies: How to move from what works in principle to what works in practice. *Journal of the Learning Sciences, 24*(1), 176–186. doi:10.1080/10508406.2014.954751

Keenihan, S. (2018, December 5). *New awards, new ambassador: Australian women in STEM look in 2019*. Retrieved from The Conversation: https://theconversation.com/new-awards-new-ambassador-australian-women-in-stem-look-to-2019-108247

Kelley, T. (2010). Staking the claim for the 'T' in STEM. *Journal of Technology Studies, 36*(1), 2–11.

Kennedy, J., Quinn, F., & Lyons, T. (2018). Australian enrolment trends in technology and engineering: Putting the T and E back into school STEM. *International Journal of Design and Technology Education, 28*, 553–571. doi:10.1007/s10798-016-9394-8

Lowrie, T., Leonard, S., & Fitzgerald, R. (2018). STEM practices: A translational framework for large-scale STEM education design. *Educational Design Research, 2*(1), 1–20. doi:dx.doi.org/10.15460/eder.2.1.1243

Mattoon, C., Bates, A., Shifflet, R., Lathan, N., & Ennis, S. (2015). Examining computational skills in pre-kindergarteners: The effects of traditional and digital manipulatives in a prekindergarten classroom. *Early Childhood Research and Practice, 17*(1). Retrieved from http://ecrp.uiuc.edu/v17n1/mattoon.html

McKinley, E. (2016). STEM and Indigenous learners. *2009–2018 ACER Research Conference, 14*, pp. 64–68. Melbourne.

Miller, T. (2018). Developing numeracy skills using interactive technology in a play-based learning environment. *International Journal of STEM Education, 5*(39). doi:10.1186/s40594-018-0135-2

Molstad, C. E., & Kareseth, B. (2016). National curricula in Norway and Finland: The role of learning outcomes. *European Educational Research Journal, 15*(3), 329–344. doi:10.1177/1474904116639311

MCEETYA. (1998). *Australia's common and agreed goals for schooling in the twenty first century: A review of the 1989 common and agreed goals for schooling in Australia ('The 'Hobart Declaration')*. Melbourne. Retrieved from http://www.curriculum.edu.au/verve/_resources/natgoals_file.pdf

MCEETYA. (2008). *Melbourne declaration on educational goals for all Australians*. Melbourne: Ministerial Council on Education, Employment, Training and Youth Affairs.

National Science Board. (2018). *Science and engineering indicators*. Arlington. Retrieved from https://nsf.gov/statistics/2018/nsb20181/assets/nsb20181.pdf

NSW Department of Education. (2017). *STEM industry school partnerships (SISP)*. Retrieved from STEM NSW: http://stem-nsw.com.au/leading-stem/sisp

OECD. (2012). *Preparing teachers and developing school leaders for the 21st century: Lessons from around the world*. Paris: OECD Publishing. Retrieved from https://www.oecd.org/site/eduistp2012/49850576.pdf

Prinsley, R., & Johnston, E. (2015, December). *Transforming STEM teaching in Australian primary schools: Everybody's business*. Office of the Chief Scientist.

PwC. (2016). *Making STEM a primary priority*. Retrieved from PwC Australia: https://www.pwc.com.au/publications/education-stem-primary-priority.html

Queensland Government. (2016). *Advancing education: An action plan for education in Queensland*. Brisbane: Department of Education and Training.

Queensland Government. (2019, March 27). *STEM girl power*. Retrieved from STEM Hub: https://learningplace.eq.edu.au/cx/resources/file/5da759ed-285d-4132-b8e8-58198109fb03/1/html/girl-power.html

Regional Development Australia's Hunter region. (2013, November 5). *iSTEM course ready to go*. Retrieved from ME Program: http://www.meprogram.com.au/istem-course-ready-to-go/

Regional Development Australia's Hunter region. (2019, March 4). *ME program*. Retrieved from The Defence Industry Skilling Program (DISP): http://www.meprogram.com.au/meprograms/defence-industry-skilling-program/

SAGE. (2019, March 28). *The Athena SWAN accreditation framework*. Retrieved from Science in Australia Gender Equity: https://www.sciencegenderequity.org.au/the-athena-swan-accreditation-framework/

Scheicher, A. (2018, November 6). *'Want to improve education? Give teachers professional freedom'*. Retrieved from https://www.tes.com/news/want-improve-education-give-teachers-professional-freedom

Schwab, J. J. (1969). The practical: A language for curriculum. *The School Review, 78*(1), 591–621.

Science & Technology Australia. (2019, March 28). *2019 superstars of STEM*. Retrieved from Science and Technology Australia: https://scienceandtechnologyaustralia.org.au/list/2019-superstars/

Sharma, J. (2016). STEM-ification of education: The zombie reformstrikes again. *Journal for Activist Science & Technology Education, 7*(1), 42–51. Retrieved from https://jps.library.utoronto.ca/index.php/jaste/article/view/26826/19850

Sharma, J., & Yarlagadda, P. K. (2018). Perspectives of 'STEM education and policies' for the development of a skilled workforce in Australia and India. *International Journal of Science Education, 40*(16), 1999–2022. doi:10.1080/09500693.2018.1517239

Simoncini, K., & Lasen, M. (2018). Ideas about STEM among Australian early childhood professionals: How important is STEM in early childhood education? *50*, 353–369. doi:10.1007/s13158-018-0229-5

Skamp, K., & Peers, S. (2012). Implementation of science based on the 5E learning model: Insights from teacher feedback on trial Primary Connections units. *Australasian Science Education Research Association Conference, 27–30 June*. Sunshine Coast: Australian Academy of Science. Retrieved from https://www.primaryconnections.org.au/research-and-evaluation

Stoeger, H., Schirner, S., Laemmle, L., Obergriesser, S., Heilemann, M., & Ziegler, A. (2016, August). A contextual perspective on talented female participants and their development in extracurricular STEM programs. *Annals of the New York Academy of Sciences, 1377*(Beyond the IQ Test), pp. 53–66.

Tang, K.-S., & Williams, P. J. (in press). STEM literacy or literacies? Examining the empirical basis of these constructs. *Review of Education*. doi:10.1002/rev3.3162

Targeted News Service. (2018, July 9). *Birmingham's STEM solution shortcut a thought-bubble*. Washington, DC: Targeted News Service.

Tasmanian Government. (2017). *STEM framework*. Retrieved from STEM: https://stem.education.tas.gov.au/framework/

Timms, M., Moyle, K., Weldon, P., & Mitchell, P. (2018). *Challenges in STEM learning in Australian schools: Literature and policy review*. Camberwell: Australian Council for Educational Research.

TKI. (2012). *The New Zealand curriculum*. Retrieved from Ministry of Education: http://nzcurriculum.tki.org.nz/The-New-Zealand-Curriculum#collapsible5

Tynan, M., & Noon, K. (2017). *Indigenous STEM education project first evaluation report September 2014-June 2016*. Canberra: CSIRO.

University of Adelaide. (2019, March 28). *CSER professional learning program*. Retrieved from CSER Digital Technologies Education: https://csermoocs.adelaide.edu.au/professional-learning/

University of Sydney. (2017, May 8). *Structure*. Retrieved from STEM Teacher Enrichment Academy: http://sydney.edu.au/stem/academy/program/primary/structure.shtml

University of Sydney. (2019, March 3). *Program structure*. Retrieved from STEM Teacher Enrichment Academy: http://sydney.edu.au/stem/academy/program/structure.shtml

van Laar, E., van Deursen, A. J., van Dijk, J. A., & de Haan, J. (2017). The relation between 21st-century skills and digital skills: A systematic literature review. *Computer in Human Behaviour, 72*, 577–588. doi:10.1016/j.chb.2017.03.010

Vivian, R., Falkner, K., & Falkner, N. (2014). Addressing the challenges of a new digital technologies curriculum: MOOCs as a scalable solution for teacher professional development. *Research in Learning Technology, 22*, 1–19.

Waite, A. M., & McDonald, K. S. (2018). Exploring challenges and solutions facing STEM careers in the 21st century: A human resource development perspective. *Advances in Developing Human Resources, 21*(1), 3–15. doi:10.1177/1523422318814482

Weldon, P. R. (2016, June). Out-of-field teaching in Australian secondary schools. *Policy Insights*(6). Retrieved from https://research.acer.edu.au/cgi/viewcontent.cgi?article=1005&context=policyinsights

Williams, P. J. (2011). STEM education: Proceed with caution. *Design and Technology Education: An International Journal, 16*(1). Retrieved from https://ojs.lboro.ac.uk/DATE/article/view/1590

35

LATIN AMERICAN STEM POLICY

A Review of Recent Initiatives on STEM Education in four Latin American Countries

Martín Bascopé, Kristina Reiss, Mayte Morales, Claudia Robles, Pilar Reyes, Mauricio Ismael Duque and Juan Carlos Andrade

Introduction

In 2017 representatives from universities and NGOs of Chile, Perú, Colombia, México and Germany launched the "Pacific-Alliance for STEM Education", as a joint effort to promote the installation of STEM education in these Latin American countries. Their own national initiatives started separately in 2011, with the objective to promote innovative ways to teach STEM education in the countries, nowadays reaching more than 2.900 teachers from 816 preschools and schools, and approximately 280.000 students from ages 3 to 15.

Addressing the field of STEM education explicitly is a new challenge in Latin American countries. In particular, it is not yet an important issue at the policy level. Hence, research in this topic is not sufficiently developed. The following chapter combines a literature review with an expert review made by practitioners of four different countries with more than ten years' working experience in STEM education. It is based not only on research but also on evidence provided by the official webpages of the different initiatives, showing also examples of new and not completely documented initiatives recently launched.

The experience to carry out STEM professional development programs in different countries implied an interdisciplinary and multi-sectorial effort, combining public and private actors and dealing with different policy frameworks to install each program. Considering the experience of the practitioners, a comparative K-12 education policy analysis is presented in the chapter. For each country, the chapter considers: (1) existence and recent development of national standards and accountability mechanisms, comparing subject-based versus STEM education guidelines; (2) description of the main professional development and support initiatives; and (3) existence of territorial multi-sectorial alliances to foster STEM education.

We start with a description of the macro policy by describing the four educational systems and their educational results, policy environments, and curricular guidelines related to STEM. After that, we describe some public/private STEM initiatives in each country, classifying them into three groups by the characteristics of these initiatives: Inquiry-based science education programs, STEM education for gender equality, and place-based STEM education. Besides these specific programs, we mention and describe STEM territorial movements with multiple and diverse participants, coming from academia as well as from the public and private sectors in each country.

With the description of the different programs and STEM territorial movements, we give a wide picture of what policy and the civil society has built particularly in the last decade. However, the educational systems analyzed still lack proper evaluations and well-structured long-term national policies on STEM. National and cross-national movements from the civil society on STEM education are arising with partial public support, but there is still the need for more activities in the STEM area. It is an urgent demand not only to improve STEM education but to bring it into the different territories of these countries.

Overview of Historical STEM Policy and Context for Chile, Colombia, México and Perú

Latin American Educational Results and Policy Contexts

Until the 1990s the focus of educational policy in Latin America was still on educational coverage, and the main objective of the systems was that students achieved basic skills in mathematics and reading, rather than higher-order skills. Quality and diversification of educational opportunities are relatively new concepts, emerging from the fact that quality issues have to be considered in order to meet new local and global challenges.

Unfortunately, Latin American countries have systematically achieved low scores in international educational tests. In particular, the four countries analyzed here performed below average in studies like the Program for International Student Assessment (PISA) (OECD, 2016). Whereas the OECD average score was 493 (SD = 94) in science, students in Chile scored 447, in Colombia and México 416, and in Perú 397. Interpreting the standard deviation as three years of schooling suggests a difference of up to three years between the OECD average and Latin American countries in academic performance. Nevertheless, if we look only at the Latin American region, the four countries analyzed here can be considered with medium to high scores and with strong policy environments (Fiszbein & Stanton, 2018).

PISA not only describes differences in academic performance between countries or economies but also provides data within countries with respect, e.g., to socioeconomic status and gender, which are regarded as key features of inequality. However, data available from different sources are not entirely consistent. Thus, the World Development Report (World Bank, 2018) suggests that children from families with a low socioeconomic background show a lower achievement level compared to their peers from more privileged families.

Based on TERCE (Third Regional Comparative and Explanatory Study) conducted in 2013, the data reveal that children from an underprivileged background have a far higher chance to be poor readers (UNESCO, 2015). In Chile, the difference may be described by the factor 2 and is comparably low. In México and Colombia, chances for poorer children are about eight times higher to score low in reading, while in Perú, the difference is larger than a factor 10. PISA provides a somehow different picture. With respect to science, data from PISA 2015 show no significant differences regarding socioeconomic status compared to the OECD average for Chile and Colombia and indicate that México lies above average in this respect meaning that socioeconomic status hardly affects students' achievement.

Regarding gender differences, PISA 2015 provides more similar results and state that girls in all four countries score below boys in science (OECD, 2016). The differences are 14 points in Chile, 10 in Colombia and Perú and 8 in México. All these differences are above the OECD average of 4, meaning that gender differences in these countries are higher than in most OECD countries. Moreover, in Colombia, Chile and Perú, more girls than boys show a very low achievement below level 2 of 5. There is no significant difference in México. Moreover, boys and girls do not differ, e.g., in their self-efficacy, meaning that they are similarly confident in their problem-solving skills with respect to science (OECD, 2016).

There has been some progress, but things move slowly and there are even setbacks. As stated earlier, Chile, Colombia, México and Perú performed below the OECD average in science in PISA 2015.

However, all countries showed improved results as rated by average increase during the three-year period between 2012 and 2015. For Colombia (+8) and Perú (+14), this increase was significant. Other interesting data for Colombia state that the mean performance in science improved significantly between 2006 and 2015 by 28 points. During the same period, the share of high-performing students (level 4 or higher) stayed unchanged in the four countries, whereas the share of low-performing students (level 1 or lower) decreased considerably. Moreover, In Chile and México between 2006 and 2015, students' socioeconomic status became less predictive of science performance, while these countries' average levels of achievement remained stable. Colombia maintained equity levels while improving average science performance. Between 2000 and 2015, equity related to reading performance improved in Chile and México and equity related to mathematics improved in México (OECD, 2016).

Curricular Changes and Standards Towards Integrated STEM Educational Opportunities

Recent changes in national curriculum had shown a significant move towards more integrated learning, but without explicitly mentioning STEM as a concept. The international educational movement, to affront the challenges of the 21st century, implies a change in the educational systems towards a more creative, integrated and innovative way of learning, to develop skills such as creativity, communication, critical thinking and collaboration (Australian Government, 2016; Freeman, Marginson, & Russel, 2015; Royal Academy of engineering, 2016; UNESCO, 2017; World Economic Forum, 2017).

For more than two decades, some sectors in Colombia have insisted on the inconvenience of having a mandatory national curriculum despite the evidence that exists about the inappropriateness of this situation (Mourshed, Chijioke, & Barber, 2010). The country abandoned the national curriculum at the beginning of the 1990s under the premise that each educational institution in its autonomy should generate its own curricula in coherence with the context.

Given the poor results of this policy, since educational institutions and teachers do not have the training to take on this task, the Ministry of Education has tried to correct this situation with several series of documents in the areas of natural sciences, social sciences, mathematics and language, which have been superimposed on each other: curricular guidelines (MEN, 1998a, 1998b), quality standards (MEN, 2004), basic learning rights (MEN, 2015) and curricular meshes (MEN, 2017). These documents are only recommendations, although national standardized tests are designed based on them. On the other hand, there is an important level of inconsistency between these documents, which complicates their application.

Specifically on a STEM approach, Colombia does not have any official document that indicates guidelines. In addition to the previous documents, a guidance document for technology education was generated in 2008, but like the previous ones, it is not mandatory. Perú has a very recent change in their curriculum towards competences, after a whole history of a content-based curriculum. In the presentation of the National Curriculum for Primary Education in Perú, it is mentioned that this document prioritizes values and civic education, as well as the development of competencies that allow responding to the demands of current times such as proficiency in the English language, education for work and ICT (Ministerio de Educación, 2016).

In this sense, the Peruvian Ministry of Education develops the "Graduate Profile" in regular primary education as the common and integral vision of the learning that students must achieve at the end of primary education. This vision allows us to unify criteria and establish a path towards common results that respect our social, cultural and geographical diversity (Ministerio de Educación, 2016). This "Graduate Profile" was designed based on the following approaches: Rights, Inclusive, Intercultural, Gender Equality, Environmental issues, Oriented to the common good and Search for excellence.

The National Curriculum specifies explicitly the aim for a comprehensive, integrated and applied education where skills and competences are highlighted at the same level as knowledge-contents. STEAM being a competency-based approach to solving problems, the competencies prioritized in the Peruvian Curriculum show the alignment with the STEAM approach, which focuses on the challenging and changing 21st century (Ministerio de Educación, 2016).

In México, curriculum for elementary and middle school education is mandatory nationwide. It considers all the subjects and topics to be covered by teachers during the scholar year but emphasizes language and math contents as the core. Every scholar year pupils in public schools get a set of textbooks whose content is made and defined by a group of disciplinary experts invited by the National Ministry of Education. Teachers plan their instruction based on the curriculum provided with few opportunities to implement innovative approaches that could enhance a more active role of students during their instruction. When teachers decide to implement other practices or programs, they do so despite knowing their students will be evaluated on the official curricular content. This condition doesn't allow facilitating or encouraging of the implementation of STEM practices into the classrooms.

Besides, every new federal administration launches its own educational reform without a formal assessment about what is working and worth keeping. Since 2006 Mexican official curriculum for elementary and secondary education has been changed three times. The last reform, launched during the last federal administration (2012–2018), was profound and impacted the whole educational system; it took time, a large amount of public funds and lobbying among the different political parties. However, the new federal government which started in 2019 has announced a cancelation of the reform, nowadays teachers don't know what will be keep or what will be discarded. So, Mexican curricular reforms did not have the impact inside the classroom and rather responds to political compromises and agendas (Guerra, 2012).

In Chile in the last 20 years, there have being three major curriculum changes for primary and secondary science education. From 2003 to 2009, the natural science curriculum was centered in units about biology, chemistry and physics as well as science skills (Mineduc, 1998). Then in 2009, the Minister of Education presented some adaptations that changed the way to make progress with scientific core ideas, as a spiral, where the lower level was the base to go deeper within the next levels of education (Mineduc, 2009). The last change was presented in 2012, titled "Bases Curriculares" [Curricular Basis] (Mineduc, 2012). This document groups several disciplines—biology, chemistry, physics, botany, geology and astronomy—that address a wide variety of natural phenomena: living beings, matter, energy and its transformations, the solar system and Earth. Also, it is imperative that students complement the understanding of science's "big ideas" with the development of research skills, which enables them to undertake scientific projects in the school context. Therefore, the procedures are particularly important and inherent to scientific activity, such as problem solving, the formulation of hypotheses, systematic observation, conducting experiments, recording and analyzing information and putting in common of ideas collectively (Harlen, 2010).

Summing up, the curricular guidelines in Chile give space to foster an integrated STEM scope for the following reasons: for the formative value intrinsic to the enthusiasm, amazement and personal satisfaction that can come from understanding and learning about nature in a holistic way. Because the forms of thought typical of scientific research are increasingly demanded in personal, work and socio-political contexts of contemporary life, and because the scientific knowledge of nature leads to an attitude of respect and care for it. (Mineduc, 1998).

Micro Policy: Implementation of STEM Initiatives

A great variety of specific STEM programs had arisen in the last five years in the four countries considered in this chapter, with different focus and objectives but sharing an idea of the importance of promoting science-integrated and practice-based learning experiences of the school curriculum. Even though STEM as a concept is still scarce at the policy level, there are several arguments aligned to different policies and public programs to sustain the importance of implementing this integrated focus. The importance of the inclusion of women to science, critical citizenship, prepared workforce for the new markets and educational opportunities for all are frequent arguments in the official documents.

In the following sections we will revise examples of different STEM programs developed in the four countries, in public/private alliances in the recent years. These programs consider in-service and pre-service teacher training and teachers' professional development opportunities, as well as initiatives focused directly on working with students.

We made a classification showing three kinds of programs, according with their main objective: (1) programs fostering an integrated inquiry-based science approach; (2) programs aiming to narrow the gender gap on STEM; and (3) programs focused on giving more contextualized place-based opportunities on STEM to foster integration of disciplines towards concrete and real problems in the schools and their surroundings. We use this systematization to clarify the motivations behind the STEM programs in the countries reviewed, and to understand the perspectives about integrated sciences behind the different public/private endeavors on STEM in the four Latin American countries.

Integrated Inquiry–Based Science Education. The inquiry-based science education (IBSE) approach has been very popular at the policy level in the four countries studied and somehow has been the first step towards the implementation of STEM programs. The STEM acronym is relatively new for the region, and many of the former initiatives has been transiting form IBSE to an inquiry-based approach on STEM, leaving behind the natural sciences disciplinary approach that dominated in the early 2000s. The following paragraphs will briefly enunciate some of the initiatives in the four countries to understand this transit and will give details about the guidelines for the implementation of each program.

The Pequeños Científicos (Little Scientist) program started in Colombia in 1999 and has achieved high national and international acknowledgment. The program seeks to renew experimental science and technology teaching and learning in Colombia. Several institutions have been involved in the Pequeños Científicos program: 10 Colombian universities, Maloka Science and Technology Museum in Bogotá, the French Embassy, National Science Academy and several private foundations.

The program introduces active learning, applying IBSE as the pedagogical approach. The program understands that disciplines have their own nature and particular ways of building knowledge, and that it is necessary for students to recognize the points of contact between different disciplines but also the specificities of each knowledge area.

Considering the definition and the fundamentals of scientific inquiry, Pequeños Científicos has adapted this information to the Colombian context and developed four frameworks: (1) a Professional Development framework, based on the state of art on teachers, including situated professional development, effective workshops, mentoring and follow-up; (2) a learning assessment framework proposed by several researchers in science evaluation, focused on formative and summative assessment tools; (3) an IBSE framework based on four domains of scientific literacy; and (4) a curriculum framework based on guided inquiry, represented in IBSE guides for teachers covering different subjects (Duque, Hernández, Gómez, & Vásquez, 2011; Carulla, Duque, Molano, & Hernández, 2007).

In 2008 the Pequeños Científicos program expanded its spectrum of action to promote STEM education. To this end, it entered into collaboration with Canada, in order to appropriate teaching strategies that have led the Quebec region to take third place in mathematics in the world in the PISA 2015 test, as a result of the reform carried out at the beginning of the century (O'Grady, Deussing, Scerbina, Fung, & Muhe, 2016). In 2018 the program changed its name to STEM-Academia, coordinated from the Colombian Academy of Sciences.[1]

A second program, the PAUTA program, is promoted by scientists and researchers from the National Autonomous University of México (UNAM) with the purpose of encouraging scientific vocations and creating spaces where children can experience science in a different way.[2] To develop scientific skills in Mexican children, PAUTA offers a set of extracurricular educational activities such as science workshops, science clubs, support with scholarships to indigenous girls and women with outstanding skills, as well as links with the scientific community, accompaniment to networks of families and pedagogical schools. PAUTA has been recognized as an exemplary STEM practice by the STEM Program of the Organization of American States.

Another initiative in México is the SEVIC Program promoted by the Civil Association Innovation on Science Education (INNOVEC), which emerged on the initiative of the US-México Foundation for Science (FUMEC) in 2002. The SEVIC Program strengthens the teaching practice through teacher training for the use of inquiry-based methodologies aimed at improving student learning, motivating them to solve problems and develop effective communication skills and logical reasoning. To achieve this, INNOVEC established an alliance with the Smithsonian Science Education Center (SSEC) of the United States,[3] an institution that has facilitated the translation of its Science and Technology Concepts (STC). With these inputs a systemic model of intervention was implemented, which includes strategies to improve the teaching of sciences with an investigative approach in five areas: a high-quality curriculum, professional teacher development, material support in the classroom, evaluation and community support.[4] The operation of the SEVIC program is possible for a public/private collaboration by the Secretariat of Public Education of México (SEP), state governments, various companies and private foundations. The program attends annually to more than 400 thousand students and about 10 thousand professors.

The Instituto Apoyo foundation in Perú also carried out a program named "Science for All—Experimento". Its purpose was to support teachers through IBSE training, so that they can offer to students opportunities to awaken their interest in understanding and explaining phenomena of natural sciences and technology, delving into some topics central to the discipline and getting closer to scientific work (Instituto APOYO, 2018a). This program was created after a first initiative call "Mathematics for All", which aims to develop mathematical skills in children in a playful and comprehensive way, through exploration experiences and relationships with their own body and environment. It is a curricular proposal that has different play activities to ensure the development of essential mathematical skills for girls and boys during a learning session that follows the steps of a Mathematical Inquiry cycle (Instituto APOYO, 2018b).

The implementation of these programs, conducted to the creation of the "National STEAM Forum, an alliance of civil society institutions (national and international), mostly conformed by 25 Peruvian universities, technological and pedagogical institutes, as well as State authorities as counsellors. The objective of the Forum is promoting quality education in STEAM fields throughout all Peruvian education cycles, with a special emphasis on primary education. The common objective of the Peruvian STEAM Forum is the creation of networks for discussion and cooperation to multiply the actions and effect of the initiatives of its individual actors, strengthening, creating and improving STEAM education in Perú (APOYO Institute, 2018c).

In Chile, the Science Education Program based on Inquiry (ECBI), implemented at a national level by the government from 2003 and 2010, and currently functioning independently under the supervision of Universidad de Chie. It aims to generate in children, through inquiry, the ability to explain the world around them using procedures of science. The general objective, it is to strengthen the pedagogical competences of the principals, teachers and monitors of the communes in IBSE.

The ECBI methodology is focused on the new knowledge about the learning process that emerges from research and seeks to bring to the classroom the skills and attitudes associated with scientific work. By applying the inquiry methodology, children explore the natural world, and this leads them to ask questions, find explanations, test them and communicate their ideas to others (Devés & Reyes, 2007).

The purpose of establishing a program of quality sciences for all children was based on the conviction that scientific education is a right of everyone and not a restricted knowledge for those who will develop careers in the scientific-technological field. This idea was also an inspiration for the Curricular Framework of the educational reform promoted in Chile by the Ministry of Education in 2012 and current Curricular Basis 2018 of Early Childhood Education (Mienduc, 2012, 2018).

After the end of ECBI as a national governmental program, the ICEC Program (Inquiry Science for Science Education in Schools) was created. It has the purpose of contributing to children from kindergarten, primary, secondary and special needs education to the comprehension of the great ideas in sciences (Harlen et al., 2012). It aims to achieve understanding of scientific ideas in a gradual and progressive way according to the levels established, to develop scientific reasoning skills, to understand the nature of scientific knowledge, to strengthen positive attitudes towards learning and to understand the role of science in society.

For teachers, it focuses on forming their own inquiry skills so that they offer opportunities to all their students to broaden their ideas, stimulate progress and human development as well as offer opportunities to apply scientific techniques and procedures that affect their daily life as to the environment. To achieve this, they provide a course about scientific inquiry and promote collaborative work among peers to achieve the improvement of pedagogical practice, as well as involve other members of the community such as scientists and educational administrators.

The ICEC program is implemented in 13 public universities from the north to the south of Chile, along with the Ministry of Education and the educational departments from different communities. There is one special moment, where all the academic teams and teachers get together, present their experience and exchange ideas to improve their science education practices. They seek also to form a sense of identity as "ICEC teacher", giving the first steps to a Chilean professional community of teachers, which is not easy but possible.

Gender Equality in STEM

In relationship with the first Pequeños Científicos initiative, in 2018 the Colombian Academy of Sciences created STEM-ACADEMIA in order to promote a quality education in the STEM areas with support in the state of the art in the teaching of these disciplines. This initiative is boosted by the experience of 20 years of the Pequeños Científicos program (Duque, Celis, & Celis, 2011; Duque, Uzcanga, & Gómez, 2015), equally ascribed to the IBSE programs of the network of the world's academies.

This approach is based on problem solving, scaffolding in explicit teaching and learning activities, with a strong component of concrete and semi-concrete manipulation and development of spatial thinking in line with what recent research has shown (Cross, Woods, Schweingruber, & NRC, 2009; Dehaene, 2018; Kilpatrick, Swafford, & Findell, 2001), with particular benefit for women (Newcome, 2017; UNESCO, 2017). Particular emphasis has been placed on the area of mathematics for its relationship with the current gender imbalance in the preference of STEM professions, and the subsequent performance in these areas (National Research Council, 2016).

The Chilean program "Girls Can Create, Undertake and Innovate" is focused on strategic communication to foster gender equality on STEM education, led by the NGO "Women Comunidad Mujer" [Women Community] and supported by the national government, UNESCO and the European Union. Their goals are to promote scientific vocations in girls, to transform the teacher profession to one that takes gender equality to the classroom and to foster educational contexts free of gender stereotypes. Here STEM education is considered, for the current gender inequalities in the STEM professions and as a tool to integrate in a creative way.

Given the fact that in México, young girls don't visualize themselves as STEM professionals in their future, STEM Movement and INNOVEC has separately started STEM programs with a gender perspective from kindergarten to high school. STEM movement empowers young girls facilitating them opportunities to explore the sciences and work with them to expand their potential to consider engineer, math or science careers.

On the other hand, the office of UNESCO in México and Siemens Stiftung Foundation in collaboration with INNOVEC in 2017 launched an initiative based on the Experimento program whose purpose is the teaching of inquiry-based science with a gender perspective. The program is still in progress and has been refined by experts in science education and gender.

"Niñas STEM pueden" [STEM Girls Can] is another pilot initiative supported by the National Ministry of Education and some outstanding women in science and technology careers. The program seeks to promote the interest of girls and adolescents in different careers related to science, technology, engineering and mathematics, which generates a conviction of aptitude to these areas, as well as empowering them to recognize and use their knowledge and skills.[5]

In the case of Perú, there are no STEM programs with a regional or national scope focused on gender equality in STEM education. An important effort of the members of the STEAM Peruvian Foro for working cooperatively to promote equal opportunities for girls is the one made in the Emblematic Educational Institution Juana Alarco de Dammert, a public school for girls that has a population of more than 3000 students. Here they focus on the integration of STEM areas, making alliances with external public and private institutions to strength their institutional capabilities in this direction. Nevertheless, STEM education with gender perspective is still a field to be developed in Perú.

Place-Based Learning

The initiatives listed in this section can be considered as a sub-group of the integrated inquiry-based science education initiatives. We decided to highlight this kind of initiative as place-based gives the opportunity to learn in specific contexts, solving daily life problems from an interdisciplinary scope. They are related to project and problem-based methods, and each program fosters educative innovations following an integrated STEM perspective.

In Colombia, in the STEM-ACADEMIA program, a "Teacher Professional Development" strategy has been assumed in coherence with what research shows on this subject (Borko, 2004; Jayaram, Moffit, & Scott, 2012), with focus on pedagogical content knowledge (PCK) (Abell, Rogers, Deborah, & Gagnon, 2009; Davis & Krajcik, 2005; Magnusson, Krajcik, & Borko, 2002; Shulman, 1986), project-based learning from an engineering perspective in design activities, prototyping and use of ICTs to solve problems that are posed to students and promote computational thinking. These educational projects, based on the school's contexts, should serve for the application and consolidation of previous learning in each of the STEM areas and to increase understanding in aspects that imply an integrated view of the STEM areas.

In Perú the program "Mathematics for All + Communication" considers that mathematical competence is a human activity that is inserted in the culture and influenced by it, in which communicative resources are used to propose, represent and solve problems of the surrounding context, allowing students to understand the "why" behind each learning. From mathematics, the child begins to develop his oral expression from the observation and analysis of everyday situational images that are linked to STEM issues. By these means, students manage to recognize their environment and express themselves orally, ordering their thinking to be understood, to raise ideas of solution, to argue, to recognize their mistakes and to overcome them; as it also improves their vocalization, vocabulary and learning to express themselves to their peers in a proper and assertive manner.

Have Fun and Learn–UPCH is a program that aims to provide children with the educational tools and experiments to find the answers to the functioning of nature. With this program, skills such as teamwork, inquiry, innovation, answering problems, designing novel proposals and learning to learn are strengthened. There is a version of the "Have Fun and Learn with Experiments" held at open doors, that is, in public spaces where the whole community is invited to participate in an event for spreading the sciences and the STEAM approach. (Universidad Peruana Cayetano Heredia, 2018)

The SABE Project is a project financed by the government of Perú and other private resources to learn through one of the main culturally relevant activities of the country: gastronomy and food production. Through the food education methodology, the SABE Project teaches people to appreciate the cultural and social importance of food—making use of the senses, passing through the pleasure of taste, cultural identity and for cooking, until you reach the dish to understand where the agricultural products come from, who grows them and how they are produced. Considering the aforementioned, the intention to integrate STEAM areas and ancestral knowledge becomes evident. This initiative was implemented in 2017 in nine schools in the Lima region, reaching 570 students and 26 teachers at the primary level. The National Innovation Program for Competitiveness and Productivity (Innóvate Perú) drove these actions, considering the legal framework of the Science Popularization Program of the National Council of Science, Technology and Technological Innovation (CONCYTEC).

> You learn about the transformation of energy with food. We cook and reflect on the effect of the discovery of fire in our evolution. We learn about these transformations using the scientific method and approach children to science, using the kitchen as a scientific laboratory, making experiments with edible results.
>
> *(Becerra, 2018)*

In Chile, the "Experimento program" in the Araucanía region has been working for the last five years in making adaptations for inquiry-based STEM learning and its relationship with local traditional knowledge in indigenous contexts. Bascopé and Caniguan (2016) presented a pedagogical approach adapted to the Chilean national curriculum, with five dimensions of traditional knowledge that can be considered to foster place-based learning in STEM. Using this framework and with the support of the public and private sector, the project in the south of Chile developed pedagogical resources, such as inquiry-based structured activities, with instructions for teachers and students and game-based resources to foster guided and open inquiry, made by the students about their contexts, traditions and ancient knowledge (Bascopé & Gutiérrez, 2019).

Territorial Alliances: Partnerships Between ONG, Practitioners, Researchers, Civil Society and the State to Foster STEM Education

Even though it is harder to find national or federal efforts towards STEM education in Latin America, some local, regional and state-level initiatives have been created and implemented in recent years. Unlike the previous programs revised, the STEM territory focus is a multi-sectorial alliance with common objectives around STEM education, which foster exchange and collaboration among participants to strength the educational chain.

Installation of STEM territories in Latin America had been fostered by an academic and private effort rather than pushed by a specific policy. However, the idea of establishing territories is inherently a political statement to articulate private and public initiatives towards the strength of the educational chain. In this section, we will review a number of regional initiatives towards the consolidation of STEM involving local authorities, universities, NGOs and the private sector.

In the case of Chile, we will highlight three territorial STEM initiatives in three different regions of the country. A big initiative with a national scope established in 2017 was "Coalición STEAM" (STEAM Coalition), conformed by a transdisciplinary group of people coming from civil society, education, industry, academia, STEAM disciplines and the public sector. After seven months of technical working sessions, complemented with interviews with successful educational experiences and a teacher survey, six powerful ideas were proposed to foster short and mid-term action: (1) our schools can be transformed into STEAM schools (it is possible under the current legislation), (2) more active and contextualized learning is needed, (3) our teachers want to change, but they need support, (4) it is necessary to build a STEM culture, (5) we should promote lifelong learning and connect the different steps, and (6) articulation of the existent efforts (Corporación de Fomento de la Producción, 2017).

Also, in the Valparaiso region of Chile, the Latin American Observatory of Sciences' Didactics (OLADIC), a group of regional universities and the Regional Secretary of Education together, started in 2018 a round table to stablish strategic lines for action in the region towards STEAM education. The three main lines defined were: (1) education, innovation and entrepreneurship; (2) sustainability; and (3) heritage and identity. The recently created network has the objective of joining inter-sectorial efforts towards STEAM initiatives with local pertinence.[6]

In the south of Chile another multi-sectorial initiative has been launched during 2018. A group of national and international NGOs leaded by Siemens Stiftung along with Pontificia Universidad Católica de Chile started the "Alliance for Educational Innovation for Sustainable Development", with the mission of impulse and foster STEAM educational opportunities for sustainable development, articulating public and private efforts. The main line of action is teacher training and follow-up, led by the university to impulse innovation in pedagogical strategies, for the development of creativity and critical thinking, connecting the schools with their local contexts.

Perú is territorially divided into regions where the foundations of educational decentralization are contemplated. It must be noted that since 2002, the decentralization process began, including that of educational services (Law No. 27783). In this context, it is necessary to highlight the importance of the Declaration of the Tacna Region as a STEAM territory.[7] This region has implemented different programs for more than two years under the STEAM approach, such as the "implementation of Robotics at the regional level" that seeks the integration of curricular competences and areas committed to solving specific problems of the community, achieving the development of skills and competencies required in the 21st century. This type of program has been strengthened in cooperation with other actors such as the British Council, Cayetano Heredia University, Instituto APOYO and Fab Lab, among others.

Another evidence of STEAM education in public policy is the Municipality of the District of Miraflores in Lima that has presented its Local Education Project, which has as its main axis the STEAM approach and territorial criteria to develop and promote educational innovation and the development of 21st-century competencies. This project provides opportunities to learn to think, investigate, reflect and create at the school level (Municipality of Miraflores, 2018).

In Colombia, Medellín, one of the most important cities in the country, declared in 2016 to be a STEM+H territory.[8] With a focus mainly on secondary education, STEM+H scope for Medellín has the purpose of fomenting in students skills such as research, leadership, inquiry, innovation and the prospective vision to generate knowledge from the classroom in a meaningful way, where priority is not just science but human and social development.

In the case of México, a recently launched movement called "Movimiento STEM" has the mission of creating ecosystems of multiple partners towards fostering STEM by means of (1) empowering and training teachers, (2) developing vocations towards the STEM pipeline for careers and (3) linking STEM talents with companies and the industry.[9] They have recently launched a document named "Visión STEM para México" [STEM Vision for México] with an historical national and international analysis of the evolution of the STEM concept and with the pedagogical and educational concepts, to guide new efforts and to consolidate the existents (Movimiento STEM, 2019).

Similarly, INNOVEC, with the support of the educational authorities of the state of México, has very recently established the country's first STEM territory, with the purpose of coordinating efforts, offering high-quality educational resources and providing teacher training in the creation and design of STEM practices for their students. The launch of the STEM territory was carried out through an education forum in November 2018, which started with the creation of networks and alliances between different actors to promote STEM education: the state government, educational centers, parents of family, companies, private institutions of national and international character among others.

The STEM Territory in the state of México will seek to strengthen primary and higher education. It aims to develop competencies in students to generate the foundations of a society with the skills and attitudes to face the challenges of technological development and innovation and allow for an informed, critical and tolerant population that can make decisions in favor of a healthy life and respect for their environment and community.

Absence of Centralized Efforts Towards Measuring Impact at a National Level

A big debt of these countries is the implementation of systematic and longitudinal evaluations of the different initiatives. Even though the majority of the programs rely on international evidence about STEM education, the empirical and contextualized evidence of the impact of the different STEM programs published in peer-reviewed journals is still scarce. There is a prevalence on case studies and almost never refer to the STEM concept, but rather to inquiry-based science education, community-based science or science and gender equality. Not many regional or national analyses offer a clear evaluation of the impact at the national level. There is a big opportunity to learn about the many initiatives on work, but still the Research and Development national investment is very low, the lowest in the OECD countries in the case of Chile followed by México (OECD, 2018).

In México the educational crisis has been studied by many educational researchers (Ornelas, 2013; Andere, 2003). Even though the difficulties for progressing in the countries international results had different and diverse causes, one of them has been the lack of an efficient long-term public policy and the inexistence of formal evaluation of the diversity of programs in the country. On the contrary, the evidence showed how constant change in the educational models and perspectives has been the tenor of Mexican educational policy (Tirado Segura, 2005).

The evidence shows the predominance of traditional content-based lessons in science (Cofré, 2010; Cofré et al., 2010), but no further research has been made at the national level either regarding STEM, or integrated science learning, or any kind of impact evaluation of these initiatives.

One interesting result regarding place-based education can be found in the educational literature in Chile. Godoy Ossa, Varas Scheuch, Martínez Videla, Treviño, and Meyer (2016) used a national review of Chilean schools that have shown improvement in their results, on what Bellei, Vanni, Valenzuela, and Contreras (2014) have called "improvement trajectories". Those schools with good and sustained improvement trajectories have also showed in their lessons greater consideration for their students' perspectives and more student commitment. This means that these schools tend to be more flexible, give students more leadership during the lessons and, in general, consider the students' previous experiences and motivations (Godoy et al., 2016). Many of these characteristics were related with STEM approaches described in the previous sections, so this study could be a first step to go further in research about schools willing to make a change in their traditional approaches in other Latin American countries.

Another evaluation was one promoted by an international project sponsored by the Inter Academies Panel (IAP), which encourages the implementation of an IBSE approach (Harlen, 2013). The project is being implemented in 30 countries, and the IAP has proposed guidelines for its evaluation to interested countries. Among the main recommendations of the Working Group on International Collaboration in the Evaluation of IBSE, it is indicated that each country constitutes a local evaluation team to design an evaluation plan, in collaboration with and with the support of an International Oversight Committee (International Committee).

As a general conclusion from the formative assessment, the reports indicated that the ECBI program from Chile is a highly valued program that teachers positively distinguish from other governmental initiatives. The assessment is based on the resources it delivers and on the changes, observed in both the teaching practices and the learning opportunities that students' access. Children are motivated to learn science through the experimental activities proposed by ECBI. Students distinguish these classes from those they receive when there are no ECBI materials (Devés & Reyes, 2009).

The in-depth understanding of an inquiry approach to the learning and teaching of science is a complex process that takes time, particularly if teachers lack a prior scientific background. The study shows that in most teachers coexist practices and beliefs consistent with the IBSE model with beliefs aligned with the traditional model that a large majority has been implementing for years. This evaluation has shown certain critical knots regarding the devices deployed by ECBI to generate new competencies that allow greater consistency in teaching practices and beliefs based on the inquiry of primary education teachers.

However, impact evaluations at a wider level about STEM education have not been in the public agenda either at the national or at the federal/regional level, and the few evaluations available have been for programs implemented in Chile. More comprehensive research on STEM-specific programs is still a challenge to fulfill.

Future Directions for STEM Education in Latin American Countries

As shown in the chapter, a great variety of initiatives with or without public support has been developed in the countries reviewed. Even though the government support is present in different forms (Ministries of Education and Environment, specific programs to foster productivity and public universities, among others), there is no clear line of action on the part of the governments regarding STEM education. However, as the curricular guidelines do not present a big challenge and there is evidence about teachers' and schools' interest, there is a big chance to formalize and propose national guidelines with proper evaluation standards.

One possible risk related with STEM education is that the great diversity of themes and approaches related what makes it very attractive in the discourse for a wide and diverse audience but is not necessarily clear in its implementation. The hard part is to make STEM education work in practice, and to plan the proper follow-up process to evaluate the consequences and learn from the application of these programs. This effort is of public interest, and the local policy in the countries reviewed had not taken this compromise yet. It is important to evaluate impacts of integrated STEM opportunities to understand how to balance integrated versus not integrated opportunities and under which characteristics it is better to implement STEM education.

In terms of the STEM focus that has been present in the region, it is important to highlight the importance of creativity and arts in different contexts. The STEAM approach in Perú, the STEAM Coalition in Chile and other specific programs in México and Colombia had shown how arts and creativity are crucial elements to success in the challenge of integrating different areas of knowledge in a coherent and meaningful way. However, the absence of well-systematized large-scale evaluations of these programs is crucial to go beyond specific contexts or programs.

Another critical point of these programs is the focus on making STEM useful to solve problems, relating STEM skills and knowledge with the local context. A great advantage of the integrated focus promoted by STEM is the possibility of using different views, perspectives and solutions to a certain problem rather than transmitting abstract and dense content. In this direction, the focus of the revised countries on promoting inquiry and place-based education, against the traditional approach of education, is key to understanding the importance of thinking about STEM at the national level.

A study made by Fiszbein et al. (2016) showed that the proportion of students that chose STEM careers in Latin America is below the proportion observed in the European Union or in the United States and mainly concentrated in engineering over all the other fields. Hence, there is a chance to advance, in the countries reviewed, towards a bigger and more diverse field in tertiary STEM education. Again, the importance of an integrated and interdisciplinary focus starting from the school level is key for the tertiary level to growth not only in vocations but also in its diversification.

To really leverage the potential of STEM education, is very important that the Latin American governments put more resources to evaluate and generate contextualized knowledge about local initiatives. The new local and regional territorial movements form the countries analyzed in this chapter present a big opportunity to stablish guidelines and articulate efforts for a better understanding of the process of change in the educational institutions towards STEM-based integrated approaches.

Even though structural constraints might jeopardize innovation, some first steps to incorporate a more integrated approach to STEM education can be achieved at the teacher and school level. In this direction, we propose a broad approach towards education for sustainable development, which considers an integrated, interdisciplinary focus to tackle local problems, incorporating gender perspective and place-based education (Aguilar, 2018; Bascopé, Perasso, & Reiss, 2019; Buckler & Creech, 2014; Capobianco, Yu, & French, 2015; Davies, 2009; Eernstman & Wals, 2013; Hägglund & Samuelsson, 2009; Hedefalk, Almqvist, & Östman, 2015; Vare & Scott, 2007). It can serve as a common goal for teachers from different disciplines and cultural backgrounds to tackle real problems and conduct more integrated lessons. Active citizenship towards sustainability can cover a wide range of STEM issues and also helps to change subject matter based learning to new collaborative and active methodologies to affront the challenges of the 21st century.

In 2017 a cross-national "Pacific Alliance for STEM Education" was established among institutions of the four countries reviewed in this chapter, to foster a transnational movement towards more integrated STEM, articulating different actors from the academia, government and civil society in this direction. The challenge is big, but the urgency for change in the Latin American educational systems is evident. To affront forthcoming scenarios of environmental and social crisis requires both macro and micro actions, from the system to the classroom, to break the inertia and transit towards a more pertinent and coherent education for the new generations.

Notes

1. www.stem-academia.org
2. http://www.pauta.org.mx/index.php/que-hacemos/. Fecha de la consulta: 11 de enero de 2019.
3. https://ssec.si.edu/
4. Tomado de www.innovec.org.mx Fecha de consulta 11 de enero de 2018.
5. http://ninastem.aprende.sep.gob.mx/en/demo/home
6. https://experimento.lat.siemens-stiftung.org/territorio-steam-valparaiso-chile-cierra-el-ano-evaluando-las-principales-necesidades-de-la-region/, accessed January 23, 2019.
7. Formalized through Regional Executive Resolution No. 571-2018-GR / GOB.REG.TACNA.
8. https://medellin.edu.co/mediatecnica/descripcion-del-programa
9. https://movimientostem.org/

References

Abell, S., Rogers, M., Deborah, H., & Gagnon, M. (2009). Preparing the next generation of science teacher educators: a model for developing PCK for teaching science teachers. *Journal of Science Teacher Education - Springer, 20.*

Aguilar, O. M. (2018). Examining the literature to reveal the nature of community EE/ESD programs and research. *Environmental Education Research, 24*(1), 26–49.

Andere, M. E. (2003). *La educación en México: un fracaso monumental.* ¿Está México en riesgo?. México: Planeta.

Australian Government. (2016). STEM programme index 2016.

Bascopé, M., & Caniguan, N. I. (2016). Propuesta pedagógica para la incorporación de conocimientos tradicionales de Ciencias Naturales en Primaria. *Revista Electrónica de Investigación Educativa, 18*(3), 162–175. Retrieved from http://redie.uabc.mx/redie/article/view/1143

Bascopé, M., & Gutiérrez, P. (2019). Recursos educativos y dispositivos lúdicos para la indagación científica: Un diálogo entre ciencia y conocimientos tradicionales. *Antología Sobre Indagación "Enseñanza de La Ciencia En La Educación Básica," 4.* México: Innovec. Retrieved from https://www.fondation-lamap.org/sites/default/files/upload/media/minisites/international/Antolog%C3%ADa_indagacion_inclusion.pdf

Bascopé, M., Perasso, P., & Reiss, K. (2019). Systematic review of education for sustainable development at an early stage: Cornerstones and pedagogical approaches for teacher professional development. *Sustainability, 11*(3), 719. https://doi.org/10.3390/su11030719

Becerra, K. (2018). *Riquisísimo!!! Recetas de cocina peruana para los niños y para los que fueron niños.* Lima, Perú: Mallqui Books.

Bellei, C., Vanni, X., Valenzuela, J. P., & Contreras, D. (2014). Trayectorias de mejoramiento escolar:¿ Existen tipologías de mejoramiento. *Lo aprendi en la escuela.¿ Cómo se logran procesos de mejoramiento escolar,* 95–116.

Borko, H. (2004). Professional development and teacher learning: Mapping the terrain. *Educational Researcher, 33*(8), 3–15.

Buckler, C., & Creech, H. (2014). *Shaping the future we want: UN decade of education for sustainable development; final report.* Paris: UNESCO.

Capobianco, B. M., Yu, J. H., & French, B. F. (2015). Effects of engineering design–based science on elementary school science students' engineering identity development across gender and grade. *Research in Science Education, 45*(2), 275–292. https://doi.org/10.1007/s11165-014-9422-1

Carulla, C., Duque, M., Molano, A., & Hernández, J. T. (2007). The Pequeños Científicos program: Science through inquiry with coverage and quality. Special issue on trends in pre-college engineering and technology education. *International Journal of Engineering Education, 23*(1), 9–14.

Cofré, H. (2010). *Cómo mejorar la enseñanza de las ciencias en Chile: Perspectivas internacionales y desafíos nacionales.* Santiago de Chile: Ediciones Universidad Católica Silva Henríquez.

Cofré, H., Camacho, J., Galaz, A., Jiménez, J., Santibáñez, D., & Vergara, C. (2010). La educación científica en Chile: Debilidades de la enseñanza y futuros desafíos de la educación de profesores de ciencia. *Estudios Pedagógicos (Valdivia), 36*(2), 279–293.

Corporación de Fomento de la Producción, C. (2017). *Preparando a Chile para la sociedad del conocimiento: Hacia una coalición que impulse la Educación STEAM.* Santiago: Fundación Chile. Retrieved from https://www.ecosisteam.cl/2019/10/24/preparando-a-chile-para-la-sociedad-del-conocimiento-hacia-una-coalicion-que-impulse-la-educacion-steam/

Cross, C., Woods, T., Schweingruber, H., & NRC. (2009). *Mathematics learning in early childhood: Paths toward excellence and equity.* Washington, DC: NAP.

Davies, J. (2009). Revealing the research 'hole' of early childhood education for sustainability: A preliminary survey of the literature. *Environmental Education Research, 15*(2), 227–241. https://doi.org/10.1080/13504620802710607

Davis, E., & Krajcik, J. (2005). Designing educative curriculum materials to promote teacher learning. *Educational Researcher, 34*(3), 3–14.

Devés, R., & Reyes, P. (2007). Principios y Estrategias del Programa de Educación en Ciencias basada en la Indagación (ECBI). *Revista Pensamiento Educativo, 41,* 115–132.

Devés, R., & Reyes, P. (2009). *Desarrollo profesional en comunidad. Formación continua en el Programa de Educación en Ciencias Basada en la Indagación (ECBI). Libro Formación continua de profesores. ¿Cómo desarrollar competencias para el trabajo escolar?* Sotomayor y Walker editores, Editorial Universitaria Santiago, Chile.

Dehaene, S. (2018). *Apprendre ! Les talents du cerveau, le défi des machines.* Paris: Odile Jacob.

Duque, M., Hernández, J. T., Gómez, M., & Vasquez, C. (2011). *Pequeños Científicos program: STEM K12 education in Colombia.* Paper presented at the Integrated STEM education Conference ISEC2011, College of New Jersey in Ewing, NJ.

Duque, M., Celis, J., & Celis, S. (2011). Desarrollo profesional docente de profesores de ingeniería: revisión y evolución de propuestas en algunas facultades de ingeniería en Colombia. In Montoya Juny, A.-M. Truscott, & A. Mejía (Eds.), *Educación para el siglo XXI: aportes del centro de investigación y formación en educación* (Vol. 2). Bogotá: CIFE, Universidad de los Andes.

Duque, M., Uzcanga, I., & Gómez, M. (2015). *A STEM outreach program: case study of a scale up in two countries.* Paper presented at the 13th Active Learning in Engineering Education Workshop (ALE), International Symposium on Project Approaches in Engineering Education (PAEE), 5th International Research Symposium on PBL (IRSPBL), San Sebastian.

Eernstman, N., & Wals, A. E. (2013). Locative meaning-making: An arts-based approach to learning for sustainable development. *Sustainability, 5*(4), 1645–1660.

Fiszbein, A., Cosentino, C., & Cumsille, B. (2016). *El desafío del desarrollo de habilidades en América Latina: un diagnóstico de los problemas y soluciones de política pública.*

Fiszbein, A., & Stanton, S. (2018, June). The future of education in Latin America and the Caribbean: Possibilities for United States Investment and Engagement. *The Dialogue.* Retrieved from http://repositorio.minedu. gob.pe/handle/MINEDU/5879

Freeman, B., Marginson, S., & Russel, T. (2015). *The age of STEM: Educational policy practices across the word in science, technology, engineering and mathematics.* New York, NY: Routledge Research in Education.

Godoy Ossa, F., Varas Scheuch, L., Martínez Videla, M., Treviño, E., & Meyer, A. (2016). Interacciones pedagógicas y percepción de los estudiantes en escuelas chilenas que mejoran: Una aproximación exploratoria. *Estudios Pedagógicos (Valdivia), 42*(3), 149–169. https://doi.org/10.4067/S0718-07052016000400008

Guerra, T. (2012). El currículo oficial de ciencias para la educación básica y sus reformas recientes, retórica y vicisitudes. En Flores (Ed.), *La enseñanza de la ciencia en la educación básica en México* (pp.79–92). México: INEE

Hägglund, S., & Samuelsson, I. P. (2009). Early childhood education and learning for sustainable development and citizenship. *International Journal of Early Childhood, 41*(2), 49. https://doi.org/10.1007/BF03168878

Harlen, W. (2010). *Principios y grandes ideas de la educación en Ciencias.* Hatfield: Association for Science Education.

Harlen, W. (2013). *Evaluación y educación en ciencias basada en la indagación aspectos de la política y la práctica.* Global Network of Science Academies (IAP) Science Education Programme (SEP).

Harlen, W., & Cols. (2012). *Principios y Grandes Ideas en Educación en Ciencias.* Academia Chilena de Ciencias.

Hedefalk, M., Almqvist, J., & Östman, L. (2015). Education for sustainable development in early childhood education: A review of the research literature. *Environmental Education Research, 21*(7), 975–990.

Instituto APOYO. (2018a). *Ciencias para Todos EXPERIMENTO.* Lima: Instituto APOYO.

Instituto APOYO. (2018b). *Foro STEAM. Recuperado el 21 de Diciembre de 2018, de Instituto APOYO.* Retrieved from http://www.institutoapoyo.org.pe/steam/foro

Instituto APOYO. (2018c). *Matemática para todos Inicial 5 años.* Lima: Instituto APOYO.

Jayaram, K., Moffit, A., & Scott, D. (2012). Breaking the habit of ineffective professional development for teachers. *McKinsey on Society,* 1–12.

Kilpatrick, J., Swafford, J., & Findell, B. (2001). *Adding it up: Helping children learn mathematics* (NAP Ed.). Washington, DC: NAP.

Law No. 27783. (2017). Law of bases of decentralization.

Magnusson, S., Krajcik, J., & Borko, H. (2002). Nature, sources, and development of pedagogical content knowledge for science teaching. In J. Gess-Newsome, & N. G. Lederman (Eds.), *Examining pedagogical content knowledge* (pp. 95–132). Dordrecht: Springer.

MEN. (1998a). *Serie lineamientos curriculares. Ciencias Naturales y Educación Ambiental.* Colombia: Ministerio de Educación Nacional.

MEN. (1998b). *Serie lineamientos curriculares. Matemáticas.* Colombia: Ministerio de Educación Nacional.

MEN. (2004). *Estándares Básicos de Competencias en Ciencias Naturales y Ciencias Sociales: Formar en ciencias, el desafío.* Bogotá: MEN.

MEN. (2015). *Derechos Básicos de Aprendizaje.* Bogotá: MEN.

MEN. (2017). *Bases Curriculares De Educación Inicial.* Bogotá: MEN.

Mineduc. (1998). *Reforma Educacional, Objetivos Fundamentales y Contenidos Mínimos Obligatorios, Decreto 220, 1998.* Chile: Ministerio de Educación.

Mineduc. (2009). *Ministerio de Educación de Chile: Ajuste Curricular de 7° a II medio.* Santiago: Mineduc.

Mineduc. (2012). *Ministerio de Educación de Chile: Bases Curriculares de 1° a 6° año básico.* Santiago: Mineduc.

Mineduc. (2018). *Ministerio de Educación de Chile: Bases Curriculares de educación parvularia.* Santiago: Mineduc.

Ministerio de Educación. (2016). *Curriculo Nacional de la Educación Básica.* Lima: Ministerio de Educación del Perú.

Mourshed, M., Chijioke, C., & Barber, M. (2010). *How the world's most improved school systems keep getting better.* London: McKinsey & Company.

Movimiento STEM. (2019). *Visión STEM para Mexico* (1st ed.). Retrieved from https://movimientostem.org/wp-content/uploads/2019/02/Visio%CC%81n-STEM-impresio%CC%81n.pdf

Municipalidad de Miraflores. (2018). *Proyecto Educativo Local.* Miraflores: Municipalidad de Miraflores.

National Research Council. (2016). *Learning to think spatially: GIS as a support system in the K-12 curriculum.* Washington: NAP.

Newcome, N. (2017). *Harnessing spatial thinking to support stem learning.* OECD Education Working papers, Paris. Retrieved from https://www.oecd-ilibrary.org/education/harnessing-spatial-thinking-to-support-stem-learning_7d5dcae6-en

OECD. (2016). *PISA 2015 results (Volume I): Excellence and equity in education.* Paris: OECD Publishing. http://dx.doi.org/10.1787/9789264266490-en.

OECD. (2018). *Main science and technology indicators* [Text]. Organization for Economic Cooperation and Development. Retrieved from https://www.oecd-ilibrary.org/science-and-technology/main-science-and-technology-indicators_2304277x

O'Grady, K., Deussing, M.-A., Scerbina, T., Fung, K., & Muhe, N. (2016). *À la hauteur: Résultats canadiens de l'étude PISA de l'OCDE: Le rendement des jeunes du Canada en sciences, en lecture et en mathématiques.* Toronto: Conseil des ministres de l'Éducation.

Ornelas, C. (2013). *El sistema educativo mexicano.* México: Fondo de Cultura Económica.

Royal Academy of Engineering. (2016). *The UK STEM education landscape: A report for the Lloyd's register foundation from the Royal Academy of Engineering Education and Skills Committee.* Retrieved from London: https://www.raeng.org.uk/publications/reports/uk-stem-education-landscape

Shulman, L. (1986). Those who understand: knowledge growth in teaching. *Educational Researcher, 15*(2), 4–14. doi:10.3102/0013189X015002004

Tirado Segura, F. (2005, abril–junio). *Reseña de "La educación en México: un fracaso monumental. ¿Está México en riesgo?" de Eduardo Andere Martínez. Revista Mexicana de Investigación Educativa* (Vol. 10, núm. 25, pp. 597–610). México: Consejo Mexicano de Investigación Educativa, A.C. Distrito Federal.

UNESCO. (2015). *Informe de resultados TERCE: logros de aprendizaje.* Retrieved from https://unesdoc.unesco.org/ark:/48223/pf0000243532

UNESCO. (2017). *Cracking the code: Girls' and women's education in science, technology, engineering and mathematics (STEM).* Paris: UNESCO.

Universidad Peruana Cayetano Heredia. (2018). *Diviertete y Aprende. Recuperado el 21 de Diciembre de 2018, de Diviertete y Aprende.* http://www.divierteteyaprende.pe/index.html

Vare, P., & Scott, W. (2007). Learning for a change: Exploring the relationship between education and sustainable development. *Journal of Education for Sustainable Development, 1*(2), 191–198. https://doi.org/10.1177/097340820700100209

World Bank. (2018). *World development report 2018: Learning to realize education's promise.* Washington, DC: World Bank. doi:10.1596/978-1-4648-1096-1.

World Economic Forum. (2017). *White paper: Realizing human potential in the fourth industrial revolution an Agenda for leaders to shape the future of education, gender and work.* Geneva: World Economic Forum.

36

MEASURING THE IMPACT OF BUSINESS ENGAGEMENT ON STEM EDUCATION

Karen Webber, Jeffrey Robert, David Tanner,
Melinda Williams Moore and Timothy Burg

Introduction

The demand for STEM graduates has increased, as evidenced in the call for one million additional college graduates in these disciplines by 2022 (Olson & Riordan, 2012). To meet the needs of STEM employment, the global need for more science, technology, engineering, and mathematics graduates remains unfilled (Hossain & Robinson, 2012; Olson & Riordan, 2012). Although not all STEM graduates end up working in STEM–related careers, the majority do. Secondary and postsecondary educators see the value in and need to increase curricular and extracurricular activities that encourage participation in STEM activities (Perdomo & Webber, 2018), particularly for students in rural geographies (Crain & Webber, 2019), and integrate these activities into authentic assessments (Sondergeld, Burton-Peters, & Johnson, 2016). Authentic activities and assessments often lead to interest in STEM majors and careers.

The number of STEM graduates has economic and workforce implications. Compared to past hiring cycles, employers in many parts of the world perceive challenges to hiring talented STEM employees. For example, Canada's *Let's Talk Science* initiative aims to establish and deepen conversations among Canadians in efforts to establish a new vision for STEM learning in Canada (http://letstalkscience.ca). According to the McKinsey Global Institute (2012) report, "many [jobs are] going unfilled for long periods of time because approximately half of employers now claim they cannot find employees with the competencies, skills, and degrees they need" (p. 3). Simply getting students interested in STEM disciplines is not enough. Some characterize the graduation rate for STEM education as the "STEM leaky pipeline," where students fail to achieve STEM degrees and disengage from STEM careers altogether (Griffith, 2010; National Science Board, 2007).

Research indicates that business engagement may help attract students to STEM subjects and maintain their interest through degree completion (Ballen & Moles, 1994; Engeln, 2003; Stych, 2018). Direct contact between working professionals and students can improve knowledge and student outcomes (Mann & Dawkins, 2014; Strata Education Network and Gallup, 2017). To close the gap in educational preparation, businesses are showing increased interest in developing the talent pipeline through secondary and postsecondary school engagement. While it helps ensure that STEM workers are ready to meet employers' needs, engagement may counter student perceptions of gender–based inequality and provide a support network for minority and underrepresented students in STEM education and careers. Business engagement may help students identify as scientists, regardless of age or grade, which can lead to a higher likelihood of STEM degree completion and to a successful transition to a STEM career.

Business Engagement in Education

Business engagement is the process by which business employers interact with educators and/or students with the intent of influencing student educational persistence and completion. Business engagement activities can focus on future employment, marketing, or community development (Berlinsky, 2014). In addition, business engagement activities such as funding, talent recruitment, research and development, workplace learning, curriculum design, faculty development, project-based learning, and other instructional support and enhancements can have singular or multiple purposes (Mann, Stanley, & Archer, 2014).

Prior related work tends to classify business engagement into three categories: monetary, student-focused, and business-oriented (Compact & UNICEF, 2013). Monetary engagement encompasses all unrestricted and restricted donations to schools and may include financial support for programs, equipment, and academic operations. Student-focused business engagement centers on mentoring, volunteer hours, and networking with business professionals within the school environment. The final category involves business activities outside of the school setting, such as internships, tours, and teacher externships (Mann et al., 2014). Even though these activities may seem student- or teacher-focused, they occur outside of the school environment and thus are categorized separately because research indicates that student learning and perceptions may differ in external settings (Callanan & Benzing, 2004).

Business engagement is fundamental to many STEM education programs from secondary schools to research universities. Recent literature indicates that business engagement can help spark student interest in STEM and that starting in the early grades is important (e.g., Watters & Diezmann, 2013). Middle school or earlier is a critical time to introduce students to career opportunities (Tierney & Hagedorn, 2002; Wimberly & Noeth, 2005), and educators "increasingly point to middle school as a critical juncture where college readiness and access programs should be targeted" (Camblin, 2003, p. 8). In a qualitative study of 116 STEM-related graduate students and doctoral graduates, Maltese and Tai (2010) found that the initial spark of interest in science came before middle school. Females were more likely (52% compared to 33% for males) to attribute their initial interest in science to school or education-based experiences. At the college level, some associations and accreditors, such as the Association to Advance Collegiate Schools of Business (AACSB) and the Accreditation Board for Engineering and Technology (ABET), require certain programs to incorporate business input and real-world learning into their curricula (AACSB, 2015; ABET, 2013).

Business engagement can occur through a variety of activities. Engagement through academics includes activities that enhance student learning, faculty and student interactions, and study groups (Tinto, 1993). Hora, Benbow, and Oleson (2016) identified eight types of partnerships that industry can build with higher education institutions, including workplace training, employer-provided guidance regarding student projects, employer and other community members serving as expert resources for student projects, and expanding student out-of-school learning. One example of a successful business engagement with education is Boeing's multimillion-dollar donation that sought to expand STEM-based experiential learning classrooms in three European Union (EU) countries in 2013, and with an additional nine EU countries in 2018 (Boeing, 2018). Along with academic engagements, business leaders can engage through social activities including clubs, sports, and other campus life events, often with increased interest and selection of a STEM major in college (Perdomo & Webber, 2018).

History of Business Engagement in Education

Business engagement in education is happening across the globe. For example, European national governments and the European Commission are seeking to broaden business engagement in higher education. Recently, 14 university-business activities were identified as positive endeavors, particularly in research and development (Davey, Meerman, Muros, Orazbayeva, & Baaken, 2018). In South Africa, universities are being modeled as 'knowledge producers' collaborating with companies to build learning and technological capabilities for national innovations, further contributing to sustained economic growth. According to a recent report (Promoting Higher Education-Industry Partnerships and Collaborations, 2016), national policy shifts require higher education institutions to align and coordinate their strategies with the state's reprioritization of socioeconomic development goals for low-income and socially disadvantaged individuals (HESA, 2009). Due to these changes, interactions and partnerships between universities, science councils, and the private sector are even more essential to achieve these goals (Promoting Collaborations Report, 2016, p. 1).

While it has recently taken on a renewed emphasis, the United States has a long history of business engagement in education. Over the past 150 years, higher education community engagement has evolved. In 1862, the Morrill Act established the land-grant college system. Connecting the community, including industry to education, the land-grant university creed promoted public service, outreach, and extension. In 1900, 14 private and public university presidents created the American Association of Universities (AAU) to establish advanced degree standards in the sciences (Fitzgerald, Bruns, Sonka, Furco, & Swanson, 2012). One of the objectives of the AAU is to increase undergraduate teaching and learning in STEM education by fostering the collaboration of experts within academic departments (Association of American Universities, 2019). To achieve defense and national security goals in the 1900s, industrial engagement within universities flourished. The space race and Cold War era accelerated cooperative research activities between universities, national labs, and federal agencies. Symbiotic relationships between industry and universities grew through the mutual interest in commercialization of university research. The Bayh-Dole Act of 1980 enabled universities to better facilitate commercialization of their research. The expansion of patent rights and royalties to universities was a turning point for campus administrators and their pursuit of a greater return on academic research (Bok, 2009). The act allowed universities, researchers, and investors to benefit from products developed on American university campuses. Since that time, researchers have been able to capitalize on inventions through corporate spinoffs and retain industry positions on corporate boards (Kenney & Patton, 2009). Not only are businesses and industrial organizations focused on university-based research and commercialization of new technologies, they are also interested in developing a talent pipeline to meet future hiring demands (Hasselmo & McKinnell, 2003).

Business Engagement Activities

One of the most common and beneficial academic engagements is internships, which enhance students' employment opportunities and help develop their skills base (Knouse & Fontenot, 2008). Internship success is generally defined in terms of technical and interpersonal skill acquisition, career-related benefits, career focus, and outcomes of a practical nature (Beard & Morton, 1998). On-site mentoring has been shown to increase the quality of an internship (Callanan & Benzing, 2004). Students benefit from clear expectations and tasks (Rothman, 2007), interesting and challenging assignments, and active employer participation in the process (Narayana, Olk, & Fukami, 2006).

Although internships may take place more often at the postsecondary level, other hands-on and experiential activities occur at the K-12 level that help students make the connections between academic and real-world learning. The P21 Partnership for 21st Century Learning (p21.org) offers a viable framework, exemplar programs, and other resources that address the synergy between innovative thinking and how students can succeed. Resonating with Hora et al.'s (2016) advocacy for similar skills enhancement, the P21 Framework for 21st Century Learning acknowledges the value of and need for skill development in key academic subjects but also students' abilities to think critically and communicate effectively. The P21 framework suggests that 21st-century learning must also include information on a number of important topics including global awareness, civic, environmental, and health literacy (P21 Frameworks, 2019). While the framework applies to all disciplines, it is highly relevant for students in STEM. The ability to think creatively and critically are important for STEM workers of the future, especially in light of the ever-evolving advances in technology. Students' and workers' flexibility and adaptability to change will be critical, as will be the ability to work independently and with others.

There is an increasing value seen in building excitement about STEM with younger students. The FIRST Programs (For Inspiration and Recognition of Science and Technology) collaborate with business partners for volunteer assistance, equipment, and sponsorships to promote student engagement within STEM disciplines (FIRST, 2019). With a focus on elementary and middle school students, the FIRST LEGO League programs promote greater awareness of STEM and student interest in jobs that use science and technology. In addition, the FIRST company offers technology-based challenges for students in grades 7–12 and robotics competitions for students in grades 9–12. Another business to include significant ties to education, the Wonderful Company, reinvested significant resources in STEM-related education. Based in California, the company sponsors two charter schools and sponsors an Ag Prep partnership that connects six feeder middle schools to seven public high schools and three community colleges. The company combines real-world work experience through paid internships with a dedicated educational curriculum to help students enter the skilled workforce (The Wonderful Company, 2018).

In addition to these education-industry partnerships, research projects are another form of business engagement that promote student learning. Business members provide feedback on research that enhances learning and provides meaningful contributions to relevant research projects. Through research projects, students learn procedures, methods, and/or theories of the discipline, and the experience culminates in a tangible product assessed by members of the field. As such, research projects increase student understanding, confidence, and awareness (Huileman & Harachiewicz, 2009; Russell, Hancock, & McCullough, 2007).

Because student mentoring is a vital factor in college retention (Habley, 2004), individuals who possess career-specific knowledge, skills, and wisdom, can promote career development with students with whom they work (D'Abate & Eddy, 2008), allowing students to get "a glimpse at life in a business setting" (Schlee, 2000, p. 332). It can lower student anxiety (Allen, McManus, & Russell, 1999), can improve career success, and can raise employment satisfaction (Tenenbaum, Crosby, & Gliner, 2001). One study found that even informal mentoring improves the likelihood that a young adult will find full-time work by 25% compared to non-mentored young adults (McDonald, Erickson, Johnson, & Elder, 2007).

Guest speakers are a form of business engagement in which industry practitioners with a particular expertise instruct students on a concept or topic in the classroom (Smith, Rayfield, & McKim, 2015; Tanner et al., 2018). As well, co-instruction can assist in content delivery and provide a spark of interest for students. The content delivered by business representatives serving as co-teachers may increase the opportunities for math and science inquiry as well as decrease the student-to-teacher ratio (Moorehead & Grillo, 2013).

Another form of business engagement is project or competition judging. Industry experts volunteer their knowledge, wisdom, and skills to identify superior student work. By judging a student project or portfolio, industry experts help faculty identify metrics for success that may influence course content and program offerings (Dillon, 1997). In a study of science fair and Science Olympiad participants—activities typically judged by industry professionals—students reported that taking part in these STEM competitions enhanced learning, helped them learn new concepts, and increased their motivation (Abernathy & Vineyard, 2001).

Facility tours are another popular form of business engagement. For students, such tours connect classroom content and real-world application (Harper, 2004). As a result of facility tours, students report higher subject interest and curiosity and display better long-term content retention (Powis, 1999). From a curriculum perspective, tours keep educators informed about new industry practices (Bone & Watson, 2007). There are challenges associated with facility tours, but new technology applications may reduce these barriers. With the widespread adoption of technology in classrooms, virtual facility tours have gained traction. Although virtual tours are less effective than physical tours, they are cheaper for educational institutions, require no transportation coordination, and avoid safety concerns for industrial or medical facilities (Qiu & Hubble, 2002).

Industry practitioners can also serve on voluntary advisory boards that support and guide STEM programs in various ways. Curriculum input is considered an integral role of advisory board members; as possible future employers, industry practitioners are able to best assess program and curriculum quality (Rooney & Puerzer, 2002). A board's effectiveness in assisting student success often depends on having clearly delineated member expectations and responsibilities. In a 2007 case study, effective advisory boards had strong school leadership, experienced board members from a variety of backgrounds, well-organized board meetings, and explicit fundraising initiatives (Genheimer & Shehab, 2009). Board members closely engaged with students are more likely to support the educational institution and help promote the school.

Curriculum enhancements, too, are a form of business engagement in which businesses provide hands-on materials that allow for problem- or project-based learning opportunities. Often students who participate in hands-on learning are more engaged and interested in engineering degrees or career pathways than those instructed in a traditional lecture method (e.g., Zastavker, Ong, & Page, 2006). In a 2001 study, Olds and Miller compared first-year undergraduate engineering students instructed via project-based learning, other hands-on methods, and traditional lecture methods; students that received hands-on instruction had higher graduation rates and expressed greater overall satisfaction with their program upon graduation. Problem- and project-based learning methods allow students to make connections to real-world applications, which increases their interest and persistence to degree completion (Kuh, O'Donnell, & Reed, 2013).

Closely aligned with curriculum, business partners can be instrumental in promoting school and student success through teacher professional development in one of four ways: developing knowledge of a new strategy; understanding the rationale and theory underlying the new strategy; modeling the new skill; and practicing the skill with peer coaching (Joyce & Showers, 2002). The structure of the activity (workshop vs. study group), demographic profile of participation of teachers, and the duration of the activities significantly influences the professional training experience and outcome (Garet, Porter, Desimone, Birman, & Yoon, 2001).

One of the most straightforward forms of business involvement in education is philanthropy, which can encompass monetary donations or fundraising or both. Businesses typically engage with educational institutions for four main reasons: to increase brand recognition, to engage in local community development, to spur research and innovation, and to develop talent for industry or company demand (McCarthy, Contardo, & Eckert, 2010). These strategies signal perceived value by leaders in business and education.

Measuring Business Engagement

Increasingly, business leaders seek to quantify their return on investment and compare their company's efforts to those of other businesses. As McCarthy et al. (2010) note in their report on corporate investments during the recession, companies want to "utilize data to provide evidence of impact, previous success or reasonable expectation of success for new innovation" (p. 263). Typically, corporations, foundations, and other philanthropies are focused on the return on their investment (Erisman & Looney, 2008). These donors endeavor to analyze their return on investment in research, development, and talent recruitment (Clevenger & MacGregor, 2016; Garber, 2017). One way that return on investment can be realized is by increasing the number of students pursuing STEM majors. Similarly, administrators and STEM educators continually seek better records of business engagement efforts, which will allow them to compare efforts to that of their peers and track student interest, enrollment, persistence in STEM majors, and employment. Having easy-to-understand measures of business engagement can help distinguish the educational institution and increase student recruitment.

Though it can be difficult to measure the effectiveness of business involvement in education and the health of a workforce development system (Barnow & King, 2005), officials in university associations who work with donors and corporate partners are currently developing frameworks and models to help illustrate their effectiveness. Universities and their corporate donors are interested in quantifying the return on investment in education. For example, the University Industry Demonstration Partnership (UIDP) is a project-oriented organization that identifies barriers to universities, promotes business partnerships, and creates ways to measure strategic partnerships (see http://uidp.org).

Due to the decrease in corporate spending on research and development, Lutchen (2018) sees positive externalities resulting from more partnerships between companies and universities. Examples include collaborations between Silicon Valley industries and universities for technology, Proctor & Gamble's Modeling and Simulation Center at the University of Cincinnati, and the partnership between Philips Healthcare and Boston University to advance personalized medicine (Lutchen, 2018). Cities like Boston are home to a number of research-intensive universities that offer the combination of resources that help synergize these partnerships.

As institution officials seek to strengthen relationships with business leaders for students' experiential learning, networking groups are of growing interest. The Network of Academic Corporate Relations Officers (NACRO) is one such organization that seeks to strengthen ties between academic institutions and companies to ensure awareness of resources on college campuses as well as to make connections for student recruitment, research collaborations, specialized training, and leadership development opportunities.

NACRO has identified five levels of business engagement in education. The lowest level of commitment for a company is termed a single point of engagement and involves a one-time interaction or activity between an educational institution and a business entity. Afterwards, the partnership terminates. When an educational institution and a business have several points of contact, they have what NACRO calls a managed or transaction-level relationship, which requires greater coordination between partners. A tailored partnership is the third level of engagement, with coordinated investments that target deeper relationships. Compared to the first two levels, the third level adds managed, more intensive direction to the business engagement. NACRO defines the fourth level of engagement as broad-based engagement. Activities include company executive-level employees, who engage with multiple campus entities or departments. Partnership activities are varied but coordinated to achieve a medium-term strategy. The fifth level of engagement NACRO calls a "strategic partnership." This partnership includes a portfolio of investments and activities, such as long-term financial contributions, sponsored research, gifts, and many points of engagement on campus (see: http://nacrocon.org). In addition, NACRO has envisioned several metrics schemes that can help business leaders and academic officials consider partner relationships and are seen by NACRO officials as relevant and appealing to a broad array of industry-education partnerships.

Measuring Influence Through an Engagement Tool

Various levels of investment are ideal, such as those in the NACRO model, because a business's capacity for investment of time and money is different for each type of business engagement activity. Conversely, each type of business engagement activity also has a varying level of influence on student persistence in STEM. The development of a matrix that plots the position for each engagement activity represents an innovative opportunity to visualize business influence on student persistence in STEM education. Researchers at the University of Georgia developed a two-factor engagement model arranged as a matrix of perceived influential engagement activities plotted against their relative capacity requirements (Tanner et al., 2018). Participants were asked to score ten potential business engagement activities on a scale from 0 to 20 for the amount of capacity needed by a business and the respective activity's perceived influence on student persistence.

This business engagement matrix (BEM) was constructed with the continuum of influence across the bottom (the X axis), with low influence being at left and high influence being at the other end of the axis, on the right. The Y axis indicates the continuum of capacity raising up the Y axis, from low capacity being at the bottom of the axis and moving up to high capacity at the top of the Y axis. The resulting matrix thus has four quadrants. The top right quadrant depicts the business engagement activities that are high influence and high capacity. These are the activities that are likely to have the most influence on student persistence in STEM education and work. However, these activities require the highest level of employer engagement or capacity. Top right quadrant activities includes internships, projects, and faculty professional development. The bottom right quadrant represents activities with lower business engagement requirements, but activities with high influence on student persistence. Activities in the bottom left quadrant include mentoring, and facility tours. The other two quadrants, top left and bottom left, are characterized by focus group respondents as having lower perceived influence on student persistence. In the top left quadrant of high capacity and low influence are activities like serving on a program advisory committee. The bottom left quadrant of low capacity and lower influence include activities such as judging a student competition or donating equipment. The focus group and survey data showed that the more personal the engagement, the greater the influence on students. As noted, engagement activities in the top right quadrant were also rated as having the greatest demand on the capacity or resources of the business partner. For more details, see Tanner et al. (2018).

Need for Future Research

In Lutchen's (2018) advocacy for greater business-university partnerships, he offers that cities such as Boston and Cincinnati with nearby research-intensive universities hold promise for strong partnerships. Furthermore, non-research-intensive postsecondary institutions have students and faculty with skills that are valued by businesses as well. Due to quickly changing technologies, employers seek students who will continue learning and adapt to new knowledge and business practices. As Hora, Benbow and Oleson (2016) noted, employers are looking for students with a wide combination of higher-order cognitive competencies, including the ability to learn new skills and adapt to new situations. The goal of business engagement is to unite these overlapping, yet often independently pursued missions; the collaboration between industry and academia can help students understand industry career paths, develop a talent pipeline for employers, increase the number of minorities in STEM, enhance brands awareness, or signal a business's commitment to school and community initiatives.

The works discussed in this chapter align with NACRO's (2012) five levels of business engagement and support NRC's (2012) vision that the relationship between business and higher education should evolve to peer-to-peer relationships. An effective business engagement assessment tool can help business and education administrators talk with clarity about the business' capacity for engagement and the level of influence their investments in STEM may have. Using an engagement matrix can help optimize their collaborations by developing strategies that align the needs of the students with the goals and capacity of the business. However, with limited capacity, business managers and education personnel need to know how and where to allocate resources effectively. Peter Drucker's (1954) comment, "What gets measured gets managed," is a reminder of the value of metrics in the work environment. The research described in the chapter indicates that activities have different levels of perceived impact on student persistence and success in STEM. Just as authentic assessment (Sondergeld et al., 2016) guides effective instruction, tools measuring the academic and career impact of any specific business engagement activity should be developed.

A fundamental challenge in creating peer-to-peer cooperation is to define a common medium with which to align business goals and objectives with those of the educational institution. A universal business engagement tool can provide a common language that business and educators both understand. The business engagement assessment tool must recognize the capacity and resources of the business partner and also the influence on student persistence. More thought is needed to consider the time, cost, and quality of business engagement in STEM education. Business leaders often use cost and time to evaluate the value of an investment. It will be very beneficial to find a common point where worth of an activity to a business can be compared to the worth of that activity to students and the educational institution. More research is needed to determine the optimal way to measure the quality of the business engagement in terms of student persistence and ultimately graduation and employment in a STEM career.

Finally, it is important to note that the path through or to degree completion is not always linear. As highlighted in a recent National Research Council (NRC) report on engineering pathways, a hidden challenge remains in knowing a STEM degree, even a professional degree like engineering, may not lead to employment or a career in that field of study (National Academy of Engineering, 2018). Using data from the 2013 *National Survey of College Graduates*, the NRC report relays that less than half of degreed engineers were employed in a position related to their degree. The report contains further refinements that examine the closeness of work activities to defined engineering occupations and provides the suggestion that certain skills are important in the larger employment view. The risk to business engagement metric development assumes that appropriate business or university partners have been identified to pursue specific goals. Following identification of the partnerships is a next step that can enhance a broader picture of the engagement and should include information on where graduates work. Indeed, there are ways to further our understanding for the impact of business engagement on students and their success.

References

Abernathy, T. V., & Vineyard, R. N. (2001). Academic competitions in science: What are the rewards for students? *Clearing House, 74*(5), 269–276. https://doi.org/10.1080/00098650109599206

Accreditation Board for Engineering and Technology (ABET). (2013). *Criteria for accrediting computing programs.* Retrieved from nsse.indiana.edu/institute/documents/accred/spec_2013/ABET_COMPSCI2013.pdf.

Allen, T. D., McManus, S. E., & Russell, J. E. A. (1999). Newcomer socialization and stress: Formal peer relationships as a source of support. *Journal of Vocational Behavior, 54*, 453–470. https://doi.org/10.1006/jvbe.1998.1674

Association to Advance Collegiate Schools of Business (AACSB). (2015). *AACSB business accreditation standards.* Retrieved from nsse.indiana.edu/institute/documents/accred/2015/AACSB%20Toolkit%202015%20%20 Business.pdf

Association of American Universities (AAU). (2019). *Undergraduate STEM education initiative.* Retrieved from https://www.aau.edu/education-community-impact/undergraduate-education/undergraduate-stem-education-initiative-3

Ballen, J., & Moles, O. (1994). *Strong families, strong schools: Building community partnerships for learning.* Washington, DC: US Department of Education. Retrieved from www.ncjrs.gov/pdffiles1/Digitization/154491NCJRS.pdf

Barnow, B. S., & King, C. T. (2005). *The workforce investment act in eight states: Overview of findings from a field network study.* ETA Occasional Paper, Washington, DC.

Beard, F., & Morton, L. (1998). Effects of internship predictors on successful field experience. *Journalism and Mass Communication Educator, 53*(4), 42–53. https://doi.org/10.1177/107769589805300404

Berlinsky, O. (2014). *Aligned pathways* (Doctoral dissertation). Harvard University.

Boeing. (2018). *Boeing donates $5 million to launch European STEM education effort.* Retrieved from https://boeing.mediaroom.com/2018-07-15-Boeing-donates-5-million-to-launch-European-STEM-education-effort

Bok, D. (2009). *Universities in the marketplace: The commercialization of higher education* (Vol. 39). Princeton, NJ: Princeton University Press.

Bone, Z., & Watson, G. (2007). Realizing the educational potential of student tours. *International Journal of Learning, 14*(8), 43–49. https://doi.org/10.18848/1447-9494/CGP/v14i08/45413

Callanan, G., & Benzing, C. (2004). Assessing the role of internships in the career-oriented employment of graduating college students. *Education + Training, 46*(2), 82–89. https://doi.org/10.1108/00400910410525261

Camblin, S. J. (2003). *The middle grades: Putting all students on track for college.* Washington, DC: Pacific Resources for Educational Learning and the Pathways to College Network.

Clevenger, M. R., & MacGregor, C. J. (2016). The role of corporate and foundation relations development officers (CFRs). In *Facilitating higher education growth through fundraising and philanthropy* (pp. 256–293). IGI Global. https://doi.org/10.4018/978-1-4666-9664-8.ch011

Compact, U. G., & UNICEF. (2013). The smartest investment: A framework for business engagement in education. *UN Global Compact Reports, 5*(1), 50–85.

Crain, A., & Webber, K. (2019). *Across the urban divide: STEM pipeline engagement among non-metropolitan students.* Manuscript submitted to peer-reviewed journal. Previous version: Crain, A., Webber, K., & Perdomo, R. (2019, April). *Across the urban divide.* Scholarly Paper presented at the American Educational Research Association, Toronto.

D'Abate, C. P., & Eddy, E. R. (2008). Mentoring as a learning tool: Enhancing the effectiveness of an undergraduate business-mentoring program. *Mentoring and Tutoring: Partnership in Learning, 16*(4), 363–378. doi: 10.1080/13611260802433692

Davey, T., Meerman, A., Muros, V., Orazbayeva, B., & Baaken, T. (2018). *The state of university-business cooperation in Europe.* Document prepared for the European Commission. Retrieved from https://www.ub-cooperation.eu/pdf/final_report2017.pdf

Dillon, W. T. (1997). Corporate advisory boards, portfolio assessment, and business and technical writing program development. *Business Communication Quarterly, 60*(1), 41–58. https://doi.org/10.1177/108056999706000104

Drucker, P. F. (1954). *The practice of management.* New York, NY: Harper & Collins Publishers.

Engeln, J. T. (2003). Guiding school/business partnerships. *Education Digest, 68*(7), 36–40.

Erisman, W., & Looney, S. M. (2008). *Corporate investments in college readiness and access. institute for higher education policy.* Retrieved from files.eric.ed.gov/fulltext/ ED518025.pdf.

FIRST. (2019). *FIRST vision and mission.* Retrieved from https://www.firstinspires.org/about/vision-and-mission

Fitzgerald, H. E., Bruns, K., Sonka, S., Furco, A., & Swanson, L. (2012). The centrality of engagement in higher education. *Journal of Higher Education Outreach and Engagement, 16*(3), 7–28.

Garber, R. C. (2017). *Academic-corporate relations at a research university: Options for engagement practices and organization.* (Master's thesis). Retrieved from jschola rship.library.jhu.edu/bitstream/handle/1774.2/40618/Garber%2C%20Robert%20C..pdf?sequence=1andisAllowed=y

Garet, M. S., Porter, A. C., Desimone, L., Birman, B. F., & Yoon, K. S. (2001). What makes professional development effective? Results from a national sample of teachers. *American Educational Research Journal, 38*(4), 915–945. https://doi.org/10.3102/00028312038004915

Genheimer, S. R., & Shehab, R. (2009). A survey of industry advisory board operation and effectiveness in engineering education. *Journal of Engineering Education, 98*(2), 169–180. https://doi.org/10.1002/j.2168-9830.2009.tb01015.x

Griffith, A. L. (2010). Persistence of women and minorities in STEM field majors: Is it the school that matters? *Economics of Education Review, 29*(6), 911–922. https://doi.org/10.1016/j.econedurev.2010.06.010

Habley, W. R. (Ed.). (2004). *The status of academic advising: Findings from the ACT sixth national survey.* [Monograph no. 10]. National Academic Advising Association, Manhattan, KS.

Harper, R. (2004). The use of group work and presentations on field trips to facilitate active learning experience. In M. Healey & J. Roberts (Eds.), *Engaging students in active learning: Case studies in geography, environment and related disciplines.* School of Environment, Cheltenham, England: University of Gloucestershire.

Hasselmo, N., & McKinnell, H. (2003). Working together, creating knowledge: The university-industry research collaborative initiative. *Business-Higher Education Forum*, Washington, DC. Retrieved from www.bhef.com/sites/default/files/BHEF_2001_working_together.pdf

HESA. (2009). *Pathways to a diverse and effective South African higher education system. Strategic Framework 2010–2020*. Pretoria: Higher Education South Africa.

Hora, M. T., Benbow, R., & Oleson, K. (2016). *Beyond the skills gap: Preparing college students for life and work*. Cambridge, MA: Harvard Education Press.

Hossain, M., & Robinson, M. (2012). How to motivate U.S. students to pursue STEM (science, technology, engineering, and mathematics) careers. *US-China Education Review, 4*, 442–451.

Huileman, C., & Harachiewicz, J. (2009). Promoting interest and performance in high school science classes. *Science, 326*(5958), 1410–1412.

Joyce, B. R., & Showers, B. (2002). *Student achievement through staff development*. National College for School Leadership. Retrieved from https://www.nationalcollege.org.uk/cm-mc-ssl-resource-joyceshowers.pdf

Kenney, M., & Patton, D. (2009). Reconsidering the Bayh-Dole Act and the current university invention ownership model. *Research Policy, 38*, 1407–1422. https://doi.org/10.1016/j.respol.2009.07.007

Knouse, S. B., & Fontenot, G. (2008). Benefits of the business college internship: A research review. *Journal of Employment Counseling, 45*(2), 61–66. https://doi.org/10.1002/j.2161-1920.2008.tb00045.x

Kuh, G. D., O'Donnell, K., & Reed, S. (2013). *Ensuring quality and taking high-impact practices to scale*. Washington, DC: Association of American Colleges and Universities.

Lutchen, K. R. (2018, January 24). Why companies and universities should forge long-term collaborations. *Harvard Business Review*. Retrieved from https://hbr.org/2018/01/why-companies-and-universities-should-forge-long-term-collaborations

Maltese, A. V., & Tai, R. H. (2010). Eyeballs in the fridge: Sources of early interest in science. *International Journal of Science Education, 32*(5), 669–685.

Mann, A., & Dawkins, J. (2014). *Employer engagement in education: Literature review*. Reading, England: CFBT Education Trust.

Mann, A., Stanley, J., & Archer, L. (Eds.). (2014). *Understanding employer engagement in education: Theories and evidence*. New York, NY: Routledge. https://doi.org/10.1187/cbe.07-06-0039

McCarthy, K., Contardo, J., & Eckert, L. M. (2010). Corporate investments in education during an economic downturn. *International Journal of Educational Advancement, 9*(4), 251–265. https://doi.org/10.1057/ijea.2009.44

McDonald, S., Erickson, L. D., Johnson, M. K., & Elder, G. H. (2007). Informal mentoring and young adult employment. *Social Science Research, 36*, 1328–1347. https://doi.org/10.1016/j.ssresearch.2007.01.008

McKinsey Global Institute. (2012). *The world at work: Jobs, pay, and skills for 3.5 billion people*. Retrieved from www.mckinsey.com/global-themes/employment-and-growth/the-world-at-work.

Moorehead, T., & Grillo, K. (2013). Celebrating the reality of inclusive STEM education: Co-teaching in science and mathematics. *Teaching Exceptional Children, 45*(4), 50–57.

Narayanan, V. K., Olk, P., & Fukami, C. (2006). Determinants of internship effectiveness: An exploratory model. In *Academy of management proceedings* (Vol. 2006, No. 1, pp. E1–E6). Briarcliff Manor, NY: Academy of Management.

National Academy of Engineering. (2018). *Understanding the educational and career pathways of engineers*. Washington, DC: The National Academies Press. https://doi.org/10.17226/25284

National Research Council. (2012). *Research universities and the future of America: Ten breakthrough actions vital to our nation's prosperity and security*. Washington, DC: The National Academies Press. https://doi.org/10.17226/13396

National Science Board. (2007). *A national action plan for addressing the critical needs of the U.S. science, technology, engineering, and mathematics education system*. Arlington, VA: National Science Foundation.

Olson, S., & Riordan, D. G. (2012). *Engage to excel: Producing one million additional college graduates with degrees in science, technology, engineering, and mathematics*. Report to the President. Executive Office of the President. Retrieved from obamawhitehouse.archives.gov/sites/default/files/microsites/ostp/pcast-engage-to-excel-final_2–25–12.pdf

P21 frameworks for 21st century learning definitions. (2019). *Battelle for kids*. Retrieved from P21_Framework_DefinitionsBFK.pdf

Perdomo, R., & Webber, K. (2018, December). *Participation matters: The benefits of extracurricular activities in high school to choice of STEM major in college*. Manuscript under review.

Powis, K. (1999). The field trip as an active learning strategy. *Teaching Options, 3*(1), 1–2. Teaching Technologies, Center for University Teaching, University of Ottawa.

Promoting Higher Education-Industry Partnerships and Collaborations. (2016). *A report to the research and innovation strategy group higher education South Africa*. Retrieved from http://www.usaf.ac.za/wp-content/uploads/2017/08/Promoting-Higher-Education_Industry-Partnerships_2012.pdf

Qiu, W., & Hubble, T. (2002). The advantages and disadvantages of virtual field trips in geoscience education. In M. Peat (Ed.), *The China papers: Tertiary science and mathematics teaching for the 21st century* (Vol. 1, p. 75). Sydney: The University of Sydney.

Rooney, D. M., & Puerzer, R. J. (2002). The smaller engineering school and its industrial advisory board: An effective partnership? In *32nd Annual ASEE/IEEE Frontiers in Education* (Vol. 2, pp. F1B16–F1B21).

Rothman, M. (2007). Lessons learned: Advice to employers from interns. *Journal of Education for Business, 82*, 140–144. https://doi.org/10.3200/JOEB.82.3.140-144

Russell, S. H., Hancock, M. P., & McCullough, J. (2007). Benefits of undergraduate research experiences. *Science, 316*(5824), 548–549. https://doi.org/10.1126/science.1140384

Schlee, R. P. (2000). Mentoring and the professional development of business students. *Journal of Management Education, 24*(3), 322–337. https://doi.org/10.1177/105256290002400304

Smith, K., Rayfield, J., & McKim, B. (2015). Effective practices in STEM integration: Describing teacher perceptions and instructional method use. *Journal of Agricultural Education, 56*, 182–201. https://doi.org/10.5032/jae.2015.04183

Sondergeld, T., Burton-Peters, E., & Johnson, C. (2016). Integrating the three dimensions of next generation science standards. *School Science and Mathematics, 116*(2). https://doi.org/10.1111/ssm.12160

Strata Education Network and Gallup. (2017). *Major influence: Where students get valued advice on what to study in college*. Retrieved from news.gallup.com/reports/219236/major-influence-students-valued-advice-study-college.aspxinsey.com/insights/employment_and_growth/the_world_at_work

Stych, A. (2018). Tech companies pledge $300M to STEM education. *American City Business Journals*. Retrieved from https://www.bizjournals.com/bizwomen/news/latest-news/2017/09/major-tech-companies-pledge-300m-to-stem-education.html?page=all

Tanner, D., Burg, T., Webber, K., Leach, C., . . . Tomlin, V. (2018). *Business engagement in STEM workforce development: How business engagement in high schools and college programs impacts student persistence in STEM education and STEM careers*. Athens, GA: University of Georgia Office of Research Report.

Tenenbaum, H. R., Crosby, F. J., & Gliner, M. D. (2001). Mentoring relationships in graduate School. *Journal of Vocational Behavior, 59*, 326–341. https://doi.org/10.1006/jvbe.2001.1804

Tierney, W., & Hagedorn, L. S. (2002). *Increasing access to college: Extending possibilities for all students*. Albany, NY: State University of New York Press.

Tinto, V. (1993). Building community. *Liberal Education, 79*(4), 16–21.

Watters, J. J., & Diezmann, C. M. (2013). Community partnerships for fostering student interest and engagement in STEM. *Journal of STEM Education: Innovations and Research, 14*(2), 47.

Wimberly, G., & Noeth, R. (2005). *College readiness begins in middle school*. ACT Policy Report. Retrieved from https://files.eric.ed.gov/fulltext/ED483849.pdf

(The) Wonderful Company. (2018). *Social responsibility: Education*. Retrieved from https://www.wonderful.com/social-responsibility/education.htm

Zastavker, Y. V., Ong, M., & Page, L. (2006, October). Women in engineering: Exploring the effects of project-based learning in a first-year undergraduate engineering program. In *Frontiers in Education Conference, 36th Annual* (pp. S3G1–6). Piscataway, NJ: Institute of Electrical and Electronics Engineers.

37

STEM TEACHER LEADERSHIP IN POLICY

*Rebecca Hite, Rebecca E. Vieyra, Jeff Milbourne, Remy Dou,
Timothy Spuck and John F. Smith*

Introduction

Research on teacher leadership tends to emphasize improving teachers' instructional performance (e.g., Smylie & Eckert, 2018; Yarger & Lee, 1994; York-Barr & Duke, 2004). Less attention has been paid to the wider impact that classroom teachers have on influencing education in ways that go beyond local contexts and into state, regional, and/or national settings (Neumerski, 2013). In this chapter, we explore a particular version of teacher leadership in policy that involves actions taken by K-12 science, technology, engineering, and mathematics (STEM) teachers who specifically target STEM education policies created at state and federal levels. STEM teacher leadership invites our attention in light of intensifying international discourse and policies around economic competitiveness, development, and demands for STEM workers. In the United States, for example, STEM education has remained a top priority for recent U.S. presidents (White House, 2012, 2018), and prominent international agencies have highlighted STEM as essential to address global environmental, economic, and social challenges (Organisation for Economic Co-operation and Development [OECD], 2018; United Nations Educational, Scientific and Cultural Organization, [UNSECO], 2017). In this chapter, we focus on the ways in which STEM teacher leaders contribute to the creation of high-level policies and programs.

STEM teacher policy leadership may include activities that explicitly lead groups of other STEM teachers toward policy action, as well as activities whereby individual teachers represent or speak on behalf of the STEM teaching profession. This form of STEM teacher leadership in policy, at state or national levels, has implications for other STEM teachers—implications that are not restricted to individual teachers, schools, or districts (e.g., translating state policy within a school, which inevitably leads to some transformation of that original policy). Our perspective also moves beyond collective bargaining of discipline-agnostic teacher groups (e.g., union-based advocacy for action on matters such as teacher salary or working conditions). In addition to the focus on STEM teacher leaders' contributions to high-level policies and programs, this chapter focuses on the highest levels of educational policymaking, which typically occurs at a state or federal level of government and may include the STEM teacher leader individually who moves past building-level instructional leadership into larger policy spaces.

K-12 Teacher Leadership in Policy

To explore K-12 STEM teacher leadership in policy, one must situate this perspective within the broad milieu of research on teacher leadership (see Chapter 30, "Teacher Leadership for STEM

Programming"). Given previous findings, teacher leadership has the potential to inform teachers' expertise development and vice versa (Berkowicz & Myers, 2017)—a potential reflected in the newly reauthorized Every Student Succeeds Act (ESSA) in the United States, which recommends developing teacher leadership to improve education outcomes (Government Track, 2015). Experiences in leadership are also being incorporated internationally into teacher performance evaluation systems in places like Singapore (Darling-Hammond & Rothman, 2011) and domestically in North Carolina (State Board of Education, 2015). Despite teacher leadership taking on a more prominent role in education reform, the lack of consensus on definitions and frameworks persists (Hunzicker, 2017).

The U.S. Department of Education (U.S. DoED) has identified that K–12 teachers who pursue opportunities to exercise leadership are more confident in their instructional abilities and more satisfied in their jobs, compared to teachers who do not engage in leadership. In response, the *Teach to Lead* initiative was convened by the National Board for Professional Teaching Standards (NBPTS), Association for Supervision and Curriculum Development (ASCD), and U.S. DoED to ensure that "teachers are valued as the foremost experts in instruction and, as such, are leaders of informing, developing, and implementing education policy and practice to steer systematic improvements to benefit student learning" (US DoED, 2019, homepage, para. 5; Teach to Lead, 2019).

Any research on teacher leadership must consider variations in national K–12 education systems. Education policy development and implementation differs drastically based upon two broad categories: centralized and decentralized systems. While these are admittedly generalized and oversimplified terms, centralized education systems tend to empower a national institution (e.g., a ministry of education) with the authority to create curriculum, policy, and/or processes that schools must adopt. This central authority may provide the majority of educational funding and holds significant power over the curriculum, pacing, and pedagogy of classrooms, such as in Turkey (Kayaoglu, 2015), China (Tan, 2015), and Uruguay (Bogliaccini & Rodríguez, 2015).

Decentralized education systems tend to hand more control over education curriculum, policy, and processes to local or district governance, although funding tends to be sourced from local revenues. Decentralization is a "process by which decision-making responsibilities are transferred from higher levels of government to lower levels and even to the schools themselves" (Bernbaum, 2011, p. 8). The U.S. has a decentralized education system, in which state departments of education and school districts have much more control over what gets taught than a sole federal ministry or department of education. Alternatively, one can think of the U.S. education system as a hybrid where individual U.S. states (notably some are as large as European countries) can act as their own centralized system.

Regardless of system type, the multi-layered policy infrastructure of any education system presents a variety of opportunities for teachers to influence policy creation and implementation. Yet, few teachers participate in higher-level policy spaces. This lack of participation may reflect the lack of instructional experiences in teacher preparation programs to engage in policy discussions and development. However, history illustrates the need for teacher leadership in these contexts and may provide some vital perspective on the importance of STEM teacher leadership in this domain.

A Brief History of K-12 STEM Teacher Policy Leadership

Arguably, the need for teacher leadership is not relegated to a particular content area, yet the impetus has remained on teachers and schools to develop the STEM pipeline given its framing as a factor of global economic competitiveness (National Science Board, 2018). Recently, some stakeholders have moved toward a less outward-facing goal for the STEM education enterprise in favor of a more inward-facing one, that is, the betterment of students both in terms of their civic understanding as well as career options available to them (OECD, 2018). Moreover, STEM is often a centerpiece in education discourse, investment, and policies at local, state, and federal levels. As such, there are questions to answer about the efficacy of these understudied investments, particularly the short- and long-term impacts of teacher leadership in policy programs.

Teachers have historically participated as supporters in national policy conversations initially through collective bargaining with unions and later through collaborative entities, such as disciplinary professional societies and advisory boards. Pennington (2013) has written on this history, pointing out that the teacher voice in policymaking began with unions like the American Federation of Teachers (AFT; established in 1916) and the National Education Association (NEA; established in 1857). In the U.S., entities such as the National Council of Teachers of Mathematics (NCTM; established in 1920), the International Technology and Engineering Educators Association (ITEEA; established in 1939), the National Science Teachers Association (NSTA; established in 1944), and the International Society for Technology in Education (ISTE; established in 1979) have had long-established position and policy statements used as points of advocacy for teachers in their respective STEM disciplines. Although historically American teacher unions (i.e., NEA, AFT) focused on teacher working conditions and wages, Pennington describes a watershed moment in the 1980s, attributed to then AFT president Al Shanker, when he pronounced that teachers *themselves* (individually) should engage in advocacy to improve education. This proclamation was made in light of the *A Nation at Risk* report (Gardner, 1983).

The maturation of teacher unions, coupled with a laser focus on improving STEM education, precipitated federal investment in K–12 STEM educational reform in the mid-to-late 20th century. Most of this reform was focused on curriculum (DeBoer, 1991), whereas investments in teachers would be later realized in the early 21st century. That national call, arousing the attention of STEM educators, occurred with the release of the report, *Prepare and Inspire,* from the President's Council of Advisors on Science and Technology (2010). These advisors called for the recognition of a corps of experienced K–12 STEM teachers who, among other roles, could "provide a voice for their profession in educational policy and . . . be effective advocates for STEM in their schools, school districts, and communities" (p. 76).

While Congress has not yet allocated funds to realize a national STEM Master Teacher Corps, dozens of existing efforts have engaged teachers in policy (Johnson & Brady, 2018), including programs like Math for America and New York State's STEM Master Teacher Program. Additionally, the U.S. Department of Education has convened stakeholders to discuss K–12 STEM teacher leadership, including their engagement in policy (US DoEd, 2019).

Further Recognition of Teachers as Leaders in Policy

When *Prepare and Inspire* was released in 2010, world education leaders, too, were coming together to identify emerging issues in math and science education policymaking. In 2009, UNESCO formed the International Group of Experts on Science and Mathematics Education Policies. This group identified a coherent and pervasive set of emerging math and science education policy issues that transcend culture. These issues included math and science literacy, promoting change in instruction, aligning formal and informal education, supporting systemic change, addressing language and gender diversity, and promoting disciplinary research (UNESCO, 2010, 2012). Although teachers were identified as primary agents of change, the committee fell short of recognizing teachers as potential policy advocates or supporting professional development of teachers that might increase their understanding of policy. On the other hand, the *Strategic Plan for 2018–2021* by the UN's International Task Force on Teachers for Education 2030 fully recognized teachers as important contributors to policy in stating that "the efficient implementation of teacher policies requires dialogue and extensive participation of all stakeholders—starting with teachers themselves" (2018, p. 10).

Recognizing the growing attention to the "E" and "T" in STEM, the U.S. National Academies of Science, Engineering, and Medicine's Board on Science Education (NASEM-BOSE) held an additional convening focused on teacher policy leadership in technology and engineering education. In 2017, STEM educators and professional societies gathered to address *Increasing the Roles and Significance of Teachers in Policymaking for K-12 Engineering Education* (National Research Council [NRC], 2017). A theme throughout the convening was that many of the attendees—nearly two-thirds of whom were teachers—felt that policies that negatively affected their classrooms could have been avoided had teachers been consulted. Teachers and other stakeholders identified how they could contribute to policy dialogue: (1) synthesizing basic engineering education research for use by teachers, (2) building public-private partnerships to improve educational offerings, (3) improving teacher preparation and professional development to better meet the disciplinary needs of teachers, (4) developing holistic student assessments, and (5) improving teacher certification procedures and requirements.

Last but not least, STEM teachers have begun to speak out on their desire and capacity for leadership in policy with significant support from NASEM-BOSE. In a convening entitled *Exploring Opportunities for STEM Teacher Leadership* (NRC, 2014), teachers called for leadership opportunities beyond the scope of instruction, with examples including state policy licensure, credentialing, and certification. Teachers also called for professional development to include leadership support and a recognition of the assets they bear when contributing to curriculum and standards development, as well as when advising state boards of education. A separate report on evidence-based practices for science teacher professional development emphasized the need for teacher leadership and how teachers can be engaged in shaping policy (NASEM, 2015).

Programmatic Exemplars of K-12 STEM Teacher Leadership

The NRC (2014) report resulting from the meeting organized by NASEM-BOSE identified programmatic exemplars that reveal potential relationships between STEM teacher participation in policy leadership activities and valuable outcomes, including improved instructional practices, retention, and persistence. These programs were the Albert Einstein Distinguished Educator Fellowship (AEF) and the Knowles Teacher Initiative (Knowles). Other extant national programs like the AEF and Knowles include the Noyce Scholars program (Noyce) and the Presidential Awards for Excellence in Mathematics and Science Teaching (PAEMST). These programs engage STEM teachers in a variety of leadership activities, some more focused on early career teachers (e.g., Knowles) and others on well-experienced teachers (e.g., PAEMST). Moreover, some of these programs specifically facilitate teacher engagement in policymaking (e.g., AEF), while others focus on developing supportive teacher communities in high-need districts and schools (e.g., Noyce).

The NRC (2014) report concluded that teachers who participate in these capacity-building programs develop skills relevant to the classroom and leverage their expertise while participating in leadership activities at the district, state, and/or national levels. Pennington (2013) states that the reason "why so many new teacher-voice organizations [and fellowships] have sprung up in the past few years . . . [is due to] the effect of federal policy requiring collaboration among teachers, administrators, school boards, and state-education officials around the improvement of education" (p. 9). This included references to additional teacher-voice programs (i.e., Teach Plus, Educators for Excellence, VIVA Teachers, the Center for Teaching Quality, and the National Network of State Teachers of the Year [NNSTOY]). The list of programs does not stop there. Groups like America Achieves, the Hope Street Group, the NSTA/NCTM STEM Ambassador Fellowship, and the US DoED School Ambassador Fellowship create teacher experiences (e.g., fellowships) that advance the teacher voice in policy.

Present Research

Despite the recognized importance of STEM teacher leadership in policy, significant literature gaps exist. International models of teacher leadership development (e.g., Poekert, Alexandrou, & Shannon, 2016) exist; however, these models relegate teacher leadership and consequent activity to the classroom, school, or local community. Further, a dearth of models exploring nuances within the policy space and understanding, perhaps even quantifying, the impact of their input is also evident (Hite & Milbourne, 2018; NASEM, 2015).

This lack of viable models creates a problem space to originate, adapt, and evaluate conceptual frameworks for STEM teacher leadership development in policy. The research community is presented with important questions such as the following: Who are K-12 STEM teacher leaders? What specific knowledge and skills are needed to foster development of a K-12 STEM teacher leader in policy? While data exist from some of the aforementioned groups, that data's purpose and collection focus not on framework development, but rather on programmatic evaluation. It is unclear how teachers' participation in the policy space actually impacts the education system, both structurally (e.g., influencing policy and funding streams) and in reform-based efforts (e.g., improving student outcomes and teacher retention).

Recent surveys of teachers suggest that the lack of broader policy-engagement opportunities is having a negative impact on teacher retention and job satisfaction. A 2017 study on teacher turnover reported two significant factors in teachers' decisions to leave the classroom: (1) lack of opportunity for input, and (2) dissatisfaction with current testing and accountability policies (Carver-Thomas & Darling-Hammond, 2017). These results echo other teacher surveys (e.g., Berry, Daughtrey, & Wieder, 2010) that identify overly prescriptive policies and lack of input into policymaking, even at the school level, as significant obstacles to teacher efficacy.

These literature gaps are consistent with similar gaps in the larger body of scholarship on teacher leadership. The "research base on teacher leadership is not robust" (NASEM, 2015, p. 196) and replete with small cottage industry studies that have yet to address how teacher leaders define themselves and how they impact instruction at scale (Neumerski, 2013). Hence, recent research has explored the creation of theory-driven conceptual frameworks to define teacher leadership (Berg & Zoellick, 2019) and sequence teacher leadership development (Hite & Milbourne, 2018). This research brings clarity to how discipline-specific culture and context mediate the teacher leadership experience and its impact within and beyond the classroom (Wenner & Campbell, 2017). As an example, Scotland's recent teacher-led revision of national curriculum provided opportunities to study how classroom teachers navigate decisions about prioritizing content and process skills that will influence the whole country (Wallace & Priestley, 2016).

Within the broader teacher leadership literature, scholarship on STEM teachers participating in policy is even more limited. Wenner and Campbell (2017) performed a meta-analysis of high-quality studies on teacher leadership in general. Only seven studies out of a total of 54 were focused specifically on STEM leadership. All seven of these studies focused on teachers' action as instructional leaders; none focused on teachers as policy leaders. A scan of specialized literature databases on math and science teaching, such as the National Science Foundation (NSF)-sponsored Math and Science Partnership Network website (MSPNet, 2019), likewise provides little in the way of scholarship beyond instructional leadership. Some research examining programs like the Robert Noyce Teacher Scholarship Program (2019) shows promise in moving toward a vision of policy engagement. However, such programs are often hosted at institutions that primarily serve pre-service teachers, focus on the early stages of teacher leadership, such as supporting teacher inductees (Alemdar, Cappelli, Criswell, & Rushton, 2018), and rarely reference policy engagement. One such Noyce program awardee and his team (Criswell, Rushton, McDonald, & Gul, 2017; Criswell et al., 2018) describe an allegory for "professional vision" with implications that teachers have the capacity to influence the system beyond their or their colleagues' instructional practices. But again, explicit programmatic foci on policy is rare.

Further, most research on STEM teacher leadership in general is limited to the U.S. The authors have performed several systematic reviews of international literature that focused on science and STEM teachers' leadership beyond the district level that yielded no results. The literature were either not outside of the U.S. or related to participation in teachers' unions. Other than the previously cited international references (UNESCO, 2010, 2012), few international policy documents even reference the value of teacher leadership, suggesting a lack of international scholarship and policy action in the STEM teacher leadership space.

Recognizing the underutilized potential of educational research, Fensham (2009) identified a gap between policy and practice in STEM education. Fensham argues that while researchers often contribute to curricular materials and new findings, these products are neither always used as intended nor useful in more complex environments. While Fensham does not explicitly call for teachers as interlocutors, he calls for a deeper research investigation into "policy as values" and "policy as authority" (p. 1081) as factors that influence instructional change. NNSTOY (2016, p. 27) has recommended that teachers learn about policymaking during their teacher preparation programs, trained with skills in advocacy, communication with lawmakers, and policy assessment.

Existing Programs Focused on K-12 STEM Education Policy Leadership

Among the limited studies of STEM teacher leadership development are a series of research reports funded by the NSF (Galosy, Mohan, Mohan, Miller, & Bintz, 2017a, 2017b, 2017c). In these reports, 18 research articles and 15 program abstracts were reviewed that covered the majority of well-known and well-established STEM teacher leadership programs. The team used a broad view of teacher leadership defined by Holland, Eckert, and Allen (2014) that included teacher influence on policymakers and focused on teacher leadership programs that focus on teachers as "change agents who not only improve their own classrooms, but also drive continuous improvement in their schools and beyond" (Galosy et al., 2017b, p. 4). The review identified just two programs that explicitly address STEM education policy or advocacy in their leadership content or pedagogy: the AEF program (US DoE, 2019) and the Kenan Fellows Program for Teacher Leadership (2019). (It is worth noting that all six of this chapter's authors served as AEF fellows, and two of the six had previously served as Kenan Fellows.)

The AEF is a federally mandated program that places K-12 STEM educators in offices on Capitol Hill and federal agencies. A recent program evaluation of the fellowship reports that AEF fellows develop better awareness of how federal agencies, including Congress, operate and make substantive contributions to their sponsoring agencies (Gareis, Priedeman, Manning, & Goodman, 2011). However, the majority of the 11-month experience is unique to the office where fellows are placed. As a result, fellows' policy engagement is more a product of their pre-existing leadership experience and independent exposure to the policy environment than any focused leadership development.

While the Kenan Fellowship provides background on how state-level policy works specific to North Carolina (NC), the program is not centered on policy engagement per se, instead providing participants with opportunities to collaborate with university and industry partners on STEM projects to foster external relationships and develop K-12 STEM curriculum from those collaborations. However, due to a lack of opportunities for NC teachers to participate in leadership with local stakeholders, the program has pivoted to provide more foundational knowledge on the nature of schooling in NC, the strategy of communicating with school board members, and opportunities to weigh in on regional educational policy issues (L. Hibler, personal communication, January 22, 2019).

An international initiative to engage STEM teachers in policy is also occurring in other parts of the Western Hemisphere. In early 2019, the Inter-American Teacher Education Network (ITEN) of the Organization of American States launched the ITEN Teacher Fellowship. This fellowship is composed of practicing STEM teachers nominated by their respective Ministries of Education in Latin America and the Caribbean who participate in multi-year collaborative teams with policymakers to address some of the most pressing needs of the region, from STEM teacher recruitment to career pathways. This program quantifies growth in teacher leadership self-efficacy, as well as their leadership impact on national educational systems. This initiative is notably different from the type of policy engagement that has up ticked in Latin America over the past two decades, which has been led primarily by teachers' unions and focused on more general issues, such as educational funding (Finger & Gindin, 2015).

A Case of an Intentional Teacher Leadership Program in Policy

In 2018, the American Association of Physics Teachers and the American Institute of Physics Teachers established the inaugural class of AAPT/AIP Master Teacher Policy Fellows (Bundy et al., 2019). This program was built on a teacher leadership framework developed by the AAPT Master Teacher Leader Task Force (2017) that includes policy leadership as one core pillar. This fellowship cohort is composed of 23 teachers in eight teams that are working on state-level policy issues related to the equitable access of K–12 physics education for all students. Their goals address issues as diverse as advocating for legislation to provide funds for teachers to recertify in higher-needs STEM fields and building support to advocate for dedicated science instructional time in elementary classrooms. These teachers participate in an eight-day summit in Washington, D.C., to define their policy issue and create a year-long advocacy plan. Over the course of the following school year, they engage their advocacy plan, supported by monthly group meetings. Preliminary data analysis of the inaugural cohort suggests that the D.C. summit facilitated observable changes in teacher policy leadership self-efficacy and policy-specific communication skills.

Extant Theories on STEM Teacher Leadership Development in Policy

Both York-Barr and Duke (2004) and Wenner and Campbell (2017) emphasized the lack of theory-driven conceptual frameworks undergirding teacher leadership programs. Several works have started to address this gap by looking at teacher leadership development more broadly and STEM teacher policy leadership more specifically. Two recent case studies examined teachers' development as instructional leaders (Hunzicker, 2017; Sinha & Hanuscin, 2017). Huggins, Lesseig, and Rhodes (2017) examined professional development structures that supported emerging leadership identities in early-career mathematics teachers, yet again focusing on instructional leadership, not policy leadership.

A recently published conceptual framework by Hite and Milbourne (2018) provides theoretical guidance for K–12 STEM teacher development specific to policy leadership. The K–12 STEM Master Teacher (STEMMaTe) model leverages a communities-of-practice framework, based on situative theory, that identifies five sequential dimensions of K–12 STEM teacher development. The model builds off Lave and Wenger's (1991) notion of legitimate peripheral participation (LPP), whereby novices develop mastery through increasingly meaningful experiences (i.e., participation) within a community. STEMMaTe depicts teachers moving from school-focused leadership to state-level and national leadership.

STEMMaTe applies the concept of LPP to STEM educational contexts by describing STEM teacher leadership development as performance within a scalable professional learning environment (e.g., classroom → school → regional → state → national) whereby the learner's unique *situated expertise* (i.e., STEM teaching) is applied incrementally through *community practices* (e.g., leadership, advocacy) in a novel activity space that extends beyond day-to-day classroom activities. In short, the

STEMMaTe framework suggests that as K–12 STEM teachers participate in professional development experiences that expand their expertise within various communities of practice in and beyond the classroom, they may also progress along the following dimensions of participation:

1. **Scholastic Effectiveness.** Leading classroom-based activities that have positive effects on student performance (e.g., standardized test scores), affect (e.g., attitudes toward STEM), and 21st-century skills (e.g., working well with others).
2. **Institutional Knowledge and Memory.** Contributing to school-level STEM curriculum implementation (e.g., department chair, math coach) and broader school culture around STEM (e.g., participation in regional or national competition).
3. **Adaptability/Flexibility.** Interacting with district teachers and administrators across schools (e.g., leading teacher professional development, contributing to local teacher-support communities).
4. **Emergent Leadership.** Starting to grow beyond their role as a classroom teacher to include regional, state, and national levels of contribution to the broader STEM education community. This may include presenting at national conferences, participating in online teaching communities, and engaging in advocacy that favors better educational practices and outcomes.
5. **Strategic Leadership.** Operationalizing their systems-wide understanding of STEM education across local, regional, state, and national levels, with varying impact across each level. Strategic leaders may serve as advisors to state boards of education, serve as leaders for national organizations like the National Science Teachers Association (NSTA), or inform teacher leadership programs.

Overall, the framework suggests that effective leadership development requires a continuum of experiences spanning across multiple programs over the course of a STEM teacher's career. This may help to explain why the Kenan Fellows Program has begun to provide more experiences in dimension 2 such that their fellows may be ready for the activities to develop their skills in dimension 3 (adaptability and flexibility). This idea of a continuum also presents an opportunity to sequence existing programs like Knowles, AEF, and similar programs so that those programs may work together in a coordinated fashion. These national program sequences could be backwards mapped to serve as models for local, state, and regional leadership development opportunities.

Future Research

Given the recognized importance of STEM teacher leadership in policy by groups like NRC and NASEM, as well as the significant literature gaps, this area is primed for further exploration. The literature has explicitly identified several questions that are ready for active and robust exploration by researchers. For example, the NASEM convening on teacher policy leadership in engineering (NRC, 2017) detailed three questions: (1) What is the evidence that teacher engagement in policy is good for education? (2) What models for teacher engagement in policy exist? And (3) what communication is needed to help people understand the role of teachers in policy? Hite and Milbourne (2018) also raise questions about STEM teacher leadership development: How could existing leadership development programs work in concert to create a continuum of experiences beginning during pre-service/induction and culminating in state/national policy leadership engagement? Given the traditional conceptions of a teacher's role, including time constraints, how can individual schools and school districts effectively leverage the skill sets of STEM teacher leaders?

In addition to these fundamental questions, this area also presents a series of tensions that need further exploration. As the last question suggests, teacher policy leaders may experience tension when trying to incorporate their policy skills into their role as a classroom educator. That tension could manifest itself as a lack of time to pursue policy activity, given the constraints associated with classroom teaching. However, that tension could also present itself in a more negative fashion if a teacher's administrator does not think that policy work is appropriate. This could lead to what some in the field have dubbed the "re-entry problem," whereby teachers experience a rich, external professional development program like AEF, go back to their classrooms, and are unable to leverage their newfound skill sets because of the limitations of their context.

Conclusion

Research on K-12 STEM teacher policy leadership presents a challenge for researchers not only in definition, design, and implementation, but also measurement and assessment of impact. While influences of teacher leadership can be observed within classrooms, schools, or even districts, impacts of policy leadership may be more difficult to measure. While teachers can engage with policy, the effects may or may not be measurable (or attributable to a teacher's engagement in policy) through traditional academic assessments. Further, because policy is often perceived as being systemic, policy teacher leaders might find themselves drawn to a policy sphere far beyond their district or even their state, thereby distancing themselves from places where they are often most highly valued—classrooms. This concern was vocalized by Steve Robinson, a Washington, D.C.-based STEM teacher, stating that "enabling teachers to get involved in policy does sometimes mean that they leave a school, which is a loss to that school" (NRC, 2014, p. 21). This sentiment is consistent with the findings of Galosy et al. (2017a) about AEF. While the program "had positive impacts on participants' teacher leadership development, 50 percent of them did not return to classroom teaching, which was not an outcome the program intended" (p. 28). It is unclear whether teachers leaving classrooms to pursue careers in education policy or program development weaken education systems or instead create a stronger system for all.

While teachers who are responsible for implementing education policy should have a role in shaping that policy, teachers' activity in the policy space has political implications. Policy and politics, while separate entities in theory, are often intertwined in practice, raising questions about what level of policy activity is appropriate for classroom teachers. Some pundits referred to the 2018 election as "the year of the teacher." It is estimated that a record number of teachers, including those who previously taught, ran for public office, and many of them were successful. The coming decade may present a unique opportunity to help us more clearly understand the impact these new policymakers, and others like them, can have.

References

AAPT Master Teacher Leader Task Force. (2017). *Aspiring to lead: Engaging K-12 teachers as agents of national change in physics education.* Retrieved from https://www.aapt.org/K12/upload/PMTL-Report-2017__aapt_fina.pdf

Alemdar, M., Cappelli, C. J., Criswell, B. A., & Rushton, G. (2018). Evaluation of a Noyce program: Development of teacher leaders in STEM education. *Evaluation and Program Planning, 71*, 1–11. https://doi.org/10.1016/j.evalprogplan.2018.06.005

Berg, J. H., & Zoellick, B. (2019). Teacher leadership: Toward a new conceptual framework. *Journal of Professional Capital and Community, 4*(1), 2–14. https://doi.org/10.1108/JPCC-06–2018–0017

Berkowicz, J., & Myers, A. (2017). *Spatial skills: A neglected dimension of early STEM education.* Retrieved from blogs.edweek.org/edweek/leadership_360/2017/02/spatial_skills_a_neglected_dimension_of_ea lY_stem_education.html

Bernbaum, M. (2011). *EQUIP2 lessons learned in education decentralization: A guide to education project design, implementation, and evaluation based on experiences from EQUIP2 projects in Egypt, Georgia, Mali, and Malawi.* Retrieved from https://www.epdc.org/sites/default/files/documents/EQUIP2%20LL%20Decentraliza tion%20AAR.pdf

Berry, B., Daughtrey, A., & Wieder, A. (2010). *Teacher leadership: Leading the way to effective teaching and learning.* Carrboro, NC: Center for Teaching Quality.

Bogliaccini, J. A., & Rodríguez, F. (2015). Education system institutions and educational inequalities in Uruguay. *CEPAL Review, 116,* 85–99.

Bundy, B., Dahl, J., Guiñals-Kupperman, S., Hengesbach, J., Martino, K., Metzler, J., Smith, J. F., Vargas, M., Vieyra, R., & Whitehurst, A. (2019). Physics teacher leaders influencing science education policy. *The Physics Teacher, 58*(3), 210–213.

Carver-Thomas, D., & Darling-Hammond, L. (2017). *Teacher turnover: Why it matters and what we can do about it.* Palo Alto, CA: Learning Policy Institute.

Criswell, B., Rushton, G. T., McDonald, S. P., & Gul, T. (2017). A clearer vision: Creating and evolving a model to support the development of science teacher leaders. *Research in Science Education, 48*(4), 811–837.

Criswell, B., Rushton, G., Nachtigall, D., Staggs, S., Alemdar, M., & Cappelli, C. (2018). Strengthening the vision: Examining the understanding of a framework for teacher leadership development by experienced science teachers. *Science Teacher Education, 102*(6), 1265–1287.

Darling-Hammond, L., & Rothman, R. (2011). Teacher and leader effectiveness in high-performing education systems. Washington, DC: Alliance for Excellent Education (ED517673). Retrieved from https://eric.ed.gov/?id=ED517673

DeBoer, G. E. (1991). *A history of ideas in science education: Implications for practice.* New York, NY: Teachers College Press.

Fensham, P. J. (2009). The link between policy and practice in science education: The role of research. *Science Education Policy, 93*(6), 1076–1095.

Finger, L., & Gindin, J. (2015). From proposal to policy: Social movements and teachers' unions in Latin America. *Prospects, 45*(3), 365–378.

Galosy, J., Mohan, L., Mohan, A., Miller, B., & Bintz, J. (2017a). *Math and science teacher leadership development: Findings from research and program reviews.* (Research Report No. 2017–02). BSCS, Colorado Springs, CO.

Galosy, J., Mohan, L., Mohan, A., Miller, B., & Bintz, J. (2017b). *Math and science teacher leadership development: Findings from research and program reviews.* (Research Report No. 2017–03). BSCS, Colorado Springs, CO.

Galosy, J., Mohan, L., Mohan, A., Miller, B., & Bintz, J. (2017c). *Math and science teacher leadership development: Findings from research and program reviews.* (Research Report No. 2017–04). BSCS, Colorado Springs, CO.

Gardner, D. P. (1983). *A nation at risk.* Washington, DC: The National Commission on Excellence in Education, US Department of Education.

Gareis, K., Priedeman, M., Manning, C., & Goodman, I. (2011). *Albert Einstein distinguished educator fellowship program: Final report on comprehensive and 2009–10 cohort evaluations.* Cambridge, MA: Goodman Research Group.

Government Track. (2015). *S. 1177–114th Congress: Every Student Succeeds Act.* Retrieved from https://www.govtrack.us/congress/bills/114/s1177

Hite, R., & Milbourne, J. (2018). A proposed conceptual framework for K–12 STEM Master Teacher (STEM-MaTe) development. *Education Sciences, 8*(4). https://doi.org/10.3390/educsci8040218

Holland, J. M., Eckert, J., & Allen, M. M. (2014). From preservice to teacher leadership: Meeting the future in educator preparation. *Action in Teacher Education, 36*(5–6), 433–445.

Huggins, K. S., Lesseig, K., & Rhodes, H. (2017). Rethinking teacher leader development: A study of early career mathematics teachers. *International Journal of Teacher Leadership, 8*(2), 28–48.

Hunzicker, J. (2017). From teacher to teacher leader: A conceptual model. *International Journal of Teacher Leadership, 8*(2), 1–27.

International Task Force for Teachers on Education 2030. (2018). *Strategic plan 2018–2021.* Retrieved from http://www.teachersforefa.unesco.org/v2/index.php/en/ressources/file/395-strategic-plan-2018-2021

Johnson, S., & Brady, M. (2018). *Interactive: Nationwide efforts to elevate the teaching profession.* Retrieved from https://www.americanprogress.org/issues/education-k-12/news/2018/02/05/445879/interactive-nationwide-efforts-elevate-teaching-profession/

Kayaoglu, M. N. (2015). Teacher researchers in action research in a heavily centralized education system. *Educational Action Research, 23*(2), 140–161.

Kenan Fellows. (2019). *Kenan Fellows program for teacher leadership.* Retrieved from https://kenanfellows.org/

Lave, J., & Wenger, E. (1991). *Situated learning: Legitimate peripheral participation.* Cambridge, UK: Cambridge University Press.

MSPNet. (2019). *Library.* Retrieved from http://hub.mspnet.org/index.cfm/library

National Academies of Sciences, Engineering, and Medicine. (2015). *Science teacher's learning: Enhancing opportunities, creating supportive contexts.* Washington, DC: The National Academies Press.

National Network of State Teachers of the Year. (2016). *ENGAGED: Educators and the policy process.* Retrieved from http://www.nnstoy.org/wp-content/uploads/2015/06/Engaged-FINAL.pdf

National Research Council. (2014). *Exploring opportunities for STEM teacher leadership: Summary of a convocation.* Washington, DC: The National Academies Press.

National Research Council. (2017). *Increasing the roles and significance of teachers in policymaking for K-12 engineering education: Proceedings of a convocation.* Washington, DC: The National Academies Press.

National Science Board. (2018). *Our nation's future competitiveness relies on building a STEM-capable U.S. workforce: A policy companion statement to Science and Engineering Indicators 2018.* Retrieved from https://www.nsf.gov/nsb/sei/companion-brief/NSB-2018-7.pdf

Neumerski, C. M. (2013). Rethinking instructional leadership, a review: What do we know about principal, teacher, and coach instructional leadership, and where should we go from here? *Educational Administration Quarterly, 49*(2), 310–347.

OECD. (2018). *The future of education and skills: Education 2030.* Retrieved from https://www.oecd.org/education/2030/E2030%20Position%20Paper%20(05.04.2018).pdf

Pennington, K. (2013). *New organizations, new voices: The landscape of today's teachers shaping policy.* Washington, DC: Center for American Progress. Retrieved from https://files.eric.ed.gov/fulltext/ED561062.pdf

Poekert, P., Alexandrou, A., & Shannon, D. (2016). How teachers become leaders: An internationally validated theoretical model of teacher leadership development. *Research in Post-Compulsory Education, 21*(4), 307–329. https://doi.org/10.1080/13596748.2016.1226559

President's Council of Advisors on Science and Technology. (2010). *Prepare and inspire: K-12 education in science, technology, engineering, and math (STEM) for America's future.* Retrieved from http://stelar.edc.org/sites/stelar.edc.org/files/pcast-stem-ed-final.pdf

Robert Noyce Teacher Scholarship Program. (2019). *The Robert Noyce teacher scholarship program.* Retrieved from http://www.nsfnoyce.org/

Sinha, S., & Hanuscin, D. L. (2017). Development of teacher leadership identity: A multiple case study. *Teaching and Teacher Education, 63*, 356–371.

Smylie, M. A., & Eckert, J. (2018). Beyond superheroes and advocacy: The pathway of teacher leadership development. *Educational Management Administration & Leadership, 46*, 556–577.

State Board of Education. (2015). *North Carolina teacher evaluation process.* Raleigh, NC: Department of Public Instruction.

Tan, C. (2015). Education policy borrowing and cultural scripts for teaching in China. *Comparative Education, 51*(2), 196–211.

Teach to Lead. (2019). *About teach to lead.* Retrieved from http://teachtolead.org/about/

UNESCO. (2010). *Current challenges in basic science education.* A report of the International Group of Experts on Science and Mathematics Education Policies, Paris, 2009. Retrieved from https://unesdoc.unesco.org/ark:/48223/pf0000191425?posInSet=3&queryId=N-EXPLORE-a7418951-eeab-4561-84af-536baee21f69

UNESCO. (2012). *Challenges in basic mathematics education.* A report of the International Group of Experts on Science and Mathematics Education Policies, Paris, 2009. Retrieved from https://unesdoc.unesco.org/ark:/48223/pf0000191776_eng?posInSet=1&queryID=N-EXPLORE- a7418951-eeab-4561-84af-536baee21f69

UNESCO. (2017). *Cracking the code: Girls' and women's education in science, technology, engineering and mathematics (STEM).* Retrieved from https://unesdoc.unesco.org/ark:/48223/pf0000253479

US DoE. (2019). *Albert Einstein distinguished educator fellowship (AEF) program.* Retrieved from https://science.energy.gov/wdts/einstein/

US DoED. (2019). *Transforming teaching and leading.* Retrieved from https://www.ed.gov/teaching

Wallace, C. S., & Priestly, M. R. (2016). Secondary science teachers as curriculum makers: Mapping and designing Scotland's new curriculum for excellence. *Journal of Research in Science Teaching, 54*(3), 324–349.

Wenner, J. A., & Campbell, T. (2017). The theoretical and empirical basis of teacher leadership: A review of the literature. *Review of Educational Research, 87*(1), 134–171.

White House. (2012, July 17). *President Obama announces plans for a new national corps to recognize and reward leading educators in STEM.* Retrieved from https://www.whitehouse.gov/the-press-office/2012/07/17/presidentobama-announces-plans-new-national-corps-recognize-and-reward-

White House. (2018). *Charting a course for success: America's strategy for STEM education.* Retrieved from https://www.whitehouse.gov/wp-content/uploads/2018/12/STEM-Education-Strategic-Plan-2018.pdf

Yarger, S. J., & Lee, O. (1994). The development and sustenance of instructional leadership. In D. R. Walling (Ed.), *Teachers as leaders: Perspectives on the professional development of teachers* (pp. 223–237). Bloomington, IN: Phi Delta Kappa Educational Foundation.

York-Barr, J., & Duke, K. (2004). What do we know about teacher leadership? Findings from two decades of scholarship. *Review of Educational Research, 74*(3), 255–316.

INDEX

Note: Page numbers in *italic* indicate a figure on the corresponding page. Page numbers in **bold** indicate a table on the corresponding page.

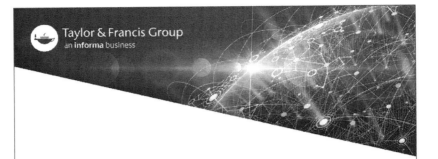